12th International Conference on Parsing Technologies 2011

(IWPT 2011)

Dublin, Ireland
5 – 7 October 2011

ISBN: 978-1-61839-238-1

Printed from e-media with permission by:

Curran Associates, Inc.
57 Morehouse Lane
Red Hook, NY 12571

Some format issues inherent in the e-media version may also appear in this print version.

Printed by Curran Associates, Inc. (2011)

For permission requests, please contact the Association for Computational Linguistics at the address below.

Association for Computational Linguistics
209 N. Eighth Street
Stroudsburg, Pennsylvania 18360

Phone: 1-570-476-8006
Fax: 1-570-476-0860

acl@aclweb.org

Additional copies of this publication are available from:

Curran Associates, Inc.
57 Morehouse Lane
Red Hook, NY 12571 USA
Phone: 845-758-0400
Fax: 845-758-2634
Email: curran@proceedings.com
Web: www.proceedings.com

Preface

Welcome to the 12th International Conference on Parsing Technologies (IWPT 2011) in Dublin, Ireland. IWPT 2011 continues the tradition of biennial conferences organized by SIGPARSE, ACL's Special Interest Group on Parsing, serving as the primary specialized forum for research on natural language parsing.

This year we received a total of 64 valid submissions, 42 long papers and 22 short papers, 6 of which were later withdrawn after being accepted for publication elsewhere. Of the remaining 58 submissions, 28 were accepted for presentation at the conference, which gives an acceptance rate of 48%. After notification, 2 more papers were withdrawn, which brings the final number of accepted papers to 26, all of which are published in these proceedings and presented at the conference in one of two ways: (i) as a long talk (long papers only) or (ii) as a short talk and a poster (short papers and some long papers). In this way, we were able to accommodate as many papers as possible and still give all the authors the opportunity of an oral presentation.

In addition to the contributed papers, IWPT 2011 will as usual feature invited talks on topics relevant to natural language parsing. This year we are delighted to welcome three very distinguished researchers: Ina Bornkessel-Schlesewsky, Michael Collins, and Mark Steedman. You will find the abstracts of their talks in the proceedings. There will also be a special workshop devoted to parsing of morphologically rich languages on the second day of the conference, a workshop that has had its own program committee and selection process.

Organizing IWPT 2011 would not have been possible without the dedicated work of a number of people. First and foremost, we would like to thank the local organizing committee, chaired by Özlem Çetinoğlu, who has done an outstanding job in taking care of all the local and practical organization. We are also grateful to the members of the program committee, who worked hard to review and discuss papers in the middle of the holiday season, and to the staff of SoftConf for support in managing the START system. Finally, thanks are due to the sponsors whose support helped to make IWPT 2011 possible: the Science Foundation Ireland, Dublin City University, the Centre for Next Generation Localisation, Springer Publishers, and Fáilte Ireland.

Enjoy the conference!

Harry Bunt	Joakim Nivre
General Chair	Program Chair

Organizers

General Chair:

Harry Bunt, Tilburg University

Program Chair:

Joakim Nivre, Uppsala University

Local Arrangements Chair:

Özlem Çetinoğlu, Dublin City University

Program Committee:

Timothy Baldwin, University of Melbourne
Srinivas Bangalore, AT&T
Philippe Blache, CNRS/Provence University
Harry Bunt, Tilburg University
Aoife Cahill, University of Stuttgart
John Carroll, University of Sussex
Eugene Charniak, Brown University
David Chiang, USC Information Sciences Institute
Stephen Clark, Cambridge University
Eric Villemonte de la Clergerie, INRIA Rocquencourt
Michael Collins, Columbia University
Özlem Çetinoğlu, Dublin City University
Jennifer Foster, Dublin City University
Josef van Genabith, Dublin City University
Carlos Gómez-Rodríguez, University of La Coruña
James Henderson, University of Geneva
Julia Hockenmaier, University of Illinois at Urbana-Champaign
Liang Huang, University of Southern California
Wenbin Jiang, Chinese Academy of Sciences
Mark Johnson, Macquarie University
Ronald Kaplan, Microsoft Corp
Martin Kay, Stanford University
Terry Koo, Google Inc
Sandra Kübler, Indiana University
Marco Kuhlmann, Uppsala University
Jonas Kuhn, University of Stuttgart
Sadao Kurohashi, Kyoto University
Alon Lavie, Carnegie Mellon University
Yuji Matsumoto, Nara Institute of Science and Technology
David McClosky, Stanford University
Ryan McDonald, Google Inc
Paola Merlo, University of Geneva
Yusuke Miyao, University of Tokyo
Mark-Jan Nederhof, University of St. Andrews
Joakim Nivre, University of Uppsala (chair)

Stephan Oepen, University of Oslo
Lilja Øvrelid, University of Oslo
Gerald Penn, University of Toronto
Slav Petrov, Google Inc
Owen Rambow, Columbia University
Kenji Sagae, Institute for Creative Technologies
Vijay Shanker, University of Delaware
Khalil Sima'an, University of Amsterdam
David Smith, University of Massachusetts
Noah Smith, Carnegie Mellon University
Mark Steedman, University of Edinburgh
Ivan Titov, Saarland University
Reut Tsarfaty, Uppsala University
Shuly Wintner, University of Haifa
Dekai Wu, Hong Kong University of Science and Technology
Yi Zhang, Saarland University
Yue Zhang, Cambridge University

Invited Speakers:

Ina Bornkessel-Schlesewsky, Philipps-Universität Marburg
Michael Collins, Columbia University
Mark Steedman, University of Edinburgh

Table of Contents

Conference Program

Wednesday October 5, 2011

09:15-09:30 Opening

09:30-10:30 Invited Talk

Computing Scope in a CCG Parser
Mark Steedman

10:30-11:00 Break

11:00-12:30 Long Talks 1

A Generalized View on Parsing and Translation
Alexander Koller and Marco Kuhlmann

Tree Parsing with Synchronous Tree-Adjoining Grammars
Matthias Büchse, Mark-Jan Nederhof and Heiko Vogler

Finding the Most Probable String and the Consensus String: an Algorithmic Study
Colin de la Higuera and Jose Oncina

12:30-14:00 Lunch

14:00-15:30 Short Talks 1

A Word Clustering Approach to Domain Adaptation: Effective Parsing of Biomedical Texts
Marie Candito, Enrique Henestroza Anguiano and Djamé Seddah

Sentence-Level Instance-Weighting for Graph-Based and Transition-Based Dependency Parsing
Anders Søgaard and Martin Haulrich

Analysis of the Difficulties in Chinese Deep Parsing
Kun Yu, Yusuke Miyao, Takuya Matsuzaki, Xiangli Wang and Junichi Tsujii

On the Role of Explicit Morphological Feature Representation in Syntactic Dependency Parsing for German
Wolfgang Seeker and Jonas Kuhn

Bayesian Network Automata for Modelling Unbounded Structures
James Henderson

Model-Theory of Property Grammars with Features
Denys Duchier, Thi-Bich-Hanh Dao and Yannick Parmentier

Wednesday October 5, 2011 (continued)

15:30-16:30 Break and Poster Session

16:30-18:00 Long Talks 2

Learning Structural Dependencies of Words in the Zipfian Tail
Tejaswini Deoskar, Markos Mylonakis and Khalil Sima'an

One-Step Statistical Parsing of Hybrid Dependency-Constituency Syntactic Representations
Kais Dukes and Nizar Habash

PLCFRS Parsing of English Discontinuous Constituents
Kilian Evang and Laura Kallmeyer

Thursday October 6, 2011

09:30-10:30 Invited Talk

Towards a Neurobiologically Plausible Model of Human Sentence Comprehension Across Languages
Ina Bornkessel-Schlesewsky

10:30-11:00 Break

11:00-12:30 Long Talks 3

Minimally Supervised Domain-Adaptive Parse Reranking for Relation Extraction
Feiyu Xu, Hong Li, Yi Zhang, Hans Uszkoreit and Sebastian Krause

Simple Semi-Supervised Learning for Prepositional Phrase Attachment
Gregory F. Coppola, Alexandra Birch, Tejaswini Deoskar and Mark Steedman

Active Learning for Dependency Parsing Using Partially Annotated Sentences
Seyed Abolghasem Mirroshandel and Alexis Nasr

12:30-13:30 Lunch

13:30-17:30 SPMRL Workshop

Friday October 7, 2011

09:30-10:30 Invited Talk

Lagrangian Relaxation for Inference in Natural Language Processing
Michael Collins

10:30-11:00 Break

11:00-12:30 Long Talks 4

Prefix Probabilities for Linear Context-Free Rewriting Systems
Mark-Jan Nederhof and Giorgio Satta

Efficient Matrix-Encoded Grammars and Low Latency Parallelization Strategies for CYK
Aaron Dunlop, Nathan Bodenstab and Brian Roark

Efficient Parallel CKY Parsing on GPUs
Youngmin Yi, Chao-Yue Lai, Slav Petrov and Kurt Keutzer

12:30-14:00 Lunch

14:00-15:30 Short Talks 2

CuteForce – Deep Deterministic HPSG Parsing
Gisle Ytrestøl

Large-Scale Corpus-Driven PCFG Approximation of an HPSG
Yi Zhang and Hans-Ulrich Krieger

Features for Phrase-Structure Reranking from Dependency Parses
Richàrd Farkas, Bernd Bohnet and Helmut Schmid

Comparing the Use of Edited and Unedited Text in Parser Self-Training
Jennifer Foster, Özlem Çetinoğlu, Joachim Wagner and Josef van Genabith

Beyond Chart Parsing: An Analytic Comparison of Dependency Chart Parsing Algorithms
Meixun Jin, Hwidong Na and Jong-Hyeok Lee

Parser Evaluation Using Elementary Dependency Matching
Rebecca Dridan and Stephan Oepen

15:30-16:30 Break and Poster Session

Friday October 7, 2011 (continued)

16:30-17:30 Long Talks 5

Parsing of Partially Bracketed Structures for Parse Selection
Mark-Jan Nederhof and Ricardo Sánchez-Sáez

Detecting Dependency Parse Errors with Minimal Resources
Markus Dickinson and Amber Smith

17:30-17:45 Closing

Computing Scope in a CCG Parser

Mark Steedman
School of Informatics
University of Edinburgh
steedman@inf.ed.ac.uk

Abstract

Ambiguities arising from alternations of scope in interpretations for multiply quantified sentences appear to require grammatical operations that compromise the strong assumptions of syntactic/semantic transparency and monotonicity underlying the Frege-Montague approach to the theory of grammar. Examples that have been proposed include covert movement at the level of logical form, abstraction or storage mechanisms, and proliferating type-changing operations. The paper examines some interactions of scope alternation with syntactic phenomena including coordination, binding, and relativization. Starting from the assumption of Fodor and Sag, and others, that many expressions that have been treated as generalized quantifiers are in fact referential expressions, and using Combinatory Categorial Grammar (CCG) as a grammatical framework, the paper presents an account of quantifier scope ambiguities according to which the available readings are projected directly from the lexicon by the combinatorics of the syntactic derivation, without any independent manipulation of logical form and without recourse to otherwise unmotivated type-changing operations. As a direct result, scope ambiguity can be efficiently processed using packed representations from which the available readings can be simply enumerated.

A Generalized View on Parsing and Translation

Alexander Koller
Dept. of Linguistics
University of Potsdam, Germany
koller@ling.uni-potsdam.de

Marco Kuhlmann
Dept. of Linguistics and Philology
Uppsala University, Sweden
marco.kuhlmann@lingfil.uu.se

Abstract

We present a formal framework that generalizes a variety of monolingual and synchronous grammar formalisms for parsing and translation. Our framework is based on regular tree grammars that describe derivation trees, which are interpreted in arbitrary algebras. We obtain generic parsing algorithms by exploiting closure properties of regular tree languages.

1 Introduction

Over the past years, grammar formalisms that relate pairs of grammatical structures have received much attention. These formalisms include *synchronous grammars* (Lewis and Stearns, 1968; Shieber and Schabes, 1990; Shieber, 1994; Rambow and Satta, 1996; Eisner, 2003) and *tree transducers* (Comon et al., 2007; Graehl et al., 2008). Weighted variants of both of families of formalisms have been used for machine translation (Graehl et al., 2008; Chiang, 2007), where one tree represents a parse of a sentence in one language and the other a parse in the other language. Synchronous grammars and tree transducers are also useful as models of the syntax-semantics interface; here one tree represents the syntactic analysis of a sentence and the other the semantic analysis (Shieber and Schabes, 1990; Nesson and Shieber, 2006).

When such a variety of formalisms are available, it is useful to take a step back and look for a generalized model that explains the precise formal relationship between them. There is a long tradition of such research on monolingual grammar formalisms, where e.g. linear context-free rewriting systems (LCFRS, Vijay-Shanker et al. (1987)) generalize various mildly context-sensitive formalisms. However, few such results exist for synchronous formalisms. A notable exception is the work by Shieber (2004), who unified synchronous tree-adjoining grammars with tree transducers.

In this paper, we make two contributions. First, we provide a formal framework – *interpreted regular tree grammars* – which generalizes both synchronous grammars, tree transducers, and LCFRS-style monolingual grammars. A grammar of this formalism consists of a regular tree grammar (RTG, Comon et al. (2007)) defining a language of derivation trees and an arbitrary number of *interpretations* which map these trees into objects of arbitrary algebras. This allows us to capture a wide variety of (synchronous and monolingual) grammar formalisms. We can also model heterogeneous synchronous languages, which relate e.g. trees with strings; this is necessary for applications in machine translation (Graehl et al., 2008) and in parsing strings with synchronous tree grammars.

Second, we also provide parsing and decoding algorithms for our framework. The key concept that we introduce is that of a *regularly decomposable algebra*, where the set of all terms that evaluate to a given object form a regular tree language. Once an algorithm that computes a compact representation of this language is known, parsing algorithms follow from a generic construction. All important algebras in natural language processing that we are aware of – in particular the standard algebras of strings and trees – are regularly decomposable.

In summary, we obtain a formalism that pulls together much existing research under a common formal framework, and makes it possible to obtain parsers for existing and new formalisms in a modular, universal fashion.

Plan of the paper. The paper is structured as follows. We start by laying the formal foundations in Section 2. We then introduce the framework of interpreted RTGs and illustrate it with some simple examples in Section 3. The generic parsing and decoding algorithms are described in Section 4. Section 5 discusses the role of binarization in our framework. Section 6 shows how interpreted RTGs can be applied to existing grammar formalisms.

2 Formal Foundations

For $n \geq 0$, we define $[n] = \{ i \mid 1 \leq i \leq n \}$.

A *signature* is a finite set Σ of function symbols f, each of which has been assigned a non-negative integer called its *rank*. Given a signature Σ, we can define a *(finite constructor) tree* over Σ as a finite tree whose nodes are labeled with symbols from Σ such that a node with a label of rank n has exactly n children. We write T_Σ for the set of all trees over Σ. Trees can be written as *terms*; $f(t_1, \ldots, t_n)$ stands for the tree with root label f and subtrees $t_1, \ldots, t_n$. The *nodes* of a tree can be identified by paths $\pi \in \mathbb{N}^*$ from the root: The root has address ϵ, and the i-th child of the node at path π has the address πi. We write $t(\pi)$ for the symbol at path π in the tree t.

A *Σ-algebra* $\mathcal{A}$ consists of a non-empty set A called the *domain* and, for each symbol $f \in \Sigma$ with rank n, a total function $f^\mathcal{A} : A^n \to A$, the *operation* associated with f. We can *evaluate* a term $t \in T_\Sigma$ to an object $[\![t]\!]_\mathcal{A} \in A$ by executing the operations:

$$[\![f(t_1, \ldots, t_n)]\!]_\mathcal{A} = f^\mathcal{A}([\![t_1]\!]_\mathcal{A}, \ldots, [\![t_n]\!]_\mathcal{A}) \, .$$

Sets of trees can be specified by *regular tree grammars (RTGs)* (Gécseg and Steinby, 1997; Comon et al., 2007). Formally, such a grammar is a structure $\mathcal{G} = (N, \Sigma, P, S)$, where N is a signature of nonterminal symbols, all of which are taken to have rank 0, Σ is a signature of terminal symbols, $S \in N$ is a distinguished start symbol, and P is a finite set of productions of the form $B \to t$, where B is a nonterminal symbol, and $t \in T_{N \cup \Sigma}$. The productions of a regular tree grammar are used as rewriting rules on terms. More specifically, the *derivation relation* of $\mathcal{G}$ is defined as follows. Let $t_1, t_2 \in T_{N \cup \Sigma}$ be terms. Then $\mathcal{G}$ derives t_2 from t_1 in one step, denoted by $t_1 \Rightarrow_\mathcal{G} t_2$, if there exists a production of the form $B \to t$ and t_2 can be obtained by replacing an occurrence of B in t_1 by t. The *(regular) language* $L(\mathcal{G})$ generated by $\mathcal{G}$ is the set of all terms $t \in T_\Sigma$ that can be derived, in zero or more steps, from the term S.

A *(tree) homomorphism* is a total function $h \colon T_\Sigma \to T_\Delta$ which expands symbols of Σ into trees over Δ while following the structure of the input tree. Formally, h is specified by pairs $(f, h(f))$, where $f \in \Sigma$ is a symbol with some rank n, and $h(f) \in T_{\Delta \cup \{x_1, \ldots, x_n\}}$ is a term with variables. Given $t \in T_\Sigma$, the value of t under h is defined as

$$h(f(t_1, \ldots, t_n)) = h(f)\{ h(t_i)/x_i \mid i \in [n] \} \, ,$$

where $\{ t_i/x_i \mid i \in [n] \}$ represents the substitution that replaces all occurrences of x_i with the respective t_i. A homomorphism is called *linear* if every term $h(f)$ contains each variable at most once; and a *delabeling* if every term $h(f)$ is of the form $g(x_{\pi(1)}, \ldots, x_{\pi(n)})$ where n is the rank of f and π a permutation of $\{1, \ldots, n\}$.

3 Interpreted Regular Tree Grammars

We will now present a generalized framework for synchronous and monolingual grammars in terms of regular tree grammars, tree homomorphisms, and algebras. We will illustrate the framework with two simple examples here, but many other grammar formalisms can be seen as special cases too, as we will show in Section 6.

3.1 An Introductory Example

The derivation process of context-free grammar is usually seen as a string-rewriting process in which nonterminals are successively replaced by the right-hand sides of production rules. The actual parse tree is explained as a post-hoc description of the rules that were applied in the derivation.

However, we can alternatively view this as a two-step process which first computes a derivation tree and then interprets it as a string. Say we have the CNF grammar G in Fig. 2, and we want to derive the string $w =$ "Sue watches the man with the telescope". In the first step, we use G to generate a *derivation tree* like the one in Fig. 2a. The nodes of this tree are labeled with names of the production rules in G; nodes with labels r_7 and r_3 are licensed by G to be the two children of r_1 because r_1 has the two nonterminals NP and VP in its right-hand side, and the left-hand sides of r_7 and r_3 are NP and VP, respectively. In a second step, we can then *interpret* the derivation tree into w by interpreting each leaf labeled with a terminal production (say, r_7) as the string on its right-hand side ("Sue"), and each internal node as a string concatenation operation which arranges the string yields of its subtrees in the order given by the right-hand side of the production rule.

This view differs from the traditional perspective on context-free grammars in that it makes the derivation tree the primary participant in the derivation process. The string is only one particular interpretation of the derivation tree, and instead of a string we could also have interpreted it as some other kind of object. For instance, if we had inter-

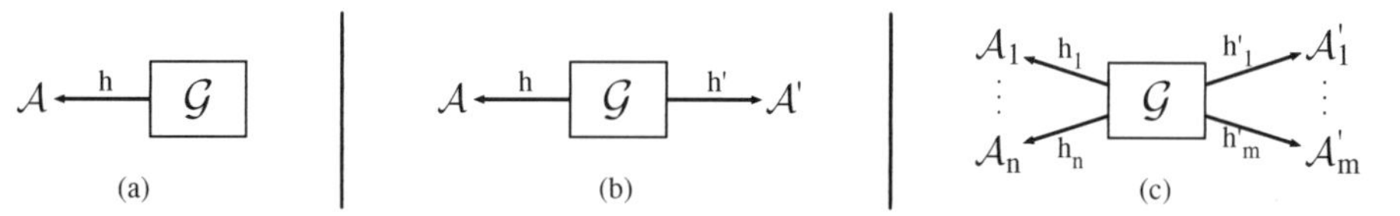

Figure 1: Interpreted tree grammars: (a) monolingual; (b) synchronous; (c) multiple "inputs" and "outputs".

preted r_7 as the *tree* N(Sue) and a rule like r_1 as a *tree operation* which takes the tree yields of its two subtrees and inserts them as the children of a root with label S, etc., the interpretation of a derivation tree would now be a tree; namely, an ordinary parse tree of G. We could even interpret the same derivation tree simultaneously as a string and as a tree using two different interpretation functions.

3.2 Interpreted Regular Tree Grammars

While this view is unnecessarily complex for explaining context-free grammars alone, the separation into two different generative processes (first derivation, then interpretation) is widely applicable. In particular, the derivation part can be independent of whether w is a string or some other algebra of objects. We formalize our view as follows. First, we need an interpretative component that maps derivation trees to terms of the relevant object algebra:

Definition 1 Let Σ be a signature. A *Σ-interpretation* is a pair $\mathcal{I} = (h, \mathcal{A})$, where $\mathcal{A}$ is a Δ-algebra, and $h\colon T_\Sigma \to T_\Delta$ is a homomorphism. □

We then capture the derivation process with a single regular tree grammar, and connect it with (potentially multiple) interpretations as follows:

Definition 2 An *interpreted regular tree grammar (IRTG)* is a structure $\mathbb{G} = (\mathcal{G}, \mathcal{I}_1, \ldots, \mathcal{I}_n)$, $n \geq 1$, where $\mathcal{G}$ is a regular tree grammar with terminal alphabet Σ, and the $\mathcal{I}_i$ are Σ-interpretations. □

Let $\mathcal{I}_i = (h_i, \mathcal{A}_i)$ be the ith interpretation. If we apply the homomorphism h_i to any tree $t \in L(\mathcal{G})$, we obtain a term $h_i(t)$, which we can evaluate to an object of $\mathcal{A}_i$. Based on this, we define the *language* generated by $\mathbb{G}$ as follows. We write $[\![t]\!]_{\mathcal{I}_i}$ as a shorthand for $[\![h_i(t)]\!]_{\mathcal{A}_i}$.

$$L(\mathbb{G}) = \{\, \langle [\![t]\!]_{\mathcal{I}_1}, \ldots, [\![t]\!]_{\mathcal{I}_n} \rangle \mid t \in L(\mathcal{G}) \,\}$$

Given this notion, we can define an obvious *membership problem*: For a given tuple of objects $\vec{a} = \langle a_1, \ldots, a_n \rangle$, is $\vec{a} \in L(\mathbb{G})$? We can also define a *parsing task*: For every element $\vec{a} \in L(\mathbb{G})$, compute (some compact representation of) the set

$$\mathsf{parses}_{\mathbb{G}}(\vec{a}) = \{\, t \in L(\mathcal{G}) \mid \forall i.\ [\![t]\!]_{\mathcal{I}_i} = a_i \,\}$$

We call the trees in this set the *derivation trees* of $\vec{a}$.

3.3 Monolingual Grammars

Let us use these definitions to make our example with context-free grammars as string-generating devices precise. This is a case with a single interpretation ($n = 1$), as illustrated in Fig. 1a.

We can adapt a standard construction (Goguen et al., 1977). Let G be a context-free grammar with nonterminals N, terminals T, and productions P. We start by defining a regular tree grammar $\mathcal{G}$. For a string $\alpha \in (N \cup T)^*$, let $\mathit{nt}(\alpha)$ denote the string of nonterminals in α, in the same order. We include into $\mathcal{G}$ all (and only) productions of the form $A \to p(A_1, \ldots, A_m)$, where $p = A \to \alpha$ is a production of G, and $A_1 \cdots A_m = \mathit{nt}(\alpha)$. Note that by doing so, we view p as a symbol of rank $|\mathit{nt}(\alpha)|$. The nonterminals and the start symbol of $\mathcal{G}$ are as for G. We now interpret the trees generated by $\mathcal{G}$ over the *string algebra* over T, which we denote by T^*. The domain of this algebra is the set of all strings over T, and we have constants for the symbols in T and the empty string, as well as a single binary concatenation operation $\bullet$. As a last step, we use a homorphism *rb* to map each rule of G into a term over the signature of T^*: For each production p of the form above, $\mathit{rb}(p)$ is the right-branching tree obtained from decomposing α into a series of concatenation operations, where the nonterminal A_i is replaced with the variable x_i. Thus we have constructed an IRTG grammar $\mathbb{G} = (\mathcal{G}, (\mathit{rb}, T^*))$. It can be shown that under this construction $L(\mathbb{G})$ is exactly $L(G)$, the string language of the original grammar.

Consider the context-free grammar in Fig. 2. The RTG $\mathcal{G}$ contains production rules such as $\mathrm{S} \to r_1(\mathrm{NP}, \mathrm{VP})$; it generates an infinite language of trees, including the derivation trees shown in Fig. 2a and 2b. These trees can now be interpreted using *rb* with $\mathit{rb}(r_1) = x_1 \bullet x_2$,[1] $\mathit{rb}(r_7) = \mathit{Sue}$, etc. This maps the tree in Fig. 2a to the term

$$\mathit{Sue} \bullet (\mathit{watches} \bullet (\mathit{the} \bullet (\mathit{man} \bullet (\mathit{with} \bullet (\mathit{the} \bullet \mathit{telescope})))))$$

over the signature of T^*, which evaluates in the algebra T^* to the string w mentioned earlier. Similarly, *rb* maps the tree in Fig. 2b to the term

[1] Here and below, we write $\bullet$ in infix notation.

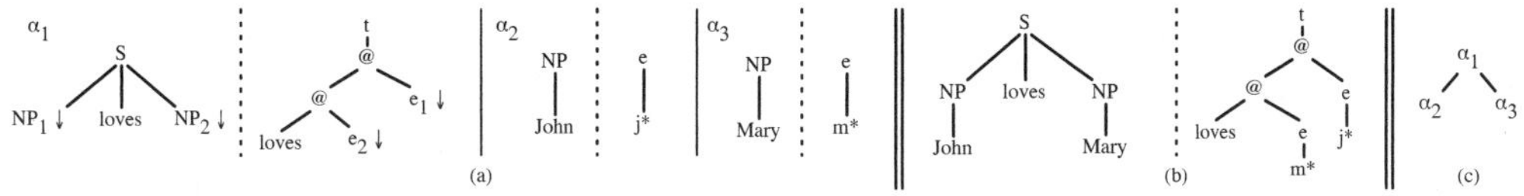

Figure 3: Synchronous TSG: (a) a lexicon consisting of three tree pairs; (b) a derived tree; (c) a derivation tree.

r_1 :	S	$\rightarrow$	NP VP
r_2 :	NP	$\rightarrow$	Det N
r_3 :	VP	$\rightarrow$	V NP
r_4 :	N	$\rightarrow$	N PP
r_5 :	VP	$\rightarrow$	VP PP
r_6 :	PP	$\rightarrow$	P NP
r_7 :	NP	$\rightarrow$	Sue
r_8 :	Det	$\rightarrow$	the
r_9 :	N	$\rightarrow$	man
r_{10} :	N	$\rightarrow$	telescope
r_{11} :	V	$\rightarrow$	watches
r_{12} :	P	$\rightarrow$	with

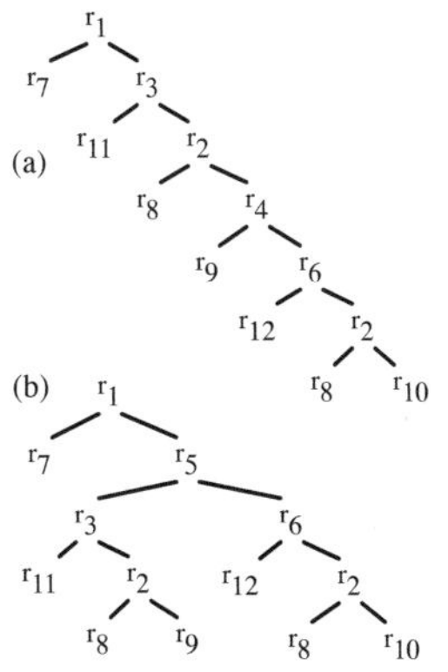

Figure 2: A CFG and two of its derivation trees.

$$Sue \bullet ((watches \bullet (the \bullet man)) \bullet (with \bullet (the \bullet telescope)))$$

This means that $L(\mathbb{G})$ is a set of strings which includes w. The tree language $L(\mathcal{G})$ contains further trees, which map to strings other than w. Therefore $L(\mathbb{G})$ includes other strings, but the trees in Fig. 2a and b are the only two derivation trees of w.

3.4 Synchronous Grammars

We can quite naturally represent grammars that describe binary relations between objects, i.e. synchronous grammars, as IRTGs with two interpretations ($n = 2$). We write these interpretations as $\mathcal{I}_L = (h_L, \mathcal{A}_L)$ ("left") and $\mathcal{I}_R = (h_R, \mathcal{A}_R)$ ("right"); see Fig. 1b.

Parsing with a synchronous grammar means to compute (a compact representation of) the set of all derivation trees for a given pair (a_L, a_R) from the set $\mathcal{A}_L \times \mathcal{A}_R$. This is precisely the parsing task that we defined in Section 3.2. A related task is *decoding*, in which we take the grammar $\mathbb{G} = (\mathcal{G}, \mathcal{I}_L, \mathcal{I}_R)$ as a translation device for mapping input objects $a_L \in \mathcal{A}_L$ to output objects $a_R \in \mathcal{A}_R$. We define the decoding task as the task of computing, for a given $a_L \in \mathcal{A}_L$, (a compact representation of) the following set, where $\mathbb{G}_L = (\mathcal{G}, \mathcal{I}_L)$:

$$\mathsf{decodes}_{\mathbb{G}}(a_L) = \{ [\![t]\!]_{\mathcal{I}_R} \mid t \in \mathsf{parses}_{\mathbb{G}_L}(a_L) \}$$

To illustrate this with an example, consider the case of synchronous tree-substitution grammars (STSGs, Eisner (2003)). An STSG combines lexicon entries, as shown in Fig. 3a, into larger *derived trees* by replacing corresponding substitution nodes with trees from other lexicon entries. In the figure, we have marked the correspondence with numeric subscripts. The trees in Fig. 3a can be combined into the derived tree in Fig. 3b in two steps; this process is recorded in the derivation tree in Fig. 3c.

We capture an STSG G_S as an IRTG $\mathbb{G}$ by interpreting the (regular) language of derivation trees in appropriate *tree algebras*. The tree algebra T_Δ over some signature Δ consists of all trees over Δ; every symbol $f \in \Delta$ of rank m is interpreted as an m-place operation that returns the tree with root symbol f and its arguments as subtrees. To model STSG, we use the two tree algebras over all the symbols occurring in the left and right components of the lexicon entries, respectively. We can obtain an RTG $\mathcal{G}$ for the derivation trees using a standard construction (Schmitz and Le Roux, 2008; Shieber, 2004); its nonterminals are pairs $\langle A_L, A_R \rangle$ of nonterminals occurring in the left and right trees of G_S. To encode a lexicon entry α with root nonterminals A_L and A_R, left substitution nodes $A_L^1, \dots, A_L^n$, and right substitution nodes $A_R^1, \dots, A_R^n$, we add an RTG rule of the form

$$\langle A_L, A_R \rangle \rightarrow \alpha(\langle A_L^1, A_R^1 \rangle, \dots, \langle A_L^n, A_R^n \rangle) .$$

We also let $h_L(\alpha)$ and $h_R(\alpha)$ be the left and right tree of α, with substitution nodes replaced by variables; h_L and h_R interpret derivation trees into derived trees in tree algebras T_Σ and T_Δ of appropriate (and possibly different) signatures. In the example, we obtain

$$\begin{aligned} \langle S, t \rangle &\rightarrow \alpha_1(\langle \mathrm{NP}, e \rangle, \langle \mathrm{NP}, e \rangle) , \\ h_L(\alpha_1) &= \mathrm{S}(x_1, \mathrm{loves}, x_2) , \qquad \text{and} \\ h_R(\alpha_1) &= t(@(@(\mathrm{loves}, x_2), x_1)) . \end{aligned}$$

The variables reflect the corresponding substitution nodes. So if we let $\mathbb{G} = (\mathcal{G}, (h_L, T_\Sigma), (h_R, T_\Delta))$, $L(\mathbb{G})$ will be a language of pairs of derived trees, including the pair in Fig. 3b.

Parsing as defined above amounts to computing a common derivation tree for a given pair of derived trees; given only a left derived tree, the decoding problem is to compute the corresponding right derived trees. However, in an application of STSG to machine translation or semantic construction, we are typically given a *string* as the left input and want to decode it to a right output tree. We can support this by left-interpreting the derivation trees directly as strings: We use the appropriate string algebra T^* (consisting of the symbols of Σ with arity zero) for $\mathcal{A}_L$, and map every lexicon entry to a term that concatenates the string yields of the elementary trees. In the example grammar, we can let $h'_L(\alpha_1) = ((x_1 \bullet \text{loves}) \bullet x_2)$, $h'_L(\alpha_2) = \text{John}$, and $h'_L(\alpha_3) = \text{Mary}$. With this local change, we obtain a new IRTG $\mathbb{G}' = (\mathcal{G}, (h'_L, T^*), (h_R, T_\Delta))$, whose language contains pairs of a (left) string and a (right) tree. One such pair has the string "John loves Mary" as the left and the right-hand tree in Fig. 3b as the right component. Therefore decodes("John loves Mary"), i.e. the set of right derived trees that are consistent with the input string, contains the right-hand tree in Fig. 3b.

We conclude this section by remarking that decoding can be easily generalized to n input objects and m output objects, all of which can be taken from different algebras (see Fig. 1c).

4 Algorithms

In the previous section, we have taken a view on parsing and translation in which languages and translations are obtained as the interpretation of regular tree grammars. One advantage of this way of looking at things is that it is possible to define completely generic parsing algorithms by exploiting closure properties of regular tree languages.

4.1 Parsing

The fundamental problem that we must solve is to compute, for a given IRTG $\mathbb{G} = (\mathcal{G}, (h, \mathcal{A}))$ and object $a \in \mathcal{A}$, a regular tree grammar $\mathcal{G}_a$ such that $L(\mathcal{G}_a) = \mathsf{parses}_{\mathbb{G}}(a)$. A parser for IRTGs with multiple interpretations follows from this immediately. Assume that $\mathbb{G} = (\mathcal{G}, \mathcal{I}_1, \ldots, \mathcal{I}_n)$; then

$$\mathsf{parses}_{\mathbb{G}}(a_1, \ldots, a_n) = \bigcap_{i=1}^{n} \mathsf{parses}_{(\mathcal{G},\mathcal{I}_i)}(a_i)\,.$$

Because regular tree languages are closed under intersection, we can parse the different a_i separately and then intersect all the $\mathcal{G}_{a_i}$.

The general idea of our parsing algorithm is as follows. Suppose we were able to compute the set $\mathsf{terms}_{\mathcal{A}}(a)$ of all possible terms t over $\mathcal{A}$ that evaluate to a. Then $\mathsf{parses}_{\mathbb{G}}(a)$ can be written as $h^{-1}(\mathsf{terms}_{\mathcal{A}}(a)) \cap L(\mathcal{G})$. Of course, $\mathsf{terms}_{\mathcal{A}}(a)$ may be a large or infinite set, so computing it in general algebras is infeasible. But now assume an algebra $\mathcal{A}$ in which $\mathsf{terms}_{\mathcal{A}}(a)$ is a regular tree language for every $a \in \mathcal{A}$, and in which we can compute, for each a, a regular tree grammar $D(a)$ with $L(D(a)) = \mathsf{terms}_{\mathcal{A}}(a)$. Since regular tree languages are effectively closed under both inverse homomorphisms and intersections (Comon et al., 2007), we obtain a parsing algorithm which first computes $D(a)$, and then $\mathcal{G}_a$ as the grammar for $h^{-1}(L(D(a))) \cap L(\mathcal{G})$.

Formally, this can be done for the following class of algebras.

Definition 3 A Σ-algebra $\mathcal{A}$ is called *regularly decomposable* if there is a computable function $D(\cdot)$ which maps every object $a \in \mathcal{A}$ to a regular tree grammar $D(a)$ such that $L(D(a)) = \mathsf{terms}_{\mathcal{A}}(a)$.□

Consider the example of context-free grammars. We have shown in Section 3.3 how these can be seen as an IRTG with an interpretation into T^*. The string algebra T^* is regularly decomposable because the possible term representations of a string simply correspond to its bracketings: For a string $w = w_1 \cdots w_n$, the grammar $D(w)$ consists of a rule $A_{i-1,i} \to w_i$ for each $1 \le i \le n$, and a rule $A_{i,k} \to A_{i,j} \bullet A_{j,k}$ for all $0 \le i < j < k \le n$. In our example "Sue watches the man with the telescope" from Section 3.2, these are rules such as $A_{2,3} \to \text{the}$, $A_{3,4} \to \text{man}$, $A_{2,4} \to A_{2,3} \bullet A_{3,4}$, and so on. The grammar generates a tree language consisting of the 132 binary bracketings of the sentence, including the two mentioned in Section 3.3.

Tree algebras are an even simpler example of a regularly decomposable algebra. For a given tree $t \in T_\Sigma$, the grammar $D(t)$ consists of the rules $A_\pi \to f(A_{\pi 1}, \ldots, A_{\pi n})$ for all nodes π in t with label f. $D(t)$ generates a language that contains a single tree, namely t itself. Thus we can use the parsing algorithm to parse tree inputs (say, in the context of an STSG) just as easily as string inputs.

4.2 Computing Inverse Homomorphisms

The performance bottleneck of the parsing algorithm is the computation of the inverse homomorphisms. The input of this problem is h and $D(a)$; the task is to compute an RTG $\mathcal{H}'$ that uses terminal symbols from the signature Σ of $\mathcal{G}$ and the same nonterminals as $D(a)$, such that $h(L(\mathcal{H}')) = L(D(a))$. This problem is nontrivial

$$\frac{h(f)(\pi) = x_i \quad A \in N_{D(a)}}{[f, \pi, A, \{A/x_i\}]} \; (var)$$

$$\frac{\begin{array}{c} A \to g(A_1, \ldots, A_n) \text{ in } \mathcal{H} \quad h(f)(\pi) = g \\ [f, \pi 1, A_1, \sigma_1] \quad \cdots \quad [f, \pi n, A_n, \sigma_n] \\ \sigma = \text{merge}(\sigma_1, \ldots, \sigma_n) \neq \textbf{fail} \end{array}}{[f, \pi, A, \sigma]} \; (up)$$

Figure 4: Algorithm for computing $h^{-1}(\mathcal{H})$.

because h may not be a delabeling, so a term $h(f)$ may have to be parsed by multiple rule applications in $D(a)$ (see e.g. $h'_L(\alpha_1)$ in Section 3.4), and we cannot simply take the homomorphic pre-images of the production rules of $D(a)$. One approach (Comon et al., 2007) is to generate all possible production rules $A \to f(B_1, \ldots, B_m)$ out of terminals $f \in \Sigma$ and $D(a)$-nonterminals and check whether $A \Rightarrow^*_{D(a)} h(f(B_1, \ldots, B_m))$. Unfortunately, this algorithm blindly combines arbitrary tuples of nonterminals. For parsing with context-free grammars in Chomsky normal form, this approach leads to an $O(n^4)$ parsing algorithm.

The problem can be solved more efficiently by the algorithm in Fig. 4. This algorithm computes an RTG $\mathcal{H}'$ for $h^{-1}(L(\mathcal{H}))$, where $\mathcal{H}$ is an RTG in a normal form in which every rule contains a single terminal symbol; bringing a grammar into this form only leads to a linear size increase (Gécseg and Steinby, 1997). The algorithm derives items of the form $[f, \pi, A, \sigma]$, stating that $\mathcal{H}$ can generate the subtree of $h(f)\sigma$ at node π if it uses A as the start symbol; the substitution σ is responsible for replacing the variables in $h(f)$ by nonterminal symbols. It starts by guessing all possible instantiations of each variable in $h(f)$ (rule *var*). It then computes items bottom-up, deriving an item $[f, \pi, A, \sigma]$ if there is a rule in $\mathcal{H}$ that can combine the nonterminals derived for the children $\pi 1, \ldots, \pi n$ of π into A (rule *up*). The substitution σ is obtained by merging all mappings in the $\sigma_1, \ldots, \sigma_n$; if some σ_i, σ_j assign different nonterminals to the same variable, the rule fails.

Whenever the algorithm derives an item of the form $[f, \epsilon, A, \sigma]$, it has processed a complete tree $h(f)$, and we add a production $A \to f(\sigma(x_1), \ldots, \sigma(x_n))$ to $\mathcal{H}'$; for variables x_i on which σ is undefined, we let $\sigma(x_i) = \$$ for the special nonterminal $\$$. We also add rules to $\mathcal{H}'$ which generate any tree from T_Σ out of $\$$.

The complexity of this algorithm is bounded by the number of instances of the *up* rule (McAllester, 2002). For parsing with context-free grammars, *up* is applied to rules of the form $A_{l,r} \to A_{l,k} \bullet A_{k,r}$ of $D(w)$; the premises are $[f, \pi 1, A_{l,k}, \sigma_1]$ and $[f, \pi 2, A_{k,r}, \sigma_2]$ and the conclusion $[f, \pi, A_{l,r}, \sigma]$. The substitution σ defines a segmentation of the substring between positions l and r into $m-1$ smaller substrings, where m is the number of variables in the domain of σ. So the instances of *up* are uniquely determined by at most $m+1$ string positions, where m is the total number of variables in the tree $h(f)$; the parsing complexity is $O(n^{m+1})$. By our encoding of context-free grammars into IRTGs, m corresponds to the maximal number of nonterminals in the right-hand side of a production of the original grammar. In particular, the generic algorithm parses Chomsky normal form grammars (where $m = 2$) in cubic time, as expected.

4.3 Parse Charts

We will now illustrate the operation of the parsing algorithm with our example context-free grammar from Fig. 2 and our example sentence $w =$ "Sue watches the man with the telescope". We first compute $D(w)$, which generates all bracketings of the sentence. Next, we use the algorithm in Fig. 4 to compute a grammar $\mathcal{H}'$ for $h^{-1}(L(D(w)))$ for the language of all derivation trees that are mapped by h to a term evaluating to w. $\mathcal{H}'$ contains rules such as $A_{2,4} \to r_2(A_{2,3}, A_{3,4})$, $A_{3,5} \to r_2(A_{3,4}, A_{4,5})$, and $A_{3,4} \to \text{man}$. That is, $\mathcal{H}'$ uses terminal symbols from Σ, but the nonterminals from $D(w)$. Finally, we intersect $\mathcal{H}'$ with $\mathcal{G}$ to retain only derivation trees that are grammatical according to $\mathcal{G}$. We obtain a grammar $\mathcal{G}_w$ for parses(w), which is shown in Fig. 5 (we have left out unreachable and unproductive rules). The nonterminals of $\mathcal{G}_w$ are pairs of the form $(N, A_{i,k})$, i.e. nonterminals of $\mathcal{G}$ and $\mathcal{H}'$; we abbreviate these pairs as $N_{i,k}$. Note that $L(\mathcal{G}_w)$ consists of exactly two trees, the derivation trees shown in Fig. 2.

There is a clear parallel between the RTG in Fig. 5 and a parse chart of the CKY parser for the same input. The RTG describes how to build larger parse items from smaller ones, and provides exactly the same kind of structure sharing for ambiguous sentences that the CKY chart would. For all intents and purposes, the RTG $\mathcal{G}_w$ *is* a parse chart. When we parse grammars of other formalisms, such as STSG, the nonterminals of $\mathcal{G}_a$ generally record nonterminals of $\mathcal{G}$ and positions in the input objects, as encoded in the nonterminals of $D(a_1), \ldots, D(a_n)$; the spans $[i, k]$ occurring in CKY parse items simply happen to be the nonterminals of the $D(a)$ for the string algebra.

In fact, we maintain that the fundamental purpose of a chart is to act as a device for generating the set of derivation trees for an input. This tree-generating nature of parse charts is made explicit by modeling them directly as RTGs; the well-known view of parse charts as context-free grammars (Billot and Lang, 1989) captures the same intuition, but abuses context-free grammars (which are primarily string-generating devices) as tree description formalisms. One difference between the two views is that regular tree languages are closed under intersection, which means that parse charts that are modeled as RTGs can be easily restricted by external constraints (see Koller and Thater (2010) for a related approach), whereas this is hard in the context-free view.

4.4 Decoding

We conclude this section by explaining how to solve the decoding problem. Suppose that in the scenario of Fig. 1c, we have obtained a parse chart $\mathcal{G}_{\vec{a}}$ for a tuple $\vec{a} = \langle a_1, \ldots, a_n \rangle$ of inputs, if necessary by intersecting the individual parse charts $\mathcal{G}_{a_i}$. Decoding means that we want to compute RTGs for the languages $h'_j(L(\mathcal{G}_{\vec{a}}))$ where $j \in [m]$. The actual output objects can be obtained from these languages of terms by evaluating the terms.

In the case where the homomorphisms h'_j are linear, we can once again exploit closure properties: Regular tree languages are closed under the application of linear homomorphisms (Comon et al., 2007), and therefore we can apply a standard algorithm to compute the output RTGs from the parse chart. In the case of non-linear homomorphisms, the output languages are not necessarily regular, so decoding exceeds the expressive capacity of our framework. However, linear output homomorphisms are frequent in practice; see e.g. the analysis of synchronous grammar formalisms in (Shieber, 2004; Shieber, 2006). Some of the workload of a non-linear homomorphism may also be carried by the output algebra, whose operations may copy or delete material freely (as long as the algebra remains regularly decomposable). Notice that non-linear *input* homomorphisms are covered by the algorithm in Fig. 4.

$\mathrm{S}_{0,7}$	$\rightarrow$	$r_1(\mathrm{NP}_{0,1}, \mathrm{VP}_{1,7})$	$\mathrm{NP}_{5,7}$	$\rightarrow$	$r_2(\mathrm{Det}_{5,6}, \mathrm{N}_{6,7})$
$\mathrm{VP}_{1,7}$	$\rightarrow$	$r_3(\mathrm{V}_{1,2}, \mathrm{NP}_{2,7})$	$\mathrm{NP}_{0,1}$	$\rightarrow$	r_7
$\mathrm{VP}_{1,7}$	$\rightarrow$	$r_5(\mathrm{VP}_{1,4}, \mathrm{PP}_{4,7})$	$\mathrm{V}_{1,2}$	$\rightarrow$	r_{11}
$\mathrm{NP}_{2,7}$	$\rightarrow$	$r_2(\mathrm{Det}_{2,3}, \mathrm{N}_{3,7})$	$\mathrm{Det}_{2,3}$	$\rightarrow$	r_8
$\mathrm{N}_{3,7}$	$\rightarrow$	$r_4(\mathrm{N}_{3,4}, \mathrm{PP}_{4,7})$	$\mathrm{N}_{3,4}$	$\rightarrow$	r_9
$\mathrm{VP}_{1,4}$	$\rightarrow$	$r_3(\mathrm{V}_{1,2}, \mathrm{NP}_{2,4})$	$\mathrm{P}_{4,5}$	$\rightarrow$	r_{12}
$\mathrm{NP}_{2,4}$	$\rightarrow$	$r_2(\mathrm{Det}_{2,3}, \mathrm{N}_{3,4})$	$\mathrm{Det}_{5,6}$	$\rightarrow$	r_8
$\mathrm{PP}_{4,7}$	$\rightarrow$	$r_6(\mathrm{P}_{4,5}, \mathrm{NP}_{5,7})$	$\mathrm{N}_{6,7}$	$\rightarrow$	r_{10}

Figure 5: A "parse chart" RTG for the sentence "Sue watches the man with the telescope".

5 Membership and Binarization

A *binarization* transforms an m-ary grammar into an equivalent binary one. Binarization is essential for achieving efficient recognition algorithms, in particular the usual $O(n^3)$ time algorithms for context-free grammars, and $O(n^6)$ time recognition of synchronous context-free grammars. In this section, we discuss binarization in terms of IRTGs.

5.1 Context-Free Grammars

We start with a discussion of parsing context-free grammars. Let $\mathbb{G} = (\mathcal{G}, (rb, T^*))$ be a CFG as we defined it in Section 3.3. We have shown in Section 4.2 that our generic parsing algorithm processes a sentence $w = w_1 \ldots w_n$ in time $O(n^{m+1})$, where m is the maximal number of nonterminal symbols in the right-hand side of the grammar. To achieve the familiar cubic time complexity, an algorithm needs to convert the grammar into a binary form, either explicitly (by converting it to Chomsky normal form) or implicitly (as in the case of the Earley algorithm, which binarizes on the fly).

Strictly speaking, no algorithm that works on the binarized grammar is a parsing algorithm in the sense of 'parsing' as we defined it above. Under our view of things, such an algorithm does not compute the set $\mathrm{parses}_{\mathbb{G}}(w)$ of derivation trees of w according to the grammar $\mathbb{G}$, but according to a second, binarized grammar $\mathbb{G}' = (\mathcal{G}', (rb, T^*))$. The binarization then takes the form of a function *bin* that transforms terms over the signature of the RTG $\mathcal{G}$ into terms over the binary signature of the RTG $\mathcal{G}'$. For a binarized grammar, we have $m = 2$, and so the parsing complexity is $O(n^3)$ plus whatever time it takes to compute $\mathbb{G}'$ from $\mathbb{G}$ and w. Standard binarization techniques of context-free grammars are linear in the size of the grammar.

Although binarization does not simplify parsing in the sense of this paper, it *does* simplify the membership problem of $\mathbb{G}$: Given a string

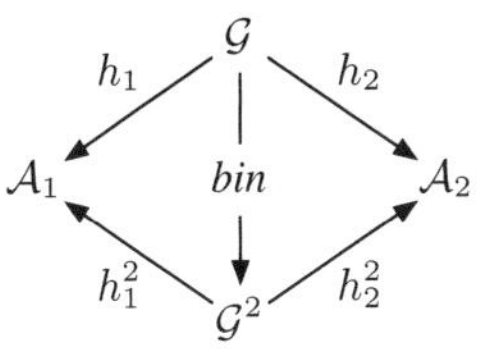

Figure 6: Binarization.

$w \in T^*$, is there some derivation tree $t \in \mathcal{G}$ such that $[\![h(t)]\!] = w$? Because $L(\mathbb{G}) = L(\mathbb{G}')$, this question can be decided by testing the emptiness of $\mathsf{parses}_{\mathbb{G}'}(w)$, without the need to compute $\mathsf{parses}_{\mathbb{G}}(w)$. Furthermore, the set $\mathsf{parses}_{\mathbb{G}'}(w)$ is useful not only for deciding membership in $L(\mathbb{G})$, but also for computing other quantities, such as inside probabilities of derivation trees of $\mathbb{G}$.

5.2 Synchronous Context-Free Grammars

Synchronous context-free grammars can be represented as IRTGs along the same lines as STSG grammars in Section 3.4. The resulting grammar $\mathbb{G} = (\mathcal{G}, (h_1, T_1^*), (h_2, T_2^*))$ consists of two 'context-free' interpretations of the RTG $\mathcal{G}$ into string algebras T_1^* and T_2^*; as above, the synchronization is ensured by requiring that related strings in T_1^* and T_2^* are interpretations of the same derivation tree $t \in L(\mathcal{G})$. As above, we can parse synchronously by parsing separately for the two interpretations and intersecting the results. This yields a parsing complexity for SCFG parsing of $O(n_1^{m+1} \cdot n_2^{m+1})$, where n_1 and n_2 are the lengths of the input strings and m is the rank of the RTG $\mathcal{G}$. Unlike in the monolingual case, this is now consistent with the result that the membership problem of SCFGs is NP-complete (Satta and Peserico, 2005).

The reason for the intractability of SCFG parsing is that SCFGs, in general, cannot be binarized. However, Huang et al. (2009) define the class of *binarizable* SCFGs, which can be brought into a weakly equivalent normal form in which all production rules are binary and the membership problem can be solved in time $O(n_1^3 \cdot n_2^3)$. The key property of binarizable SCFGs, in our terms, is that if r is any production rule pair of the SCFG, $h_1(r)$ and $h_2(r)$ can be chosen in such a way that they can be transformed into each other by locally swapping the subterms of a node. For instance, an SCFG rule pair $\langle A \to A_1\ A_2\ A_3\ A_4, B \to B_3\ B_4\ B_2\ B_1 \rangle$ can be represented by $h_1(r) = (x_1 \bullet x_2) \bullet (x_3 \bullet x_4)$ and $h_2(r) = (x_4 \bullet x_3) \bullet (x_1 \bullet x_2)$, and $h_2(r)$ can be obtained from $h_1(r)$ by swapping the children of the nodes ϵ and 2. In such a situation, we can binarize the rule $\langle A, B \rangle \to r(\langle A_1, B_1 \rangle, \ldots, \langle A_4, B_4 \rangle)$ in a way that follows the structure of $h_1(r)$, e.g.

$$\begin{aligned} \langle A, B \rangle &\to r_1^\epsilon(\langle A_1^r, B_1^r \rangle, \langle A_2^r, B_2^r \rangle) \\ \langle A_1^r, B_1^r \rangle &\to r_1^1(\langle A_1, B_1 \rangle, \langle A_2, B_2 \rangle) \\ \langle A_2^r, B_2^r \rangle &\to r_1^2(\langle A_3, B_3 \rangle, \langle A_4, B_4 \rangle) \end{aligned}$$

We can then encode the local rotations in two new left and right homomorphisms h_1^2 and h_2^2, i.e. $h_1^2(r_1^\epsilon) = h_1^2(r_1^1) = h_1^2(r_1^2) = h_2^2(r_1^2) = x_1 \bullet x_2$, $h_2^2(r_1^\epsilon) = h_2^2(r_1^1) = x_2 \bullet x_1$. To determine membership of some (a_1, a_2) in $L(\mathbb{G})$, we compute the pre-images of $D(a_1)$ and $D(a_2)$ under h_1^2 and h_1^2 and intersect them with the binarized version, $\mathcal{G}^2$, of $\mathcal{G}$. This can be done in time $O(n_1^3 \cdot n_2^3)$.

5.3 A Generalized View on Binarization

The common theme of both examples we have just discussed is that binarization, when it is available, allows us to solve the membership problem in less time than the parsing problem. A lower bound for the membership problem of a tuple $\langle a_1, \ldots, a_n \rangle$ of inputs is $O(|D(a_1)| \cdots |D(a_n)|)$, because the pre-images of the $D(a_i)$ grammars are at least as big as the grammars themselves, and the intersection algorithm computes the product of these. This means that a membership algorithm is optimal if it achieves this runtime.

As we have illustrated above, the parsing algorithm from Section 4 is not optimal for monolingual context-free membership, because the RTG $\mathcal{G}$ has a higher rank than $D(a)$, and therefore permits too many combinations of input spans into rules. The binarization constructions above indicate one way towards a generic optimal membership algorithm. Assume that we have algebras $\mathcal{A}_1, \ldots, \mathcal{A}_n$, all of which over signatures with maximum rank k, and an IRTG $\mathbb{G} = (\mathcal{G}, (h_1, \mathcal{A}_1), \ldots, (h_n, \mathcal{A}_n))$, where $\mathcal{G}$ is an RTG over some signature Σ. Assume further that we have some other signature Δ, of maximum rank k, and a homomorphism $\mathit{bin} : T_\Sigma \to T_\Delta$. We can obtain a RTG $\mathcal{G}^2$ with $L(\mathcal{G}^2) = \mathit{bin}(L(\mathcal{G}))$ as in the SCFG example above. Now assume that there are delabelings $h_i^2 : T_\Delta \to T_{\mathcal{A}_i}$ such that $h_i^2(L(\mathcal{G}^2)) = h_i(L(\mathcal{G}))$ for all $i \in [n]$ (see Fig. 6). Then we can decide membership of a tuple $\langle a_1, \ldots, a_n \rangle$ by intersecting $\mathcal{G}^2$ with all the $(h_i^2)^{-1}(L(D(a_i)))$. Because the h_i^2 are delabelings, computing the pre-images can be done in linear time; therefore this membership algorithm is optimal. Notice that if the result of the intersection is the RTG $\mathcal{H}$, then we can obtain parses$(a_1, \ldots, a_n) = bin^{-1}(L(\mathcal{H}))$; this is where the exponential blowup can happen.

The constructions in Sections 5.1 and 5.2 are both special cases of this generalized approach, which however also maintains a clear connection to the strong generative capacity. It is not obvious to us that it is necessary that the homomorphisms h_i^2 must be delabelings for the membership algorithm to be optimal. Exploring this landscape, which ties in with the very active current research on binarization, is an interesting direction for future research.

6 Discussion and Related Work

We conclude this paper by discussing how a number of different grammar formalisms from the literature relate to IRTGs, and use this discussion to highlight a number of features of our framework.

6.1 Tree-Adjoining Grammars

We have sketched in Section 3.4 how we can capture tree-substitution grammars by assuming an RTG for the language of derivation trees and a homomorphism into the tree algebra which spells out the derived trees; or alternatively, a homomorphism into the string algebra which computes the string yield. This construction can be generalized to tree-adjoining grammars (Joshi and Schabes, 1997).

Assume first that we are only interested in the string language of the TAG grammar. Unlike in TSG, the string yield of a derivation tree in TAG may be discontinuous. We can model this with an algebra whose elements are strings and pairs of strings, along with a number of different concatenation operators that represent possible ways in which these elements can be combined. (These are a subset of the operations considered by Gómez-Rodríguez et al. (2010).) We can then specify a homomorphism, essentially the binarization procedure that Earley-like TAG parsers do on the fly, that maps derivation trees into terms over this algebra. The TAG string algebra is regularly decomposable, and $D(a)$ can be computed in time $O(n^6)$.

Now consider the case of mapping derivation trees into derived trees. This cannot easily be done by a homomorphic interpretation in an ordinary tree algebra. One way to deal with this, which is taken by Shieber (2006), is to replace homomorphisms by a more complex class of tree translation functions called *embedded pushdown tree transducers*. A second approach is to interpret homomorphically into a more powerful algebra. This approach is taken by Maletti (2010), who uses an ordinary tree homomorphism to map a derivation tree t into a tree t' of 'building instructions' for a derived tree, and then applies a function $\cdot^E$ to execute these building instructions and build the TAG derived tree. Maletti's approach fits nicely into our framework if we assume an algebra in which the building instruction symbols are interpreted according to $\cdot^E$.

Synchronous tree-adjoining grammars (Shieber and Schabes, 1990) can be modeled simply as an RTG with two separate TAG interpretations. We can separately choose to interpret each side as trees or strings, as described in Section 3.4.

6.2 Weighted Tree Transducers

One influential approach to statistical syntax-based machine translation is to use *weighted transducers* to map parse trees for an input language to parse trees or strings of the output language (Graehl et al., 2008). Bottom-up tree transducers can be modeled in terms of *bimorphisms*, i.e. triples $(h_L, \mathcal{G}, h_R)$ of an RTG $\mathcal{G}$ and two tree homomorphisms h_L and h_R that map a derivation $t \in L(\mathcal{G})$ into the input tree $h_L(t)$ and the output tree $h_R(t)$ of the transducer (Arnold and Dauchet, 1982). Thus bottom-up transducers fit into the view of Fig. 1b. Although Graehl et al. use extended top-down transducers and not bottom-up transducers, a first inspection of their transducers leads us to believe that nothing hinges on this specific choice for their application. The exact situation bears further investigation.

Graehl et al.'s transducers further differ from the setup we have presented above in that they are *weighted*, i.e. each derivation step is associated with a numeric weight (e.g., a probability), and we can ask for the optimum derivation for a given input. Our framework can be straightforwardly extended to cover this case by assuming that the RTG $\mathcal{G}$ is a weighted RTG (wRTG, Knight and Graehl (2005)). The parsing algorithm from Section 4.1 generalizes to an algorithm for computing a weighted chart RTG, from which the best derivation can be extracted efficiently (Knight and Graehl, 2005). Similarly, the decoding algorithm from Section 4.4 can be used to compute a weighted RTG for the output terms, and an algorithm for EM training can be defined directly on the weighted charts. In general, every grammar formalism that can be captured as an IRTG has a canonical weighted variant in this way. As probabilistic grammar formalisms, these assume that all RTG rule applications are statistically independent. That is, the canonical probabilistic version of context-free grammars is PCFG, and the canonical probabilistic version of tree-adjoining grammar is PTAG (Resnik, 1992).

A final point is that Graehl et al. invest considerable effort into defining different versions of their transducer training algorithms for the tree-to-tree and tree-to-string translation cases. The core of their paper, in our terms, is to define synchronous parsing algorithms to compute an RTG of derivation trees for (tree, tree) and (tree, string) input pairs. In their setup, these two cases are formally completely different objects, and they define two separate algorithms for these problems. Our approach is more modular: The training and parsing algorithms can be fully generic, and all that needs to be changed to switch between tree-to-tree and tree-to-string is to replace the algebra and homomorphism on one side, as in Section 3.4. In fact, we are not limited to interpreting derivation trees into strings or trees; by interpreting into the appropriate algebras, we can also describe languages of graphs (Eaton et al., 2007), pictures (Drewes, 2006), 3D models (Bokeloh et al., 2010), and other objects with a suitable algebraic structure.

6.3 Generalized Context-Free Grammars

Finally, the view we advocate here embraces a tradition of grammar formalisms going back to generalized context-free grammar (GCFG, Pollard (1984)), which follows itself research in theoretical computer science (Mezei and Wright, 1967; Goguen et al., 1977). A GCFG grammar can be seen as an RTG over a signature Σ whose trees are evaluated as terms of some Σ-algebra $\mathcal{A}$. This is a special case of an IRTG, in which the homomorphism is simply the identical function on T_Σ, and the algebra is $\mathcal{A}$. In fact, we could have equivalently defined an IRTG as an RTG whose trees are interpreted in multiple Σ-algebras; the mediating homomorphisms do not add expressive power. We go beyond GCFG in three ways. First, the fact that we map the trees described by the RTG into terms of other algebras using different homomorphisms means that we can choose the signatures of these algebras and the RTG freely; in particular, we can reuse common algebras such as T^* for many different RTGs and homomorphisms. This is especially important in relation to the second advance, which is that we offer a generic parsing algorithm for arbitrary regularly decomposable algebras; because the algebras and RTGs are modular, we can reuse algorithms for computing $D(a)$ even when we change the homomorphism. Finally, we offer a more transparent view on synchronous grammars, which separates the different dimensions clearly.

An important special case of GCFG is that of *linear context-free rewrite systems* (LCFRS, Vijay-Shanker et al. (1987)). LCFRSs are essentially GCFGs with a "yield" homomorphism that maps objects of $\mathcal{A}$ to strings or tuples of strings. Therefore every grammar formalism that can be seen as an LCFRS, including certain dependency grammar formalisms (Kuhlmann, 2010), can be phrased as string-generating IRTGs. One particular advantage that our framework has over LCFRS is that we do not need to impose a bound on the length of the string tuples. This makes it possible to model formalisms such as combinatory categorial grammar (Steedman, 2001), which may be arbitrarily discontinuous (Koller and Kuhlmann, 2009).

7 Conclusion

In this paper, we have defined *interpreted RTGs*, a grammar formalism that generalizes over a wide range of existing formalisms, including various synchronous grammars, tree transducers, and LCFRS. We presented a generic parser for IRTGs; to apply it to a new type of IRTG, we merely need to define how to compute decomposition grammars $D(a)$ for input objects a. This makes it easy to define synchronous grammars that are heterogeneous both in the grammar formalism and in the objects that each of its dimensions describes.

The purpose of our paper was to pull together a variety of existing research and explain it in a new, unified light: We have not shown how to do something that was not possible before, only how to do it in a uniform way. Nonetheless, we expect that future work will benefit from the clarified formal setup we have proposed here. In particular, we believe that the view of parse charts as RTGs may lead to future algorithms which exploit their closure under intersection, e.g. to reduce syntactic ambiguity (Schuler, 2001).

Acknowledgments

We thank the reviewers for their helpful comments, as well as all the colleagues with whom we have discussed this work—especially Martin Kay for a discussion about the relationship to chart parsing.

References

A. Arnold and M. Dauchet. 1982. Morphismes et bimorphismes d'arbres. *Theoretical Computer Science*, 20(1):33–93.

Sylvie Billot and Bernard Lang. 1989. The structure of shared forests in ambiguous parsing. In *Proceedings of the 27th ACL*.

M. Bokeloh, M. Wand, and H.-P. Seidel. 2010. A connection between partial symmetry and inverse procedural modeling. In *Proceedings of SIGGRAPH*.

David Chiang. 2007. Hierarchical phrase-based translation. *Computational Linguistics*, 33(2):201–228.

H. Comon, M. Dauchet, R. Gilleron, C. Löding, F. Jacquemard, D. Lugiez, S. Tison, and M. Tommasi. 2007. Tree automata techniques and applications. Available on: `http://www.grappa.univ-lille3.fr/tata`.

Frank Drewes. 2006. *Grammatical picture generation: a tree-based approach*. EATCS. Springer.

Nancy Eaton, Zoltán Füredi, Alexandr V. Kostochka, and Jozef Skokan. 2007. Tree representations of graphs. *European Journal of Combinatorics*, 28(4):1087–1098.

Jason Eisner. 2003. Learning non-isomorphic tree mappings for machine translation. In *Proceedings of the 41st ACL*.

Ferenc Gécseg and Magnus Steinby. 1997. Tree languages. In Grzegorz Rozenberg and Arto Salomaa, editors, *Handbook of Formal Languages*, volume 3, pages 1–68. Springer.

Joseph A. Goguen, James W. Thatcher, Eric G. Wagner, and Jesse B. Wright. 1977. Initial algebra semantics and continuous algebras. *Journal of the Association for Computing Machinery*, 24(1):68–95.

Carlos Gómez-Rodríguez, Marco Kuhlmann, and Giorgio Satta. 2010. Efficient parsing of well-nested linear context-free rewriting systems. In *Proceedings of NAACL-HLT*.

Jonathan Graehl, Kevin Knight, and Jonathan May. 2008. Training tree transducers. *Computational Linguistics*, 34(4):391–427.

Liang Huang, Hao Zhang, Daniel Gildea, and Kevin Knight. 2009. Binarization of synchronous context-free grammars. *Computational Linguistics*, 35(4):559–595.

Aravind K. Joshi and Yves Schabes. 1997. Tree-Adjoining Grammars. In Grzegorz Rozenberg and Arto Salomaa, editors, *Handbook of Formal Languages*, volume 3, pages 69–123. Springer.

Kevin Knight and Jonathan Graehl. 2005. An overview of probabilistic tree transducers for natural language processing. In *Computational linguistics and intelligent text processing*, pages 1–24. Springer.

Alexander Koller and Marco Kuhlmann. 2009. Dependency trees and the strong generative capacity of CCG. In *Proceedings of the 12th EACL*.

Alexander Koller and Stefan Thater. 2010. Computing weakest readings. In *Proceedings of the 48th ACL*.

Marco Kuhlmann. 2010. *Dependency structures and lexicalized grammars: An algebraic approach*, volume 6270 of *Lecture Notes in Computer Science*. Springer.

P. M. Lewis and R. E. Stearns. 1968. Syntax-directed transduction. *Journal of the ACM*, 15(3):465–488.

Andreas Maletti. 2010. A tree transducer model for synchronous tree-adjoining grammars. In *Proceedings of the 48th ACL*.

David McAllester. 2002. On the complexity analysis of static analyses. *Journal of the Association for Computing Machinery*, 49(4):512–537.

Jorge E. Mezei and Jesse B. Wright. 1967. Algebraic automata and context-free sets. *Information and Control*, 11(1–2):3–29.

Rebecca Nesson and Stuart M. Shieber. 2006. Simpler TAG semantics through synchronization. In *Proceedings of the 11th Conference on Formal Grammar*.

Carl J. Pollard. 1984. *Generalized Phrase Structure Grammars, Head Grammars, and Natural Language*. Ph.D. thesis, Stanford University.

Owen Rambow and Giorgio Satta. 1996. Synchronous models of language. In *Proceedings of the 34th ACL*.

Philip Resnik. 1992. Probabilistic tree-adjoining grammar as a framework for statistical natural language processing. In *Proceedings of COLING*.

Giorgio Satta and Enoch Peserico. 2005. Some computational complexity results for synchronous context-free grammars. In *Proceedings of Human Language Technology Conference and Conference on Empirical Methods in Natural Language Processing (HLT/EMNLP)*.

Sylvain Schmitz and Joseph Le Roux. 2008. Feature unification in tag derivation trees. In *Proceedings of the 9th TAG+ Workshop*.

William Schuler. 2001. Computational properties of environment-based disambiguation. In *Proceedings of the 39th ACL*.

Stuart Shieber and Yves Schabes. 1990. Synchronous tree-adjoining grammars. In *Proceedings of the 13th COLING*.

Stuart Shieber. 1994. Restricting the weak generative capacity of synchronous tree-adjoining grammars. *Computational Intelligence*, 10(4):371–386.

Stuart M. Shieber. 2004. Synchronous grammars as tree transducers. In *Proceedings of the Seventh International Workshop on Tree Adjoining Grammar and Related Formalisms (TAG+ 7)*.

Stuart M. Shieber. 2006. Unifying synchronous tree-adjoining grammars and tree transducers via bimorphisms. In *Proceedings of the 11th EACL*.

Mark Steedman. 2001. *The Syntactic Process*. MIT Press.

K. Vijay-Shanker, David J. Weir, and Aravind K. Joshi. 1987. Characterizing structural descriptions produced by various grammatical formalisms. In *Proceedings of the 25th ACL*.

Tree Parsing with Synchronous Tree-Adjoining Grammars

Matthias Büchse [a] and **Mark-Jan Nederhof** [b] and **Heiko Vogler** [a]

[a] Department of Computer Science
Technische Universität Dresden
D-01062 Dresden, Germany

[b] School of Computer Science
University of St Andrews
North Haugh, St Andrews, KY16 9SX, UK

Abstract

Restricting the input or the output of a grammar-induced translation to a given set of trees plays an important role in statistical machine translation. The problem for practical systems is to find a compact (and in particular, finite) representation of said restriction. For the class of synchronous tree-adjoining grammars, partial solutions to this problem have been described, some being restricted to the unweighted case, some to the monolingual case. We introduce a formulation of this class of grammars which is effectively closed under input and output restrictions to regular tree languages, i.e., the restricted translations can again be represented by grammars. Moreover, we present an algorithm that constructs these grammars for input and output restriction, which is inspired by Earley's algorithm.

1 Introduction

Many recent systems for statistical machine translation (SMT) (Lopez, 2008) use some grammar at their core. Chiang (2007), e. g., uses synchronous context-free grammars (SCFG) that derive pairs of translationally equivalent sentences. Huang et al. (2006) use tree-to-string transducers (called xRLNS) that describe pairs of the form (phrase-structure tree, string). Other systems, such as (Eisner, 2003; Zhang et al., 2008; Nesson et al., 2006; DeNeefe and Knight, 2009), use variants of synchronous tree-adjoining grammars (STAGs) (Abeille et al., 1990; Joshi and Schabes, 1997) that derive pairs of dependency or phrase-structure trees. Common variants of STAGs are synchronous tree-substitution grammars (STSGs) and synchronous tree-insertion grammars (STIGs).

For grammar-based systems, a variety of tasks can be described using the general concepts of *input product* and *output product* (Maletti, 2010b). Roughly speaking, these products restrict the translation described by the grammar to a given tree or string language on the input or output side. For practical purposes, the derivations of the restricted translation are represented in a compact way, e.g., using a weighted regular tree grammar (WRTG) (Alexandrakis and Bozapalidis, 1987). The process of obtaining this representation is called *tree parsing* or *string parsing*, depending on the type of restriction. We illustrate the importance of input and output product by considering its role in three essential tasks of SMT.

Grammar Estimation. After the rules of the grammar have been obtained from a sample of translation pairs (rule extraction), the probabilities of the rules need to be determined. To this end, two approaches have been employed.

Some systems such as those by Chiang (2007) and DeNeefe and Knight (2009) hypothesize a canonical derivation for each translation pair, and apply relative-frequency estimation to the resulting derivations to obtain rule probabilities. While this procedure is computationally inexpensive, it only maximizes the likelihood of the training data under the assumption that the canonical derivations are the true ones.

Other systems such as those by Eisner (2003), Nesson et al. (2006), and Graehl et al. (2008) use a variant of the EM algorithm (Dempster et al., 1977) called Inside-Outside. This algorithm requires that the set of derivations for a given translation pair be representable by a WRTG. In most cases, this can be computed by restricting the grammar at hand to the given translation pair, that is, by applying input and output product. Note that the pair can contain strings or trees or even some combination thereof.

Feature Weight Estimation. In the systems mentioned at the beginning of this section, a probability distribution of the form $p(e, d \mid f)$ is chosen from a log-linear model (Berger et al., 1996; Och and Ney, 2002), where e, d, and f are an English sentence, a derivation, and a foreign sentence, respectively. Such a distribution combines information from different sources, called features, such as the grammar or a probability distribution over English sentences. The features are represented by real-valued functions $h_i(e, d, f)$. For said combination, each feature gets a weight λ_i.

The feature weights are usually estimated using minimum-error-rate training (Och, 2003). For this it is necessary to compute, for a given f, the set D_f of n highest ranking derivations generating f on the foreign side. Roughly speaking, this set can be computed by applying the input product with f, and then applying the n-best algorithm (Huang and Chiang, 2005; Büchse et al., 2010). We note that, while f is usually a string, it can in some circumstances be a phrase-structure tree, as in (Huang et al., 2006).

Decoding. The actual translation, or decoding, problem amounts to finding, for a given f,

$$\hat{e} = \mathrm{argmax}_e \sum_d \prod_i h_i(e, d, f)^{\lambda_i} .$$

Even for the simplest grammars, this problem is NP hard (Casacuberta and de la Higuera, 2000). As a result, SMT systems use approximations such as crunching or variational decoding (Li et al., 2009). Here we focus on the former, which amounts to restricting the sum in the equation to the set D_f. Since this set is finite, the sum is then zero for almost all e, which makes the computation of $\hat{e}$ feasible. As mentioned before, the input product can be used to compute D_f.

As we have seen in these tasks, tree parsing is employed in recent SMT systems. Table 1 lists five relevant contributions in this area. These contributions can be classified according to a number of characteristics indicated by the column headings. One of these characteristics is the abstraction level (AL), which we categorize as follows:

1. language-theoretic result,
2. construction,
3. algorithm,
4. implementation.

The first three entries of Tab. 1 deal with contributions that are restricted to tree substitution. Huang et al. (2006) show an algorithm for computing the best derivation of the input product of an xRLNS with a single tree. Graehl et al. (2008) present an algorithm for computing the derivation WRTG for the input and output product of a tree-to-tree transducer (called xRLN) with a single pair of trees. Eisner (2003) describes an algorithm for computing the set of derivations for the input and output product of an STSG with a single pair of trees.

We note that the grammar classes covered so far are strictly less powerful than STAGs. This is due to the fact that STAGs additionally permit an operation called adjoining. As Nesson et al. (2006) and DeNeefe and Knight (2009) point out, the adjoining operation has a well-founded linguistic motivation, and permitting it improves translation quality.

There are two papers approaching the problem of tree parsing for STAGs, given in the fourth and fifth entries of the table. These papers establish closure properties, that is, their constructions yield a grammar of the same type as the original grammar. Since the resulting grammars are compact representations of the derivations of the input product or output product, respectively, these constructions constitute tree parsing.

Nederhof (2009) shows that weighted linear index grammars (WLIGs) are closed under weighted intersection with tree languages generated by WRTGs. WLIGs derive phrase-structure trees, and they are equivalent to tree-adjoining grammars (TAGs). His construction can be extended to some kind of synchronous WLIG without problems. However, synchronization interacts with the height restriction present for WLIG rules in a way that makes synchronous WLIGs less powerful than STAGs.

Maletti (2010a) uses an alternative representation of STAG, namely as extended tree transducers (XTT) with explicit substitution. In this framework, adjoining is encoded into the phrase-structure trees by introducing special symbols, to be evaluated in a separate step. He indicates that his representation of STAG is closed under input and output product with regular tree languages by providing a corresponding construction. However, in his setting, both the translations and the languages are unweighted.

The advantage of closure properties of the above kind is that they allow cascades of input and output products to be constructed in a uniform way, as well as applying further operations on the grammars, such as projection. Ultimately, SMT tasks may be described in this framework, as witnessed by toolboxes that exist for WFSTs (Mohri, 2009) and XTTs (May and Knight, 2006).

paper	AL	grammar	characteristics restriction type	result
(Huang et al., 2006)	3–4	xRLNS	tree	best derivation
(Graehl et al., 2008)	3–4	xRLN	(tree, tree)	derivation WRTG
(Eisner, 2003)	3–4	STSG	(tree, tree)	derivations
(Nederhof, 2009)	2	WLIG	regular tree language	WLIG
(Maletti, 2010a)	2	XTT	regular tree language	XTT
(this paper)	1–3	WSTAG	regular tree language	WSTAG

Table 1: Tree-parsing algorithms published so far in comparison with this paper.

In this paper, we propose a weighted formulation of STAGs which is closed under input and output product with WRTGs, and we present a corresponding tree-parsing algorithm. This paper is organized as follows.

In Sec. 2, we introduce our formulation of STAGs, which is called weighted synchronous tree-adjoining grammar (WSTAG). The major difference with respect to the classical STAGs is two-fold: (i) we use states and (ii) we encode substitution and adjoining sites as variables in the tree. The states make intersection with regular properties possible (without the need for relabeling as in (Shieber, 2004) and (Maletti, 2010a)). In addition, they permit implementing all features of conventional STAG/STIG, such as potential adjoining and left/right adjoining. The variables are used for synchronization of the input and output sides.

In Sec. 3, we show that WSTAGs are closed under input and output product with tree languages generated by WRTGs (cf. Theorem 1). We do this by means of a direct construction (cf. Sec. 4). Our construction is based on the standard technique for composing two top-down tree transducers (cf. page 195 of (Baker, 1979)). This technique has been extended in Theorem 4.12 of (Engelfriet and Vogler, 1985) to the composition of a macro tree transducer and a top-down tree transducer (also cf. (Rounds, 1970)); in fact, our direct construction is very similar to the latter one.

Section 5 contains Algorithm 1, which computes our construction (modulo reduction). It is inspired by a variant of Earley's algorithm (Earley, 1970; Graham et al., 1980). In this way we avoid computation of a certain portion of useless rules, and we ensure that the complexity is linear in the size of the input WSTAG. The algorithm is presented in the framework of deductive parsing (Goodman, 1999; Nederhof, 2003).

In Sections 6 and 7, we discuss the correctness of our algorithm and its complexity, respectively.

2 Formalisms

We denote the set of all unranked, ordered, labeled trees over some alphabet Σ by U_Σ. We represent trees as well-formed expressions, e.g., $\mathrm{S}(\mathrm{Adv}(\mathrm{yesterday}), *)$; a graphical representation of this tree occurs at the very bottom of Fig. 1(a). Sometimes we assign a *rank* (or: *arity*) $k \in \mathbb{N}$ to a symbol $\sigma \in \Sigma$ and then require that every σ-labeled position of a tree has exactly k successors. We denote the set of all positions of a tree $t \in U_\Sigma$ by $\mathrm{pos}(t)$. A position is represented as a finite sequence of natural numbers (Gorn notation). If $w \in \mathrm{pos}(t)$, then $t(w)$ denotes the label of t at w, and $\mathrm{rk}_t(w)$ denotes the number of successors of w.

2.1 Weighted Regular Tree Grammars

A *weighted regular tree grammar* (for short: WRTG) is a tuple $H = (P, \Sigma, r_0, R, p)$ where P is a finite set of *states*, Σ is an alphabet, $r_0 \in P$ is the *initial state*, and R is a finite set of *rules*; every rule ρ has the form $r \to \sigma(r_1, \ldots, r_k)$ where $k \in \mathbb{N}$, $r, r_1, \ldots, r_k \in P$, and $\sigma \in \Sigma$ (note that $\sigma(r_1, \ldots, r_k)$ is a tree over $\Sigma \cup P$); finally, $p : R \to \mathbb{R}_{\geq 0}$ is the *weight assignment*, where $\mathbb{R}_{\geq 0}$ is the set of all non-negative real numbers.

A *run (of H)* is a tree $\kappa \in U_P$. Let $t \in U_\Sigma$ and let κ be a run. We say that κ is a *run on t* if $\mathrm{pos}(\kappa) = \mathrm{pos}(t)$ and for every position $w \in \mathrm{pos}(t)$ the rule $\rho(\kappa, t, w)$ is in R, where $\rho(\kappa, t, w)$ is defined as

$$\kappa(w) \to t(w)\Big(\kappa(w1), \ldots, \kappa(w\,\mathrm{rk}_t(w))\Big).$$

The *weight of a run κ on t* is the value $\mathrm{wt}(\kappa, t) \in \mathbb{R}_{\geq 0}$ defined by

$$\mathrm{wt}(\kappa, t) = \prod_{w \in \mathrm{pos}(t)} p(\rho(\kappa, t, w)) \ .$$

The *weighted tree language generated by* WRTG H is the mapping $L(H) : U_\Sigma \to \mathbb{R}_{\geq 0}$

defined by

$$L(H)(t) = \sum_{\substack{\kappa \text{ run on } t \\ \kappa(\varepsilon)=r_0}} \mathrm{wt}(\kappa, t) \ .$$

The *support* $\mathrm{supp}(L(H))$ of $L(H)$ is the set of all $t \in U_\Sigma$ such that $L(H)(t) \neq 0$.

2.2 Weighted Tree-Adjoining Grammars

In our formulation of STAGs we use states (cf. Fülöp et al. (2010) for the use of states in STSGs). The states make intersection with devices of finite-state power possible. More specifically, they allow for a product construction as is common in automata theory (cf. Sec. 4). Moreover, they permit implementing all features of conventional STAG/STIG, such as potential adjoining and left/right adjoining. In contrast to the traditional setting, substitution sites and adjoining sites are formalized as explicit positions in the right-hand sides of rules; these positions are labeled by variables. For this, we assume that $x_1, x_2, \dots$ and $z_1, z_2, \dots$ are two fixed infinite and disjoint sequences of pairwise distinct variables. We assume that every x_j has rank 0 and every z_j has rank 1. We use $x_1, x_2, \dots$ to denote substitution sites and $z_1, z_2, \dots$ to denote adjoining sites. The foot node is labeled by an additional nullary symbol $*$. The input and output components are synchronized via these sites and the corresponding states.

A *weighted synchronous tree-adjoining grammar with states* (for short: WSTAG) is a tuple $G = (Q, F, \Sigma, q_0, R, p)$ where

- Q and F are disjoint finite sets (of *nullary* and *unary states*, respectively, each denoted by variants of q and f, respectively),
- Σ is an alphabet (*terminal alphabet*),
- q_0 is a nullary state (*initial state*),
- R is a finite set of *rules* of either of the following forms:

$$q \to \langle \zeta\zeta', q_1 \cdots q_m, f_1 \cdots f_l \rangle \qquad (\alpha)$$
$$f(*) \to \langle \zeta\zeta', q_1 \cdots q_m, f_1 \cdots f_l \rangle \qquad (\beta)$$

  where ζ and ζ' are trees over $\Sigma \cup V$ and

$$V = \{x_1, \dots, x_m, z_1, \dots, z_l\} \qquad (\alpha)$$
$$V = \{x_1, \dots, x_m, z_1, \dots, z_l, *\} \qquad (\beta)$$

  and every element of V occurs exactly once in each of ζ and ζ', and
- $p : R \to \mathbb{R}_{\geq 0}$ is the *weight assignment*.

Rules of the forms (α) and (β) are called (m, l)-rules; ζ and ζ' are called the *input tree* and the *output tree* of the rule, respectively. For fixed q and f, the sets of all rules of the form (α) and (β) are denoted by R_q and R_f, resp. Figure 1(a) shows an example of a WSTAG. In the following, let $G = (Q, F, \Sigma, q_0, R, p)$ be a WSTAG.

We define the semantics in terms of bimorphisms (Shieber, 2006). For this we define a WRTG $\mathcal{H}_G$ that generates the weighted tree language of derivation trees of G, and two tree homomorphisms h_1 and h_2 that retrieve from a derivation tree the derived input tree and output tree, respectively.

The *derivation tree WRTG of G* is the WRTG $\mathcal{H}_G = (Q \cup F, R, q_0, R', p')$ where

- we assign the rank $m + l$ to every (m, l)-rule,
- R' is the set of all rules $D(\rho)$ with $\rho \in R$ and
  - if ρ is of the form (α), then $D(\rho) = q \to \rho(q_1, \dots, q_m, f_1, \dots, f_l)$,
  - if ρ is of the form (β), then $D(\rho) = f \to \rho(q_1, \dots, q_m, f_1, \dots, f_l)$,
- and $p'(D(\rho)) = p(\rho)$.

Recall that $L(\mathcal{H}_G)$ is the weighted tree language generated by $\mathcal{H}_G$. We call the trees in $\mathrm{supp}(L(\mathcal{H}_G))$ *derivation trees*. For instance, with the WSTAG of Fig. 1(a), the tree $d_{\mathrm{ex}} = \rho_1(\rho_2, \rho_3(\rho_4), \rho_5)$ is a derivation tree of the derived trees shown in Fig. 1(b) and Fig. 1(c).

Formally, the derived trees are obtained by the tree homomorphisms h_1 and h_2, each of type $\mathrm{supp}(L(\mathcal{H}_G)) \to U_\Sigma$, which we define inductively as follows:

$$h_1(\rho(d_1, \dots, d_m, d'_1, \dots, d'_l)) = \zeta[\vec{x}/h_1(\vec{d})][\![\vec{z}/h_1(\vec{d'})]\!]$$

where $[\vec{x}/h_1(\vec{d})]$ abbreviates the m first-order substitutions $[x_1/h_1(d_1)] \dots [x_m/h_1(d_m)]$, and $[\![\vec{z}/h_1(\vec{d'})]\!]$ abbreviates the l second-order substitutions $[\![z_1/h_1(d'_1)]\!] \dots [\![z_l/h_1(d'_l)]\!]$. The first-order substitution $[x/s]$ replaces every occurrence of x by s, and the second-order substitution $[\![z/s]\!]$ is defined inductively in Fig. 2. The tree homomorphism h_2 is defined in the same way as h_1, but with ζ' instead of ζ. We call d a derivation tree of the pair $(h_1(d), h_2(d))$.

In continuation of our running example, we calculate $h_1(d_{\mathrm{ex}})$, where we use [1], [2], and $[\![3]\!]$ as abbreviations for the substitutions $[x_1/h_1(\rho_2)]$,

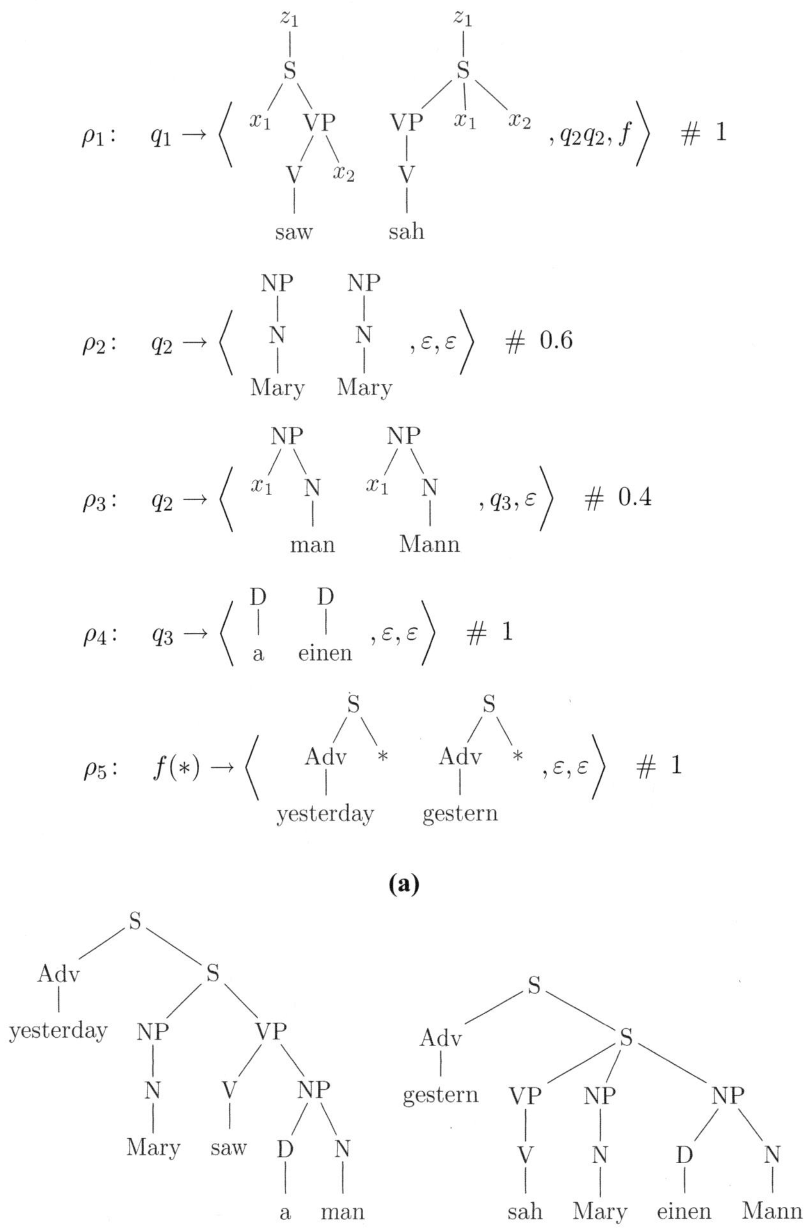

Figure 1: (a) Example of a WSTAG (following (Joshi and Schabes, 1997)), (b) input tree, and (c) output tree.

$$\sigma(\zeta_1, \ldots, \zeta_k)[\![z/s]\!] = \sigma(\zeta_1[\![z/s]\!], \ldots, \zeta_k[\![z/s]\!]) \qquad x_j[\![z/s]\!] = x_j \qquad *[\![z/s]\!] = *$$

$$z_j(\zeta)[\![z/s]\!] = \begin{cases} s' & \text{if } z = z_j \text{ and } s' \text{ is obtained from } s \text{ by replacing the } * \text{ by } \zeta \\ z_j(\zeta[\![z/s]\!]) & \text{otherwise.} \end{cases}$$

Figure 2: Second-order substitution $[\![z/s]\!]$, where $\sigma \in \Sigma$, x_j is a nullary variable, and z_j is a unary variable.

$[x_2/h_1(\rho_3(\rho_4))]$, and $[\![z_1/h_1(\rho_5)]\!]$, respectively:

$$\begin{aligned}
&h_1(d_{\text{ex}}) \\
&= z_1(\text{S}(x_1, \text{VP}(\text{V}(\text{saw}), x_2)))[1][2][\![3]\!] \\
&= z_1(\text{S}(h_1(\rho_2), \text{VP}(\text{V}(\text{saw}), x_2)))[2][\![3]\!] \\
&= z_1(\underbrace{\text{S}(h_1(\rho_2), \text{VP}(\text{V}(\text{saw}), h_1(\rho_3(\rho_4)))))}_{\xi})[\![3]\!] \\
&= \text{S}(\text{Adv}(\text{yesterday}), \xi) ,
\end{aligned}$$

which evaluates to the tree of Fig. 1(b).

The *weighted tree transformation specified by WSTAG G* is $T(G) : U_\Sigma \times U_\Sigma \to \mathbb{R}_{\geq 0}$ defined by

$$T(G)(s,t) = \sum_{d \text{ derivation tree of } (s,t)} L(\mathcal{H}_G)(d).$$

We note that for every derivation tree d there is a unique run κ_d of $\mathcal{H}_G$ on d: $\kappa_d(w)$ is the state occurring in the left-hand side of the rule $d(w)$, for every $w \in \text{pos}(d)$.

As an example, we reconsider d_{ex}, which is a derivation tree of the translation pair (s, t), given by Fig. 1(b) and Fig. 1(c). Then we have $L(\mathcal{H}_G)(d_{\text{ex}}) = \text{wt}(\kappa_{d_{\text{ex}}}, d_{\text{ex}}) = \prod_{i=1}^{5} p(\rho_i) = 0.24$. Since d_{ex} is the only derivation tree of (s,t), we have that $T(G)(s,t) = 0.24$.

STSGs as defined in Fülöp et al. (2010) are WSTAGs which only have nullary states. Also classical STAGs (Abeille et al., 1990; Shieber and Schabes, 1990) and STIGs (Nesson et al., 2005; Nesson et al., 2006; DeNeefe and Knight, 2009) can be viewed as particular WSTAGs. In particular, potential adjoining as it occurs in classical STAGs can be simulated, as the following excerpt of a WSTAG shall illustrate:

$$\begin{aligned}
q &\to \langle z_1(A(x_1))\,\zeta', q', f\rangle \\
f(*) &\to \langle *\,*, \varepsilon, \varepsilon\rangle \\
f(*) &\to \langle z_1(*)\, z_1(*), \varepsilon, f'\rangle
\end{aligned}$$

Moreover, the left-/right adjoining restriction of STIGs can be handled by keeping appropriate finite information in the states.

3 Closure Result

First we define the input product and output product of a weighted tree transformation $T: U_\Sigma \times U_\Sigma \to \mathbb{R}_{\geq 0}$ and a weighted tree language $L: U_\Sigma \to \mathbb{R}_{\geq 0}$. Formally, the *input product of T and L* is the weighted tree transformation $L \lhd T: U_\Sigma \times U_\Sigma \to \mathbb{R}_{\geq 0}$ such that

$$(L \lhd T)(s,t) = L(s) \cdot T(s,t) \ .$$

Similarly, we define the *output product of T and L* as $T \rhd L: U_\Sigma \times U_\Sigma \to \mathbb{R}_{\geq 0}$ such that

$$(T \rhd L)(s,t) = T(s,t) \cdot L(t) \ .$$

We note that the input product and output product can be considered as a kind of composition of weighted relations by viewing L as mapping $L' : U_\Sigma \times U_\Sigma \to \mathbb{R}_{\geq 0}$ with $L'(s,t) = L(s)$ if $s = t$, and $L'(s,t) = 0$ otherwise.

Here we prove that WSTAGs are closed under input product (and output product) with WRTGs.

Theorem 1 *For every WSTAG G and WRTG H there are WSTAGs $H \lhd G$ and $G \rhd H$ such that*

- $T(H \lhd G) = L(H) \lhd T(G)$ *and*
- $T(G \rhd H) = T(G) \rhd L(H)$.

We will only prove the closure under input product, because the proof for the output product is similar.

For the unweighted case, the closure result follows from classical results. The unweighted case is obtained if we replace the algebra in Sec. 2 by another one: $\mathbb{R}_{\geq 0}$ is replaced by the set $\mathbb{B} = \{\mathit{true}, \mathit{false}\}$ and the operations $+$ and $\cdot$ are replaced by disjunction and conjunction, respectively. In other words, we replace the inside semiring $(\mathbb{R}_{\geq 0}, +, \cdot, 0, 1)$ by the Boolean semiring $(\mathbb{B}, \vee, \wedge, \mathit{false}, \mathit{true})$. Then $L(H)$ and $T(G)$ become sets $L(H) \subseteq U_\Sigma$ and $T(G) \subseteq U_\Sigma \times U_\Sigma$. In this setting and using $h : \text{supp}(L(\mathcal{H}_G)) \to U_\Sigma \times U_\Sigma$ defined by $h(d) = (h_1(d), h_2(d))$, we have that

$$L(H) \lhd T(G) = h(h_1^{-1}(L(H))) \ .$$

Note that $h_1^{-1}(L(H)) \subseteq \text{supp}(L(\mathcal{H}_G))$. Now we observe that h_1 can be computed by a particular macro tree transducer (Engelfriet, 1980; Courcelle and Franchi-Zannettacci, 1982); we note that in (Shieber, 2006) such macro tree transducers were called embedded tree transducers.

Engelfriet and Vogler (1985) proved in Theorem 7.4 that the class of regular tree languages is closed under the inverse of macro tree transducers. Thus, since $L(H)$ is a regular tree language, also $h_1^{-1}(L(H))$ is a regular tree language. Thus $L(H) \lhd T(G) = h(L(\bar{H}))$ for some regular tree grammar $\bar{H}$. Now it is easy to construct (using h_1 and h_2) a STAG $H \lhd G$ from $\bar{H}$ such that $T(H \lhd G) = h(L(\bar{H}))$.

For the weighted case, we give a direct construction in the next section.

4 Direct Construction

We now provide our construction of the WSTAG $H \lhd G$ in Theorem 1 where $G = (Q, F, \Sigma, q_0, R, p)$ is a WSTAG and $H = (P, \Sigma, r_0, R_H, p_H)$ is a WRTG.

First we define an enrichment of H that can generate trees like ζ as they occur in rules of G, that is, including variables x_j, z_j, and possibly $*$. To this end, let $\rho \in R$. A *(state) assignment for* ρ is a mapping θ that maps each nullary variable in ρ to a state of H and each unary variable in ρ to a pair of such states. Likewise, if $*$ occurs in ζ, then θ maps it to a state of H. For every $r \in P$ and assignment θ, we define the WRTG $H(r, \theta)$, which is obtained from H by using r as initial state and adding the following rules with weight 1 for every $r, r' \in P$:

$$
\begin{aligned}
&r \to x_j && \text{if } \theta(x_j) = r, \\
&r \to z_j(r') && \text{if } \theta(z_j) = (r, r'), \text{ and} \\
&r \to * && \text{if } \theta(*) = r\,.
\end{aligned}
$$

Roughly speaking, for every rule $\rho \in R$, we let $H(r, \theta)$ "run" on the input tree ζ of ρ. Formally, we define the *product WSTAG of H and G* as the WSTAG $H \lhd G =$

$$(Q \times P, F \times (P \times P), \Sigma, (q_0, r_0), R', p')$$

as follows. Let $\rho \in R$, $r \in P$, and θ an assignment for ρ. Then, depending on whether ρ has the form (α) or (β), the rule

$$(q, r) \to \langle \zeta\zeta', u, v\rangle \qquad (\alpha)$$
$$(f, (r, \theta(*))) \to \langle \zeta\zeta', u, v\rangle \qquad (\beta)$$

is in R' where

- $u = (q_1, \theta(x_1)) \cdots (q_m, \theta(x_m))$ and
- $v = (f_1, \theta(z_1)) \cdots (f_m, \theta(z_l))$.

We denote this rule by (ρ, r, θ). Its weight is $p'(\rho, r, \theta) = p(\rho) \cdot L(H(r, \theta))(\zeta)$. There are no further elements in R'.

We omit a proof for $T(H \lhd G) = L(H) \lhd T(G)$.

We have that $|R'| \in O(|R| \cdot |P|^C)$ where $C = \max\{m + 2 \cdot l + y \mid \exists \rho\colon \rho \text{ is an } (m, l)\text{-rule}, y = 1 \text{ in case } (\alpha), y = 2 \text{ in case } (\beta)\}$.

5 Algorithm

Now we present Algorithm 1, which performs the construction of $H \lhd G$. It uses a strategy similar to that of Earley's algorithm to construct at least all useful rules of $H \lhd G$ while avoiding construction of a certain portion of useless rules. A rule is *useful* if it occurs in some derivation tree; otherwise it is *useless*.

Algorithm 1 Product construction algorithm

Require: $G = (Q, F, \Sigma, q_0, R, p)$ a WSTAG and $H = (P, \Sigma, r_0, R_H, p_H)$ a WRTG,
Ensure: R_u contains at least the useful rules of $H \lhd G$, p_u coincides with the weight assignment of $H \lhd G$ on R_u

```
                                       ▷ step 1: compute 𝓘
𝓘 ← ∅
repeat
    add items to 𝓘 by applying the rules in Fig. 3
until convergence
                                       ▷ step 2: compute rules
R_u ← ∅
for [ρ, ε, r, θ] ∈ 𝓘 do
    R_u ← R_u ∪ {(ρ, r, θ)} as in Sec. 4
                                 ▷ step 3 (optional): reduce
perform reachability analysis to remove useless
    rules from R_u
                                 ▷ step 4: compute weights
for (ρ, r, θ) ∈ R_u do
    p_u(ρ, r, θ) ← p(ρ) · 𝒲([ρ, ε, r, θ])
                                       ▷ defined in Fig. 4
```

Conceptually, the algorithm proceeds in four steps. Note that, in practice, some of these steps may be implemented interleaved in order to reduce constants in the runtime complexity.

The first step is based on a deductive system, or deductive parsing schema, which is given in Fig. 3. Its central notion is that of an *item*, which is a syntactic representation of a proposition. We say that an item *holds* if the corresponding proposition is true. In Sec. 6 we will explain the meaning of the items in detail. Roughly speaking, the items drive a depth-first left-to-right simulation of H on the trees on the input side of rules of G. Items with round brackets are responsible for top-down traversal and items with square brackets for horizontal and bottom-up traversal. The deductive system contains inference rules which are, as usual, syntactic representations of conditional implications (Goodman, 1999; Nederhof, 2003).

The first step of the algorithm computes the least set $\mathcal{I}$ of items that is closed under application of the inference rules. This is done in the usual iterative way, starting with the empty set and applying rules until convergence. Since there are only finitely many items, this process will terminate. Note that, given the soundness of the infer-

$$(1)\quad \frac{}{(q_0, r_0)}$$

$$(2q)\quad \frac{(q,r)}{(\rho,\varepsilon,r)}\ \{\ \rho \in R_q \qquad (2f)\quad \frac{(f,r)}{(\rho,\varepsilon,r)}\ \{\ \rho \in R_f$$

$$(3q)\quad \frac{(q,r) \qquad [\rho,\varepsilon,r,\theta]}{[q,r]}\ \{\ \rho \in R_q \qquad (3f)\quad \frac{(f,r) \qquad [\rho,\varepsilon,r,\theta]}{[f,r,\theta(*)]}\ \{\ \rho \in R_f$$

$$(4)\quad \frac{(\rho,w,r)}{[\rho,w,0,r,r_1\cdots r_k,\emptyset]}\ \begin{cases} \zeta(w)\in\Sigma \quad k=\mathrm{rk}_\zeta(w) \\ p_H(r\to\zeta(w)(r_1,\ldots,r_k))>0 \end{cases}$$

$$(5)\quad \frac{[\rho,w,j,r,r_1\cdots r_k,\theta]}{(\rho,w(j+1),r_{j+1})}\ \{\ \zeta(w)\in\Sigma \quad k=\mathrm{rk}_\zeta(w) \quad 1\le j+1\le k$$

$$(6)\quad \frac{[\rho,w,j,r,r_1\cdots r_k,\theta] \qquad [\rho,w(j+1),r_{j+1},\theta']}{[\rho,w,j+1,r,r_1\cdots r_k,\theta\cup\theta']}\ \{\ \zeta(w)\in\Sigma \quad k=\mathrm{rk}_\zeta(w)$$

$$(7)\quad \frac{[\rho,w,k,r,r_1\cdots r_k,\theta]}{[\rho,w,r,\theta]}\ \{\ \zeta(w)\in\Sigma \quad k=\mathrm{rk}_\zeta(w)$$

$$(8x)\quad \frac{(\rho,w,r)}{(q_j,r)}\ \{\ \zeta(w)=x_j \qquad (8z)\quad \frac{(\rho,w,r)}{(f_j,r)}\ \{\ \zeta(w)=z_j$$

$$(9x)\quad \frac{(\rho,w,r) \qquad [q_j,r]}{[\rho,w,r,\{x_j\mapsto r\}]}\ \{\ \zeta(w)=x_j \qquad (9z)\quad \frac{(\rho,w,r) \qquad [f_j,r,r']}{(\rho,w1,r')}\ \{\ \zeta(w)=z_j$$

$$(10)\quad \frac{(\rho,w,r) \qquad [f_j,r,r'] \qquad [\rho,w1,r',\theta]}{[\rho,w,r,\theta\cup\{z_j\mapsto(r,r')\}]}\ \{\ \zeta(w)=z_j$$

$$(11)\quad \frac{(\rho,w,r)}{[\rho,w,r,\{*\mapsto r\}]}\ \{\ \zeta(w)=*$$

Note: whenever ρ is mentioned, we implicitly assume that
$\rho = q \to \langle\zeta\zeta', q_1\cdots q_m, f_1\cdots f_l\rangle$ or
$\rho = f(y) \to \langle\zeta\zeta', q_1\cdots q_m, f_1\cdots f_l\rangle$.

Figure 3: Deductive parsing schema for the input product.

If $\zeta(w)\in\Sigma$, with $k=\mathrm{rk}_\zeta(w)$, and θ_j is the restriction of θ to variables below node wj in ρ, then:

$$\mathcal{W}([\rho,w,r,\theta]) = \sum_{\substack{r_1,\ldots,r_k:\\ [\rho,w1,r_1,\theta_1],\ldots,[\rho,wk,r_k,\theta_k]\in\mathcal{I}}} p_H(r\to\zeta(w)(r_1,\ldots,r_k))\cdot\prod_j \mathcal{W}([\rho,wj,r_j,\theta_j])$$

If $\zeta(w)\in\{*,x_1,\ldots,x_m\}$, then $\mathcal{W}([\rho,w,r,\theta])=1$.

If $\zeta(w)=\{z_j\}$, with $\theta(z_j)=(r,r')$, then $\mathcal{W}([\rho,w,r,\theta])=\mathcal{W}([\rho,w1,r',\theta\setminus\{z_j\mapsto(r,r')\}])$

Figure 4: Computing the weights of rules in the product grammar $H \lhd G$.

ence rules (cf. Sec. 6), all items in $\mathcal{I}$ hold.

In the second step, for each $[\rho, \varepsilon, r, \theta]$ in $\mathcal{I}$ we construct one rule of $H \lhd G$ as in (α) or as in (β) in Sec. 4, depending on whether $\rho \in R_q$ or $\rho \in R_f$.

The third step is a reachability analysis to remove useless rules. This step is optional—it depends on the application whether the runtime spent here is amortized by subsequent savings.

In the fourth step, we determine the weight of each of the rules we have. For a rule (ρ, r, θ) this is $p(\rho) \cdot \mathcal{W}([\rho, \varepsilon, r, \theta])$, where $\mathcal{W}$ is defined in Fig. 4. The computation can be sped up by storing "back pointers" for each item, i.e., the items which were used for its generation. Alternatively, it is possible to compute the weights on-the-fly during the first step, thus alleviating the need for a separate recursive computation.

To this end, items should be prioritized to make sure that they are generated in the right order for the computation. To be more precise, one has to ensure that all items referred to on the right-hand sides of the equations in Fig. 4 are generated before the items on the left-hand sides.

6 Meaning of Items

The meaning of the items can best be illustrated by the concepts of enriched derivation tree and partial enriched derivation tree.

An *enriched derivation tree* is a modified derivation tree in which the labels have the form (ρ, c) for some rule ρ and some decoration mapping c; c maps every position of the input tree ζ of ρ to a state of the WRTG H. Moreover, c must be consistent with the rules of H, and positions that coincide in the derived tree must be decorated with the same state (cf. Fig. 5, dashed lines). A *partial enriched derivation tree* (for short: pedt) is an enriched derivation tree in which subtrees can still be missing (represented by $\perp$) or the decoration with states from H is not yet complete (i.e., some positions are mapped to ?).

Figure 5 shows an example pedt d, where we represent the decoration at each position of d by annotating the corresponding input tree. This pedt can be viewed as representing application of the following rules:

$$(1), (2q), (8z), (2f), (4), (5), (4), (5), (4), (7), \ldots$$

Now we make our description of pedts more precise. Let n be a position of d, ρ be the rule occurring in the label $d(n)$, and ζ be the input

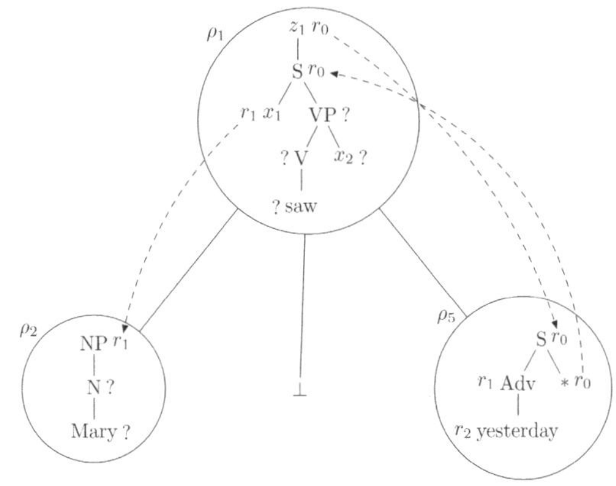

$$R_H: \quad r_0 \to \mathrm{S}(r_1, r_3)$$
$$r_1 \to \mathrm{Adv}(r_2)$$
$$r_2 \to \text{yesterday}$$
$$\vdots$$

Figure 5: Partial enriched derivation tree.

tree of ρ. Then there is a position w of ζ such that (1) every position u which is lexicographically smaller than w is decorated by a state and, if $\zeta(u)$ is a variable x_j or z_j, then the subtree of n which corresponds to the variable does not contain $\perp$ or ?, and (2) every position v which is lexicographically greater than w is decorated by ? and, if $\zeta(v)$ is a variable x_j or z_j, then the child of n which corresponds to the variable is $\perp$. For instance, if we consider the root $n = \varepsilon$ of the pedt in Fig. 5, then $w = 11$ (i.e., the position with label x_1).

Finally we can describe the meaning of the items by referring to properties of pedts.

$(\boldsymbol{q}, \boldsymbol{r})$ (and $(\boldsymbol{f}, \boldsymbol{r})$): There are a pedt d, a position n of d, a rule ρ, and a decoration c such that $d(n) = (\rho, c)$, $\rho \in R_q$ (resp., $\rho \in R_f$), and $c(\varepsilon) = r$.

$[\boldsymbol{q}, \boldsymbol{r}]$: There are a pedt d, a position n of d, a rule ρ, and a decoration c such that $d(n) = (\rho, c)$, $\rho \in R_q$, $c(\varepsilon) = r$, and c is a complete decoration.

$[\boldsymbol{f}, \boldsymbol{r}, \boldsymbol{r'}]$: There are a pedt d, a position n of d, a rule ρ, and a decoration c such that $d(n) = (\rho, c)$, $\rho \in R_f$, $c(\varepsilon) = r$, c is a complete decoration, and c maps the $*$-labeled position of the input tree of ρ to r'.

$(\boldsymbol{\rho}, \boldsymbol{w}, \boldsymbol{r})$: There are a pedt d, a position n of d, and a decoration c such that $d(n) = (\rho, c)$ and $c(w) = r$.

$[\boldsymbol{\rho}, \boldsymbol{w}, \boldsymbol{r}, \boldsymbol{\theta}]$: There are a pedt d, a position n of d, and a decoration c such that $d(n) = (\rho, c)$,

$c(w) = r$ and, if a position u below w of the input tree ζ of ρ is labeled by x_j, then $c(u) = \theta(x_j)$, and if it is labeled by z_j, then $(c(u), c(u1)) = \theta(z_j)$, and if it is labeled by $*$, then $c(u) = \theta(*)$.

$[\boldsymbol{\rho}, \boldsymbol{w}, \boldsymbol{j}, \boldsymbol{r}, \boldsymbol{r_1} \cdots \boldsymbol{r_k}, \boldsymbol{\theta}]$: There are a pedt d, a position n of d, and a decoration c such that $d(n) = (\rho, c)$, $c(w) = r$, and, if a position u of the input tree ζ of ρ is labeled by some variable y and u is lexicographically smaller than wj, c and θ agree in the same way as in the preceding item.

Given this semantics of items, it is not difficult to see that the inference rules of the deduction system are sound. The completeness of the system can be derived by means of a small proof by contradiction.

7 Complexity Analysis

In this section, we analyse the worst-case space and time complexity of step 1 of Algorithm 1.

The space complexity is

$$O\big(|G|_{\text{in}} \cdot |R_H| \cdot |P|^C\big) ,$$

which is determined by the number of possible items of the form $[\rho, w, j, r, r_1 \cdots r_k, \theta]$. The first factor, $|G|_{\text{in}}$, denotes the *input size of G*, defined by $\sum_{\rho \in R} |\text{pos}(\zeta(\rho))|$, where $\zeta(\rho)$ is the input tree of ρ. It captures the components ρ, w, and j in said items, which together identify exactly one node of an input tree of G. The factor $|R_H|$ captures the components r and $r_1 \cdots r_k$. The final factor, $|P|^C$, captures the θ, where C is given at the end of Sec. 4.

Following McAllester (2002) we determine the time complexity by the number of instantiations of the inference rules. In our case the time complexity coincides with the space complexity.

8 Conclusion

We have introduced a formulation of STAGs that is closed under input product and output product with regular weighted tree languages. By the result of Maletti and Satta (2009), this implies closure under input product and output product with regular weighted string languages. We have provided a direct construction of the STAG that generates said input product (and, mutatis mutandis, the output product). No such construction has been published before that deals with both weights and synchronization. Moreover, we have presented a novel algorithm for computing our construction. This algorithm is inspired by Earley's algorithm to the effect that computation of a certain portion of useless rules is avoided.

The next step towards an implementation would be to consider pruning. This amounts to partitioning the set $\mathcal{I}$ of items and imposing a bound on the size of each partition. Such a technique has already been presented by Chiang (2007) for his cube-pruning algorithm.

Another possible future contribution could be an algorithm specifically tailored to the input product with a regular weighted string language. For this scenario, several contributions exist, requiring additional restictions however. For instance, Nesson et al. (2006) show a CYK-like algorithm for intersecting a STIG with a pair of strings. Their algorithm requires that the trees of the grammar be binarized. As DeNeefe and Knight (2009) point out, this makes the grammar strictly less powerful. They in turn propose a construction which converts the STIG into an equivalent tree-to-string transducer, and they use corresponding algorithms for parsing, such as the one by DeNero et al. (2009). However, their construction relies on the fact that tree-insertion grammars are weakly equivalent to context-free grammars. Thus, it is not applicable to the more general STAGs.

Acknowledgments

We are grateful to the referees for thorough remarks and helpful suggestions. The first author was financially supported by DFG VO 1011/6-1.

References

A. Abeille, Y. Schabes, A.K. Joshi. 1990. Using lexicalized TAGs for machine translation. In *Proc. of COLING*, vol. 3, pp. 1–6, Helsinki, Finland.

A. Alexandrakis, S. Bozapalidis. 1987. Weighted grammars and Kleene's theorem. *Inform. Process. Letters*, 24(1):1–4.

B.S. Baker 1979. Composition of top-down and bottom-up tree transductions *Inform. and Control*, 41(2):186–213.

A.L. Berger, V.J. Della Pietra, S.A. Della Pietra. 1996. A maximum entropy approach to natural language processing. *Comp. Ling.*, 22:39–71.

M. Büchse, D. Geisler, T. Stüber, H. Vogler. 2010. n-best parsing revisited. In: F. Drewes,

M. Kuhlmann (eds.), *Proc. of Workshop on ATANLP*, pp. 46–54. ACL.

F. Casacuberta, C. de la Higuera. 2000. Computational complexity of problems on probabilistic grammars and transducers. In: A.L. Oliveira (ed.), *Proc. of ICGI*, LNAI 1891, pp. 15-24, Springer-Verlag.

D. Chiang. 2007. Hierarchical phrase-based translation. *Comp. Ling.*, 33(2):201–228.

B. Courcelle, P. Franchi-Zannettacci. 1982. Attribute grammars and recursive program schemes I and II. Theoret. Comput. Sci. 17, 163-191 and 235-257.

A. P. Dempster, N. M. Laird, D. B. Rubin. 1977. Maximum likelihood from incomplete data via the EM algorithm. *J. of the Royal Statistical Society. Series B (Methodological)*, 39(1):1–38.

S. DeNeefe, K. Knight. 2009. Synchronous tree adjoining machine translation. In: P. Koehn, R. Mihalcea (eds.), *Proc. of EMNLP*, pp. 727–736. ACL.

S. DeNeefe, K. Knight, H. Vogler. 2010. A decoder for probabilistic synchronous tree insertion grammars. In: F. Drewes, M. Kuhlmann (eds.), *Proc. of Workshop on ATANLP*, pp. 10–18. ACL.

J. DeNero, M. Bansal, A. Pauls, and D. Klein. 2009. Efficient parsing for transducer grammars. In *Proc. NAACL*, pp. 227–235.

J. Earley. 1970. An efficient context-free parsing algorithm. *Communications of the ACM*, 13(2):94–102.

J. Eisner. 2003. Learning non-isomorphic tree mappings for machine translation. In *Proc. of 41st ACL - Volume 2*, ACL, pages 205–208, Stroudsburg, PA, USA. Association for Computational Linguistics.

J. Engelfriet. 1980. Some open questions and recent results on tree transducers and tree languages. In: R.V. Book (ed.), *Formal language theory; perspectives and open problems*, New York, Academic Press, 241-286.

J. Engelfriet, H. Vogler. 1985. Macro tree transducers. J. Comput. System Sci. 31, 71–146.

Z. Fülöp, A. Maletti, H. Vogler. 2010. Preservation of recognizability for synchronous tree substitution grammars. In: F. Drewes, M. Kuhlmann (eds.), *Proc. of Workshop on ATANLP*, pp. 1–9. ACL.

M. Galley, M. Hopkins, K. Knight, D. Marcu. 2004. What's in a translation rule? In: D. Marcu, S. Dumais, S. Roukos (eds.), *Proc. of HLT-NAACL*, pp. 273–280, ACL.

F. Gécseg, M. Steinby. 1997. Tree languages. In: G. Rozenberg, A. Salomaa (eds.), *Handbook of Formal Languages*, vol. 3, chapter 1, pp. 1–68. Springer-Verlag.

J. Goodman. 1999. Semiring parsing. *Comput. Linguist.*, 25(4):573–605.

J. Graehl, K. Knight, J. May. 2008. Training tree transducers. *Comput. Linguist.*, 34(3):391–427.

S. L. Graham, M. Harrison, and W. L. Ruzzo. 1980. An improved context-free recognizer. *ACM Trans. Program. Lang. Syst.*, 2:415–462, July.

L. Huang, D. Chiang. 2005. Better k-best parsing. In *Proc. of IWPT*, pp. 53–64, ACL.

L. Huang, K. Knight, and A. Joshi. 2006. Statistical syntax-directed translation with extended domain of locality. In *Proc. AMTA*, pages 66–73.

A.K. Joshi, L.S. Levy, M. Takahashi. 1975. Tree adjunct grammars. *Journal of Computer and System Sciences*, 10(1):136–163.

A.K. Joshi, Y. Schabes. 1997. Tree-adjoining grammars. In: *Handbook of Formal Languages*. Chapter 2, pp. 69–123, Springer-Verlag.

K. Knight. 2007. Capturing practical natural language transformations. Machine Translation 21, 121–133.

Z. Li, J. Eisner, S. Khudanpur. 2009. Variational decoding for statistical machine translation. In: *Proc. of ACL-IJCNLP*, pp. 593–601, ACL.

A. Lopez. 2008. Statistical Machine Translation. ACM Computing Surveys 40(3), 8:1–8:49.

A. Maletti. 2010a. A tree transducer model for synchronous tree-adjoining grammars. In J.-S. Chang and P. Koehn, eds., *Proc. ACL*, pp. 1067–1076. ACL.

A. Maletti. 2010b. Input and output products for weighted extended top-down tree transducers. In Y. Gao, H. Lu, S. Seki, and S. Yu, eds., *Proc. DLT*, LNCS, vol. 6224, pp. 316–327. Springer-Verlag.

A. Maletti and G. Satta. 2009. Parsing algorithms based on tree automata. In: *Proc. IWPT*, pp. 1–12. ACL.

D.F. Martin and S.A. Vere. 1970. On syntax-directed transduction and tree transducers. In: *Proc. 2nd ann. Assoc. Comput. Sci. Symp. Theory of Comp.*, pp. 129–135.

J. May and K. Knight. 2006. Tiburon: a weighted tree automata toolkit. In O.H. Ibarra and H.-C. Yen, editors, *CIAA 2006*, volume 4094 of *Lecture Notes in Comput. Sci.*, pages 102–113. Springer-Verlag.

D. McAllester. 2002. On the complexity analysis of static analyses. *J. ACM*, 49:512–537, July.

M. Mohri. 2009. Weighted automata algorithms. In M. Droste, W. Kuich, and H. Vogler, editors, *Handbook of Weighted Automata*, chapter 6, pages 213–254. Springer-Verlag.

M.-J. Nederhof. 2003. Weighted deductive parsing and Knuth's algorithm. *Computational Linguistics*, 29(1):135–143.

M.-J. Nederhof. 2009. Weighted parsing of trees. In: *Proc. of IWPT*, pp. 13–24. ACL.

R. Nesson, S.M. Shieber, A. Rush. 2005. Induction of probabilistic synchronous tree-insertion grammars. Technical Report TR-20-05, Computer Science Group, Harvard University, Cambridge, Massachusetts.

R. Nesson, S.M. Shieber, A. Rush. Induction of probabilistic synchronous tree-inserting grammars for machine translation. In: *Proc. of the 7th AMTA*, 2006.

F.J. Och. 2003. Minimum error rate training in statistical machine translation. In: *Proc. of Annual Meeting of ACL*, pp. 160–167.

F.J. Och, H. Ney. 2002. Discriminative training and maximum entropy models for statistical machine translation. In: *Proc. of Annual Meeting of ACL*, pp. 295–302. ACL.

W.C. Rounds. 1969. Context-free grammars on trees. In: *Proc. of STOC*, pp. 143–148.

W.C. Rounds. 1970. Tree-oriented proofs of some theorems on context-free and indexed languages In: *2nd Ann. ACM STOC*, pp. 109–116.

S.M. Shieber. 2004. Synchronous grammars and tree transducers. In: *Proc. 7th Workshop on Tree Adjoining Grammars and Related Formalisms*, pp. 88–95. ACL.

S.M. Shieber. 2006. Unifying synchronous tree-adjoining grammars and tree transducers via bimorphisms. In: *Proc. of EACL*, pp. 377–384. ACL.

S.M. Shieber, Y. Schabes. 1990. Synchronous tree-adjoining grammars. In: *Proc. of COLING*, vol. 3, pp. 253–258, ACL.

M. Zhang, H. Jiang, A. Aw, H. Li, C.L. Tan, S. Li. 2008. A tree sequence alignment-based tree-to-tree translation model. In: J.D. Moore, S. Teufel, J. Allan, S. Furui, *Proc. of Annual Meeting of ACL*, pp. 559–567. ACL.

Finding the Most Probable String and the Consensus String: an Algorithmic Study

Colin de la Higuera* and **Jose Oncina****
*Université de Nantes, CNRS, LINA, UMR6241, F-44000, France
cdlh@univ-nantes.fr
**Departamento de Lenguajes y Sistemas Informaticos
Universidad de Alicante, Alicante, Spain
oncina@dlsi.ua.es

Abstract

The problem of finding the most probable string for a distribution generated by a weighted finite automaton or a probabilistic grammar is related to a number of important questions: computing the distance between two distributions or finding the best translation (the most probable one) given a probabilistic finite state transducer. The problem is undecidable with general weights and is $\mathcal{NP}$-hard if the automaton is probabilistic. We give a pseudo-polynomial algorithm which computes the most probable string in time polynomial in the inverse of the probability of the most probable string itself, both for probabilistic finite automata and probabilistic context-free grammars. We also give a randomised algorithm solving the same problem.

1 Introduction

When using probabilistic machines to define distributions over sets of strings, the usual and best studied problems are those of parsing and of finding the most probable explanation of a given string (the most probable parse). These problems, when dealing with probabilistic (generating) finite state automata, hidden Markov Models (HMMs) or probabilistic context-free grammars depend on the ambiguity of the machine: indeed, if there can be different parses for the same string, then the probability of the string is obtained by summing over the different parses.

A more difficult problem we study here is that of finding the most probable string; this string is also known as the *consensus* string.

The problem of finding the most probable string was first addressed in the computational linguistics community by Sima'an (1996): he proved the problem to be $\mathcal{NP}$-hard if we consider tree grammars, and as a corollary he gave the same result for context-free grammars. Goodman (1998) showed that, in the case of HMMs, the problem of finding whether the most most probable string of a given length n is at least p is $\mathcal{NP}$-Complete. Moreover, he points that his technique cannot be applied to show the $\mathcal{NP}$-completeness of the problem when n is not prespecified because the most probable string can be exponentially long. Casacuberta and de la Higuera (2000) proved the problem to be $\mathcal{NP}$-hard, using techniques developed for linguistic decoding (Casacuberta and de la Higuera, 1999): their result holds for probabilistic finite state automata and for probabilistic transducers even when these are acyclic: in the transducer case the related (and possibly more important) question is that of finding the most probable translation. The problem was also addressed with motivations in bioinformatics by Lyngsø and Pedersen (2002). Their technique relies on reductions from maximal cliques. As an important corollary of their hardness results they prove that the L_1 and L_∞ distances between distributions represented by HMMs are also hard to compute: indeed being able to compute such distances would enable to find (as a side product) the most probable string. This result was then applied on probabilistic finite automata in (Cortes et al., 2006; Cortes et al., 2007) and the L_k distance, for each odd k was proved to be intractable.

An essential consequence of these results is that finding the most probable translation given some probabilistic (non deterministic) finite state transducer is also at least as hard. It can be shown (Casacuberta and de la Higuera, 1999; Vidal et al., 2005) that solving this problem consists in finding the most probable string inside the set of all acceptable translations, and this set is structured as a probabilistic finite automaton. Therefore, the most probable translation problem is also $\mathcal{NP}$-hard.

On the other hand, in the framework of multiplicity automata or of *accepting* probabilistic finite automata (also called Rabin automata), the problem of the existence of a string whose weight is above (or under) a specific threshold is known to be undecidable (Blondel and Canterini, 2003). In the case where the weight of each individual edge is between 0 and 1, the score can be interpreted as a probability. The differences reside in the fact that in multiplicity automata the sum of the probabilities of all strings does not need to be bounded; this is also the case for Rabin automata, as each probability corresponds to the probability for a given string to belong to the language.

In this paper we attempt to better understand the status of the problem and provide algorithms which find a string of probability higher than a given threshold in time polynomial in the inverse of this threshold. These algorithms give us pragmatic answers to the consensus string problem as it is possible to use the probabilistic machine to define a threshold and to use our algorithms to find, in this way, the most probable string.

We will first (Section 2) give the different definitions concerning automata theory, distributions over strings and complexity theory. In Section 3 we show that we can compute the most probable string in time polynomial in the inverse of the probability of this most probable string but in the bounded case, *i.e.* when we are looking for a string of length smaller than some given bound. In Section 4 we show how we can compute such bounds. In Section 5 the algorithms are experimentally compared and we conclude in Section 6.

2 Definitions and Notations

2.1 Languages and Distributions

Let $[n]$ denote the set $\{1, \ldots, n\}$ for each $n \in \mathbb{N}$. An *alphabet* Σ is a finite non-empty set of symbols called *letters*. A *string* w over Σ is a finite sequence $w = a_1 \ldots a_n$ of letters. Let $|w|$ denote the length of w. In this case we have $|w| = |a_1 \ldots a_n| = n$. The *empty string* is denoted by λ. When decomposing a string into substrings, we will write $w = w_1 \ldots w_n$ where $\forall i \in [n]\ w_i \in \Sigma^\star$.

Letters will be indicated by $a, b, c, \ldots$, and strings by $u, v, \ldots, z$.

We denote by $\Sigma^\star$ the set of all strings, by Σ^n the set of those of length n, by $\Sigma^{<n}$ (respectively $\Sigma^{\leq n}$, $\Sigma^{\geq n}$) the set of those of length less than n (respectively at most n, at least n).

A *probabilistic language* $\mathcal{D}$ is a probability distribution over $\Sigma^\star$. The probability of a string $x \in \Sigma^\star$ under the distribution $\mathcal{D}$ is denoted as $Pr_{\mathcal{D}}(x)$ and must verify $\sum_{x \in \Sigma^\star} Pr_{\mathcal{D}}(x) = 1$.

If the distribution is modelled by some syntactic machine $\mathcal{M}$, the probability of x according to the probability distribution defined by $\mathcal{M}$ is denoted $Pr_{\mathcal{M}}(x)$. The distribution modelled by a machine $\mathcal{M}$ will be denoted by $\mathcal{D}_{\mathcal{M}}$ and simplified to $\mathcal{D}$ if the context is not ambiguous.

If L is a language (thus a set of strings, included in $\Sigma^\star$), and $\mathcal{D}$ a distribution over $\Sigma^\star$, $Pr_{\mathcal{D}}(L) = \sum_{x \in L} Pr_{\mathcal{D}}(x)$.

2.2 Probabilistic Finite Automata

The probabilistic finite automata (PFA) (Paz, 1971) are generative devices:

Definition 1. *A* Probabilistic Finite Automaton (PFA) *is a tuple* $\mathcal{A} = \langle \Sigma, Q, S, F, \delta \rangle$, *where:*

- Σ *is the alphabet;*
- $Q = \{q_1, \ldots, q_{|Q|}\}$ *is a finite set of* states;
- $S : Q \rightarrow \mathbb{R}^+ \cap [0, 1]$ *(initial probabilities);*
- $F : Q \rightarrow \mathbb{R}^+ \cap [0, 1]$ *(final probabilities);*
- $\delta : Q \times (\Sigma \cup \{\lambda\}) \times Q \rightarrow \mathbb{R}^+$ *is a transition function; the function is complete:* $\delta(q, a, q') = 0$ *can be interpreted as "no transition from* q *to* q' *labelled with* a*".*

S, δ and F are functions such that:

$$\sum_{q \in Q} S(q) = 1, \tag{1}$$

and $\forall q \in Q$,

$$F(q) + \sum_{a \in \Sigma \cup \{\lambda\},\, q' \in Q} \delta(q, a, q') = 1. \tag{2}$$

Let $x \in \Sigma^\star$. $\Pi_{\mathcal{A}}(x)$ is the set of all paths accepting x: a path is a sequence $\pi = q_{i_0} x_1 q_{i_1} x_2 \ldots x_n q_{i_n}$ where $x = x_1 \cdots x_n$, $x_i \in \Sigma \cup \{\lambda\}$, and $\forall j \leq n$, $\exists p_j \neq 0$ such that $\delta(q_{i_{j-1}}, x_j, q_{i_j}) = p_j$. The probability of the path π is

$$S(q_{i_0}) \cdot \prod_{j \in [n]} p_j \cdot F(q_{i_n})$$

And the probability of the string x is obtained by summing over all the paths in $\Pi_{\mathcal{A}}(x)$. Note that this may result in an infinite sum because of λ-transitions (and more problematically λ-cycles.

An effective computation can be done by means of the Forward (or Backward) algorithm (Vidal et al., 2005).

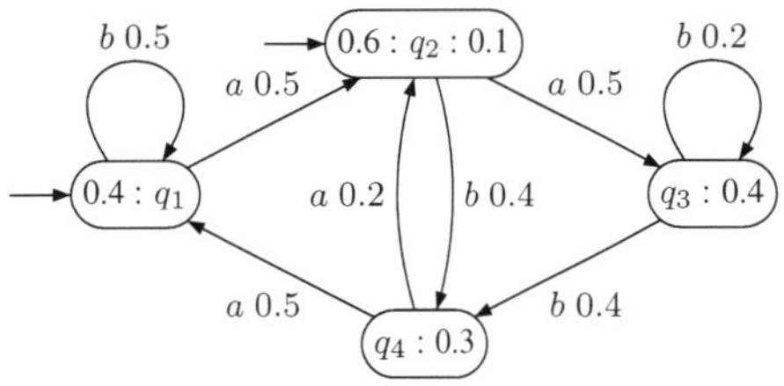

Figure 1: Graphical representation of a PFA.

Alternatively, a PFA (with n states) is given when the following matrices are known:

- $\mathbf{S} \in \mathrm{R}^{1\times n}$ represents the probabilities of starting at each state. $\mathbf{S}[i]{=}S(q_i)$;
- $\mathbf{M} = \{\mathbf{M}_a \in \mathrm{R}^{n\times n} | a \in \Sigma \cup \{\lambda\}\}$ represents the transition probabilities. $\mathbf{M}_a[i,j] = \delta(q_i, a, q_j)$;
- $\mathbf{F} \in \mathrm{R}^{n\times 1}$ represents the probabilities of ending in each state. $\mathbf{F}[i]{=}F(q_i)$.

Given a string $x = a_1 \cdots a_k$ we compute $Pr_{\mathcal{A}}(x)$ as:

$$Pr_{\mathcal{A}}(x) = \mathbf{S} \prod_{i=1}^{|x|} [\mathbf{M}_\lambda^* \mathbf{M}_{a_i}] \, \mathbf{M}_\lambda^* \mathbf{F} \qquad (3)$$

where

$$\mathbf{M}_\lambda^* = \sum_{i=0}^{\infty} M_\lambda^i = (I - \mathbf{M}_\lambda)^{-1}$$

Then, equations 1 and 2 can be written as:

$$\mathbf{S}\mathbf{1} = 1 \qquad (4)$$

$$\sum_{a\in\Sigma\cup\{\lambda\}} \mathbf{M}_a \mathbf{1} + \mathbf{F} = \mathbf{1} \qquad (5)$$

where $\mathbf{1} \in \mathrm{R}^n$ is such that $\forall i \; \mathbf{1}[i] = 1$.
Note that

$$Pr_{\mathcal{A}}(\lambda) = \mathbf{S}\mathbf{M}_\lambda^*\mathbf{F} \in [0,1] \qquad (6)$$

This implies that $\mathbf{M}_\lambda^*$ should be a non singular matrix.

Moreover, in order for $Pr_{\mathcal{A}}$ to define a distribution probability over Σ^* it is required that:

$$\sum_{x\in\Sigma^*} Pr_{\mathcal{A}}(x) = \sum_{i=0}^{\infty} \mathbf{S}\mathbf{M}_\lambda^*\mathbf{M}_\Sigma^i\mathbf{M}_\lambda^*\mathbf{F}$$
$$= \mathbf{S}\mathbf{M}_\lambda^*(I - \mathbf{M}_\Sigma)^{-1}\mathbf{M}_\lambda^*\mathbf{F} = 1$$

where I is the identity matrix and $\mathbf{M}_\Sigma = \sum_{a\in\Sigma} \mathbf{M}_a$. Note that as a consequence of that, $(I - \mathbf{M}_\Sigma)$ is a non singular matrix.

2.3 Hidden Markov Models

Hidden Markov models (HMMs) (Rabiner, 1989; Jelinek, 1998) are finite state machines defined by (1) a finite set of states, (2) a probabilistic transition function, (3) a distribution over initial states, and (4) an output function.

An HMM generates a string by visiting (in a hidden way) states and outputting values when in those states. Typical problems include finding the most probable path corresponding to a particular output (usually solved by the Viterbi algorithm). Here the question of finding the most probable output has been addressed by Lyngsø and Pedersen (2002). In this paper the authors prove that the hardness of this problem implies that it is also hard to compute certain distances between two distributions given by HMMs.

Note that to obtain a distribution over $\Sigma^\star$ and not each Σ^n the authors introduce a unique final state in which, once reached, the machine halts. An alternative often used is to introduce a special symbol (♯) and to only consider the strings terminating with ♯: the distribution is then over $\Sigma^\star$ ♯.

Equivalence results between HMMs and PFA can be found in (Vidal et al., 2005).

2.4 Probabilistic Context-free Grammars

Definition 2. *A probabilistic context-free grammar (PCFG) G is a quintuple $< \Sigma, V, R, P, N >$ where Σ is a finite alphabet (of terminal symbols), V is a finite alphabet (of variables or non-terminals), $R \subset V \times (\Sigma \cup V)^*$ is a finite set of production rules, and N $(\in V)$ is the axiom. $P : R \to \mathrm{R}^+$ is the probability function.*

A PCFG is used to generate strings by rewriting iteratively the non terminals in the string, starting from the axiom. A string may be obtained by different derivations. In this case the problem is called ambiguity. Parsing with a PCFG is usually done by adapting the Earley or the CKY algorithms.

Particularly appealing is a very efficient extension of the Early algorithm due to Stolcke (1995) that can compute:

- the probability of a given string x generated by a PCFG G;
- the single most probable parse for x;
- the probability that x occurs as a prefix of some string generated by G, which we denote by $Pr_G(x\,\Sigma^\star)$.

2.5 Probabilistic Transducers

There can be different definitions of probabilistic transducers. We use the one from (Vidal et al., 2005):

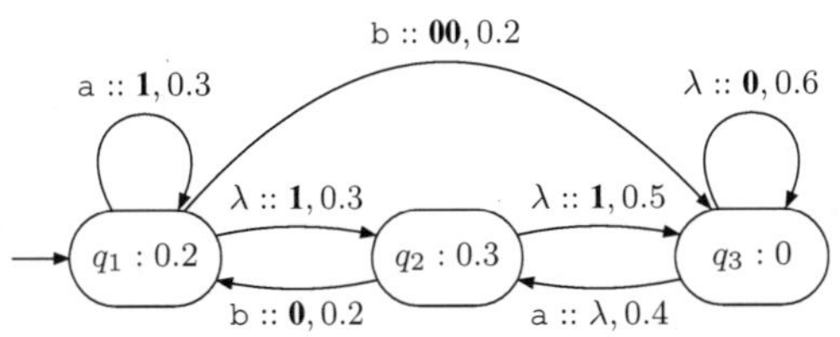

Figure 2: Transducer.

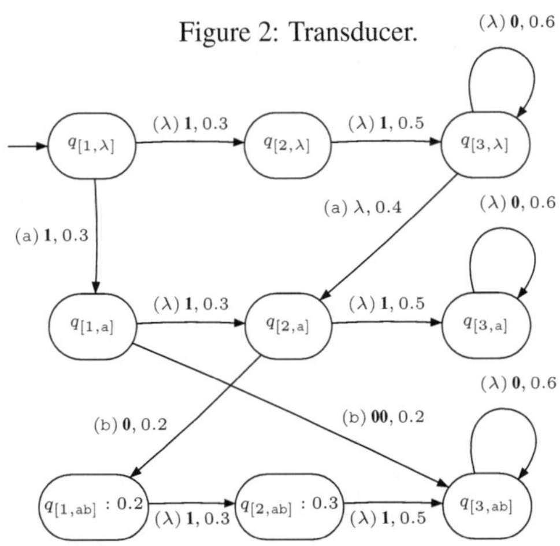

Figure 3: Corresponding non normalized PFA for the translations of ab. Each state indicates which input prefix has been read. Between the brackets, on the transitions, the input symbol justifying the transition.

Probabilistic finite-state transducers (PFST) are similar to PFA, but in this case two different alphabets (source Σ and target Γ) are involved. Each transition in a PFST has attached a symbol from the source alphabet (or λ) and a string (possible empty string) of symbols from the target alphabet. PFSTs can be viewed as graphs, as for example in Figure 3.

Definition 3 (Probabilistic transducer). *A probabilistic finite state* transducer *(*PFST*) is a 6-tuple* $\langle Q, \Sigma, \Gamma, S, E, F\rangle$ *such that:*

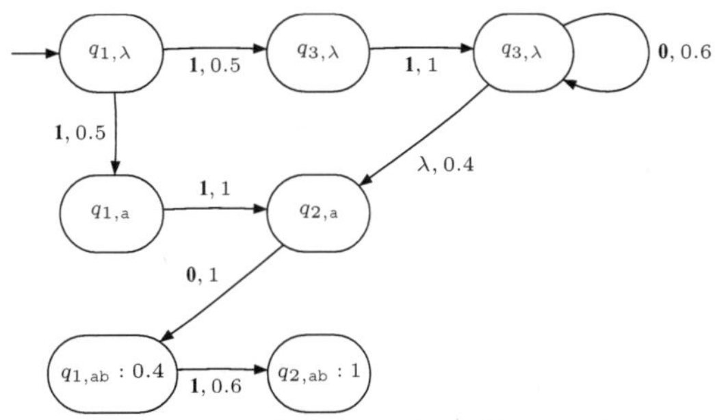

Figure 4: Corresponding normalized PFA for the translations of ab. The most probable string (**111**) has probability 0.54.

- *Q is a finite set of* states*; these will be labelled $q_1,\ldots,q_{|Q|}$;*
- $S : Q \rightarrow \mathrm{R}^+ \cap [0,1]$ *(initial probabilities);*
- $F : Q \rightarrow \mathrm{R}^+ \cap [0,1]$ *(halting probabilities);*
- $E \in Q \times (\Sigma \cup \{\lambda\}) \times \Gamma^\star \times Q \times \mathrm{R}^+$ *is the set of transitions;*

S, δ and F are functions such that:

$$\sum_{q\in Q} S(q) = 1,$$

and $\forall q \in Q$,

$$F(q) + \sum_{a\in\Sigma\cup\{\lambda\},\ q'\in Q} p : (q, a, w, q', p) \in E = 1.$$

Let $x \in \Sigma^\star$ and $y \in \Gamma^\star$. Let $\Pi_{\mathcal{T}}(x, y)$ be the set of all paths accepting (x, y): a path is a sequence $\pi = q_{i_0}(x_1, y_1)q_{i_1}(x_2, y_2)\ldots(x_n, y_n)q_{i_n}$ where $x = x_1\cdots x_n$ and $y = y_1\cdots y_n$, with $\forall j \in [n]$, $x_j \in \Sigma\cup\{\lambda\}$ and $y_j \in \Gamma^\star$, and $\forall j \in [n]$, $\exists p_{i_j}$ such that $(q_{i_{j-1}}, x_j, y_j, q_{i_j}, p_{i_j}) \in E$. The probability of the path is

$$S(q_{i_0}) \cdot \prod_{j\in[n]} p_{i_j} \cdot F(q_{i_n})$$

And the probability of the translation pair (x, y) is obtained by summing over all the paths in $\Pi_{\mathcal{T}}(x, y)$.

Note that the probability of y given x (the probability of y as a translation of x, denoted as $Pr_{\mathcal{T}}(y|x)$) is $\frac{Pr_{\mathcal{T}}(x,y)}{\sum_{z\in\Sigma^\star} Pr_{\mathcal{T}}(x,z)}$.

Probabilistic finite state transducers are used as models for the the *stochastic translation problem* of a source sentence $x \in \Sigma^\star$ that can be defined as the search for a target string y that:

$$\operatorname*{argmax}_y Pr(y \mid x) = \operatorname*{argmax}_y Pr(y, x).$$

The problem of finding this optimal translation is proved to be a $\mathcal{NP}$-hard by Casacuberta and de la Higuera (2000).

An approximate solution to the stochastic translation can be computed in polynomial time by using an algorithm similar to the Viterbi algorithm for probabilistic finite-state automata (Casacuberta, 1995; Picó and Casacuberta, 2001).

The stochastic translation problem is computationally tractable in particular cases. If the PFST $\mathcal{T}$ is *non-ambiguous in the translation sense* ($\forall x \in \Sigma^\star$ there are not two target sentences $y, y' \in \Gamma^\star$, $y \neq y'$, such that $Pr_\mathcal{T}(x, y) > 0$ and $Pr_\mathcal{T}(x, y') > 0$), the translation problem is polynomial. If the PFST $\mathcal{T}$ is simply *non-ambiguous* ($\forall x \in \Sigma^\star$ there are not two different paths that deal with (x, y) and with probability different to zero), the translation problem is also polynomial. In both cases, the computation can be carried out using an adequate version of the Viterbi algorithm (Vidal et al., 2005).

Alternative types of PFSTs have been introduced and applied with success in different areas of machine translation. In (Mohri, 1997; Mohri et al., 2000), *weighted finite-state transducers* are studied.

2.6 Complexity Classes and Decision Problems

We only give here some basic definitions and results from complexity theory. A *decision problem* is one whose answer is **true** or **false**. A decision problem is *decidable* if there is an algorithm which, given any specific instance, computes correctly the answer and halts. It is *undecidable* if not. A decision problem is in $\mathcal{P}$ if there is a polynomial time algorithm that solves it.

A decision problem is *$\mathcal{NP}$-complete* if it is both $\mathcal{NP}$-hard and in the class $\mathcal{NP}$: in this case a polynomial time non-deterministic algorithm exists that always solves this problem. Alternatively, a problem is in $\mathcal{NP}$ if there exists a *polynomial certificate* for it. A polynomial certificate for an instance I is a short (polynomial length) string which when associated to instance I can be checked in polynomial time to confirm that the instance is indeed positive. A problem is *$\mathcal{NP}$-hard* if it is at least as hard as the satisfiability problem (SAT), or either of the other $\mathcal{NP}$-complete problems (Garey and Johnson, 1979).

A randomized algorithm makes use of random bits to solve a problem. It *solves a decision problem with one-sided error* if given any value δ and any instance, the algorithm:

- makes no error on a negative instance of a problem (it always answers no);
- makes an error in at most δ cases when working on a positive instance.

If such an algorithm exists, the problem is said to belong to the class $\mathcal{RP}$. It should be noticed that by running such a randomized algorithm n times the error decreases exponentially with n: if a positive answer is obtained, then the instance had to be positive, and the probability of not obtaining a positive answer (for a positive instance) in n tries is less than δ^n. A randomized algorithm which solve a decision problem in the conditions above is called a *Monte Carlo algorithm*.

When a decision problem depends on an instance containing integer numbers, the fair (and logical) encoding is in base 2. If the problem admits a polynomial algorithm whenever the integers are encoded in base 1, the problem (and the algorithm) are said to be *pseudo-polynomial*.

2.7 About Sampling

One advantage of using PFA or similar devices is that they can be effectively used to develop randomised algorithms. But when generating random strings, the fact that the length of these is unbounded is an issue. Therefore the termination of the algorithm might only be true *with probability 1*: this means that the probability of an infinite run, even if it cannot be discarded, is of null measure.

In the work of Ben-David et al. (1992) which extends Levin's original definitions from (Levin, 1986), a distribution over $\{0, 1\}^*$ is considered *samplable* if it is generated by a randomized algorithm that runs in time polynomial in the length of its output.

We will require a stronger condition to be met. We want a distribution represented by some machine $\mathcal{M}$ to be *sampable in a bounded way*, ie, we require that there is a randomized algorithm which, when given a bound b, will either return any string w in $\Sigma^{\leq b}$ with probability $Pr_\mathcal{M}(w)$ or return *fail* with probability $Pr_\mathcal{M}(\Sigma^{>b})$. Furthermore, the algorithm should run in time polynomial in b.

As we also need parsing to take place in polynomial time, we will say that a machine $\mathcal{M}$ is *stronly sampable* if

- one can parse an input string x by $\mathcal{M}$ and return $Pr_{\mathcal{M}}(x)$ in time polynomial in $|x|$;
- one can sample $\mathcal{D}_{\mathcal{M}}$ in a bounded way.

2.8 The Problem

The question is to find the most probable string in a probabilistic language. An alternative name to this string is the *consensus* string.

Name: Consensus string (CS)
Instance: A probabilistic machine $\mathcal{M}$
Question: Find in $\Sigma^\star$ a string x such that $\forall y \in \Sigma^\star\ Pr_{\mathcal{M}}(x) \geq Pr_{\mathcal{M}}(y)$.

With the above problem we associate the following decision problem:

Name: Most probable string (MPS)
Instance: A probabilistic machine $\mathcal{M}$, a $p \geq 0$
Question: Is there in $\Sigma^\star$ a string x such that $Pr_{\mathcal{M}}(x) \geq p$?

For example, if we consider the PFA from Figure 1, the most probable string is a.

Note that p is typically encoded as a fraction and that the complexity of our algorithms is to depend on the size of the encodings, hence of $\log \frac{1}{p}$.

The problem MPS is known to be $\mathcal{NP}$-hard (Casacuberta and de la Higuera, 2000). In their proof the reduction is from SAT and uses only acyclic PFA. There is a problem with MPS: there is no bound, in general, over the length of the most probable string. Indeed, even for regular languages, this string can be very long. In Section 4.4 such a construction is presented.

Of interest, therefore, is to study the case where the longest string can be bounded, with a bound given as a separate argument to the problem:

Name: Bounded most probable string (BMPS)
Instance: A probabilistic machine $\mathcal{M}$, a $p \geq 0$, an integer b
Question: Is there in $\Sigma^{\leq b}$ a string x such that $Pr_{\mathcal{M}}(x) \geq p$?

In complexity theory, numbers are to be encoded in base 2. In BMPS, it is necessary, for the problem not to be trivially unsolvable, to consider a unary encoding of b, as strings of length up to b will have to be built.

3 Solving BMPS

In this section we attempt to solve the bounded case. We first solve it in a randomised way, then propose an algorithm that will work each time the prefix probabilities can be computed. This is the case for PFA and for probabilistic context free grammars.

3.1 Solving by Sampling

Let us consider a class of **strongly sampable** machines.

Then BMPS, for this class, belongs to $\mathcal{RP}$:

Theorem 1. *If a machine $\mathcal{M}$ is strongly sampable,* BMPS *can be solved by a Monte Carlo algorithm.*

Proof. The idea is that any string s whose probability is at least p, should appear (with high probability, at least $1-\delta$) in a sufficiently large randomly drawn sample (of size m), and have a relative frequency $\frac{f}{m}$ of at least $\frac{p}{2}$.

Algorithm 1 therefore draws this large enough sample in a bounded way and then checks if any of the more frequent strings (relative frequency $\frac{f}{m}$ of at least $\frac{p}{2}$) has real probability at least p.

We use multiplicative Chernov bounds to compute the probability that an arbitrary string whose probability is at least p has relative frequency $\frac{f}{m}$ of at least $\frac{p}{2}$:

$$Pr(\frac{f}{m} < \frac{p}{2}) \leq 2e^{-mp/8}$$

So for a value of $\delta \leq 2e^{-mp/8}$ it is sufficient to draw a sample of size $m \geq \frac{8}{p} \ln \frac{2}{\delta}$ in order to be certain (with error δ) that in a sample of size m any probable string is in the sample with relative frequency $\frac{f}{m}$ of at least $\frac{p}{2}$.

We then only have to parse each string in the sample which has relative frequency at least $\frac{p}{2}$ to be sure (within error δ) that s is in the sample.

If there is no string with probability at least p, the algorithm will return **false**. □

The complexity of the algorithm depends on that of bounded sampling and of parsing. One can check that in the case of PFA, the generation is in $\mathcal{O}(b \cdot \log |\Sigma|)$ and the parsing (of a string of length at most b) is in $\mathcal{O}(b \cdot |Q|^2)$.

3.2 A Direct Computation in the Case of PFA

When the machine is a probabilistic finite automaton, we can do a bit better by making use of simple properties concerning probabilistic languages.

Data: a machine $\mathcal{M}$, $p \geq 0$, $b \geq 0$
Result: $w \in \Sigma^{\leq b}$ such that $Pr_{\mathcal{M}}(w) \geq p$, **false** if there is no such w

```
begin
    Map f;
    m = (8/p) ln (2/δ);
    repeat m times
        w = bounded_sample(M, b);
        f[w]++;
    foreach w: f[w] ≥ pm/2 do
        if Pr_M(w) ≥ p then
            return w;
    return false
```

Algorithm 1: Solving BMPS in the general case

We are given a $p > 0$ and a PFA $\mathcal{A}$. Then we have the following properties:

Property 1. $\forall u \in \Sigma^\star$, $Pr_{\mathcal{A}}(u\,\Sigma^\star) \geq Pr_{\mathcal{A}}(u)$.

Property 2. *For each $n \geq 0$ there are at most $\frac{1}{p}$ strings u in Σ^n such that $Pr_{\mathcal{A}}(u\,\Sigma^\star) \geq p$.*

Both proofs are straightforward and hold not only for PFA but for all distributions. Notice that a stronger version of Property 2 is Property 3:

Property 3. *If X is a set of strings such that (1) $\forall u \in X, Pr_{\mathcal{A}}(u\,\Sigma^\star) \geq p$ and (2) no string in X is a prefix of another different string in X, then $|X| \leq \frac{1}{p}$.*

Analysis and complexity of Algorithm 2. The idea of the algorithm is as follows. For each length n compute the set of viable prefixes of length n, and keep those whose probability is at least p. The process goes on until either there are no more viable prefixes or a valid string has been found. We use the fact that $Pr_{\mathcal{A}}(ua\,\Sigma^\star)$ and $Pr_{\mathcal{A}}(u)$ can be computed from $Pr_{\mathcal{A}}(u\,\Sigma^\star)$ provided we memorize the value in each state (by a standard dynamic programming technique). Property 2 ensures that at every moment at most $\frac{1}{p}$ valid prefixes are open.

If all arithmetic operations are in constant time, the complexity of the algorithm is in $\mathcal{O}(\frac{b|\Sigma|\cdot|Q|^2}{p})$.

3.3 Sampling Vs Exact Computing

BMPS can be solved with a randomized algorithm (and with error at most δ) or by the direct Algorithm 2. If we compare costs, and assuming that bounded sampling a string can be done in time linear in b, and that all arithmetic operations take constant time we have:

Data: a PFA : $\mathcal{A} = \langle \Sigma, \mathbf{S}, \mathbf{M}, \mathbf{F} \rangle$, $p \geq 0$, $b \geq 0$
Result: $w \in \Sigma^{\leq b}$ such that $Pr_{\mathcal{A}}(u) \geq p$, **false** if there is no such w

```
begin
    Queue Q;
    p_λ = SF;
    if p_λ ≥ p then
        return p_λ;
    push(Q, (λ, F));
    while not empty(Q) do
        (w, V) = pop(Q);
        foreach a ∈ Σ do
            V' = V M_a;
            if V'F ≥ p then
                return V'F;
            if |w| < b and V'1 ≥ p then
                push(Q, (wa, V'));
    return false
```

Algorithm 2: Solving BMPS for automata

- Complexity of (randomized) Algorithm 1 for PFA is in $\mathcal{O}(\frac{8b}{p}\ln\frac{2}{\delta}\cdot\log|\Sigma|)$ to build the sample and $\mathcal{O}(\frac{2b}{p}\cdot|Q|^2)$ to check the $\frac{2}{p}$ most frequent strings.
- Complexity of Algorithm 2 is in $\mathcal{O}(\frac{b|\Sigma|\cdot|Q|^2}{p})$.

Therefore,for the randomized algorithm to be faster, the alphabet has to be very large. Experiments (see Section 5) show that this is rarely the case.

3.4 Generalising to Other Machines

What is really important in Algorithm 2 is that the different $Pr_{\mathcal{M}}(u\,\Sigma^\star)$ can be computed. If this is a case, the algorithm can be generalized and will work with other types of machines. This is the case for context-free grammars (Stolcke, 1995).

For classes which are strongly sampable, we propose the more general Algorithm 3.

4 More about the Bounds

The question we now have to answer is: how do we choose the bound? We are given some machine $\mathcal{M}$ and a number $p \geq 0$. We are looking for a value n_p which is the smallest integer such that $Pr_{\mathcal{M}}(x) \geq p \implies |x| \leq n_p$. If we can compute this bound we can run one of the algorithms from the previous section.

```
Data: a machine M, p ≥ 0, b ≥ 0
Result: w ∈ Σ^{≤b} such that Pr_M(w) ≥ p,
   false if there is no such w
begin
    Queue Q;
    p_w = Pr_M(λ);
    if p_w ≥ p then
        return p_w;
    push(Q, λ);
    while not empty(Q) do
        w = pop(Q);
        foreach a ∈ Σ do
            if Pr_M(wa) ≥ p then
                return Pr_M(wa);
            if |w| < b and Pr_M(waΣ*) ≥ p
            then
                push(Q, wa);
    return false
```

Algorithm 3: Solving BMPS for general machines

4.1 Computing Analytically n_p

If given the machine $\mathcal{M}$ we can compute the mean μ and the variance σ of the length of strings in $\mathcal{D}_{\mathcal{M}}$, we can use Chebychev's inequality:

$$Pr_{\mathcal{M}}\big(\big||x| - \mu\big| > k\sigma\big) < \frac{1}{k^2}$$

We now choose $k = \frac{1}{\sqrt{p}}$ and rewrite:

$$Pr_{\mathcal{M}}\big(|x| > \mu + \frac{\sigma}{\sqrt{p}}\big) < p$$

This means that, if we are looking for strings with a probability bigger than p, it is not necessary to consider strings longer than $\mu + \frac{\sigma}{\sqrt{p}}$.

In other words, we can set $b = \lceil \mu + \frac{\sigma}{\sqrt{p}} \rceil$ and run an algorithm from Section 3 which solves BMPS.

4.2 Computing Analytically n_p for PFA

We consider the special case where the probabilistic machine is a PFA $\mathcal{A}$. We are interested in computing the mean and the variance of the string length. It can be noted that the fact the PFA is deterministic or not is not a problem.

The mean string length of the strings generated by $\mathcal{A}$ can be computed as:

$$\begin{aligned}\mu &= \sum_{i=0}^{\infty} i\, Pr_{\mathcal{A}}(\Sigma^i)\\ &= \sum_{i=0}^{\infty} i\, \mathbf{S}\mathbf{M}_\lambda^*\mathbf{M}_\Sigma^i\mathbf{M}_\lambda^*\mathbf{F}\\ &= \mathbf{S}\mathbf{M}_\lambda^*\mathbf{M}_\Sigma(I - \mathbf{M}_\Sigma)^{-2}\mathbf{M}_\lambda^*\mathbf{F}\end{aligned}$$

Moreover, taking into account that:

$$\begin{aligned}&\sum_{i=0}^{\infty} i^2 Pr_{\mathcal{A}}(\Sigma^i) = \sum_{i=0}^{\infty} i^2 \mathbf{S}\mathbf{M}_\lambda^*\mathbf{M}_\Sigma^i\mathbf{M}_\lambda^*\mathbf{F}\\ &= \mathbf{S}\mathbf{M}_\lambda^*\mathbf{M}_\Sigma(I + \mathbf{M}_\Sigma)(I - \mathbf{M}_\Sigma)^{-3}\mathbf{M}_\lambda^*\mathbf{F}\end{aligned}$$

The variance can be computed as:

$$\begin{aligned}\sigma^2 &= \sum_{i=0}^{\infty}(i-\mu)^2 Pr_{\mathcal{A}}(\Sigma^i)\\ &= \sum_{i=0}^{\infty} i^2 Pr_{\mathcal{A}}(\Sigma^i) - \mu^2\\ &= \mathbf{S}\mathbf{M}_\lambda^*\mathbf{M}_\Sigma(I + \mathbf{M}_\Sigma)(I - \mathbf{M}_\Sigma)^{-3}\mathbf{M}_\lambda^*\mathbf{F}\\ &\quad - \left[\mathbf{S}\mathbf{M}_\lambda^*\mathbf{M}_\Sigma(I - \mathbf{M}_\Sigma)^{-2}\mathbf{M}_\lambda^*\mathbf{F}\right]^2\end{aligned}$$

Then, both values are finite since $(I - \mathbf{M}_\Sigma)$ is non singular.

4.3 Computing $n_{p,\delta}$ via Sampling

In certain cases we cannot draw an analytically obtained value for the mean and the variance. We have to resort to sampling in order to compute an estimation of n_p.

A sufficiently large sample is built and used by Lemma 1 to obtain our result. In that case we have the following:

- If the instance is negative, it is anyhow impossible to find a string with high enough probability, so the answer will always be **false**.
- If the instance is positive, the bound returned by the sampling will be good in all but a small fraction (less than δ) of cases. When the sampling has gone correctly, then the algorithm when it halts has checked all the strings up to length n. And the total weight of the remaining strings is less than p.

The general goal of this section is to compute, given a strogly sampable machine $\mathcal{M}$ capable of generating strings following distribution

$\mathcal{D}_{\mathcal{M}}$ and a positive value p, an integer $n_{p,\delta}$ such that $Pr_{\mathcal{D}_{\mathcal{M}}}(\Sigma^{n_{p,\delta}}) < p$. If we do this by sampling we will of course have the result depend also on the value δ covering the case where the sampling process went abnormally wrong.

Lemma 1. *Let $\mathcal{D}$ be a distribution over $\Sigma^\star$. Then if we draw, following distribution $\mathcal{D}$, a sample S of size at least $\frac{1}{p}\ln\frac{1}{\delta}$, given any $p > 0$ and any $\delta > 0$, the following holds with probability at least 1-δ: the probability of sampling a string x longer than any string seen in S is less than p.*

Alternatively, if we write $n_S = \max\{|y| : y \in S\}$, then, with probability at least $1-\delta$, $Pr_{\mathcal{D}}(|x| > n_S) < p$.

Proof. Denote by m_p the smallest integer such that the probability for a randomly drawn string to be longer than m_p is less than p: $Pr_{\mathcal{D}}(\Sigma^{>m_p}) < p$.

We need now to compute a large enough sample to be sure (with a possible error of at most δ) that $\max\{|y| : y \in S\} \geq m_p$. For $Pr_{\mathcal{D}}(|x| > m_p) < p$ to hold, a sufficient condition is that we take a sample large enough to be nearly sure (*i.e.* with probability at least $1-\delta$) to have at least one string as long as m_p. On the contrary, the probability of having all (k) strings in S of length less than m_p is at most $(1-p)^k$. Using the fact that $(1-p)^k > \delta$ implies that $k > \frac{1}{p}\ln\frac{1}{\delta}$, it follows that it is sufficient, once we have chosen δ, to take $n_{p,\delta} > \frac{1}{p}\ln\frac{1}{\delta}$ to have a correct value. □

Note that in the above, all we ask is that we are able to sample. This is indeed the case with HMM, PFA and (well defined) probablistic context-free grammars, provided these are not expansive. Lemma 1 therefore holds for any of such machines.

4.4 The Most Probable String Can Be of Exponential Length

If the most probable string can be very long, how long might it be? We show now an automaton for which the most probable string is of exponential length with the size of the automaton. The construction is based on (de la Higuera, 1997). Let us use a value $\gamma > 0$ whose exact value we will compute later.

We first note (Figure 5) how to build an automaton that only gives non null probabilities to strings whose length are multiples of ψ for any value of ψ (and of particular interest are the prime numbers). Here, $Pr(a^{k\psi}) = \gamma(1-\gamma)^k$.

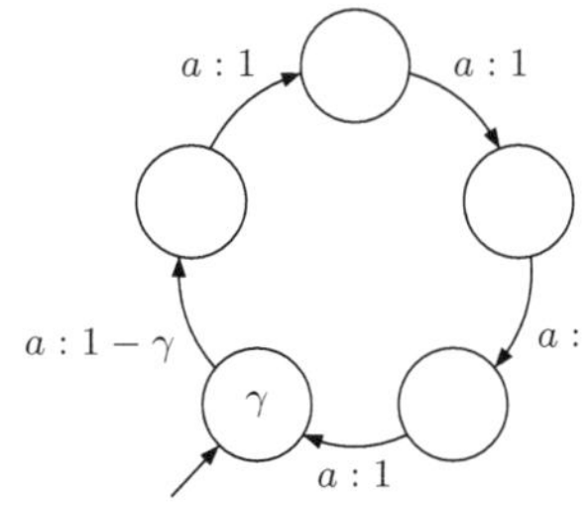

Figure 5: Automaton for $(a^5)^*$.

We now extend this construction by building for a set of prime numbers $\{\psi_1, \psi_2, \ldots, \psi_z\}$ the automaton for each ψ_i and adding an initial state. When parsing a non empty string, a sub-automaton will only add to the mass of probabilities if the string is of length multiple of ψ_i. This PFA can be constructed as proposed in Figure 6, and has $1 + \sum_{i=1}^{i=z}\psi_i$ states.

The probability of string a^k with $k = \prod_{i=1}^{i=z} p_i$ is $\sum_{i=1}^{i=z}\frac{1}{z}\gamma(1-\gamma)^{\frac{k}{\psi_i}-1} = \frac{\gamma}{z}\sum_{i=1}^{i=z}(1-\gamma)^{\frac{k}{\psi_i}-1}$.

First consider a string of length less than k. This string is not accepted by at least one of the sub-automata so it's probability is at most $\gamma\frac{z-1}{z}$.

On the other hand we prove now that for a good value of γ, $Pr(a^k) > \gamma\frac{z-1}{z}$.

We simplify by noticing that since $\frac{k}{\psi_i} - 1 \leq k$, $(1-\gamma)^{\frac{k}{\psi_i}-1} > (1-\gamma)^k$.

So $Pr(a^k) > \frac{\gamma}{z}\sum_{i=1}^{i=z}(1-\gamma)^k = \gamma(1-\gamma)^k$.

$$(1-\gamma)^k > \frac{z-1}{z}$$
$$1-\gamma > \sqrt[k]{\frac{z-1}{z}}$$
$$\gamma < 1 - \sqrt[k]{\frac{z-1}{z}}$$

no shorter string can have higher probability.

5 Experiments

We report here some experiments in which we compared both algorithms over probabilistic automata.

In order to have languages where the most probable string is not very short, we generated a set of random automata with a linear topology, only one initial state and one final state, and where transitions were added leading from each state to all

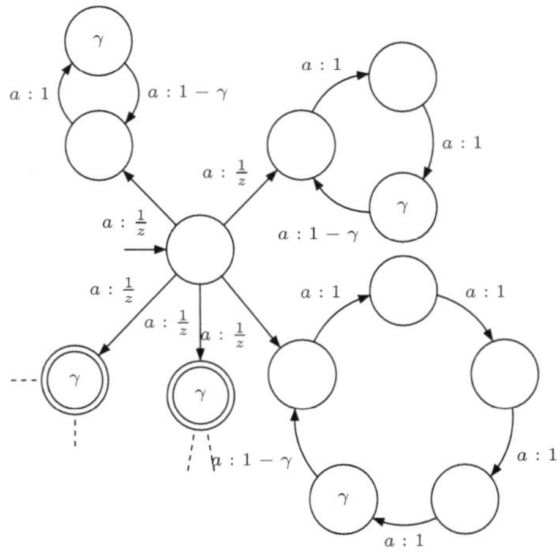

Figure 6: An automaton whose smallest 'interesting string' is of exponential length.

previous states labelled by all the symbols of the vocabulary.

The probabilities on the edges and the final state were set assigning to them randomly (uniformly) distributed numbers in the range $[0, 1]$ and then normalizing.

Voc size	Sampling (s)	Exact (s)
2	0.34	0.00
4	13.26	0.00
6	13.80	0.01
8	31.85	0.02
10	169.21	0.09
12	156.58	0.10

Table 1: Execution time of Algorithm 1 (sampling) and Algorithm 2 (exact) for 4 state automata

In our experiments, the exact algorithm is systematically faster than the one that uses sampling.

Alternative settings which would be favourable to the randomized algorithm are still to be found.

6 Conclusion

We have proved the following:

1. There exists a PFA whose most probable string is not of polynomial length.

2. If we can sample and parse (strongly samplable distribution), then we have a randomised algorithm which solves MPS.

3. If furthermore we can analytically compute the mean and variance of the distribution, there is an exact algorithm for MPS. This means that the problem is decidable for a PFA or HMMs.

4. In the case of PFA the mean and the variance are polynomially computable, so MPS can be solved in time polynomial in the size of the PFA and in $\frac{1}{p}$.

5. In the case of PFA, we can use practical algorithms:

   (a) randomly draw a sample S of n strings following distribution $\mathcal{D}_{\mathcal{A}}$;

   (b) let $p = \max\{p(u) : u \in S\}$ and $b = \max\{|u| : u \in S\}$;

   (c) run Algorithm 2 using p and b.

Practically, the crucial problem may be CS; A consensus string can be found by either sampling to obtain a lower bound to the probability of the most probable string and solving MPS, or by some form of binary search.

Further experiments are needed to see in what cases the sampling algorithm works better, and also to check its robustness with more complex models (like probabilistic context-free grammars).

Finally, in Section 4.4 we showed that the length of the most probable string could be exponential, but it is unclear if a higher bound to the length can be obtained.

Acknowledgement

Discussions with Pascal Koiran during earlier stages of this work were of great help towards the understanding of the nature of the problem. The first author also acknowledges partial support by the Région des Pays de la Loire. The second author thanks the Spanish CICyT for partial support of this work through projects TIN2009-14205-C04-C1, and the program CONSOLIDER INGENIO 2010 (CSD2007-00018).

References

S. Ben-David, B. Chor, O. Goldreich, and M. Luby. 1992. On the theory of average case complexity. *Journal of Computer and System Sciences*, 44(2):193—-219.

V. D. Blondel and V. Canterini. 2003. Undecidable problems for probabilistic automata of fixed dimension. *Theory of Computer Systems*, 36(3):231–245.

F. Casacuberta and C. de la Higuera. 1999. Optimal linguistic decoding is a difficult computational problem. *Pattern Recognition Letters*, 20(8):813–821.

F. Casacuberta and C. de la Higuera. 2000. Computational complexity of problems on probabilistic grammars and transducers. In *Proceedings of* ICGI *2000*, volume 1891 of LNAI, pages 15–24. Springer-Verlag.

F. Casacuberta. 1995. Probabilistic estimation of stochastic regular syntax-directed translation schemes. In R. Moreno, editor, *VI Spanish Symposium on Pattern Recognition and Image Analysis*, pages 201–297. AERFAI.

C. Cortes, M. Mohri, and A. Rastogi. 2006. On the computation of some standard distances between probabilistic automata. In *Proceedings of* CIAA *2006*, volume 4094 of LNCS, pages 137–149. Springer-Verlag.

C. Cortes, M. Mohri, and A. Rastogi. 2007. l_p distance and equivalence of probabilistic automata. *International Journal of Foundations of Computer Science*, 18(4):761–779.

C. de la Higuera. 1997. Characteristic sets for polynomial grammatical inference. *Machine Learning Journal*, 27:125–138.

M. R. Garey and D. S. Johnson. 1979. *Computers and Intractability*. Freeman.

Joshua T. Goodman. 1998. *Parsing Inside–Out*. Ph.D. thesis, Harvard University.

F. Jelinek. 1998. *Statistical Methods for Speech Recognition*. The MIT Press, Cambridge, Massachusetts.

L. Levin. 1986. Average case complete problems. *SIAM Journal on Computing*, 15(1):285–286.

R. B. Lyngsø and C. N. S. Pedersen. 2002. The consensus string problem and the complexity of comparing hidden markov models. *Journal of Computing and System Science*, 65(3):545–569.

M. Mohri, F. C. N. Pereira, and M. Riley. 2000. The design principles of a weighted finite-state transducer library. *Theoretical Computer Science*, 231(1):17–32.

M. Mohri. 1997. Finite-state transducers in language and speech processing. *Computational Linguistics*, 23(3):269–311.

A. Paz. 1971. *Introduction to probabilistic automata*. Academic Press, New York.

D. Picó and F. Casacuberta. 2001. Some statistical-estimation methods for stochastic finite-state transducers. *Machine Learning Journal*, 44(1):121–141.

L. Rabiner. 1989. A tutorial on hidden Markov models and selected applications in speech recoginition. *Proceedings of the* IEEE, 77:257–286.

K. Sima'an. 1996. Computational complexity of probabilistic disambiguation by means of tree-grammars. In COLING, pages 1175–1180.

A. Stolcke. 1995. An efficient probablistic context-free parsing algorithm that computes prefix probabilities. *Computational Linguistics*, 21(2):165–201.

E. Vidal, F. Thollard, C. de la Higuera, F. Casacuberta, and R. C. Carrasco. 2005. Probabilistic finite state automata – part I and II. *Pattern Analysis and Machine Intelligence*, 27(7):1013–1039.

A Word Clustering Approach to Domain Adaptation: Effective Parsing of Biomedical Texts

Marie Candito†, Enrique Henestroza Anguiano† & Djamé Seddah†‡
† Alpage (Univ. Paris Diderot & INRIA), 175 rue du Chevaleret, 75013 Paris, France
‡ Univ. Paris Sorbonne, 28, rue Serpente, 75006 Paris, France
marie.candito@linguist.jussieu.fr, henestro@inria.fr, djame.seddah@paris-sorbonne.fr

Abstract

We present a simple and effective way to perform out-of-domain statistical parsing by drastically reducing lexical data sparseness in a PCFG-LA architecture. We replace terminal symbols with unsupervised word clusters acquired from a large newspaper corpus augmented with biomedical target-domain data. The resulting clusters are effective in bridging the lexical gap between source-domain and target-domain vocabularies. Our experiments combine known self-training techniques with unsupervised word clustering and produce promising results, achieving an error reduction of 21% on a new evaluation set for biomedical text with manual bracketing annotations.

1 Introduction

If Natural Language Processing were the Olympics, statistical parsing would be the combination of "long jump" and "100 meters": a discipline where performance is evaluated in light of raw metric data in a very specific arena. Leaving aside this far-fetched metaphor, it is a fact that statistical constituent-based parsing has long been subjected to an evaluation process that can almost be qualified as *addicted* to its own test set (Gildea, 2001; McClosky et al., 2006; Foster, 2010). However, the gap between this intrinsic evaluation methodology, which is only able to provide a ranking of some parser/treebank pairs using a given metric, and the growing need for accurate wide coverage parsers suitable for coping with an unlimited stream of new data, is currently being tackled more widely. Thus, the task of parsing out-of-domain text becomes crucial.

Various techniques have been proposed to adapt existing parsing models to new genres: domain adaptation via self training (Bacchiani et al., 2006; McClosky et al., 2006; Sagae, 2010), co-training (Steedman et al., 2003), treebank and target transformation (Foster, 2010), source-domain target data matching prior to self-training (Foster et al., 2007), and recently, uptraining techniques (Petrov et al., 2010). Although very diverse in practice, these techniques are all designed to overcome the syntactic and lexical gaps that exist between source domain and target domain data. Interestingly, the lexical gap found for English (Sekine, 1997) can only be wider for out-of-domain parsing of languages that are morphologically richer. Indeed, the relatively small size of their annotated treebanks and their levels of lexical variation are already a stress case for most statistical parsing models, without adding the extreme challenges caused by lexical out-of-domain variation.

In this paper, we take the PCFG-LA framework (Petrov and Klein, 2007), implemented by Attia et al. (2010), and explore a combination of known self-training techniques with a novel application of unsupervised word clustering (Koo et al., 2008) that was successfully used to reduce lexical data sparseness for French parsing (Candito and Crabbé, 2009; Candito and Seddah, 2010).

2 Target Domain Corpus

For our work on domain adaptation, we used the French Treebank (FTB) (Abeillé and Barrier, 2004) as the *source domain* corpus, which consists of 12,351 sentences from the *Le Monde* newspaper. For the *target domain*, we used biomedical texts from the European Medicines Agency, specifically the French part of the EMEA section[1] of the OPUS corpus (Tiedemann, 2009). Although we chose the biomedical domain for this paper, our approach can be used for any target domain.

2.1 Corpus Characteristics

The EMEA corpus includes documents related to medicinal products: it mostly consists of summaries of European public assessment reports (EPAR), each on a specific medicine. The French

[1] opus.lingfil.uu.se/EMEA.php

part we used (hereafter EmeaFr) was taken from the English-French aligned bi-text of the EMEA corpus, which consists of raw text converted from PDF files. We estimate that the French part contains around 1000 documents. According to the Standard Operating Procedure of the EMEA for EPARs[2], these documents are first written in English, in a "language understandable by someone not an expert in the field". The translation into all official European languages is managed by the Translation Centre for the Bodies of the European Union (CdT), with standardized terminology for biomedical lay language. As far as we can judge, the quality of the French translation is very good.

This corpus is challenging for domain adaptation: though it contains well-formed sentences, it uses specialized terminology (protocols to test and administrate medicines, and descriptions of diseases, symptoms and counter-indications), and its writing style is very different from that used in the journalistic domain. There are many uses of imperative verbs (in the instructions for use), numerous dosage descriptions, and frequent information within brackets (containing abreviations, glosses of medical terms, and frequency information).

2.2 Corpus Preprocessing

The original EmeaFr corpus contains approximately 14 million words. We corrected some obvious errors from the PDF to text conversion, such as missing quotes after elided tokens (j' for elided "I", n' for elided "not", etc.). We then performed tokenization, segmentation into sentences, and recognition of multiword expressions using the BONSAI package[3], in order to obtain tokenized text that resembles the tokenization of the FTB. Finally we removed lines (sentences) not containing any alphabetical character, as well as duplicated sentences (we kept only one occurrence of each unique tokenized sentence). This resulted in a drastic reduction of the corpus, as many sentences provide general information or recommendations that are repeated in every EPAR document. In the end, the resulting preprocessed corpus (hereafter EmeaFrU) contains approximately 5.3 million tokens and 267 thousand sentences.

2.3 Manual Bracketing Annotation

To evaluate parsing performance, we manually annotated two extracts of the EmeaFrU corpus, corresponding to two EPAR documents: one for development and one for final tests. We removed them from EmeaFrU. In order to obtain gold parses for the development and test sets, we first parsed them using the BONSAI package, which contains the Berkeley parser (Petrov and Klein, 2007), and a French model as described in (Candito et al., 2010). We retained only the POS tags, and had them validated by an expert. Then we reparsed the sets in pre-tagged mode, and had them validated by the same expert, using the WORDFREAK tool (Morton and LaCivita, 2003) that we adapted to French. We removed section numbers starting or ending sentences, table cells, and also a few obviously incomplete sentences.[4]

	Test Set	Dev Set
# of sentences	544	574
avg sent. length	21.5	16.2
# of tokens	11,679	9,346
Stats for any type of token		
# of tokens (% unknown)		9,346 (23%)
# of types (% unknown)		1,917 (42%)
Stats for alpha-lc tokens		
# of tokens (% unknown)		8,109 (22%)
# of types (% unknown)		1,608 (36%)

Table 1: Statistics on the EMEA dev and test sets. *alpha-lc* stands for tokens converted to lowercase and containing at least one letter. *Unknown* tokens/types are those absent from the FTB training set.

Table 1 shows a few statistics for the evaluation sets, and a comparison of the dev set vocabulary with that of the FTB standard training set. Focusing on non-punctuation, non-numeric tokens, we see that more than $1/3$ of the vocabulary is unknown (36%), representing 22% of the token occurrences. This strongly motivates a domain adaptation technique focused on lexical variation between the source domain and the target domain.

3 Lexical Domain Adaptation

In our approach to domain adaption, we use unsupervised word clustering performed on a mixture of target-domain (biomedical) and source-domain (journalistic) text. The objective is to obtain clusters grouping together source-domain and target-domain words, thus bridging the two vocabularies.

We build on the work of Candito and Crabbé (2009), who proposed a technique to improve in-domain parsing by reducing lexical data sparse-

[2]Document 3131, at: www.ema.europa.eu

[3]alpage.inria.fr/statgram/frdep/fr_stat_dep_parsing.html

[4]We plan to make the manually-annotated corpus freely available, following a final validation step.

ness: (i) replace tokens with unsupervised word clusters both in training and test data; (ii) learn a grammar from the word-clustered sentences in the training set; (iii) parse the word-clustered sentences in the test set; (iv) reintroduce the original tokens into the test sentences to obtain the final parsed output. The clustering is performed in two steps: (i) a morphological clustering is applied using the *Lefff* morphological lexicon (Sagot et al., 2006), where plural and feminine suffixes are removed from word forms and past/future tenses are mapped to present tense (provided this does not change the part-of-speech ambiguity of the form); (ii) an unsupervised clustering algorithm (Brown et al., 1992) is run on a large unlabeled corpus to learn clusters over the desinflected forms. Both clustering steps proved to be beneficial for parsing in-domain French text using the Berkeley parser.

We apply a similar unsupervised word clustering technique to lexical domain adaptation, with the difference being that clusters are learned over a mixture of source-domain and target-domain text (hereafter *mixed clusters*). We test this technique when training a parser on the FTB training set as well as in self-training mode (McClosky and Charniak, 2008), where the parser is trained on both the source-domain training set and automatically parsed sentences from the target domain.

4 Experiments

For our parsing experiments, we used the PCFG-LA algorithm of Petrov and Klein (2007), implemented by Attia et al. (2010).[5] The treebank used was the FTB (cf. Section 2). More precisely, we used the version of the treebank as defined by Candito and Crabbé (2009), which has a 28 POS tagset and some multiword expressions replaced by regular syntactic structures. We used the standard training (80%), dev (10%), and test (10%) split, containing respectively 9881, 1235 and 1235 sentences from the *Le Monde* newspaper.

For unsupervised clustering, we first systematically applied the desinflection process of Candito and Crabbé (2009), using the Bonsai tool. We obtained *source clusters* by applying Percy Liang's implementation[6] of the Brown clustering algorithm to the *L'Est Républicain* corpus (herafter ER), a 125 million word journalistic corpus,

[5]Our experiments were run using five split-merge cycles and tuned suffixes for handling French unknown words.

[6]www.eecs.berkeley.edu/~pliang/software

	F-Measure on EMEA test set (≤ 40)	
Symbols	No self-training	200k self-training
raw	81.25	84.75
dfl	81.82	84.72
clt-er	82.65	85.09
clt-er-emea	83.53	85.19

Table 2: F-Measure for sentences $\leq$ 40 tokens on the EMEA test set, both with self-training (200k auto-parsed sentences from EmeaFrU) and without.

freely available at CNRTL[7]. Though this newspaper is less formal than *Le Monde*, it is still journalistic, so we consider it as being in the source domain. The *mixed clusters* were obtained by concatenating the *L'Est Républicain* corpus and the EmeaFrU (cf. Section 2), herafter ER+EMEA. We did not investigate any weighting techniques for building the source corpus for mixed clusters. On both the ER and ER+EMEA corpora, we ran Brown clustering with 1000 clusters for the desinflected forms appearing at least 60 times.

Having performed desinflection and different types of clustering, we trained PCFG-LA grammars on the FTB training set using four settings for terminal symbols: *raw* uses original word forms; *dfl* uses desinflected word forms; *clt-er* uses clusters of desinflected forms computed over the ER corpus, with a process described in detail by Candito and Crabbé (2009); *clt-er-emea* is the same as *clt-er*, but with mixed clusters over the ER+EMEA corpus. Having obtained these initial grammars, we used each to parse the EmeaFrU unlabeled corpus (with appropriate desinflection and clustering preprocessing for each of the four terminal symbol settings). We then performed self-training experiments adding up to 200k predicted parses from EmeaFrU to the FTB training set, and training new grammars for each such enlarged training set.

4.1 Results

Figure 1 shows the effect of self-training on parsing the EMEA and FTB dev sets. Unsurprisingly, the baseline parser (*raw* setting without self-training) has a 5 point drop in F-measure when parsing the EMEA compared to the FTB. Consistent with previous results on English biomedical texts (Lease and Charniak, 2005; McClosky and Charniak, 2008), self-training helps in parsing the EMEA, with more predicted parses generally leading to better performance on the EMEA (and worse performance on the FTB).

[7]www.cnrtl.fr/corpus/estrepublicain

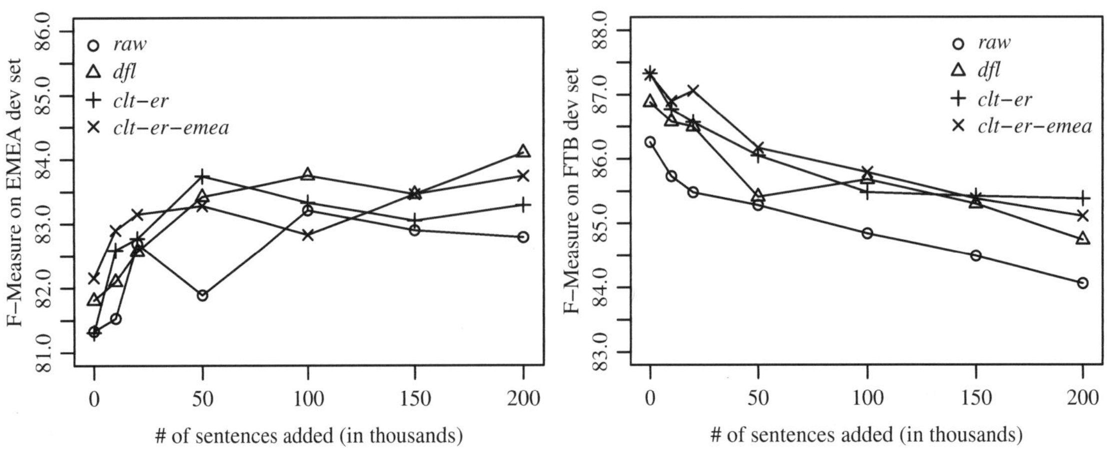

Figure 1: F-Measure for sentences of length ≤ 40 on the EMEA (left) and FTB (right) dev sets using self-training (with different amounts of auto-parsed sentences from EmeaFrU), by terminal symbol setting.

Concerning the different settings for terminal symbols, for source-domain data we reproduce (right side of Figure 1) the findings of Candito and Crabbé (2009): parsing desinflected forms (*dfl*) increases performance, and parsing unsupervised clusters of desinflected forms (*clt-er* and *clt-er-emea*) is even better. For target-domain data, we find that desinflection does help, and even achieves better performance than source clusters. This can be explained by the fact that the desinflection process provides forms that still follow French morphology, so the general handling of unknown words (with classes of suffixes) does apply. In contrast, terminological tokens are (hopefully) more frequently absent from the ER corpus than the ER+EMEA corpus, and they are replaced by the UNK token more often for source clusters (*clt-er*) than for mixed clusters (*clt-er-emea*). Indeed, for the EMEA dev set, 1,466 tokens are UNK in the *clt-er* setting, while only 729 tokens are UNK in the *clt-er-emea* setting.

Table 2 shows final parsing results on the EMEA test set for each of the four terminal symbol settings, with and without self-training (using 200k parses from EmeaFrU). We evaluated using F-Measure on labeled precision and recall, ignoring punctuation, and calculated the significance of differences between settings.[8] The *clt-er-emea* setting gives the best overall performance, with or without self-training. When comparing *clt-er-emea* with self-training (best overall) to *raw* without self-training (baseline), we obtain a 21% error reduction. This result is encouraging, given the small amount of raw target-domain data added to the ER corpus (5M added to 125M words). However, self-training produces the most pronounced increase in performance (statistically significant improvement over no self-training for each terminal symbol setting), and attenuates the improvement attained by clustering: while *clt-er-emea* is significantly better than *raw* or *dfl* without self-training, the differences are not significant with self-training. More raw target-domain data may be needed for mixed clusters to be fully effective.

5 Conclusion

We have proposed a technique of parsing word clusters for domain adaptation, clustering together source and target-domain words. We have shown this to be beneficial for parsing biomedical French texts, though it did not provide significant additional improvement over self-training.

Our perspectives for future work are to investigate: (i) producing mixed clusters with a larger unlabeled target-domain corpus; (ii) using lexicon-informed part-of-speech taggers; (iii) supplementing our approach with other techniques like reranking, known to improve self-training for domain adaptation (McClosky and Charniak, 2008), or uptraining (Petrov et al., 2010).

Acknowledgements

Thanks to J. Foster, D. Hogan and J. Le Roux for making the LORG parser available to us and to the French National Research Agency (SEQUOIA project ANR-08-EMER-013).

[8] Significance at $p = 0.05$, using Bikel's Statistical Significance Tester: www.cis.upenn.edu/~dbikel/software.html

References

Anne Abeillé and Nicolas Barrier. 2004. Enriching a french treebank. In *Proc. of LREC'04*, Lisbon, Portugal.

Mohammed Attia, Jennifer Foster, Deirdre Hogan, Joseph Le Roux, Lamia Tounsi, and Josef van Genabith. 2010. Handling unknown words in statistical latent-variable parsing models for arabic, english and french. In *Proceedings of the NAACL/HLT Workshop on Statistical Parsing of Morphologically Rich Languages (SPMRL 2010)*, Los Angeles, CA.

M. Bacchiani, M. Riley, B. Roark, and R. Sproat. 2006. Map adaptation of stochastic grammars. *Computer speech & language*, 20(1):41–68.

Peter F. Brown, Vincent J. Della, Peter V. Desouza, Jennifer C. Lai, and Robert L. Mercer. 1992. Class-based n-gram models of natural language. *Computational linguistics*, 18(4):467–479.

Marie Candito and Benoît Crabbé. 2009. Improving generative statistical parsing with semi-supervised word clustering. In *Proceedings of the 11th International Conference on Parsing Technologies (IWPT'09)*, pages 138–141, Paris, France, October. Association for Computational Linguistics.

Marie Candito and Djamé Seddah. 2010. Parsing word clusters. In *Proceedings of the NAACL/HLT Workshop on Statistical Parsing of Morphologically Rich Languages (SPMRL 2010)*, Los Angeles, CA.

Marie Candito, Joakim Nivre, Pascal Denis, and Enrique Henestroza Anguiano. 2010. Benchmarking of statistical dependency parsers for french. In *Proceedings of COLING 2010*, Beijing, China.

J. Foster, J. Wagner, D. Seddah, and J. Van Genabith. 2007. Adapting wsj-trained parsers to the british national corpus using in-domain self-training. In *Proceedings of the Tenth IWPT*, pages 33–35.

Jennifer Foster. 2010. "cba to check the spelling": Investigating parser performance on discussion forum posts. In *Human Language Technologies: The 2010 Annual Conference of the North American Chapter of the Association for Computational Linguistics*, pages 381–384, Los Angeles, California, June. Association for Computational Linguistics.

Daniel Gildea. 2001. Corpus variation and parser performance. In *Proceedings of the First Conference on Empirical Methods in Natural Language Processing (EMNLP)*, pages 167–202.

Terry Koo, Xavier Carreras, and Michael Collins. 2008. Simple semi-supervised dependency parsing. In *Proceedings of ACL-08*, pages 595–603, Columbus, USA.

M. Lease and E. Charniak. 2005. Parsing biomedical literature. *Natural Language Processing–IJCNLP 2005*, pages 58–69.

David McClosky and Eugene Charniak. 2008. Self-training for biomedical parsing. In *Proceedings of ACL-08: HLT, Short Papers*, pages 101–104, Columbus, Ohio, June. Association for Computational Linguistics.

D. McClosky, E. Charniak, and M. Johnson. 2006. Reranking and self-training for parser adaptation. In *Proceedings of the 21st International Conference on Computational Linguistics and the 44th annual meeting of the Association for Computational Linguistics*, pages 337–344. Association for Computational Linguistics.

T. Morton and J. LaCivita. 2003. Wordfreak: an open tool for linguistic annotation. In *Proceedings of the 2003 Conference of the North American Chapter of the Association for Computational Linguistics on Human Language Technology: Demonstrations-Volume 4*, pages 17–18. Association for Computational Linguistics.

Slav Petrov and Dan Klein. 2007. Improved inference for unlexicalized parsing. In *Human Language Technologies 2007: The Conference of the North American Chapter of the Association for Computational Linguistics; Proceedings of the Main Conference*, pages 404–411, Rochester, New York, April. Association for Computational Linguistics.

S. Petrov, P.C. Chang, M. Ringgaard, and H. Alshawi. 2010. Uptraining for accurate deterministic question parsing. In *Proceedings of the*

2010 Conference on Empirical Methods in Natural Language Processing, pages 705–713. Association for Computational Linguistics.

Kenji Sagae. 2010. Self-training without reranking for parser domain adaptation and its impact on semantic role labeling. In *Proceedings of the 2010 Workshop on Domain Adaptation for Natural Language Processing*, pages 37–44, Uppsala, Sweden, July. Association for Computational Linguistics.

Benoît Sagot, Lionel Clément, Eric V. de La Clergerie, and Pierre Boullier. 2006. The lefff 2 syntactic lexicon for french: Architecture, acquisition, use. *Proc. of LREC 06, Genoa, Italy.*

S. Sekine. 1997. The domain dependence of parsing. In *Proceedings of the fifth conference on Applied natural language processing*, pages 96–102. Association for Computational Linguistics.

M. Steedman, R. Hwa, S. Clark, M. Osborne, A. Sarkar, J. Hockenmaier, P. Ruhlen, S. Baker, and J. Crim. 2003. Example selection for bootstrapping statistical parsers. In *Proceedings of the 2003 Conference of the North American Chapter of the Association for Computational Linguistics on Human Language Technology-Volume 1*, pages 157–164. Association for Computational Linguistics.

Jörg Tiedemann. 2009. News from OPUS - A collection of multilingual parallel corpora with tools and interfaces. In N. Nicolov, K. Bontcheva, G. Angelova, and R. Mitkov, editors, *Recent Advances in Natural Language Processing*, volume V, pages 237–248. John Benjamins, Amsterdam/Philadelphia, Borovets, Bulgaria.

Sentence-Level Instance-Weighting for Graph-Based and Transition-Based Dependency Parsing

Anders Søgaard
Center for Language Technology
University of Copenhagen
soegaard@hum.ku.dk

Martin Haulrich
ISV Computational Linguistics Group
Copenhagen Business School
mwh.isv@cbs.dk

Abstract

Instance-weighting has been shown to be effective in statistical machine translation (Foster et al., 2010), as well as cross-language adaptation of dependency parsers (Søgaard, 2011). This paper presents new methods to do instance-weighting in state-of-the-art dependency parsers. The methods are evaluated on Danish and English data with consistent improvements over unadapted baselines.

1 Introduction

The default assumption in theoretical machine learning is that training and test data are independently and identically (iid) drawn from the same distribution. If the distributions differ, we face what is referred to as sample selection bias in the statistical literature. Sample selection bias is typically ignored in machine learning, but it occurs often in practice.

In natural language processing, the problem shows up in almost any real-world application. Machine translation systems are trained on large amounts of parallel text, but typically this text comes from a small set of sources or institutions, e.g. the Europarl corpora of transcribed debates from the European Parliament (Koehn, 2005). Machine translation systems are used to translate many different kinds of texts, however. In machine translation, which can be seen as a structured learning problem of predicting target sentence y given a source sentence x, we typically see a bias in $P(y)$ and $P(\mathbf{x})$, but not in $P(y|\mathbf{x})$. Statistical parsers for English are typically trained on annotated text from the Wall Street Journal corpus of newspaper articles (Marcus et al., 1993), but are used to process many different kinds of text. Since the problem of sample selection bias in natural language processing is typically related to differences in textual domains, computational linguists typically refer to the problem as domain adaptation.

Domain adaptation is one of the most fundamental yet-to-be-solved problems in natural language processing. While statistical parsers have accuracies of 90-92% parsing newspaper articles, accuracy on transcribed telephone conversations or child-directed speech often drop to 60-70% (Nivre et al., 2007a). Domain adaptation is therefore also receiving more and more attention, and it has recently been studied in the context of named entity recognition (Daume III, 2007), sentiment analysis (Blitzer et al., 2007), dependency parsing (Sagae and Tsujii, 2007; Kawahara and Uchimoto, 2009), text classification (Chen et al., 2009), context-free parsing (McClosky et al., 2010) and machine translation (Foster et al., 2010).

Domain adaptation is the problem of learning a target distribution from a labeled sample of source data with a similar, but different distribution. The problem comes in two variants; one where we also have a small amount of labeled target domain data, and one in which we only have labeled source domain data and must rely on unlabeled source and target domain data to do the actual adaptation of the model that can be learned from source domain data. Much work in natural language processing has assumed a small amount of labeled target domain data (Daume III, 2007; Foster et al., 2010), but we consider the more difficult case where none is available. This is sometimes referred to as unsupervised domain adaptation.

How domain adaptation is tackled depends much on the assumptions we may have about the similarities and differences between the two distributions. One line of approaches to domain adaptation is to change the feature representation of the source domain data, typically focusing on the features that are also predictive in the target domain (Ben-David et al., 2007). Such approaches assume a bias in $P(\mathbf{x})$, but may also try to deal with scenarios where there is a bias in $P(y|\mathbf{x})$. Others have proposed using priors to encode knowledge about one domain in a model induced from data in another domain, or they have promoted frequent target domain classes if they were less frequent in the source domain. Such approaches assume a bias in $P(y)$ and have become popular in word sense disambiguation (Zhu and Hovy, 2007), for example, where a particular reading of *bank* may be much more frequent in some domains rather than others. Classes can be promoted using instance weighting, but instance weighting can also be used to change the marginal distribution of data. The first case is typically referred to as solving class imbalance, while the second case is called covariate shift (Shimodaira, 2000). We will, assuming a bias in $P(\mathbf{x})$, consider the covariate shift scenario. A fourth line of research in domain adaptation applies semi-supervised or transductive learning algorithms to domain adaptation problems, using unlabeled data from the target domain.

In dependency parsing, domain adaptation received attention in the CoNLL 2007 Shared Task. While semi-supervised learning and structural correspondence learning were used by participants in the CoNLL 2007 Shared Task, none of the participants used instance-weighting techniques. In this paper, we follow suggestions in the related literature on learning under sample selection bias to transform the density ratio estimation problem in co-variate shift into a problem of predicting whether an instance is from the source domain or from the target domain (Zadrozny, 2004; Bickel and Scheffer, 2007). We show how to do this in the context of graph-based and transition-based dependency parsing.

Related work includes Søgaard (2011) who uses perplexity per word to select the source data most similar to the target data, so a form of instance weighting with weights 0 and 1, but applies the technique to cross-language adaptation of dependency parsers; but also Plank and van Noord (2011) who in a similar fashion use topic similarity measures to select articles rather than sentences.

Our instance-weighted parsers are evaluated primarily on a new data set, namely a partitioning of the Danish treebank (Buch-Kromann, 2003) into four different textual domains. We do experiments with all pair-wise combinations of the four domain-specific treebanks. Our results are supplemented by a subset of the CoNLL 2007 Shared Task data. It has been noted in several places that there were annotation differences between the source and target data in the original data which makes domain adaptation almost impossible (Dredze et al., 2007). Consequently, we only use the three small target domain evaluation datasets, which were annotated more consistently, and do experiments with all pair-wise combinations of these datasets. Our experiments can also be seen as transductive learning experiments, since no target data other than the data used for evaluation is used.

2 Sentence-Based Instance-Weighting in Dependency Parsing

2.1 Using Text Classification for Instance-Weighting

The source and target plain text corpora are first extracted, and each sentence is assigned a label saying whether the sentence was sampled from source or target data. The idea is then to train a text classifier on the data and use the probability that a sentence comes from the target domain to weight the source instances. This is also the approach to learning under sample selection bias suggested by Zadrozny (2004).

Our text classifier was a logistic regression classifier implemented in Mallet. It represents each sentence by a vector representing occurrences of n-grams in the sentence ($n \leq 3$). No stop word lists were used. The text classifier was used to approximate the probability that each source sentence was sampled from the target domain. The weights are obtained using ten-fold cross-validation. We store one weight for each sentence in the labeled source data.

2.2 Graph-Based Dependency Parsing

Graph-based dependency parsing is a heterogeneous family of approaches to the dependency parsing algorithms, each of which couples a learning algorithm and a parsing algorithm. Some of these algorithms assume dependency trees are projective (Eisner, 1996), while others allow for non-projective dependency trees (McDonald et al., 2005).

One approach to graph-based parsing of non-projective dependency trees is applying minimum spanning tree algorithms to matrices of weighted head-dependent candidate pairs. The learning al-

	Malt-bl	Malt-sys	MST-bl	MST-sys
law-lit	63.55	**64.22**	62.57	**65.31**
law-magz	60.8	**61.34**	**58.65**	58.59
law-news	60.23	**60.58**	58.84	**62.07**
lit-laws	78.34	**79.31**	77.58	**78.06**
lit-magz	**80.22**	80.04	**80.61**	80.55
lit-news	77.31	**77.6**	79.79	**80.14**
magz-law	72.04	**73.98**	73.84	**74.74**
magz-lit	75.74	**76.63**	77.27	**77.78**
magz-news	**73.73**	73.42	**74.42**	73.91
news-law	77.85	**79.65**	80.69	**82.7**
news-lit	85.33	**85.49**	**88.25**	88.22
news-magz	84.93	**85.65**	87.81	87.81
AV	74.17	**74.86**	75.02	**75.82**

Table 1: Unlabeled attachment scores for Danish.

gorithm used in McDonald et al. (2005) and the publicly available MSTParser[1] to learn candidate weights is MIRA (Crammer and Singer, 2003). The MIRA algorithm considers one sentence at each update of the weight vector, and the successive values of the vector are accumulated to later produce an averaged weight vector in a way similar to using averaged perceptron. Unlike using averaged perceptron, MIRA aggressively maximizes the margin between the correct dependency structure and the parser's prediction enforcing it to be larger than the loss of that prediction.

In our experiments we weight the margin such that a large margin between the correct and predicted structures is less aggressively enforced when learning from distant data points. This is achieved by weighting the loss of incorrect classifications by the probability that the sentence was sampled from the target domain.

2.3 Transition-Based Dependency Parsing

Transition-based parsing reduces the problem of finding the most likely dependency tree for a sentence to a series of classification problems by seeing parsing as transitions between configurations. Parsing is incremental and left-to-right. A configuration typically consists of the next couple of words to be read, the first couple words on a stack storing previously read words, and part of the dependency structure already build. Each configuration is a feature vector used to predict the parser's next transition. The guiding classifier is trained on canonical derivations of the dependency trees in the labeled training data.

[1]http://sourceforge.net/projects/mstparser/

The most widely used transition-based dependency parser is the MaltParser (Nivre et al., 2007b).[2] The parser comes with several parsing algorithms, but uses a projective and very efficient algorithm by default. MaltParser is bundled with LibSVM 2.91, implementing a wide range of support vector machine algorithms that are used to learn classifiers to guide parsing. LibSVM 2.91 does not allow for instance weighting. However, LibSVM 3.0 does. In our experiments with the MaltParser, we use LibSVM 3.0 in conjunction with the MaltParser providing it with sentence-level instance weights from our Mallet text classifier. This means that configuration-transition pairs in the canonical derivations of a sentence with weight w will have weight w when training the support vector machine used by our parser.

3 Data

We evaluate our instance-weighted parsers on two domain adaptation data sets from English and Danish annotated corpora, one of which (Danish) has not previously been used in the literature. The Danish corpus is a balanced corpus, annotated building the Danish Dependency Treebank (DD (Buch-Kromann, 2003) and used in the CoNLL-X Shared Task (Buchholz and Marsi, 2006). The DDT comes with metadata revealing the original source of each sentence. This metadata was used to split the DDT into four domains: law (77 sent.), literature (lit; 984 sent.), magazines (magz; 190 sent.) and newspapers (news; 5052 sent.).

The second dataset was also used for the CoNLL 2007 Shared Task on domain adaptation

[2]http://maltparser.org

	Malt-bl	Malt-sys	MST-bl	MST-sys
childes-pbiotb	43.11	**43.91**	46.03	**48.86**
childes-pchemtb	38.01	**39.69**	**44.89**	44.41
pbiotb-childes	**50.35**	49.91	59.07	**61.37**
pbiotb-pchemtb	**75.64**	75.26	**77.26**	77.16
pchemtb-childes	49.63	**50.69**	60.89	**60.91**
pchemtb-pbiotb	**75.28**	75.06	76.39	**76.73**
AV	55.34	**55.75**	60.76	**61.57**

Table 2: Unlabeled attachment scores for English.

for dependency parsers (Nivre et al., 2007a). In the shared task, the Penn-III treebank (Marcus et al., 1993) was used as source domain, and test domains were chemical and biomedical research articles and transcribed child-directed speech. The quality of the shared task data was questioned by participants (Dredze et al., 2007), and there is some consensus today that annotation styles were too different for evaluation results to be useful. We therefore use data from the target domains only: biomedical literature (160 sent.), chemical literature (195 sent.) and child-directed speech (666 sent.). We consider all pairwise combinations of datasets within the two languages.

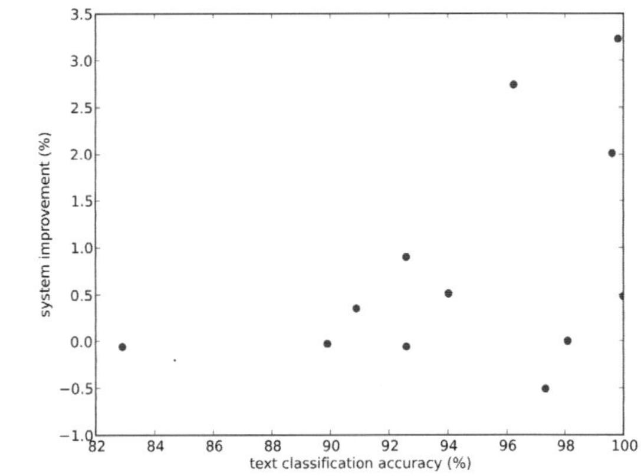

Figure 1: Correlation between text classification accuracy and system improvement (Danish).

4 Results

Our results for both Danish and English (see Table 1 and 2), reporting unlabeled attachment scores including punctuation, show rather consistent improvements across all pairwise combinations of datasets. Error reductions vary greatly from dataset to dataset, however. The average error reduction on the Danish data is $\geq 3\%$ for the instance-weighted MSTParser, and $\geq 2.5\%$ for the instance-weighted MaltParser.

It is interesting to note that there were no significant improvements when English input data was weighted by a text classifier trained on biomedical and chemical literature. These two text types are of course more similar to each other than to child-directed speech. This is reflected in the text classification accuracy, which is as high as 98–99% when comparing sentences sampled from technical literature and sentences sampled from child-directed speech, but considerably lower ($\sim$93.5%) when trying to differentiate biomedical sentences from chemical ones. Table 1 plots the correlation between system improvements and text classification accuracy for the Danish data. It is easy to see that high text classification accuracy is necessary for substantial improvements over the non-weighted baseline system.

Finally we note that we did similar experiments on the Penn-III treebank using the metadata also used by Webber (2009), with less robust results and smaller average improvements. The distribution of text types is very skewed in the Wall Street Journal, however, making text classification on this data alone a difficult job.

5 Conclusion

We have presented ways of implementing instance-weighting in transition-based and graph-based dependency parsing based on text classification and showed that this leads to consistent improvements over non-adapted baselines in domain adaptation scenarios, especially across very different domains.

References

Shai Ben-David, John Blitzer, Koby Crammer, and Fernando Pereira. 2007. Analysis of representations for domain adaptation. *Advances in Neural Information Processing Systems*, 19:137–144.

Steffen Bickel and Tobias Scheffer. 2007. Dirichlet-enhanced spam filtering based on biased samples. *Advances in Neural Information Processing Systems*, 19:161–168.

John Blitzer, Mark Dredze, and Fernando Pereira. 2007. Biographies, bollywood, boom-boxes and blenders: Domain adaptation for sentiment classification. In *ACL*.

Matthias Buch-Kromann. 2003. The Danish Dependency Treebank and the DTAG Treebank Tool. In *TLT*.

Sabine Buchholz and Erwin Marsi. 2006. CoNLL-X shared task on multilingual dependency parsing. In *CoNLL*.

Bo Chen, Wai Lam, Ivor Tsang, and Tak-Lam Wong. 2009. Extracting discriminative concepts for domain adaptation in text mining. In *KDD*.

Koby Crammer and Yoram Singer. 2003. Ultraconservative algorithms for multiclass problems. In *JMLR*.

Hal Daume III. 2007. Frustratingly easy domain adaptation. In *ACL*.

Mark Dredze, John Blitzer, Partha Pratim Talukdar, Kuzman Ganchev, João Graca, and Fernando Pereira. 2007. Frustratingly hard domain adaptation for dependency parsing. In *EMNLP-CoNLL*.

Jason Eisner. 1996. Three new probabilistic models for dependency parsing. In *COLING*.

George Foster, Cyril Goutte, and Roland Kuhn. 2010. Discriminative instance weighting for domain adaptation in statistical machine translation. In *EMNLP*.

Daisuke Kawahara and Kiyotaka Uchimoto. 2009. Learning reliability of parses for domain adaptation of dependency parsing. In *IJCNLP*.

Philipp Koehn. 2005. Europarl: a parallel corpus for statistical machine translation. In *MT-Summit*.

Mitchell Marcus, Mary Marcinkiewicz, and Beatrice Santorini. 1993. Building a large annotated corpus of English: the Penn Treebank. *Computational Linguistics*, 19(2):313–330.

David McClosky, Eugene Charniak, and Mark Johnson. 2010. Automatic domain adaptation for parsing. In *NAACL-HLT*.

Ryan McDonald, Fernando Pereira, Kiril Ribarov, and Jan Hajič. 2005. Non-projective dependency parsing using spanning tree algorithms. In *HLT-EMNLP*.

Joakim Nivre, Johan Hall, Sandra Kübler, Ryan McDonald, Jens Nilsson, Sebastian Riedel, and Deniz Yuret. 2007a. The CoNLL 2007 shared task on dependency parsing. In *EMNLP-CoNLL*.

Joakim Nivre, Johan Hall, Jens Nilsson, Atanas Chanev, Gülsen Eryigit, Sandra Kübler, Svetoslav Marinov, and Erwin Marsi. 2007b. MaltParser: a language-independent system for data-driven dependency parsing. *Natural Language Engineering*, 13(2):95–135.

Barbara Plank and Gertjan van Noord. 2011. Effective measures of domain similarity for parsing. In *ACL*.

Kenji Sagae and Jun'ichi Tsujii. 2007. Dependency parsing and domain adaptation with lr models and parser ensembles. In *EMNLP-CoNLL*.

Hidetoshi Shimodaira. 2000. Improving predictive inference under covariate shift by weighting the log-likelihood function. *Journal of Statistical Planning and Inference*, 90:227–244.

Anders Søgaard. 2011. Data point selection for cross-language adaptation of dependency parsers. In *ACL*.

Bonnie Webber. 2009. Genre distinctions for discourse in the Penn Treebank. In *ACL-IJCNLP*.

Bianca Zadrozny. 2004. Learning and evaluating classifiers under sample selection bias. In *ICML*.

Jingbo Zhu and Eduard Hovy. 2007. Active learning for word sense disambiguation with methods for addressing the class imbalance problem. In *EMNLP-CoNLL*.

Analysis of the Difficulties in Chinese Deep Parsing

Kun Yu[1] **Yusuke Miyao**[2] **Takuya Matsuzaki**[1] **Xiangli Wang**[3] **Junichi Tsujii**[4]

1. The University of Tokyo, Tokyo, Japan
{kunyu, matuzaki}@is.s.u-tokyo.ac.jp
2. National Institute of Informatics, Tokyo, Japan
yusuke@nii.ac.jp
3. Japan Patent Information Organization, Tokyo, Japan
xiangli_wang@japio.or.jp
4. Microsoft Research Asia, Beijing, P.R.China
jtsujii@microsoft.com

Abstract

This paper discusses the difficulties in Chinese deep parsing, by comparing the accuracy of a Chinese HPSG parser to the accuracy of an English HPSG parser and the commonly used Chinese syntactic parsers. Analysis reveals that deep parsing for Chinese is more challenging than for English, due to the shortage of syntactic constraints of Chinese verbs, the widespread *pro-drop*, and the large distribution of ambiguous constructions. Moreover, the inherent ambiguities caused by verbal coordination and relative clauses make semantic analysis of Chinese more difficult than the syntactic analysis of Chinese.

1 Introduction

Syntactic parsing provides only the syntactic structure of text, while deep parsing offers richer information, such as the semantic roles. With the advancement of research in natural language processing, this rich information has become important for many applications, including statistical machine translation, information extraction, and question answering.

Performing semantic role labeling (Marquez et al., 2009) with shallow parsing is one way to fulfill deep parsing. Another alternative to semantic role labeling is to perform deep parsing based on lexicalized grammar theories, such as Head-Driven Phrase Structure Grammar (HPSG) (Pollard and Sag, 1994), Lexical Functional Grammar (LFG) (Dalrymple et al., 1995), Combinatory Categorial Grammar (CCG) (Steedman, 2000), and Lexicalized Tree Adjoining Grammar (LTAG) (O'Donovan et al., 2005). Many research projects have been done successfully in this way, such as is the case in parsing English with HPSG (Miyao and Tsujii, 2008; Matsuzaki et al., 2007), CCG (Clark and Curran, 2004), and LFG (Kaplan et al., 2004).

However, obtaining the deep analysis of Chinese has proven to be more difficult. We evaluated an existing HPSG parser, which has been used successfully for English deep parsing (Miyao and Tsujii, 2008), on the Chinese HPSG Treebank constructed by Yu et al. (2010). The results indicated that compared to English, this parser obtained a 12.97% decrease in semantic F1-score on Chinese deep parsing.

Therefore, this paper focuses on investigating the difficulties in Chinese deep parsing, by comparing the parsing results of this HPSG parser on both Chinese and English, with the parsing results from commonly used Chinese syntactic parsers. This is the first time that the difficulties in Chinese deep parsing were analyzed; the resulting analysis provides insight into future research for Chinese deep parsing.

2 Linguistic Properties of Chinese

As discussed in Guo (2009), Chinese has little inflectional morphology, compared with Indo-European languages. There is no tense, case, and number marker in Chinese, and in sequence, there are fewer syntactic constraints; such as the case with the agreement in English. Therefore, in Chinese, word order plays an important role in determining the sentence meaning.

吃/eat 过 苹果/apple 了 。
((Somebody) has eaten the apple.)

(a) A Chinese sentence with subject *pro-drop*

吃/eat 过 了 。

((Somebody) has eaten (something).)

(b) A Chinese sentence with both subject and object *pro-drop*

Figure 1: Examples of *pro-drop* in Chinese

The other significant linguistic property in Chinese is the frequent *pro-drop* phenomena. For example, Levy and Manning (2003) showed that unlike English, the subject *pro-drop* (the null realization of uncontrolled pronominal subjects) is widespread in Chinese; this is exemplified in Figure 1 (a). Huang (1989) further provided a detailed analysis to show that subjects as well as objects may drop from finite Chinese sentences (as shown in Figure 1 (b)).

3 Chinese Deep Parsing based on HPSG

3.1 Parsing Model

In this paper, we used an HPSG parser - Enju[1], which was successfully applied in English deep parsing, to obtain the deep analysis of Chinese. This HPSG parser uses the feature forest model proposed by Miyao and Tsujii (2008), which is a maximum entropy model that is defined over feature forests, as a parsing disambiguation model. The feature forest model provides a solution to the problem of probabilistic modeling of complex data structures. Moreover, in order to reduce the search space and further increase the parsing efficiency, in this parser, a supertagger (Matsuzaki et al. 2007) is applied before parsing. This supertager provides the maybe-parsable supertag (i.e. lexical template) sequences to the parser.

In short, in the HPSG parser, the probability, $p(t|w)$, of producing a parse tree t for a given sentence w is defined by Equation 1. Here, Z_w is a normalization constraint; $p(l|w)$ is a maxent supertagging model in which l is the supertag sequence for sentence w; $f_i(t,l,w)$ is a feature function that represents the characteristics of t, l, and w; and λ_i is its weight. When performing Chinese HPSG parsing, the feature functions (i.e. $f_i(t,l,w)$) were borrowed from the English parser without any change, but the weights (i.e. λ_i) were tuned by using the development data.

$$p(t \mid w) = \frac{1}{Z_w} p(l \mid w) \exp(\sum_i \lambda_i f_i(t,l,w)) \quad (1)$$

[1] http://www-tsujii.is.s.u-tokyo.ac.jp/enju/index.html

The parsing procedure of this HPSG parser can be explained in the following way:

Given a segmented and pos-tagged input sentence,

(1) the supertagger offers all the maybe-parsable supertag (i.e. lexical template) sequences with scores to the parser;

(2) the feature forest model applies beam threshold on the scored supertag sequences, and then obtains a well-formed HPSG parse tree.

Figure 2 shows a supertag sequence provided by the supertagger for a Chinese sentence, in which the supertag of the word '写(wrote)' indicates a lexical template for the transitive verb with an extracted object. Figure 3 illustrates the HPSG parse tree output from the parser with this supertag sequence.

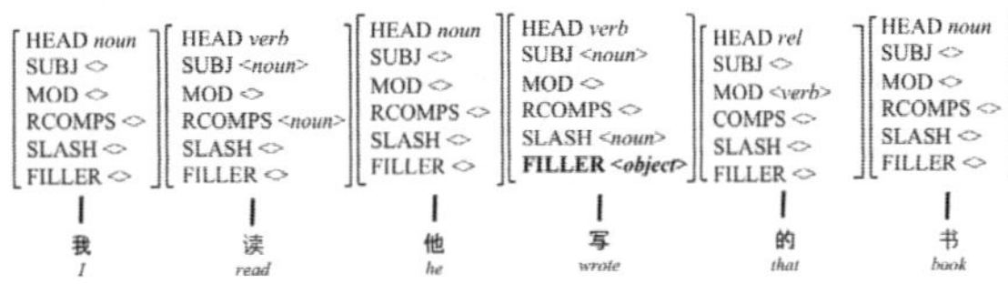

(I read the book that he wrote.)

Figure 2: A supertag sequence provided by the supertagger

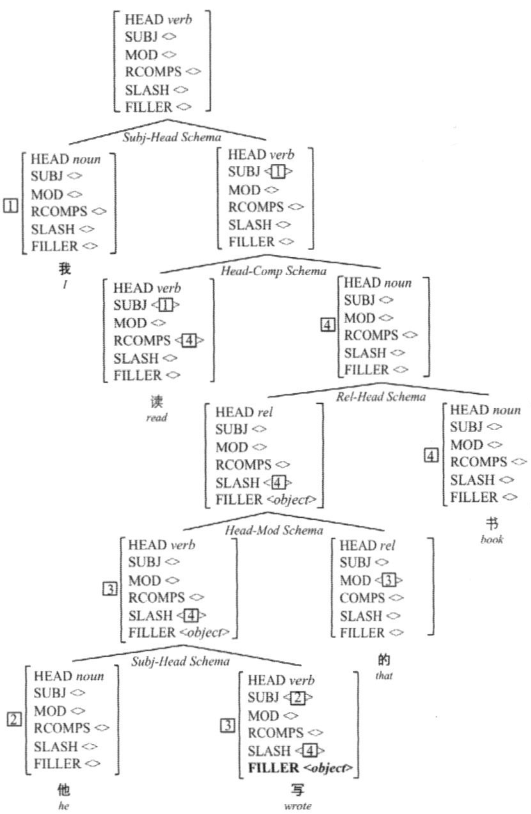

(I read the book that he wrote.)

Figure 3: The HPSG tree created from Figure 2

3.2 Training Data

In order to apply the HPSG parser to Chinese deep parsing, we used the Chinese HPSG Treebank developed by Yu et al. (2010) to train the parser.

This Chinese HPSG Treebank is based on the Chinese HPSG grammar designed in (Yu et al., 2010). 25,724 (95.66%) trees in the Penn Chinese Treebank 6.0 were successfully converted into HPSG trees, with 97.24% accuracy (Yu et al., 2010). For the details concerning the construction phase, please refer to (Yu et al., 2010).

From the syntactic point-of-view, in addition to the phrase structure of the Penn Chinese Treebank, this HPSG Treebank records the syntactic dependency relations, which are identified with the head rules similar to the head rules provided by Yuan Ding[2].

This treebank uses 51 types of predicate-argument dependencies to represent the semantic structures among 13 classes of words. A predicate-argument dependency is defined as $<w_p, w_a, r, l>$, where w_p is the head word of the predicate and w_a is the head word of the argument. r is the type of predicate-argument dependency between w_p and w_a. l is the argument label, such as *ARG1* and *ARG2*.

3.3 Experimental Setting

By using the Chinese HPSG Treebank described above, we re-trained the feature forest model and the supertagger, and built a Chinese HPSG parser. The treebank was split into development, testing, and training data sets, following the recommendation from the authors of the Penn Chinese Treebank. The training data was used to train the HPSG parser, and the testing data was used for parsing evaluation; the development data was used for parameter tuning. Table 1 shows the statistics that resulted from the different data sets.

Data Set	# Total Tree	# Success Tree	# Word	# Template
Train	22,224	21,186	557,447	2,185
Test	2,635	2,530	71,921	863
Dev	2,067	2,042	56,736	783

Table 1: Statistics for the Chinese HPSG Treebank

In the experiments performed with for the HPSG parser, the gold-standard word boundaries and POS tags were supplied.

[2] http://w3.msi.vxu.se/~nivre/research/chn_headrules.txt

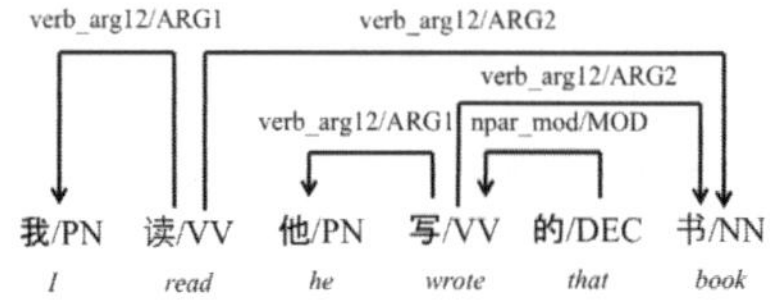

(I read the book that he wrote.)

Figure 4: A predicate-argument dependency parse tree output by the Chinese HPSG parser

The Chinese HPSG parser offers predicate-argument dependencies as the output of semantic parsing. Figure 4 illustrates a parse tree with a predicate-argument dependency that has been built by the Chinese HPSG parser, in which the label of each dependency is the combination of r and l in a predicate-argument dependency $<w_p, w_a, r, l>$. As an example, the predicate-argument dependencies of the verb '写(writes)' shown in Figure 4 indicates that the verb is a transitive verb (*verb_arg12*), and has a subject (*ARG1*) '他(he)', and an object (*ARG2*) '书(book)'.

Therefore, we evaluated the performance of the Chinese HPSG parser on semantic parsing by analyzing the accuracy of the predicate-argument dependencies. Six evaluation metrics used by Miyao and Tsujii (2008) were selected for the evaluation. *LP* and *LR* refer to the labeled precision and recall of the predicate-argument dependencies, while *UP* and *UR* refer to the unlabeled precision and recall, respectively. *Sem.F1* is the semantic F1-score calculated based on *LP* and *LR*. *Sent.acc.* is the accuracy of the sentences with the correct predicate-argument dependencies.

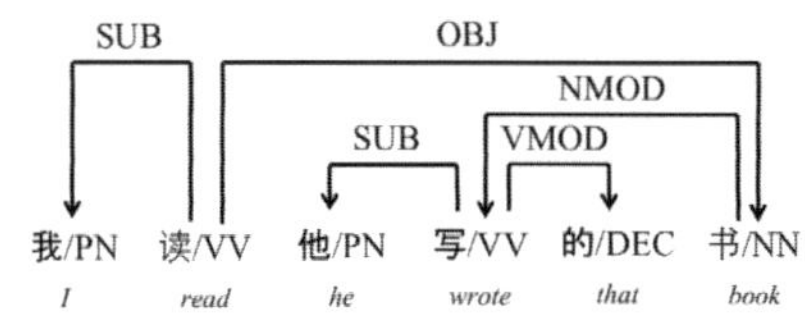

(I read the book that he wrote.)

Figure 5: A syntactic dependency parse tree corresponding to Figure 4

Besides of semantic analysis, the Chinese HPSG parser also provides the syntactic head for each branch in an HSPG parse tree and the schemas used to construct the branch, which can be used to extract the labeled syntactic dependency as the output of syntactic parsing. In order to evaluate the syntactic analysis of the Chinese HPSG parser, we used the similar dependency labels as the CoNLL dependency labels (Nivre et al., 2007 (b)). Figure 5 shows the labeled syntactic dependency tree output by the parser, in which the label *SUB* and *OBJ* refer to the subject and object, respectively. The common metrics used in CoNLL-2007 shared task (Nivre et al., 2007 (b)) were applied in the evaluation of the syntactic parsing. These metrics include the labeled attachment score (*LAS*), unlabeled attachment score (*UAS*), and the complete sentence accuracy (*COMP*) with labeled dependency.

3.4 Evaluation Results

The accuracy of both syntactic parsing and semantic parsing of the Chinese HPSG parser was 83.75% *LAS and* 77.55% *Sem.F1*, and is listed in Table 2 and Table 3.

To compare the performance of the Chinese HPSG parser on syntactic parsing with other related works, we evaluated two commonly used syntactic dependency parsers: MaltParser (Nivre et al., 2007 (a)) and MstParser (McDonald et al., 2006); the same syntactic dependency converted from the Chinese HPSG Treebank was used. In this experiment, the MaltParser and MstParser used both the gold-standard word boundaries and gold-standard POS tags, like the HPSG parser. Table 2 displays the results. The Chinese HPSG parser achieved a comparable accuracy to the MaltParser and the MstParser with 1st order features, but the Chinese HPSG parser's accuracy was slightly lower than the accuracy of the MstParser with 2nd order features.

Parser	*LAS*	*UAS*	*COMP*
Chinese HPSG	83.75%	85.57%	29.67%
Malt	83.74%	84.17%	29.01%
MST (1st order)	84.75%	85.22%	25.99%
MST (2nd order)	86.44%	86.95%	30.54%

Table 2: Accuracy of syntactic parsing

LP	*LR*	*UP*	*UR*
77.14%	77.97%	81.82%	82.70%
Sem.F1		*Sentence acc.*	
77.55%		23.84%	

Table 3: Accuracy of semantic parsing by the Chinese HPSG parser

Parser	*Sem.F1*
(Bjorkelund et al., 2009)	78.60%
(Meza-Ruiz and Riedel, 2009)	77.73%
(Zhao et al., 2009)	77.72%

Table 4: Accuracy of the top three systems in CoNLL-2009 Shared Task on Chinese Data

Since there has been no previous work conducted on the same Chinese HPSG formalism as used in the HPSG parser, comparing our semantic parsing results against the results of the existing approaches would not be accurate. However, a closely related work on joint syntactic and semantic parsing was done in the CoNLL-2009 shared task (Hajic et al., 2009). In this shared task, the Penn Chinese Treebank and the Chinese Proposition Bank (Xue and Palmer, 2009) were merged to serve as the training and testing data, and a semantic labeled F1-score *(Sem.F1)* was applied to evaluate the performance of semantic role labeling (Hajic et al., 2009). While the CoNLL-2009 shared task only applied gold-standard word boundaries, our experiment used both gold-standard word boundaries and gold-standard POS tags.

Table 4 lists the performance of the top three systems on the closed challenge for Chinese in the CoNLL-2009 shared task. Unfortunately, we cannot compare the result of the Chinese HPSG parser to the results of the top three systems in the CoNLL-2009 shared task, because of the different experimental settings. However, all the top systems in the shared task performed semantic role labeling after the syntactic parsing from the state-of-the-art parsers took place, whereas in our experiment, the Chinese HPSG parser applied a joint model that performed syntactic parsing and semantic parsing at the same time.

4 Discussion Concerning the Difficulties in Chinese Deep Parsing

4.1 Chinese Deep Parsing vs. English Deep Parsing

The HPSG parser that we used for Chinese deep parsing was also applied for English deep parsing (Miyao and Tsujii, 2008). Thus, we first compared the performance of the HPSG parser on parsing Chinese and English. In this experiment, we applied the same supertagging model with the same definition of supertags and feature sets, and the same parsing disambiguation model with the same feature sets, to the two treebanks.

To parse English, we used the English HPSG Treebank, which has been developed by Miyao et al. (2006), to train and evaluate the parser. The design of this treebank basically followed the definition in (Pollard and Sag, 1994). The HPSG trees converted from Sections 02-21 (39,832 sentences) of the Penn Treebank were used for training. The HPSG trees transformed from Section 23 (2,416 sentences) of the Penn Treebank were used for evaluation, and the HPSG trees converted from Section 22 (2,067 sentences) were used to tune parameters.

Parser	English	Chinese
HPSG	90.52%	77.55% (-12.97%)
HPSG + gold supertag	95.66%	92.52% (-3.14%)

Table 5: *Sem.F1* of the HPSG parser on both English and Chinese, with different models

We evaluated two different parsers in this experiment: the HPSG parser introduced in Section 3, and the HPSG parser with the gold-standard supertag sequence as input. Table 5 lists the evaluation results for both English and Chinese data. The results indicate that compared to English, the HPSG parser obtained 12.97% decrease in *Sem.F1* when parsing Chinese. Furthermore, this result shows that when given the exact supertag sequence of an input sentence, the HPSG parser still achieved a lower (3.14%) accuracy on Chinese than on English.

Data	# Ave. Parses	# Ave. Words	# Ave. Verbs	Sentence Distribution (#Verb>3)
Eng. Dev.	10,988. 74	23.20	2.97	35.88%
Chi. Dev.	37,200, 740.79	26.37	4.66	59.36%

Table 6: Average number of parses, words, and verbs per sentence in the English and Chinese development data

Training data deficiency may account for the low accuracy when parsing Chinese. However, the learning curve shown in (Miyao and Tsujii, 2008) indicates that even with half of the size of the full training data (i.e. 24,000 sentences), the HPSG parser obtained similar accuracy values on English deep parsing. Furthermore, we counted the average number of parses per sentence when given the exact supertag sequence for both Chinese and English on the development data. The numbers (as listed in Table 6) indicate that the parsing disambiguation is more difficult for Chinese than for English, because Chinese sentences have much more parses averagely than English sentences given the exact supertag sequence. A possible reason for the large average number of parses in Chinese is that Chinese sentences contain more verbs than English (as shown in Table 6). Due to the shortage of syntactic constraints of Chinese verbs, such as the agreement in English, it is easier for Chinese sentences with verbs to create ambiguous parses than for English.

Moreover, the comparison of the overall supertagging accuracy on Chinese and English (as shown in the left-most column in Figure 6) reveals that besides of the difficulty in Chinese parsing disambiguation, Chinese supertagging is also more difficult than for English. Following displays the possible reasons.

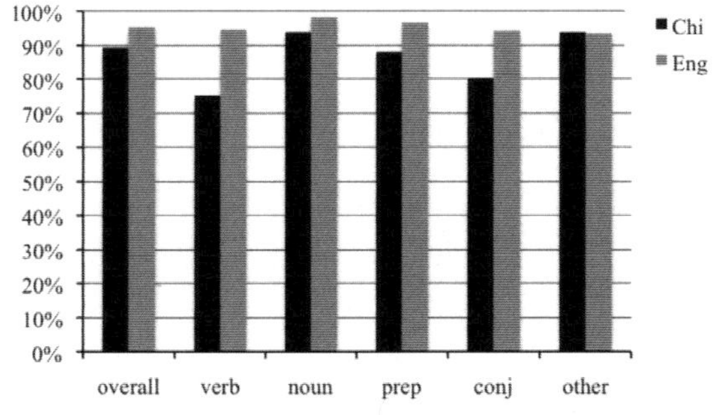

Figure 6: Supertagging accuracy on both English and Chinese testing data

(1) In comparison with English words, Chinese words have a much larger averaged number of supertags, especially for verbs.

Table 7 lists the total number of supertags and the average number of supertags per word in both the English HPSG Treebank and the Chinese HPSG Treebank. These numbers reveal that with the same granularity of supertags, although the total number of supertags is similar for both English and Chinese, the Chinese words have almost twice the average number of supertags than English words have. This difference makes it difficult for the supertagger to assign correct supertags for Chinese sentences.

Treebank	# Total Supertag	# Ave. Supertag for all words	# Ave. Supertag for verb
English	1,368	12.46	27.61
Chinese	1,279	21.57	87.82

Table 7: Statistics of the supertags in the English and Chinese HPSG Treebank

In addition, the analysis indicates that compared to other word types, the supertags of verbs in Chinese have more variations than verbs in English. As shown in Table 7, in the English HPSG Treebank, a verb has an average of 27.61 different supertags. By contrast, in the Chinese HPSG Treebank, a verb has an average of 87.82 different supertags. Table 8 lists the main reasons for the various verb supertags in Chinese and the sentence percentage with corresponding phenomena in the Chinese HPSG Treebank, of which the widespread subject *pro-drop* is the most predominant. The restrictions of the modifiee and topic in the supertag definition also brings about a large variation to the verb supertags. Changing the granularity of supertags of Chinese verbs is a possible way to solve this problem. Experimental results showed that by removing the restrictions of modifiee and topic in the definition of verb supertags, the *Sem.F1* could be improved by 0.3%.

Reason	Percentage
Subject *pro-drop*	34.75%
With/without modifiee	23.19%
With/without Topic	10.51%
Auxiliary verb	2.19%
Non-local dependency	0.30%

Table 8: Distribution of the main reasons for various verb supertags in Chinese

(2) The ambiguous constructions in supertagging have a larger distribution in the Chinese HPSG Treebank than in the English HPSG Treebank.

The supertagger's performance on different types of words, as shown in Figure 6, implicates that compared to English, Chinese verbs obtained the largest decrease in the accuracy of supertagging; 21.23% of the errors were related to the relative clause. Figure 6 also shows that in addition to verbs, coordination conjunctions decreased the accuracy of supertagging in Chinese.

However, there is not much difference in the supertagging ambiguity of coordination and relative clause in the two languages. For example, for both Chinese and English, in the supertagging of a verb in the relative clause, there is ambiguity as to whether assigning extracted predicate-argument dependency to this verb; the supertagging of a comma between verb phrases, has ambiguity in whether this comma will be treated as a coordination conjunction. Therefore, we further calculated the percentage of the sentences, including the verbal coordination with a comma conjunction and the relative clause in the two treebanks.

Treebank	Relative clause	Verbal Coordination with comma conj
English	14.31%	9.31%
Chinese	33.26%	52.95%

Table 9: Distribution of constructions in the English and Chinese HPSG Treebank

The statistics data is shown in Table 9. It reveals that in the Chinese HPSG Treebank, there are much more relative clauses than in the English HPSG Treebank. Moreover, the proportion of verbal coordination with comma conjunction in Chinese was also much larger than the proportion in English. Therefore, although the supertagging ambiguities of verbal coordination and relative clauses are similar for the two languages, the large distribution of these constructions increased the difficulty of Chinese supertagging.

4.2 Chinese Semantic Parsing vs. Chinese Syntactic Parsing

In comparing the accuracy of both the semantic parsing and syntactic parsing, as shown in Table 2 and Table 3, it is clear that although the performance on the syntactic analysis of the parser still has room for further improvement, the accuracy of predicate-argument dependencies was significantly lower than the accuracy of syntactic dependencies. Therefore, in this section, we focus on this gap by comparing the syntactic and semantic parsing results from the Chinese HPSG parser.

Error	# Occur
Subject of transitive verb	84
Left conjunct in coordination	84
Modifiee of punctuation	70
Root of sentence	51
Object of transitive verb	49
Right conjunct in coordination	46
Modifiee of noun	43
Modifiee of adverb	41
Subj. of intransitive verb	31
Missed object of transitive verb	28

Table 10: Occurrence of top 10 frequently occurring errors

We chose 93 sentences from the development data, which obtained a higher accuracy on syntactic parsing (i.e. with more than 85% *LAS*) and lower accuracy on semantic parsing (i.e. with less than 75% *Sem.F1*); the detailed errors were analyzed. The top 10 frequently occurring errors with their occurrence were documented in Table 10. The table indicates that there are two main difficulties in Chinese semantic parsing, in comparison to syntactic parsing.

- **Difficulty in Analyzing the Semantics of Parallel Verb Phrases**

As indicated in Table 10, the top nine errors were attachment errors; for a predicate-argument dependency $<w_p, w_a, r, l>$, only w_a is incorrect. There were 499 incorrect predicate-argument dependencies with the top nine errors. Of them,

59.12% of the errors were related to the semantic analysis of parallel verb phrases.

When two verb phrases are parallel, there are two possible semantic analyses for them:

(1) The two verb phrases are treated as coordination, and consequently share the same subject. Figure 7 shows the predicate-argument dependency tree created by this analysis.

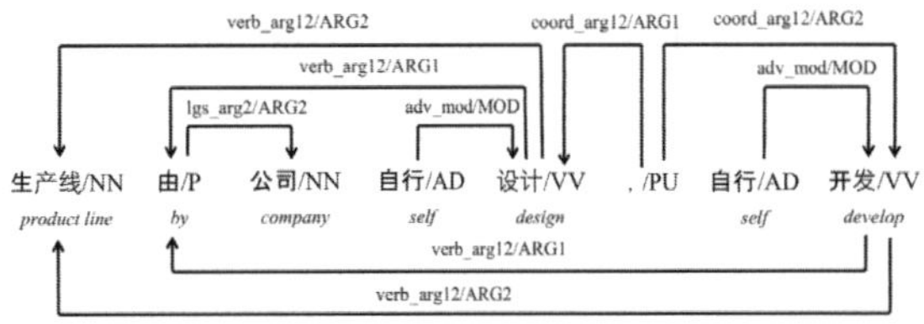

(The product line is self-designed and self-developed by this company)

Figure 7: The predicate-argument dependency tree when treating parallel VPs as coordination

(2) Treating the second verb phrase as a modifier of the first verb phrase. Figure 8 shows the corresponding predicate-argument dependency tree, in which the dependency *verb_arg12/ARG1* and *verb_arg12/ARG2* for verb '开发(develop)' are missed.

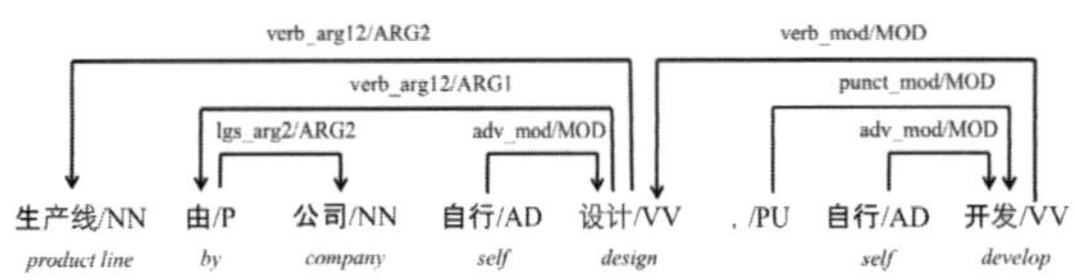

(The product line is self-designed and self-developed by this company)

Figure 8: The predicate-argument dependency tree when treating parallel VPs as modification

However, the above such ambiguity in semantic analysis does not exist in the syntactic analysis of this type of construction. For example, no matter which type of semantic analysis the parser chooses, the syntactic dependency trees for the sentences shown in Figure 7 and Figure 8 are the same (as shown in Figure 9).

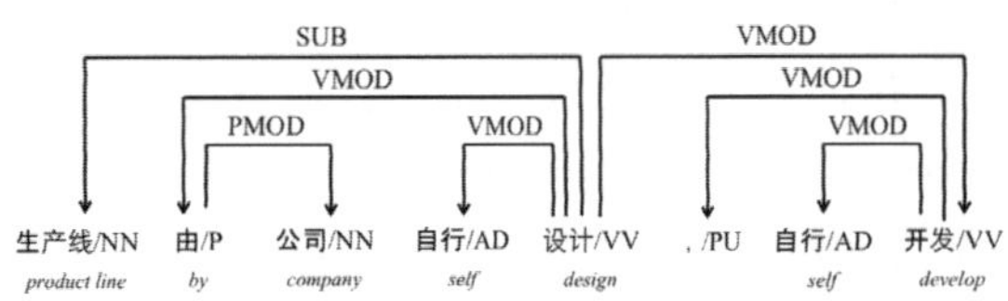

(The product line is self-designed and self-developed by this company)

Figure 9: The syntactic dependency tree corresponding to Figure 7 and Figure 8

- **Difficulty in Analyzing the Semantics of Relative Clause**

The tenth error shown in Table 10 was a type of relation error, in which the parser failed to find the object for a transitive verb. The error analysis shows that among the 28 incorrect predicate-argument dependencies with this type of error, 71.43% of the incorrect predicate-argument dependencies were from the incorrect semantic analysis of the relative clause.

There are two possible ways to analyze the semantics of a relative clause. The first way is to analyze the extracted noun in a relative clause as a moved argument of the predicate. The second way is to treat the relative clause as an apposition of the following noun, such that the extracted noun has no semantic relation with the predicate. For example, among the relative clauses in the Chinese HPSG Treebank, about 81% of the clauses were analyzed in the first way, and the remaining 19% were analyzed in the second way.

In reference to the relative clauses shown below, for the relative clause '写书的人(the person who wrote the book)', the semantics should be created by the first analysis (as shown in Figure 10), in which there is a predicate-argument dependency *verb_arg12/ARG1* between '写(wrote)' and '人(person)'. However, for another relative clause '写书的原因 (the reason that someone wrote the book)', the clause should be analyzed as an apposition (as shown in Figure 11). This is because the head noun '原因(reason)' has no predicate-argument relation with the verb '写(wrote)'.

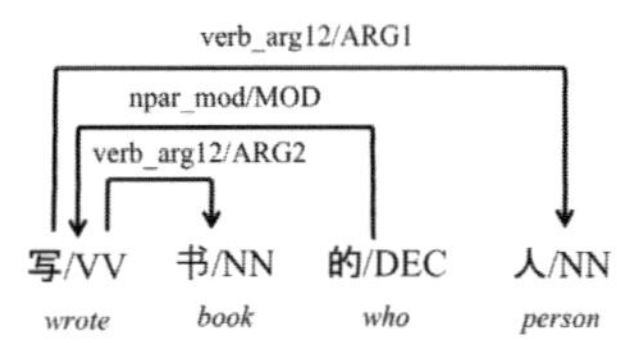

(the person who wrote the book)

Figure 10: The predicate-argument dependency tree when analyzing a relative clause with extracted argument

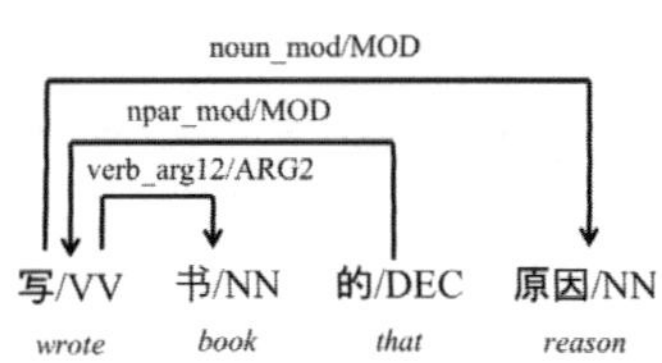

(the reason that someone wrote the book)

Figure 11: The predicate-argument dependency tree when treating a relative clause as an apposition

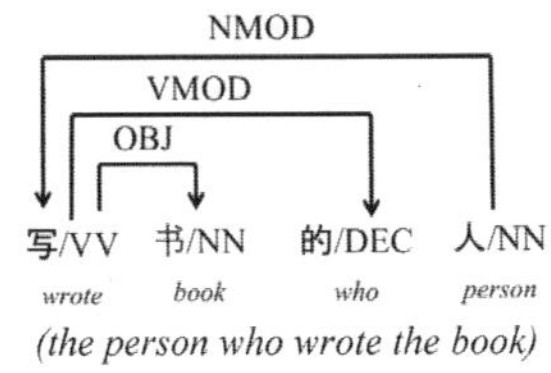

Figure 12: The syntactic dependency tree corresponding to Figure 10

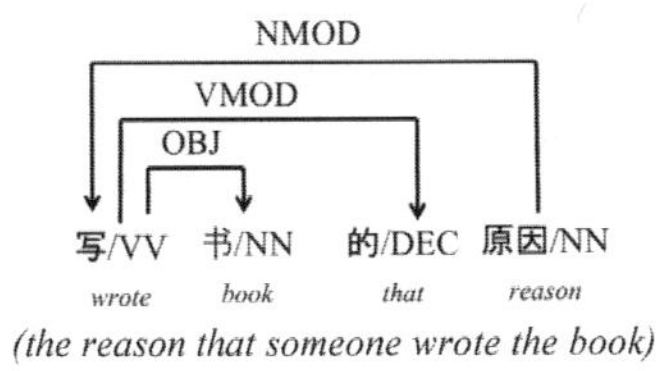

Figure 13: The syntactic dependency tree corresponding to Figure 11

However, since the syntactic analysis does not consider predicate-argument dependencies, such an ambiguity in semantic parsing does not exist in syntactic parsing. For instance, for both the two semantic analyses listed in Figure 10 and Figure 11, the syntactic dependencies are similar, as shown in Figure 12 and Figure 13.

5 Related Works

One related work was done by Levy and Manning (2003) on analyzing the difficulties in Chinese PCFG parsing. In this work, the authors applied a factored-model statistical parser on both the Penn Treebank (Marcus et al., 1994) and the Penn Chinese Treebank (Xue et al., 2005), and investigated the major sources of syntactic parsing errors and the corresponding causes in the two treebanks. The authors found that among the major error types in Chinese PCFG parsing, the coordination scope errors with verbal conjunct and the adjunction errors into IP are special for Chinese, due to the subject *pro-drop*. Guo (2009) presented the other related work; Guo discussed the language-specific properties of Chinese, including the shortage of syntactic constraints, the *pronoun-dropping* and the *topic-prominence*.

In our work, we focused on the difficulties faced in Chinese deep parsing, and drew similar conclusions to the previous two related works. We revealed that the following three aspects brought difficulties to Chinese deep parsing: (1) the large distribution of Chinese verbs and their shortage of syntactic constraints; (2) the large variety of supertags for Chinese verbs, for which the subject *pro-drop* was considered to be the main reason; (3) the large numbers of relative clauses and verbal coordination in Chinese, and the ambiguity in their analysis.

In addition to analyzing the parsing difficulty in Chinese deep parsing, some researchers focused on developing Chinese deep parsers.

Guo et al. (2007) built an LFG-based parser using wide-coverage LFG approximations induced from the Penn Chinese Treebank. This is the only previous work that had been conducted on Chinese deep parsing based on lexicalized grammars, although many related works had been done on English. Instead of training a parser based on the obtained LFG resources, Guo used an external PCFG parser to create c-structure trees, and then mapped the c-structure trees into f-structures using their annotation rules (Guo, 2009).

Besides of Guo's work, some researchers worked on joint dependency parsing and semantic role labeling to fulfill Chinese deep parsing (Li et al., 2010; Morante et al., 2009; Gesmundo et al., 2009; Dai et al., 2009; Lluis et al., 2009); other researchers focused on performing semantic role labeling after syntactic parsing (Fung et al., 2007; Sun and Jurafsky, 2004; Bjorkelund et al., 2009; Meza-Ruiz and Riedel, 2009; Zhao et al., 2009).

There were also some previous works that focused on building the language resources with lexicalized grammars, but not parsing with these resources. With the hand-crafted conversion rules, Yu et al. (2010) built a Chinese HPSG Treebank semi-automatically from the Penn Chinese Treebank. Guo (2009) also used rules to convert the Penn Chinese Treebank into LFG resources. Moreover, Tse and Curran (2010) built a Chinese CCGbank, which was also automatically induced from the Penn Chinese Treebank.

6 Conclusion and Future Work

In this paper, we discussed the prevalent difficulties in Chinese deep parsing, based on a lexicalized grammar theory – HPSG. All of the discussions were based on the analysis of a Chinese HPSG parser, which was trained on a Chinese HPSG Treebank, developed from the Penn Chinese Treebank. The analysis shows that since in Chinese, verbs have less syntactic constraints; the subject *pro-drop* appears frequently; furthermore, there is a larger distribution of ambiguous constructions, such as the relative clause and verbal coordination, deep parsing on Chinese is more difficult than on English. In addition, compared with Chinese syntactic parsing, Chinese semantic parsing is more difficult, because of the inherent ambiguities caused by both verbal coordination and relative clauses.

To our current knowledge, it is the first work that makes a detailed analysis of the difficulty in Chinese deep parsing based on lexicalized grammars. The conclusions drawn in this work will be useful to other related works on Chinese deep parsing, by providing the possible future research directions. Moreover, the conclusions will also help us to improve the performance of the Chinese HPSG parser, by enhancing coordination disambiguation with the method proposed in (Kurohashi and Nagao, 1994); reducing the granularity of verb supertags, and so on. In addition, the Chinese HPSG parser, which had been applied in this work for comparison, will also be released this year.

References

Anders Bjorkelund, Love Hafdell and Pierre Nugues. 2009. Multilingual Semantic Role Labeling. *Proceedings of the 13th Conference on Computational Natural language Learning (CoNLL): Shared task.*

Stephen Clark and James R. Curran. 2004. Parsing the WSJ Using CCG and Log-linear Models. *Proceedings of the 42nd Annual Meeting of the Association for Computational Linguistics (ACL 2004).*

Qifeng Dai, Enhong Chen and Liu Shi. 2009. An Iterative Approach for Joint Dependency Parsing and Semantic Role Labeling. *Proceedings of the 13th Conference on Computational Natural Language Learning (CoNLL 2009).*

Mary Dalrymple, Ronald M. Kaplan, John T. Maxwell and Annie Zaenen. 1995. *Formal Issues in Lexical-Functional Grammar.* Cambridge University Press, Stanford, CA.

Ruth O'Donovan, Michael Burke, Aoife Cahill, Josef Van Genabith and Andy Way. 2005. Large-Scale Induction and Evaluation of Lexical Resources from the Penn-II and Penn-III Treebanks. Computational Linguistics: 329 – 366.

Pascale Fung, Zhaojun Wu, Yongsheng Yang and Dekai Wu. 2007. Learning Bilingual Semantic Frames: Shallow Semantic Parsing vs. Semantic Role Projection. *Proceedings of the 11th Conference on Theoretical and Methodological Issues in Machine Translation (TMI 2007).* 75-84.

Yuqing Guo. 2009. *Treebank-based acquisition of Chinese LFG Resources for Parsing and Generation.* Ph.D. Thesis. Dublin City University.

Yuqing Guo, Josef van Genabith and Haifeng Wang. 2007. Acquisition of Wide-Coverage, Robust, Probabilistic Lexical-Functional Grammar Resources for Chinese. *Proceedings of the 12th International Lexical Functional Grammar Conference (LFG 2007).* 214-232.

Jan Hajic, Massimiliano Ciaramita, Richard Johansson, Daisuke Kawahara, Maria Antònia Martí, Lluís Màrquez, Adam Meyers, Joakim Nivre, Sebastian Padó, Jan Štepánek, Pavel Straňák, Mihai Surdeanu, Nianwen Xue and Yi Zhang. 2009. The CoNLL-2009 Shared Task: Syntactic and Semantic Dependencies in Multiple Languages. *Proceedings of the 13th Conference on Computational Natural language Learning (CoNLL): Shared task.* 1-18.

C. T. James Huang. 1989. Pro-drop in Chinese: A Generalized Control Theory. *O. Jaeggli and K. Safir (eds.). The Null Subject Parameter.* 185-214.

Ronald M. Kaplan, Stefan Riezler, Tracy H. King, John T. Maxwell III and Alexander Vasserman. 2004. Speed and Accuracy in Shallow and Deep Stochastic Parsing. *Proceedings of Human Language Technology conference / North American chapter of the Association for Computational Linguistics annual meeting (HLT/NAACL 2004).*

Sadao Kurohashi and Makoto Nagao. 1994. A Syntactic Analysis Method of Long Japanese Sentences based on the Detection of Conjunctive Structures. *Computational Linguistics.* 20(4): 507-534.

Roger Levy and Christopher Manning. 2003. Is it Harder to Parse Chinese, or the Chinese Treebank? *Proceedings of the 41st Annual Meeting of the Association for Computational Linguistics (ACL 2003).*

Junhui Li, Guodong Zhou and Hwee Tou Ng. 2010. Joint Syntactic and Semantic Parsing of Chinese. Proceedings of the 48th Annual Meeting of the Association for Computational Linguistics (ACL 2010). 1108-1117.

Xavier Lluis, Stefan Bott and Lluis Marquez. 2009. A Second-order Joint Eisner Model for Syntactic and Semantic Dependency Parsing. *Proceedings of the 13th Conference on Computational Natural Language Learning (CoNLL 2009).*

Mitchell P. Marcus, Beatrice Santorini and Mary Ann Marcinkiewicz. 1994. Building a Large Annotated Corpus of English: the Penn Treebank. *Computational Linguistics.* 19(2): 313-330.

Takuya Matsuzaki, Yusuke Miyao and Junichi Tsujii. 2007. Efficient HPSG Parsing with Supertagging and CFG-filtering. *Proceedings of the 20th International Joint Conference on Artificial Intelligence (IJCAI 2007).*

Lluis Marquez, Xavier Carreras, Kenneth C. Litkowski and Suzanne Stevenson. 2009. Semantic

Role Labeling: An Introduction to the Special Issue. *Computational Linguistics*. 34(2): 145-159.

Ryan McDonald, Kevin Lerman and Fernando Pereira. 2006. Multilingual Dependency Analysis with a Two-stage Discriminative Parser. *Proceedings of the 10th Conference on Computational Natural Language Learning (CoNLL-X)*.

Ivan Meza-Ruiz and Sebastian Riedel. 2009. Multilingual Semantic Role Labeling with Markov Logic. *Proceedings of the 13th Conference on Computational Natural language Learning (CoNLL): Shared task*.

Yusuke Miyao. 2006. *From Linguistic Theory to Syntactic Analysis: Corpus-oriented Grammar Development and Feature Forest Model*. Ph.D. Thesis. The University of Tokyo.

Yusuke Miyao and Junichi Tsujii. 2008. Feature Forest Models for Probabilistic HPSG Parsing. *Computational Linguistics*. 34(1): 35-80.

Roser Morante, Vincent Van Asch and Antal van den Bosch. 2009. A Simple Generative Pipeline Approach to Dependency Parsing and Semantic Role Labeling. *Proceedings of the 13th Conference on Computational Natural Language Learning (CoNLL 2009)*.

Andrea Gesmundo, James Henderson, Paola Merlo and Ivan Titov. 2009. A Latent Variable Model of Synchronous Syntactic-semantic Parsing for Multiple Languages. *Proceedings of the 13th Conference on Computational Natural Language Learning (CoNLL 2009)*.

Joakim Nivre, Johan Hall, Jens Nilsson, Atanas Chanev, Gulsen Eryigit, Sandra Kubler, Svetoslav Marinov and Erwin Marsi. 2007 (a). MaltParser: A Language-independent System for Data-driven Dependency Parsig. *Natural Language Engineering*. 13(2): 95-135.

Joakim Nivre, Johan Hall, Sandra Kubler, Ryan T. McDonald, Jens Nilsson, Sebastian Riedel and Deniz Yuret. 2007 (b). The CoNLL 2007 Shared Task on Dependency Parsing. *Proceedings of the CoNLL Shared Task Session of EMNLP-CoNLL 2007*. 915-932.

Carl Pollard and Ivan A. Sag. 1994. *Head-Driven Phrase Structure Grammar*. The University of Chicago Press and CSLI Publications, Chicago, IL and Stanford, CA.

Mark Steedman. 2000. *The Syntactic Process*. The MIT Press.

Honglin Sun and Daniel Jurafsky. 2004. Shallow Semantic Parsing of Chinese. *Proceedings of Human Language Technology conference / North American chapter of the Association for Computational Linguistics annual meeting (HLT/NAACL 2004)*.

Daniel Tse and James R. Curran. 2010. Chinese CCGbank: Extracting CCG Derivations from the Penn Chinese Treebank. *Proceedings of the 23rd International Conference on Computational Linguistics (COLING 2010)*.

Nianwen Xue and Martha Palmer. 2009. Adding Semantic Rules to the Chinese Treebank. *Natural Language Engineering*. 15(1): 143-172.

Nianwen Xue, Fei Xia, Fudong Chiou and Martha Palmer. 2005. The Penn Chinese Treebank: Phrase Structure Annotation of a Large Corpus. *Natural Language Engineering*. 11(2): 207-238.

Kun Yu, Yusuke Miyao, Xiangli Wang, Takuya Matsuzaki, Junichi Tsujii. 2010. Semi-automatically Developing Chinese HPSG Grammar from the Penn Chinese Treebank for Deep Parsing. *Proceedings of the 23rd International Conference on Computational Linguistics (COLING 2010)*.

Hai Zhao, Wenliang Chen, Chunyu Kity and Guodong Zhou. 2009. Multilingual Dependency Learning: a Huge Feature Engineering Method to Semantic Dependency Parsing. *Proceedings of the 13th Conference on Computational Natural language Learning (CoNLL): Shared task*.

On the Role of Explicit Morphological Feature Representation in Syntactic Dependency Parsing for German

Wolfgang Seeker and Jonas Kuhn
Institut für Maschinelle Sprachverarbeitung
University of Stuttgart
{seeker,jonas}@ims.uni-stuttgart.de

Abstract

We investigate the question whether an explicit feature representation for morphological features is necessary when parsing German with a fully lexicalized, statistical dependency parser. We use two morphosyntactic phenomena of German to show that while lexicalization does indeed suffice to a large extent when recovering the internal structure of noun phrases, an accurate explicit representation can support the correct selection of its grammatical function.

1 Introduction

German is usually considered a border case between morphologically rich languages like Czech and morphologically poor languages like English. It does show phenomena that are typical for morphologically rich languages, e. g. a rich nominal and verbal inflection system and hence a relatively free word order. However, compared to Czech or other morphologically rich languages, the morphological system is less elaborate and characterized by a large amount of form syncretism, which introduces a lot of ambiguity.

A lot of work investigated the best way to utilize morphological information in statistical PCFG parsers for German, mostly by transforming the treebank making morphological information more accessible (Schiehlen, 2004; Dubey, 2005). Lexicalization of PCFGs has been a controversial subject of research in German, where some found no effect (Dubey and Keller, 2003) while others did (Kübler et al., 2006; Rafferty and Manning, 2008). However, this work concentrated on constituent parsing. While there are many parsing results of dependency parsers on German (Buchholz and Marsi, 2006; Kübler, 2008; Hajič et al., 2009), the investigation of morphological representations and their interplay with dependency parsing algorithms has been started only recently (cf. Tsarfaty et al. (2010)). In this paper, we pursue the question of how important it is to mark morphological information explicitly for a data-driven lexicalized dependency parser when applied to German. We therefore investigate the performance of the parser on two morphosyntactic phenomena of German, namely the agreement within a noun phrase[1] and the recognition of the grammatical function of a noun that is marked by its case value.

2 Morphology of German Noun Phrases

Three morphological categories participate in the agreement of a German noun phrase: gender, number, and case.[2] Number and gender values are governed by the noun, and the case value is determined by the grammatical function of the noun. The dependents of a noun (determiners, adjectives, attributive pronouns) need to agree with their head noun in these three categories.

(1)	*die*	*Öl*
	ART+nom/acc.sg.fem	NN+acc.sg.neut
	the	oil
	verarbeitende	*Industrie*
	ADJ+nom/acc.sg.fem	NN+nom/acc.sg.fem
	processing	industry
	'the oil processing industry'	

Example 1 shows a German noun phrase consisting of a determiner (*die*), an adjective (*verarbeitende*), and a noun (*Industrie*). Additionally, the noun *Öl* is an argument of the adjective. Without morphological information we might in principle be dealing with two separate noun phrases here, which just happen to appear in adjacent position. However, agreement tells us that the determiner is not depending on the first noun because morphologically it marks either singular feminine

[1]We use the term noun phrase to denote a noun and all its direct dependents although strictly speaking there are no phrases in dependency syntax.

[2]German has three gender values, two number values, and four case values.

or plural for all genders, but it cannot mark singular neuter. It is thus morphologically incompatible with the first noun.

According to Eisenberg (2006, 142), the inflectional paradigms of the parts of the German noun phrase have developed such that they mark morphological information with diverging explicitness. The declension patterns of nouns tend to use different forms to mark number but show form syncretism in marking case while determiners (and adjectives) show more form syncretism for marking number than for marking case. Eisenberg therefore argues for what he calls function sharing (*Funktionsteilung*) in the German noun phrase. In Example 1, the determiner by itself can mark nominative or accusative case for feminine singular nouns, or for plural nouns of every gender. The second noun, to which the determiner is attached, is ambiguous for all four cases but cannot be plural. This shows the importance of the agreement relation because only by agreement, determiner and noun disambiguate each other for nominative or accusative feminine singular.

Example 1 also demonstrates an inherent problem of the German nominal paradigms as a whole. Because of the vast amount of syncretism in the system, there are some ambiguities that can never be resolved by formal means, but need to be disambiguated by their semantic context. This affects the distinction between nominative and accusative for all feminine, neuter, and plural nouns as well as the distinction between genitive and dative case for feminine singular nouns. In Example 1, we therefore cannot tell without further context which one of the two possible case values is correct.

(2) *den Löwen sieht der Hund*
OBJ+acc SUBJ+nom
the lion see the dog
'the dog sees the lion'

While morphological information by agreement helps us recover the internal structure of a noun phrase, it also plays a role when determining the grammatical function of the whole phrase. German uses its four case values to mark the arguments of verbs, adpositions, and adjectives. Example 2 shows a transitive sentence where the subject is marked by nominative case and the object is marked by accusative case. In German, the subject of a sentence will always be in the nominative case, while the structural object receives accusative case. In ditransitive sentences, the direct object gets accusative case while the indirect object receives dative case.[3]

The relation between a case system and the grammatical functions in a language is usually not a one-to-one mapping (Blake, 2001, 48ff). In German, nominative encodes subjects and predicates, accusative mostly marks objects and some adjuncts, dative also marks objects, and genitive mostly marks possessive constructions but can also mark objects and some adjuncts. Since the mapping is not one-to-one, a certain amount of ambiguity remains (e. g. both subject and predicate are marked by nominative case), but it also restricts the choice for a lot of nouns. A noun in accusative case cannot end up being subject and a noun in dative case cannot mark a possessor.

To summarize, we deal with three kinds of ambiguity: the first one is the diverging explicitness of feature marking in different nominal inflectional paradigms, as discussed for determiners and nouns. This ambiguity can often be resolved by taking agreement into account, which then leads to mutual disambiguation. The second kind of ambiguity is inherent to the morphological system and affects all paradigms alike. I. e. certain distinctions simply cannot be made in the system, e. g. the distinction between genitive and dative feminine singular. The third ambiguity concerns the mapping between case values and grammatical functions. Since a particular case value can signal more than one grammatical function, the final decision between those functions must be made using non-morphological information.

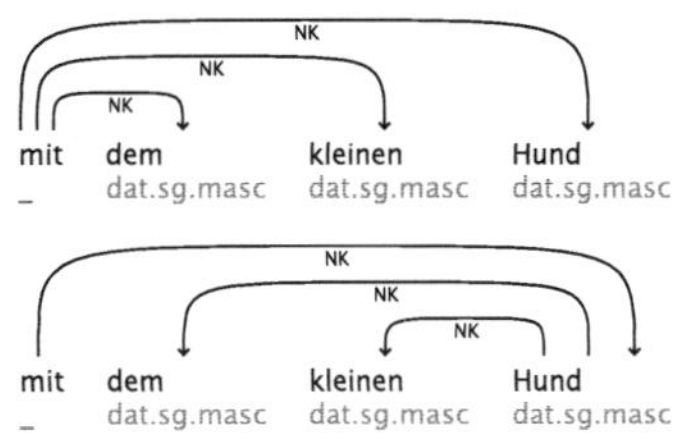

Figure 1: A prepositional phrase in the CoNLL 2009 data and in our version for the phrase *mit dem kleinen Hund* (with the little dog)

3 Data

For our experiments, we use the CoNLL 2009 Shared Task data (Hajič et al., 2009), which has been derived automatically from the German TiGer treebank (Brants et al., 2002). In order to

[3]However, a big group of transitive verbs assigns lexical dative or genitive case to its direct object.

get more consistent data we semi-automatically changed the annotation of prepositional phrases: in the original treebank, prepositional phrases have been analysed as flat structures without an embedded noun phrase. We introduced additional structure as shown in Figure 1 to achieve a consistent annotation for all noun phrases where agreement is represented by direct links labelled by *NK* (noun kernel element). This excludes any effects caused by the otherwise inconsistent annotation of noun phrases and we can evaluate the agreement relation more directly.

4 Evaluation

We evaluate the data-driven dependency parser described in Bohnet (2010), a state-of-the-art second-order maximum spanning tree parser performing second on German in the CoNLL 2009 Shared Task. The parser uses a rich feature model (Bohnet, 2009) and is fully lexicalized. We used statistical tools[4] to automatically lemmatize, part-of-speech tag, and morphologically annotate the training section (36k sentences) of the data by using ten-fold cross annotation. We parsed the whole corpus creating three different models: one using the gold morphology, one using predicted morphology, and one using no explicit morphology. Morphological information was represented as in the CoNLL 2009 Shared Task.

In the following two experiments we test, whether the parser does need explicit morphological information to correctly recover noun phrases and their grammatical function. Since the parser is fully lexicalized, we expect the parser to learn at least some morphological information even when it is not explicitly given.

4.1 Agreement

In order to evaluate how well the parser learns the agreement between a noun and its dependents, we measure the number of times, a parser correctly establishes all links labelled by *NK* between a noun (NN) and its dependent determiners (ART), adjectives (ADJA), and attributive pronouns (PDAT, PIAT, PPOSAT). The total number of these edges is 115,136, the total number of words involved is 206,026. The accuracy of the morphological tagger on gender, number, and case values of these words is 92.79%. Table 1 shows the results in terms of precision, recall, and f-score.

All three models perform very well and close to each other. Even the model without any explicit morphology achieves an f-score of over 99%. We conclude that lexicalization and configurational information seem to suffice to a large extent for a second-order parser when recovering the internal structure of noun phrases. However, all the differences in f-score between the three models turn out to be statistically significant,[5] so there seems to be a small number of cases where morphology can help in disambiguation. Noun phrases like in Example 1 illustrate these cases where, in principle, arbitrarily many phrases can appear between the determiner and the head noun.

	prec	rec	f1
gold-morph	99.34	99.78	99.56
pred-morph	98.83	99.66	99.24
no-morph	98.77	99.62	99.19

Table 1: Evaluation of NK-edges between ART, ADJA, PIAT, PDAT, PPOSAT, and NN, which represent the agreement relation inside a noun phrase.

4.2 Case – Function Mapping

The second phenomenon we evaluate is the ability of the parser to learn the case – function mapping of German. If the parser is able to learn it, we expect it to only make errors that are related to either the inherent syncretism of the morphological system or to mapping ambiguities between a case value and the functions that it signals.

We evaluate nouns, proper nouns, adjectives, and substituting pronouns (marked for case) for f-score on the functions related to case.[6]

Table 2 shows a clear ranking of the three models:[7] the model using gold morphology outperforms the one using predicted morphology which itself outperforms the third model that uses no explicit morphology. The good performance of the gold morphology model can to a big extent be explained by the fact that in the gold morphology even those ambiguities are resolved that are inherent to the case system of German (see discussion above) and would normally need syntactic or semantic information to be resolved. The biggest difference between the model without morphology and the one using predicted morphology appears for *DA* and *OG*. These two functions are indicated by dative and genitive case respectively. For the

[4] `http://code.google.com/p/mate-tools/`

[5] measured on sentence level with a sign test, $\alpha = 0.001$

[6] SB – subject, PD – predicate, OA – accusative object, DA – dative obj., OG – genitive obj., AG – genitive adjunct

[7] All differences are statistically significant except for *PD*, and between pred-m and no-m for *OG*, test see Footnote 5

other functions, the difference in performance is not as high.

	gold-m	pred-m	no-m
SB	95.85	90.85	89.36
PD	76.51	75.40	74.73
OA	94.63	85.22	83.04
DA	88.55	71.59	62.79
OG	58.40	40.98	36.54
AG	96.36	94.05	91.94
total	94.73	88.80	86.82

Table 2: Evaluation of grammatical function assignment to case marked elements (nouns, proper nouns, adjectives, and pronouns) in terms of f-score.

One ambiguity the parser has to deal with is that the same case value can be mapped to two or more different functions. This happens with nominative case, which can be mapped to either *SB* or *PD*, and with genitive case, which can be mapped either to *OG* or *AG*. We expect this ambiguity to pose problems to all models, especially for the one that uses gold morphology. Table 3 shows the fraction of the recall errors for one function where it has been confused with the other possible one. Here we get an interesting picture: while *PD* and *OG* most of the time get confused with their counterpart, the effect is less strong the other way around. Knowing, that *PD* and *OG* are much less frequent than their counterparts may explain the results and gives us a first hint that the mapping learnt by the parser is probably skewed by frequency effects.

SB – PD	23.77	PD – SB	71.55
OG – AG	51.95	AG – OG	2.11

Table 3: Confusion of ambiguous case mappings (in percent) for the model using gold morphology.

The inherent ambiguity of the case system is resolved in the model using gold morphology. We would however expect the model using predicted morphology to additionally have problems to tell apart *SB/PD* (nominative) from *OA* (accusative), and *DA* (dative) from *OG/AG* (genitive).

Table 4 shows the top three functions that the model using predicted morphology confused a function with. For *SB* and *OA* we get the expected picture: without the oracle disambiguation of case, the parser makes the expected errors. For *DA* on the other hand, the parser seems to have problems to recognize the dative as such and so confuses it with *SB* and *OA*, both functions that cannot be marked by dative case. We used a finite state morphology (Schiller, 1994) to annotate every case-bearing word (nouns, determiners, adjectives, pronouns, proper nouns, determined by the automatically assigned part-of-speech tag) with every possible gender, number, and case value that this word form might have. We then disambiguated this annotation further by taking intra-noun phrase agreement into account and found out that 19.63% of the errors could have been fully disambiguated to dative case. This shows that the parser does not learn the mapping between dative case and the label *DA* well enough. A likely reason for that is the lower frequency of *DA*, which occurs 8 times less than *OA*. For *OG*, Table 4 shows a frequent confusion with *AG* and *DA*, which is predicted by the case syncretism in the system.

	1.		2.		3.	
SB	OA	45.86	NK	11.57	PD	9.76
OA	SB	56.82	NK	10.36	CJ	5.17
DA	SB	28.98	OA	20.30	AG	11.88
OG	AG	33.03	DA	21.10	OA	13.76

Table 4: Top three functions that a function has been confused with (in percent) by the model using predicted morphology.

5 Discussion

Recovering the internal structure of a German noun phrase does not seem to pose a big problem for the parser. For most cases, lexicalization and configurational information seem to suffice, although a small portion of the noun phrases can be better disambiguated when explicit feature representations are given.

Good accuracy on the noun phrase's internal structure should then provide a good basis for determining its grammatical function in a broader sentential context because a second-order parser has all the information even though it is distributed on different parts of the phrase (function sharing). However, our second experiment indicates problems for the parser that exceed those caused by inherent ambiguities. A clear sign is the *DA* function, which should only appear with dative case but is frequently confused with other functions that cannot be marked by dative. The low frequency of *DA* might explain the confusion with e.g. *SB* and *OA*, which occur much more often.

Our next steps will include determining an upper bound on gold morphology that is not disambiguated for its inherent syncretism and investigating verbal frames, which may contribute independent information to function selection.

References

Barry J. Blake. 2001. *Case*. Cambridge University Press, Cambridge, New York, 2nd edition.

Bernd Bohnet. 2009. Efficient Parsing of Syntactic and Semantic Dependency Structures. In *Proceedings of the Thirteenth Conference on Computational Natural Language Learning (CoNLL 2009): Shared Task*, volume 2007, Boulder, Colorado. Association for Computational Linguistics.

Bernd Bohnet. 2010. Very high accuracy and fast dependency parsing is not a contradiction. In *Proceedings of the 23rd International Conference on Computational Linguistics*, pages 89–97, Beijing, China. Association for Computational Linguistics.

Sabine Brants, Stefanie Dipper, Silvia Hansen, Wolfgang Lezius, and George Smith. 2002. The TIGER treebank. In *Proceedings of the Workshop on Treebanks and Linguistic Theories*, pages 24–41.

Sabine Buchholz and Erwin Marsi. 2006. CoNLL-X shared task on multilingual dependency parsing. In *Proceedings of the Tenth Conference on Computational Natural Language Learning*, pages 149–164, Morristown, NJ, USA. Association for Computational Linguistics.

Amit Dubey and Frank Keller. 2003. Probabilistic parsing for German using sister-head dependencies. In *Proceedings of ACL 2003*, pages 96–103, Morristown, NJ, USA. Association for Computational Linguistics.

Amit Dubey. 2005. What to do when lexicalization fails: parsing German with suffix analysis and smoothing. In *Proceedings of ACL 2005*, pages 314 - 321, Ann Arbor, Michigan. Association for Computational Linguistics.

Peter Eisenberg. 2006. *Grundriss der deutschen Grammatik: Der Satz*. J.B. Metzler, Stuttgart, 3 edition.

Jan Hajič, Massimiliano Ciaramita, Richard Johansson, Daisuke Kawahara, Maria Antònia Martí, Lluís Màrquez, Adam Meyers, Joakim Nivre, Sebastian Padó, Jan Stepánek, Pavel Stranák, Mihai Surdeanu, Nianwen Xue, and Yi Zhang. 2009. The CoNLL-2009 shared task: Syntactic and Semantic dependencies in multiple languages. In *Proceedings of the 13th CoNLL Shared Task*, pages 1–18, Boulder, Colorado.

Sandra Kübler, Erhard W. Hinrichs, and Wolfgang Maier. 2006. Is it really that difficult to parse German? In *Proceedings of the 2006 Conference on Empirical Methods in Natural Language Processing - EMNLP '06*, page 111, Morristown, NJ, USA. Association for Computational Linguistics.

Sandra Kübler. 2008. The PaGe 2008 shared task on parsing German. In *Proceedings of the Workshop on Parsing German*, pages 55–63, Morristown, NJ, USA. Association for Computational Linguistics.

Anna N. Rafferty and Christopher D. Manning. 2008. Parsing three German treebanks: Lexicalized and unlexicalized baselines. In *Proceedings of the Workshop on Parsing German*, pages 40–46. Association for Computational Linguistics.

Michael Schiehlen. 2004. Annotation strategies for probabilistic parsing in German. In *Proceedings of the 20th international conference on Computational Linguistics*, pages 390–397. Association for Computational Linguistics.

Anne Schiller. 1994. Dmor - user's guide. Technical report, University of Stuttgart.

Reut Tsarfaty, Djamé Seddah, Yoav Goldberg, Sandra Kübler, Marie Candito, Jennifer Foster, Yannick Versley, Ines Rehbein, and Lamia Tounsi. 2010. Statistical parsing of morphologically rich languages (SPMRL): what, how and whither. In *Proceedings of the NAACL HLT 2010 First Workshop on Statistical Parsing of Morphologically-Rich Languages*, pages 1–12. Association for Computational Linguistics.

Bayesian Network Automata for Modelling Unbounded Structures

James Henderson
Department of Computer Science
University of Geneva
Geneva, Switzerland
James.Henderson@unige.ch

Abstract

This paper proposes a framework which unifies graphical model theory and formal language theory through automata theory. Specifically, we propose Bayesian Network Automata (BNAs) as a formal framework for specifying graphical models of arbitrarily large structures, or equivalently, specifying probabilistic grammars in terms of graphical models. BNAs use a formal automaton to specify how to construct an arbitrarily large Bayesian Network by connecting multiple copies of a bounded Bayesian Network. Using a combination of results from graphical models and formal language theory, we show that, for a large class of automata, the complexity of inference with a BNA is bounded by the complexity of inference in the bounded Bayesian Network times the complexity of inference for the equivalent stochastic automaton. This illustrates that BNAs provide a useful framework for developing and analysing models and algorithms for structure prediction.

1 Introduction

Work in Computational Linguistics has developed increasingly sophisticated probabilistic models of language. For example, Latent Probabilistic Context-Free Grammars (LPCFGs) (Matsuzaki et al., 2005) have been developed with latent head labels (Prescher, 2005), multiple latent variables decorating each nonterminal (Musillo and Merlo, 2008), and a hierarchy of latent nonterminal subcategories (Liang et al., 2007). In this paper we propose a general framework which facilitates the specification and parsing of such complex models by exploiting graphical models to express local bounded statistical relationships, while still allowing the use of grammar formalisms to express the unbounded nature of natural language.

Graphical models were developed as a unification of probability theory and graph theory. They have proved a powerful framework for specifying and reasoning about probabilistic models. Dynamic Bayesian Networks (Ghahramani, 1998) extend this framework to models which describe arbitrarily long sequences. There has been work applying ideas from graphical models to more complex unbounded structures, such as natural language parse trees (e.g. (Henderson and Titov, 2010)), but the power of the architectures proposed for such extensions have not been formally characterised.

The formal power of systems for specifying arbitrarily large structures has been studied extensively in the area of formal language theory. Formal language theory has proved a wide range of equivalences and subsumptions between grammar formalisms, the most well known example being the Chomsky hierarchy (i.e. finite languages $<$ regular languages $<$ context-free languages $<$ context-sensitive languages $<$ recursively enumerable languages). It has also demonstrated the equivalence between formal grammars and formal automata (e.g. finite state automata generate regular languages, push-down automata generate context-free languages, Turing machines generate recursively enumerable languages). While grammar formalisms are generally more readable than automata, they appear in a wide variety of notational variants, whereas automata provide a relatively consistent framework in which different grammar formalisms can be compared. Automata also provide a clearer connection to Dynamic Bayesian Networks. For these reasons, this paper uses automata theory rather than grammars, although many of the ideas are trivially transferable to grammars.

We propose Bayesian Network Automata (BNAs) as a framework for specifying stochastic automata which generate arbitrarily large (i.e. unbounded) structures. A BNA is a standard stochastic automaton, but uses a Bayesian Network (BN) to specify its stochastic transition function. For example, the specification of a stochastic push-down automaton (PDA) requires a specification of the conditional probability distribution over *push(X)* and *pop* actions given the current state, input symbol, and top stack symbol. This distribution can be specified in a BN. While not changing the theoretical properties of the stochastic automaton, this use of BNs allows us to merge algorithms and theoretical results from BNs with those for the stochastic automaton, and thereby with those for the equivalent probabilistic grammar formalism. In the PDA example, the algorithm discussed in section 5.2 allows us to sum over all possible values for X in *push(X)* while at the same time summing over all possible parse tree structures, as is used in unsupervised grammar induction. We argue that this merging with graphical model theory simplifies the specification of more complex stochastic transition functions or grammar rules (e.g. (Musillo and Merlo, 2008)), and reduces the need for adhoc solutions to such inference problems.

BNAs can also be seen as a generalisation of Dynamic Bayesian Networks to more complex unbounded structures. BNAs simplify the specification and analysis of these more complex BNs by drawing a distinction between a finite set of statistical relationships, represented in a Bayesian Network, and the recursive nature of the unbounded structures, represented by the control mechanisms of the automaton. To illustrate the usefulness of this framework, we exploit the separation between the automaton and the Bayesian Network to provide bounds on the complexity of inference in some classes of BNAs. In particular, for a large class of grammar formalisms, the complexity of marginalising over variables in the Bayesian Network and the complexity of marginalising over structures from the automaton are independent factors in the complexity of inference with the BNA. We also exploit results from formal language theory to characterise the power of previously proposed models in terms of the generative capacity of their automata.

In the rest of this paper, we first define the framework of Bayesian Network Automata, and discuss its key properties. This provides the formal mechanisms we need to compare various Bayesian Network architectures that have been previously proposed. We then provide results on the efficiency of inference in BNAs.

2 Bayesian Network Automata

Bayesian Network Automata is a framework for specifying stochastic automata which generate unbounded structures. Formally, a BNA is simply an alternative notation for its equivalent stochastic automaton. In this section, we provide a formal definition of BNAs, without limiting ourselves to any specific class of automata.

2.1 Generating Unbounded Structures with BNAs

The purpose of a BNA is to specify a probability distribution over an infinite set of unboundedly large structures. It does this by specifying an equivalent stochastic automaton. Each complete run of the automaton generates a single structure, which is derived from the semantics of the operations performed by the automaton. The sequence of operations performed in a complete run of the automaton is called a *derivation* for its associated structure. Typically automata are designed so that derivations are isomorphic to structures, but even if multiple derivations map to the same structure, to specify a probability distribution over structures it is enough to specify a probability distribution over derivations. Stochastic automata do this in terms of a generative process for derivations, generating each operation incrementally conditioned on the derivation prefix of preceding operations.

Standard specifications of stochastic automata include specific operations acting over specific data structures. These data structures are used to represent each state of the automaton (called the *configuration*) as it proceeds through the computation. For example, the configuration of a finite state machine is a single state symbol, and the configuration of a push-down automaton is a single state symbol plus an arbitrarily deep stack of stack symbols.[1] Here we do not want to restrict attention to any specific class of automata, so the operations and data structures of BNAs are necessarily abstract (see the top half of table 1 below). For concreteness, we will illustrate the definitions with the example of push-down automata for Probabilistic Context-Free Grammars (PCFGs), illustrated

[1]Normally the configuration of an automaton includes an input tape, whose string is either accepted or rejected by the automaton. Because we are using stochastic automata as a generative process, this string is considered part of the automaton's output and therefore is not included in the configuration.

in figure 1. The left side of figure 1(a) illustrates the data structures used in a PDA's configuration.

Standard non-stochastic automata specify how to choose which operation to apply in a given configuration using a nondeterministic mapping specified in a finite transition table. The symbols input to this mapping are determined by pointers into the configuration, called *read-heads*.[2] Stochastic automata simply add a probability distribution over each nondeterministic choice of operation given read-head values. Thus, the probabilistic transition table defines the conditional distribution over operations used in each step of generating a derivation.

The central difference between BNAs and stochastic automata is that a BNA specifies its probabilistic transition table in a Bayesian Network (BN) (T in table 1). Such a BN is illustrated on the right side of figure 1(a), discussed below. To determine the probability distribution to be used for generating the next operation, the values for the BN's input variables must be set to the values pointed to by the associated read-heads in the automaton's current configuration. Since these values were themselves determined by previous operations, setting the input variable values is equivalent to equating the input variables with the relevant previous output variables from these previous operations. The resulting compound Bayesian network is illustrated in figure 1(b) as the graph of circles and arrows.

2.2 BNA Configurations

The configurations of BNAs make use of this compound BN in specifying the intermediate states of derivations. Each configuration includes a compound BN that has been constructed by instantiating copies of the transition table BN T and equating their input variables with the appropriate previous output variables. To be more precise, this compound BN g_t is iteratively constructed by taking the BN g_{t-1} from the previous configuration, setting the values $\langle b_{t-1}, w_{t-1}, v_{1t-1}, \ldots, v_{kt-1}\rangle$ chosen in the previous operation, adding a new instantiation of the transition table BN T, and equating its input variables with the appropriate variables from g_{t-1}. This construction process is performed by the *inst* function in table 1. In the example in figure 1, the BN in (b) includes four copies

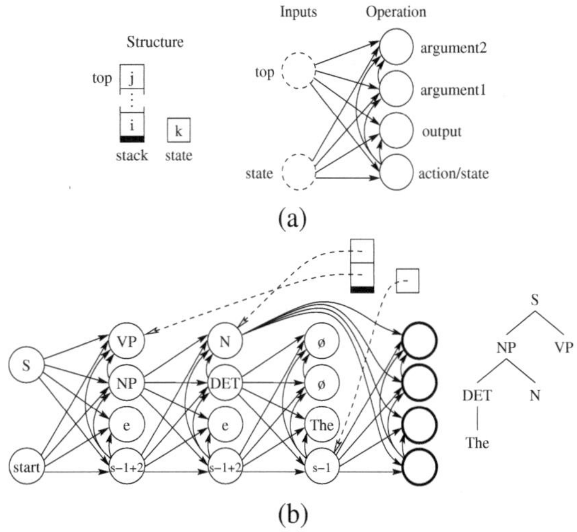

Figure 1: Illustrations of (a) a BNA specification and (b) its configuration after generating a partial tree

of the BN in (a). It includes all the instances of variables needed to specify the generation of the portion of tree shown on the right of figure 1(b), plus one set for choosing the next operation. The actions are "s-1" for popping one symbol from the stack and "s-1+2" for popping one and pushing two symbols. The pattern of edges reflects which variable instance was pointed to by the top of the stack at the time when each copy of the BN in (a) was added to the configuration's BN.

To determine which variables from g_{t-1} should be equated with each input variable in the new instantiation of T, BNA configurations include a second component that records information for the read-heads. This structural component c_t is equivalent to the data structures employed in standard automata, such as the stack of a PDA. The difference is that, instead of including symbols directly, these data structures include indices of variables in the compound BN g_t. The values of these variables are the symbols of the equivalent configuration in a standard automaton. This structural component is illustrated at the top of figure 1(b), where the indices are shown as dashed arrows. The read-heads R read indexes from c_{t-1} and pass them to the function *inst* so that it knows where to equate the associated variables from the new instantiation of T.

After constructing a new compound BN g_t, we can use it to determine the distribution over the possible next operations by looking at the output variables in the new instantiation of T. For book-

[2] For consistency, we generalise the notion of read-head to include all inputs to the transition function, including the state.

Table 1: Bayesian Network Automata specifications

Γ	a finite set of symbols
Σ	a subset of Γ which are output symbols
B	a finite set of actions
f	a halt action, $f \in B$
O	a finite set of operations $\langle b, w, v_1, \ldots, v_k \rangle$, s.t. $b \in B$, $w \in \Sigma^*$, $v_i \in \Gamma \cup \{\emptyset\}$
s_c	a start configuration structure
trans	a mapping from configuration-structure,action,$\mathbb{I}^{k+2}$ triples to configuration structures
R	a mapping from configurations to read-head vectors of indices $\mathbb{I}^r$
s_g	a start configuration BN specifying $P(b, w, v_1, \ldots, v_k)$, s.t. $\langle b, w, v_1, \ldots, v_k \rangle \in O$
s_I	The $k+2$ indices in s_g of the variables $b, w, v_1, \ldots, v_k$
T	a Bayesian Network specifying $P(b, w, v_1, \ldots, v_k \| u_1, \ldots, u_r)$, s.t. $\langle b, w, v_1, \ldots, v_k \rangle \in O$ and $u_i \in \Gamma \cup \{\emptyset\}$
inst	a mapping from BN,BN,$\mathbb{I}^r$,$\mathbb{I}^{k+2}$ quadruples to BNs, where *inst*(T, g, H, I) instantiates T in g with $u_1, \ldots, u_r$ indexed by H and $b, w, v_1, \ldots, v_k$ indexed by I

keeping purposes, the indices I_t of these output variables are stored in a third component of a BNA configuration. These variables are shown in figure 1(b) as bold circles.

In summary, a BNA configuration consists of three components $\langle c_t, g_t, I_t \rangle$, the structure c_t, the BN g_t, and the next operation variables I_t in g_t.

2.3 BNA Specifications

A formal definition of the generative process for BNA derivations is given in figure 2, according to the definitions given in table 1. The step of stochastically generating an operation of the automaton is given in line 3, which chooses a completely specified operation from the finite set of operations, O, which the equivalent stochastic automaton can perform. These operations specify the basic action b (e.g. *push* or *pop*), any arguments to that action $v_1, \ldots, v_k$, and any string w which should be concatenated to the output of the automaton.[3] The semantics of operations is de-

[3]In addition to generating the elements of a standard automaton's "input tape", this specification is notationally different from standard ones in that there is a distinction between the action b and the arguments to that action $v_1, \ldots, v_k$. As discussed below, this is to distinguish between decisions which change the structure of statistical dependencies (the actions) and decisions which only change the labels which decorate that structure (the arguments).

$\langle c_0, g_0, I_0 \rangle \leftarrow \langle s_c, s_g, s_I \rangle$
For $t = 0, 1, 2, \ldots$
  Stochastically generate an operation $\langle b_t, w_t, v_{1t}, \ldots, v_{kt} \rangle$ from distribution defined by variables I_t in g_t
  Write w_t to the output
  If $b_t = f$, then halt
  $c_{t+1} \leftarrow$ *trans*(c_t, b_t, I_t)
  Deterministically generate unique $I_{t+1} \in \mathbb{I}^{k+2}$
  $g_{t+1} \leftarrow$ *inst*$(T, g_t, R(c_{t+1}), I_{t+1})$
  Set the values of variables I_t in g_{t+1} to $\langle b_t, w_t, v_{1t}, \ldots, v_{kt} \rangle$

Figure 2: Pseudo-code for generating BNA derivations

fined by the function *trans*. As indicated in figure 2, *trans*(c_t, b_t, I_t) computes the next configuration structure c_{t+1} given the previous configuration structure c_t, the operation's action b_t, and the indices I_t of the variables $b_t, w_t, v_{1t}, \ldots, v_{kt}$ which select the action and its arguments. Any complete sequence of allowable operations is a derivation.

When choosing the next operation to perform, the stochastic automaton's transition function can only look at those symbols pointed to by its read-heads, specified in R in table 1. For example, the read-heads for a PDA identify the top of the stack and the state. In a BNA, this transition function is specified in the BN T, which has as many input variables as there are read-heads (r), and as many output variables as there are terms in an operation ($k + 2$). Conditioning on the variables pointed to by the automaton's read-heads is achieved by the *inst* function. As indicated in figure 2, *inst*$(T, g_t, R(c_{t+1}), I_{t+1})$ computes the next configuration BN g_{t+1} by adding to the previous configuration BN g_t an instance of T, such that the input variables of T are equated with the variables $R(c_{t+1})$ in g_t pointed to by the read-heads, and the output variables of T are assigned the new unique indices I_{t+1}. Any other variables in T are also assigned new unique indices.

The BN T is required to have no edges whose

destination is one of the input variables, so as to prevent edges whose direction conflicts with the temporal order of the automaton's operations. This property is important for efficient inference in BNAs, as will be discussed in the next section.

3 Bounded Versus Unbounded Generalisations

Bayesian networks capture generalisations by using the same parameters for more than one pattern of variable values. By specifying how parameters are reused across different cases, they specify how to generalise from data on one pattern to previously unseen patterns. This specification is done in the BN's model structure. Because this model structure is finite, BN's can only express generalisations over a bounded number of cases.

In contrast, formal language theory captures generalisations with formalisms that can handle an infinite number of patterns. By proving that a formalism can handle an infinite number of cases for some variation, one proves that the formalism must be capable of generalising across that variation. For example, we know that regular grammars and finite state automata can generalise across positions in a string, because they can generate arbitrarily large strings despite having a finite specification. They can model a finite number of specific string positions, but there will always be a larger string position for which they have no special case, and therefore they must treat it in the same way as some other smaller string position. Proofs of this form are called pumping lemmas. Context-Free Grammars and push-down automata generalise to arbitrarily long dependencies within a string, using arbitrarily deep tree structures. Tree Adjoining Grammars generalise to arbitrarily long dependencies within these trees, using arbitrarily deep trees which themselves generate trees.

3.1 Conditionally Bounded Models

Previous work has developed formalisms for specifying graphical models that generalise to an infinite number of cases. Dynamic Bayesian Networks (DBNs) (Ghahramani, 1998), such as Hidden Markov Models, and linear-chain Conditional Random Fields (Lafferty et al., 2001) generalise to unbounded string lengths. These models specify both a template model structure which is used for each position in the string, and the model structure which connects two adjacent position in the string (or any finite window of contiguous positions). In addition, the strings are padded with start and stop symbols, with the constraint that no positions can exist beyond these symbols. These symbols act like the halt action for BNAs, and are used to ensure a proper probability distribution over sequence lengths. Given a string of a specific length, it is possible to construct the entire relevant model structure for that string, and then apply normal graphical model inference techniques to this constructed model.

If you are given the string length, it is sometimes possible to take this approach even for more complex models, such as Probabilistic Context Free Grammars. It is common practice with PCFGs to transform them into a form where the depth of the tree is bounded by the length of the string. This transformation (such as binarisation, or Chomsky normal form) does not generate the same tree structures, but it does generate the same strings. With the transformed PCFG, given the string length, it is possible to construct the whole relevant bounded-depth model structure for that string, for example using case-factor diagrams (McAllester et al., 2004), or sum-product networks (Poon and Domingos, 2011). Inference can then be done, for example, using belief propagation (Smith and Eisner, 2008).

However, this approach is limited to inference problems where the string length is known, which in turn limits the potential training methods. We cannot necessarily use this pre-construction method if we want to take a generative approach, where the string length is determined by a generative process, or if we want to do incremental interpretation, where we want to do inference on prefixes of the string without knowing to total string length. In this situation, we might need to consider an infinite amount of model structure, for all the possible string lengths. In particular, this is true for undirected graphical models, such as Conditional Random Fields, which are globally normalised (c.f. (Rohanimanesh et al., 2009)).

3.2 Model Structure Prediction

BNAs allow us to do generative, incremental inference because they use directed graphical models, in particular Bayesian Networks. Because BNs are locally normalised, it is possible to solve some inference problems independently of the infinite unconstrained portion of the model structure. For example, a Hidden Markov Model can be applied to any string prefix to infer the probability distribution over the following element of the string, without needing to know the length of the total string. In general, an inference can be done independently of the unconstrained portion of the model structure provided there are no edges directed from the unconstrained portion to the portion where information is given. More precisely, consider the set $\mathcal{G}$ of complete model structures consistent with the given visible variables V, and let G be the intersection of all the $G' \in \mathcal{G}$. If for all $G' \in \mathcal{G}$, for all $h \in (G' - G)$, and for all $v \in V$, there is no directed path from h to v, then for all $G' \in \mathcal{G}$, $P(V|G') = P(V|G)$. This follows directly from well known properties of BNs, which rely on the fact that normalising $P(V|G)$ can be done locally to G. Thus $\sum_{G'} P(G')P(V|G') = P(V|G)$, and therefore we can do inference looking only at the known portion G of the model structure.[4]

For BNAs, this means that, given a prefix of an automaton's derivation, we can determine a unique model structure which is sufficient to compute the probability distribution for the automaton's next operation. There is no need to consider all possible future derivations.

Interestingly, not all variables in the derivation prefix must be given in order to determine a finite specification of the model structure. In some formalisms, it is sufficient to know the length of the string generated by the derivation prefix. But this approach may not take full advantage of existing algorithms for doing inference with grammars or automata. On the other extreme, the approach we took in section 2 of completely specifying all variables does not take full advantage of existing algorithms for doing inference in graphical models. As we will see in section 5.2, BNAs provide a framework where these two types of algorithms can be combined in a conceptually and computationally modular way.

More specifically, BNA derivations make a distinction between variables b_t which specify the action and variables $w_t, v_{1t}, \ldots, v_{kt}$ which specify the arguments to the action. The action (e.g. *push* versus *pop*) must be sufficient to determine the structure c_t of the configuration. The configuration structure in turn determines the placement of the read-heads $R(c_t)$, which determines the model structure of the configuration's BN g_t. Therefore, the sequence of derivation actions $b_0, \ldots b_n$ is sufficient to uniquely determine the model structure of the final configuration's BN g_{n+1}.

In BNA derivations, the arguments (e.g. *push*(A) versus *push*(B)) only affect the labels in the configuration's BN g_t. We can exploit this fact by only choosing specific values for the action variables, and leaving the argument variables unspecified. The constructed BN g_t will then specify a distribution over values for the argument variables. For example, a BNA configuration for a PDA must specify a specific depth for the stack, but could specify a distribution over the symbols in each position on a stack of that depth.

To illustrate this distinction between actions and arguments, consider an alternative two-pass generative process for BNA derivations. In the first pass of the generative process, it chooses the sequence of actions $b_0, \ldots b_n$ for a derivation, which predicts the model structure of the final configuration's BN g_{n+1}. The probability distributions for generating this sequence is defined by marginalising out the values for the argument variables. The probability distribution over argument variables defined by the final configuration's BN g_{n+1} then defines a distribution over argument variable values. In the second pass of the generative process, the argument values are chosen according to this distribution. This two-pass generative process will generate the same distributions over derivations as the characterisation in section 2.3.

4 Related Architectures and Grammars

In this section we discuss how BNAs are related to some previous proposals for the probabilistic modelling of unbounded structures.

Dynamic Bayesian Networks extend BNs to arbitrarily long sequences. A DBN specifies a bounded BN that models one position in the sequence, including input and output variables. A new instance of this BN is created for each position in the given sequence, with the outputs for one position's BN equated with the inputs of the subsequent position's BN. DBNs are equivalent to BNAs with finite state automata. The bounded BN of the DBN corresponds to the T of the BNA. The DBN has no need for an explicit representation of the BNA's configuration structure because

[4] This argument for directed models was recognised previously in (Titov and Henderson, 2007). Garg and Henderson (2011) proposes a model which mixes directed and undirected edges, but which still has this property because undirected edges are all local to individual derivation steps.

the configuration of a finite state automaton consists only of a state variable with a bounded number of values, so all information about the configuration can be encoded in the bounded BN. The only structure-modifying actions which are necessary are *continue* versus *stop*, which are used to generate the length of the sequence.

Switching DBNs (Ghahramani, 1998; Murphy, 2002) are DBNs which include variables that switch between multiple BN models during each position in the sequence. They are also covered by finite state BNAs, by the same argument. Although different BN models may be chosen for different positions, there are only a bounded number of possible BNs, so they can all be included in a single T. The switching decisions must be encoded in the structure-modifying actions.

The previous work on graphical models which is closest to our proposal is Incremental Sigmoid Belief Networks (ISBNs) (Henderson and Titov, 2010). Sigmoid Belief Networks (SBNs) (Neal, 1992) are a type of Bayesian Network, and ISBNs use the same technique as here for modelling arbitrarily large structures, namely incrementally constructing an SBN that generates the derivation of the structure. Henderson and Titov (2010) used this framework to reinterpret previous work on neural network parsing (Henderson, 2003) as an approximation to inference in ISBNs, and proposed another approximate inference method for natural language parsing. However, the control mechanism needed to construct an SBN for a derivation was not formalised.

Without any formal specification of how to construct an SBN for a derivation, it is hard to determine the power of the ISBN architecture. The specific ISBN models developed for natural language parsing cannot be expressed with a finite state controller, and thus they are not DBNs. They require at least a push-down automaton. The derivations modelled in (Henderson and Titov, 2010) are predictive LR derivations, which are equivalent in power to context-free derivations. However, the statistical dependencies which are specified as edges in their constructed SBN are not restricted to the context-free structure of the derivations. Edges may refer to any "structurally local" variables decorating the derived tree, even if they are not immediately local (such as the leftmost sibling). To translate such a model into a BNA, the read-head R would have to have access to symbols which are not on the top of the stack, and therefore the derivation structure would not be context-free. Given the restriction of locality, it is probably possible to devise chains of variables which pass the necessary information through the context-free structure of the tree. But without such a transformation, our analysis of inference algorithms in the next section suggests that it would be difficult to devise efficient algorithms for exact inference with this model. Henderson and Titov (2010) avoid this question by only considering approximate inference methods, since inference in the bounded SBN of their model is already intractable even before combining it with a parsing algorithm.

Koller et al. (1997) propose a framework for specifying complex recursive probabilistic models in terms of a stochastic functional programming language. As with BNAs, these models are locally normalised. They propose an inference algorithm for this framework, and discuss Bayesian networks and context-free grammars as examples of what can be implemented in it. The use of a functional programming language suggests a close relationship to the context-free derivation structures discussed in the next section.

From the grammar formalism side, the model that is closest to our proposal is Latent Probabilistic Context-Free Grammars (LPCFGs) (Matsuzaki et al., 2005). LPCFGs are PCFGs where the nonterminal labels are augmented with a latent variable. There has been much work recently on different training methods and different restrictions to the pattern of values which the latent variables are allowed to take (e.g. (Matsuzaki et al., 2005; Prescher, 2005; Petrov et al., 2006; Musillo and Merlo, 2008)). LPCFGs can be modelled as BNAs with push-down automata. The bounded BN of the equivalent BNA includes both a variable for the visible nonterminal label of the LPCFG and a variable for the latent extension of the nonterminal label. As a more specific example, the latent head labels of (Prescher, 2005) could be specified using a BN with a switching variable that selects which child's head variable is propagated to the head variable of the parent. Musillo and Merlo (2008) extend LPCFGs to include multiple latent variables decorating each nonterminal, with linguistically motivated constraints on how they can be related to each other. The BN of BNAs would provide a more perspicuous method to express these constraints.

5 Inference in Bayesian Network Automata

To illustrate the usefulness of the BNA framework, we look at algorithms for exact inference in BNAs. The way in which BNAs allow us to separate issues of structure from issues of labelling greatly facilitates the analysis and design of algorithms for calculating probabilities and exploring the space of derivations. In many important cases, previous algorithms for grammars can be combined directly with previous algorithms for Bayesian Networks, and the resulting algorithm has a complexity where the complexity of its two components are independent factors.

A BNA is a specification of a generative probabilistic model, and as such can be used to answer many questions about the probability distributions for some variables given others. We might want to find the most probable derivation given some sequence of output symbols (as in statistical parsing, or decoding), to marginalise over the derivations (as in language modelling), or to find the most probable values for a subset of the variables while marginalising over others (as in latent variable models of parsing). Although in some ways the most interesting, this last class of problems is in general NP-hard. Even for models based on finite state automata (e.g. HMMs), mixing the maximisation of some probabilities with the sum over others results is an NP-hard problem (Lyngsø and Pedersen, 2002). Because for reasons of space we are limiting our discussion to exact inference, we therefore also limit our discussion to the first two types of problems. However, the arguments given in section 5.2 for marginalising over all the unknown variables can also be applied to many approximations to latent variable models of parsing.

5.1 Fully-Specified BN Computation

The first case we consider is when the space of inputs and operations of the BN T is small enough that it is feasible to compute the complete conditional probability distribution of all possible operations given each possible input. In this case, the conditional probability distribution can be precomputed and used to fill the transition table for the equivalent stochastic automaton. Then any standard algorithm for the stochastic automaton can be applied. Under this assumption, if the complexity of inferring the complete conditional probability distribution for T is $O(F_B)$, and the complexity of the standard algorithm is $O(F_A)$, then the complexity of the complete problem is $O(F_B + F_A)$. In other words, computation time is dominated by whichever of these complexities is worse. For most previously proposed statistical parsing models, the parsing complexity does dominate and this pre-compilation strategy is in effect adopted. However, the interest of the BNA framework is in allowing the specification of more complicated models, where inference in the BN T is not so simple.

The second case we consider also uses any standard algorithm for the stochastic automaton, but computes probabilities with the BN T on-line during the running of the algorithm. This strategy may require forward inference of the distribution over operations given a specific input, or backward inference of the distribution over inputs given a specific operation, but in general it avoids the need to compute the complete joint distribution over both. In this case, if the complexity of the necessary inference in T is $O(F'_B)$, and the complexity of the standard algorithm is $O(F_A)$, then the complexity of the complete problem is $O(F'_B F_A)$. This is a good strategy if $O(F'_B)$ is much smaller than $O(F_B)$ from the previous case, as might be the case for lexicalised models, where $O(F_B)$ is a function of the vocabulary size but $O(F'_B)$ is only a function of the number of words in the sentence.

5.2 Marginalisation in the BN

Both of the above cases require computing probabilities given completely-specified values for all the inputs and/or all the outputs of the BN T. To fully exploit previous work on inference in BNs, we would like to develop inference algorithms which work directly with probability distributions over values for both the inputs and outputs of T. A full treatment of such algorithms is beyond the scope of this paper, but here we provide some results on cases where inference algorithms for BNs can be extended to BNAs. In particular, we look at what classes of automata can be combined with belief propagation (Pearl, 1988).

Belief propagation is a general method for efficiently computing marginal probabilities in Bayesian Networks (i.e. summing over latent variables). Provided that the BN has a tree structure (ignoring the directionality of the edges), this algorithm is guaranteed to stop with the exact marginal probability in time linear in the size of the BN. Therefore, if we can guarantee that the configuration BN g_t constructed by a BNA is always a tree, then we can apply belief propagation to inference in g_t, or in any sub-graph of g_t.

The structure of g_t reflects the structure of conditioning allowed by the derivations of the automaton. In formal language theory, this is called the derivation structure. If necessary, we can abstract away from any undirected cycles that might be introduced by the specific form of the BN T by collapsing all the non-input non-action variables in T into a single variable. By using this collapsed version of T to construct g_t, the structure of g_t becomes isomorphic to the derivation structure.[5] Thus, we can guarantee that (a version of) g_t will have a tree structure if the derivation structures of the automaton are trees, or more precisely, if the automaton has context-free derivation structures.

The most important class of grammar formalisms which have context-free derivation structures is Linear Context-Free Rewriting Systems (LCFRS) (Weir, 1988). In addition to Context-Free Grammars, popular examples of LCFRS include Synchronous Context-Free Grammars and Tree Adjoining Grammars (Joshi, 1987). This latter grammar formalism can specify classes of languages much larger than context-free languages, and Synchronous CFGs express languages over pairs of strings. For our purposes, the observations can be of any form and the formalism can have any method for combining the observations generated by sub-derivations, provided the derivation structures are context-free and there exists an algorithm for marginalising over the derivation structures given an observation.

Given an automaton whose derivations have a context-free tree structure, we can apply belief propagation to compute the marginal probability for any derivation generated by that automaton (if necessary collapsing the non-input non-action variables in T into a single variable). This will be feasible if it is feasible to propagate beliefs through one instance of T. This requirement is different from the one in the previous subsection in that the given information is a probability distribution (the belief), whereas above it was assumed to

$$
\begin{aligned}
&In(i-1,i,a) = P(a \Rightarrow w_i|a)\\
&In(i,k,a) =\\
&\quad \sum_{j=i+1}^{k-1} \sum_{b,c} P(a \Rightarrow bc|a) In(i,j,b) In(j,k,c)\\
&Out(0,|w|,c) = \text{ 1 if } c = S;\ \text{ 0 otherwise}\\
&Out(i,k,c) =\\
&\quad \sum_{j=0}^{i-1} \sum_{a,b} Out(j,k,a) In(j,i,b) P(a \Rightarrow bc|a) +\\
&\quad \sum_{j=k+1}^{|w|} \sum_{a,b} Out(i,j,a) P(a \Rightarrow cb|a) In(k,j,b)
\end{aligned}
$$

Figure 3: The Inside-Outside algorithm for PCFGs, where a, b, c are symbols, i, j, k are indices in string w, and $a \Rightarrow bc$, $a \Rightarrow w_i$ are CFG rules

be completely specified values. So, assuming that it is feasible to propagate beliefs through T and given an automaton with context-free derivations, we can feasibly compute the marginal probability of any derivation using belief propagation.

So far in this subsection we have only considered inference for a given derivation structure. In general, inference in BNAs requires marginalising both over labellings and over the structure itself, as is commonly required for unsupervised or partially-supervised grammar induction. Marginalising over structures can be done with the inside-outside algorithm for Context-Free Grammars (Baker, 1979) (given in figure 3) or the inside-outside algorithm for Tree-Adjoining Grammars (Schabes, 1992). These are dynamic programming algorithms. The inside calculations are very similar to bottom-up parsing algorithms such as CKY (Younger, 1967), except they compute sums of probabilities instead of taking the maximum probability. The outside calculations are also done in a single pass, but top-down.

Both inside and outside calculations work by incrementally considering equivalence classes of increasingly large sub-graphs of the derivation structure. For example in the equations in figure 3, each step computes a sum over the various ways that an operation can be used to construct a larger sub-derivation out of smaller ones, such that they all have the same start i, end k and label. As discussed at the end of section 3.2, with BNAs we can easily represent $In(i,k,\cdot)$ and $Out(i,k,\cdot)$ as distributions over labels, i.e. the beliefs. The sums over symbols in these equa-

[5]Note that all action variables $b_{t'}$ in g_t will have known values, because this is necessary in order to know the model structure. Thus, the concern here is the structure of the interdependencies between the possibly-unknown variables $w_{t'}, v_{1t'}, \ldots, v_{kt'}$ in g_t, because these are the variables we need to marginalise over using belief propagation.

tions ($\sum_{b,c} P(a \Rightarrow bc|a)In(i,j,b)In(j,k,c)$ and $\sum_{a,b} Out(i,j,a)P(a \Rightarrow cb|a)In(k,j,b)$) can then be done using belief propagation through the BN representation of $P(a \Rightarrow cb|a)$.

If the configuration BN g_t is a tree, then any connected sub-graph of g_t will also be a tree, so we can apply belief propagation to the sub-graph of g_t for any of the sub-derivations. In addition, belief propagation can be applied either forward or backward through the edges of g_t, so the probability distribution for any node in a sub-graph of g_t can be computed in a single pass over the sub-graph by propagating beliefs towards the desired node. This allows belief propagation to be integrated into an inside-outside algorithm; whenever the inside-outside algorithm considers building larger sub-derivations out of smaller ones, belief propagation is applied to continue the propagation of beliefs out of the smaller sub-derivations' graphs and into the instance of T for the operation used in the combination. This belief propagation can then be interleaved with the sums over structural alternatives (the sums over j in figure 3).

Because each use of an operation considered by the inside-outside algorithm corresponds to belief propagation through a single instance of T, the time complexity of performing belief propagation through T is a constant factor in the complexity of the entire algorithm. For the inside part of the algorithms, only backward inference through T is required, and then for the outside computations forward inference is required. Thus, given an $O(F_A)$ inside-outside inference algorithm and an $O(F''_B)$ inference algorithm for propagating beliefs (forward or backward) through T, the complexity of parsing will be $O(F''_B F_A)$. As with the results from the previous subsection, this complexity result factors the two components of the algorithm.

6 Conclusions

In this article we have proposed a framework for specifying and reasoning with complex probabilistic models of unbounded structures, called Bayesian Network Automata. The BNA framework combines the theory of graphical models with automata theory and formal language theory. It uses Bayesian Networks to provide a perspicuous representation of local statistical generalisations. It uses automata to provide a precise specification of how to generalise to arbitrarily large model structures, even when the model structure must be predicted during inference. Together they provide a precise and perspicuous representation of probability distributions over unbounded structures.

Using this framework, we have clarified the power of various previously proposed probabilistic models of unbounded structures. Without any additional control structure, Dynamic Bayesian Networks are equivalent to BNAs with finite state automata. This limited power also applies to switching DBNs. Incremental Sigmoid Belief Networks potentially have greater power, but previous work did not formally characterise the nature of the additional control structure which they employ. The model of parsing which has been proposed for ISBNs appears to be a BNA with a push-down automaton, but the nature of the BN used prevents direct application of the efficient parsing methods we have discussed.

We have also used this framework to explore how the complexity of inference with the bounded Bayesian Network interacts with the complexity of inference with the automaton. We have shown that for a large class of automata (which can generate more than just context-free languages), the complexity of inference with a BNA is simply the multiplication of the complexity of inference in the Bayesian Network times the complexity of inference with the automaton.

BNAs have the potential to greatly expand the class of problems which we can effectively model with graphical models, through their simple mechanism for increasing the power of these models and the large body of existing theory and algorithms that help us limit this power in ways that retain tractability. They provide a useful framework for future work on many issues, including approximate inference methods that interface well with parsing algorithms. We believe that the BNA framework will be most useful with large Bayesian Networks where only approximate inference methods are tractable.

Acknowledgements

The author would like to thank the many reviewers that have contributed to making this a better paper. This work was partly funded by European Community FP7 grant 216594 (CLASSiC, www.classic-project.org) and Swiss NSF grant 200021 125137.

References

J. K. Baker. 1979. Trainable grammars for speech recognition. *The Journal of the Acoustical Society of America*, 65(S1):S132–S132.

Nikhil Garg and James Henderson. 2011. Temporal restricted boltzmann machines for dependency parsing. In *Proc. 49th Annual Meeting of the Association for Computational Linguistics: Human Language Technologies*, pages 11–17.

Zoubin Ghahramani. 1998. Learning dynamic bayesian networks. In C. Giles and M. Gori, editors, *Adaptive Processing of Sequences and Data Structures*, pages 168–197. Springer-Verlag, Berlin, Germany.

James Henderson and Ivan Titov. 2010. Incremental sigmoid belief networks for grammar learning. *Journal of Machine Learning Research*, 11(Dec):3541–3570.

James Henderson. 2003. Inducing history representations for broad coverage statistical parsing. In *Proc. joint meeting of North American Chapter of the Association for Computational Linguistics and the Human Language Technology Conf.*, pages 103–110.

Aravind K. Joshi. 1987. An introduction to tree adjoining grammars. In Alexis Manaster-Ramer, editor, *Mathematics of Language*. John Benjamins, Amsterdam.

D. Koller, D. McAllester, and A. Pfeffer. 1997. Effective Bayesian inference for stochastic programs. In *Proc. 14th National Conf. on Artificial Intelligence (AAAI 1997)*, pages 740–747.

John Lafferty, Andrew McCallum, and Fernando Pereira. 2001. Conditional random fields: Probabilistic models for segmenting and labeling sequence data. In *Proc. 18th International Conf. on Machine Learning*, pages 282–289. Morgan Kaufmann, San Francisco, CA.

Percy Liang, Slav Petrov, Michael Jordan, and Dan Klein. 2007. The infinite PCFG using hierarchical dirichlet processes. In *Joint Conf. on Empirical Methods in Natural Language Processing and Computational Natural Language Learning*, pages 688–697, Prague, Czech Republic.

Rune B. Lyngsø and Christian N.S. Pedersen. 2002. The consensus string problem and the complexity of comparing hidden markov models. *Journal of Computer and System Sciences*, 65:545–569.

Takuya Matsuzaki, Yusuke Miyao, and Jun'ichi Tsujii. 2005. Probabilistic CFG with latent annotations. In *Proc. 43rd Annual Meeting on Association for Computational Linguistics*, pages 75–82.

David McAllester, Michael Collins, and Fernando Pereira. 2004. Case-factor diagrams for structured probabilistic modeling. In *Proc. 20th Conf. on Uncertainty in Artificial Intelligence*, pages 382–391.

Kevin P. Murphy. 2002. *Dynamic Belief Networks: Representation, Inference and Learning*. Ph.D. thesis, University of California, Berkeley, CA.

Gabriele Musillo and Paola Merlo. 2008. Unlexicalised hidden variable models of split dependency grammars. In *Proc. 46th Annual Meeting of the Association for Computational Linguistics: Human Language Technologies*, pages 213–216.

Radford Neal. 1992. Connectionist learning of belief networks. *Artificial Intelligence*, 56:71–113.

Judea Pearl. 1988. *Probabilistic Reasoning in Intelligent Systems: Networks of Plausible Inference*. Morgan Kaufmann.

Slav Petrov, Leon Barrett, Romain Thibaux, and Dan Klein. 2006. Learning accurate, compact, and interpretable tree annotation. In *Proc. 44th annual meeting of the ACL and the 21st Int. Conf. on Computational Linguistics*, pages 433–440.

Hoifung Poon and Pedro Domingos. 2011. Sum-product networks: A new deep architecture. In *Proc. 12th Conf. on Uncertainty in Artificial Intelligence*, pages 337–346.

Detlef Prescher. 2005. Head-driven PCFGs with latent-head statistics. In *Proc. 9th Int. Workshop on Parsing Technologies*, pages 115–124.

Khashayar Rohanimanesh, Michael Wick, and Andrew McCallum. 2009. Inference and learning in large factor graphs with adaptive proposal distributions and a rank-based objective. Technical Report UM-CS-2009-008, University of Massachusetts.

Yves Schabes. 1992. Stochastic Tree-Adjoining Grammars. In *Proc. workshop on Speech and Natural Language*, pages 140–145.

David A. Smith and Jason Eisner. 2008. Dependency parsing by belief propagation. In *Proc. 2008 Conference on Empirical Methods in Natural Language Processing*, pages 145–156.

Ivan Titov and James Henderson. 2007. Incremental bayesian networks for structure prediction. In *Proc. 24th International Conf. on Machine Learning*, pages 887–894.

David Weir. 1988. *Characterizing Mildly Context-Sensitive Grammar Formalisms*. Ph.D. thesis, University of Pennsylvania, Philadelphia, PA.

Daniel H. Younger. 1967. Recognition and parsing of context-free languages in time n^3. *Information and Control*, 10(2):189–208.

Model-Theory of Property Grammars with Features

Denys Duchier
LIFO - Université d'Orléans
Orléans, France

Thi-Bich-Hanh Dao
LIFO - Université d'Orléans
Orléans, France

Yannick Parmentier
LIFO - Université d'Orléans
Orléans, France

firstname.lastname@univ-orleans.fr

Abstract

In this paper, we present a model-theoretic description of Property Grammar (PG) with features. Our approach is based on previous work of Duchier *et al.* (2009), and extends it by giving a model-theoretic account of feature-based properties, which was lacking in the description of Duchier *et al.*

On top of providing a formal definition of the semantics of feature-based PG, this paper also discusses the various possible interpretations of features (*e.g.*, within the requirement and agreement properties), and show how these interpretations are represented in our framework. This work opens the way for a constraint-based implementation of a parser for PG with features.

1 Introduction

Many formal descriptions of natural language syntax rely on rewriting systems (*e.g.*, Tree-Adjoining Grammar). They specify how to generate the syntactic structures (hence the strings) belonging to a given (natural) language, by applying successive derivations (rewritings). Such syntactic descriptions are called generative-enumerative syntax. They provide a procedural view of language that naturally leads to the development of parsing algorithms. Nonetheless, as advocated by Pullum and Scholz (2001), such descriptions fail in accounting for ungrammatical sentences, such as those regularly produced by humans.

An alternative description of syntax, called model-theoretic syntax, focuses on syntactic properties that the structures (and strings) of a language are supposed to follow (*e.g.*, Property Grammar).In other terms, such descriptions do not give any information about how to produce these structures, they "simply" give a declarative specification of them. The grammar can thus be seen as a set of constraints, and syntactic structures as models satisfying these constraints. If one allows for the violation of some specific constraints, it then becomes possible to account for ungrammatical sentences, that is, to build *quasi-models* that are linguistically motivated and formally computed.[1]

Duchier *et al.* (2009) proposed a model-theoretic semantics of Property Grammar (PG), where models are trees labeled with syntactic categories. Their formalization was then converted into a constraint optimization problem to implement a parser for PG (Duchier et al., 2010). In their formalization, the authors did not account for features, thus omitted some properties such as *agreement*[2]. In this paper, we propose to fill this gap, by giving a model-theoretic semantics of feature-based PG. This semantics makes it possible to implement a constraint-based parser for the full class of PG in a similar way to that of Duchier *et al.* (2010).

The paper is organized as follows. In section 2, we introduce (feature-based) PG. Then, in section 3, we present our logical specification of PG. Finally, in section 4, we discuss the different interpretations of feature-based properties and their representations in our specification.

2 Property Grammar

As mentioned above, Property Grammar (Blache, 2000) is a formalism belonging to model-theoretic syntax. It describes the relations between syntactic constituents in terms of local constraints (the so-called *properties*). These properties come from linguistic observations (*e.g.*, order between words, co-occurrence, facultativity, *etc*). In

[1]This ability to describe ungrammatical sentences by means of violable constraints is also present in Optimality Theory (Prince and Smolensky, 1997).

[2]In her PhD thesis, Guénot (2006) proposed to replace dependency (as introduced in Blache (2000)) with a more specialized property named agreement.

a first approximation, these properties can be seen as local constraints on categories labeling syntactic trees. A property $A : \psi$ specifies, for a given node labeled A, the constraint ψ to be applied on the categories of A's daughter nodes (written B, C hereafter). ψ is one of the following:

Obligation	$A : \triangle B$	at least one B
Uniqueness	$A : B!$	at most one B
Linearity	$A : B \prec C$	B precedes C
Requirement	$A : B \Rightarrow C$	if $\exists\, B$, then $\exists\, C$
Exclusion	$A : B \not\Leftrightarrow C$	not both B and C
Constituency	$A : S?$	all children $\in S$
Agreement	$A : B \leadsto C$	feat. constraints

As mentioned above, in PG, properties are not restricted to syntactic categories, they actually handle feature structures. That is, the above properties do not only constrain atomic categories labeling syntactic nodes, but feature-based labels. In order to give a logical specification of PG, we first need to formally define these feature-based properties.

Let $\mathcal{F}$ be a finite set of features $\{f_1, \dots, f_n\}$, where each feature f_i takes its values in a finite upper semilattice D_i. We write $\top_i$ for D_i's greatest element ($\top_i$ will be used in our specification to refer to features that do not apply within a given property). Since the syntactic category has a special status (it is mandatory within properties), we suppose that among the features f_i, there is one called `cat` to encode the category. Attribute-value matrices (AVM) of type $\mathcal{M} = [f_1{:}D_1, \dots, f_n{:}D_n]$ also form a finite upper semilattice, equipped with the usual "product order" (written $\sqsubseteq$). This will allows us to compare AVM values. We write $\mathcal{M}_\downarrow$ for the minimal elements of $\mathcal{M}$. Within AVM values, we omit f_i if its value is $\top_i$. We also use AVM expressions, where features can be associated with variables (thus allowing for coreferences).[3] If S is an AVM expression, then S^v is the corresponding value obtained by replacing any occurrence of $f_i{:}X$ by $f_i{:}\top_i$ because f_i's value is constrained only by coreference equations. If S_0, S_1, S_2 are AVM expressions, then $E(S_0, S_1, S_2)$ is the set of coreference equations $(i, f) \doteq (j, g)$ for all $f{:}X$ in S_i and $g{:}X$ in S_j.

We can now define properties as being either of the form $S_0{:}r(S_1)$ or $S_0{:}r(S1, S2)$, where $S_0, S_1, S2$ are AVM expressions, and r one of the relations introduced above ($\triangle, \Rightarrow, \dots$). That is, property literals are formed in one of the following ways (s_1 refers to a set of AVM expressions): $S_0 : \triangle S_1$, $S_0 : S_1!$, $S_0 : S_1 \prec S_2$, $S_0 : S_1 \Rightarrow S_2$, $S_0 : S_1 \not\Leftrightarrow S_2$, $S_0 : s_1?$, $S_0 : S_1 \leadsto S_2$. We write $\mathcal{P}$ for the set of all possible property literals over $\mathcal{F}$. Let $\mathcal{W}$ be a set of elements called *words*. A lexicon is a subset of $\mathcal{W} \times \mathcal{M}$ (that is, a lexicon maps words with AVM types). A *property grammar* G is a pair (P_G, L_G) where P_G is a set of properties (*i.e.*, a subset of $\mathcal{P}$) and L_G a lexicon.

When describing natural language, the properties of P_G are encapsulated within *linguistic constructions*, which typically describe syntactic constituents. As an illustration, consider Fig. 1 containing an extract of the PG for French of (Prost, 2008). In this figure, the `NP` construction describes noun phrases. It can be read as follows. In a noun phrase, there must be either a noun or a pronoun. If there is a determiner, a noun, a prepositional phrase or a pronoun, it must be unique. The determiner (if any) precedes the noun, pronoun, prepositional and adjective phrase (if any). A noun must come with a determiner, so does an adjective phrase with a noun. There cannot be both a noun and a pronoun. There must be gender and number agreements between the noun and the determiner.

3 Model-Theoretic Semantics

We will now extend the logical specification of PG of Duchier *et al.* (2009) using the above definition of feature-based properties.

Class of models. Following (Duchier et al., 2009), the strong semantics (*i.e.*, no property violation is allowed) of property grammars is given by interpretation over the class of syntactic trees τ. We write $\mathbb{N}_0$ for $\mathbb{N}\backslash\{0\}$. A *tree domain* D is a finite subset of $\mathbb{N}_0^*$ which is closed for prefixes and left-siblings; in other words, $\forall \pi, \pi' \in \mathbb{N}_0^*, \forall i, j \in \mathbb{N}_0$:

$$\begin{array}{lcl} \pi\pi' \in D & \Rightarrow & \pi \in D \\ i < j \wedge \pi j \in D & \Rightarrow & \pi i \in D \end{array}$$

A syntax tree $\tau = (D_\tau, L_\tau, R_\tau)$ consists of a tree domain D_τ, a labeling function $L_\tau : D_\tau \to \mathcal{M}_\downarrow$ assigning a *minimal* AVM value (w.r.t. $\sqsubseteq$) to each node, and a function $R_\tau : D_\tau \to \mathcal{W}^*$ assigning to each node its surface realization.

For convenience, we define the arity function $A_\tau : D_\tau \to \mathbb{N}$ as follows, $\forall \pi \in D_\tau$:

$$A_\tau(\pi) = \max\{0\} \cup \{i \in \mathbb{N}_0 \mid \pi i \in D_\tau\}$$

Instances. Following (Duchier et al., 2009), a property instance is a pair of a property and a tuple of nodes (paths) to which it is applied (see Fig. 2).

[3] In our PG specification, coreferences are only allowed within agreement properties.

NP (Noun Phrase)

obligation : $\triangle$(N $\sqcup$ Pro)
uniqueness : D!
: N!
: PP!
: Pro!
linearity : D $\prec$ N
: D $\prec$ Pro
: D $\prec$ AP
: N $\prec$ PP
requirement : N $\Rightarrow$ D
: AP $\Rightarrow$ N
exclusion : N $\not\Leftrightarrow$ Pro
agreement : $\mathrm{N}_{\begin{bmatrix}\text{gend} & \boxed{1}\\ \text{num} & \boxed{2}\end{bmatrix}} \leadsto \mathrm{D}_{\begin{bmatrix}\text{gend} & \boxed{1}\\ \text{num} & \boxed{2}\end{bmatrix}}$

VP (Verb Phrase)

obligation : $\triangle$V
uniqueness : $\mathrm{V}_{[\text{mode:past-part}]}!$
: NP!
: PP!
linearity : V $\prec$ NP
: V $\prec$ Adv
: V $\prec$ PP
requirement : $\mathrm{V}_{[\text{mode:past-part}]} \Rightarrow \mathrm{V}_{[\text{aux:+}]}$
exclusion : $\mathrm{Pro}_{[\text{case:acc}]} \not\Leftrightarrow$ NP

Figure 1: Extract of a Property Grammar for French

$$
\begin{aligned}
\mathcal{I}_\tau[\![G]\!] &= \cup\{\mathcal{I}_\tau[\![p]\!] \mid \forall p \in P_G\}\\
\mathcal{I}_\tau[\![S_0 : S_1 \prec S_2]\!] &= \{(S_0 : S_1 \prec S_2)@\langle\pi, \pi i, \pi j\rangle \mid \forall \pi, \pi i, \pi j \in D_\tau,\ i \neq j\}\\
\mathcal{I}_\tau[\![S_0 : \triangle S_1]\!] &= \{(S_0 : \triangle S_1)@\langle\pi\rangle \mid \forall \pi \in D_\tau\}\\
\mathcal{I}_\tau[\![S_0 : S_1!]\!] &= \{(S_0 : S_1!)@\langle\pi, \pi i, \pi j\rangle \mid \forall \pi, \pi i, \pi j \in D_\tau,\ i \neq j\}\\
\mathcal{I}_\tau[\![S_0 : S_1 \Rightarrow S_2]\!] &= \{(S_0 : S_1 \Rightarrow S_2)@\langle\pi, \pi i\rangle \mid \forall \pi, \pi i \in D_\tau\}\\
\mathcal{I}_\tau[\![S_0 : S_1 \not\Leftrightarrow S_2]\!] &= \{(S_0 : S_1 \not\Leftrightarrow S_2)@\langle\pi, \pi i, \pi j\rangle \mid \forall \pi, \pi i, \pi j \in D_\tau,\ i \neq j\}\\
\mathcal{I}_\tau[\![S_0 : s_1?]\!] &= \{(S_0 : s_1?)@\langle\pi, \pi i\rangle \mid \forall \pi, \pi i \in D_\tau\}\\
\mathcal{I}_\tau[\![S_0 : S_1 \leadsto S_2]\!] &= \{(S_0 : S_1 \leadsto S_2)@\langle\pi, \pi i, \pi j\rangle \mid \forall \pi, \pi i, \pi j \in D_\tau,\ i \neq j\}
\end{aligned}
$$

Figure 2: Property instances of a grammar G on a syntactic tree τ

Pertinence. Since we created instances of all properties in P_G for all nodes in τ, we must distinguish properties which are truly pertinent at a node from those which are not. For this purpose, we define the predicate P_τ over instances as in Fig. 3. This evaluation of property pertinence extends (Duchier et al., 2009) by comparing AVM expressions.

Satisfaction. When an instance is pertinent, it should also (preferably) be satisfied. For this purpose, we extend the predicate S_τ over instances of (Duchier et al., 2009) as in Fig. 4. For agreement, satisfaction relies on satisfaction of coreference equations, defined as follows. We say that the triple of values M_0, M_1, M_2 satisfies the coreference equations of expressions S_0, S_1, S_2, and write $M_0, M_1, M_2 \models E(S_0, S_1, S_2)$, iff $M_i.f{=}M_j.g$ for all $(i, f) \doteq (j, g)$ in $E(S_0, S_1, S_2)$. As in (Duchier et al., 2009), we write $I^0_{G,\tau}$ for the set of pertinent instances, $I^+_{G,\tau}$ for its subset that is satisfied, and $I^-_{G,\tau}$ for its subset that is violated:

$$
\begin{aligned}
I^0_{G,\tau} &= \{r \in \mathcal{I}_\tau[\![G]\!] \mid P_\tau(r)\}\\
I^+_{G,\tau} &= \{r \in I^0_{G,\tau} \mid S_\tau(r)\}\\
I^-_{G,\tau} &= \{r \in I^0_{G,\tau} \mid \neg S_\tau(r)\}
\end{aligned}
$$

Admissibility. A syntax tree τ is admissible as a candidate model for grammar G iff it satisfies the projection property, *i.e.* $\forall \pi \in D_\tau$:

$$
\begin{aligned}
A_\tau(\pi) = 0 \text{ (leaf node)} &\Rightarrow \quad \langle L_\tau(\pi), R_\tau(\pi)\rangle \in L_G\\
A_\tau(\pi) \neq 0 \text{ (inner node)} &\Rightarrow R_\tau(\pi) = \textstyle\sum_{i=1}^{i=A_\tau(\pi)} R_\tau(\pi i)
\end{aligned}
$$

where $\sum$ represents the concatenation of sequences. In other words, leaf nodes must conform to the lexicon, and inner nodes pass upward the ordered realizations of their daughters.

Strong and loose models. The definition of strong and loose models stated by Duchier *et al.* (2009) are applied directly in this extension. A syntax tree τ is a strong model of a property grammar G iff it is admissible and $I^-_{G,\tau} = \emptyset$. A syntax tree τ is a loose model of G iff it is admissible and it maximizes the ratio $F_{G,\tau}$ defined as $F_{G,\tau} = I^+_{G,\tau}/I^0_{G,\tau}$.

4 About the Interpretation of Features

Let us now discuss the model-theoretic semantics of feature-based PG introduced above, by looking at some examples. In particular, let us see what is the meaning of features and how do these affect property pertinence and satisfaction. Let us first consider the requirement property of VP in Fig. 1.

$$
\begin{aligned}
P_\tau((S_0 : S_1 \prec S_2)@\langle \pi, \pi i, \pi j\rangle) &\equiv (L_\tau(\pi) \sqsubseteq S_0^v) \wedge (L_\tau(\pi i) \sqsubseteq S_1^v) \wedge (L_\tau(\pi j) \sqsubseteq S_2^v) \\
P_\tau((S_0 : \triangle S_1)@\langle \pi\rangle) &\equiv L_\tau(\pi) \sqsubseteq S_0^v \\
P_\tau((S_0 : S_1!)@\langle \pi, \pi i, \pi j\rangle) &\equiv (L_\tau(\pi) \sqsubseteq S_0^v) \wedge (L_\tau(\pi i) \sqsubseteq S_1^v) \wedge (L_\tau(\pi j) \sqsubseteq S_1^v) \\
P_\tau((S_0 : S_1 \Rightarrow S_2)@\langle \pi, \pi i\rangle) &\equiv (L_\tau(\pi) \sqsubseteq S_0^v) \wedge (L_\tau(\pi i) \sqsubseteq S_1^v) \\
P_\tau((S_0 : S_1 \not\Leftrightarrow S_2)@\langle \pi, \pi i, \pi j\rangle) &\equiv (L_\tau(\pi) \sqsubseteq S_0^v) \wedge ((L_\tau(\pi i) \sqsubseteq S_1^v) \vee (L_\tau(\pi j) \sqsubseteq S_2^v)) \\
P_\tau((S_0 : s_1?)@\langle \pi, \pi i\rangle) &\equiv L_\tau(\pi) \sqsubseteq S_0^v \\
P_\tau((S_0 : S_1 \leadsto S_2)@\langle \pi, \pi i, \pi j\rangle) &\equiv (L_\tau(\pi) \sqsubseteq S_0^v) \wedge (L_\tau(\pi i) \sqsubseteq S_1^v) \wedge (L_\tau(\pi j) \sqsubseteq S_2^v)
\end{aligned}
$$

Figure 3: Property pertinence on a syntactic tree τ

$$
\begin{aligned}
S_\tau((S_0 : S_1 \prec S_2)@\langle \pi, \pi i, \pi j\rangle) &\equiv i < j \\
S_\tau((S_0 : \triangle S_1)@\langle \pi\rangle) &\equiv \vee\{(L_\tau(\pi i) \sqsubseteq S_1^v) \mid 1 \leq i \leq A_\tau(\pi)\} \\
S_\tau((S_0 : S_1!)@\langle \pi, \pi i, \pi j\rangle) &\equiv i = j \\
S_\tau((S_0 : S_1 \Rightarrow S_2)@\langle \pi, \pi i\rangle) &\equiv \vee\{(L_\tau(\pi j) \sqsubseteq S_2^v) \mid 1 \leq j \leq A_\tau(\pi)\} \\
S_\tau((S_0 : S_1 \not\Leftrightarrow S_2)@\langle \pi, \pi i, \pi j\rangle) &\equiv (L_\tau(\pi i) \not\sqsubseteq S_1^v) \vee (L_\tau(\pi j) \not\sqsubseteq S_2^v) \\
S_\tau((S_0 : s_1?)@\langle \pi, \pi i\rangle) &\equiv L_\tau(\pi i) \sqsubseteq x \quad \text{for some } x \text{ in } s_1 \\
S_\tau((S_0 : S_1 \leadsto S_2)@\langle \pi, \pi i, \pi j\rangle) &\equiv L_\tau(\pi), L_\tau(\pi i), L_\tau(\pi j) \models E(S_0, S_1, S_2)
\end{aligned}
$$

Figure 4: Property satisfaction on a syntactic tree τ

This property states that, within a verb phrase, a past-participle requires an auxiliary. That is, in a model, a V node labeled with [mode:past-part] must come with a sister V node labeled with [aux:+]. As shown in Fig. 3, for this property to be *pertinent* for a couple of nodes $\langle \pi, \pi i\rangle$ with π the mother node of πi, these need to have category VP and V respectively, and πi needs to be labeled with [mode:past-part] ($L_\tau(\pi i) \sqsubseteq S_1^v$). For this property to be *satisfied*, a sister node of πi, say πj, needs to be labeled with [aux:+] ($L_\tau(\pi j) \sqsubseteq S_2^v$), as shown in Fig. 4. In other words, the `cat` and `mode` features affect pertinence and `aux` satisfaction.

Let us now consider the agreement property of `NP` in Fig. 1. Such a property ensures that, within a noun phrase, there are gender and number agreements between the determiner and the noun. For this property to be pertinent, we only consider the categories of the triple of nodes $\langle \pi, \pi i, \pi j\rangle$ (*i.e.*, omitting variables), see Fig. 3. For it to be satisfied, one need the coreferences to hold ($L_\tau(\pi), L_\tau(\pi i), L_\tau(\pi j) \models E(S_0, S_1, S_2)$). Here, all but the `cat` feature affect satisfaction.

Let us finally consider the following property:

$$
\texttt{VP} : \texttt{V}\begin{bmatrix} \text{mode} & \text{past-part} \\ \text{gend} & \boxed{1} \\ \text{num} & \boxed{2} \\ \text{pers} & \boxed{3} \end{bmatrix} \leadsto \texttt{Pro}\begin{bmatrix} \text{case} & \text{acc} \\ \text{gend} & \boxed{1} \\ \text{num} & \boxed{2} \\ \text{pers} & \boxed{3} \end{bmatrix}
$$

which constrains the gender, number and person agreements between a past-participle and an accusative pronoun (*e.g.*, *je l'ai aimée* / I loved her). For this property to be pertinent at a triple of nodes $\langle \pi, \pi i, \pi j\rangle$, one needs (a) π to have category VP ($L_\tau(\pi) \sqsubseteq S_0^v$), (b) πi to have category V and to be labeled with [mode:past-part] ($L_\tau(\pi i) \sqsubseteq S_1^v$), and (c) πj to have category Pro and to be labeled with [case:acc] ($L_\tau(\pi j) \sqsubseteq S_2^v$). For it to be satisfied, one needs the additional constraint that the coreferences hold ($L_\tau(\pi), L_\tau(\pi i), L_\tau(\pi j) \models E(S_0, S_1, S_2)$). In this example, the property mixes features affecting pertinence (`cat`, `mode`, `case`) and features affecting satisfaction (`gend`, `num`, `pers`). Thanks to our definition of AVM, and of $\sqsubseteq$ only checking for ground values, and $\models$ checking for coreferences, our representation supports the various interpretations of features.

5 Conclusion

We presented a model-theoretic semantics of PG that supports the various interpretations of features. Forthcoming work concerns the implementation of a PG parser by converting this semantics into a constraint optimization problem following Duchier *et al.* (2010). The motivation behind this is to provide the linguist with a device to implement her/his theories and check the logical consequences of these on syntactic analyzes.

References

Philippe Blache. 2000. *Constraints, Linguistic Theories and Natural Language Processing*. Lecture Notes in Artificial Intelligence Vol. 1835. Springer-Verlag.

Denys Duchier, Jean-Philippe Prost, and Thi-Bich-Hanh Dao. 2009. A model-theoretic framework for grammaticality judgements. In *Conference on Formal Grammar (FG2009)*, Bordeaux, France, July.

Denys Duchier, Thi-Bich-Hanh Dao, Yannick Parmentier, and Willy Lesaint. 2010. Property Grammar Parsing Seen as a Constraint Optimization Problem. In *Proceedings of the 15th International Conference on Formal Grammar (FG 2010)*, Copenhagen, Denmark.

Marie-Laure Guénot. 2006. *Éléments de grammaire du français pour une théorie descriptive et formelle de la langue*. Ph.D. thesis, Université de Provence.

Alan Prince and Paul Smolensky. 1997. Optimality: From neural networks to universal grammar. *Science*, 275(5306):1604–1610, March.

Jean-Philippe Prost. 2008. *Modelling Syntactic Gradience with Loose Constraint-based Parsing*. Cotutelle Ph.D. Thesis, Macquarie University, Sydney, Australia, and Université de Provence, Aix-en-Provence, France, December.

Geoffrey Pullum and Barbara Scholz. 2001. On the Distinction Between Model-Theoretic and Generative-Enumerative Syntactic Frameworks. In Philippe de Groote, Glyn Morrill, and Christian Rétoré, editors, *Logical Aspects of Computational Linguistics: 4th International Conference*, number 2099 in Lecture Notes in Artificial Intelligence, pages 17–43, Berlin. Springer Verlag.

Learning Structural Dependencies of Words in the Zipfian Tail

Tejaswini Deoskar
School of Informatics
University of Edinburgh
tdeoskar@inf.ed.ac.uk

Markos Mylonakis
ILLC
University of Amsterdam
m.mylonakis@uva.nl

Khalil Sima'an
ILLC
University of Amsterdam
k.simaan@uva.nl

Abstract

Using semi-supervised EM, we learn fine-grained but sparse lexical parameters of a generative parsing model (a PCFG) initially estimated over the Penn Treebank. Our lexical parameters employ *supertags*, which encode complex structural information at the pre-terminal level, and are particularly sparse in labeled data – our goal is to learn these for words that are unseen or rare in the labeled data. In order to guide estimation from unlabeled data, we incorporate both structural and lexical priors from the labeled data. We get a large error reduction in parsing ambiguous structures associated with unseen verbs, the most important case of learning lexico-structural dependencies. We also obtain a statistically significant improvement in labeled bracketing score of the treebank PCFG, the first successful improvement via semi-supervised EM of a generative structured model already trained over large labeled data.

1 Introduction

Computational models of natural language trained on labeled data contain many parameters that are not estimated accurately, due to the data sparsity inherent in labeled data. This is especially true of complex structured models like parsers, which contain a large number of parameters, and where labeled training data is expensive to create.These models employ various forms of parameter smoothing to deal with overfitting and with unknown or low-frequency words. However, it is desirable, and in many cases necessary, to augment supervised models using readily available unlabeled data, such as raw news-wire or from the web. Semi-supervised methods have therefore received a lot of attention in recent years.

In this paper, we present a method for semi-supervised training of a large-scale structured model (a Penn Treebank PCFG) using the Expectation Maximization algorithm (Dempster et al., 1977). We focus on learning only those parameters of the model that are particularly difficult or impossible to obtain from labeled data, namely parameters related to *low-frequency* and *unseen* words (the Zipfian tail). Words are important determiners of structural information for parsers; for instance, verb subcategorization information improved the Collins' parser (Collins, 1997). However, this data is very sparse in even the largest labeled dataset available today, i.e., the Penn Treebank (Marcus et al., 1993). To illustrate the severity of the problem, consider the fact that close to 40% of verb types in the training sections of the Penn Treebank have occurred only *once* therein. Thus, modelling the structural properties of these verbs that may be useful for disambiguation in a parser (such as subcategorization properties) is simply not possible from labeled data, and one has to look to unlabeled data.

From the machine learning point of view, semi-supervised learning in general, and semi-supervised EM in particular, has been successful for classification-based NLP tasks (e.g. Nigam et al. (1998), Blum and Mitchell (1998), Yarowsky (1995)). For more structured tasks such as part-of-speech tagging and grammar learning, semi-supervised learning has worked largely in the case where the labeled data is small in size (Klein and Manning, 2004; Steedman et al., 2003; Druck et al., 2009a; Ganchev et al., 2010; Reichart and Rappoport, 2007). There have been some instances of successful large-scale semi-supervised learning for structured models (McClosky et al., 2006; Deoskar, 2008; Koo et al., 2008; Bansal and Klein, 2011), where a grammar model trained on a large amount of labeled data such as the full Penn Treebank has shown further improvement from unlabeled data. These methods have typically depended on the complementarity of multiple views of the data (a discriminative reranking model over a generative model as in (McClosky et al., 2006)), and/or complex or heuristic objective functions (as in Deoskar (2008); Koo et al. (2008)) or simply by incorporating surface counts from unlabeled data (as in a recent paper by Bansal and Klein (2011)). A contribution of this paper is that we show that using EM in a semi-supervised manner with a simple objective function can improve a parser, contrary to common belief in the field.

The PCFG model used in this paper is trained on the Penn Treebank. It contains fine-grained structural information marked on pre-terminal categories, making them similar in spirit to *supertags* for strongly lexicalised formalisms like LTAG (Bangalore and Joshi, 1999) and CCG (Steedman, 2000). A supertag encodes structure that is distributed over the tree and localises it onto a single parameter of the model. Our learning problem is cast very simply as estimating the parameters $p(w|\tau)$ (where w is a word and τ a supertag) from labeled and unlabeled data. The problem is, however, more complex than a sequence labeling task because these supertags are highly ambiguous and encode argument-adjunct distinctions as well as long-distance dependencies (illustrated later in examples). Semi-supervised EM is known to often give models that are worse than the supervised model (Merialdo, 1994; Charniak, 1993; Ng and Cardie, 2003). To address this, we incorporate probabilistic constraints on unsupervised estimation by using labeled data to derive prior knowledge at two levels: (a) structural constraints in the form of higher PCFG rules (b) preferences over the distributions $p(w|\tau)$ themselves. We obtain large improvements in assigning correct structures to unseen verbs, and also a statistically significant improvement in labeled bracketing over a smoothed supervised model.

The rest of the paper is structured as follows: a description of the Treebank PCFG model and its smoothing is in §2. §3 describes the semi-supervised method, the constraints derived from labeled data, and their theoretical interpretation. §4 contains experiments and §5 evaluations. A discussion of related literature is in §6. §7 concludes.

2 The PCFG Model

We work with a probabilistic context-free grammar (PCFG) model, since it is easy to analyse and most other more sophisticated parsing models can be understood as refinements of it (Charniak, 1997). The Penn Treebank PCFG used in this work is based on Deoskar and Rooth (2008) and Deoskar (2009) . It has pre-terminal categories that are complex and fine-grained, especially for open-class words. The PCFG is obtained by a process that effectively results in node-relabelling transformations of Penn Treebank II trees (Johnson, 1998), and counting relative frequencies of context-free rules in the transformed trees. We illustrate the nature of complex preterminal categories in the grammar with some examples below. These complex categories are intended to encode structure selected by/associated with a word onto the preterminal-tag of the word. Fig. 1 shows fragments of Penn Treebank (henceforth, PTB) sentences along with their annotation (empty categories are slightly simplified). In (a), the verb *add* has two arguments – an NP *four more Boeings* and a PP-CLR *to the two units*. The -CLR label indicates that the PP is an argument.

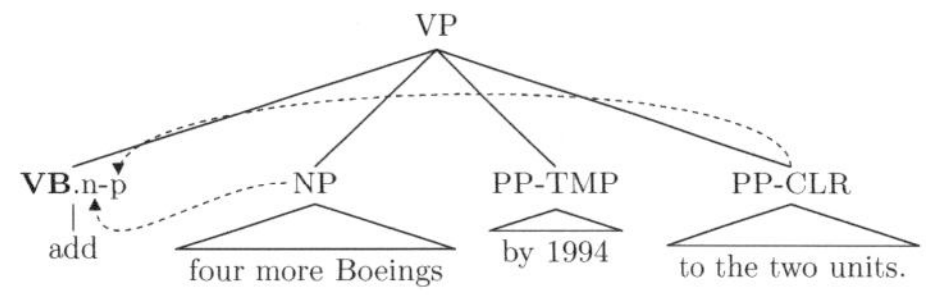

(a) An NP PP subcategorization frame on the verb 'add'.

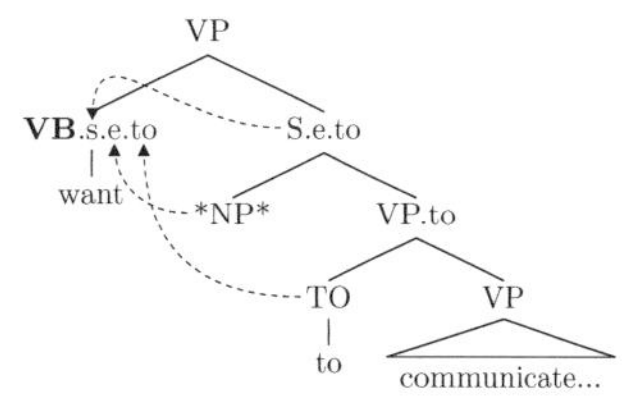

(b) An S frame on the verb 'want' (*NP* is the empty subject)

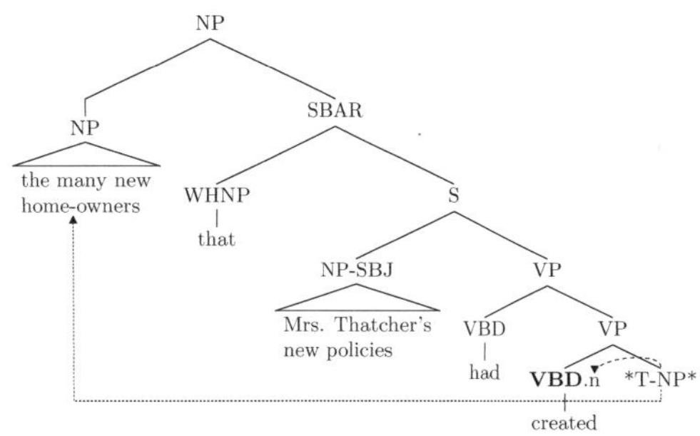

(c) Long-distance. (*T-NP* is the trace of NP)

Figure 1: Some verbal supertags.

These arguments are encoded in the supertag on the verb as `n-p` giving the new pre-terminal category '**VB**.`n-p`', made of the original PTB POS-tag VB, followed after a dot by its refinement `n-p` indicating the NP and PP-CLR arguments. The temporal PP (PP-TMP) is considered an adjunct and is not included in the supertag. Fig. 1(b) shows a more complex supertag on the verb *want* – this supertag encodes the complement S as `s`, the empty subject of the S as `e` and the TO further down the tree as `to`, together forming `s.e.to`. The `e` serves to distinguish this structure from others like *expect them to communicate*, while the `to` distinguishes it from finite subordinate clauses like *set the economy moving* or *help meet increasing demand*. The final example in 1(c) shows an object relative clause. The verb of interest is 'created', which has a transitive supertag `n` indicating an NP complement. Notice that this verb is assigned the transitive supertag even though the complement NP is quite far removed from its original position (indicated by *T-NP*), thus capturing a long-distance dependency between the verb *created* and the NP *the many new home-owners*.

Our supertags are quite fine-grained – there are 81 sub-categories for verbs[1]. The additional marking on the original PTB POS tag is determined automatically and unambiguously by (solely) using information available in the treebank tree, such as the structure of the tree and functional tag marking. As seen above, these supertags distinguish arguments from adjuncts and localise onto a single parameter, long distance information that may be spread across different levels of the tree.

For space reasons, we do not describe aspects of the PCFG that are not directly relevant to this work (but see Deoskar (2009)). Importantly, the PCFG does not contain lexicalisation at higher levels of the tree, except for function words such as prepositions and determiners (as in (Klein and Manning, 2003)). As far as content-words (non-functional words) are concerned, word or head-word information is not part of any parameter of the PCFG except pre-terminal rules. Thus the unlexicalised PCFG has a clean division between complex lexical parameters (pre-terminal rules) and non-lexical ones (the rest). We exploit this in our semi-supervised method to constrain unsupervised estimation (§3). Another consideration in using an unlexicalised PCFG for this work is that it would be significantly more computationally expensive to use a lexicalized one, due to the larger number of parameters.

The (smoothed) PCFG performs close to the best reported results for a simple unlexicalised Treebank PCFG (without splitting and merging of categories as in Petrov and Klein (2007)), with a labeled bracketing f-score of 87.4% ($<$ 40 words) and 86.5% (all sentences) on Section 23 of the PTB. While this is not the highest-performing grammar trained on the Penn Treebank (Petrov and Klein, 2007; Charniak and Johnson, 2005), note that it is trained on PTB trees that retain all functional categories as well as empty categories originally present in the PTB. Most treebank parsers remove functional tags and empty categories, thereby reducing sparsity and improving scores. Including functional categories and traces enables our PCFG to make finer distinctions and recover traces, but makes our training data much sparser than usual. Empty category recovery of the PCFG is 84%, at par with the state-of-the-art (Schmid, 2006). Functional tag recovery is comparable to Blaheta and Charniak (2000); Blaheta (2004) (the only other reported results that use all functional tags in the PTB [2]). Our non-null f-scores for the categories described in Blaheta's work are as follows (with the best scores from Blaheta and Charniak (2000) or Blaheta (2004) in brackets) – Grammatical: 94.78 (95.55), Semantic: 77.96 (78.63), Topicalization: 96.26 (95.28), Miscellaneous: 61.97 (58.99).

2.1 Smoothing the treebank PCFG based on POS tagging: creating a baseline.

Most treebank parsers are required to smooth their estimates to deal with over-fitting and with unknown words. This is usually done by backing off from a more articulated level (such as words) to a less articulated one (such as POS-tags), or by interpolating between the two. In the case of fine-grained lexical categories (supertags), the problem of smoothing becomes more severe. In some other generative models containing fine-grained lexical categories, such as CCG, smoothing is done by replacing unseen words and words below a cut-off

[1]This number holds for the case when lexicalized prepositions are not projected into the supertag. The complete list is available in Deoskar (2009) (Appendix D).

[2]Merlo and Musillo (2005)'s work uses a subset of the functional tags in the PTB, and hence their results are not comparable to ours.

frequency with POS tags. This cut-off frequency is in fact very high – for instance, Hockenmaier and Steedman (2002) find that the optimal cut-off is 30 for their generative parser. In our work, such a method is not an option: we are interested precisely in learning supertags for low frequency and unseen words from the unlabeled corpus. Secondly, POS tags are not a parameter of the PCFG, only supertags are.

We adopt a smoothing method first described in Deoskar (2008), that specifically aims at introducing parameters for unseen words from the unlabeled corpus into the PCFG[3]. In this method, every word from the unlabeled corpus is assigned with all those supertags that have been seen in the labeled corpus with the POS tag of the word. Thus, each verb is assigned all supertags that are associated with verbs in the labeled corpus. This applies both to words that are seen and unseen in the labeled data, thus taking care of the case where a word may have been seen in the labeled data, but may not have been seen with all relevant categories (an issue when dealing with fine-grained categories). A small probability mass is taken from the supervised distribution and redistributed amongst the newly introduced parameters. Equations and more details are in Deoskar (2008).

The unlabeled corpus is first POS-tagged by an off-the-shelf POS tagger to give counts of words and POS-tags. The count of a (word, POS-tag) pair from the unlabeled corpus is divided amongst all supertags (for that POS-tag) based on the ratio of supertags in the *labeled* data. For unseen words, this gives an initial estimate that is informed by marginal counts, counted over all words (with the given POS tag) in the labeled data. For instance, in the case of an unseen verb, the method will result, say, in the transitive supertag being more common than a ditransitive one, since transitive supertags are overall more common than ditransitive ones across all verbs in the labeled data. This model thus gives us an informed baseline to evaluate models learnt from the semi-supervised process, a baseline that is more informed than backing off to the part-of-speech of the word. This smoothed model also forms the initial model for the EM estimation described in the section below.

[3]It is important for unsupervised estimation that the PCFG contain non-zero lexical parameters for all words in the unlabeled corpus. If not, sentences with unseen words will not get an analysis and parameters for those words will never be induced.

3 Semi-Supervised Learning of Lexical Parameters

3.1 The Learning Problem

EM is notoriously fickle for learning structured models in semi-supervised settings, needing tricky initialisation and careful constraining (Mann and McCallum, 2010) (e.g. Charniak (1993) for parsing, Merialdo (1994) for POS-tagging). In our case, the initial model is a highly-accurate, smoothed model obtained from labeled data (§2.1). Our task is to retrieve an estimate from the joint corpus of labelled and unlabeled data that performs better than a smoothed estimate from labeled data alone. In our unlexicalised PCFG, grammatical parameters (i.e., non-lexical rules) from the labeled data are fairly accurate [4]. We do not re-estimate these from unlabeled data (following Deoskar (2008)). Instead, we solely re-estimate lexical parameters, which are complex and contain a lot of structural information localised onto the pre-terminal level of the tree (recall the examples in Fig. 1). This allows us to learn syntactic information, while keeping the learning problem adjacent to the lexical surface.

In the following sections, we describe two ways in which we use the labeled data to constrain our latent variable (preterminal supertag sequences): structural constraints in the form of non-lexical rules, and distributions over lexical parameters $p(w|\tau)$ themselves. These constraints are included in a well-founded manner: a structural probabilistic prior over supertag sequences, and Dirichlet priors over conditional distributions $p(w|\tau)$ (as seen later in §3.5, by interpreting the learning process as a maximum a posteriori unsupervised estimator). These priors direct the estimator towards more promising parameter spaces, creating a strong learning environment with a clear objective function.

3.2 A Prior Over Supertag Sequences

Notation:

w : terminal (word)	TB : labeled corpus
τ : pre-terminal	UC : unlabeled corpus

$\mathbf{w}$: sequence of terminals

$\boldsymbol{\tau}$: sequence of pre-terminals

$p(\boldsymbol{\tau})$: distribution over $\boldsymbol{\tau}$

$\hat{p}(\boldsymbol{\tau})$: relative frequency estimate of $p(\boldsymbol{\tau})$

[4]This assumption is justified to a large extent in the case of an unlexicalised grammar; however, grammar rules are also subject to sparsity and may benefit from re-estimation.

$\tau := \langle T, \iota \rangle$ consists of a POS-tag T and a sequence of features ι.

A PCFG, apart from defining a language and distribution over terminal strings, *also* does so for strings of pre-terminal symbols [5]. If we consider derivations down to the level of pre-terminals, the (syntactic part of the) PCFG provides a distribution $p(\boldsymbol{\tau})$ over sequences of pre-terminals $\boldsymbol{\tau}$. If $\mathcal{T}(\boldsymbol{\tau})$ is the set of trees with $\boldsymbol{\tau}$ as their leaves, then $p(\boldsymbol{\tau})$ is the sum of probabilities of all such trees $p(\boldsymbol{\tau}) = \sum_{T \in \mathcal{T}(\boldsymbol{\tau})} p(T)$.

We are concerned with estimating the conditional probabilities $p(w|\tau)$, i.e., the parameters of the conditional model $p(\mathbf{w}|\boldsymbol{\tau})$. We use Maximum-Likelihood Estimation (MLE) for this purpose. For the labeled part of the data TB, MLE boils down to simply getting the relative-frequency estimate. For the unlabeled data UC however, we need to marginalise over all plausible pre-terminal sequences $\boldsymbol{\tau}$. As a consequence, $p(\boldsymbol{\tau})$ directly emerges as a *prior* over the latent variable $\boldsymbol{\tau}$. The likelihood of the concatenation of the two corpora can then be written as follows, with θ the set of lexical parameters $p(w|\tau)$:

$$\mathcal{L}(TB, UC;\ \theta, p(\boldsymbol{\tau})) = \prod_{\langle \mathbf{w}, \boldsymbol{\tau} \rangle \in TB} p(\mathbf{w}|\boldsymbol{\tau};\theta) p(\boldsymbol{\tau}) * \prod_{\mathbf{w} \in UC} \sum_{\boldsymbol{\tau}} p(\mathbf{w}|\boldsymbol{\tau};\theta) p(\boldsymbol{\tau}) \quad (1)$$

In general, this approach allows semi-supervised MLE training of a model conditioning on a latent variable, by introducing a prior over the latent variable which can be directly estimated from the labeled part of the training data. For our model, after computing a PCFG relative-frequency estimate for the parameters $\hat{p}(\boldsymbol{\tau})$ on TB, we can shift our focus away from the syntactical analyses in TB and effectively treat this part of the data as a corpus of sentences labeled with pre-terminal sequences.

3.3 MLE with Semi-Supervised EM

We estimate the parameter set θ of the conditional model $p(\mathbf{w}|\boldsymbol{\tau})$ by maximising the likelihood of the concatenation of the labeled and unlabeled corpus. During the estimation we employ the estimate $\hat{p}(\boldsymbol{\tau})$ that we retrieve from the labeled corpus TB as a prior over $\boldsymbol{\tau}$, i.e., its parameters are not a subject of the estimation process and remain constant. On the contrary, $\hat{p}(\boldsymbol{\tau})$ *guides* the estimation process, showing a strong preference towards supertag sequences which are syntactically justified.

[5]Most PCFGs used in parsing employ pre-terminals, i.e., non-terminals which are the only ones which expand to terminal symbols and only terminal symbols. Even if a PCFG does not satisfy this requirement, it can be converted to an equivalent Chomsky Normal Form grammar which does so. Without loss of generality, we will here confine ourselves to a grammar making use of pre-terminals.

Initialise θ_0
for $i = 1$ to N iterations **do**
  E-step {Find expected complete-data log-likelihood, given current estimate}
  $Q(\theta|\theta_{i-1}) =$
  $E[log(\mathcal{L}(TB, \langle UC, UC_{\boldsymbol{\tau}} \rangle; \theta, \hat{p}(\boldsymbol{\tau})))|TB, UC, \theta_{i-1}]$
  M-step {Maximise Q in respect to θ}
  $\theta_i = \arg\max_{\theta} Q(\theta|\theta_{i-1})$
end for

Figure 2: The EM algorithm for the semi-supervised learning of $p(w|\tau)$

Since $\boldsymbol{\tau}$ is a latent variable for the unlabeled corpus UC, $\arg\max_\theta \mathcal{L}(TB, UC; \theta, \hat{p}(\boldsymbol{\tau}))$ cannot be found analytically. Instead, we use the Expectation-Maximization (EM) algorithm (Dempster et al., 1977). We start with an initialisation point θ_0, which, since we have labeled data available, is the (smoothed) relative-frequency estimate of these parameters on TB.

E-step In the *Expectation* step, we find the expected value $Q(\theta|\theta_{i-1})$ of the complete data log-likelihood (with UC completed with missing pre-terminal sequences $UC_{\boldsymbol{\tau}}$) with respect to the missing data (pre-terminal sequences), given the observed data (sentences in UC, $\langle \mathbf{w}, \boldsymbol{\tau} \rangle$ pairs in TB) and the current estimate of the parameters θ_{i-1}. Since the sentences in TB already have supertags, in practice this step relates only to UC.

M-step In the *Maximization* step, the new estimate θ_i is retrieved by maximising the expectation of the E-step. The M-step under the constraints $\sum_w p(w|\tau) = 1$ can be performed analytically. This involves computing the expected counts of word-supertag pairs $c_{i-1}(w, \tau)$ over the combined corpus of labeled and unlabeled data, given θ_{i-1}. This is equivalent to adding the observed word-supertag counts from the labeled data to the expected counts from the unlabeled part, which can be efficiently computed using the Inside-Outside algorithm (Lari and Young, 1990). The update rule for the parameters of the new estimate θ_i are:

$$\theta_i(w|\tau) = \frac{c^{UC}_{i-1}(w, \tau) + c^{TB}_{i-1}(w, \tau)}{\sum_{w'} c^{UC}_{i-1}(w', \tau) + c^{TB}_{i-1}(w', \tau)} \quad (2)$$

3.4 Corpora Scaling Factors and Additional Constraints

The impact of the labeled part of the data can be fine-tuned as follows: since the training data is seen as a concatenation of the labeled and unlabeled part, we can scale them before concatenating them, i.e., take a 'copies' of the unlabeled data together with b 'copies' of the labeled data. This operation can be understood as merely altering the input training corpus and has no effect on the existing analysis. In the new update formula, the scaling factors of the corpora trickle down as scaling factors of the (expected) counts:

$$\theta_i(w|\tau) = \frac{a * c_{i-1}^{UC}(w,\tau) + b * c_{i-1}^{TB}(w,\tau)}{\sum_{w'} a * c_{i-1}^{UC}(w',\tau) + b * c_{i-1}^{TB}(w',\tau)} \tag{3}$$

Secondly, we might also want to constrain the estimation objective by limiting the number of parameters of the conditional model $p(\mathbf{w}|\boldsymbol{\tau})$ to be estimated. Many lexical parameters are estimated accurately from the treebank (for example, those related to function words and other high-frequency words), and estimation from unlabeled data might hurt them. For each distribution $p(w|\tau)$, we choose to retain values from TB for some of the parameters which we assume are less affected by sparsity issues (i.e., we keep these parameters fixed) while estimating the rest. Under the same analysis as above, we end up with a similar update formula as before. For each conditional distribution given τ, if π_{fixed} is the sum of the fixed probability values and W_{free}^{τ} the set of words for which we wish to estimate $p(w|\tau)$, the remaining (i.e., not fixed) probability mass is $(1 - \pi_{\text{fixed}})$ and is distributed to the free parameters in proportion to the related (expected) counts $c(w, \tau)$. We skip the proof due to space limitations.

$$\theta_i(w|\tau) = (1-\pi_{\text{fixed}}) \frac{a * c_{i-1}^{UC}(w,\tau) + b * c_{i-1}^{TB}(w,\tau)}{\sum_{w' \in W_{\text{free}}^{\tau}} a * c_{i-1}^{UC}(w',\tau) + b * c_{i-1}^{TB}(w',\tau)} \tag{4}$$

3.5 Semi-Supervised Learning as Maximum A Posteriori Estimation

In this subsection, we discuss an interpretation of our learning method (i.e. maximum-likelihood of the concatenated labeled and unlabeled corpora) as *Maximum a Posteriori* (MAP) estimation solely on the unlabeled corpus employing a prior $p(\theta)$ over the parameter set θ. This is useful in order to understand the role that the labeled data plays in guiding estimation from unlabeled data. For each of the multinomials $p(\mathbf{w}|\boldsymbol{\tau})$, consider a Dirichlet conjugate prior with hyper-parameters α providing a distribution over the possible multinomial parameter sets.

$$p(\mathbf{w}, \boldsymbol{\tau}; \theta) = p(\mathbf{w}|\boldsymbol{\tau}; \theta)p(\boldsymbol{\tau})p(\theta) \tag{5}$$

The hyper-parameters α of the Dirichlet can be interpreted as prior counts of the events that the multinomial tracks, with each α_w^{τ} corresponding to word w emitted by pre-terminal τ. We take advantage of this feature[6] to introduce relevant counts from the labeled corpus in the Dirichlet hyper-parameters, setting each $\alpha_w^{\tau} = c^{TB}(w,\tau) + 1$.

Dempster et al. (1977) show that EM can also be used under MAP to climb towards the posterior mode of the parameter space θ. Due to the Dirichlet being conjugate to the multinomial distribution, it is easy to show that the new quantity that we wish to maximise has the same functional form as $Q(\theta|\theta_{i-1})$. Interestingly, for the Dirichlet priors in Eq. (5), MAP estimation boils down to the same update formula as in (2), establishing an equivalent interpretation of the estimation process which clarifies how the labeled training data 'guide' EM estimation on the unlabeled part of the corpus at two distinct levels: (a) a structural prior $p(\boldsymbol{\tau})$ preferring syntactically correct pre-terminal sequences, considering the interdependencies between pre-terminals in a sentence and (b) priors over the parameter space itself $p(\theta)$, considering lexical choice for each pre-terminal separately.

4 Experiments

We report experiments using a treebank PCFG trained on approximately 36,000 sentences from sections 0-22 of the Wall Street Journal (WSJ) portion of the PTB, with about 5000 sentences held-out for testing and development. Semi-supervised training is carried out using 4, 8, 12 and 16 million words of unlabeled WSJ data, after limiting sentence length to <25 words. Inside-outside estimation is implemented in Bitpar (Schmid, 2004). The corpus scaling factor for labeled data is set to 8 (i.e., $a = 1$ and $b = 8$ in Eq. 3; this value makes our labeled data (1 million words) weigh about twice as much as our smallest unlabeled corpus of 4 million words. We experimented with setting the scaling factor to 4, making the labeled corpus of 1

[6]Starting from an uninformed Dirichlet prior $p(\theta)$ with $\alpha_w^{\tau} = 1$ for all w, τ, the posterior $p(\theta|TB)$ after observing the labeled data TB also takes the form of a Dirichlet distribution with updated hyper-parameters $\alpha_w^{\tau} = c^{TB}(w,\tau) + 1$.

	4M	8M	12M	16M
t_{smooth}	29.86	29.86	29.86	29.86
t_{parse}	27.80	27.82	27.80	27.80
It 1	28.44	28.12	27.16	27.64
2	27.72	27.08	26.13	25.73
3	27.40	26.53	25.89	25.34
4	27.40	26.21	25.97	25.18
5	27.24	**25.89**	25.66	24.7
6	**27.08**	26.05	25.81	24.78
7	27.08	26.05	25.50	24.7
8	-	-	25.42	24.62
9	-	-	25.42	**24.62**
10	-	-	**25.18**	-
11	-	-	25.42	-
% Err.reduc	9.31	12.76	15.67	**17.5**

Table 1: Supertag error for *unseen* verbs in test Viterbi parses, for different sizes of unlabeled training data

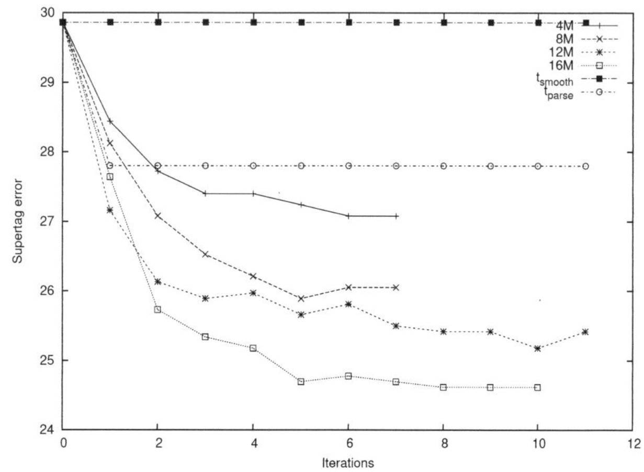

Figure 3: Supertag error for unseen verbs in Viterbi parses, for different sizes of unlabeled training data.

million words effectively equal in size to the unlabeled corpus of 4 million words; however, a value of 8 gives better results, and we report only these.

5 Evaluations

Learning lexico-syntactic information

We evaluate the learning of lexico-syntactic dependencies by measuring the accuracy of supertag assignment in Viterbi (maximum-probability) parses of test sentences. We report this number for verbs, since they are the most important lexical determiners of structure in a sentence, as well as the most ambiguous. To evaluate unseen verbs, we created a separate testset of 1200 sentences with about 1250 token occurrences of unseen verbs (about 110 types), by holding out all sentences with occurrences of these verbs from the labeled data. These verbs have a wide variety of ambiguous subcategorization frames and are thus representative of typical verbs in the lexicon of a language. This evaluation is a parsing-based evaluation and gives us a focused way of measuring the learning of syntactic structures associated with unseen words (verbs in this case). Note that each supertag is associated with a local or nonlocal structure, and hence counting supertag accuracy in effect measures the accuracy of getting this subtree-structure right. Since these supertags encode empty categories and functional tags, it is not possible to compare other standard state-of-the-art parsers on this metric, since they do not contain either in their output. Table 1 shows the error in identifying the correct supertag for these unseen verbs in Viterbi parses of test sentences, for unlabeled training data of sizes 4, 8, 12 and 16 million words. The baseline model is the smoothed treebank PCFG t_{smooth} (§2.1), with an error of 29.86%. This model does not contain lexical information specific to these verbs (being unseen). Thus, in about 70% of the cases the parser assigns a correct supertag without verb-specific information. We create a second baseline by parsing the unlabeled corpus with the model t_{smooth} and obtaining Viterbi parses – this parsed corpus is merged with the labeled data, keeping corpus scaling factors same as before, and a PCFG t_{parse} extracted from it. This model is thus a self-trained model – it improves the supertag error over t_{smooth} to 27.8%, and does not change subsequently.

Semi-supervised EM training improves the error rate over t_{smooth} in the first iteration, and t_{parse} in the second. This improvement is already significant ($p < 0.01$, using McNemar's test). The error rate goes on to further improve in subsequent iterations. The error rate also improves with increasing sizes of unlabeled data. The best obtained error is 24.62% with 16M words ($p < 0.0001$), a substantial error reduction of 17.5% over the smoothed supervised model. Since these verbs have not occurred in the labeled data, the improvements are solely the result of learning from unlabeled data. We also evaluated seen but low-frequency verbs (frequency 1 to 5 in the training corpus). We see a benefit for these as well, with an error reduction of 8.97% (from 23.51 for the baseline t_{smooth} to 21.40 for 16M words of unlabeled data).

Figure 3 shows the learning curves for different sizes of unlabeled data. The distance between the 12M and 16M curves suggests that further improvements may be obtained by adding even more

	t_{smooth}	It 1	2	3	4	5	6	7	8
Recall	86.49	86.74	***86.83	86.79	86.79	86.78	86.80	86.79	86.79
Precision	86.84	86.84	**86.90	**86.90	86.83	86.86	86.88	86.88	86.87
f-score	86.56	86.79	**86.87	86.83	86.82	86.82	86.82	86.84	86.83

Table 2: Labeled bracketing f-scores on Sec. 23 of PTB (4M words, $f < 5$). *** p<0.001, ** p<0.01

unlabeled data.

Labeled bracketing

The PARSEVAL metric is not the best metric for evaluating the lexico-syntactic learning that is the focus of this paper, for two reasons. Firstly, it is a coarse metric, known to be insensitive to lexico-syntactic (i.e. subcategorization) information (Briscoe et al., 1998), in addition to not counting argument/adjunct distinctions, functional tags or empty categories. Secondly, and more importantly, our method is targeted towards the learning of rare/low-frequency events, which do not have enough of a token count in Section 23 to make a big impact. However, we do see a statistically significant improvement in labeled bracketing scores on Section 23 of the PTB (Table 2) (statistical significance calculated using a randomised version of the paired-sample t-test).

The improvements are not large, however they are the first improvements to be obtained using semi-supervised EM for a large-scale Penn Treebank grammar. This is the result solely of learning lexical parameters of low-frequency words ($f < 5$). It is not surprising that the improvements are small – the total token count of words that our method impacts (i.e., words with a frequency less than 5 in the training data) constitute only 6.1% tokens in Section 23 (excluding numbers, but including proper nouns, for which it is not useful to learn structural dependencies). However, they correspond to about 34.2% types, relevant for a obtaining a broad-coverage lexicon, but not relevant for a token-based evaluation like labelled bracketing. It should be noted that while models in later iterations are not better than the baseline, nor are they significantly *worse*.

Another important point is that the f-score on Section 23 remains stable when the value of the cut-off frequency f is increased, and when unlabeled data size is increased to 16M words (not shown in table). Thus, although we obtain large improvements in learning about unseen words (as shown in the previous evaluation), the overall quality of the models, as measured by labeled bracketing does not degrade. This is an important consideration for semi-supervised learning, since adding large amounts of unlabeled data tends to have a negative impact on the supervised model.

It	$f < 5$	$f < 10$	$f < 20$	$f < 50$	$f < 1000$
t_{smooth}	18.13	18.13	18.13	18.13	18.13
1	17.78	17.82	17.79	17.68	17.65
2	18.14	17.63	17.63	17.65	17.65
3	18.43	17.65	17.70	17.67	17.65
4	18.14	17.74	17.75	17.67	17.70
5	**17.53**	17.72	17.74	17.81	17.68
6	17.65	17.81	17.84	17.79	17.75
7	17.68	17.81	17.87	17.84	17.84

Table 3: Overall verbal supertag error, 4M words unlabeled data. (It=iteration)

Making more parameters free

We experimented with making more and more lexical parameters free, by changing the cut-off frequency f[7]. Surprisingly, this does not affect the learning process much. The best model is obtained with $f < 5$, in terms of labeled bracketing scores, supertag accuracy for unseen verbs, as well as overall supertag accuracy for verbs (seen and unseen). Table 3 shows the overall supertag error for all verbs (seen and unseen) for different values of f. When high-frequency parameters are subject to unsupervised estimation, the error rate degrades by a small amount, but not much, even for $f < 1000$. Thus, the structural constraints plus the current corpus scaling factor (of eight) that scales up the size of labeled data are together sufficient to keep these estimates in the right ballpark, with the cut-off frequency not playing much of a role. This will be relevant to future work since it opens up the possibility of learning even mid-to-high frequency lexical items using this methodology.

5.1 Analysis

We present some examples of incorrect parses by the baseline model t_{smooth}, and corresponding improved parses by a semi-supervised EM-trained model (10 iterations, 12M words unlabeled data). These examples also serve to illustrate exactly what is captured by measuring supertag accuracy (our main evaluation). Fig. 4 shows improve-

[7] f is the occurrence freq. of words in TB above which parameters are *fixed* i.e. estimates from unlabeled data are not used.

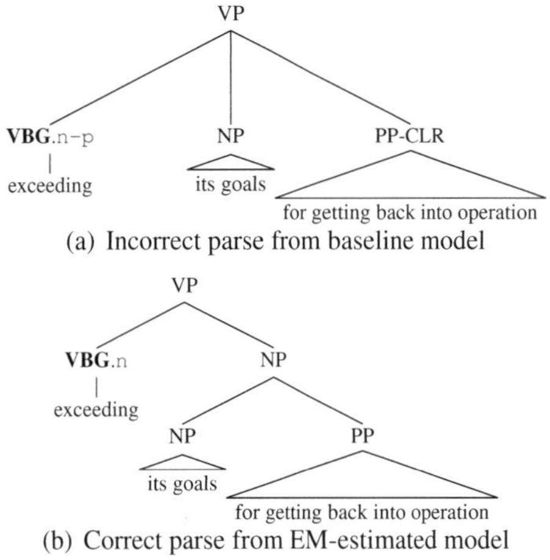

(a) Incorrect parse from baseline model

(b) Correct parse from EM-estimated model

Figure 4: Improvement in PP attachment.

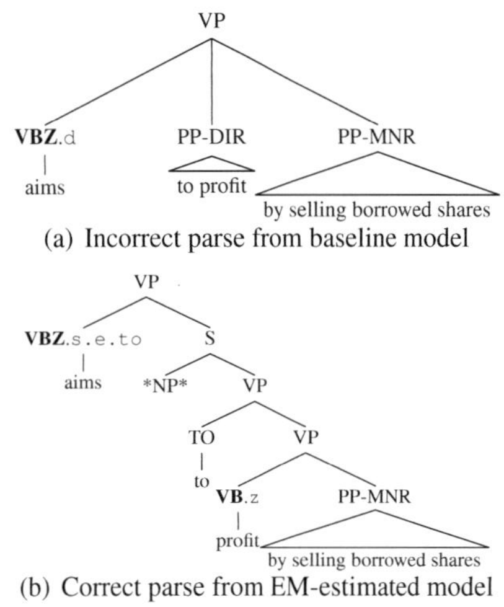

(a) Incorrect parse from baseline model

(b) Correct parse from EM-estimated model

Figure 5: Detection of an S structure for *aims*

ments in a common PP attachment case (some categories are simplified for clarity). This improvement is due to learning a distribution for the unseen verb *exceeding* that represents its subcategorization preference for 'NP' rather than 'NP PP' (**VBG**.n supertag in (b) as opposed to **VBG**.n-p in (a)). Fig. 5 shows the improvement in assigning a more complex supertag. In (a), *to profit* is incorrectly parsed as a directional PP, and the verb *aims* is assigned an incorrect supertag **VBZ**.d (*d*irectional complement). The EM-trained grammar gives the correct parse – the correct supertag **VBZ**.s.e.to is assigned to *aims*, with the associated structure of an S with a empty subject *NP* and an infinitival (to) VP. Additionally, *profit* is now correctly detected as a verb and assigned an intransitive supertag (**VB**.z in our notation).

6 Related Work

We compare our work to prior research along several dimensions: for instance, the use of semi-supervised EM for a complex structured model, the aspect of using labeled data to constrain or guide estimation from unlabeled data, and the use of unlabeled data to improve an already accurate, high baseline treebank parser.

Semi-supervised learning for a generative model employing the EM-algorithm was already introduced in (Miller and Uyar, 1996). It has been applied to text classification before (Nigam et al., 1998, 2006) (we derive our inspiration from this work), but has not been successful with more complex NLP tasks such as parsing. In contrast to text classification, where the latent variable is the document class (amongst a few tens of classes), our latent variable (pre-terminal supertag sequences) is much richer in nature and takes an unbounded number of values. While in Nigam et al. (2006) a simple multinomial prior over document classes is part of the joint model and is itself trained, we have a rich structural prior obtained from labeled data which is kept fixed. In addition, Nigam et al. (2006) make use of a uniform Dirichlet prior over the model parameters. Instead, we utilise the labeled corpus to impose an informed Dirichlet prior over model parameters with a preference for configurations closer to the relative-frequency estimate of the labeled data.

Recently, there has been a lot of focus on semi-supervised methods that can incorporate constraints on latent variables based on prior knowledge, either in the form of labeled data or by other forms of indirect supervision. Ganchev et al. (2010); Graca et al. (2007) present the Posterior Regularization framework, which incorporates data-dependent constraints encoded as model posteriors on the observed data. The Generalized Expectation criteria (Mann and McCallum, 2010, 2007) incorporates weakly labeled data or 'side-information' such as marginal label distributions to inform estimation from unlabeled data. These methods have been shown to work for some structured tasks but have not been applied to a large scale grammar yet, and whether they can be used to improve a high baseline model is an open question.

There is also a substantial body of work on supertagging (Bangalore and Joshi (1999); Clark and Curran (2004), amongst several others), but their focus has been on improving parsing *efficiency*. Some other work focuses on unsupervised learning, but not for high-baseline supervised models (for instance, Dridan and Baldwin (2010); Ravi et al. (2010)).

The current work is most similar to Deoskar (2008) who used a treebank PCFG with Inside-outside to obtain ML estimates from an unlabeled corpus with an intention similar to ours: to learn lexico-syntactic dependencies. Their method gave improved results, with error reductions of up to 31.6% on the supertag detection task (we are not able to compare absolute numbers, since their treebank model is different from ours). Their approach was based on frequency transformations of inside-outside counts at each iteration: these transformations ensured that unsupervised estimates did not diverge far from the original treebank estimates, playing the same role as our priors. Their method did not have an interpretation in terms of a well-understood objective function; it is therefore not clear whether it has general applicability, or will extend to larger unlabeled data. The current work, although it shows somewhat more modest improvements, overcomes these shortcomings.

McClosky et al. (2006) enhance the performance of a state-of-the-art parser-reranker combination by self-training on large amounts of unlabeled data. Much of the improvement in their case comes from the ability of an external maximum-entropy Parse Reranker (Charniak and Johnson, 2005) to select parses from the parser's output for the unannotated sentences. Our work differs from McClosky et al. (2006) in that, firstly, they employ a fully lexicalized parser, whereas our parser is unlexicalised with supertags as pre-terminals. We are thus isolating lexico-syntactic dependencies, rather than word-word dependencies. All our improvements come from enhancing the lexical component of the PCFG. They find in their analysis that lexical learning does not play a large role in the improvements they obtain. Secondly, in contrast with their somewhat complex self-training objective, we retrain the parser under a well known and simple Maximum-likelihood objective. Koo et al. (2008) improved a dependency parser by using word clusters learnt from unlabeled data (an idea similar in some ways to learning supertag-word dependencies, since supertags form finer classes of words that POS tags do, but coarser than words), showing the utility of learning such statistics from unlabeled data. Most recently, Bansal and Klein (2011) improved the Berkeley parser (Petrov and Klein, 2007) by using surface counts from Google n-grams. The method proved very useful for some cases of parser disambiguation, but it is unlikely that surface counts alone can be used to learn long-distance or complex structural properties.

7 Conclusions

We have used semi-supervised EM to learn complex, ambiguous lexico-structural dependencies, obtaining large improvements for the hardest case of unseen verbs, as well as low-frequency verbs. We used a parser that uses all the information in the Penn Treebank, viz functional tags and empty categories. Learning such information is crucial for semantic analysis, besides being useful for syntactic disambiguation, but falls in the long Zipfian tail of linguistic events for which unlabeled data is the only learning source. We used labeled data to derive priors that guided estimation from unlabeled data to both the structural and lexical level in a principled manner. Our structural prior took the form of a PCFG; however it may be replaced by alternative, more complex models employing a different view on the labeled data.

This is the first instance of semi-supervised EM improving a complex structured model, and we believe the success is due to tightly constraining estimation from unlabeled data, as well as due to our complex lexical parameters that isolate structural information spread across a tree onto localised parameters of the model. The method has direct applicability to statistical grammars for strongly lexicalised formalisms like CCG and LTAG, of which statistical models suffer from severe sparsity and have not been successfully trained using semi-supervised methods. Another area of future work will be to incorporate supertags that encode other forms of lexico-structural dependencies, such as noun subcategorization or adverb attachment.

Acknowledgements

We thank Alexandra Birch, Mark Steedman, and three anonymous reviewers for detailed comments and suggestions. This research was supported by the VIDI grant 639.022.604 from The Netherlands Organisation for Scientific Research (NWO). The first author was further supported by the ERC Advanced Fellowship 249520 GRAMPLUS.

References

Srinivas Bangalore and Aravind K. Joshi. 1999. Supertagging: An Approach to Almost Parsing. *Computational Linguistics*, 25:237–265.

Mohit Bansal and Dan Klein. 2011. Web-Scale Features for Full-Scale Parsing. In *Proceedings of ACL 2011*.

Don Blaheta. 2004. *Functional Tagging*. Ph.D. thesis, Department of Computer Science, Brown University.

Don Blaheta and Eugene Charniak. 2000. Assigning Function Tags to Parsed Text. In *ANLP'00*.

A. Blum and T. Mitchell. 1998. Combining labeled and unlabeled data with co-training. In *Proceedings of Conference on Computational Learning Theory (COLT) 1998*.

Ted Briscoe, John Carroll, and Sanfilippo. 1998. Parser evaluation: a survey and a new proposal. In *1st Language Resources and Evaluation Conference*. Granada, Spain.

E. Charniak. 1997. Statistical parsing with a context-free grammar and word statistics. In *Proceedings of the 14th National Conference on Artificial Intelligence*, pages 598–603. AAAI Press/MIT Press, Menlo Park.

Eugene Charniak. 1993. *Statistical Language Learning*. MIT Press.

Eugene Charniak and Mark Johnson. 2005. Coarse-to-fine n-best parsing and MaxEnt discriminative reranking. In *Proceedings of 43rd ACL*. Ann Arbor, Michigan.

Stephen Clark and James R. Curran. 2004. The Importance of Supertagging for Wide-Coverage CCG Parsing. In *Proceedings of COLING-04*, pages 282–288. Geneva, Switzerland.

Michael Collins. 1997. Three generative, lexicalised models for statistical parsing. In *Proceedings of the 35th ACL*.

A. P. Dempster, N. M. Laird, and D. B. Rubin. 1977. Maximum likelihood estimation from incomplete data via the EM algorithm. *J. Royal Statistical Society*, 39(B):1–38.

Tejaswini Deoskar. 2008. Re-estimation of Lexical Parameters for Treebank PCFGs. In *Proceedings of COLING 2008*.

Tejaswini Deoskar. 2009. *Induction of fine-grained lexical parameters of treebank PCFGs with inside-outside estimation and frequency transformations*. Ph.D. thesis, Cornell University.

Tejaswini Deoskar and Mats Rooth. 2008. Induction of Treebank-Aligned Lexical Resources. In *Proceedings of 6th LREC, Marrakech, Morocco*.

Rebecca Dridan and Timothy Baldwin. 2010. Unsupervised Parse Selection for HPSG. In *Proceedings of the 2010 Conference on Empirical Methods in Natural Language Processing*, pages 694–704. Association for Computational Linguistics, Cambridge, MA.

G. Druck, G. Mann, and A. McCallum. 2009a. Semi-supervised learning of dependency parsers using generalized expectation criteria. In *ACL/IJCNLP*.

Kuzman Ganchev, Joao Graca, Jennifer Gillenwater, and Bill Taskar. 2010. Posterior Regularization for Structured Latent Variable Models. *Journal of Machine Learning Research*, 11:2001–2049.

J Graca, K Ganchev, and B Taskar. 2007. Expectation Maximization and posterior constraints. In *NIPS 2007*.

Julia Hockenmaier and Mark Steedman. 2002. Generative Models for Statistical Parsing with Combinatory Categorial Grammar. In *ACL40*.

Mark Johnson. 1998. PCFG models of linguistic tree representations. *Computational Linguistics*, 24(4).

D. Klein and C. Manning. 2004. Corpus-based induction of syntactic structure: Models of dependency and constituency. In *ACL 2004*.

Dan Klein and Christopher Manning. 2003. Accurate unlexicalized parsing. In *ACL 41*. Sapporo, Japan.

Terry Koo, Xavier Carreras, and Michael Collins. 2008. Simple Semi-supervised Dependency Parsing. In *Proceedings of ACL-08: HLT*, pages 595–603. Association for Computational Linguistics, Columbus, Ohio.

K. Lari and S. J. Young. 1990. The estimation of stochastic context-free grammars using the Inside-Outside algorithm. *Computer Speech and Language*, 4:35–56.

G. Mann and A. McCallum. 2007. Simple, robust, scalable semi-supervised learning via expectation regularization. In *ICML 2007*.

Gideon Mann and Andrew McCallum. 2010. Generalized Expectation Criteria for Semi-Supervised LEarning with Weakly Labeled Data. *Journal of Machine Learning Research*, 11:955–984.

M. P. Marcus, B. Santorini, and M. A. Marcinkiewicz. 1993. Building a Large Annotated Corpus of English: The Penn Treebank. *Computational Linguistics*, 19(2):313–330.

D. McClosky, E. Charniak, and M. Johnson. 2006. Effective Self-Training for Parsing. In *Proceedings of HLT-NAACL 2006*.

Bernard Merialdo. 1994. Tagging English Text with a Probabilistic Model. *Computational Linguistics*, 20(2):155–171.

Paola Merlo and Gabriele Musillo. 2005. Accurate Function Parsing. In *Proceedings of Human Language Technology Conference and Conference on Empirical Methods in Natural Language Processing*.

David J. Miller and Hasan S. Uyar. 1996. A Mixture of Experts Classifier with Learning Based on Both Labelled and Unlabelled Data. In *Advances in Neural Information Processing Systems (NIPS)*, pages 571–577.

Vincent Ng and CLaire Cardie. 2003. Weakly supervised natural language learning without redundant views.

Kamal Nigam, Andrew Mccallum, and Tom Mitchell. 1998. Learning to Classify Text from Labeled and Unlabeled Documents. In *Fifteenth National Conference on Artificial Intelligence (AAAI-98)*, pages 792–799. AAAI Press.

Kamal Nigam, Andrew Mccallum, and Tom Mitchell. 2006. *Semi-Supervised Learning*, chap. 3. MIT Press, Cambridge, Massachusetts.

Slav Petrov and Dan Klein. 2007. Improved Inference for Unlexicalized Parsing. In *HLT- NAACL 07*.

Sujith Ravi, Jason Baldridge, and Kevin Knight. 2010. Minimized Models and Grammar-Informed Initialization for Supertagging with Highly Ambiguous Lexicons. In *Proceedings of the 48th Annual Meeting of the Association for Computational Linguistics*, pages 495–503. Association for Computational Linguistics, Uppsala, Sweden.

Roi Reichart and Ari Rappoport. 2007. Self-Training for Enhancement and Domain Adaptation of Statistical Parsers Trained on Small Datasets. In *ACL2007*.

Helmut Schmid. 2004. Efficient Parsing of Highly Ambiguous Context-Free Grammars with Bit Vectors. In *COLING 2004*.

Helmut Schmid. 2006. Trace Prediction and Recovery with Unlexicalised PCFGs and Slash Features. In *21st COLING and 44th Annual Meeting of the ACL*, pages 177–184. Sydney, Australia.

Mark Steedman. 2000. *The Syntactic Process*. MIT Press/Bradford Books.

Mark Steedman, Miles Osborne, Anoop Sarkar, Stephen Clark, Rebecca Hwa, Julia Hockenmaier, Paul Ruhlen, Steven Baker, and Jeremiah Crim. 2003. Bootstrapping statistical parsers from small datasets. In *Proceedings of EACL03*.

D. Yarowsky. 1995. Unsupervised Word Sense Disambiguation Rivaling Supervised Methods. In *ACL95*.

One-Step Statistical Parsing of Hybrid Dependency-Constituency Syntactic Representations

Kais Dukes
Institute for Artificial Intelligence
University of Leeds, United Kingdom
sckd@leeds.ac.uk

Nizar Habash
Center for Computational Learning Systems
Columbia University, New York, USA
habash@ccls.columbia.edu

Abstract

In this paper, we describe and compare two statistical parsing approaches for the hybrid dependency-constituency syntactic representation used in the Quranic Arabic Treebank (Dukes and Buckwalter, 2010). In our first approach, we apply a multi-step process in which we use a shift-reduce algorithm trained on a pure dependency preprocessed version of the treebank. After parsing, the dependency output is converted into the hybrid representation. This is compared to a novel one-step parser that is able to learn the hybrid representation without preprocessing. We define an extended labelled attachment score (ELAS) as our performance metric for hybrid parsing, and report 87.47% (F1 score) for the multi-step approach, and 89.03% (F1 score) for the one-step integrated algorithm. We also consider the effect of using different sets of morphological features for parsing the Quran, comparing our results to recent work on Modern Standard Arabic.

1 Introduction

Research into statistical parsing for English has resulted in over a decade of high-performance results (Collins, 1999; Charniak, 2000), with most work focusing on the Penn English Treebank (Marcus et al., 1993). However, adapting these parsing models to other languages has been less successful. Results from the CoNLL-X shared task on multilingual dependency parsing showed that Arabic is one of the most challenging languages to parse, due to its rich morphology and relatively free word order (Nivre et al., 2007b).

In this paper we consider statistical parsing for Classical Arabic, the direct ancestor of Modern Standard Arabic (MSA). As a training and test data source, we use the online Quranic Arabic Corpus (http://corpus.quran.com). This website is a useful study aid for understanding the Quran through grammatical annotation, and is used by 100,000 people monthly. In contrast to other recent annotation efforts for MSA (Maamouri et al., 2004; Habash and Roth, 2009), Quranic Treebank annotators have cross-checked their analyses against historical works based on the traditional Arabic grammar known as *i'rāb* (إعراب) (Salih, 2007; Dukes et al., 2011; Dukes and Buckwalter, 2010). To provide annotation that closely follows traditional grammar, the treebank creators used a hybrid representation that supports relations between morphemes, as well as between phrases, clauses and sentences. The treebank also includes empty nodes for pro-drop and for semantic elision.

This representation presents several challenges to statistical parsing. Possible pipeline approaches include converting to pure constituency or to pure dependency as a preprocessing step. The alternative we pursue is using an integrated model to parse the hybrid representation. For other parsing tasks, integrated models have been shown to out-perform pipeline approaches, e.g., Goldberg and Tsarfaty (2008) integrate morphological and syntactic disambiguation for Hebrew, and report improved parsing performance.

In the next section, we review the Treebank. In Section 3, we survey related work. Section 4 describes our parsing algorithm. We present our parsing approaches and evaluate in Sections 5 and 6, respectively.

2 The Quranic Arabic Treebank

For our parsing experiments we use version 0.5 of the Quranic Treebank, containing 37,578 word-forms (~ 49% of the full Quranic text), segmented into 47,220 tokens (Dukes and Buckwalter, 2010). A common scheme for en-

<table>
<tr><th>Node</th><th>Type</th><th>Extent</th><th>Form</th><th>Tag</th><th>Head</th><th>Dep</th><th>Features</th></tr>
<tr><td>1</td><td>T</td><td>_</td><td>qaAla</td><td>V</td><td>_</td><td>_</td><td>PERF|LEM:qaAla|ROOT:qwl|3MS</td></tr>
<tr><td>2</td><td>E</td><td>_</td><td>Huwa</td><td>PRON</td><td>1</td><td>subj</td><td>_</td></tr>
<tr><td>3</td><td>T</td><td>_</td><td>ha`*aA</td><td>DEM</td><td>_</td><td>_</td><td>LEM:ha`*aA|MS</td></tr>
<tr><td>4</td><td>T</td><td>_</td><td>rab~i</td><td>N</td><td>3</td><td>pred</td><td>LEM:rab~|ROOT:rbb|M|NOM</td></tr>
<tr><td>5</td><td>T</td><td>_</td><td>Y</td><td>PRON</td><td>4</td><td>poss</td><td>PRON:1S|SUFFIX</td></tr>
<tr><td>6</td><td>P</td><td>3-5</td><td>_</td><td>NS</td><td>1</td><td>obj</td><td>_</td></tr>
</table>

Figure 1: Example hybrid graph in extended CoNLL-X format. Node types: T = Terminal node, E = Elided word / Empty category, P = Phrase node; Tags: V = Verb, PRON = Pronoun, DEM = Demonstrative, N = Noun, NS = Nominal Sentence; Dependencies: subj = subject, pred = predicate, poss = possessive construction, obj = object.

coding dependency treebanks is the CoNLL-X format (Nivre et al., 2007b). The Quranic Treebank uses an extension of this to support phrases and elided words. Figure 1 shows an example sentence illustrating common tags used in the treebank. The extended format adds two new columns: TYPE indicates the different types of nodes, and EXTENT defines a phrase by specifying start and end terminal nodes. Head nodes, dependency labels, and morphological features are shown in separate columns. On the treebank's website, this information is represented visually using dependency graphs (Figure 2). Read from right-to-left, this graph uses a convention that dependent nodes point towards their heads, and edges are labelled with roles in Arabic. The second Arabic word in parenthesis is an implied elided subject pronoun that has been syntactically annotated, and is not in the original Quranic verse. The last word on the left has been segmented into two tokens, resulting in a total of five terminal nodes in the graph.

This hybrid representation is based on the traditional *i'rāb* analysis found in Salih (2007), a 12-volume work collating previous historical analyses, e.g., the analysis for Figure 2 states:

> In this verse, 'said' is a perfective verb, whose subject is an elided pronoun of the form 'he'. The noun 'lord' is in the nominative case and is the predicate of the demonstrative pronoun 'this'. The suffixed pronoun 'my' attached to the noun is a possessive clitic. The nominal sentence, headed by the demonstrative pronoun, acts as the object of the verb 'said'.

The example sentence shown in Figures 1 and 2 illustrates several linguistic aspects of the Quranic Treebank which make it challenging for statistical parsing: rich morphology, phrase structure, and elision. We discuss various aspects of the Treebank next.

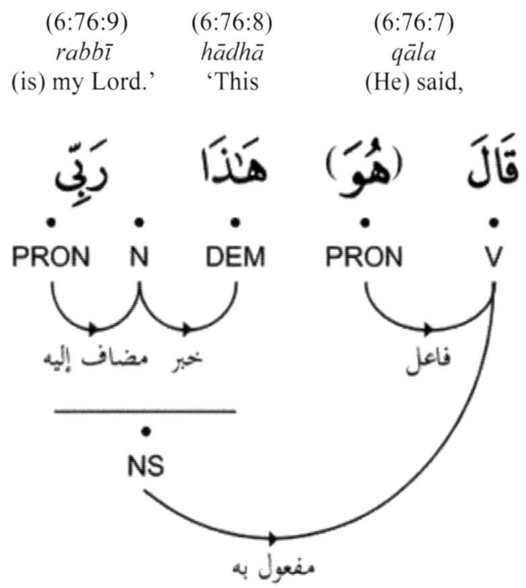

Figure 2: Hybrid graph in presentation form for the annotated example: *He said, 'This is my Lord.'*

Dependency: Although traditional Arabic grammar developed independently from modern European linguistics, it uses the concepts of heads (*āmil*) and dependents (*ma'mūl fī-hi*). Along with Panini's grammar for Classical Sanskrit, it is considered to be one of the origins of modern dependency grammar (Owens, 1988; Bohas et al., 1990).

Morphemes: The basic unit of analysis in traditional Arabic grammar is the morphological segment. Compound word-forms in Classical Arabic are tokenized into independent grammatical units. This agrees with other recent treebanking efforts for MSA such as the Columbia Arabic Treebank (Habash and Roth, 2009), the Prague Arabic Dependency Treebank (Smrž, et al., 2008), and the Penn Arabic Treebank (Maamouri et al., 2004). This also compares with recent parsing work for other morphological rich languages. For example, Eryiğit et al. (2008) show that for Turkish using groups of morphemes as the basic unit instead of words improves parsing accuracy.

However, in contrast to other Arabic treebanks that define their own segmentation schemes, morphological annotation in the Quranic Treebank closely follows segmentation rules from *i'rāb* (Dukes and Habash, 2010). In addition to part-of-speech, the grammar describes multiple features for each morpheme, including person, gender, number, verb mood, noun case and state. The treebank also includes roots and lemmas. A root is a sequence of three or four radicals that are used to group words with related derivational morphology. The lemma is a further subdivision that groups forms varying only in inflectional morphology (Habash, 2010). In our experiments, we consider how different combinations of these rich morphological features affect the accuracy of statistical parsing.

Phrases: Most dependencies in the treebank relate morphological segments. The treebank also includes dependencies between these units and phrases, and between pairs of phrases. In accordance with traditional Arabic grammar, the Quranic Treebank annotates five phrase types: nominal sentences (جملة اسمية), verbal sentences (جملة فعلية), conditionals (جملة شرطية), preposition phrases (جار ومجرور) and subordinate clauses (تأويل مصدر). There are simple rules for distinguishing between these phrase types in the grammar.

Phrase nodes are used to model constituency structure. In a pure dependency representation, the grammatical relationship between a pair of phrases is implicit in the edge that connects the head words of the two phrases. In the traditional Arabic grammar of the Quran, phrase-level relations such as conjunction and apposition are made explicit in syntactic analysis. Since the grammatical rules that determine these phrase structures allow recursion, the Quranic Treebank includes hybrid graphs that contain multiple levels of nested consistency structure.

Elision: In the Penn English Treebank, empty categories are used for constructions such as null complementizers: 'The man (0) I saw', and for *wh*-movement: 'What$_1$ do you want (NP *T*-1)?'. The Quranic Treebank distinguishes between morphological, syntactic and semantic elision. Like MSA, Classical Arabic is a pro-drop language. A verb's dropped subject pronoun is implied through its morphology. Syntactic elision arises in order to satisfy constraints in the grammar. For example, in certain cases preposition phrases are attached to nouns via an elided adjective. Semantic elision involves elided words, used to explain the reason for case markers in certain verses of the Quran. Dukes, Atwell and Sharaf (2010) provide a more detailed description of elision in the Quranic Treebank. In our parsing experiments in this paper, we handle the three types of elision separately as they form different edge patterns in dependency graphs.

3 Previous Related Work

Related computational work includes statistical parsing for other morphologically rich languages, as well as recent parsing work for hybrid representations, and for recovering elision.

Hebrew, another Semitic language, faces a similar set of challenges in comparison to parsing Arabic. Both feature relatively free word order and require morphological disambiguation for syntactic parsing. For dependency grammar, Goldberg and Elhadad (2010), apply a pipeline approach by disambiguating morphology and syntax in two separate steps. They report a 84.2% labelled attachment score using gold morphological disambiguation, and 76.2% when using automatic morphological analysis.

For Arabic, Kulick et al. (2006) discuss parsing the Penn Arabic Treebank using phrase structure grammar. One conclusion that can be drawn from their results is that parsing using a constituency representation leads to lower accuracy for Arabic in comparison to English. They report a Parseval F1-score of 74% for version 1 of the Penn Arabic treebank, and 88% for English using a similar sized corpus, trained using Bikel's parser (Bikel, 2004).

More recent work for Modern Arabic has focused on dependency grammar. Marton et al. (2010) use MaltParser for parsing the CATiB treebank, and experiment with different combinations of rich morphological features. Like the Quranic Arabic Treebank, CATiB is also based on traditional Arabic grammar, although it uses a subset of the full traditional syntactic roles and only six POS tags. Another related Arabic treebank that uses a dependency representation is the Prague Arabic Dependency Treebank (Smrž, et al., 2008). Hall et al. (2007) use MaltParser to parse ten different languages, including data from the Prague Arabic Treebank. They compare this to an ensemble system that combines six different strategies to boost parsing performance.

In addition to parsing Arabic, MaltParser is ideally suited to parsing morphologically rich languages, due to its integration of flexible feature sets during training (Nivre, et al., 2007a).

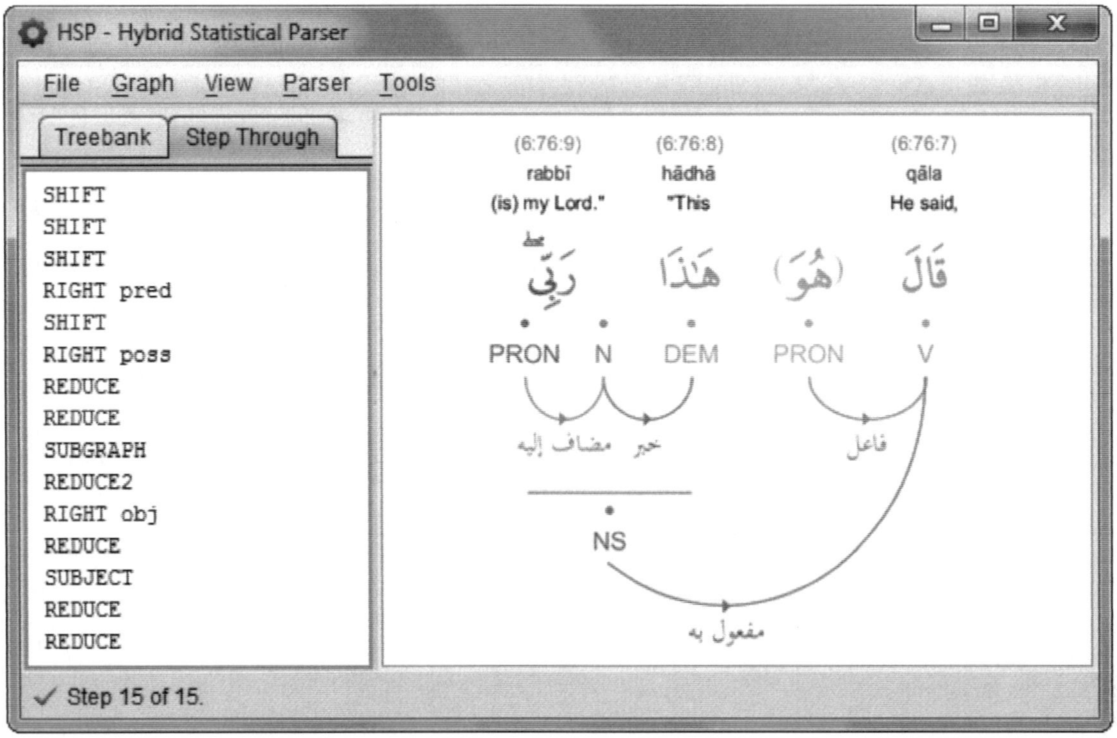

Figure 3: Custom Java application for HSP showing the steps in an example parsing program for Arabic. The various operations on the left panel are described in Section 4.1.

For example, Bengoetxea and Gojenola (2010) use MaltParser for version 2 of Basque Dependency Treebank, although to simplify the syntactic representation this latest version no longer includes empty nodes for ellipsis and coordination. Most statistical parsers do not handle elision. However, Gabbard et al. (2006) show that it is possible to fully recover Penn Treebank-style trees for English including empty categories, by training a cascade of statistical classifiers.

For parsing hybrid representations, Hall and Nivre (2008) adapt MaltParser to the German TIGER and TüBa-D/Z treebanks, reporting a labelled attachment score close to 90%. Similarly, Hall et al. (2007) adapt MaltParser for hybrid constituency-dependency parsing of the Swedish Talbanken05 treebank. These treebanks are hybrid in a different sense to the Quranic Treebank. For each sentence, they include dual annotation in both constituency and dependency grammar, in contrast to combining these into a single representation. A related example is the Hindi/Urdu multi-representational treebank (Bhatt et al., 2009). For the baseline experiment that we describe in section 5, we use a dependency-based encoding similar to the scheme Hall et al. (2007) use for parsing the hybrid German and Swedish treebanks.

4 Hybrid Statistical Parser

In this section we describe the Hybrid Statistical Parser (HSP) that we use for our parsing experiments. Instead of using MaltParser, we implemented a new parser in Java using a similar algorithm, along with a new graphical user interface (Figure 3). We made this decision to allow us to extend the parsing architecture, and created the user interface to help debug the parser. As with previous work that uses MaltParser for other morphologically rich languages, we assume that input sentences to HSP have been tokenized and already annotated with part-of-speech tags and features. We use gold-standard tokenization and POS tags.

HSP outputs both pure and hybrid dependency graphs. Each of these have a formal definition. Let $(t_1, ..., t_n)$ be an input sentence that has been morphologically tokenized, and let R denote the set of dependency relations. A pure dependency graph is defined as $G = (V, E, L)$, where $V = \{t_1, ..., t_n\}$ are the vertices formed from the input tokens, $E \subseteq V \times V$ are the graph's edges, and $L : E \to R$ are the edge labels. For hybrid graphs, we extend the set of vertices to include phrase nodes. Let $p_{ij} = (t_i, t_j)$ denote the phrase that spans the tokens from t_i to t_j inclusively, and let P denote the set of all possible phrases. We define a hybrid dependency graph as $G' = (V', E', L')$ where $V' = \{t_1, ..., t_n\} \cup P'$ and $P' \subseteq P$. As before, the edges are $E' \subseteq V' \times V'$ with labels $L' : E' \rightarrow R$. For elision, we further extend the set of vertices to include empty categories as additional terminal nodes.

4.1 Parsing Algorithm

HSP uses a shift-reduce algorithm similar to Nivre's. Two data structures are used for parsing: a stack S for temporary storage and a queue Q to buffer input. In its initial configuration, the parser has all input tokens placed onto the queue with the stack empty: $Q = (t_1, \ldots, t_n)$ and $S = \emptyset$. The parser reads from the queue and finishes when the queue and stack are both empty ($Q = \emptyset \wedge S = \emptyset$). To construct a dependency graph, a sequence of operations are executed by the parser, analogous to the instructions in a computer program. Figure 3 shows the operations used to parse the example sentence used previously in Figures 1 and 2.

In contrast to MaltParser, HSP uses an extended instruction set. To define these operations, let $Q = (q_1, \ldots, q_A)$ and $S = (s_1, \ldots, s_B)$ be the state of the parser at an intermediate stage of the program, and Q' and S' be the state after executing the next instruction. The operations are:

1. SHIFT reads the next token from the queue and moves this to the top of the stack: $Q' = (q_2, \ldots, q_A)$ and $S' = (q_1, s_1, \ldots, s_B)$.

2. REDUCE pops the stack: $S' = (s_2, \ldots, s_B)$.

3. LEFT adds an edge to the graph, with s_1 as the head node and s_2 as the dependent node.

4. RIGHT adds an edge to the graph, with s_2 as the head node and s_1 as the dependent node.

5. REDUCE2 pops the second node on the stack: $S' = (s_1, s_3, \ldots, s_B)$.

6. EMPTY adds an empty node e to the graph after s_1. The elided node e is pushed onto the stack: $S' = (e, s_1, \ldots, s_B)$.

7. SUBJECT is only applicable if s_1 is a verb. An elided pronoun e is inserted after s_1, and a *subj* edge is added with s_1 as the head node, and e as the dependent node. e is pushed onto the stack: $S' = (e, s_1, \ldots, s_B)$.

8. SUBGRAPH adds a phrase node p to the graph spanning the terminal nodes from s_1 to the end of the subgraph with root s_1. p is pushed onto the stack: $S' = (p, s_1, \ldots, s_B)$.

Three of these instructions are parameterized. LEFT and RIGHT take an edge relation $r \in R$, and EMPTY takes a part-of-speech as a parameter. The last four instructions are extensions compared to MaltParser. EMPTY is used to add elided nodes with a specific part-of-speech. SUBJECT is similar to the combination EMPTY then LEFT , but takes into consideration the morphology of the verb to produce a correctly inflected subject pronoun. REDUCE2 is useful in the situation where an edge should be formed between the first and third elements of the stack, so that the second element can be easily discarded. After a SUBGRAPH operation, it is possible to use REDUCE2 to discard the head of the subgraph, which would now be at the second element of the stack. See the parsing run in Figure 3 for an example of this. Only the first four instructions listed above are used for pure dependency graphs. In hybrid mode, the parser uses all eight instructions.

4.2 Machine Learning

Like MaltParser, HSP uses supervised learning during training. For each graph in the training data, an oracle driven by a small set of rules is used to deduce the sequence of actions required to construct the graph. For machine learning, we use support vector machines, implemented by the Java version of LIBSVM (Chang and Lin, 2001). For each step in the parsing programs, a collection of SVM classifiers learn to predict the next operation, given the feature vector associated with the first few nodes at the top of the queue and stack. Feature selection is described in more detail in the next section.

We apply the standard technique of binarization of input features in the training data, so that a single symbolic feature is represented using many binary predicates (Yamada and Matsumoto, 2003). To reduce learning time, the training set is partitioned using the part-of-speech at the top of the stack, and one statistical classifier is trained for each part-of-speech. We use the same LIBSVM settings that Hall and Nivre (2008) use for parsing the German TIGER and TüBa-D/Z treebanks: $\gamma = 0.2$ and $r = 0$ for kernel parameters, $C = 0.5$ for penalty and $\varepsilon = 1$ for termination. We also use the same quadratic kernel:

$$K(x_i, x_j) = (\gamma x_i^T x_j + r)^2.$$

5 Parsing Experiments

We compare two approaches to parsing the treebank. First, we use HSP in pure dependency mode and recover the hybrid representation through a post-processing step. The second experiment uses an integrated approach that builds phrase structure and elided nodes during parsing. Both of these experiments are repeated using different sets of morphological features.

5.1 Multi-step Parsing

In our first experiment, we perform the following steps:

1. The training data is converted to pure dependency by encoding additional information using new complex edge labels.

2. In the learning phase, we restrict HSP to using only the four operations that are required for pure dependency parsing: SHIFT, REDUCE, LEFT and RIGHT.

3. The parser's output is pure dependency. We recover the hybrid representation by reversing the transformations in step 1.

The size of the unconverted dataset is 50,955 tokens, including 3,775 empty categories. The dependency graphs in the treebank contain 9,847 phrase nodes and 38,642 edges. After conversion, all phrase nodes and empty categories were removed, resulting in 47,220 tokens and a total of 34,849 edges. The number of edges dropped due to collapsing edges between empty categories.

For conversion, we use a similar process to Hall et al. (2007, 2008)'s approach for German and Swedish, but adapt this to the representation used for traditional Arabic grammar. During the conversion process, we apply graph transformations to encode information about phrase structure and elision:

Phrases: Let $p = (t_i, t_j)$ be a phrase node in the hybrid graph covering the terminal nodes from t_i to t_j inclusively. The conversion for the phrase node p is based on the observation that the phrase covers a subgraph with root ω_0. If p is a dependent node with edge E, head h, and dependency relation r, we remove E and p and add a new edge E' with dependent ω_0, head h, and label $+r$. Similarly, if p is a head node, we add a new edge with label $r+$. For the inverse transformation, $+r$ and $r+$ denote expanding the edge's dependent or head into a subgraph respectively. The label $+r+$ indicates that both head and dependent nodes for that edge should be expanded, to produce an edge between a pair of phrases. Figure 4 illustrates this conversion process. As with the dependency graphs displayed on the treebank's website, the convention in these diagrams is that dependents point towards heads.

Elision: For verbs with elided subject pronouns, we simply remove these from the converted graph as they are easily recovered through the verb's rich morphology. To keep the transformation rules simple, for syntactic elision we consider only the most common case where two

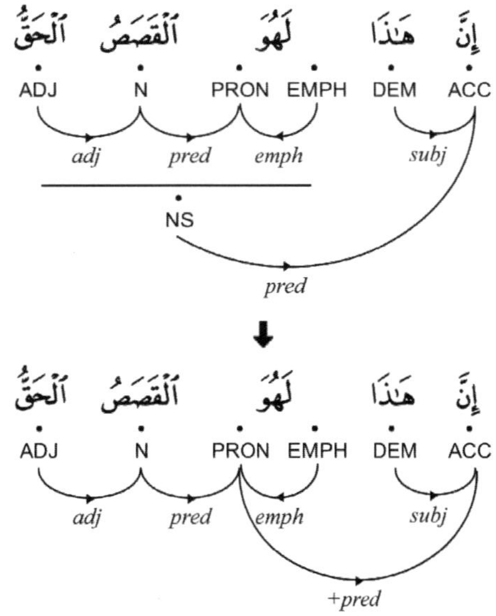

Figure 4: Conversion of phrase structure.

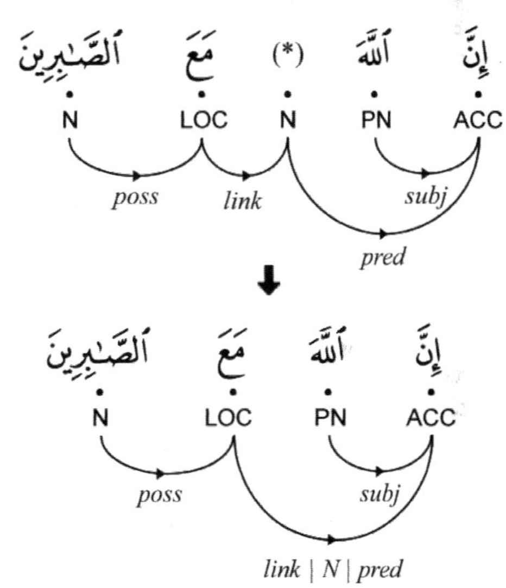

Figure 5: Conversion of syntactic elision.

tokens are connected via an empty category (Figure 5). If a depends on an elided node e with part-of-speech pos and relation r_1, and e depends on b with relation r_2, we remove e and the two edges. We add a new edge with dependent a, head b and complex label $r_1 \mid pos \mid r_2$.

As we discuss in the evaluation section, the performance of the baseline approach to parsing is affected by the coverage of the conversion process. However, the small set of rules above for phrases and elision allow us to correctly recover nearly all edges in the hybrid graphs through this process.

5.2 Integrated Parsing

The integrated approach is simpler because there are no conversion steps. We train HSP using the treebank's full hybrid representation without preprocessing. In this experiment, we add to the instruction set the four parser actions that are required to build hybrid graphs: REDUCE2, EMPTY, SUBJECT and SUBGRAPH. Although in both cases the same set of features are available during the training phase, the two approaches lead to different machine learning problems. In the first experiment, the parser has to learn more complex edge labels. In the second experiment, there are fewer classes for classification, and phrase structure and elision are integrated directly into the parsing process.

5.3 Feature Selection

The parser uses graph features as well as morphological features, taken from the top three nodes on the stack and the top from the queue. The graph features are DEPREL, IS ROOT and IS EDGE. The first of these is a compound feature: For each relation $r \in R$, a binary predicate is set if the node has a dependent with that relation. IS ROOT is set if the node is the root of a well-formed subgraph, and IS EDGE is set if s_1 and s_2 form a previously parsed edge.

After initial work using a subset of the data, we decided to use five different sets of morphological features, which we grouped together to simplify the number of parsing experiments (Figure 6). A more detailed description of these features is given in the treebank's annotation guidelines (Dukes, Atwell and Sharaf, 2010). Each feature set also includes the same graph features. For our parsing experiments, we use gold-standard morphological data for the parser's input.

Features	POS	MORPH6	MORPH9	LEMMA	PHI
POS	Y	Y	Y	Y	Y
PHRASE	Y	Y	Y	Y	Y
VOICE	-	Y	Y	Y	Y
MOOD	-	Y	Y	Y	Y
CASE	-	Y	Y	Y	Y
STATE	-	Y	Y	Y	Y
PRONTYPE	-	-	Y	Y	Y
SEGTYPE	-	-	Y	Y	Y
COPULA	-	-	Y	Y	Y
LEMMA	-	-	-	Y	Y
PERSON	-	-	-	-	Y
GENDER	-	-	-	-	Y
NUMBER	-	-	-	-	Y

Figure 6: Morphological features used for parsing.

In comparison, Marton et al. (2010) show that for modern Arabic using predicted features or gold-standard morphological features for parsing achieves similar results. Our different feature sets are described below:

POS: This baseline feature set includes the part-of-speech and phrase tags for the selected nodes.

MORPH6: This set adds the core morphological features that might help with parsing, based on domain knowledge of traditional Arabic grammar: VOICE, MOOD, CASE and STATE. State is either not-specified, definite (for the Arabic definite article *al-* prefix) or indefinite (for *tanween*).

MORPH9: Adds a further three morphological features. PRONTYPE marks a pronoun clitic as either an object pronoun or subject pronoun. Due to Arabic's rich morphology, these different types of clitics are common, and they form either subject or object dependency relations when attached to verbs. The feature SEGTYPE indicates if a token is a prefix, stem or suffix. The COPULA feature is used for a subset of copular verbs known as *kāna wa akhwātaha* (كان واخواتها). Although assigned the same part-of-speech tag as normal verbs, in traditional Arabic grammar these words form subject and predicate relations instead of subject and object.

LEMMA: To test the effect of lexicalization on the parser, this feature set adds lemmas.

PHI: This feature set includes the so-called phi-features of person, gender and number.

6 Evaluation

6.1 Metrics and Methodology

Two standard metrics for evaluating parsing performance are LAS (labelled attachment score) for pure dependency parsing, and Parseval for constituency parsing. LAS is a single measure, while Parseval defines three measures: precision, recall, and F1-score, where F1-score is the harmonic mean of precision and recall. For hybrid parsing, we combine both LAS and Parseval into a new metric which we call ELAS (extended labelled attachment score). We first define the two existing metrics in set-theoretic terms, and then show how they can be combined.

In the CoNLL-X shared task on multilingual dependency parsing (Nivre, et al. 2007b), LAS was used an official accuracy metric. Let $(t_1, ..., t_n)$ be an input sentence that has been morphologically tokenized, $G = (V, E, L)$ be an expected graph from the reference data, and $G' = (V', E', L')$ be the corresponding pure dependency graph output by the parser. Let $H(t)$ be the expected head of the token $t \in \{t_1, ..., t_n\}$, or ϕ if t is headless. Similarly, if $H(t) \neq \phi$, let $l(t) \in L$ denote the expected label of the edge $e \in E$ from t to $H(t)$. The LAS metric for the dependency parse pair (G, G') is then defined as the cardinality ratio:

$$\frac{|\{t : H(t) \neq \phi \wedge H(t) = H'(t) \wedge l(t) = l'(t)\}|}{|\{t : H(t) \neq \phi\}|}$$

For a pure dependency graph, this is the fraction of tokens that are assigned the correct head node and dependency label. This token-based definition does not easily generalize to hybrid parsing since hybrid graphs can contain edges between phrase nodes. Therefore, we provide a second definition of LAS by shifting focus from tokens to edges. For a well-formed pure dependency graph, the number of tokens with heads is the same as the number of edges. We define the edge equivalence relation $e \equiv e'$ to be true if and only if e and e' both connect t to $H(t)$ and if $l(e) = l(e')$. We then have the following edge-based definition:

$$\text{LAS} = \frac{|\{e' \in E' : \exists e \in E \ (e \equiv e')\}|}{|E|}$$

For constituency phrase structure, the Parseval metric (Black et al., 1991) can also be defined using a similar equivalence relation. Let C denote the set of constituency labels. Given a sentence $(t_1, ..., t_n)$, we let $p_{ij} = (t_i, t_j)$ be the phrase that spans the tokens from t_i to t_j inclusively with label $c(p) \in C$. Let P denote the set of non-terminal phrases in a parse tree from the reference data, and P' be the corresponding set of phrases output by a pure constituency parser. A phrase $p' \in P'$ is considered to be correct if there exists an equivalent phrase $p \in P$ with the same label that spans the same tokens. We define the phrase equivalence relation $p \equiv p' \Leftrightarrow \exists i, j : p = p_{ij} \wedge p' = p'_{ij} \wedge c(p) = c(p')$. For the constituency parse pair (P, P') we define Parseval precision and recall scores as:

$$\text{Precision} = \frac{|\{p' \in P' : \exists p \in P \ (p \equiv p')\}|}{|P'|}$$

$$\text{Recall} = \frac{|\{p' \in P' : \exists p \in P \ (p \equiv p')\}|}{|P|}$$

For hybrid parsing, we consider an edge in a parsed graph $G' = (V', E', L')$ to be correct if it has an equivalent edge in the reference graph $G = (V, E, L)$. Two edges are equivalent if they have the same edge label, and connect equivalent vertices. A vertex $v \in V$ may represent a token, a phrase node or elision. We define the vertex equivalence relation $v \equiv v'$ to be true when v and v' are both the same token. For two vertices that are phrases $(v = p \wedge v' = p')$, we use the same phrase equivalence relation $p \equiv p'$ in the Parseval metric. For elision, two vertices are equivalent if they have the same POS tag and surface form. For two edges, e from v to $H(v)$, and e' from v' to $H'(v')$, we define the edge equivalence relation as $e \equiv e' \Leftrightarrow v \equiv v' \wedge H(v) \equiv H'(v') \wedge l(e) = l(e')$. We then define ELAS precision and recall scores as:

$$\text{Precision} = \frac{|\{e' \in E' : \exists e \in E \ (e \equiv e')\}|}{|E'|}$$

$$\text{Recall} = \frac{|\{e' \in E' : \exists e \in E \ (e \equiv e')\}|}{|E|}$$

and the F1-score as the harmonic mean of precision and recall. This metric combines LAS and Parseval. For pure dependency graphs, ELAS recall is the same as vanilla labelled attachment score. For an edge between two phrase nodes in a hybrid graph, the metric uses a Parseval-like measure of correctness for the two phrases.

Feature Set	Multi-step Parser			Integrated Parser			F1-Diff.
	Precision	Recall	F1-Score	Precision	Recall	F1-Score	
POS	76.73	74.38	75.54	78.28	75.01	76.61	+1.07
MORPH6	82.52	79.74	81.10	84.62	80.64	82.58	+1.48
MORPH9	86.98	85.32	86.14	89.42	86.35	87.86	+1.72
LEMMA	**88.42**	**86.54**	**87.47**	**90.98**	**87.16**	**89.03**	**+1.56**
PHI	88.23	86.35	87.28	90.87	87.02	88.90	+1.62

Figure 7: Extended labelled attachment scores (ELAS) for parsing the treebank using different feature sets.

6.2 Results

We use ELAS as our evaluation metric for measuring the performance of HSP in both the one-step and two-step parsing experiments. To reduce sample bias, we use 10-fold cross-validation. Our F1-scores are calculated by aggregating the total number of true positives and false positives across the ten folds, as per method three in Forman and Scholz (2009).

Figure 7 shows the results for the two parsing approaches. Using the best performing feature set, HSP achieves an F1-score of 87.47% for the multi-step approach, and 89.03% for the integrated approach. This high performance may not only be due to the treebank being annotated with rich morphological features or our choice of algorithm. The Quranic text contains many examples of syntactic and stylistic repetition (Salih, 2007). Repetition leads to an easier machine learning problem, as fewer non-standard cases are encountered during training.

For statistical parsing, the five feature sets above each give different results. It is surprising that the POS feature set is already a good baseline. Using no morphological features and only part-of-speech tags, this feature set produces scores of 75.54% and 76.61% for the two approaches respectively. Our explanation for this is the fact that the treebank uses a detailed part-of-speech tagset, with 45 tags. However, we note that all five feature sets use the same graph features defined in the previous section. Without these graph features, accuracy for the baseline POS feature set drops to only 21.64%. The graph features provide constraints on possible dependencies. For example, the DEPREL features stop additional edges being formed where these would not make sense based on examples in the training data, such as multiple subjects for the same verb.

The next feature set MORPH6 adds voice, mood, case and state. The improvement over the POS feature set is 5.56% for the multi-step approach and 5.97% for the integrated approach. This is consistent with recent work for parsing Modern Standard Arabic. Marton et al. (2010) use a similar set of morphological features to improve parsing accuracy for CATiB (Habash and Roth, 2009). The next set MORPH9 similarly improves performance using further morphological features.

In comparison to parsing Modern Standard Arabic, the best feature set is LEMMA, which boosts performance by a further 1.33% and 1.17% respectively over MORPH9. However, the feature set PHI that adds person, gender and number, surprisingly degrades performance by 0.19% and 0.13% for the two approaches. This contrasts with recent work for parsing CATiB, where the phi-features have been shown to be helpful. We conclude that adding these features may not be statistically significant for parsing the Quran using 10-fold cross-validation, or that this last feature set possibly includes too many features for our SVM model, given the relatively small size of the current version of the treebank.

6.3 Effect of the Conversion Process

The results above show that the integrated parser outperforms the multi-step parser for all of the five feature sets. However, it is interesting that the absolute difference between the two F1-scores consistently lies in the narrow band 1.4 ± 0.32. This suggests that the two parsers have similar sensitivities to feature selection.

Another factor affecting the performance of the multi-step parser is the accuracy of the conversion process from the hybrid representation to pure dependency, and then back to hybrid. The rule-based conversion algorithm outlined in section 5.1 correctly recovers 94.81% of edges. Although it might have been possible to improve the accuracy of the conversion process, this would have required a larger set of more complex rules for uncommon structures, such as the few cases of non-projective edges in the treebank, or for semantic elision.

To measure the effect of the conversion process, we performed a further experiment. We excluded from the treebank all dependency graphs that did not have a perfect reversible conversion to pure dependency (~ 8% of all graphs). We then repeated the 10-fold cross-validation tests using the best performing configuration for both approaches, the LEMMA feature set. On this subset of the data, the multi-step parser achieved an F1-score of 88.89% (89.33 precision, 88.45 recall), and the integrated parser's F1-score was 90.24% (91.48 precision, 89.03 recall). The difference between the two F1-scores was +1.35, which lies in the same narrow band of 1.4 ± 0.32.

These results suggest that the absence of a conversion process is not the largest contributing factor to integrated parser's improved performance. Although additional investigation into optimizing the two-step parsing algorithm could be further pursued, we choose not to. Instead, we argue that the integrated approach is not only simpler as there is no conversion, but is also better suited to the hybrid representation in the treebank.

7 Conclusion and Future Work

In this paper we presented HSP, a Hybrid Statistical Parser, trained using data from the Quranic Treebank. This treebank is a resource for studying the Quran online, and uses a hybrid representation that closely follows the traditional Arabic grammar known as *i'rāb* (إعراب). The treebank's syntactic representation includes phrase nodes and elided words, and presents a special challenge to statistical parsing.

We described two approaches to parsing using different sets of rich morphological features, and compared this to recent work for Modern Standard Arabic. Our shift-reduce algorithm is able to parse hybrid syntactic representations using a one-step process. We concluded that our novel integrated architecture is not only more elegant, but that encoding information this way also improves performance, resulting in a 1.6% ELAS absolute increase over the multi-step baseline for the integrated approach. To the best of our knowledge, this is the first work on statistical parsing for the Classical Arabic language of the Quran.

In the future, we plan to continue our work on hybrid parsing by focusing on three key areas: integrating morphological disambiguation into the parser, comparing HSP to other statistical parsers, and extending the parser to other related languages.

Morphological disambiguation is an important component of our proposed architecture. In this paper, we focused on parsing using only gold standard morphological input. However, Marton et al. (2010) show that parsing Arabic using predicted instead of gold morphological input gives similar results for different feature sets. For Hebrew, Goldberg and Tsarfaty (2008) show that joint morphological and syntactic disambiguation outperforms a pipeline approach. We plan to determine if the same applies to parsing the Quran. Another area of future work is to compare HSP to other statistical parsers. Since our two-step approach converts the hybrid representation to pure dependency, we could in principle parse the Quranic Treebank using any pure dependency parser. For example, MSTParser (McDonald, et al., 2006) could be used to compare one-step hybrid parsing to two-step pure dependency parsing using an alternative graph-based parsing algorithm.

We also plan to extend HSP to parse other languages and treebanks. Classical languages such as Quranic Arabic are sometimes easier to parse statistically compared to modern languages, since vocabulary size and the number of linguistic constructions in such languages is smaller. We are interested to determine if our approach generalizes to other classical languages such as Biblical Hebrew, as well as modern texts, beyond this particular dataset.

Acknowledgments

The authors would like to thank the three anonymous reviewers who provided invaluable feedback to improve the quality of this paper. We thank Eric Atwell at Institute for Artificial Intelligence, University of Leeds for reviewing this paper and providing numerous useful suggestions. We also acknowledge the hard work of the volunteer collaborators involved in online annotation of the Quranic Treebank.

References

Kepa Bengoetxea and Koldo Gojenola. 2010. Application of Different Techniques to Dependency Parsing of Basque. In *Proceedings of the NAACL/HLT Workshop on Statistical Parsing of Morphologically Rich Languages (SPMRL 2010)*, Los Angeles, California.

Rajesh Bhatt, Bhuvana Narasimhan, Martha Palmer, Owen Rambow, Dipti Misra Sharma and Fei Xia. 2009. Multi-Representational and Multi-Layered Treebank for Hindi/Urdu. In *Proceedings of the Third Linguistic Annotation Workshop at the conference of the Association for Computational Linguistics (ACL-IJCNLP)*, Suntec, Singapore.

Daniel Bikel. 2004. On the Parameter Space of Lexicalized Statistical Parsing Models. *PhD thesis, Department of Computer and Information Sciences*. University of Pennsylvania.

Ezra Black et al. 1991. A Procedure for Quantitatively Comparing the Syntactic Coverage of English Grammars. In *Proceedings of the February 1991 DARPA Speech and Natural Language Workshop*.

Georges Bohas, Jean-Patrick Guillaume, and Djamel Eddin Kouloughli. 1990. The Arabic linguistic tradition. *Arabic Thought and Culture*. Routledge.

Chih-Chung Chang and Chih-Jen Lin. 2001. LIBSVM: A Library for Support Vector Machines. *Technical Report, Department of Computer Science and Information Engineering*, National Taiwan University.

Eugene Charniak. 2000. A Maximum-entropy-inspired Parser. In *Proceedings of the 1st Annual Meeting of the North American Chapter of the ACL (NAACL)*, Seattle.

Michael Collins. 1999. *Head-driven Statistical Models for Natural Language Parsing*. Ph.D. thesis, University of Pennsylvania.

Kais Dukes, Eric Atwell and Nizar Habash. 2011. Supervised Collaboration for Syntactic Annotation of Quranic Arabic. To appear in *Language Resources and Evaluation Journal (LREJ): Special Issue on Collaboratively Constructed Language Resources*.

Kais Dukes, Eric Atwell and Abdul-Baquee Sharaf. 2010. Syntactic annotation guidelines for the Quranic Arabic Dependency Treebank. In *Proceedings of the Language Resources and Evaluation Conference (LREC)*. Valletta, Malta.

Kais Dukes and Timothy Buckwalter. 2010. A Dependency Treebank of the Quran using Traditional Arabic Grammar. In *Proceedings of the 7th international conference on Informatics and Systems (INFOS)*. Cairo, Egypt.

Kais Dukes and Nizar Habash. 2010. Morphological Annotation of Quranic Arabic. In *Proceedings of the Language Resources and Evaluation Conference (LREC)*. Valletta, Malta.

Gülsen Eryiğit, Joakim Nivre and Kemal Oflazer. 2008. Dependency Parsing of Turkish. *Computational Linguistics*.

George Forman and Martin Scholz. 2009. Apples-to-apples in Cross-validation Studies: Pitfalls in Classifier Performance Measurement. *HP technical Reports*, HPL-2009-359.

Ryan Gabbard, Seth Kulick, and Mitchell Marcus. 2006. Fully parsing the Penn Treebank. In *Proceedings of the Human Language Technology Conference of the NAACL*, New York.

Yoav Goldberg and Michael Elhadad. 2010. Easy-First Dependency Parsing of Modern Hebrew. In *Proceedings of the NAACL/HLT Workshop on Statistical Parsing of Morphologically Rich Languages (SPMRL 2010)*, Los Angeles, California.

Yoav Goldberg and Reut Tsarfaty. 2008. A Single Generative Model for Joint Morphological Segmentation and Syntactic Parsing. In *Proceedings of ACL-HLT*. Columbus, Ohio.

Nizar Habash and Ryan Roth. 2009. CATiB: The Columbia Arabic Treebank. In *Proceedings of the ACL-IJCNLP 2009 Conference Short Papers*. Suntec, Singapore, August.

Nizar Habash. 2010. Introduction to Arabic Natural Language Processing. Morgan & Claypool Publishers.

Johan Hall, Jens Nilsson, Joakim Nivre, Gülsen Eryiğit, Beáta Megyesi, Mattias Nilsson, and Markus Saers. 2007. Single Malt or Blended? A Study in Multilingual Parser Optimization. In *Proceedings of EMNLP-CoNLL*.

Johan Hall and Joakim Nivre. 2008. A Dependency-driven Parser for German Dependency and Constituency Representations. In *Proceedings of the ACL Workshop on Parsing German (PaGe08)*, Columbus, Ohio.

Johan Hall, Joakim Nivre and Jens Nilsson. 2007. A Hybrid Constituency-dependency Parser for Swedish. In *Proceedings of NODALIDA*, Tartu, Estonia.

Seth Kulick, Ryan Gabbard, and Mitchell Marcus. 2006. Parsing the Arabic Treebank: Analysis and Improvements. In *Proceedings of Treebanks and Linguistic Theories Conference*. Prague, Czech Republic.

Mohamed Maamouri, Ann Bies, Timothy Buckwalter, and Wigdan Mekki. 2004. The Penn Arabic Treebank: Building a Large-scale Annotated Arabic Corpus. In *Proceedings of the NEMLAR Confer-*

ence on Arabic Language Resources and Tools. Cairo, Egypt.

Mitchell Marcus, Beatrice Santorini, and Mary Ann Marcinkiewicz. 1993. Building a Large Annotated corpus of English: The Penn Treebank. *Computational Linguistics*.

Yuval Marton, Nizar Habash, and Owen Rambow. 2010. Improving Arabic Dependency Parsing with Lexical and Inflectional Morphological Features. In *Proceedings of the NAACL/HLT Workshop on Statistical Parsing of Morphologically Rich Languages (SPMRL 2010)*, Los Angeles, California.

Ryan McDonald, Kevin Lerman, and Fernando Pereira. 2006. Multilingual Dependency Analysis with a Two-stage Discriminative Parser. In *Proceedings of CoNLL*. New York.

Joakim Nivre, Johan Hall, Jens Nilsson, Atanas Chanev, Gülşen Eryiğit, Sandra Kübler, Svetoslav Marinov, and Erwin Marsi. 2007a. MaltParser: A Language Independent System for Data-driven Dependency Parsing. *Natural Language Engineering*.

Joakim Nivre, Johan Hall, Sandra Kübler, Ryan McDonald, Jens Nilsson, Sebastian Riedel and Deniz Yuret. 2007b. The CoNLL 2007 Shared Task on Dependency Parsing. In *Proceedings of EMNLP-CoNLL*.

Jonathan Owens. 1988. The Foundations of Grammar: An Introduction to Medieval Arabic Grammatical Theory. *Amsterdam Studies in the Theory and History of Linguistic Science*. John Benjamins.

Bahjat Salih. 2007. *al-i'rāb al-mufassal li-kitāb allāh al-murattal* ('A Detailed Grammatical Analysis of the Recited Quran using *i'rāb*'). Dar Al-Fikr, Beirut.

Otakar Smrž, Viktor Bielický, Iveta Kourilová, Jakub Kráčmar, Jan Hajic, and Petr Zemánek. 2008. Prague Arabic Dependency Treebank: A Word on the Million Words. In *Proceedings of the Workshop on Arabic and Local Languages (LREC 2008)*. Marrakech, Morocco.

Hiroyasu Yamada and Yuji Matsumoto. 2003. Statistical Dependency Analysis with Support Vector Machines. In *Proceedings of International Conference on Parsing Technologies (IWPT 2003)*.

PLCFRS Parsing of English Discontinuous Constituents

Kilian Evang
Humanities Computing
University of Groningen
k.evang@rug.nl

Laura Kallmeyer
Institut für Sprache und Information
University of Düsseldorf
kallmeyer@phil.uni-duesseldorf.de

Abstract

This paper proposes a direct parsing of non-local dependencies in English. To this end, we use probabilistic linear context-free rewriting systems for data-driven parsing, following recent work on parsing German. In order to do so, we first perform a transformation of the Penn Treebank annotation of non-local dependencies into an annotation using crossing branches. The resulting treebank can be used for PLCFRS-based parsing. Our evaluation shows that, compared to PCFG parsing with the same techniques, PLCFRS parsing yields slightly better results. In particular when evaluating only the parsing results concerning long-distance dependencies, the PLCFRS approach with discontinuous constituents is able to recognize about 88% of the dependencies of type *T* and *T*-PRN encoded in the Penn Treebank. Even the evaluation results concerning local dependencies, which can in principle be captured by a PCFG-based model, are better with our PLCFRS model. This demonstrates that by discarding information on non-local dependencies the PCFG model loses important information on syntactic dependencies in general.

1 Introduction

Discontinuous constituents as exemplified in (1) are more frequent than generally assumed, even in languages such as English that display a rather rigid word order. In (1), the NP *areas of the factory where the crocidolite was used* is separated into two non-adjacent parts. (1) is an example from the Penn Treebank (PTB). More generally, all constructions where head-argument or head-modifier dependencies are non-local, such as *wh*-movement, can be seen as instances of discontinuous constituency. Such instances appear in about 20% of the sentences in the PTB. They constitute a particular challenge for parsing.

(1) *Areas of the factory* were particularly dusty *where the crocidolite was used.*

In the past, data-driven parsing has largely been dominated by Probabilistic Context-Free Grammar (PCFG). This is partly due to the annotation formats of treebanks such as the Penn Treebank (PTB) (Marcus et al., 1994), which are used as a data source for grammar extraction. Their annotation generally relies on the use of trees without crossing branches, augmented with a mechanism that accounts for non-local dependencies. In the PTB, e.g., labeling conventions and trace nodes are used which establish additional implicit edges in the tree beyond the overt phrase structure.

However, given the expressivity restrictions of PCFG, work on data-driven parsing has mostly excluded non-local dependencies. When using treebanks with PTB-like annotation, labeling conventions and trace nodes are often discarded.

Some work has however been done towards incorporating non-local information into data-driven parsing. One general way to do this is (non-projective) dependency parsing where parsers are not grammar-based and the notion of constituents or phrases is not employed, see e.g. McDonald et al. (2005) or Nivre (2009). Within the domain of grammar-based constituent parsing, we can distinguish three approaches (Nivre, 2006): 1. Non-local information can be reconstructed in a post-processing step after PCFG parsing (Johnson, 2002; Levy and Manning, 2004; Jijkoun and de Rijke, 2004; Campbell, 2004; Gabbard et al., 2006). 2. Non-local information can be incorpo-

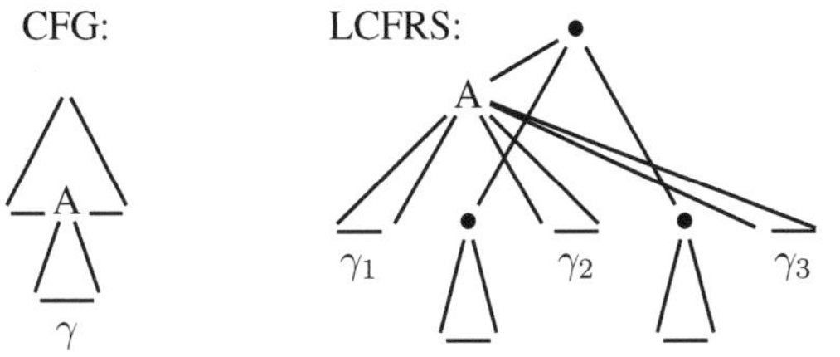

Figure 1: Different domains of locality

rated into the PCFG model (Collins, 1999) or into complex labels (Dienes and Dubey, 2003; Hockenmaier, 2003; Cahill et al., 2004). 3. A formalism can be used which accommodates the direct encoding of non-local information (Plaehn, 2004; Maier and Kallmeyer, 2010; Kallmeyer and Maier, 2010). This paper pursues the third approach.

Our work is based on recent research in using Linear Context-Free Rewriting Systems (LCFRS) (Vijay-Shanker et al., 1987) for data driven parsing. LCFRSs extend CFGs such that non-terminals can span tuples of possibly non-adjacent strings (see Fig. 1). This enables them to describe discontinuous constituents and non-projective dependencies (Kuhlmann and Satta, 2009; Maier and Lichte, 2009). Furthermore, they are able to capture synchronous derivations, something that is empirically attested in treebanks (Kallmeyer et al., 2009). In order to parse German, a language where discontinuities are particularly frequent, Kallmeyer and Maier (2010); Maier and Kallmeyer (2010) use probabilistic LCFRSs (PLCFRSs). As a data source, they use the German NEGRA and TIGER treebanks that annotate discontinuous constituents by using crossing branches.

We adapt this approach for German to English, using the PTB. For this, we first need to transform the trace-based annotation of discontinuous constituents into an annotation with crossing branches which requires a careful treatment of the different types of traces that occur in the PTB. Then we extract a PLCFRS from the resulting treebank and we use the PLCFRS parser from Kallmeyer and Maier for our parsing experiments.

The paper is structured as follows. Section 2 introduces PLCFRS and the parsing algorithm. The next section explains the transformation of the PTB into an annotation format where non-local dependencies are annotated with crossing branches. Section 4 describes further transformations we apply to the resulting treebanks, in particular binarization and category splitting. Finally, section 5 reports the results or our parsing experiments with a detailed evaluation of the way the different types of long-distance dependencies are captured. Section 6 concludes.

2 PLCFRS Parsing

2.1 PLCFRS

LCFRSs are an extension of CFG where the non-terminals can span not only single strings but, instead, tuples of strings (see Fig. 1). An LCFRS (Vijay-Shanker et al., 1987) is a tuple $\langle N, T, V, P, S\rangle$ where

a) N is a finite set of non-terminals with a function dim: $N \rightarrow \mathbb{N}$; $dim(A)$ is called the *fan-out* of A and determines the dimension of the tuples in the yield of A;

b) T and V are disjoint finite sets of terminals and variables;

c) $S \in N$ is the start symbol with $dim(S) = 1$;

d) P is a finite set of rules

$$A(\alpha_1, \dots, \alpha_{dim(A)}) \rightarrow A_1(X_1^{(1)}, \dots, X_{dim(A_1)}^{(1)}) \cdots A_m(X_1^{(m)}, \dots, X_{dim(A_m)}^{(m)})$$

for $m \geq 0$ where $A, A_1, \dots, A_m \in N$, $X_j^{(i)} \in V$ for $1 \leq i \leq m, 1 \leq j \leq dim(A_i)$ and $\alpha_i \in (T \cup V)^*$ for $1 \leq i \leq dim(A)$. For all $r \in P$, it holds that every variable X occurring in r occurs exactly once in the left-hand side (LHS) and exactly once in the right-hand side (RHS).

A rewriting rule describes how the yield of the LHS non-terminal can be computed from the yields of the RHS non-terminals. The rules $A(ab, cd) \rightarrow \varepsilon$ and $A(aXb, cYd) \rightarrow A(X, Y)$ for instance specify that 1. $\langle ab, cd\rangle$ is in the yield of A and 2. one can compute a new tuple in the yield of A from an already existing one by wrapping a and b around the first component and c and d around the second.

For every $A \in N$ in a LCFRS G, we define the yield of A, $yield(A)$ as follows:

a) For every $A(\vec{\alpha}) \rightarrow \varepsilon$, $\vec{\alpha} \in yield(A)$;

b) For every rule

$$A(\alpha_1, \dots, \alpha_{dim(A)}) \rightarrow A_1(X_1^{(1)}, \dots, X_{dim(A_1)}^{(1)}) \cdots A_m(X_1^{(m)}, \dots, X_{dim(A_m)}^{(m)})$$

and all $\vec{\tau_i} \in yield(A_i)$ for $1 \leq i \leq m$, $\langle f(\alpha_1), \dots, f(\alpha_{dim(A)})\rangle \in yield(A)$ where f is defined as follows: (i) $f(t) = t$ for all $t \in T$, (ii) $f(X_j^{(i)}) = \vec{\tau_i}(j)$ for all $1 \leq i \leq m, 1 \leq j \leq dim(A_i)$ and (iii) $f(xy) = f(x)f(y)$ for all $x, y \in (T \cup V)^+$. f is the *composition function* of the rule.

c) Nothing else is in $yield(A)$.

The language is then $\{w \mid \langle w \rangle \in yield(S)\}$.

The *fan-out* of an LCFRS G is the maximal fan-out of all non-terminals in G. An LCFRS with a fan-out of n is called an n-LCFRS. Furthermore, the RHS length of a rewriting rules $r \in P$ is called the *rank* of r and the maximal rank of all rules in P is called the *rank* of G. We call a LCFRS *monotone* if for every $r \in P$ and every RHS non-terminal A in r and each pair X_1, X_2 of arguments of A in the RHS of r, X_1 precedes X_2 in the RHS iff X_1 precedes X_2 in the LHS.

A *probabilistic LCFRS* (PLCFRS) (Kato et al., 2006) is a tuple $\langle N, T, V, P, S, p \rangle$ such that $\langle N, T, V, P, S \rangle$ is a LCFRS and $p : P \rightarrow [0..1]$ a function such that for all $A \in N$: $\Sigma_{A(\vec{x}) \rightarrow \vec{\Phi} \in P} p(A(\vec{x}) \rightarrow \vec{\Phi}) = 1$.

2.2 CYK Parsing

We use the parser from Kallmeyer and Maier (2010); Maier (2010), Maier and Kallmeyer (2010) which is a probabilistic version of the CYK parser from Seki et al. (1991), applying techniques of weighted deductive parsing (Nederhof, 2003).

LCFRSs can be binarized (Gómez-Rodríguez et al., 2009) and ε-components in the LHS of rules can be removed (Boullier, 1998). We can therefore assume that all rules are of rank 2 (in section 4.1, we explain our binarization technique) and do not contain ε components in their LHSs. Furthermore, we assume POS tagging to be done before parsing. POS tags are non-terminals of fan-out 1. The rules are then either of the form $A(a) \rightarrow \varepsilon$ with A a POS tag and $a \in T$ or of the form $A(\vec{\alpha}) \rightarrow B(\vec{x})$ or $A(\vec{\alpha}) \rightarrow B(\vec{x})C(\vec{y})$ where $\vec{\alpha} \in (V^+)^{dim(A)}$, i.e., only the rules for POS tags contain terminals in their LHSs.

For every $w \in T^*$, we call every pair $\langle l, r \rangle$ with $0 \leq l \leq r \leq |w|$ a *range* in w. The *concatenation* of two ranges $\rho_1 = \langle l_1, r_1 \rangle, \rho_2 = \langle l_2, r_2 \rangle$ is defined as follows: if $r_1 = l_2$, then $\rho_1 \cdot \rho_2 = \langle l_1, r_2 \rangle$; otherwise $\rho_1 \cdot \rho_2$ is undefined.

For a given rule $p : A(\alpha_1, \dots, \alpha_{dim(A)}) \rightarrow B(X_1, \dots, X_{dim(B)})C(Y_1, \dots, X_{dim(C)})$ we now extend the composition function f to ranges, given an input w: for all vectors of ranges $\vec{\rho_B}$ and $\vec{\rho_C}$ of dimensions $dim(B)$ and $dim(C)$ respectively, $f_r(\vec{\rho_B}, \vec{\rho_C}) = \langle g(\alpha_1), \dots, g(\alpha_{dim(A)}) \rangle$ is defined as follows: $g(X_i) = \vec{\rho_B}(i)$ for all $1 \leq i \leq dim(B)$, $g(Y_i) = \vec{\rho_C}(i)$ for all $1 \leq i \leq dim(C)$ and $g(xy) = g(x) \cdot g(y)$ for all $x, y \in V^+$. $p : A(f_r(\vec{\rho_B}, \vec{\rho_C})) \rightarrow B(\vec{\rho_B})C(\vec{\rho_C})$ is then called an *instantiated rule*.[1]

Scan: $\dfrac{}{0 : [A, \langle\langle i, i+1 \rangle\rangle]}$ $\quad A$ POS tag of w_{i+1}

Unary: $\dfrac{in : [B, \vec{\rho}]}{in + |log(p)| : [A, \vec{\rho}]}$ $\quad p : A(\vec{\alpha}) \rightarrow B(\vec{\alpha}) \in P$

Binary: $\dfrac{in_B : [B, \vec{\rho_B}], in_C : [C, \vec{\rho_C}]}{in_B + in_C + log(p) : [A, \vec{\rho_A}]}$

where $p : A(\vec{\rho_A}) \rightarrow B(\vec{\rho_B})C(\vec{\rho_C})$ is an instantiated rule.

Goal: $[S, \langle\langle 0, n \rangle\rangle]$

Figure 2: Weighted CYK deduction system

add SCAN results to $\mathcal{A}$
while $\mathcal{A} \neq \emptyset$
  remove best item $x : I$ from $\mathcal{A}$
  add $x : I$ to $\mathcal{C}$
  if I goal item
  then stop and output true
  else
    for all $y : I'$ deduced from $x : I$ and items in $\mathcal{C}$:
      if there is no z with $z : I' \in \mathcal{C} \cup \mathcal{A}$
      then add $y : I'$ to $\mathcal{A}$
      else if $z : I' \in \mathcal{A}$ for some z
        then update weight of I' in $\mathcal{A}$ to $max(y, z)$

Figure 3: Weighted deductive parsing

For a given input w, our items have the form $[A, \vec{\rho}]$ where $A \in N$, $\vec{\rho}$ a vector of ranges with $|\vec{\rho}| = dim(A)$. $\vec{\rho}$ characterizes the span of A. We specify the set of weighted parse items via the deduction rules in Fig. 2. The parser performs a weighted deductive parsing (Nederhof, 2003), based on this deduction system. It uses a chart $\mathcal{C}$ and an agenda $\mathcal{A}$, both initially empty, and proceeds as in Fig. 3.

3 Treebank Transformation

The PTB annotation guidelines (Bies et al., 1995, Section 1.1) specify a set of rules that determine where arguments and adjuncts are attached with respect to their head words. For example, subjects are attached at clause level, most other arguments and adjuncts of verbs are attached at VP level, and phrases modifying nouns such as PPs and relative clauses are adjoined at NP level. Knowing these

[1]This corresponds to the *instantiated clauses* in simple Range Concatenation Grammars (Boullier, 1998; Boullier, 2000).

rules, head-argument and head-adjunct dependencies can be read off the trees easily, e.g. for semantic interpretation.

Non-local head-argument and head-adjunct dependencies constitute exceptions to these rules. Following the rules would lead to discontinuous constituents with crossing branches, containing the head and the argument or adjunct, but not containing some intervening tokens. Examples of non-locally dependent arguments and adjuncts include *wh*-moved phrases, fronted phrases, extraposed modifiers, *it*-extraposition, and right-node-raised phrases (Fig. 4a-d). Such phrases are attached at locations in the tree that avoid discontinuity, thus the heads on which they depend cannot easily be determined from the tree structure alone. The PTB instead uses the null elements *T*, *ICH*, *EXP* and *RNR* to mark the position where the phrases would be attached according to the general rules and indices in node labels to indicate which null element stands for which phrase (shown by arcs in the tree diagrams). Null elements are embedded in "placeholder phrases" of the same category (but without WH prefixes) as the non-locally dependent phrase. This representation of non-local dependencies is not suitable for PCFG parsing since null elements pose a serious combinatorial problem and PCFG has no mechanism for dealing with indexed category labels. Null elements and indices are therefore usually removed before training PCFG parsers, resulting in parse trees that do not contain information on non-local dependencies.

We use the approach proposed and tested on the German treebanks NEGRA and TIGER in Maier and Kallmeyer (2010): permit discontinuous constituents, attach non-locally dependent arguments and adjuncts according to the general rules, resulting in a uniform representation for local and non-local dependencies, and use PLCFRS for parsing. While NEGRA and TIGER already use such a uniform representation, training and testing data for English can be obtained by removing placeholder phrases with *T*, *ICH*, *EXP* and *RNR* null elements from their locations in the PTB trees and reattaching the coindexed phrases to those locations, removing indices from node labels (Fig. 5). Other types of null elements are used to indicate control and other relations with no immediate bearing on non-local head-adjunct and head-argument dependencies. We remove these from the treebank along with corresponding indices.

type	instances	trees	trees with gap-degree 0	1	2
T	18759	15452	7292	7924	236
T-PRN	843	843	0	71	772
ICH	1268	1240	7	1200	33
EXP	658	651	1	630	20
RNR	210	208	131	67	10
any reattachment	21738	17187	7397	8996	794
no reattachment	n/a	32021	32021	0	0
total	n/a	49208	39418	8996	794

Table 1: Reattachment types and gap-degrees of resulting trees

Two types of cases require special treatment. First, some arguments and adjuncts are shared between two or more heads, marked by two or more null elements with the same index (Fig. 4(d)). Since a phrase cannot be attached to more than one location in a tree even with crossing branches, the phrase must either remain in place, where no relation to any head can be immediately read off the tree, or be attached according to the general rules with respect to only one of the heads, leaving the others with no trace of the argument or adjunct. For now, we decided to put consistency in the way arguments and adjuncts are attached first and always attach phrases with multiple heads as depending on the head which is closest (Fig. 5(d)). The other special case concerns phrases, typically quotations, that surround the matrix phrase containing the head on which they depend. In the PTB annotation, the matrix phrase is embedded into such arguments under a node labeled PRN for *parenthesis* (Fig. 4(e)). To avoid cycles after the transformation, such matrix phrases are detached from within the argument and reattached to the node where the argument was originally attached, if any (Fig. 5(e)).

Table 1 gives an overview of the tendency of each type of null element[2] to introduce gaps when so transformed as indicated by *gap-degree* (Holan et al., 1998; Maier and Lichte, 2009), i.e. the maximal number of gaps in any constituent of the resulting trees. Most typically, one gap is introduced since there is a single phrase non-adjacent to the rest of the phrase to which it is attached. No gap at all is introduced by the reattachment of most *wh*-moved subjects and *EXP*-type phrases in object position. Gap degrees of 2 are almost exclusively accounted for by surrounding phrases where the

[2]Those instances of *T* reattachments where the dependent element is a surrounding phrase are given separately as *T*-PRN.

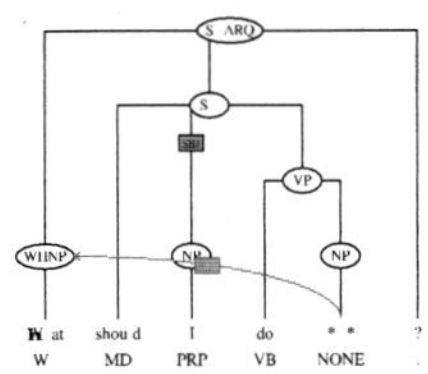
S ARQ
S
VP
WHNP
NP
NP
shou d
I
do
MD
PRP
VB
NONE

VP of the surrounded matrix clause is typically interrupted by two commas and the subject of the matrix clause. On the whole, about 20% of the trees in the transformed PTB contain discontinuities – less than the c. 30% reported by Maier and Lichte (2009) for the German treebanks NEGRA and TIGER, but still a considerable percentage.

An LCFRS is extracted from the transformed treebank using the algorithm of Maier and Søgaard (2008), simplified using the fact that leaves do not have siblings and their parents are labeled with POS tags: every leaf is represented as a variable. Every internal node n is represented as a term $A_i(X_{11} \dots X_{1j_1}, \dots, X_{i1} \dots X_{ij_i})$ where $X_{11}, \dots, X_{1j_1}, \dots, X_{i1} \dots X_{ij_1}$ represent the leaves dominated by n in order, there is an argument boundary between two variables iff the corresponding leaves are non-adjacent, A is the label of n and i is the number of arguments, used to obtain a unique non-terminal A_i with fan-out i. A rule $\alpha \rightarrow \beta_1 \dots \beta_m$ is extracted for each internal node n such that α is the term representing n and $\beta_1, \dots, \beta_m$ are the terms representing its children, conventionally ordered by leftmost dominated terminal. For parents of leaves, m is 0, and the single variable in α is replaced with the terminal labeling the corresponding leaf. For other nodes, every sequence of variables that occurs as a right-hand side argument is replaced with a single new variable on both sides. Fig. 6 shows an example. Rules are equivalent if equal up to renaming variables. The resulting LCFRS rules are ε-free and they are monotone. The latter means that the order of the arguments of a RHS element is the same as the order of these variables in the LHS. Both properties facilitate parsing.

The number of occurrences of the rules are counted and the probabilities of RHSs conditioned on LHSs are then calculated using MLE. In this way, a PLCFRS is obtained. This is a very simple probability model, much like a vanilla PCFG. In the following section, we discuss techniques we used to refine the probability model.

4 Grammar Annotation

4.1 Binarization

Similarly to the transformation of a CFG into Chomsky Normal Form (CNF), we binarize the LCFRS extracted from the treebank. The result is an LCFRS of rank 2. A binarization technique that results in horizontal Markovization of

Non-binary tree:

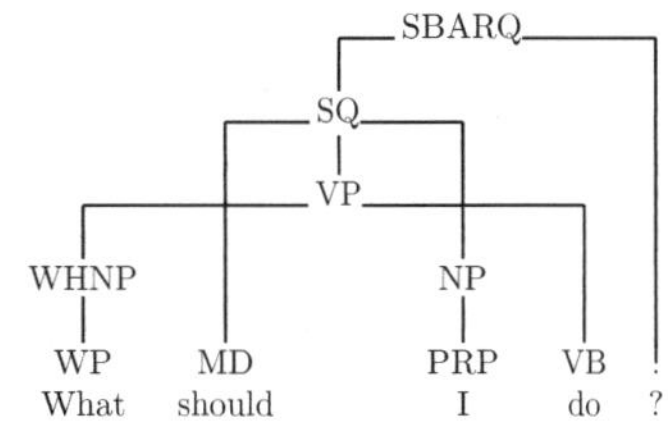

Extracted LCFRS rules:

$$
\begin{aligned}
\text{SBARQ}_1(XY) &\rightarrow \text{SQ}_1(X)\text{.}_1(Y)\\
\text{SQ}_1(XYZU) &\rightarrow \text{VP}_2(X,U)\text{MD}_1(Y)\text{NP}_1(Z)\\
\text{VP}_1(X,Y) &\rightarrow \text{WHNP}_1(X)\text{VB}_1(Y)\\
\text{WHNP}_1(X) &\rightarrow \text{WP}_1(X)\\
\text{NP}_1(X) &\rightarrow \text{PRP}_1(X)\\
\text{WP}_1(\text{What}) &\rightarrow \varepsilon\\
\text{MD}_1(\text{should}) &\rightarrow \varepsilon\\
\text{PRP}_1(\text{I}) &\rightarrow \varepsilon\\
\text{VB}_1(\text{do}) &\rightarrow \varepsilon\\
\text{.}_1(?) &\rightarrow \varepsilon
\end{aligned}
$$

Figure 6: LCFRS extraction from trees

the grammar is proposed and successfully used for parsing NEGRA and TIGER in Kallmeyer and Maier (2010). However, our experiments have shown that the beneficial effect of this horizontal Markovization technique does not carry over to parsing the PTB, presumably because compared to the two German treebanks, the PTB has a more hierarchical annotation scheme, extracted grammars have rules with shorter RHSs to begin with and can thus profit less from additional factorization; the adverse effect of wrong independence assumptions predominates. We thus use a *deterministic* binarization technique that does not change the probability model. Specifically, we introduce a *unique* new non-terminal for each right-hand side longer than 2 and split the rule into two rules, using this new intermediate non-terminal. This is repeated until all right-hand sides are of length 2. The transformation algorithm is inspired by Gómez-Rodríguez et al. (2009) and it is also specified in Kallmeyer (2010). Fig. 7 shows an example.

$$
\begin{aligned}
\text{SBARQ}_1(XY) &\rightarrow \text{SQ}_1(X)\text{.}_1(Y)\\
\text{SQ}_1(XYZ) &\rightarrow \text{VP}_1(X,Z)\text{C}_1(Y)\\
\text{C}_1(XY) &\rightarrow \text{MD}_1(X)\text{NP}_1(Y)\\
\text{VP}_1(X,Y) &\rightarrow \text{WHNP}_1(X)\text{VB}_1(Y)\\
\text{WHNP}_1(X) &\rightarrow \text{WP}_1(X)\\
\text{NP}_1(X) &\rightarrow \text{PRP}_1(X)
\end{aligned}
$$

Figure 7: Binarized grammar equivalent to the grammar in Figure 6, not showing terminal rules.

Note however that the fan-out of the LCFRS can increase because of the binarization.

4.2 Category Splits

Category splitting, i.e. relabeling certain nodes in the training data depending on context, has been used to improve the performance of PCFG parsing (Klein and Manning, 2003) and also PLCFRS parsing (Kallmeyer and Maier, 2010). Our experiments have shown that a combination of three splits for the PTB annotation improved performance considerably: S nodes are relabeled to SWH if a *wh*-element is extracted from the sentence. In order to make this split more effective, SBAR nodes that have only one child after transformation to the discontinuous format are removed. VP nodes are relabeled to VPHINF if their head is labeled VB, to VPHTO if their head is labeled TO and to VPHPART if their head is labeled VBN or VBG. S nodes rooting infinitival clauses (head child labeled VPHINF or VPHTO) are relabeled to SINF.

5 Evaluation

We use the Wall Street Journal sections 1-22 of the Penn Treebank (version 2.0) as training data and sections 23-24 as test data. Due to time constraints and the complexity of PLCFRS parsing, sentences with more than 25 tokens (not counting null elements) are excluded, resulting in 25801 training sentences and 2233 test sentences. After a small number of corrections to the annotation, concerning chiefly wrong indices and missing PRN nodes, we create discontinuous versions of the training and test set by carrying out the reattachment operations described in Section 3 while also keeping context-free versions. All four sets are then preprocessed by removing all (remaining) indices, null elements and empty constituents. We call the resulting context-free training and test set Tr and Te, and the resulting discontinuous training and test set Tr' and Te'.

5.1 EVALB-Style Evaluation

Since the structure in Te' encodes local as well as non-local dependencies, it serves as our primary gold standard. In a first step, we use the standard EVALB metric, generalized to trees with discontinuous constituents as in Maier and Kallmeyer (2010), to measure how much of the structure in the gold standard is captured by different parsers. We compare Maier and Kallmeyer's parser trained on Tr' (resulting in a 3-PLCFRS) with three parsers that do *not* produce discontinuous structures: the Berkeley parser (Petrov et al., 2006; Petrov and Klein, 2007) trained on Tr using our manual category splits but no automatic splitting/merging/smoothing, the Berkeley parser trained on Tr using its default setting of six iterations of split/merge/smooth, and Maier and Kallmeyer's parser with a grammar extracted from Tr (a 1-PLCFRS, i.e. a PCFG). The upper half of Table 2 shows the results. For comparison, we also evaluated the three context-free parsers on the untransformed context-free test set Te. These figures are given in the lower half of the table. For Maier and Kallmeyer's parser, the number of rules in the grammar before and after binarizing is also given, as well as the number of items created during parsing as an indicator of parsing complexity.

Across these experiments, the most crucial factor for parsing accuracy seems to be splitting/merging/smoothing. As the comparison between the two parsing experiments with the Berkeley parser shows, this technique is key to achieving its state-of-the-art results. We plan to transfer this technique to discontinuous constituent parsing in future work. For now, we must compare discontinuous to context-free constituent parsing on a level below the state of the art. Comparison between the two experiments with Maier and Kallmeyer's parser shows that it works with about the same accuracy when trained and tested on discontinuous data as when trained and tested on context-free data, although parsing complexity is considerably higher in the discontinuous experiment as evidenced by the number of items produced. Note that scores would presumably be lower if sentences with more than 25 tokens were included.

Even when trained on the context-free data, both parsers get most of the structure in Te' right since only a relatively small fraction of constituents is discontinuous. However, for those test sentences that do contain discontinuous constituents (Te'_D), context-free parsers fare much worse than for sentences that do not (Te'_C). For Maier and Kallmeyer's parser trained on Tr' they seem to be only slightly harder to parse. Although its scores for Te'_D with discontinuous parsing are lower than for Te_D with context-free parsing, the former may be considered a better parse result than the latter since the Te'_D gold standard con-

Parser		Berkeley		Maier&Kallmeyer	
Training set		Tr	Tr	Tr	Tr'
Split/merge		6 it.	man.	man.	man.
Test set					
Te'	LP	87.29	72.86	78.13	80.36
	LR	86.89	67.88	74.60	77.61
	LF_1	87.09	70.28	76.33	78.96
	UP	90.40	77.70	82.59	83.74
	UR	89.98	72.39	78.86	80.00
	UF_1	90.19	74.95	80.68	82.29
Te'_C	LP	89.43	74.55	79.97	80.66
	LR	89.37	69.75	76.57	77.81
	LF_1	89.40	72.07	78.23	79.21
	UP	91.85	78.63	83.91	83.95
	UR	91.78	73.57	80.34	80.99
	UF_1	91.82	76.02	82.09	82.44
Te'_D	LP	77.06	64.76	69.42	78.90
	LR	75.31	59.14	65.44	76.61
	LF_1	76.17	61.82	67.37	77.74
	UP	83.48	73.23	76.31	82.77
	UR	81.58	66.88	71.93	80.37
	UF_1	82.52	69.91	74.06	81.55
Te	LP	89.82	74.88	80.37	-
	LR	89.64	69.94	76.94	
	LF_1	89.73	72.32	78.61	
	UP	91.89	78.80	83.91	
	UR	91.70	73.60	80.33	
	UF_1	91.80	76.11	82.08	
Te_C	LP	89.90	74.94	80.36	-
	LR	89.85	70.12	76.95	
	LF_1	89.88	72.45	78.62	
	UP	91.90	78.63	83.92	
	UR	91.84	73.57	80.36	
	UF_1	91.87	76.02	82.10	
Te_D	LP	89.43	74.58	80.40	-
	LR	88.64	69.08	76.87	
	LF_1	89.03	71.73	78.60	
	UP	91.86	79.61	83.85	
	UR	91.05	73.74	80.16	
	UF_1	91.46	76.56	81.96	
Rules				8892	9761
Bin. rules				27809	29218
Items				580M	1056M

Table 2: EVALB-style evaluation of parsing experiments (scores in %). Tr and Te are the context-free training and test sets, Tr' and Te' the discontinuous transformed versions. The D and C subscripts indicate the subsets of the test sets containing the sentences that actually have (D) resp. do not have (C) one or more discontinuities in Te'. For Maier and Kallmeyer's parser, the number of rules in the unbinarized and binarized grammar as well as the number of parse items produced is given.

Parser		Maier&Kallmeyer
Training set		Tr''
Split/merge		man.
Test set		
Te''	LP	80.71
	LR	77.85
	LF_1	79.26
	UP	84.07
	UR	81.09
	UF_1	82.55
Te''_C	LP	80.82
	LR	77.90
	LF_1	79.33
	UP	84.12
	UR	81.07
	UF_1	82.57
Te''_D	LP	78.87
	LR	76.38
	LF_1	77.60
	UP	82.49
	UR	79.88
	UF_1	81.16
Rules		9653
Bin. rules		29096
Items		852M

Table 3: Results of a second discontinuous parsing experiment where *ICH* and *EXP* transformations have been omitted in the transformation

tains information on non-local dependencies while Te_D does not.

5.2 Dependency Evaluation

In order to assess to what degree this is the case, we perform a *dependency evaluation* (Lin, 1995), first used for evaluating discontinuous constituent parser output in Maier (2010). This method requires a conversion of constituent trees to sets of word-word dependencies. We use Lin's dependency conversion method, where each phrase is represented by its lexical head. To determine the head of each phrase, we use the head-finding algorithm of Collins (1999), ordering the children of each node by leftmost dominated terminal.

Under this standard dependency conversion method, the transformation described in Section 3 introduces new word-word (head-argument/head-adjunct) dependencies that are relevant to semantic interpretation. Word-word dependencies lost in the transformation are not normally relevant since they result from attachment of phrases outside of the domains of their heads. We therefore choose Te' as the gold standard against which to evaluate both context-free and discontinuous parsing results. Table 4 shows that discontinuous parsing as compared to context-free parsing boosts the unlabeled attachment score (i.e. recall on word-word dependencies) slightly for local dependencies and considerably for non-local dependencies. The lat-

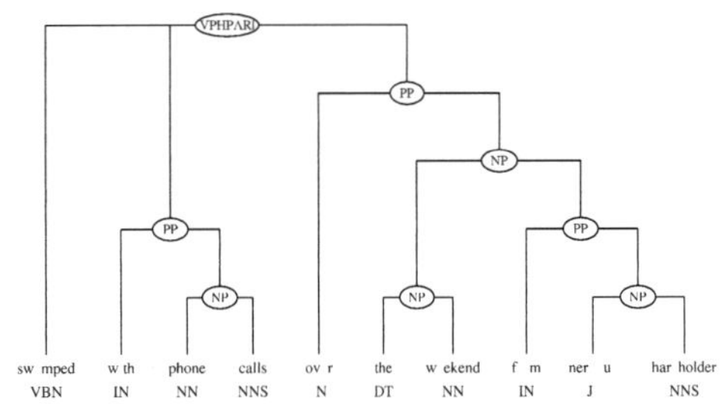

Figure 8: Failure to recognize the discontinuous NP *phone calls from nervous shareholders*

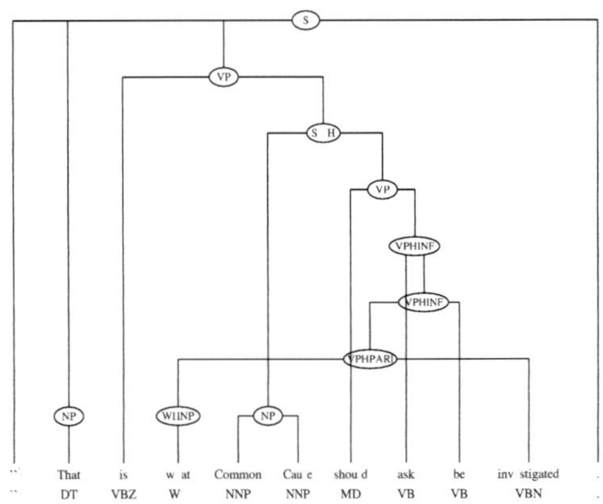

	gold	Maier&Kallmeyer			MSTParser	
		Tr	*Tr'*	*Tr''*	*Tr'* unlabeled	*Tr'* Hall&Nivre
T	436	134	386	380	374	379
T-PRN	32	8	26	26	25	26
ICH	31	3	5	4	10	9
EXP	18	0	1	0	8	9
RNR	4	2	3	3	3	3
other	35918	29785	30252	30241	32452	32457
total	36439	29932	30673	30654	32872	32883
		82.14%	84.18%	84.12%	90.21%	90.24%

Table 4: Unlabeled attachment scores in dependency evaluation on the dependency-converted Te'

be tackled by factoring rules into an expansion part (what RHS categories) and a separation part (where the gap is), similar to the factorization proposed in Levy (2005, Section 4.8). Note also that there is nothing in the present model to prevent LCFRS rules associated with different constructions, such as *wh*-movement and fronting, from recombining, producing nonsensical parses in a few cases. Finally, it should be noted that attaching commas surrounding parentheses inside surrounding quotations rather than to the PRN node could reduce the fan-out of the grammar from 3 to 2, benefiting parsing efficiency.

6 Conclusion and Future Work

This paper pursues an approach of direct parsing of discontinuous constituents. We have applied data-driven PLCFRS parsing to English. To this end, we have first transformed the trace-based Penn Treebank annotation format into a format with crossing branches and explicit discontinuous constituents. The latter can then be used for PLCFRS parsing.

Our evaluation has shown that, compared to PCFG parsing with the same techniques, PLCFRS parsing yields slightly better results. In particular when evaluating only the parsing results concerning long-distance dependencies, the PLCFRS approach with discontinuous constituents is able to recognize about 88% of the dependencies of type *T* and *T*-PRN. Even the results concerning local dependencies, which can in principle be captured by a CFG-based model, are better with the PLCFRS model. This demonstrates that by discarding information on non-local dependencies the PCFG model loses important information on syntactic dependencies in general.

Our results show that data-driven PLCFRS parsing is a promising and feasible strategy not only for so-called free word order languages such as German but also for English where we obtain competitive parsing results.

However, our experiments also reveal some shortcomings of the chosen probabilistic model. A general problem is that some decisions, for instance on PP-attachments, cannot be taken solely based on the syntactic information we have used. This problem occurs independent from the choice of PLCFRS. A careful integration of more lexical information can help to overcome this problem. A shortcoming that is specific to LCFRS is the assumption that the expansions of the same category with different fan-outs (for instance a continuous VP and a discontinuous VP) are independent from each other. This bears two problems. Firstly, since categories of higher fan-out are rather rare, we have a sparse data problem. Secondly, the independence assumption is probably wrong. In order to tackle this problem, we plan to develop models that factor rules into an expansion part and a separating part that introduces gaps. We leave this issue for future work.

Acknowledgments

We would like to thank Wolfgang Maier for fruitful discussions and help with implementation, and the anonymous reviewers for their valuable suggestions on improving the paper.

References

Ann Bies, Mark Ferguson, Karen Katz, and Robert MacIntyre. 1995. Bracketing Guidelines for Treebank II Style Penn Treebank Project. University of Pennsylvania.

Pierre Boullier. 1998. A Proposal for a Natural Language Processing Syntactic Backbone. Technical Report 3342, INRIA.

Pierre Boullier. 2000. Range Concatenation Grammars. In *Proceedings of the Sixth International Workshop on Parsing Technologies (IWPT2000)*, pages 53–64, Trento, Italy, February.

Aoife Cahill, Michael Burke, Ruth O'Donovan, Josef Van Genabith, and Andy Way. 2004. Long-distance dependency resolution in automatically acquired wide-coverage PCFG-based LFG approximations. In *Proceedings of the 42nd Meeting of the Association for Computational Linguistics (ACL'04), Main Volume*, pages 319–326, Barcelona, Spain, July.

Richard Campbell. 2004. Using linguistic principles to recover empty categories. In *Proceedings of the 42nd Meeting of the Association for Computational Linguistics (ACL'04), Main Volume*, pages 645–652, Barcelona, Spain, July.

Michael Collins. 1999. *Head-Driven Statistical Models for Natural Language Parsing*. Ph.D. thesis, University of Pennsylvania.

Pétr Dienes and Amit Dubey. 2003. Deep syntactic processing by combining shallow methods. In *Proceedings of the 41st Annual Meeting of the Association for Computational Linguistics*, pages 431–438, Sapporo, Japan, July. Association for Computational Linguistics.

Ryan Gabbard, Seth Kulick, and Mitchell Marcus. 2006. Fully parsing the Penn Treebank. In *Proceedings of the Human Language Technology Conference of the NAACL, Main Conference*, pages 184–191, New York City, USA, June. Association for Computational Linguistics.

Carlos Gómez-Rodríguez, Marco Kuhlmann, Giorgio Satta, and David Weir. 2009. Optimal reduction of rule length in linear context-free rewriting systems. In *Proceedings of the North American Chapter of the Association for Computational Linguistics - Human Language Technologies Conference (NAACL'09:HLT)*, pages 539–547, Boulder, Colorado.

Johan Hall and Joakim Nivre. 2008. Parsing discontinuous phrase structure with grammatical functions. In *Proceedings of the 6th International Conference on Natural Language Processing (GoTAL)*, pages 169–180.

Julia Hockenmaier. 2003. *Data and models for statistical parsing with Combinatory Categorial Grammar*. Ph.D. thesis, School of Informatics, University of Edinburgh.

Tom Holan, Vladislav Kubo, Karel Oliva, and Martin Pltek. 1998. Two useful measures of word order complexity. In *Workshop on Processing of Dependency-Based Grammars*, pages 21–29, Montreal, Canada.

Valentin Jijkoun and Maarten de Rijke. 2004. Enriching the output of a parser using memory-based learning. In *Proceedings of the 42nd Meeting of the Association for Computational Linguistics (ACL'04), Main Volume*, pages 311–318, Barcelona, Spain, July.

Mark Johnson. 2002. A simple pattern-matching algorithm for recovering empty nodes and their antecedents. In *Proceedings of 40th Annual Meeting of the Association for Computational Linguistics*, pages 136–143, Philadelphia, Pennsylvania, USA, July. Association for Computational Linguistics.

Laura Kallmeyer and Wolfgang Maier. 2010. Data-driven parsing with probabilistic Linear Context-Free Rewriting Systems. In *Proceedings of the 23rd International Conference on Computational Linguistics (COLING 2010)*, Beijing, China.

Laura Kallmeyer, Wolfgang Maier, and Giorgio Satta. 2009. Synchronous rewriting in treebanks. In *Proceedings of IWPT 2009*.

Laura Kallmeyer. 2010. *Parsing Beyond Context-Free Grammars*. Springer, Berlin. Textbook.

Yuki Kato, Hiroyuki Seki, and Tadao Kasami. 2006. Stochastic multiple context-free grammar for RNA pseudoknot modeling. In *Proceedings of The Eighth International Workshop on Tree Adjoining Grammar and Related Formalisms (TAG+8)*, pages 57–64, Sydney, Australia, July.

Dan Klein and Christopher D. Manning. 2003. Accurate unlexicalized parsing. In *Proceedings of the 41st Annual Meeting of the Association for Computational Linguistics*, pages 423–430,

Sapporo, Japan, July. Association for Computational Linguistics.

Marco Kuhlmann and Giorgio Satta. 2009. Treebank grammar techniques for non-projective dependency parsing. In *Proceedings of EACL*.

Roger Levy and Christopher Manning. 2004. Deep dependencies from context-free statistical parsers: Correcting the surface dependency approximation. In *Proceedings of the 42nd Meeting of the Association for Computational Linguistics (ACL'04), Main Volume*, pages 327–334, Barcelona, Spain, July.

Roger Levy. 2005. *Probabilistic models of word order and syntactic discontinuity*. Ph.D. thesis, Stanford University.

Dekang Lin. 1995. A dependency-based method for evaluating broad-coverage parsers. In *Proceedings of the Fourteenth International Joint Conference on Artificial Intelligence (IJCAI 1995)*, Montreal, Quebec, Canada.

Wolfgang Maier and Laura Kallmeyer. 2010. Discontinuity and non-projectivity: Using mildly context-sensitive formalisms for data-driven parsing. In *Proceedings of the Tenth International Workshop on Tree Adjoining Grammars and Related Formalisms (TAG+10)*, New Haven.

Wolfgang Maier and Timm Lichte. 2009. Characterizing discontinuity in constituent treebanks. In *Proceedings of Formal Grammar 2009*, Bordeaux, France, July. To appear in Lecture Notes in Computer Science, Springer.

Wolfgang Maier and Anders Søgaard. 2008. Treebanks and mild context-sensitivity. In Philippe de Groote, editor, *Proceedings of the 13th Conference on Formal Grammar (FG-2008)*, pages 61–76, Hamburg, Germany. CSLI Publications.

Wolfgang Maier. 2010. Direct parsing of discontinuous constituents in German. In *Proceedings of the NAACL HLT 2010 First Workshop on Statistical Parsing of Morphologically-Rich Languages*, pages 58–66, Los Angeles, CA, USA, June. Association for Computational Linguistics.

Mitchell Marcus, Grace Kim, Mary Ann Marcinkiewicz, Robert MacIntyre, Ann Bies, Mark Ferguson, Karen Katz, and Britta Schasberger. 1994. The penn treebank: annotating predicate argument structure. In *HLT '94: Proceedings of the workshop on Human Language Technology*, pages 114–119, Morristown, NJ, USA. Association for Computational Linguistics.

Ryan McDonald and Fernando Pereira. 2006. Online learning of approximate dependency parsing algorithms. In *11th Conference of the European Chapter of the Association for Computational Linguistics*.

Ryan McDonald, Fernando Pereira, Kiril Ribarov, and Jan Hajic. 2005. Non-projective dependency parsing using spanning tree algorithms. In *Proceedings of Human Language Technology Conference and Conference on Empirical Methods in Natural Language Processing*, pages 523–530, Vancouver, British Columbia, Canada, October. Association for Computational Linguistics.

Mark-Jan Nederhof. 2003. Weighted Deductive Parsing and Knuth's Algorithm. *Computational Linguistics*, 29(1):135–143.

Joakim Nivre. 2006. Constraints on non-projective dependency parsing. In *11th Conference of the European Chapter of the Association for Computational Linguistics*, pages 73–80, Trento, Italy. Association for Computational Linguistics.

Joakim Nivre. 2009. Non-projective dependency parsing in expected linear time. In *Proceedings of the Joint Conference of the 47th Annual Meeting of the ACL and the 4th International Joint Conference on Natural Language Processing of the AFNLP*, pages 351–359, Suntec, Singapore, August. Association for Computational Linguistics.

Slav Petrov and Dan Klein. 2007. Improved inference for unlexicalized parsing. In *Human Language Technologies 2007: The Conference of the North American Chapter of the Association for Computational Linguistics; Proceedings of the Main Conference*, pages 404–411, Rochester, New York, April. Association for Computational Linguistics.

Slav Petrov, Leon Barrett, Romain Thibaux, and Dan Klein. 2006. Learning accurate, compact, and interpretable tree annotation. In *Proceedings of the 21st International Conference on Computational Linguistics and 44th Annual Meeting of the Association for Computational Linguistics*, pages 433–440, Sydney, Australia, July. Association for Computational Linguistics.

Oliver Plaehn. 2004. Computing the most probable parse for a discontinuous phrase-structure grammar. In *New developments in parsing technology*. Kluwer.

Hiroyuki Seki, Takahashi Matsumura, Mamoru Fujii, and Tadao Kasami. 1991. On multiple context-free grammars. *Theoretical Computer Science*, 88(2):191–229.

K. Vijay-Shanker, David J. Weir, and Aravind K. Joshi. 1987. Characterizing structural descriptions produced by various grammatical formalisms. In *Proceedings of ACL*, Stanford.

Towards a Neurobiologically Plausible Model of Human Sentence Comprehension Across Languages

Ina Bornkessel-Schlesewsky
Institut für Germanistische Sprachwissenschaft
Philipps-Universität Marburg
`iboke@staff.uni-marburg.de`

Abstract

Among human cognitive abilities, language is singular in the diversity of its manifestations: over 6000 languages are spoken in the world today. Some of the major challenges in modelling how language is processed by the human brain thus lie in explaining (a) how this diversity is handled, and (b) whether there are nevertheless some underlying generalisations that recur across languages of different types. Furthermore, an adequate model should be neurobiologically plausible, i.e., respect what we know about the structure and function of the human brain. In this presentation, I will describe a line of research in which we have attempted to take up these challenges at the level of sentence comprehension. Based on the results of neurophysiological experiments in a range of typologically varied languages, I will argue for a comprehension architecture that is actor-centred, i.e., focused on identifying the participant primarily responsible for the state of affairs under discussion. I will introduce the latest version of a comprehension model (extended Argument Dependency Model, eADM; Bornkessel and Schlesewsky, 2006), the architecture of which is built around actor-centrality as a design principle, and will describe how it accounts for potential universals of comprehension and critical dimensions of variation.

References

Ina Bornkessel and Matthias Schlesewsky. 2006. The Extended Argument Dependency Model: A neurocognitive approach to sentence comprehension across languages. *Psychological Review*, 113, 787–821.

Minimally Supervised Domain-Adaptive Parse Reranking for Relation Extraction

Feiyu Xu, Hong Li, Yi Zhang, Hans Uszkoreit, Sebastian Krause

DFKI, LT-Lab, Germany

{feiyu,lihong,Yi.Zhang,uszkoreit,sebastian.krause}@dfki.de

Abstract

The paper demonstrates how the generic parser of a minimally supervised information extraction framework can be adapted to a given task and domain for relation extraction (RE). For the experiments a generic deep-linguistic parser was employed that works with a largely hand-crafted head-driven phrase structure grammar (HPSG) for English. The output of this parser is a list of n best parses selected and ranked by a MaxEnt parse-ranking component, which had been trained on a more or less generic HPSG treebank. It will be shown how the estimated confidence of RE rules learned from the n best parses can be exploited for parse reranking. The acquired reranking model improves the performance of RE in both training and test phases with the new *first* parses. The obtained significant boost of recall does not come from an overall gain in parsing performance but from an application-driven selection of parses that are best suited for the RE task. Since the readings best suited for successful rule extraction and instance extraction are often not the readings favored by a regular parser evaluation, generic parsing accuracy actually decreases. The novel method for task-specific parse reranking does not require any annotated data beyond the semantic seed, which is needed anyway for the RE task.

1 Introduction

Domain adaptation is a central research topic for many language technologies including information extraction (IE) and parsing (e.g., (Grishman and Sundheim, 1996; Muslea, 1999; Hara et al., 2005; McClosky et al., 2010; Miwa et al., 2010)). The largest challenge is to develop methods that exploit domain knowledge with minimal human effort.

Many IE systems benefit from combining generic NLP components with task-specific extraction methods. Various machine learning approaches have been employed for adapting the IE methods to new domains and extraction tasks (e.g., (Yangarber, 2001; Sudo et al., 2003; Greenwood and Stevenson, 2006)). The IE framework extended in this paper utilizes minimally supervised learning of extraction rules for the detection of relation instances (Xu et al., 2007). Since the minimally supervised learning starts its bootstrapping from a few semantic examples, no treebanking or any other annotation is required for new domains. In addition to this inherently domain-adaptable rule-learning component, the framework also employs two language analysis modules: a named-entity (NE) recognizer (Drozdzynski et al., 2004) and a parser (Lin, 1998; de Marneffe and Manning, 2008). NE recognizers are adapted to new domains–if needed–by adding rules for new NE types and extending the gazetteers. The employed generic data-driven dependency parsers or deep-linguistic handcrafted parsers have not yet been adapted to IE domains and tasks.

The new work presented here concerns the adaptation of a generic parser to a given relation extraction (RE) task and domain without actually changing the parser itself. For the experiments a generic deep-linguistic parser was used together with a hand-crafted HPSG (Pollard and Sag, 1994) grammar for English (ERG) (Flickinger, 2000). The output of this parser is a list of n best parses selected and ranked by a MaxEnt parse-ranking component (Toutanova et al., 2005b), which had been trained on a generic HPSG treebank (Oepen et al., 2002). The parse ranking had attracted our attention because the first RE tests with the hand-crafted grammar revealed recall problems even for the parsable relation mentions. Our suspicion to partially blame the generic parse selection was confirmed by our experiments.

In this paper we will show how the estimated confidence of rules learned from the n best parses can be exploited for task-specific parse reranking. The acquired reranking model improves the performance of RE both in training and test phases. The task-driven reranking leads to significantly better RE recall by boosting readings that are better suited for RE rule extraction and rule application. The beneficial reranking does not improve the quality of parsing measured by task-independent performance criteria, not even for the IE domain. The validation of the adapted parser using a hand-checked HPSG treebank of in-domain texts rather shows a deterioration of parsing accuracy. But often the incorrect parses selected over less faulty parses support the correct detection of instance mentions.

The novel method for task-specific parse reranking does not require any annotated data beyond the semantic seed, needed anyway for the RE task. Thus it does not require a domain-specific treebank.

The paper is organized as follows. Section 2 describes the grammar and the associated parse selection model. Section 3 introduces the RE framework. Section 4 explains the new task/domain-oriented reranking approach. Section 5 presents the experiments and evaluations. Special emphasis is placed on the role of reranking for the performance of the RE system. Section 6 discusses related work. Finally, Section 7 summarizes the results and suggests directions for further research.

2 HPSG and Parse Selection Model

Recent progress in parsing has several sources. The most noticeable trend is the shift from pure symbolic rule-based approaches toward statistical parsing. The availability of large-scale treebanks has enabled the training of powerful data-driven parsers, some based on constituency others on dependency. Meanwhile, existing hand-crafted precision oriented linguistic grammars have also benefitted from empirical methods through new disambiguation models trained on treebanks.

Among the available deep linguistic grammars, ERG is a good representative of the state of the art. Its lexicon contains $\sim$35K entries. The 1004 release of the grammar we use is accompanied by a maximum-entropy-based parse disambiguation model trained on the Redwoods Treebank (Oepen et al., 2002), a treebank of $\sim$20K sentences with mixed genre texts (dialogs, tourist information, emails, etc). The discriminative log-linear disambiguation model scores each parse by the following (Toutanova et al., 2005b),

$$P(t|w) = \frac{\exp \sum_{i=1}^{n} \lambda_i f_i(t, w)}{\sum_{t' \in T(w)} \exp \sum_{i=1}^{n} \lambda_i f_i(t', w)} \quad (1)$$

where w is the given input sentence and t is the HPSG reading; $T(w)$ is the set of all possible readings for a given sentence w licensed by the grammar; $\langle f_1, \ldots, f_n \rangle$ and $\langle \lambda_1, \ldots, \lambda_n \rangle$ are feature functions and their corresponding weights. In practice, the effective features are defined on the HPSG derivation trees (without details from the feature structures), and the best readings are decoded efficiently from a packed parse forest with dynamic programming (Zhang et al., 2007).

Although there are indications that parsers with hand-written grammars usually suffer less from the shift of domain than statistical parsers (Zhang and Wang, 2009; Plank and van Noord, 2010), the effect can still be observed, say in the preference of lexical selection. The issue is not that the correct analysis would be ruled out by the constraints in the treebank-induced grammar, but rather that it is not favored by the statistical ranking model, since the statistical distribution of the syntactic structures in the training corpus is different from the target application domain. This issue is recently acknowledged in most parsing systems and known as the domain adaptation task.

3 DARE and Confidence Estimation

DARE (Xu et al., 2007; Xu, 2007) is a minimally supervised machine learning system for RE for free texts consisting of two major parts: 1) rule learning, 2) relation extraction (RE). DARE provides a recursive extraction-rule representation, which can deal with relations of varying complexity. Rule learning and RE feed each other in a bootstrapping framework. The bootstrapping starts from so-called "semantic seed" as a search query, which is a small set of instances of the target relation. The rules are extracted from found sentences with annotations of semantic entities and parsing results. RE applies acquired rules to texts in order to discover more relation instances, which in turn are employed as seed for further iterations. The confidence values of the newly acquired rules and instances are calculated in the spirit of the "Duality principle" (Brin, 1998; Agichtein and Gravano, 2000; Yangarber, 2001), i.e., the confidence values of the rules are dependent on the truth value of their extracted instances and on the seed instances from which they stem. The confidence value of an extracted instance makes use of the confidence value of its ancestor seed instances. The core system architecture of DARE is depicted in Figure 1. The entire bootstrapping stops when no new rules or new instances can be detected.

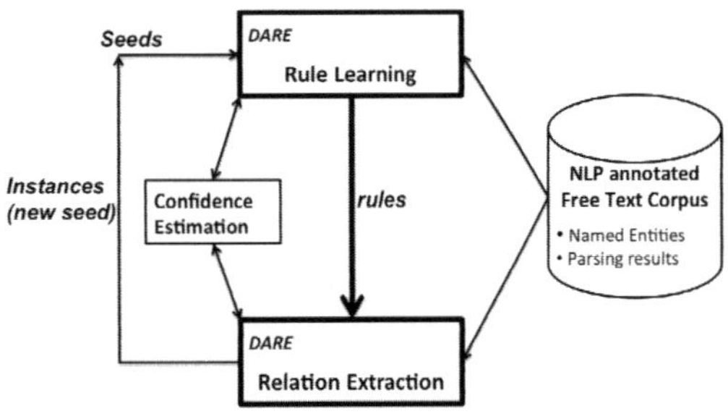

Figure 1: DARE core architecture

Relying entirely on semantic seeds as domain knowledge, DARE can accommodate new relation types and domains with minimal effort. Since we had already reported on experiments applying the framework to different relation types and corpora including MUC-6 data in the cited papers, including comparisons with other ML approaches to RE (Xu, 2007; Uszkoreit et al., 2009), we omit a comparative discussion here.

For confidence estimation, the method proposed by Xu et al. (2010) is adopted.[1] Actually, in (2) we propose an extended version of the rule scoring, since the rule scoring in (Xu et al., 2010) did not consider the case when a learned rule does not extract any new instances. Thus, given the scoring of instances, the confidence value of a rule is the average score of all instances ($\mathbb{I}_{extracted}$) extracted by this rule or the average score of seed instances (I_{rule}) from which they are learned. Through the factor δ we reduce the score of rules that have not proven yet their potential for extracting instances.

[1]The actual confidence estimation is slightly more complex because it further improves the scoring by utilizing implicit negative evidence provided by closed-world seeds, a method proposed by (Xu et al., 2010). As this mechanism is not relevant in the context of this paper, we omit a description.

$$\textbf{confidence}(rule) = \begin{cases} \frac{\sum_{i \in \mathbb{I}_{extracted}} \textbf{score}(i)}{|\mathbb{I}_{extracted}|} & \text{if } \mathbb{I}_{extracted} \neq \phi \\ \frac{\sum_{j \in I_{rule}} \textbf{score}(j)}{|I_{rule}|} \times \delta & \text{if } \mathbb{I}_{extracted} = \phi \end{cases}$$
$$\text{where } \mathbb{I}_{extracted} = \textbf{getInstances}(rule), \quad I_{rule} = \textbf{getMotherInstancesOf}(rule), \quad \delta = 0.5 \qquad (2)$$

This method allows DARE to estimate the confidence value of a rule according to its extraction performance or the confidence value of its origin.

4 Domain Adaptive Parse Reranking

4.1 Basic Idea

In our research, we observe that there is a strong connection between the RE task and the parser via the learned extraction rules, because these rules are derived from the parse readings. The confidence values of the extraction rules imply the domain appropriateness of the parse readings. Therefore, the confidence values can be utilized as feedback to the parser to help it to rerank its readings.

4.2 Reranking Architecture and Method

Figure 2 depicts the overall architecture of our experimental system. We utilize the HPSG to parse our experimental corpus and keep the first n readings of each sentence (e.g., 256) delivered by the parser. During bootstrapping DARE tries to learn extraction rules from all readings of sentences containing a seed instance or newly detected instances. At each iteration the extracted rules are applied to all readings of all sentences. When bootstrapping has terminated, the obtained rules are assigned confidence values based on the DARE ranking method described in Section 3.

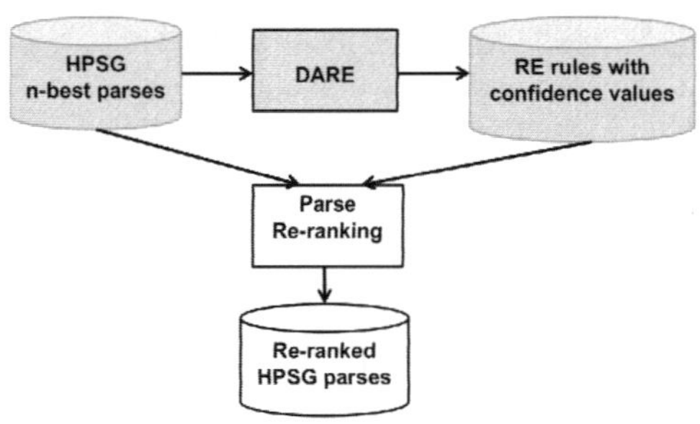

Figure 2: DARE and Parse Reranking

The parse reranking component scores the alternative parses of each sentence based on the confidence values of the rules matching these parses, i.e., all rules that could have been extracted from a parse or successfully applied to it.

For each reading from the HPSG parser, the reranking model assigns a numeric score by the following formula:

$$S(t) = \begin{cases} \sum_{r \in R(t)} (\textbf{confidence}(r) - \phi\textbf{confidence}) & if R(t) \neq \phi, \\ 0 & if R(t) = \phi. \end{cases} \quad (3)$$

$R(t)$ is the set of RE rules matching parse reading t, and ϕ**confidence** is the average confidence score among all rules. The score of the reading will be increased if the matching rule has an above-average confidence score. And the matching of low-confidence rules will decrease the reading's reranking score. If a reading has no matching DARE rule, it will be assigned the lowest score 0, for no potential relation can be extracted from that reading.

After the calculation, the top-n readings are sorted in descending order. In case two or more readings received the same reranking score (e.g. by matching the same set of DARE rules), the original maximum entropy-based disambiguation scores are used as a tie-breaker. The sort comparison function is shown below:

Algorithm 1 compare_readings(r_i, r_j)

```
if compare(S(r_i), S(r_j)) ≠ 0 then
    return compare(S(r_i), S(r_j))
else # Tie-breaking with MaxEnt scores
    return compare(MaxEnt(r_i), MaxEnt(r_j))
end if
```

In practice, most readings will have no more than two matching DARE rules. And many readings from the HPSG parser do not affect the RE task. A consequence is that the reranking model can only partially disambiguate and have an effect only on particular subsets of the readings. As we are only evaluating RE performance, the remaining ambiguity is not an issue.

5 Experiments and Evaluation

5.1 Experiment and Evaluation Setup

Data For several reasons we decided to conduct our experiments on the Nobel Prize award corpus used also in (Xu et al., 2007). Previous results have shown that

1. not every data collection is suited for the minimally supervised approach to RE (Xu, 2007);
2. freely available Nobel Prize award corpus actually has the required properties (Uszkoreit et al., 2009).

Moreover, the availability of a version of the corpus in which all relation mentions are labelled and a treebank for a subset of the corpus have greatly facilitated the evaluation.

The target relation is *prize-awarding event*, namely, a relation among four arguments: WINNER, PRIZE_NAME, PRIZE_AREA and YEAR. We take the same seed example as utilized in (Xu et al., 2007), namely, the 1999 Nobel Chemistry winner Ahmed H Zewail in our experiments[2]. The seed looks like an database recond:

$\langle$*Ahmed H Zewail*, *Nobel*, *Chemistry*, 1999$\rangle$

The corpus contains 2864 documents from BBC, CNN and NYT, together 143289 sentences. ERG covers around 70% sentences of the total corpus. For our experiments we randomly divide the parsable corpus into two parts: training and test corpus, each containing the same number of sentences. The average sentence length of the total corpus is around 20 words. If we look at the domain relevant sentences, namely, those contain both person name mentions and prize name mentions, they have an average length of around 30. Among those relevant ones, the average length of the sentences parsable by ERG is around 25.

Experiments Two phases of experiments are conducted. In the *training* phase, we show that reranking improves RE performance. The *test* phase applies the reranking model resulting from the training phase to the test corpus. In both phases, two different experiments are conducted *1) Baseline*: without reranking; *2) reranking*: with parse reranking. In the baseline experiment, we

[2]Uszkoreit et al. (2009) show that for the given dataset the particular choice of the single seed instance does not have any affect on the performance.

keep the first n readings of all sentences and run DARE for rule learning and RE on top of these readings. The aim is to observe whether correct relation instances can also be detected in lower-ranked readings. In the second experiments, we aim to investigate whether reranking based on task-feedback and domain knowledge is useful for better extraction performance. These experiments are conducted only with the best reading after reranking, i. e. the normal setting of RE application. In none of the experiments, confidence thresholds are employed for improving precision by filtering out less confident rules or instances. As we are mainly interested in the effects of reranking on RE recall, we are trying to avoid any other factors that may influence the recall. Thus in our experiments confidence estimation scores are only used for reranking.

Qualitative Analysis Given the experimental results, we carry out various qualitative analysis on the results of both parsing and RE. With respect to parsing, we evaluate the results against the gold-standard treebank before and after reranking. In addition we evaluate the quality of the extraction rules before and after the reranking.

5.2 Experiments

5.2.1 Training

Baseline Figure 4 shows the baseline evaluation results. In this case, no confidence thresholds are applied, therefore we have neither reranking nor filtering. In order to monitor the contribution of lower-ranked parses to RE, we add readings in logarithmic increments. We start with one reading, namely the best reading proposed by the parser and then in steps go up to 500. From each reading, DARE tries to learn rules and to extract relation instances. When DARE only works with the best reading, the precision is very high, namely, 87.83%, but with a very low recall of 45.18%. When we increase the number of readings, we observe that precision drops while recall increases. This confirms our suspicion that many good readings are among the lower ranked ones in the current maximum entropy-based parse model. Therefore, reranking is important for lifting the good readings to the top.

Reranking In the training phase, we learn DARE rules from all 500 readings from all sentences in the training corpus. Given the rules and their confidence values, we rerank the 500 read-

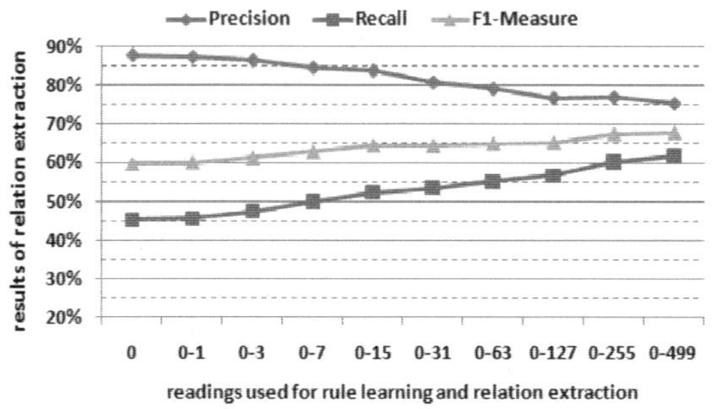

Figure 4: Training phase (baseline): RE performance w.r.t. the increase of readings

ings of each sentence in this corpus.

Reading 0	Precision	Recall	F1-Measure
Baseline (no reranking)	87.83%	45.18%	59.66%
After reranking	83.87%	56.19%	67.29%

Table 1: Training phase: Comparison of RE performance before and after reranking.

Table 1 compares the RE performance with just the first reading before reranking (baseline experiment) and after reranking. As indicated, the reranking strongly improves the recall value (56.19% vs. 45.18%) and also yields a significantly better F-measure (67.29% vs. 59.66%).

Figure 5 illustrates the behavior of parse readings with respect to the respective frequencies of matches with extraction rules (indicating their usefulness for rule or instance extraction). After reranking, the number of the higher ranked readings that match with the RE rules is increased significantly. This indicates that the higher ranked readings after reranking are better suited for the RE task.

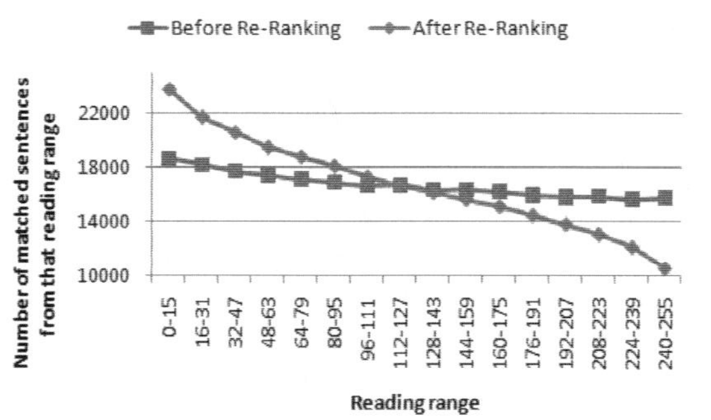

Figure 5: Training phase: Distribution of parse readings from 0 to 255 and their frequency of matching rules before and after reranking

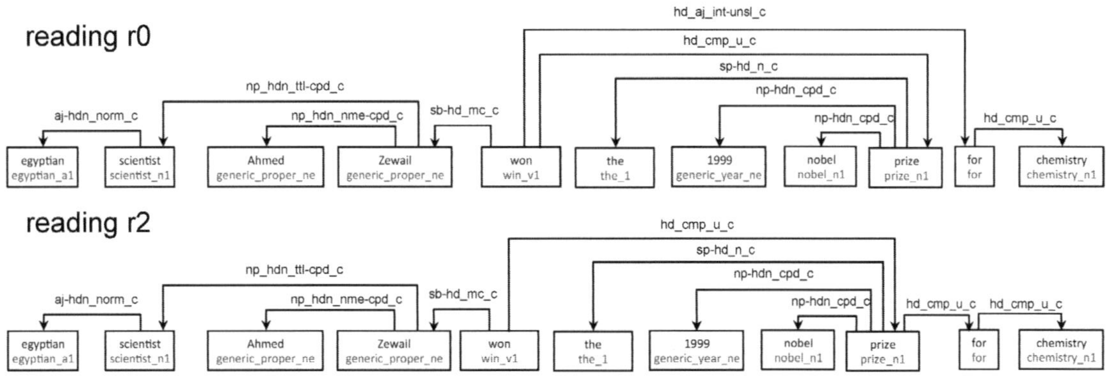

Figure 3: An example of ambiguous parses with PP attachment

reranking Examples In our experiment, we utilize the syntactic derivation tree of the HPSG analysis. Figure 3 shows two derivation trees of a sentence (4) from the experimental domain corpus.

(4) *Egyptian scientist Ahmed Zewail won the 1999 Nobel Prize for Chemistry*

In Figure 3, in the first reading *r0* the PP *"for chemistry"* is wrongly attached to the verb *"win"*, while *r2* (the third reading) is more appropriate since the PP here modifies the noun *"prize"*. The DARE rule in Figure 6 is presented as a typed feature structure, which is learned from HPSG parses. The value of its feature *PATTERN* contains the derivation tree structures relevant for the target relation, while the value of the feature *OUTPUT* represents the co-indexing between the semantic arguments of the target relation and the linguistic arguments in *PATTERN*. Since this rule has a high confidence value and it matches the reading *r2*, *r2* is pushed to the top after reranking.

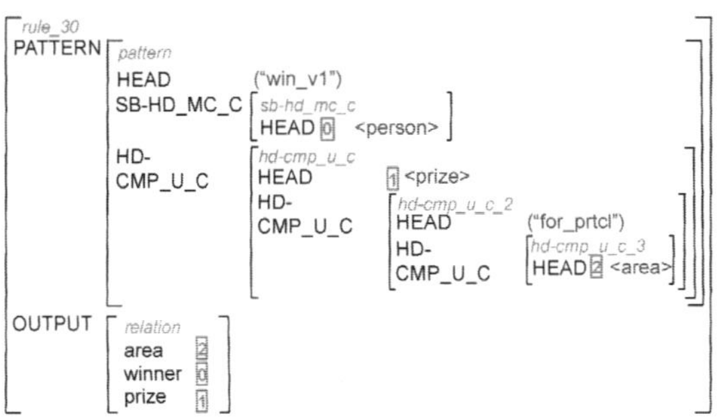

Figure 6: An example DARE rule derived from HPSG derivation trees

5.2.2 Testing

In the test phase, we apply the reranking model trained in the training phase to the parsing of the test corpus when performing RE. The reranking model consists of RE rules with their respective confidence values. These rules work as classifiers that add their confidence values to the ranking scores of matching readings.

Baseline First, we evaluate the performance of the baseline system, i.e., parsing the test corpus without reranking. Similar to the experiments on the training corpus, we first examine the performance of RE on different reading sets. The results are shown in Figure 7. Similar to the training phase results, the recall and F-measure values increase when more readings are taken into account.

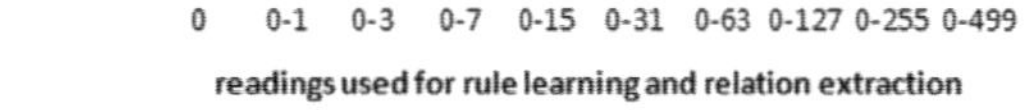

Figure 7: Test phase (baseline): RE performance with respect to the increase of readings.

Reranking Table 2 presents the extraction performance after application of the trained reranking model to the test corpus, using only the highest-ranked reading. Similar to the training phase results, both recall and F-measure also improve significantly in comparison to the baseline system before reranking.

Reading 0	**Precision**	**Recall**	**F1-Measure**
Baseline (no reranking)	82.93%	45.37%	58.56%
after reranking	80.33%	53.41%	64.16%

Table 2: Test phase: Comparison of RE performance before and after reranking.

Model	$LB_{f_1}(full)$	$LB_{f_1}(subtree)$
MaxEnt	0.8613	0.8918
Reranked	0.7966	0.8132

Table 3: Labeled bracketing f-score

5.3 Qualitative Analysis

Experiments in both training and test phases confirm that our reranking improves RE recall and F-measure. A further observation is that the reranked best readings are much more compatible with the learned extraction rules. Naturally, the question arises whether reranking also improves overall parsing accuracy.

5.3.1 Parsing before and after Reranking

Finally, we evaluate the general parsing accuracy before and after reranking. More specifically, we compare the syntactic structures against a high-quality gold-standard treebank annotated by the ERG grammar developer Dan Flickinger. This evaluation indicates the general correctness of the parser (or in particular the disambiguation model).[3]

Table 3 reveals that the general parsing performance suffers from reranking both with respect to full trees and subtrees. To further narrow down the effect of reranking, we manually marked the regions (sub-strings in sentences) most relevant for the target relations and calculated the parser scores within those subtrees.[4] The degradation of parser performance (against gold annotation) is more significant within these local regions.

Further error analyses show the breakdown of the differences: Of the 113 test sentences, 68 show a difference w.r.t. reranking. The labeled bracketing accuracy (on relevant subtrees) increased for 13 sentences. Among these, 3 are due to better *appositions*, 2 to better selection of *verb subcat frames*, 6 to better *PP attachments*. Of the 55 cases of degradation, main causes are: incorrect *compounding in NPs* (24 cases), bad *coordinations* (7 cases), wrong *lexical categories* (2 cases).

	"good" for RE
Before reranking	50%
After reranking	85%

Table 4: "Good" readings for RE among 68 reranked sentences

A careful study has been conducted on these 68 cases with respect to their effect on RE performance. It turns out that after reranking more of the parses are "good" for RE, i.e., leading to good rules. A "good" rule is defined by us as a rule which extracts correct instances. Table 4 shows that after reranking 85% of the 68 have good parses as opposed to 50% before reranking.

An explanation for the drop of linguistic quality is that linguistically "wrong" analyses nevertheless lead to consistent extraction of rules and instances. For example, the gold-standard bracketing of the compound noun "Nobel Peace Prize laureate" is *((Nobel (Peace Prize)) laureate)*. The reranking reading is *((Nobel Peace) (Prize laureate))*, which is wrong. However, the rule derived from this wrong reading can be applied to all equally incorrect readings of similar compound nouns such as "Nobel Chemistry/Physics/Economics Prize laureate" to successfully extract two arguments of the target relation, namely, PRIZE_NAME and PRIZE_AREA. Thus the increased consistency in the re-ranked parses does help improve the RE process.

5.3.2 Extraction Rules after Reranking

In the above analysis, we can learn the lessons that a good reading for RE task is not necessary a linguistically correct parse. The major contribution of reranking is not the improvement of general lin-

[3]Since manual treebanking of HPSG derivation trees is very expensive, the gold-standard treebank only contains 500 randomly selected domain relevant sentences in which both persons and prizes are mentioned. Among these 500 sentences, 113 are in the test corpus. Although this treebank was developed independent from our research approach, the 113 sentences turn out to be useful because they are potential candidates for RE rules and thus their readings can be more effected by reranking than sentences which are irrelevant for the target relation.

[4]We also evaluated the parsing performance on the subtrees selected by the relation extraction rules, whose results are consistent with the above findings.

guistic parse selection but the improvement of selection of good readings for RE tasks.

Table 5 shows a comparison of the distribution of the good readings before and after reranking in test corpus. Bad readings are readings where bad rules are learned, namely, rules which extract only incorrect instances. Useless readings are readings from which useless rules are learned. Useless rules are rules which do not extract any instance. Table 5 clearly demonstrates that the porportion of good readings increases significantly after reranking, while the number of bad readings and useless readings drop.

	Good Reading	Bad Reading	Useless Reading
before reranking	29.2%	1.3%	69.5%
after reranking	42.4%	0.8%	56.8%

Table 5: Test corpus: distribution of good readings before and after reranking

We also compare the number of the learned good rules and their extraction productivity. After reranking, not only the number of good rules increases, but also the average number of the instances extracted by each good rule is grown to 4.3 in comparison to 3.5 before reranking. The growth of good readings and rules and the productivity of rule extraction performance explains the recall improvement after the parse reranking.

6 Related Work

Various attempts have been made to improve the cross-domain performance of statistical parsing models. McClosky et al. (2006) uses self-training to improve Charniak's parser by feeding large amount of unannotated texts to the parser. Plank (2009) utilize structural-correspondence learning to improve the accuracy of the Dutch Alpino parser on the Wikipedia texts. Rimell and Clark (2008) show that a small set of annotated in-domain data can significantly improve the CCG parser's performance. Hara et al. (2007) improves the Enju HPSG parser performance in the biomedical domain by a low-cost retraining of the lexical disambiguation model. Nearly all approaches evaluate the parsing quality against a "gold-standard" treebank. Miwa et al. (2010) compares five parsers for bio-molecular event extraction to investigate the correlation between the performance on a gold-stand treebank and the usefulness in real-world applications. All four domain-adapted parsers achieve similar IE performance and are better than the one not adapted.

The idea of reranking parses for better disambiguation is not new. Charniak and Johnson (2005) presents a discriminative model for capturing the linguistically motivated global properties of the candidate parses proposed by the first-stage generative parser. As the reranking model operates on a relatively small set of candidates, it is able to more accurately find the best reading. In the same spirit, several applications such as named-entity extraction (Collins, 2002), semantic parsing (Toutanova et al., 2005a) and semantic labeling (Ge and Mooney, 2006) have taken advantage of reranking approaches based on discriminative models.

In contrast to the above proposals, our approach does not need the annotated "gold-standard" data for domain adaptation or training of the reranking model. Our system exploits application feedback for reranking. In a sense, the approach is akin in spirit to the joint learning of multiple types of linguistic structures with non-jointly labeled data (Finkel and Manning, 2010), although in our case the emphasis is entirely put on the application performance.

7 Conclusion and Future Work

The main contribution of our work is a method for adapting generic parsers to the tasks and domains of relation extraction by parse reranking. Our reranking is based on feedback from the application. We could show that for one generic parser/grammar, recall and f-measure could be considerably improved and hope that this effect can also be obtained for other generic parsers. We do not worry much about the collateral decrease in precision, because precision will be tightened again when we employ confidence estimation thresholds for filtering out less promising rules and instances.

A side result of the work was the insight that a better parse ranking for the purpose of relation extraction does not necessarily correspond to a better parse ranking for other purposes or for generic parsing. This should not be surprising since relation extraction in contrast to text understanding does not need the entire and correct syntactic structure for the detection of relation instances. The ease and consistency of rule extraction and rule application counts more than the linguistically correct analysis. The gained new insight that the consistency of parse selection is more relevant than parsing accuracy, we consider worth sharing.

The presented results may also be viewed as a step forward toward making deep linguistic grammars useful for relation extraction, whereas up to now most minimally supervised approaches to RE have employed shallower robust parsers. The hope behind these attempts is to improve precision without losing too much recall. After reclaiming recall through our parse reranking, next steps in this line of research will be dedicated to balancing off the deficits in coverage by data-driven lexicon extension in the spirit of (Zhang et al., 2010) and by exploiting the chart for partial parses involving the relevant types of named entities. Furthermore, the approach of (Dridan and Baldwin, 2010) to learning a parse selection model in an unsupervised way by utilizing the constraints of HSPG grammars might also be interesting for domain adaptive parse selection for relation extraction. At some point we may then be in a position to conduct a fair empirical comparison between deep-linguistic parsing with hand-crafted grammars on the one hand and purely statistical parsing on the other. An error analysis may then indicate the chances for hybrid approaches. However, before targeting these medium-term goals we plan to investigate whether our approach can also be applied to other parsers with inherent generic parse ranking and whether the set of learned RE rules with their confidence values can be directly used as features in the statistical parse disambiguation models instead of in the post-processing step by a separate re-ranker.

Acknowledgements

This research was conducted in the context of the German DFG Cluster of Excellence on Multimodal Computing and Interaction (M2CI), projects Theseus Alexandria and Alexandria for Media (funded by the German Federal Ministry of Economy and Technology, contract 01MQ07016), and project TAKE (funded by the German Federal Ministry of Education and Research, contract 01IW08003). Many thanks go to Peter Adolphs and Dan Flickinger for providing us the treebank of the Nobel Prize award corpus.

References

Eugene Agichtein and Luis Gravano. 2000. Snowball: Extracting relations from large plain-text collections. In *Proceedings of the 5th ACM International Conference DL'00*, San Antonio, TX, June.

Sergey Brin. 1998. Extracting patterns and relations from the world wide web. In *WebDB Workshop at EDBT 98*.

Eugene Charniak and Mark Johnson. 2005. Coarse-to-fine n-best parsing and maxent discriminative reranking. In *Proceedings of ACL 05*, pages 173–180, Ann Arbor, Michigan, June. Association for Computational Linguistics.

Michael Collins. 2002. Ranking algorithms for named-entity extraction: Boosting and the voted perceptron. In *Proceedings of ACL '02*.

Marie-Catherine de Marneffe and Christopher D. Manning. 2008. The stanford typed dependencies representation. In *Proceedings of the workshop on Cross-Framework and Cross-Domain Parser Evaluation at COLING08*, Manchester, UK.

Rebecca Dridan and Timothy Baldwin. 2010. Unsupervised parse selection for hpsg. In *Proceedings of the 2010 Conference on Empirical Methods in Natural Language Processing*, EMNLP '10, pages 694–704, Stroudsburg, PA, USA. Association for Computational Linguistics.

Witold Drozdzynski, Hans-Ulrich Krieger, Jakub Piskorski, Ulrich Schäfer, and Feiyu Xu. 2004. Shallow processing with unification and typed feature structures — foundations and applications. *Künstliche Intelligenz*, 1.

Jenny Rose Finkel and Christopher D. Manning. 2010. Hierarchical joint learning: Improving joint parsing and named entity recognition with non-jointly labeled data. In *Proceedings of ACL '10*, pages 720–728, Uppsala, Sweden.

Dan Flickinger. 2000. On building a more efficient grammar by exploiting types. *Natural Language Engineering*, 6(1):15–28.

Ruifang Ge and Raymond J Mooney. 2006. Discriminative reranking for semantic parsing. In

Proceedings of COLING and ACL 06), pages 263–270. Association for Computational Linguistics.

Mark A. Greenwood and Mark Stevenson. 2006. Improving semi-supervised acquisition of relation extraction patterns. In *Proceedings of the Workshop on Information Extraction Beyond The Document*, pages 29–35, Sydney, Australia, July. Association for Computational Linguistics.

Ralph Grishman and Beth Sundheim. 1996. Message understanding conference - 6: A brief history. In *Proceedings of COLING 96*, Copenhagen, June.

Tadayoshi Hara, Yusuke Miyao, and Jun'ichi Tsujii. 2005. Adapting a probabilistic disambiguation model of an HPSG parser to a new domain. In *Proceedings of IJCNLP 05*.

Tadayoshi Hara, Yusuke Miyao, and Jun'ichi Tsujii. 2007. Evaluating impact of re-training a lexical disambiguation model on domain adaptation of an hpsg parser. In *Proceedings of the Tenth International Conference on Parsing Technologies*, pages 11–22, Prague, Czech Republic, June. Association for Computational Linguistics.

Dekan Lin. 1998. Dependency-based evaluation of MINIPAR. *Workshop on the Evaluation of Parsing Systems*.

David McClosky, Eugene Charniak, and Mark Johnson. 2006. Reranking and self-training for parser adaptation. In *Proceedings of COLING and ACL 06*, pages 337–344, Sydney, Australia.

David McClosky, Eugene Charniak, and Mark Johnson. 2010. Automatic domain adaptation for parsing. In *Proceedings of HLT and NAACL '10*, pages 28–36, Los Angeles, California, June. Association for Computational Linguistics.

Makoto Miwa, Sampo Pyysalo, Tadayoshi Hara, and Jun'ichi Tsujii. 2010. A comparative study of syntactic parsers for event extraction. In *Proceedings of the 2010 Workshop on Biomedical Natural Language Processing*, pages 37–45, Uppsala, Sweden, July. Association for Computational Linguistics.

Ion Muslea. 1999. Extraction patterns for information extraction tasks: A survey. In *AAAI Workshop on Machine Learning for Information Extraction*, Orlando, Florida, July.

Stephan Oepen, Kristina Toutanova, Stuart Shieber, Christopher Manning, Dan Flickinger, and Thorsten Brants. 2002. The LinGO Redwoods treebank: motivation and preliminary applications. In *Proceedings of COLING 2002: The 17th International Conference on Computational Linguistics: Project Notes*, Taipei, Taiwan.

Barbara Plank and Gertjan van Noord. 2010. Grammar-driven versus data-driven: Which parsing system is more affected by domain shifts? In *Proceedings of the 2010 Workshop on NLP and Linguistics: Finding the Common Ground*, Uppsala, Sweden, July.

Barbara Plank. 2009. A comparison of structural correspondence learning and self-training for discriminative parse selection. In *Proceedings of the NAACL HLT 2009 Workshop on Semi-supervised Learning for Natural Language Processing*, pages 37–42, Boulder, Colorado, June. Association for Computational Linguistics.

Carl J. Pollard and Ivan A. Sag. 1994. *Head-Driven Phrase Structure Grammar*. University of Chicago Press, Chicago, USA.

Laura Rimell and Stephen Clark. 2008. Adapting a lexicalized-grammar parser to contrasting domains. In *Proceedings of EMNLP 08*, pages 475–484, Honolulu, Hawaii, October. Association for Computational Linguistics.

K. Sudo, S. Sekine, and R. Grishman. 2003. An improved extraction pattern representation model for automatic IE pattern acquisition. *Proceedings of ACL 2003*.

Kristina Toutanova, Aria Haghighi, and Christopher D. Manning. 2005a. Joint learning improves semantic role labeling. In *Proceedings of ACL 05*, page 589 596. Association for Computational Linguistics.

Kristina Toutanova, Christoper D. Manning, Dan Flickinger, and Stephan Oepen. 2005b. Stochastic HPSG parse selection using the Redwoods corpus. *Journal of Research on Language and Computation*, 3(1):83–105.

Hans Uszkoreit, Feiyu Xu, and Hong Li. 2009. Analysis and improvement of minimally supervised machine learning for relation extraction. In *14th International Conference on Applications of Natural Language to Information Systems*. Springer.

Feiyu Xu, Hans Uszkoreit, and Hong Li. 2007. A seed-driven bottom-up machine learning framework for extracting relations of various complexity. In *Proceedings of ACL 2007*, Prague, Czech Republic, 6.

Feiyu Xu, Hans Uszkoreit, Sebastian Krause, and Hong Li. 2010. Boosting relation extraction with limited closed-world knowledge. In *Proceedings of COLING '10, Poster Session*. Association for Computational Linguistics.

Feiyu Xu. 2007. *Bootstrapping Relation Extraction from Semantic Seeds*. Phd-thesis, Saarland University.

Roman Yangarber. 2001. *Scenarion Customization for Information Extraction*. Dissertation, Department of Computer Science, New York University, New York, USA.

Yi Zhang and Rui Wang. 2009. Cross-domain dependency parsing using a deep linguistic grammar. In *Proceedings of the Joint Conference ACL and AFNLP 09*, Suntec, Singapore, August.

Yi Zhang, Stephan Oepen, and John Carroll. 2007. Efficiency in unification-based N-best parsing. In *Proceedings of the 10th International Conference on Parsing Technologies (IWPT 2007)*, pages 48–59, Prague, Czech.

Yi Zhang, Timothy Baldwin, Valia Kordoni, David Martinez, and Jeremy Nicholson. 2010. Chart mining-based lexical acquisition with precision grammars. In *Proceedings of HLT and NAACL '10*, HLT '10, pages 10–18, Stroudsburg, PA, USA. Association for Computational Linguistics.

Simple Semi-Supervised Learning for Prepositional Phrase Attachment

Gregory F. Coppola, Alexandra Birch, Tejaswini Deoskar and Mark Steedman
School of Informatics
University of Edinburgh
Edinburgh, EH8 9AB, UK
g.f.coppola@sms.ed.ac.uk
{abmayne, tdeoskar, steedman}@inf.ed.ac.uk

Abstract

Prepositional phrase attachment is an important subproblem of parsing, performance on which suffers from limited availability of labelled data. We present a semi-supervised approach. We show that a discriminative lexical model trained from labelled data, and a generative lexical model learned via Expectation Maximization from unlabelled data can be combined in a product model to yield a PP-attachment model which is better than either is alone, and which outperforms the modern parser of Petrov and Klein (2007) by a significant margin. We show that, when learning from unlabelled data, it can be beneficial to model the generation of modifiers of a head collectively, rather than individually. Finally, we suggest that our pair of models will be interesting to combine using new techniques for discriminatively constraining EM.

1 Introduction

Labelled data for NLP tasks will always be in short supply. Thus, a statistical parser trained with labelled data alone will always be troubled by unseen events—primarily when parsing out-of-domain data, or when faced with rare events from in-domain data. Thus, a major focus of current work is the use of cheap, abundant *unlabelled data* to improve state-of-the-art parser performance.

We focus on an important sub-problem of parsing—prepositional phrase attachment—and demonstrate a successful semi-supervised learning strategy. We show that, using a mix of labelled and unlabelled data we can improve *both* the in-domain and out-of-domain performance of a prepositional phrase attachment classifier.

Prepositional phrase attachment, for us, is the decision as to which heads a series of prepositional phrases of the form [$_{\text{PP}}$ prep NP] modify, as in, e.g.,

He ate a salad [$_{\text{PP}}$ with a fork] [$_{\text{PP}}$ of plastic]

Prepositional phrase attachment is an important sub-problem of parsing in and of itself. Structural heuristics perform poorly (cf., Collins and Brooks, 1995), and so lexical knowledge is crucial.

Moreover, the highly lexicalized nature of prepositional phrase attachment makes it a kind of microcosm of the general problem of learning dependency structure, and so acts as a computationally less-demanding testing ground on which to try out learning techniques. We have endeavoured to approach the problem with a strategy that might be likely to generalize: a mix of generative and discriminative lexical models, trained using techniques that have worked for parsers.

The main contributions of this paper are:

- We compare the performance on the prepositional phrase attachment task of natural lexicalized dependency parsing strategies, to the popular semi-lexicalized model of Petrov and Klein (2007), and show that a lexical is more effective for this problem.

- We show that a discriminative lexical model trained from labelled data and a generative lexical model learned through Expectation Maximization on unlabelled data can perform better in a *product model* than either does alone, yielding a significant improvement over our baseline reference, the parser of Petrov and Klein (2007).

- We show that, in this case, when learning from unlabelled data, a strategy of generating all modifiers of a head *collectively* works better than generating them individually.

2 Prior Work

Work on the topic of prepositional phrase attachment typically views the problem as a binary classification task. Given a 4-tuple,

$$\langle \text{verb}, \text{noun}_1, \text{prep}, \text{noun}_2 \rangle$$

the task is to decide whether the attachment of the $[_{PP}$ prep NP$]$ prepositional phrase characterized by $\langle$prep, noun$_2\rangle$ is to verb or to noun$_1$.

Human performance on this prepositional phrase attachment task has been estimated by Ratnaparkhi et al. (1994). They found that treebanking experts given the 4-tuple binary decision task choose the correct attachment 88.2% of the time. And, when then given the full context for the same examples, they choose the "correct" attachment (i.e. the same attachment that is given by the Penn Treebank) 93.2% of the time.

Approaches to training from labelled data include rule-based (Brill and Resnik, 1994), maximum-entropy (Ratnaparkhi et al., 1994), and a generative "backed-off" model (Collins and Brooks, 1995).

The state-of-the-art is an approach by Stetina and Nagao (1997). They replace each noun and verb by a WordNet sense using a custom word sense disambiguation algorithm. Then, they train a decision tree on labelled WSJ data. Their method achieves essentially a human level of accuracy on this task: 88.1%. Toutanova et al. (2004) achieve a comparable result with a method that integrates word-sense disambiguation into the generative attachment model.

There is also a variety of work that makes use of unlabelled data to learn prepositional phrase attachment. An early example in this category is Hindle and Rooth (1991). They estimate the probability that a given preposition modifies a given head using an iterative process with heterogeneous steps. Ratnaparkhi (1998) uses deterministic heuristics.

The state-of-the-art in this area is due to Pantel and Lin (2000). They, use a homespun iterative algorithm learning algorithm which bears a resemblance to EM, but it does not seem to learn a generative model. One interesting feature of this approach is that the attachment decision for a given word is allowed to make use of the statistics collected for *similar words*, which helps to the sparsity that occurs even in a large, unlabelled corpus. Their performance on the binary classification task is 84.5%.

We are aware of one case that has used a mix of labelled and unlabelled data: Volk (2002) uses a back-off strategy in which information from labelled data is used when conclusive, and information from unlabelled data otherwise. Performance on the same task on a NEGRA-based data set lags behind the others, at 81.0%.

Finally, Atterer and Schütze (2007) argue that an experimental setup that evaluates a prepositional phrase attachment with possible attachments given by an "oracle," rather than an actual parser, may make the problem appear easier than it really is. This is a good point. But, for the purposes of comparing learning techniques, we feel that the typical oracle task is better suited, as it avoids introducing the noise of parser mistakes.

3 Background

3.1 The Prediction Task

We treat prepositional phrase attachment as a structured prediction task, rather than as a binary decision. The input to the prediction procedure will be a (prepositional phrase) *attachment problem*, a string matching either the regular expression (1) or (2).

(1) verb baseNP (prep baseNP)*

(2) baseNP (prep baseNP)*

For example, some attachment problems are:

(3) sought man from Germany with expertise

(4) man from Germany with expertise

Though not indicated above, we assume that POS tags are given as part of the problem, and need not be predicted.

Our goal is to create a prediction procedure which, given an attachment problem, $\mathbf{x}$, will return a *derivation*, $\mathbf{d}$, which is a parse for $\mathbf{x}$ using the following mini CFG grammar whose initial symbol is ROOT:

(5) a. ROOT $\rightarrow$ VP
b. ROOT $\rightarrow$ NP
c. VP $\rightarrow$ verb$_H$ NP PP*
d. NP $\rightarrow$ baseNP$_H$ PP*
e. PP $\rightarrow$ prep$_H$ NP

The head of each XP is indicated with a subscripted H. All siblings to a head are called its *modifiers*.

Given a full parse tree in the style of Marcus et al. (1993), *attachment problem-derivation* pairs were extracted using a TGrep-like functional program, which is described in Appendix A.[1]

3.2 Scoring Performance

When evaluating a prediction procedure, we will give it a series of attachment problems and ask for the derivations. In most cases, the score we will focus on is what we can call the *binary decision score*, i.e., the percentage of the time in which the first prepositional phrase following a verb–direct-object pair is attached correctly. In this case, we are reporting the same score as is typically reported on this task, so as to avoid introducing a new metric.

To be clear, then, when scoring, in this way,

$$[_{\text{VP}} \text{ set } [_{\text{NP}} \text{ rate } [_{\text{PP}} \text{ on } [_{\text{NP}} \text{ refund}]] \,] \, [_{\text{PP}} \text{ at } [_{\text{NP}} \text{ 5 percent}]]]]$$

we only ask where $[_{\text{PP}}$ on $[_{\text{NP}}$ refund$]]$ attaches, and ignore the attachment decision of $[_{\text{PP}}$ at $[_{\text{NP}}$ 5 percent$]]$.

One might thus ask what the point of bothering with the whole derivation is if we are typically only intending to score a binary decision. Well, our model in §5.2 makes each attachment decision independently, and in this example from the WSJ development test set, incorrectly attaches both *on refund* and *at 5 percent* to the verb. In contrast, our model of §5.3 attaches prepositional phrases *collectively*, and rejects the derivation where *on refund* and *at 5 percent* both modify *set*. Thus, though we only score one decision in a derivation, that decision can be influenced by others, and so it does make a difference to work at the level of derivations.

3.3 Data Sets

The traditional semi-supervised learning task involves learning from two sets. The first is a set of pairs, $\{(\mathbf{x}_i, \mathbf{d}_i)\}$, of data points along with their labels. The second is a (typically much larger) set of data points alone, $\{\mathbf{x}_j\}$ (i.e. without labels). In our case, the data points are attachment problems and the labels, which are structured, are derivations.

Our experiment is interested in performance across domains. Thus, we also distinguish between in-domain labelled data, some of which we will allow ourselves to use to train model parameters, and out-of-domain labelled data, which we will not use to train model parameters.[2]

Our source of labelled data is the Penn Treebank (Marcus et al., 1993). We use sections 0-22 of the WSJ portion of the Penn Treebank for training and development and sections $23, 24$ are left for final evaluation. We variously use i) sections 2-21 as labelled training data, with sections $0, 1, 22$ as a development test set, or ii) sections $0, 1, 5$-22 as labelled data with sections 2-4 as held-out set for parameter tuning.

We split up the Brown portion of the treebank similarly to Gildea (2001)—i.e. we split it into 10 sections such that the s'th sentence is assigned to section $s \mod 10$. We then use sections 0-2 development test set, 4-6 for tuning, and sections 7-9 are left for final evaluation. Our divisions of the Penn Treebank are chosen to resemble the canonical training-test split for parsing, but we use more sections for testing, to obtain more reliable test scores, as there are far fewer decisions to test on in each section in our task, when compared to parsing.

Our source of unlabelled data is the New York Times portion of the GigaWord corpus (Graff et al., 2005). These sentences are parsed automatically using the generative semi-lexicalized parser of Petrov and Klein (2007). We did some filtering of these unlabelled sentences, removing sentences with quotations (as quoted material can be ungrammatical) and sentences over 40 words in length (to increase the chance that each automatic parse used was reasonable).

We use these automatically extracted parses only to identify *attachment problems* $(\mathbf{x})$, which we will then treat as unlabelled. That is, while there is possibly information in the *derivations* (the $\mathbf{d}$) that the parser is coming up with, we did not use this.

In terms of size, our WSJ2-21 set has $29,750$ examples. The GigaWord set has $8,038,001$ examples.

[1] Our data sets extracted from the Penn Treebank will be available on request to those with the relevant license(s) to use Penn Treebank data.

[2] However, we do appeal to the labels of a portion of the out-of-domain Brown data once, in order to fix a single experimental parameter, which is the number of iterations of EM to run on the unlabelled data, cf. note 6.

3.4 Baseline

Much past work has tested on the 4-tuple, binary decision data set of Ratnaparkhi et al. (1994). This data does not have all of the information required by our approach, and is based on a preliminary version of the Penn Treebank (version 0.75), which is incomplete and difficult to work with. Thus, we could not compare our work directly with past work.

In order to evaluate our performance, then, we will compare our model against the performance on prepositional phrase attachment of the Berkeley parser (Petrov and Klein, 2007), which is popular, readily available, and essentially state-of-art among supervised parsing methods. And, as we said, this is precisely the technology that we use to process unlabelled data, so it makes sense that our model should improve upon this in order to be of any use.

So, we need to evaluate the prepositional phrase attachment performance of the Berkeley parser. What we do is parse the test sections of the Penn Treebank using this parser (which is trained on WSJ2-21). We run our functional program to extract problem-derivation pairs from the automatic parse. Suppose we extract the pair $(\mathbf{d}_a, \mathbf{x}_a)$ from the automatic parse. We compare this to the gold tree. If the gold tree contains the pair $(\mathbf{d}_g, \mathbf{x}_g)$, and $\mathbf{x}_a = \mathbf{x}_g$, then we score $\mathbf{d}_a$ with respect to $\mathbf{d}_g$. Otherwise, we do not score $\mathbf{d}_a$.

This means the parser is not penalized for failing to identify attachment problems in the gold parse. And, this should be a favourable comparison for the parser as it is evaluated on the examples it knows most about, i.e. those for which it can identify the location of an attachment problem.

We supply the parser with gold POS tags to maximize the chance that it will find each attachment problem. In this way, we were able to assess the performance of the Berkeley parser on $\frac{3184}{3475} = 91.6\%$ of the test examples in the WSJ set, and $\frac{3091}{3509} = 88\%$ in the Brown (both dev. test and final test). Our models are tested on all examples.

An important parameter for the Berkeley parser is the number of *split-merge iterations* done during training (cf. Petrov and Klein, 2007). The documentation suggests 6 is better for parsing the WSJ, while 5 is better for parsing other English. We tried both. The results are shown in Table 1. We will use whichever parameterization did better on each data set as the baseline on that data set.[3]

	WSJ		Brown	
Parser	Dev.	Test	Dev.	Test
Berkeley 5 SM	**85.3**	**83.0**	82.4	81.1
Berkeley 6 SM	84.6	**83.0**	**83.3**	**82.7**

Table 1: Performance of the Berkeley parser on the prepositional phrase attachment task. The best scores on each data set will be our baseline.

3.5 Reduction of Open-Class Words

In all experiments, all nouns and verbs were replaced by more general forms. If applicable, nouns were replaced by their NER label, either *person*, *place* or *organization*, using the NER classifier of Finkel et al. (2005). All numeral strings of two or four digits were replaced with a symbol representing *year*, and all other numeral strings were replaced with a symbol representing *numeric value*.

A word not reduced in either of these ways was replaced by its stem using the stemmer designed by Minnen et al. (2001).[4]

Finally, this reduced form is paired with the category of the word $c \in \{\text{NOUN}, \text{VERB}\}$ to distinguish uses of words that can either be nouns or verbs. We find that these reductions improve performance slightly and also reduce the size of the generative probability table.

4 A Discriminative Model from Labelled Data

4.1 The Model

As noted, we have access to one set $\{(\mathbf{x}_i, \mathbf{d}_i)\}$ of labelled examples. We begin by discriminatively training two conditional models on this set.

Our model uses two types of features: i) structural, and ii) lexical.

The structural features exploit two characteristics of prepositional phrase attachment that are often noted in the literature. First, a prepositional phrase headed by the preposition *of* almost always attaches to the nearest available attachment site to its left. So, one feature fires whenever this is

[3]The performance of this parser depends on a random seed used to initialize the training parser. Our 6-iteration grammar was downloaded from the authors' web site. Our 5-iteration grammar is the one that resulted from our first run of the training process.

[4]We use the Java reimplementation in the Stanford NLP API, http://nlp.stanford.edu/software/index.shtml.

not the case. Second, prepositional phrases almost never attach to pronouns. So, another feature fires whenever some prepositional phrase attaches to a pronoun.

The first model, denoted $p_{\mathbf{D}_1}(\mathbf{d} \mid \mathbf{x}; \theta_{\mathbf{D}_1})$, uses these and lexical features of the form

$$\langle \mathbf{head}, \mathbf{prep} \rangle$$

Here, **head** is either a noun or a verb, and **prep** is a preposition. The feature $\langle \mathbf{head}, \mathbf{prep} \rangle$ is active in derivation $\mathbf{d}$ iff (a prepositional phrase headed by) **prep** modifies **head** in $\mathbf{d}$.

Our second model, $p_{\mathbf{D}_2}(\mathbf{d} \mid \mathbf{x}; \theta_{\mathbf{D}_2})$, has all features mentioned above, and also those of the form

$$\langle \mathbf{head}, \mathbf{prep}, \mathbf{noun}_{\text{inside}} \rangle$$

Here, **head** and **prep** are as before, and $\mathbf{noun}_{\text{inside}}$ is the head of the noun phrase inside the prepositional phrase headed by **prep**.

For example, in

$$[_{\text{NP}} \text{ salad } [_{\text{PP}} \text{ with } [_{\text{NP}} \text{ dressing}]]]$$

The active features are ⟨salad, with⟩ and ⟨salad, with, dressing⟩.

This latter type of feature represents straightforward specialization of the concept used by higher-order dependencies for parsing, especially Carreras (2007), to the problem of prepositional phrases.

Our estimates of $\theta_{\mathbf{D}_1}$ and $\theta_{\mathbf{D}_2}$ are arrived at using structured perceptron training (Collins, 2002). The models trained on all examples in our training section (i.e. those of type NP and of type VP). We pick the number of perceptron training iterations for each model by maximizing performance on a held-out set, using our parameter tuning split described in §3.3. We only use feature instances that have occurred at least twice in training.

If $\Phi(\mathbf{x}, \mathbf{d})$ is a feature vector characterizing $(\mathbf{x}, \mathbf{d})$, the perceptron algorithm will output a parameter vector $\theta_{\mathbf{D}_i}$, and the "score" assigned to a pair $(\mathbf{x}, \mathbf{d})$ under this interpretation will be $\theta_{\mathbf{D}_i} \cdot \Phi(\mathbf{x}, \mathbf{d})$, with the predicted derivation being the $\mathbf{d}$ with the highest score (in the case of any tie, we always choose attachment to the verb).

As we have suggested, we are interested in a conditional probability for $\mathbf{d}$ given $\mathbf{x}$, rather than just a linear "score". This is for use in a future section (i.e. §6). The natural way to achieve this is to interpret $\theta_{\mathbf{D}_i}$ as the parameters for a maximum entropy model, i.e.

$$p_{\mathbf{D}_i}(\mathbf{d} \mid \mathbf{x}; \theta_{\mathbf{D}_i}) = \frac{\exp\{\theta_{\mathbf{D}_i} \cdot \Phi(\mathbf{x}, \mathbf{d})\}}{\sum_{\mathbf{d}'} \exp\{\theta_{\mathbf{D}_i} \cdot \Phi(\mathbf{x}, \mathbf{d}')\}}$$

Fortunately, we will see that we never need actually compute the normalizing term in the denominator.

	WSJ		Brown	
Classifier	Dev.	Test	Dev.	Test
$p_{\mathbf{D}_2}$ (2nd-order)	**87.4**	**86.0**	**84.7**	**83.9**
$p_{\mathbf{D}_1}$ (1st-order)	86.2	**86.0**	**84.7**	83.0
Baseline	85.3	83.0	83.3	82.7

Table 2: Performance of the two discriminative classifiers.

4.2 Results

The performance of this model both in- and out-of-domain are shown in Table 2, along with the performance of the baseline Berkeley parser.

The results should be of interest to those interested the use of lexical features for parsing. The models that use lexical features outperform the semi-lexical model of Petrov and Klein (2007). Prepositional phrase attachment may be one area where lexicalized models are especially important.

We also see that the use of second-order features buys extra performance on some data sets, but not on others. A look at the dev. sets show that second-order features were active in 9 of the first 60 decisions in the WSJ, but in 0 of the first 60 in Brown. We speculate that use of word senses as features, taking after Stetina and Nagao (1997), might result in better generality across domains, but leave this to future work.

5 Two Generative Models Trained on Unlabelled Data

5.1 Common Model Structure

We now want to make use of our unlabelled data, $\{\mathbf{x}_j\}$. For this purpose, we turn to the Expectation Maximization algorithm (Dempster et al., 1977). Thus, we will estimate generative models of the data, each of the form $p_{\mathbf{G}_*}(\mathbf{x}, \mathbf{d}; \theta_{\mathbf{G}})$.

Our discriminatively trained classifier made use of both structural and lexical features. Our strategy will be to use our unlabelled examples to estimate just the *lexical* parameters.

It would seem impossible to expect that we could learn the structural features, e.g., that prepositional phrases do not attach to pronouns from unlabelled data. Nor do we need to do this, as this constraint can be encoded with little effort. What we do want to be able to estimate from unlabelled data is the strength of lexical relationships in arbitrary domains, which we could not hope to encode manually.

So, the question arises as to how to incorporate our knowledge of the structural constraints into the problem, and to constrain the EM process using these. Probably the most powerful and general purpose way to do this would be to use one of the new variants of EM that allows the specification of expectations for feature counts, such as Ganchev et al. (2010) or Druck and McCallum (2010). In this case we could specify that, e.g., we expect the average number of times we see a prepositional phrase attach to a pronoun to be 0, and the modified EM process would be encouraged or forced to converge to a solution that respects this expectation. This strategy is very general, but also much more expensive than ordinary EM, as each E-step involves an expensive optimization problem.

Here, we get by with a simpler, and much more computationally inexpensive strategy.

The structural constraints we have made use of are very robust. In our WSJ sections $2-21$, *of*-headed PPs attach to the nearest non-pronoun to their left in about 98.6% of cases. And, in 99.6% of cases, pronouns have nothing attaching to them.

Thus, we are willing to take a deterministic stance: we will assign 0 probability mass to derivations that violate our structural constraints. Let AD, intuitively the set of "admissible derivations," be the set of derivations that have: i) no attachment to a pronoun, unless there is no other choice, and ii) every *of*-pp attaching to its nearest available non-pronoun site, if it has one.

Let $\mathbf{1}_{d \in AD}$ be an indicator function, which is equal to 1 if $d \in AD$, and 0 otherwise. Then, the strategy is to let

$$p_{\mathbf{G}_*}(\mathbf{x}, \mathbf{d}) = p_{\mathbf{G}_*}(\mathbf{x}, \mathbf{d} \mid \mathbf{1}_{d \in AD}) \cdot \mathbf{1}_{d \in AD}$$

and to estimate $p_{\mathbf{G}_*}(\mathbf{x}, \mathbf{d} \mid \mathbf{1}_{d \in AD})$ from unlabelled data. The result is easily seen to be a probability distribution in which all weight is given to derivations in AD.

We will look at two model structures. In both cases, the data trained on will include all examples of type VP and NP from our GigaWord set. Examples with unambiguous attachment, such as [NP place [PP at table]], are included, so that parameters chosen must maximize likelihood over these examples as well. Also note that, since the number of derivations is never unmanageable, when summing over derivations, we do so exhaustively rather than use some form of dynamic programming such as, e.g., the inside-outside algorithm.

We will now look at two different ways to structure a model for $p_{\mathbf{G}_*}(\mathbf{x}, \mathbf{d} \mid \mathbf{1}_{d \in AD})$.

5.2 Individual Dependent Generation

The first model uses the same lexical features as our first-order discriminative model. We model a derivation as a series of sub-events, which will be draws from a pair of random variables, $(\mathbf{head}, \mathbf{prep})$. Intuitively, this corresponds to the event *the phrase headed by* $\mathbf{head}$ *generates a modifier headed by* $\mathbf{prep}$. Following the reasoning of Collins (1999, p. 46), we imagine that each head's final modifier is a special STOP symbol.

Thus, the derivation

(6) [VP ate [NP salad] [PP with [NPfork]]]

is modeled as the four events (eat, with), (eat, STOP), (salad, STOP), (fork, STOP).

Then, the probability of a problem-derivation pair, conditioned on $\mathbf{1}_{d \in AD}$, is estimated as

$$p_{\mathbf{G}_{Ind}}(\mathbf{x}, \mathbf{d} \mid \mathbf{1}_{d \in AD}; \theta_{\mathbf{G}_{Ind}}) = \prod_{h \in heads(\mathbf{d})} \prod_{p \in deps(\mathbf{head})} p_{\mathbf{G}_{Ind}}(\mathbf{prep} \mid \mathbf{head}; \theta_{\mathbf{G}_{Ind}})$$

Here $heads(\mathbf{d})$ is the set of head of NP and VP phrases in $\mathbf{d}$, and $deps(\mathbf{head})$ is the list of modifiers of $\mathbf{head}$ in $\mathbf{d}$, including the STOP symbol.

Even though our unlabelled training set was large, there were still nouns and verbs seen during test that were not seen during training. Thus, we created a GENERIC head for each category (one for VERB and one for NOUN). Each time an event $(\mathbf{head}, \mathbf{prep})$ was counted, we would also count $(\text{GENERIC}_{type(\mathbf{head})}, \mathbf{prep})$, where $type(\mathbf{head}) \in \{\text{VERB}, \text{NOUN}\}$. Thus, the generic head represents a kind of "average head." Then, if we needed the probability for some event $(\mathbf{head}', \mathbf{prep}')$ during test, and $\mathbf{head}'$ had not been seen during training, we would back off to the event $(\text{GENERIC}_{type(\mathbf{head}')}, \mathbf{prep}')$.

5.3 Collective Dependent Generation

The next strategy we try is to generate the collection of dependents for a head $\mathbf{head}$ *as a whole*. In particular, we generate each head's *multi-set* of dependents.[5]

In this case, if a verb has a direct object, the direct object is represented in the multi-set of the verbs modifiers. But, rather than put the word itself, each direct object is represented by a special symbol, DO.

So, in this model, (6) is modeled as three events, (eat, $\{\text{DO}, with\}$), (salad, $\{\}$), and (fork, $\{\}$).

Then, if $deps_{\mathbf{d}}(\mathbf{head})$ is the multi-set of modifiers of $\mathbf{head}$ in $\mathbf{d}$, our estimate of the probability of the problem-derivation pair, conditioned on $\mathbf{1}_{d \in AD}$, is

$$p_{\mathbf{G}_{Col}}(\mathbf{x}, \mathbf{d} \mid \mathbf{1}_{d \in AD}; \theta_{\mathbf{G}_{Col}}) = \prod_{\mathbf{head} \in heads(\mathbf{d})} p_{\mathbf{G}_{Col}}(deps_{\mathbf{d}}(\mathbf{head}) \mid \mathbf{head}; \theta_{\mathbf{G}_{Col}})$$

Unseen heads are handled in the same manner as in §5.2.

5.4 Initializing and Terminating the EM Process

We consider two cases for initializing the EM process. In one case, our initial guess at the posterior distribution is the uniform distribution: all derivations for a given $\mathbf{x}$ that are in AD are considered equally likely, with small random perturbations to break any symmetry (we found there to be essentially no difference from run to run).

In the second case, we make better use of our labelled data, and begin with the conditional distribution given by $p_{\mathbf{D}_1}$, the model with only first-order features, that we had estimated discriminatively from labelled data, i.e.

$$p_{\mathbf{G}_*}(\mathbf{d}|\mathbf{x}, \mathbf{1}_{d \in AD}; \emptyset) = p_{\mathbf{D}_1}(\mathbf{d}|\mathbf{x}; \theta_{\mathbf{D}_1})$$

Given that running EM to convergence can overfit the training data, to the detriment of performance (cf., Liang and Klein (2009)), we chose to run EM for a fixed number of iterations, with the number of iterations determined using a tuning test set. We picked the number of iterations to maximize performance of the best performing model (which turned out to be the collective dependent generation initialized with $p_{\mathbf{D}_1}$) on a Brown tuning set, sections 4-6.[6] The optimal number of iterations was found to be 4.

5.5 Results

The performance of these two model structures, under the two kinds of initialization methods, is shown in Table 3. Performance on the dev. test sets is plotted versus the number of iterations of the EM procedure. The fourth row is highlighted as this was determined to be the optimal number of iterations in the manner just described.

We see that the best performing method is that which generates the (multi-set of the) modifiers simultaneously, while initializing using the conditional distribution estimated from labelled data. It is also interesting to note that, models initialized with $p_{\mathbf{D}_1}$ get progressively better at parsing Brown but worse at parsing WSJ. In fact, after 6 iterations, performance at parsing the WSJ is similar for both models initialized with $p_{\mathbf{D}_1}$ and those initialized with the uniform distribution. This suggests to us that the information that we have from our valuable labelled data is being lost, and leads us to think that it may be profitable to incorporate this information more forcefully, using techniques for constraining EM with information, such as those of Ganchev et al. (2010) and Druck and McCallum (2010) already mentioned.

However, though the model may be "losing" information relevant to parsing the WSJ, the noteworthy aspect is that it ends up being able to parse the Brown data better than our discriminatively trained parsers (both with accuracy of 84.7 on Brown dev. test), and thus makes a contribution to overall parsing accuracy.

Note that we show the performance of the various models on the development test set only here. We report results on a held-out set in the next section.

[5] We also experimented with lists and sets, finding multisets to work slightly better. To avoid losing the focus of this discussion, we will only discuss multi-sets.

[6] In this case, we are using the labels from our out-of-domain data during training. We feel that this is legitimate because these are only used to tune a single experimental parameter, the number of EM iterations. Tuning a single parameter requires only a small number of examples, that does not necessarily grow with the number of lexical parameters being estimated. It is the fact that we can learn lexical model parameters from unlabelled data that will ultimately save us from having to label the entire web.

	Initialized with $p_{\mathbf{D}_1}(\mathbf{d} \mid \mathbf{x}; \theta_{\mathbf{D}_1})$				Initialized to uniform distr.			
	Independent		Collective		Independent		Collective	
EM Its.	WSJ	Brown	WSJ	Brown	WSJ	Brown	WSJ	Brown
1	85.7	83.9	86.3	85.8	82.0	83.4	81.6	84.5
2	84.2	84.9	84.9	85.7	82.4	84.4	82.7	85.2
3	83.3	84.5	84.7	86.0	82.8	84.6	82.5	85.1
4	83.0	84.6	83.8	86.3	82.9	84.6	82.5	85.4
5	82.9	84.6	83.5	86.0	82.9	84.7	82.6	85.7
6	82.8	84.6	82.8	86.0	82.9	84.7	82.4	85.8

Table 3: Performance of the two generative models. Variables are: i) the model learned, independent vs. collective modifier generation (§5.2, 5.3), ii) the intial guess at a conditional distribution for hidden variables (§5.4), and iii) the number of iterations of EM. Score is the binary decision score (cf. §3.2).

6 A Combination of Models

6.1 The Combination

We now have two models of prepositional phrase attachment. One is estimated from labelled data, and one from unlabelled data. Each performs well in isolation. But, we find that the combination of the two in a *logarithmic opinion pool* framework works better than either does alone.

With roots in Bordley (1982), a logarithmic opinion pool, as defined in Smith et al. (2005), has the form

$$p_{\mathbf{lop}}(\mathbf{d}|\mathbf{x}) = \frac{1}{Z_{\mathbf{lop}}} \prod_{\alpha} p_{\alpha}(\mathbf{d}|\mathbf{x})^{w_a}$$

In related work, Hinton (1999) describes a *product of experts*, i.e. multiple models trained to work together, so that an unweighted product, will be sensible. Petrov (2010) has success with the unweighted product of the scores of several similar parsing models. Smith et al. (2005) adjust weights by maximizing the likelihood of a labelled dataset.

Here, we weight the component models so as to maximize performance on a held out set. Where i is either 1 or 2, let

$$p_{\mathbf{lop},i}(\mathbf{d} \mid \mathbf{x}; \theta_{\mathbf{D}_i}, \theta_{\mathbf{G}_{Col}}) = \frac{1}{Z_i} \cdot p_{\mathbf{D}_i}(\mathbf{d} \mid \mathbf{x}; \theta_{\mathbf{D}_i})^{k_i} \cdot p_{\mathbf{G}_{Col}}(\mathbf{d} \mid \mathbf{x}; \theta_{\mathbf{G}_{Col}})^{1-k_i}$$

for some $k_i \in [0, 1]$. That i can be 1 or 2 signifies that we will create two combinations, one for $p_{\mathbf{D}_1}$ and one for $p_{\mathbf{D}_2}$. The Z_i are normalizing factors. The conditional distribution $p_{\mathbf{G}_{Col}}(\mathbf{d} \mid \mathbf{x}; \theta_{\mathbf{G}_{Col}})$ is obtained from the joint, in theory, by normalizing. In practice, we never actually need to compute any normalizing factors.[7]

To estimate k_i, we first train $\theta_{\mathbf{D}_1}{}'$ and $\theta_{\mathbf{D}_2}{}'$ on our WSJ tuning training sections $(0, 1, 5\text{-}22)$. We then use $\theta_{\mathbf{D}_1}{}'$ to estimate $\theta_{\mathbf{G}_{Col}}{}'$. Finally, we choose the value for k_i that maximizes the performance of the model that combines $\theta_{\mathbf{D}_i}{}'$ with $\theta_{\mathbf{G}_{Col}}{}'$ on our WSJ sections 2-4, with a simple search over values $[0, .01, \cdots, .99, 1]$. The optimal values for the k_i were $k_1 = .70$ and $k_2 = .71$.

6.2 Results

Table 4 compares our two combined models against our individuals models, and our Berkeley parser baseline. We see that the combined models outperform their component models on all tasks. That is, the $\text{LOP}_{\text{1st-order}}$ model that combines $p_{\mathbf{D}_1}$ and $p_{\mathbf{G}_{Col}}$ outperforms both $p_{\mathbf{D}_1}$ and $p_{\mathbf{G}_{Col}}$. And, the $\text{LOP}_{\text{2nd-order}}$ model that combines $p_{\mathbf{D}_2}$ and $p_{\mathbf{G}_{Col}}$ outperforms both $p_{\mathbf{D}_2}$ and $p_{\mathbf{G}_{Col}}$. This all adds up to a significant improvement over the performance of the Berkeley parser. And, we see that when parsing the out-of-domain Brown data, the first-order model performs as well or slightly better than the second-order model.

Recall that we have used a new data set. In terms of past work on the Ratnaparkhi et al. (1994) data set, recall that the state-of-the-art using labelled data alone is Stetina and Nagao (1997), with

[7]To see this, note that

$$\begin{aligned}
&\underset{\mathbf{d}}{\text{argmax}} \frac{\left(\frac{f(\mathbf{d})}{Z_1}\right)^a \cdot \left(\frac{g(\mathbf{d})}{Z_2}\right)^b}{Z_3} \\
=&\underset{\mathbf{d}}{\text{argmax}} \frac{1}{Z_1{}^a Z_2{}^b Z_3} f(\mathbf{d})^a g(\mathbf{d})^b \\
=&\underset{\mathbf{d}}{\text{argmax}}\, f(\mathbf{d})^a g(\mathbf{d})^b
\end{aligned}$$

88.1% accuracy, and with unlabelled data alone is Pantel and Lin (2000), with 84.5% accuracy. Our results compare favourably to these, though, of course, the comparison is indirect.[8]

Furthermore, both of these other author's models make use of semantic resources such as WordNet and similar words lists to combat the sparsity of combinations that occurs even in large unlabelled samples. The limited utility of second-order features based on only the stems of the $\mathbf{noun}_{\text{inside}}$ suggests to us that features based on some more general semantic concept might generalize to other domains better. What is interesting in this regard is the strength of our first-order model, $\text{LOP}_{\text{1st-order}}$, which achieves performance approaching or passing the previous work without looking at $\mathbf{noun}_{\text{inside}}$. This suggests to us that collective dependent generation is a useful technique, which can presumably be combined with the semantic resources of the authors just mentioned to make an even better model.

Returning to the results, while the performance on the out-of-domain Brown corpus looks very comparable to that on the WSJ for both our system and the Berkeley parser, it actually seems that the Brown corpus is somewhat "easier", in the sense that it contains more examples that can be settled on the basis of our two fairly reliable structural heuristics.[9] Table 5 shows the performance on examples in which the structural heuristics do not apply. Here, we see that performance on the out-of-domain Brown corpus lags significantly behind performance on the WSJ.

Those interested in the automatic grammar discovery technique of the Berkeley parser will note the significant drop in performance of that parser on this subset of the data which implies that this parser had done essentially perfectly in cases where our structural heuristics did apply, meaning it must have *learned* equivalent heuristics to those that we encoded by hand, which is noteworthy.

Finally, though we have so far reported only the binary decision score (cf. §3.2) for each derivation, Table 6 shows a more general score: the percentage of correct attachments in any example (whether headed by noun or verb) in which more than one attachment was possible. Here, we see that the general problem is, as one would expect, harder than the binary decision problem.

	WSJ		Brown	
Model	Dev.	Test	Dev.	Test
$p_{\mathbf{G}_{Col}}$ (4 EM its.)	83.8	81.6	86.3	85.4
$\text{LOP}_{\text{2nd-order}}$	**88.9**	**86.9**	86.4	**86.2**
$p_{\mathbf{D}_2}$ (2nd-order)	87.4	86.0	84.7	83.9
$\text{LOP}_{\text{1st-order}}$	87.5	86.6	**86.6**	**86.2**
$p_{\mathbf{D}_1}$ (1st-order)	86.2	86.0	84.7	83.0
Baseline	85.3	83.0	83.3	82.7

Table 4: Performance of the combined model. Score is the binary decision score (cf. §3.2).

	WSJ		Brown	
Model	Dev.	Test	Dev.	Test
$\text{LOP}_{\text{2nd-order}}$	**84.1**	**80.3**	76.0	76.2
$\text{LOP}_{\text{1st-order}}$	82.3	79.8	**76.1**	**76.3**
Baseline	78.7	74.4	70.0	69.0

Table 5: Performance of the combined model on examples that cannot be settled by our two structural constraints. I.e., examples where i) the preposition is not *of*, and ii) the direct object is not a pronoun. Score is the binary decision score (cf. §3.2)

6.3 Analysis: What does Unlabelled Data Change?

At this point, we ask what difference the unlabelled data makes. To answer this question, we consider the nature of the disagreements between the $p_{\mathbf{D}_1}$ itself, and the $\text{LOP}_{\text{1st-order}}$ model that mixes $p_{\mathbf{D}_1}$ with $p_{\mathbf{G}_{Col}}$.

In Table 7, the *Count* column shows the number of agreements and disagreements on the development test sets. One possible outcome would have been few disagreements between models and that each of these would be won by the combined model. In fact, a significant number of disagree-

	WSJ		Brown	
Model	Dev.	Test	Dev.	Test
$\text{LOP}_{\text{2nd-order}}$	**85.8**	**84.8**	**83.7**	**84.0**
$\text{LOP}_{\text{1st-order}}$	84.5	84.2	83.4	83.9
Baseline	82.6	80.1	81.2	82.2

Table 6: Performance of the combined model. Score is the percentage of prepositional phrases attached correctly in all cases in which more than one attachment was possible.

[8] While both the Ratnaparkhi et al. (1994) test set and our WSJ test set are from the essentially the same material, they are not exactly the same examples, as the Treebank has undergone reordering.

[9] On WSJ sections 0, 1, 22-24, structural features fire in 33.8% of examples, while on Brown sections 0-2, 7-9 structural features fire in 46.0% of examples.

	WSJ Dev.		Brown Dev.	
Model correct	Count	p_{D_1} neutral	Count	p_{D_1} neutral
Both	1748	134	1396	227
$LOP_{1st\text{-}order}$	117	29	105	26
p_{D_1}	87	9	72	12
Neither	176	37	161	49

Table 7: Analysis of the agreements and disagreements between the first-order discriminative classifier, p_{D_1}, and the combined model, $LOP_{1st\text{-}order}$. The second row describes examples where $LOP_{1st\text{-}order}$ was correct but p_{D_1} was wrong, and the third row describes the converse situation. The *Count* column gives the number of examples in each category. The p_{D_1}*neutral* column gives the number of examples in each category in which no features in the p_{D_1} model were active (the strategy is to pick attachment to verb in this case).

ments go each way, but the large majority are won by the combined model.

The p_{D_1} *neutral* category counts the number of times that none of p_{D_1}'s features fire. These are the examples in which p_{D_1} has no opinion whatsoever, and so the combined model should have an advantage, if the unlabelled data is contributing useful information. We see that this is indeed the case. When no features fire for p_{D_1}, the strategy, as noted, is to choose attachment to the verb, which should still lead to a large number of correct responses. Thus, it makes sense that some disagreements are won by p_{D_1}, even when none of its features fire.

7 Conclusion and Future Work

We have shown that supervised techniques based on lexical dependency parsing outperform the semi-lexicalized strategy of Petrov and Klein (2007).

We have demonstrated that a properly chosen pair of models, one trained discriminatively from labelled data, and one trained generatively from unlabelled data, can be combined in a product model to yield a model better than either is alone.

We have shown that, when learning from unlabelled data, it may be preferable to generate dependents collectively.

Finally, we have introduced a pair of models which we think will be interesting to combine using the new methods for constraining EM, e.g., a la Ganchev et al. (2010) or Druck and McCallum (2010).

Acknowledgements

We thank Ioannis Konstas, Micha Elsner, and the reviewers for helpful suggestions. This work was supported by the Scottish Informatics and Computer Science Alliance and the ERC Advanced Fellowship 249520 GRAMPLUS.

References

Michaela Atterer and Hinrich Schütze. 2007. Prepositional phrase attachment without oracles. *Computational Linguistics*, 33(4):469–476.

R. F. Bordley. 1982. A multiplicative formula for aggregating probability assessments. *Management Science*, 28:1137–1148.

Eric Brill and Philip Resnik. 1994. A rule-based approach to prepositional phrase attachment disambiguation. In *COLING*, pages 1198–1204.

Xavier Carreras. 2007. Experiments with a higher-order projective dependency parser. In *Proceedings of the CoNLL Shared Task Session of EMNLP-CoNLL 2007*, pages 957–961.

Michael Collins and James Brooks. 1995. Prepositional phrase attachment through a backed-off model. *CoRR*.

Michael Collins. 1999. *Head-Driven Statistical Models for Natural Language Parsing*. Ph.D. thesis, University of Pennsylvania.

Michael Collins. 2002. Discriminative training methods for hidden Markov models: theory and experiments with perceptron algorithms. In *EMNLP*, pages 1–8, Stroudsburg, PA, USA. Association for Computational Linguistics.

A. P. Dempster, N. M. Laird, and D. B. Rubin. 1977. Maximum likelihood from incomplete data via the EM algorithm. *Journal of the Royal Statistical Society, B*, 39.

Gregory Druck and Andrew McCallum. 2010. High-performance semi-supervised learning using discriminatively constrained generative models. In *ICML*, pages 319–326.

Jenny Rose Finkel, Trond Grenager, and Christopher D. Manning. 2005. Incorporating nonlocal information into information extraction systems by Gibbs sampling. In *ACL*.

Kuzman Ganchev, João Graça, Jennifer Gillenwater, and Ben Taskar. 2010. Posterior regularization for structured latent variable models. *Journal of Machine Learning Research*, 11:2001–2049.

Daniel Gildea. 2001. Corpus variation and parser performance. In Lillian Lee and Donna Harman, editors, *Proceedings of the 2001 Conference on Empirical Methods in Natural Language Processing*, EMNLP '01, pages 167–202, Stroudsburg. Association for Computational Linguistics.

David Graff, Junbo Kong, Ke Chen, and Kazuaki Maeda. 2005. *English Gigaword Second Edition*. Linguistic Data Consortium: Philadelphia.

Donald Hindle and Mats Rooth. 1991. Structural ambiguity and lexical relations. In *ACL'91*, pages 229–236.

Geoffrey Hinton. 1999. Product of experts. In *ICANN*.

Percy Liang and Dan Klein. 2009. Online em for unsupervised models. In *HLT-NAACL*, pages 611–619.

Mitchell P. Marcus, Beatrice Santorini, and Mary Ann Marcinkiewicz. 1993. Building a large annotated corpus of English: The Penn Treebank. *Computational Linguistics*, 19(2):313–330.

Guido Minnen, John Carroll, and Darren Pearce. 2001. Applied morphological processing of english. *Nat. Lang. Eng.*, 7:207–223, September.

Patrick Pantel and Dekang Lin. 2000. An unsupervised approach to prepositional phrase attachment using contextually similar words. In *ACL*.

Slav Petrov and Dan Klein. 2007. Improved inference for unlexicalized parsing. In *HLT-NAACL*, pages 404–411.

Slav Petrov. 2010. Products of random latent variable grammars. In *HLT-NAACL*, pages 19–27.

Adwait Ratnaparkhi, Jeffrey C. Reynar, and Salim Roukos. 1994. A maximum entropy model for prepositional phrase attachment. In *HLT*.

Adwait Ratnaparkhi. 1998. Statistical models for unsupervised prepositional phrase attachement. In *COLING-ACL*, pages 1079–1085.

Andrew Smith, Trevor Cohn, and Miles Osborne. 2005. Logarithmic opinion pools for conditional random fields. In *ACL*.

J. Stetina and M. Nagao. 1997. Corpus based pp attachment ambiguity resolution with a semantic dictionary. In *Natural Language Processing Pacific Rim Symposium*.

Kristina Toutanova, Christopher D. Manning, and Andrew Y. Ng. 2004. Learning random walk models for inducing word dependency distributions. In *ICML*.

Martin Volk. 2002. Combining unsupervised and supervised methods for pp attachment disambiguation. In *Proceedings of the 19th international conference on Computational linguistics - Volume 1*, COLING '02, pages 1–7, Stroudsburg, PA, USA. Association for Computational Linguistics.

Appendix A: Extracting Examples from Gold Trees

In this section, we describe the functional program used to extract examples from gold trees.

A *base noun phrase* is phrase labelled NP, which does not dominate any other phrases. A base noun phrase is identified with its head-word. Head words are found using the Java reimplementation of Collins (1999) head-finder in the Stanford NLP API.

Noun phrase examples extracted are those that match

$$[_{S} \ldots [_{NP_1} \text{BaseNP}_H \text{ (prep baseNP)}_i^* \ldots] \ldots]$$

NP_1 must be immediately dominated by an S, $baseNP_H$ must be the left-most descendant of NP_1, and all (prep baseNP)$_i$ substrings must be dominated by NP_1 as well.

Verb phrase examples are those that match

$$[_{VP_1} \text{ verb}_H \text{ (PRT) (ADVP) (baseNP) (prep baseNP)}_i^+ \ldots]$$

VP_1 can occur in any environment. If there is a particle (PRT), this is appended to the verb. The adverbial phrase (ADVP) is ignored.

Active Learning for Dependency Parsing Using Partially Annotated Sentences

Seyed Abolghasem Mirroshandel   Alexis Nasr
Laboratoire d'Informatique Fondamentale de Marseille- CNRS - UMR 6166
Université Aix-Marseille, Marseille, France
ghasem.mirroshandel@lif.univ-mrs.fr, alexis.nasr@lif.univ-mrs.fr

Abstract

Current successful probabilistic parsers require large treebanks which are difficult, time consuming, and expensive to produce. Some parts of these data do not contain any useful information for training a parser. Active learning strategies allow to select the most informative samples for annotation. Most existing active learning strategies for parsing rely on selecting uncertain sentences for annotation. We show in this paper that selecting full sentences is not an optimal solution and propose a way to select only subparts of sentences.

1 Introduction

Current probabilistic parsers rely on treebanks in order to estimate their parameters. Such data is known to be difficult and expensive to produce. One can also observe that the quality of parsers increase when they model complex lexico-syntactic phenomena. Unfortunately, increasing the precision of models is quickly confronted with data sparseness which prevents to reliably estimate the model parameters. Treebanks size is therefore a limit to the accuracy of probabilistic parsers. Given the cost of annotating new data with syntactic structures, it is natural to ask oneself, before annotating a new sentence and adding it to a treebank, if this new piece of information will benefit a parser trained on the treebank.

This question is at the heart of active learning which assumes that *"a machine learning algorithm can achieve greater accuracy with fewer training labels if it is allowed to choose the data from which it learns. An active learner may pose queries, usually in the form of unlabeled data instances to be labeled by an oracle (e.g. human annotator). Active learning is well-motivated in many modern machine learning problems, where unlabeled data may be abundant or easily obtained, but labels are difficult, time-consuming, or expensive to obtain."* (Settles, 2010)

Different scenarios have been proposed for active learning. The work described here is based on the Pool-Based Sampling scenario (Lewis and Gale, 1994) which is adapted to the problem at hand. Pool-based sampling scenario assumes that there is a small set of labeled data $\mathcal{L}$ and a large pool of unlabeled data $\mathcal{U}$ available. Instances are drawn from $\mathcal{U}$ according to a selection strategy. The chosen instance(s) are then labeled and added to $\mathcal{L}$. These steps are repeated until either $\mathcal{U}$ is empty or does not contain informative instances anymore.

Many selection strategies have been proposed in the literature. Uncertainty sampling, which is the strategy that has been used in this work, is the simplest and the most commonly used one. In this strategy, instances for which the prediction of the label is the most uncertain are selected by the learner. The performances of such methods heavily rely on the definition of a good confidence measure, which measures the confidence the model, in our case the parser, has in the solution it proposes.

Active learning has been used for many NLP applications, such as automatic speech recognition, information extraction, part of speech tagging or syntactic parsing. We will not detail the way active learning has been applied to those tasks, the interested reader can find two reasonably recent surveys in (Settles, 2010) and (Olsson, 2009), and concentrate on its application to statistical parsing.

(Tang et al., 2002) and (Hwa, 2004) proposed active learning techniques for training probabilistic parsers. They both used uncertainty sampling and suggested a measure of uncertainty based on the entropy of the probability distribution of the parses of a sentence. The idea being that the higher this entropy is, the more uncertain the parser is of its choice. (Tang et al., 2002) proposed to combine uncertainty with representativeness, the idea here is to make sure that the instances selected with uncertainty criterion are also representative of the data distribution. The common point to these two approaches, and most work on active learning applied to parsing is that they only consider full sentences in their instance selection.

There is something not satisfactory in considering only full sentences as instances since, in many cases, only part of the syntactic structure is uncertain. The manual annotation of this part would benefit the parser while the annotation of the remaining part of the sentence would be a waste of effort.

The main novelty of the work reported here is that we explore the other extreme position: instead of considering uncertain sentences, we consider single uncertain word tokens in a sentence. More precisely, we consider the attachment of single word tokens. In the framework of dependency parsing, which is used here, this boils down to selecting, for a token w, its governor and the label of the dependency between w and its governor. The task is therefore to select, in a sentence, the most uncertain dependencies.

Active learning for parsing using sub-sentential units has already been explored by (Sassano and Kurohashi, 2010). In their work they select unreliable dependencies predicted by a parser (a simple shift-reduce parser where dependencies are weighted using an averaged perceptron with polynomial kernels), based on the score the parser assigns to the dependencies. Such dependencies are hand labeled and, based on syntactic characteristics of Japanese syntax (dependencies are projective and oriented from left to right (the governor is always to the right of the dependent)) other dependencies are deduced and this set of dependencies are added to the training set. Our work departs from their in the uncertainty measure that we use, in the kind of parser used, on the way hand annotated single dependencies are added to the training data (without using language specific properties) as well as on the fact that we use both sentence based and dependency based uncertainty measures.

The structure of the paper is the following: in section 2, we describe, in some details, the parsing model on which this work is based, namely the graph-based dependency parsing framework. Such a detailed description is motivated by two extensions of graph based parsing that we describe. The first one is how to take into account, in the input of the parser, part of the syntactic structure of the sentence to parse, a feature that is needed when annotating only a subpart of the syntactic structure of a sentence. We will see that this can be done very easily and this is the main reason why we chose this parsing framework. The second extension concerns the production of a list of n-best candidates, which is necessary for computing our uncertainty measure and is not a standard operation for this kind of parsers, contrary to syntagmatic parsers, for example. In section 3, we report a first series of experiments in which full sentences are selected during the instance selection procedure. The techniques used here are not novel and the aim of this section is to constitute a baseline for evaluating our idea of partial annotation, which is described in section 4. Section 5 shows that better results can be reached when taking into account both uncertainty of a sentence and uncertainty of parts of it. Finally, section 6 concludes the paper.

2 Graph-Based Parsing

Graph-Based parsing (McDonald et al., 2005; Kübler et al., 2009) defines a framework for parsing that does not make use of a generative grammar. In such a framework, given a sentence $W = w_1 \dots w_l$, any dependency tree[1] for W is a valid syntactic representation of W. The heart of a graph-based parser is the scoring function that assigns a score to every tree $T \in \mathcal{T}_W$, where $\mathcal{T}_W$ denotes the set of all dependency trees of sentence W. Such scores are usually a weighted sum of the scores of subparts of W.

$$s(T) = \sum_{\psi \in \psi_T} \lambda_\psi$$

where ψ_T is the set of all the relevant subparts of tree T and λ_ψ is the score of subpart ψ.

Depending on the decomposition of the tree into subparts, different models of increasing complexity can be defined. The most simple one is the *arc factored model*, also called *first order model*, which simply decomposes a tree into single

[1] A dependency tree for sentence $W = w_1 \dots w_l$ and the dependency relation set $\mathcal{R}$ is a directed labelled tree (V, A) such that $V = \{w_1, \dots w_n\}$ and $A \subseteq V \times \mathcal{R} \times V$.

dependencies and assigns a score to a dependency, independently of its context.

The score of tree T, noted $s(T)$ in this model is therefore :

$$s(T) = \sum_{(w_i, r, w_j)} \lambda(i, r, j)$$

where (i, r, j) is the dependency that has w_i as governor, w_j as dependent and r as label, and $\lambda(i, r, j)$ is the score assigned to such a dependency.

Parsing a sentence W in such a system boils down to determining the tree that has the highest score in $\mathcal{T}_W$. Determining such a tree can be simply accomplished using the maximum spanning tree algorithm.

A maximum spanning tree or MST of a directed multigraph $G = (V, A)$ is the highest scoring subgraph G' that satisfies the following conditions:

- $V' = V$, i.e. G' spans all the original nodes of G.
- G' is a directed tree.

Given a sentence $W = w_1 \ldots w_l$, and a set of functional labels $\mathcal{R} = \{r_1, \ldots r_m\}$, a graph $G_W = (V_W, A_W)$ can be built such that:

- $V_W = \{w_1, \ldots w_l\}$
- $A_W = \{(i, r, j)\}\ \forall w_i, w_j \in V_W$ and $r \in \mathcal{R}$ and $i \neq j$

In other words, G_W is the graph composed of all the dependencies that can be defined between tokens of W. Given a scoring function λ that assigns a score to every arc of G_W, a simple Graph-Based parser can be implemented based on any MST algorithm such as Chu-Liu-Edmonds (Chu and Liu, 1965; Edmonds et al., 1968).

In order to build an actual parser, a scoring function λ is needed. Current versions of Graph-Based Parsers assume that such a function is a linear classifier. The score of a dependency is computed as follows:

$$\lambda(i, r, j) = \alpha \cdot f(i, r, j)$$

where f is a feature function that maps the dependency to a boolean vector and α is the feature weight vector that associates a weight with every feature of the model. In first order models, features describe different aspects of a dependency, such as the part of speech of the governor and the dependent, their lexical value, the length of the dependency, the part of speech of tokens between the dependent and the governor ...

Different Machine Learning techniques can be used in order to learn the weight vector. In our experiment, we used the implementation of (Bohnet, 2010) that is based on MIRA (Crammer et al., 2006), an on-line large margin classifier.

The arc factored model, described here, achieves good performances, but it relies on a very strong independence assumption which is that the score of a dependency is independent of its context. Such an independence assumption is linguistically unappealing and more elaborate models, known as second order (Carreras, 2007) and third order (Koo and Collins, 2010) models, which associate a score with pairs of adjacent dependencies in a tree or chains of two or three dependencies, have shown to give better results.

Although we have used second order models in our experiments, we will consider in the next two subsections, only first order models, which are conceptually and computationally simpler.

2.1 Constraining the Output of the Parser

The graph-based framework allows us to impose structural constraints on the parses that are produced by the parser in a straightforward way, a feature that will reveal itself to be precious for our experiments.

Given a sentence $W = w_1 \ldots w_l$, a parser with a scoring function λ and a dependency $d = (i, r, j)$ with $1 \leq i, j \leq l$. We can define a new scoring function λ_d^+ in the following way:

$$\lambda_d^+(i', r', j') = \begin{cases} -\infty & \text{if } j' = j \text{ and} \\ & (i' \neq i \text{ or } r' \neq r) \\ \lambda(i', r', j') & \text{otherwise} \end{cases}$$

When running the parser on sentence W, with the scoring function λ_d^+, one can be sure that dependency d will be part of the solution produced by the parser since it will be given a better score than any competing dependency, i.e. a dependency of the form (i', r, j') with $j = j'$ and $i' \neq i$ or $r' \neq r$. This feature will be used in section 4 in order to parse a sentence for which a certain number of dependencies are set in advance.

Symmetrically, we can define a function λ_d^- in the following way:

$$\lambda_d^-(i', r', j') = \begin{cases} -\infty & \text{if } j' = j \text{ and} \\ & i' = i \text{ and } r' = r \\ \lambda(i, r, j) & \text{otherwise} \end{cases}$$

The effect of this new scoring function when parsing sentence W is that the solution produced by the parser will not contain dependency d.

Functions λ^+ and λ^- can be extended in order to force the presence or the absence of any set of dependencies in the output of the parser. Suppose $\mathcal{D}$ is a set of dependencies, we define $\lambda_{\mathcal{D}}^+$ the following way:

$$\lambda_{\mathcal{D}}^+(i, r, j) = \begin{cases} \lambda_d^+(i, r, j) & \text{if } (\cdot, \cdot, j) \in \mathcal{D} \\ \lambda(i, r, j) & \text{otherwise} \end{cases}$$

2.2 Producing N-Best Parses

Given scoring functions $\lambda_{\mathcal{D}}^-$, we can define a simple way of producing the n-best scoring parses of a sentence. Given a scoring function λ and a sentence W, let's call $\hat{T}_1 = \{d_1, \ldots d_l\}$ the tree output by the parser, where $d_1 \ldots d_l$ are the dependencies that make up the tree $\hat{T}_1$, d_i being the dependency that has w_i as a dependent.

By definition, $\hat{T}_1$ is the tree of $\mathcal{T}_W$ with the highest score. Now let's define l functions $\lambda_{d_1}^- \ldots \lambda_{d_l}^-$ and run the parser l times on W, equipped respectively with functions $\lambda_{d_1}^- \ldots \lambda_{d_l}^-$. The result of these runs is a set of trees $\mathcal{L}_0 = \{T_1, \ldots T_l\}$ respectively produced with functions $\lambda_{d_1}^- \ldots \lambda_{d_l}^-$. These trees are such that T_i does not contain dependency d_i. Let's define $\hat{T}_2$ as follows:

$$\hat{T}_2 = \arg\max_{T \in \mathcal{L}_0} s(T)$$

It is easy to prove that $\hat{T}_2$ is the second best scoring tree in $\mathcal{T}_W$. This proposition holds because trees $T_1 \ldots T_l$ are all the best scoring trees of $\mathcal{T}_W$ that differ from $\hat{T}_1$ by at least one dependency. Among them, the tree with the highest score is therefore the second best scoring tree.

Suppose $\hat{T}_2 = \{d'_1, \ldots d'_n\}$, The process is recursively applied to $\hat{T}_2$ and produces a list of trees $\mathcal{L}$. A new list $\mathcal{L}_1$ is then defined as follows:

$$\mathcal{L}_1 = \mathcal{L}_0 - \{\hat{T}_2\} \cup \mathcal{L}$$

and the third best scoring tree $\hat{T}_3$ is defined as follows:

$$\hat{T}_3 = \arg\max_{T \in \mathcal{L}_1} s(T)$$

The process is iterated until a tree $\hat{T}_n$ has been produced, for a given value of n.

The process, as described is not computationnaly optimal since the parser is run $n \times l$ times on the same sentence and many operations are duplicated. Much of the redundant work could be avoided using dynamic programming.

We are not aware of a general method for efficiently computing n-best parses for graph-based parsing, as it is the case with context-free parsing (Huang and Chiang, 2005). Nevertheless, (Hall, 2007) describes an efficient n-best method for graph-based parsing which is unfortunately limited to first order models.

3 Selecting Full Sentences

We report in this section a first series of experiments in which full sentences are selected from the pool at every iteration of the active learning algorithm. The aim of this section is primarily to set up a baseline against which we will compare the results obtained in sections 4 and 5. In order to set up a reasonable baseline, we used successful methods described in (Tang et al., 2002) and (Hwa, 2004) but we adapted them to our framework: discriminative dependency parsing. The method described here will also prove to be interesting to combine with the model of section 4, as we will see in section 5.

The experiments have been conducted on the French Treebank (Abeillé et al., 2003) which is made of $12,350$ sentences taken from newspaper *Le Monde* and annotated with syntagmatic structures along with syntactic functions. The corpus has been divided into three parts, the labeled set $\mathcal{L}$ made of 500 sentences, the pool $\mathcal{U}$, made of $10,665$ sentences and a test set $\mathcal{T}$ made of $1,185$ sentences. The syntagmatic annotations have been converted to dependencies using the BONSAÏ converter (Candito et al., 2010).

As described in the introduction, the algorithm is Pool-Based. A first parser P_0 is trained on $\mathcal{L}$ and used to parse the sentences of $\mathcal{U}$. An uncertainty measure is then computed for every sentence of $\mathcal{U}$ and the k most uncertain sentences are labeled, removed from $\mathcal{U}$ and added to $\mathcal{L}$. A second parser P_1 is trained on $\mathcal{L}$ and the process is iterated until there is no more sentences left in $\mathcal{U}$. These different steps are illustrated in Algorithm 1.

Algorithm 1 ACTIVE LEARNING WITH FULL SENTENCES ANNOTATION

$\mathcal{L}$: Initial training set
$\mathcal{U}$: Unlabeled pool
$\varphi(S)$: Uncertainty measure of sentence S
$i = 0$;
  while $\mathcal{U}$ is not empty **do**
    $P_i = train(\mathcal{L})$;
    Build n-best parses of $\mathcal{U}$ based on P_i;
    Compute $\varphi(S)$ for $S \in \mathcal{U}$;
    $\mathcal{U}'$ = k most uncertain sentences of $\mathcal{U}$;
    $\mathcal{L}'$ = Annotate $\mathcal{U}'$;
    $\mathcal{U} = \mathcal{U} - \mathcal{U}'$;
    $\mathcal{L} = \mathcal{L} \cup \mathcal{L}'$;
    $i = i + 1$;
  end while

3.1 Sentence Entropy

The uncertainty measure we have been using, the sentence entropy, noted SE, is close to the uncertainty measures defined in (Tang et al., 2002), (Hwa, 2004) or (Sánchez-Sáez et al., 2009). Given a sentence W and the n-best parses of W with scores respectively noted $s_1 \ldots s_n$, $SE(W)$ is computed as follows:

$$SE(W) = -\sum_{i=1}^{n} p_i \log(p_i)$$

where p_i is the posterior probability:

$$p_i = \frac{s_i}{\sum_{j=1}^{n} s_j}$$

This uncertainty measure is based on the intuitive idea that when the scores of the n-best parses of a sentence are close to each other, and therefore the entropy of the distribution of the posterior probabilities is high, this indicates that the parser is "hesitating" between some of the n-best parses.

Two curves have been represented in figure 1, they show the Labeled Accuracy Score (LAS) computed on the test set against the size of the train set, given in tokens[2]. Two curves have been drawn, a curve based on the sentence entropy and a curve based on a random selection. The sentence entropy curve has two interesting features, it grows quicker than the random curve and presents an asymptotical shape which shows that it has "extracted" all the useful information present in $\mathcal{U}$ when it reaches the asymptote.

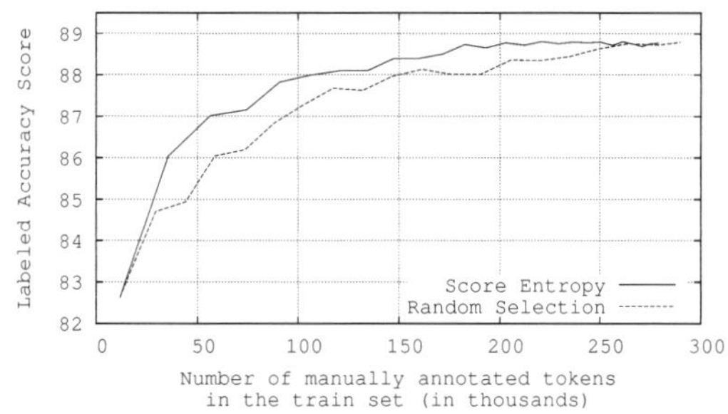

Figure 1: Learning curves with full sentences selection using sentence entropy, comparison with random selection.

The uncertainty measure of a sentence W used in this experiment is supposed to measure the difficulty of parsing sentence W. It must therefore be related to the mean error rate of the parser on sentence W. The curve of figure 2 shows the relation between labeled accuracy score and sentence entropy computed on a set of 1000 randomly selected sentences. The curve shows that on average LAS tends to decrease when sentence entropy increases. The small range in which score entropy takes its values is explained by the fact that, on average, the score of parse trees in n-best list are close to each other. Their posterior probability is therefore close to 0.01 (due to the fact that it is computed on a 100 best list). We do not have an explanation for the general shape of the curve.

(Tang et al., 2002) and (Hwa, 2004) discuss the relation between entropy and the length of sentences. The idea is that long sentences tend to have more parses than short sentences and tend to have on average higher entropy. This dependency between sentence length and entropy

[2]In all our experiments, the LAS was computed on whole sentences, including punctuation.

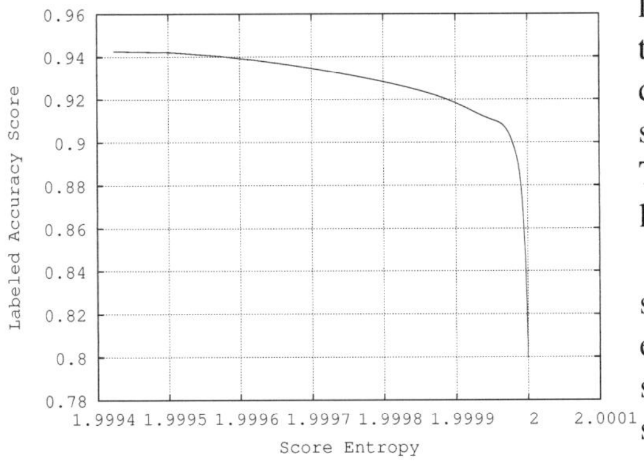

Figure 2: Relation between Labeled Accuracy Score and Sentence Entropy

will therefore bias the active learning algorithm towards selecting long sentences. They therefore propose to normalize entropy either with sentence length (Tang et al., 2002) or number of parses for a sentence (Hwa, 2004).

In our case, we did not observe any influence of sentence length on sentence entropy. That might be due to the fact that we only consider the n-best scoring parses (but that was also the case of (Tang et al., 2002)) or to the fact that the scores from which posterior probabilities are computed are not probabilities but scores given by the MIRA classifier which have different distributions than generative probabilites. We did not investigate further this difference since our goal in this section was mostly to define a reasonable baseline for evaluating the results of the selection strategy that will be described in the following section.

4 Selecting Single Tokens

The algorithm described in the preceding section associates an uncertainty measure with whole sentences and, based on this measure, decides to ask for its labeling, or not. The syntactic analysis of a sentence is a complex object, part of it can be difficult to parse and a correct analysis of this part could improve the parser while the remaining of the syntactic structure might not contain any new piece of information. The idea that we explore in this section consists in locating in a sentence some difficult parts and ask for the labeling of these parts only. More precisely, we will try to locate single difficult dependencies and ask for the labeling of just these dependencies. The partly labeled sentence is then parsed in such a way that the parser preserves the manually annotated dependencies. This is done by changing the scoring function of the parser, as described in 2.1. The output of the parser is then added to the set of labeled sentences $\mathcal{L}$.

In order to estimate the potential benefit of such a method, we conducted the following experiment: the parser P_0, trained on the 500 sentences of $\mathcal{L}$, was used to parse 1000 randomly selected sentences from $\mathcal{U}$. We will refer to this set of sentences as $\mathcal{U}_{1000}$. Among the $24,000$ dependencies created by the parser, $3,144$ were incorrect (governor or/and dependency label was incorrect for a given token). These dependencies were corrected (the right governor along with the right dependency label was restored) and the partially parsed sentences were parsed with P_0 preserving manual annotation. The output of this process was added to $\mathcal{L}$ and used to train a new parser $P_{partial}$. Eventually a third parser $P_{complete}$ was trained on a fully correct version of $\mathcal{U}_{1000}$ plus $\mathcal{L}$. The two parsers were evaluated on the test set $\mathcal{T}$. The result of these experiments are reported in table 1.

Model	LAS	UAS
$P_{complete}$	85.60	87.84
$P_{partial}$	85.71	87.91

Table 1: Performances of parsers trained with respectively a set of 1000 sentences fully annotated and the same set of sentences in which only wrong dependencies were hand annotated.

The figures reported in table 1 show that training a parser P on a corpus in which only the mistakes of P were corrected can lead to better results than training it on the fully annotated version of this same corpus. In our case, the partially annotated corpus contained only $3,144$ manually annotated dependencies and the fully annotated corpus contained $24,000$ ones.

If we were able to determine the set of wrong attachments made by a parser we would therefore be in a position to define a very efficient active learning algorithm. Although determining all and only the wrong attachments is clearly impossible, we can try to approximate this set using a dependency based confidence measure as described in the following subsection.

4.1 Attachment Entropy

Given the n-best parses of a sentence W, one indication of the confidence of the attachment of token w is the number of its possible governors in the n-best parses. We define attachment entropy of token w, noted $AE(w)$ as a simple measure of this confidence. Attachment entropy is computed as follows:

$$AE(w) = - \sum_{g \in G(w)} P(g, \cdot, w) \log P(g, \cdot, w)$$

where $G(w)$ is the set of the possible governors of token w in the n-best parses and $P(g, \cdot, w)$ is the probability that token w is governed by token g in the n-best parses. This probability is estimated as follows:

$$P(g, \cdot, w) = \frac{count(g, \cdot, w)}{n}$$

where $count(g, \cdot, w)$ counts the number of times token w was governed by token g in the n-best parses[3].

A perfect confidence measure should, in the experiments reported above, allow to select the wrong dependencies and only those. In order to evaluate the quality of attachment entropy, precision recall curves have been computed. For a given threshold τ of our confidence measure, the dependencies that are above τ (more precisely, the dependencies $(g, \cdot, w)$ of the first best parse such that $AE(w) \geq \tau$) are collected to form the set $\mathcal{D}_U$ of uncertain dependencies. This set is compared with the set $\mathcal{D}_I$ of incorrect dependencies (the set of $3,144$ dependencies described above). The comparison is realized with precision and recall, which are computed as follows:

$$Prec. = \frac{|\mathcal{D}_I \cap \mathcal{D}_U|}{|\mathcal{D}_U|} \quad Rec. = \frac{|\mathcal{D}_I \cap \mathcal{D}_U|}{|\mathcal{D}_I|}$$

Attachment entropy depends on the length of the n-best lists of parses produced by the parser. A high value of n will produce, on average, a higher number of possible governors for a token of a sentence and therefore, a potentially higher entropy. Three precision recall curves are reported in figure 3 for n best lists of lengths respectively

[3]Labelling errors of correct attachments are not taken into account for measuring attachment entropy for they did not improve the quality of the confidence measure.

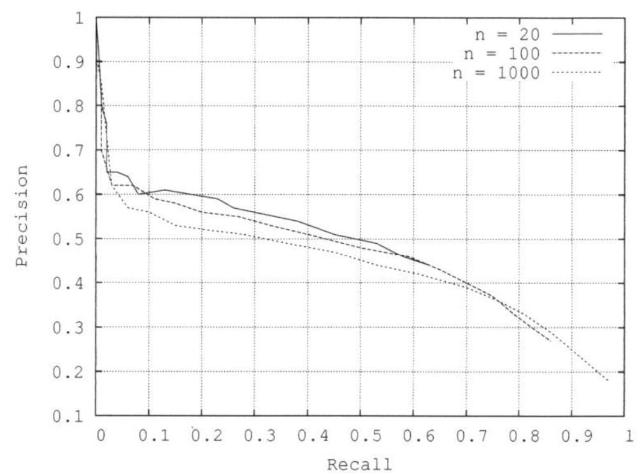

Figure 3: Precision Recall curves for attachment entropy for different n-best output of the parser.

equal to 20, 100 and 1000. Several conclusions can be drawn from these curves. The first one is that attachment entropy is quite far from the perfect confidence measure that would achieve a precision and recall of 1. High recall values can be obtained at the cost of very low precision, and inversely, high precision yields very low recall. On average, lower values of n achieve better precision recall tradeoffs but do not allow to reach high recall values.

The inability for low values of n to reach high values of recall opens the door for a discussion about the influence of the sentence length on precision recall curves. The number of parses of a sentence is, in the worse case, an exponential function of its length (Church and Patil, 1982). Computing entropy attachment on fixed length n-best parses lists only allow to consider a very limited number of possible governors of a token for longer sentences. A natural solution in order to cope with this problem is to compute variable length n-best lists, where the value of n is a function of the length (l) of the sentence being parsed. It would make sense to let n be an exponential function of l. This approach is in practice impossible since (at least in our implementation of the n best algorithm) the production of the n-best list will take an exponential time. Furthermore, our experiments showed that the value of n should not grow too fast, as reported in figure 4. Three[4] curves

[4]We have added the fixed 20-best curve, that achieved the best result for fixed length n, for comparison purpose.

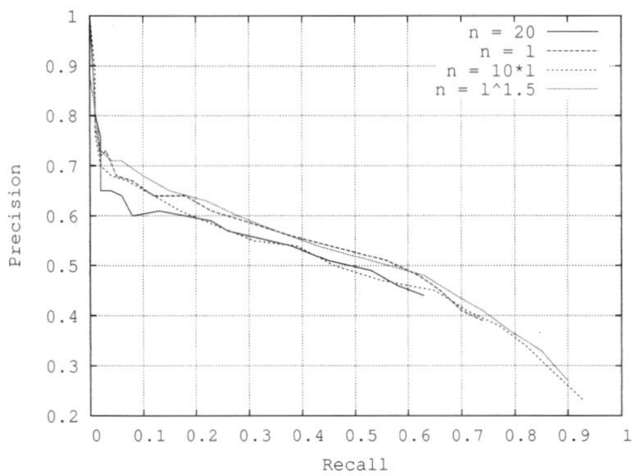

Figure 4: Precision Recall curves for attachment entropy with variable length n-best lists.

have been reported in this figure, that correspond to three functions linking n and l. The best results were obtained for the function $n = l^{\frac{3}{2}}$. Higher order function did not obtain good results, contrary to our intuition.

It is important, at this point to discuss one aspect of our attachment entropy measure. In graph-based parsing, one can compute the score of any dependency linking two tokens of a sentence. It is therefore possible to compute, for a given token w_j, the score of all the dependencies of the form $(i, \cdot, j)$, $\forall j\ 1 \leq j \leq k$ and compute attachment entropy based on this score. This method has the advantage of considering all tokens of the sentence as a potential governor and does not ask for the construction of the n-best parses. But such a method does not take into account the global score of a parse. A dependency can get a high score when considered alone but might not be part of a good (high scoring) parse. In practice, it gave very bad results[5].

4.2 Active Learning Strategy

The token based active learning algorithm is straightforward. For every iteration of the algorithm, the most uncertain tokens are selected, hand annotated and their sentences are parsed in such a way that the partial annotation is preserved. The new parses are then added to the labeled set and the process is iterated, as shown in Algorithm 2. Two different approaches can be considered when selecting most uncertain tokens. One can either select for every sentence the most uncertain token or select for the whole pool the k most uncertain tokens. In the latter case, several tokens of a single sentence could be selected for every step.

Algorithm 2 ACTIVE LEARNING WITH SINGLE DEPENDENCY ANNOTATION

$\mathcal{L}$: Initial training set
$\mathcal{U}$: Unlabeled pool
$\varphi(w)$: Uncertainty measure for token w
$i = 0$;
while There is no uncertain dependency **do**
  $P_i = train(\mathcal{L})$;
  Build n-best parses of $\mathcal{U}$ based on P_i;
  Compute $\varphi(w)$ for each token;
  $\mathcal{U}'$ = sentences containing the k most uncertain tokens;
  Annotate selected tokens;
  $\mathcal{L}'$ = Parse $\mathcal{U}'$ sentences, preserving annotation;
  $\mathcal{L} = \mathcal{L} \cup \mathcal{L}'$;
  $i = i + 1$;
end while

The result of the token selection strategy is reported in figure 5. The full sentence selection based on score entropy as well as the random selection are also reported for comparison purpose. The two strategies described above (selecting the most uncertain token per sentence or the k most uncertain tokens in the corpus) gave almost the same results. The full sentence selection strategy yielded better results for the first iterations of the algorithm but was outperformed by the token selection strategy after a while. The token selection strategy shows good asymptotical performances, it reaches the asymptote with $130,000$ manually annotated tokens (45.45% of total tokens of $\mathcal{U}$) while the full sentence strategy asks for $180,000$ tokens (62.94% of total tokens of $\mathcal{U}$) to reach it. It is unclear why full sentence selection gave better results in the first iterations, it is as if the parser needs to be trained on full sentences in the beginning and, after a while, gain better benefit from isolated difficult attachments.

[5]As suggested by one of the reviewers, for first order models, the confidence measure can be computed without producing the n-best parses, using marginal probability of an arc existing in any tree, which can be efficiently computed, via the matrix tree theorem (McDonald and Satta, 2007).

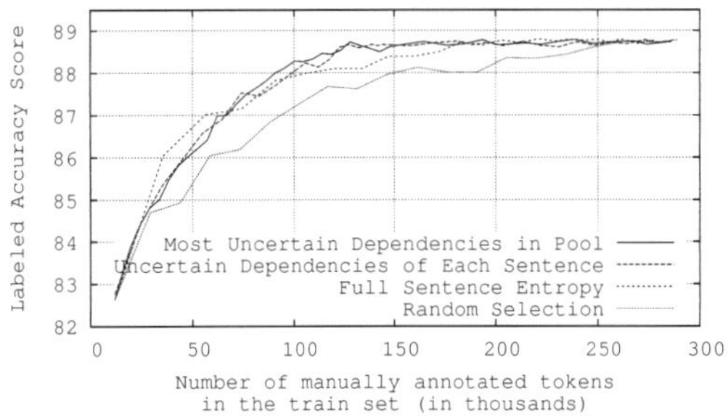

Figure 5: Learning curves with token selection strategy. Comparison with full sentence strategy and random selection.

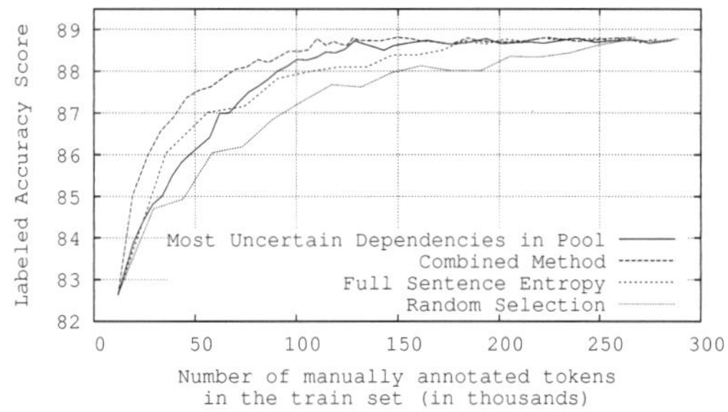

Figure 6: Learning curves for the combined strategy. Comparison with token selection strategy, full sentence strategy and random selection.

5 Selecting Uncertain Tokens of Uncertain Sentences

The results obtained when selecting uncertain sentences and those obtained for uncertain tokens showed that both strategies seem to be somehow complementary. Such conclusion opens the door for a two level strategy. In a first step uncertain full sentences are selected, then uncertain tokens of these sentences are selected, as described in Algorithm 3.

Algorithm 3 COMBINED ACTIVE LEARNING

$\mathcal{L}$: Initial training set
$\mathcal{U}$: Unlabeled pool
$\varphi(S)$: Full sentence uncertainty measure
$\psi(w)$: Single dependency uncertainty measure
$i = 0$;
while $\mathcal{U}$ is not empty **do**
  $P_i = train(\mathcal{L})$;
  Build n-best parses of $\mathcal{U}$ based on P_i;
  Compute $\varphi(S)$ for $S \in \mathcal{U}$;
  $\mathcal{U}'$ = k most uncertain sentences of $\mathcal{U}$;
  Compute $\psi(x)$ for each token of $\mathcal{U}'$;
  Select k' most uncertain tokens;
  Annotate selected tokens;
  $\mathcal{L}'$ = Partially parse $\mathcal{U}'$ sentences, preserving annotation;
  $\mathcal{U} = \mathcal{U} - \mathcal{U}'$;
  $\mathcal{L} = \mathcal{L} \cup \mathcal{L}'$;
  $i = i + 1$;
end while

Figure 6 reports the results of the combined method. The new method outperforms both the full sentence and the single token strategy for every iteration of the algorithm. It reaches the asymptote with only $109,000$ manually annotated tokens (37.98% of total tokens in $\mathcal{U}$). These result confirm the intuition that both score entropy and attachment entropy carry complementary information. One way to interpret the results obtained is that the two methods that were tested in this paper: selecting full sentences vs. selecting single tokens, are two extreme positions. We did not investigate the search space that lie between them, i.e. specifically looking for unreliable *parts* of sentences. We describe in the next section some preliminary results along this line.

6 Conclusions and Future Work

We proposed in this paper three active learning techniques for dependency parsing. The novelty of this work is to annotate only difficult attachment insead of full sentences as it is usually done in other approaches.

Although selecting single dependencies showed an improvement over selecting full sentences, in some cases, it turns out that selecting subparts of the sentence is a good strategy. A preliminary experiment was conducted on punctuation. It showed that selecting tokens that lie in a window of 6 tokens centered on punctuation yielded very good results. Such a method could be useful for difficult attachment such as PP attachment or coordination where dependencies must be considered in a larger context.

Acknowledgements

This work has been funded by the French Agence Nationale pour la Recherche, through the project SEQUOIA (ANR-08-EMER-013). The authors would like to thank the anonymous reviewers for the very high quality of their reviews.

References

Anne Abeillé, Lionel Clément, and Toussenel François, 2003. *Treebanks*, chapter Building a treebank for French. Kluwer, Dordrecht.

Bernd Bohnet. 2010. Top Accuracy and Fast Dependency Parsing is not a Contradiction. In *Proceedings of COLING.*

Marie Candito, Benoît Crabbé, and Pascal Denis. 2010. Statistical French Dependency Parsing: Treebank Conversion and First Results. In *Proceedings of LREC2010.*

X. Carreras. 2007. Experiments with a higher-order projective dependency parser. In *Proceedings of the CoNLL Shared Task Session of EMNLP-CoNLL*, volume 7, pages 957–961.

Y.J. Chu and T.H. Liu. 1965. On the shortest arborescence of a directed graph. *Science Sinica*, 14(1396-1400):270.

K. Church and R. Patil. 1982. Coping with syntactic ambiguity or how to put the block in the box on the table. *Computational Linguistics*, 8(3-4):139–149.

Koby Crammer, Ofer Dekel, Joseph Keshet, Shai ShalevShwartz, and Yoram Singer. 2006. Online Passive-Aggressive Algorithm. *Journal of Machine Learning Research.*

J. Edmonds, J. Edmonds, and J. Edmonds. 1968. *Optimum branchings.* National Bureau of standards.

K. Hall. 2007. K-best spanning tree parsing. In *Proceedings of the 45th Annual Meeting of the ACL*, page 392.

L. Huang and D. Chiang. 2005. Better k-best parsing. In *Proceedings of the 9th International Workshop on Parsing Technology*, pages 53–64.

R. Hwa. 2004. Sample selection for statistical parsing. *Computational Linguistics*, 30(3):253–276.

T. Koo and M. Collins. 2010. Efficient third-order dependency parsers. In *Proceedings of the 48th Annual Meeting of the ACL*, pages 1–11.

S. Kübler, R. McDonald, and J. Nivre. 2009. *Dependency parsing.* Synthesis Lectures on Human Language Technologies. Morgan & Claypool Publishers.

D.D. Lewis and W.A. Gale. 1994. A sequential algorithm for training text classifiers. In *Proceedings of the 17th annual international ACM SIGIR conference on Research and development in information retrieval*, pages 3–12.

R. McDonald and G. Satta. 2007. On the complexity of non-projective data-driven dependency parsing. In *Proceedings of IWPT*, pages 121–132.

R. McDonald, K. Crammer, and F. Pereira. 2005. Online large-margin training of dependency parsers. In *Proceedings of the 43rd Annual Meeting of the Association for Computational Linguistics*, pages 91–98.

F. Olsson. 2009. A literature survey of active machine learning in the context of natural language processing. Technical report, Swedish Institute of Computer Science.

R. Sánchez-Sáez, J.A. Sánchez, and J.M. Benedí. 2009. Statistical confidence measures for probabilistic parsing. In *Proceedings of RANLP*, pages 388–392.

Manabu Sassano and Sadao Kurohashi. 2010. Using smaller constituents rather than sentences in active learning for japanese dependency parsing. In *Proceedings of the 48th Annual Meeting of the ACL*, pages 356–365.

Burr Settles. 2010. Active Learning Literature Survey. Technical Report Technical Report 1648, University of Wisconsin-Madison.

M. Tang, X. Luo, and S. Roukos. 2002. Active learning for statistical natural language parsing. In *Proceedings of the 40th Annual Meeting of the Association for Computational Linguistics*, pages 120–127.

Lagrangian Relaxation for Inference in Natural Language Processing

Michael Collins
Department of Computer Science
Columbia University
mcollins@cs.columbia.edu

Abstract

There has been a long history in combinatorial optimization of methods that exploit structure in complex problems, using methods such as dual decomposition or Lagrangian relaxation. These methods leverage the observation that complex inference problems can often be decomposed into efficiently solvable sub-problems. Thus far, however, these methods are not widely used in NLP.

In this talk I will describe recent work on inference algorithms for NLP based on Lagrangian relaxation. In the first part of the talk I will describe work on non-projective parsing. In the second part of the talk I will describe an exact decoding algorithm for syntax-based statistical translation. If time permits, I will also briefly describe algorithms for dynamic programming intersections (e.g., the intersection of a PCFG and an HMM), and for phrase-based translation.

For all of the problems that we consider, the resulting algorithms produce exact solutions, with certificates of optimality, on the vast majority of examples; the algorithms are efficient for problems that are either NP-hard (as is the case for non-projective parsing, or for phrase-based translation), or for problems that are solvable in polynomial time using dynamic programming, but where the traditional exact algorithms are far too expensive to be practical.

While the focus of this talk is on NLP problems, there are close connections to inference methods, in particular belief propagation, for graphical models. Our work was inspired by recent work that has used dual decomposition as an alternative to belief propagation in Markov random fields.

This is joint work with Yin-Wen Chang, Tommi Jaakkola, Terry Koo, Sasha Rush, and David Sontag.

Prefix Probabilities for Linear Context-Free Rewriting Systems

Mark-Jan Nederhof
School of Computer Science
University of St Andrews
North Haugh, St Andrews, Fife
KY16 9SX
United Kingdom

Giorgio Satta
Dept. of Information Engineering
University of Padua
via Gradenigo, 6/A
I-35131 Padova
Italy

Abstract

We present a novel method for the computation of prefix probabilities for linear context-free rewriting systems. Our approach streamlines previous procedures to compute prefix probabilities for context-free grammars, synchronous context-free grammars and tree adjoining grammars. In addition, the methodology is general enough to be used for a wider range of problems involving, for example, several prefixes.

1 Introduction

There are a number of problems related to probabilistic grammatical formalisms that involve summing an infinite number of values. For example, if P is a probability distribution over strings defined by a probabilistic grammar, and w is a string, then the **prefix probability** of w is defined to be:

$$\sum_{v} P(wv)$$

In words, all possible suffixes v that may follow prefix w are considered, and the probabilities of the concatenations of v and w are summed.

Prefix probabilities can be exploited to predict the next word or part of speech, for incremental processing of text or speech from left to right (Jelinek and Lafferty, 1991). They can also be used in speech processing to score partial hypotheses in beam search (Corazza et al., 1991).

At first sight, it is not clear that prefix probabilities can be effectively computed, as the number of possible strings v is infinite. It was shown however by Jelinek and Lafferty (1991) that in the case of probabilistic context-free grammars, the infinite sums can be isolated from any particular w, and these sums can be computed off-line by solving linear systems of equations. For any particular w, the prefix probability can then be computed in cubic time in the length of w, on the basis of the values computed off-line. Whereas Jelinek and Lafferty (1991) consider parsing in the style of the Cocke-Kasami-Younger algorithm (Younger, 1967; Harrison, 1978), prefix probabilities for probabilistic context-free grammars can also be computed in the style of the algorithm by Earley (1970), as shown by Stolcke (1995).

This approach is not restricted to context-free grammars. It was shown by Nederhof et al. (1998) that prefix probabilities can also be effectively computed for probabilistic tree adjoining grammars. That effective computation is also possible for probabilistic synchronous context-free grammars was shown by Nederhof and Satta (2011b), which departed from earlier papers on the subject in that the solution was divided into a number of steps, namely a new type of transformation of the grammar, followed by elimination of epsilon and unit rules, and the computation of the inside probability of a string.

In this paper we focus on a much more general formalism than those mentioned above, namely that of probabilistic linear context-free rewriting systems (PLCFRS). This formalism is equivalent to the probabilistic simple RCGs discussed by Maier and Søgaard (2008) and by Kallmeyer and Maier (2010), and probabilistic extensions of multiple context-free grammars, such as those considered by Kato et al. (2006). Nonterminals in a PLCFRS can generate discontinuous constituents. For this reason, (P)LCFRSs have recently been used to model discontinuous phrase structure treebanks as well as non-projective dependency treebanks; see (Maier and Lichte, 2009; Kuhlmann and Satta, 2009; Kallmeyer and Maier, 2010).

The main contribution of this paper is a method for computing prefix probabilities for PLCFRSs. We are not aware of any existing algorithm in the literature for this task. Our method implies existence of algorithms for the computation of prefix probabilities for probabilistic versions of formalisms that are special cases of LCFRSs, such as the generalized multitext grammars of Melamed et al. (2004), which are used to model translation, and the already mentioned formalism proposed by Kuhlmann and Satta (2009) to model non-projective dependency structures.

We follow essentially the same approach as Nederhof and Satta (2011b), and reduce the problem of computing the prefix probabilities for PLCFRSs to the well-known problem of computing inside probabilities for PLCFRSs. The reduction is obtained by the composition of a PLCFRS with a special finite-state transducer. Most importantly, this composition is independent of the specific input string for which we need to solve the prefix probability problem, and can therefore be computed off-line. We also show how off-line application of a generic form of epsilon and unit rule elimination for PLCFRS can be exploited, which simplifies the computation of the inside probability.

The rest of this paper is organized as follows. In Section 2 we introduce PLCFRS and finite-state transducers. In Section 3 we discuss a general algorithm for composing a PLCFRS with a finite-state transducer. This construction will be used in several places in later sections. Section 4 shows an effective way of computing the inside probabilities for PLCFRSs, and Section 5 presents a method for the elimination of epsilon and unit rules in a PLCFRS. Section 6 combines all of the previous techniques, resulting in an algorithm for the computation of prefix probabilities via a reduction to the computation of inside probabilities. We then conclude in Section 7 with some discussion.

2 Definitions

This section summarizes the terminology and notation of linear context-free rewriting systems, and their probabilistic extension. For more detailed definitions on linear context-free writing systems, see Vijay-Shanker et al. (1987).

For an integer $n \geq 1$, we write $[n]$ to denote the set $\{1, \ldots, n\}$ and $[0] = \emptyset$. We write $[n]_0$ to denote $[n] \cup \{0\}$. A **linear context-free rewriting system** (LCFRS for short) is a tuple $G = (N, \Sigma, P, S)$, where N and Σ are finite, disjoint sets of nonterminal and terminal symbols, respectively. Each $A \in N$ is associated with an integer value $\phi(A) \geq 1$, called its **fan-out**. The nonterminal S is the **start symbol**, with $\phi(S) = 1$. Finally, P is a set of **rules**, each of the form:

$$\pi : A \rightarrow g(A_1, A_2, \ldots, A_r)$$

where $A, A_1, \ldots, A_r \in N$, and:

$$g : (\Sigma^*)^{\phi(A_1)} \times \cdots \times (\Sigma^*)^{\phi(A_r)} \rightarrow (\Sigma^*)^{\phi(A)}$$

is a linear, non-erasing function. In other words, g takes r tuples of strings as input, the j-th tuple being of size $\phi(A_j)$, and provides as output a tuple of strings of size $\phi(A)$. Each of the output strings is the concatenation of a sequence of elements, each element being an input string or a terminal symbol. Each input string is used precisely once in such a sequence. The number r is called the **rank** of the rule, and is denoted by $\rho(\pi)$ or $\rho(g)$.

The symbol π is the label of the rule, and each rule is uniquely identified by its label. For technical reasons, we allow the existence of multiple rules that are identical apart from their labels. Again for technical reasons, we assume that each function g is uniquely identified with one rule π.

The rank of LCFRS G, written $\rho(G)$, is the maximum rank among all rules of G. The fan-out of LCFRS G, written $\phi(G)$, is the maximum fan-out among all nonterminals of G.

Let a rule π be:

$$\begin{aligned}
&\pi : A \rightarrow g(A_1, A_2, \ldots, A_r), \text{ where} \\
&g(\langle x_{1,1}, \ldots, x_{1,\phi(A_1)} \rangle, \\
&\quad \ldots, \\
&\quad \langle x_{r,1}, \ldots, x_{r,\phi(A_r)} \rangle) = \\
&\qquad \langle\, y_{1,1} \cdots y_{1,m_1}, \\
&\qquad \ldots, \\
&\qquad y_{\phi(A),1} \cdots y_{\phi(A),m_{\phi(A)}} \rangle
\end{aligned}$$

where for each $k \in [\phi(A)]$ and $l \in [m_k]$, $y_{k,l}$ is from the set $\Sigma \cup \{x_{i,j} \mid i \in [r],\ j \in [\phi(A_i)]\}$. We say π is **monotone** if for each $i \in [r]$, for each $j_1, j_2 \in [\phi(A_i)]$ such that $j_1 < j_2$, and for each $k_1, k_2 \in [\phi(A)]$, $l_1 \in [m_{k_1}]$ and $l_2 \in [m_{k_2}]$ such that $y_{k_1,l_1} = x_{i,j_1}$ and $y_{k_2,l_2} = x_{i,j_2}$, we have that either $k_1 < k_2$, or $k_1 = k_2$ and $l_1 < l_2$. In other words, the order of variables associated with each of the right-hand side nonterminals is preserved in the output of function g. In this paper we will assume all rules in a LCFRS are monotone. Restriction to monotone rules preserves the generative power of LCFRS (Michaelis, 2001; Kracht, 2003; Kallmeyer, 2010). Furthermore, known techniques to extract (probabilistic) LCFRSs from treebanks all provide grammars with monotone rules (Maier and Lichte, 2009; Kuhlmann and Satta, 2009).

For each nonterminal A in a LCFRS G, there is a set of **derivations** for A, denoted $D_G(A)$, or $D(A)$ when G is understood. The simultaneous definition of $D_G(A)$ for all A is inductively as follows. Let:

$$\pi : A \rightarrow g(A_1, A_2, \ldots, A_r)$$

be a rule of G, and let $\zeta_1, \ldots, \zeta_r$ be derivations for $A_1, \ldots, A_r$. Then the expression $g(\zeta_1, \ldots, \zeta_r)$ is a derivation for A, with an *uninterpreted* function symbol g. When $r = 0$, we write the derivation as $g()$.

The **yield** of a derivation ζ for nonterminal A in grammar G is the $\phi(A)$-tuple of strings resulting from evaluating all occurrences in ζ of function symbols. It will be denoted as $\mathit{yield}_G(\zeta)$, with once more G omitted when the grammar is understood. The language **generated** by G, denoted $L(G)$, is the set of all strings w such that $\langle w \rangle$ is the yield of a derivation for S; formally, $L(G) = \{w \mid \langle w \rangle \in \mathit{yield}_G(\zeta),\ \zeta \in D_G(S)\}$.

Example 1 Consider the LCFRS G defined by the rules:

$$\begin{aligned}
&\pi_1 : S \rightarrow g_1(A), \text{ where} \\
&\qquad g_1(\langle x_{1,1}, x_{1,2} \rangle) = \langle x_{1,1} x_{1,2} \rangle \\
&\pi_2 : A \rightarrow g_2(A), \text{ where} \\
&\qquad g_2(\langle x_{1,1}, x_{1,2} \rangle) = \langle a x_{1,1} b, c x_{1,2} d \rangle \\
&\pi_3 : A \rightarrow g_3(), \text{ where} \\
&\qquad g_3() = \langle \varepsilon, \varepsilon \rangle
\end{aligned}$$

We have $\phi(S) = 1$, $\phi(A) = \phi(G) = 2$, $\rho(\pi_3) = 0$ and $\rho(\pi_1) = \rho(\pi_2) = \rho(G) = 1$. G generates the language $\{a^n b^n c^n d^n \mid n \in \mathbb{N}\}$. For instance, the string $a^3 b^3 c^3 d^3$ is obtained through the yield $\langle a^3 b^3 c^3 d^3 \rangle$ of the derivation $g_1(g_2(g_2(g_2(g_3()))))$ for S. □

Let $\pi : A \rightarrow g(A_1, A_2, \ldots, A_r)$ be a rule in G and let d_π be the number of occurrences of terminal symbols in the definition of the associated function g. We define the size of π as:

$$|\pi| = d_\pi + \phi(A) + \sum_{i \in [r]} \phi(A_i)$$

It is not difficult to see that we can encode rule π and its associated function g using space linear in $|\pi|$. We define the size of G as $|G| = \sum_{\pi \in P} |\pi|$, where P is the set of all rules in G.

A LCFRS is said to be **reduced** if the function g from each rule occurs in some derivation from $D(S)$. Because each function uniquely identifies a rule, this means that also all rules are useful for obtaining some derivation for S. A procedure for transforming a LCFRS to make it reduced will be discussed in Section 3.

A **probabilistic** LCFRS (PLCFRS for short) is a pair $\mathcal{G} = (G, p)$ where $G = (N, \Sigma, P, S)$ is a LCFRS and p is a function from P to real numbers in $[0, 1]$. We say that $\mathcal{G}$ is **proper** if for each A:

$$\sum_{\pi : A \rightarrow g(A_1, A_2, \ldots, A_{\rho(g)})} p(\pi) = 1$$

The probability of a derivation ζ in G, denoted $L_{\mathcal{G}}(\zeta)$, is obtained by multiplying the probability of the rule corresponding to each occurrence of a function symbol in ζ. The probability of a string w, denoted $L_{\mathcal{G}}(w)$, is the sum of the probabilities of all derivations in $D(S)$ of which the yield is $\langle w \rangle$. A PLCFRS $\mathcal{G}$ is **consistent** if $\sum_w L_{\mathcal{G}}(w) = 1$. It is not difficult to see that if a PLCFRS $\mathcal{G}$ is reduced, proper and consistent, then for each A, $\sum_{\zeta \in D(A)} L_{\mathcal{G}}(\zeta) = 1$.

Example 2 Consider the extension of the LCFRS from the previous example with function p defined by $p(\pi_1) = 1$, $p(\pi_2) = 0.3$ and $p(\pi_3) = 0.7$. The resulting PLCFRS $\mathcal{G}$ is proper, as the sum of probabilities of all rules with left-hand side S is 1, and so is the sum of probabilities of all rules with left-hand side A. The probability of derivation $g_1(g_2(g_2(g_2(g_3()))))$ is $1 \cdot (0.3)^3 \cdot 0.7$. This is also the probability of the string $a^3 b^3 c^3 d^3$. It can be easily shown that $\mathcal{G}$ is consistent, as:

$$\sum_{j=0}^{\infty} 1 \cdot (0.3)^j \cdot 0.7 = 1$$

□

In the following sections, we need to consider PLCFRSs $\mathcal{G}$ that are not necessarily proper or consistent, and our discussion will involve computation of values $L_{\mathcal{G}}(A)$ for each nonterminal A, defined by:

$$L_{\mathcal{G}}(A) = \sum_{\zeta \in D(A)} L_{\mathcal{G}}(\zeta)$$

In the literature, $L_{\mathcal{G}}$ is also called the **partition function** of the grammar. We can relate these values by means of the following equations, one for each nonterminal A:

$$L_{\mathcal{G}}(A) = \sum_{\pi: A \to g(A_1,\ldots,A_{\rho(g)})} p(\pi) \cdot \prod_{j \in [\rho(g)]} L_{\mathcal{G}}(A_j)$$

The above relations specify a system of polynomial, nonlinear equations. The smallest non-negative solution to this system gives us the values of $L_{\mathcal{G}}(A)$ for all A.

The sought solutions for the nonlinear system described above can be irrational and non-expressible by radicals, even if we assume that all the rules of our LCFRS have probabilities that are rational numbers, as observed by Etessami and Yannakakis (2009). Hence values $L_{\mathcal{G}}(A)$ can only be approximated.

Approximate solutions can be obtained using the fixed-point iteration method, as described for example in (Abney et al., 1999). This method is easy to implement but shows very slow convergence in the worst case, resulting in exponential time behaviour (Etessami and Yannakakis, 2009).

Alternatively, the more powerful Newton's method can be exploited; see again (Etessami and Yannakakis, 2009). It has been shown by Kiefer et al. (2007) that, after a certain number of initial iterations, each new iteration of Newton's method adds a fixed number of bits to the precision of the approximate solution, resulting in polynomial time convergence in the size of the grammar and the number of bits in the desired approximation. However, Kiefer et al. (2007) also show that, in some degenerate cases, the number of iterations needed to compute the first bit of the solution can be at least exponential in the size of the system. For further discussion of practical issues in the computation of values $L_{\mathcal{G}}(A)$, we refer the reader to Wojtczak and Etessami (2007) and Nederhof and Satta (2008).

Despite the computational limitations discussed above, there are cases in which values $L_{\mathcal{G}}(A)$ can be computed exactly, and simpler methods can be exploited. This happens when there are no cyclic dependencies in the probabilistic grammar. This is the situation we will deal with in Section 4.

In this paper, we will consider a type of **finite-state transducer** (FST) that has a single final state and that consumes exactly one input symbol in each transition. Although such restricted FSTs cannot describe all rational transductions (Berstel, 1979), they are sufficient for our purposes, and the restrictions greatly simplify the definitions in the following sections.

Hence, our type of FST can be defined by a tuple $M = (\Sigma_1, \Sigma_2, Q, q_s, q_f, T)$, where Σ_1 and Σ_2 are finite sets of input and output symbols, respectively, Q is a finite set of **states**, of which q_s is the **start state** and q_f is the **final state**, and T is a finite set of **transitions**.

Each transition has the form $s \overset{a,u}{\mapsto} s'$, where $s, s' \in Q$, $a \in \Sigma_1$ and $u \in \Sigma_2 \cup \{\epsilon\}$. This means that we can jump from s to s' by reading a from the input, and generating u as output.

The transduction generated by FST M, denoted $L(M)$, is the set of all pairs $\langle w, v\rangle$ such that there is a sequence of n transitions $s_0 \overset{a_1,u_1}{\mapsto} s_1, \ldots, s_{n-1} \overset{a_n,u_n}{\mapsto} s_n$, such that $s_0 = q_s$, $s_n = q_f$, $a_1 \cdots a_n = w$, and $u_1 \cdots u_n = v$. The definition allows $n = 0$, in which case q_f must be q_s and the transduction includes $\langle \varepsilon, \varepsilon\rangle$. We say a FST M is **unambiguous** if each pair $\langle w, v\rangle$ is obtained by at most one sequence of transitions as above.

3 Composition

Seki et al. (1991, Thm 3.9(3), pg. 203) have shown that the class of languages generated by LCFRSs are closed under intersection with regular languages.[1] The proof is a generalization of the proof that context-free languages are closed under intersection with regular languages (Bar-Hillel et al., 1964). We slightly extend this result by showing that if we point-wise map the language generated by a LCFRS G by means of a FST M, then the resulting language is generated by another LCFRS G', or formally, $L(G') = \{v \mid w \in L(G) \land \langle w, v\rangle \in L(M)\}$. As we will show below, LCFRS G' can be effectively constructed from G and M. The construction is denoted by operator $\circ$, hence $G' = G \circ M$. The construction can be extended to take as input a PLCFRS $\mathcal{G}$ and a FST M and the output is then another PLCFRS $\mathcal{G}'$, and we denote $\mathcal{G}' = \mathcal{G} \circ M$. If the FST is unambiguous, then the probabilities are preserved, or formally:

$$L_{\mathcal{G}'}(v) = \sum_{\langle w,v\rangle \in L(M)} L_{\mathcal{G}}(w)$$

This follows directly from the fact that rule probabilities from $\mathcal{G}$ are copied unchanged to $\mathcal{G}'$.

Without loss of generality, we will assume that $G = (N, \Sigma, P, S)$ and $M = (\Sigma_1, \Sigma_2, Q, q_s, q_f, T)$, with $\Sigma = \Sigma_1$. The construction produces $G' = (N', \Sigma_2, P', S')$.

[1] The result by Seki et al. (1991) is obtained for a syntactic variant of LCFRSs called multiple context-free grammars.

The nonterminals in N' are of the form $A(\langle s_1, s'_1\rangle, \ldots, \langle s_{\phi(A)}, s'_{\phi(A)}\rangle)$, where $A \in N$ and $s_1, s'_1, \ldots, s_{\phi(A)}, s'_{\phi(A)} \in Q$. The intuition behind this definition is discussed in what follows. From the derivations for A in G, we take the subset of those that have yield $\langle w_1, ..., w_{\phi(A)}\rangle$ such that for each $j \in [\phi(A)]$ it must be possible to take the automaton from state s_j to state s'_j while consuming input w_j. In addition, input symbols are replaced by the corresponding output strings, according to the relevant transitions of the automaton. The start symbol S' is naturally $S(\langle q_s, q_f\rangle)$, as the composition ultimately needs to match strings that are generated by G against those input strings that take the automaton from the start state to the final state.

The rules of G' are constructed by exhaustively applying the following procedure. Choose a rule from G of the form:

$$\begin{aligned}
&\pi : A \to g(A_1, A_2, \ldots, A_r), \text{ where}\\
&\quad g(\ \langle x_{1,1}, \ldots, x_{1,\phi(A_1)}\rangle,\\
&\quad\quad \ldots,\\
&\quad\quad \langle x_{r,1}, \ldots, x_{r,\phi(A_r)}\rangle\ ) =\\
&\quad\quad\quad \langle\ y_{1,1} \cdots y_{1,m_1},\\
&\quad\quad\quad\quad \ldots,\\
&\quad\quad\quad\quad y_{\phi(A),1} \cdots y_{\phi(A),m_{\phi(A)}}\ \rangle
\end{aligned}$$

where for each $k \in [\phi(A)]$ and $l \in [m_k]$, $y_{k,l}$ is from the set $\Sigma \cup \{x_{i,j} \mid i \in [r],\ j \in [\phi(A_i)]\}$. Further choose two states $s_{i,j}, s'_{i,j}$ from M for each $i \in [r]$ and each $j \in [\phi(A_i)]$, and choose two states $q_{k,l}, q'_{k,l}$ from M for each $k \in [\phi(A)]$ and each $l \in [m_k]$, under the following constraints, which if satisfied define $z_{k,l}$ for $k \in [\phi(A)]$ and $l \in [m_k]$:

- if $y_{k,l} = x_{i,j}$, then $q_{k,l}$ must be $s_{i,j}$ and $q'_{k,l}$ must be $s'_{i,j}$, and we let $z_{k,l} = x_{i,j}$,
- if $y_{k,l} = a \in \Sigma$ then we must be able to choose a transition $q_{k,l} \overset{a,u}{\mapsto} q'_{k,l}$, and we let $z_{k,l} = u$,
- for each $k \in [\phi(A)]$ and each $l \in [m_k - 1]$, $q'_{k,l} = q_{k,l+1}$

In words, all variables coming from right-hand side nonterminals are associated with two states, whose intended meaning was explained before. In addition, each terminal occurrence in the output of the function g must correspond to a transition between two states. Lastly, an output component of the form $y_{k,1} \cdots y_{k,m_k}$ must match a contiguous path through the automaton, with each $y_{k,l}$ representing a segment of that path from state $q_{k,l}$ to state $q'_{k,l}$.

This determines a rule in G', which is of the form:

$$\begin{aligned}
&\pi' : A' \to g'(A'_1, A'_2, \ldots, A'_r), \text{ where}\\
&\quad g'(\ \langle x_{1,1}, \ldots, x_{1,\phi(A_1)}\rangle,\\
&\quad\quad \ldots,\\
&\quad\quad \langle x_{r,1}, \ldots, x_{r,\phi(A_r)}\rangle\ ) =\\
&\quad\quad\quad \langle\ z_{1,1} \cdots z_{1,m_1},\\
&\quad\quad\quad\quad \ldots,\\
&\quad\quad\quad\quad z_{\phi(A),1} \cdots z_{\phi(A),m_{\phi(A)}}\ \rangle
\end{aligned}$$

Here A' is:

$$A(\langle q_{1,1}, q'_{1,m_1}\rangle, \ldots, \langle q_{\phi(A),1}, q'_{\phi(A),m_{\phi(A)}}\rangle)$$

and for each $i \in [r]$, A'_i is:

$$A_i(\langle s_{i,1}, s'_{i,1}\rangle, \ldots, \langle s_{i,\phi(A_i)}, s'_{i,\phi(A_i)}\rangle)$$

A new label π' and new function name g' are produced for each rule in G' that is constructed as above.

If we are dealing with probabilities, then the rules in $\mathcal{G}' = \mathcal{G} \circ M$ are constructed in the same manner, and in addition, the probability of each rule π is copied to each rule π' constructed from it.

Example 3 Assume the following is a rule in G:

$$\begin{aligned}
&\pi : A \to g(A_1, A_2), \text{ where}\\
&\quad g(\langle x_{1,1}, x_{1,2}\rangle, \langle x_{2,1}, x_{2,2}, x_{2,3}\rangle) =\\
&\quad\quad \langle x_{1,1} a x_{2,1}, x_{2,2} x_{1,2}, x_{2,3}\rangle
\end{aligned}$$

Further assume the existence of states $s_1, \ldots, s_9$ in M and the existence of a transition $s_2 \overset{a,b}{\mapsto} s_3$ for M. Then we add to G' the rule:

$$\begin{aligned}
&\pi' : A(\langle s_1, s_4\rangle, \langle s_5, s_7\rangle, \langle s_8, s_9\rangle) \to g'(\\
&\quad A_1(\langle s_1, s_2\rangle, \langle s_6, s_7\rangle),\\
&\quad A_2(\langle s_3, s_4\rangle, \langle s_5, s_6\rangle, \langle s_8, s_9\rangle)), \text{ where}\\
&\quad\quad g'(\langle x_{1,1}, x_{1,2}\rangle, \langle x_{2,1}, x_{2,2}, x_{2,3}\rangle) =\\
&\quad\quad\quad \langle x_{1,1} b x_{2,1}, x_{2,2} x_{1,2}, x_{2,3}\rangle
\end{aligned}$$

□

A LCFRS $G' = G \circ M$ (or PLCFRS $\mathcal{G}' = \mathcal{G} \circ M$) is generally not reduced. We can make it reduced by a process almost identical to the process of reduction for context-free grammars (Sippu and

Soisalon-Soininen, 1988). This consists of three phases. First, there is a bottom-up phase to identify the 'generating' nonterminals, that is, those that have derivations. Second, restricting attention to the generating nonterminals, a top-down phase identifies the possibly smaller set of nonterminals that are also reachable from the start symbol. Lastly, all rules are removed except those that are generating and reachable.

Computation Let us first relate $|G'|$ to $|G|$, where $G' = G \circ M$. To simplify the discussion, consider a rule of G of the form $\pi : A \to g(A_1, A_2, \ldots, A_r)$ without terminal symbols, or in other words $d_\pi = 0$. Let Q be the set of states of M. Then the composition construction defines a new rule in G' for each possible choice of a number of states in Q equal to $\phi(A) + \sum_{i\in[r]} \phi(A_i)$. This results in $|Q|^{|\pi|}$ new rules in G' that are derived from π, where each new rule has size $\mathcal{O}(|\pi|)$. Thus the target grammar has size exponential in $|G|$.

Our algorithm for composition can be easily implemented to run in time $\mathcal{O}(|G'|)$, that is, in linear time in the size of the output grammar. Because of the above discussion, the algorithm runs in exponential time in the size of the input. Exponential time for the composition construction is not unexpected: the problem at hand is a generalization of the parsing problem for LCFRS, and the latter problem is known to be NP-hard when the grammar is part of the input (Satta, 1992).

The critical term in the above analysis is $|\pi|$. If we can cast our LCFRS in a form in which each rule has length bounded by some constant, then composition can be carried out in polynomial time. The process of reducing the length of rules in a LCFRS is called **factorization**. It is known that not all LCFRSs can be factorized in such a way that each rule has length bounded by some constant (Rambow and Satta, 1999). However, in the context of natural language parsing, it has been observed that the vast majority of rules in real world applications can be factorized to some small length, and that excluding the worst-case rules which cannot be handled in this way does not significantly affect accuracy; see for instance (Huang et al., 2009) and (Kuhlmann and Satta, 2009) for discussion. Efficient algorithms for factorization of LCFRSs have been presented by Kuhlmann and Satta (2009), Gómez-Rodríguez and Satta (2009) and Sagot and Satta (2010).

Finally, the procedure for reducing a LCFRS that we outlined in this section can be easily implemented to run in time linear in the size of the source grammar.

4 Effective LCFRS Parsing

String parsing with LCFRS G and input $w = a_1 \cdots a_n \in \Sigma^*$ can be described in terms of composition as follows. We construct a FST M_w with states $s_0, \ldots, s_n$, of which s_0 is the start state and s_n is the final state, and transitions $s_{i-1} \overset{a_i,a_i}{\mapsto} s_i$ for each $i \in [n]$. In words, the FST describes a mapping from only one string w to itself. The composition $G' = G \circ M_w$ restricts the derivations from G to only those that have $\langle w \rangle$ as yield.

This approach is consistent with the observation by Lang (1994) that parsing is a form of intersection. In the case of very ambiguous grammars, the approach has the advantage that the set of all parse trees is represented in a compact manner by the intersection grammar, or $G' = G \circ M_w$ in our case.

Because M_w is unambiguous, the composition also has favourable properties for PLCFRS $\mathcal{G}$. In particular, the probability $L_{\mathcal{G}}(w)$ of a string w can be determined by summing the probabilities of all derivations of PLCFRS $\mathcal{G}' = \mathcal{G} \circ M_w$, or formally:

$$L_{\mathcal{G}}(w) = \textstyle\sum_v L_{\mathcal{G}'}(v) = L_{\mathcal{G}'}(S(\langle s_0, s_n \rangle))$$

We have thus reduced the problem of computing the inside probability of w under $\mathcal{G}$ to the problem of computing the values of the partition function for $\mathcal{G}'$. Because $L_{\mathcal{G}}(w)$ can be less than 1, it is clear that $\mathcal{G}'$ need not be consistent, even if we assume that $\mathcal{G}$ is.

As we have discussed in Section 2, if $\mathcal{G}'$ is any PLCFRS that may not be proper or consistent, then the values $L_{\mathcal{G}'}(A)$ for the different nonterminals of $\mathcal{G}'$ can be expressed in terms of a system of equations. Solving such equations can be computationally expensive.

A more efficient way to compute the values $L_{\mathcal{G}'}(A)$ is possible however if there are no cyclic dependencies in $\mathcal{G}'$, that is, in the system of equations specified in Section 2, no value is defined in terms of itself. This can be ensured if the functions g of the rules of the grammar are such that the multiset of non-empty strings in the output are never the same as the multiset of non-empty strings in the input arguments. This in turn is ensured if the grammar contains no epsilon rules and no unit rules.

Analogously to the theory of context-free grammars, we define an **epsilon rule** to be of the form:

$$\pi : A \rightarrow g(), \text{ where } g() = \langle \varepsilon, \ldots, \varepsilon \rangle$$

We define a **unit rule** to be of the form:

$$\pi : A \rightarrow g(A_1), \text{ where}$$
$$g(\langle x_1, \ldots, x_{\phi(A_1)} \rangle) = \langle x_1, \ldots, x_{\phi(A_1)} \rangle$$

Note that we assume that $\phi(A_1) = \phi(A)$. The reason why we do not need to consider a reordering of variables is because we have assumed that all LCFRSs are monotone, as mentioned in Section 2. In Section 5 we will show that a LCFRS can be transformed to eliminate all epsilon rules and unit rules, while preserving the language as well as the assignment of probabilities to strings. In the remainder of the present section, we discuss the computation of the values $L_{\mathcal{G}'}(A)$ under the assumption that we do not have to deal with cyclic dependencies.

We define a binary relation $\prec$ over sequences of strings by letting $\langle w_1, \ldots, w_k \rangle \prec \langle v_1, \ldots, v_m \rangle$ if and only if $|w_1 \cdots w_k| < |v_1 \cdots v_m|$ or $|w_1 \cdots w_k| = |v_1 \cdots v_m|$ and $m < k$. In words, a sequence is smaller than another if it contains fewer occurrences of symbols, and when the two sequences contain the same number of occurrences of symbols, then the first is smaller if the symbol occurrences are distributed over more strings.

Let w be any string. If LCFRS G does not contain epsilon rules or unit rules, then LCFRS $G' = G \circ M_w$ has the following property. If $\zeta = g'(\zeta_1, \ldots, \zeta_r)$ is a derivation for some nonterminal A' in G', then $\mathit{yield}(\zeta_i) \prec \mathit{yield}(\zeta)$ for every $i \in [r]$. Note that $\mathit{yield}(\zeta) = g'(\mathit{yield}(\zeta_1), \ldots, \mathit{yield}(\zeta_r))$.

If we extend this to the probabilistic case, with $\mathcal{G}' = \mathcal{G} \circ M_w$, $\mathcal{G} = (G, p)$ and $\mathcal{G}' = (G', p')$, then $L_{\mathcal{G}'}(\zeta) = p'(\pi') \cdot \prod_i L_{\mathcal{G}'}(\zeta_i)$, where π' is the label of the rule in which g' occurs. If we use the fact that multiplication distributes over addition, we derive:

$$L_{\mathcal{G}'}(A') = \sum_{\pi' : A' \rightarrow g'(A'_1, \ldots, A'_{\rho(g')})} p'(\pi') \cdot \prod_{i \in [\rho(g')]} L_{\mathcal{G}'}(A'_i)$$

Recall that M_w has the set of states $\{s_0, \ldots, s_n\}$, where $n = |w|$. Using the notation in Section 3, A' is therefore of the form:

$$A(\langle s_{b_{1,1}}, s_{b'_{1,m_1}} \rangle, \ldots, \langle s_{b_{\phi(A),1}}, s_{b'_{\phi(A),m_{\phi(A)}}} \rangle),$$

where for each $k \in [\phi(A)]$ and $l \in [m_k]$, $b_{k,l}$ and $b'_{k,l}$ are integers in $[n]_0$. Furthermore, for each $i \in [\rho(g')]$, A'_i is of the form:

$$A_i(\langle s_{c_{i,1}}, s_{c'_{i,1}} \rangle, \ldots, \langle s_{c_{i,\phi(A_i)}}, s_{c'_{i,\phi(A_i)}} \rangle),$$

where for each $j \in [\phi(A_i)]$, $c_{i,j}$ and $c'_{i,j}$ are integers in $[n]_0$.

By associating each pair $\langle s_{b_{k,l}}, s_{b'_{k,l}} \rangle$ (or $\langle s_{c_{i,j}}, s_{c'_{i,j}} \rangle$) with a corresponding substring $a_{b_{k,l}+1} \cdots a_{b'_{k,l}}$ (or $a_{c_{i,j}+1} \cdots a_{c'_{i,j}}$, respectively) of w, we obtain sequences of strings for A'_i that are smaller than those for A', by relation $\prec$. Because $\prec$ is acyclic, this means we can compute $L_{\mathcal{G}'}(A'_i)$ strictly before computing $L_{\mathcal{G}'}(A')$. All values of $L_{\mathcal{G}'}$ for different nonterminals can be obtained by enumerating all sequences of substrings from w in an order that is consistent with $\prec$. We refer to this procedure as the **inside algorithm** for PLCFRSs.

Computation It is not difficult to implement the inside algorithm in such a way that all values $L_{\mathcal{G}'}(A)$ can be computed in time linear in the size of $G' = G \circ M_w$. This is essentially a generalization of the well-known inside algorithm for probabilistic context-free grammars (Manning and Schütze, 1999) to a special kind of non-recursive PLCFRS.

5 Grammar Transformations

In this section we introduce grammar transformations that remove cyclic dependencies from LCFRS, and discuss their application to a special class of PLCFRSs.

We say a nonterminal A is **nullable** in grammar G if there is a derivation $\zeta \in D_G(A)$ with $\mathit{yield}_G(\zeta) = \langle \varepsilon, \ldots, \varepsilon \rangle$. The set E_G of nullable nonterminals in G can be found as a straightforward generalization of the algorithm to find nullable nonterminals in a context-free grammar (Sippu and Soisalon-Soininen, 1988). Similarly, we can construct the set of all nonterminals A for which at least one derivation $\zeta \in D_G(A)$ has a yield containing at least one non-empty string. We denote this set by $\overline{E}_G$.

A LCFRS G can now be transformed into a LCFRS G' without epsilon rules, by applying the following exhaustively.[2] Take a rule from G:

$$\pi : A \rightarrow g(A_1, \ldots, A_r), \text{ where}$$
$$g(\langle x_{1,1}, \ldots, x_{1,\phi(A_1)} \rangle, \ldots, \langle x_{r,1}, \ldots, x_{r,\phi(A_r)} \rangle) = \langle \alpha_1, \ldots, \alpha_{\phi(A)} \rangle$$

and determine:

$$\mathcal{U}_\pi = \{ i \mid i \in [r],\ A_i \in E_G \}$$
$$\overline{\mathcal{U}}_\pi = \{ i \mid i \in [r],\ A_i \in \overline{E}_G \}$$

and then choose any set $\mathcal{U}$ with $(\mathcal{U}_\pi \setminus \overline{\mathcal{U}}_\pi) \subseteq \mathcal{U} \subseteq \mathcal{U}_\pi$. That is, the set must contain all indices of right-hand side nonterminals that only generate yields with empty strings, and it may additionally contain the indices of other nullable nonterminal occurrences. Now construct the rule:

$$\pi_{\mathcal{U}} : A \rightarrow g_{\mathcal{U}}(B_1, \ldots, B_{r'}), \text{ where}$$
$$g_{\mathcal{U}}(\langle x'_{1,1}, \ldots, x'_{1,\phi(B_1)} \rangle, \ldots, \langle x'_{r',1}, \ldots, x'_{r',\phi(B_{r'})} \rangle) = \langle \alpha'_1, \ldots, \alpha'_{\phi(A)} \rangle$$

where $B_1, \ldots, B_{r'}$ is obtained from $A_1, \ldots, A_r$ by omitting A_i if $i \in \mathcal{U}$, where $r' = r - |\mathcal{U}|$. Similarly, $g_{\mathcal{U}}$ has only r' arguments, by omitting its i-th argument if $i \in \mathcal{U}$. Lastly, for each $k \in [\phi(A)]$, α'_k is obtained from α_k by omitting any variables of the form $x_{i,j}$ where $i \in \mathcal{U}$. The constructed rule $\pi_{\mathcal{U}}$ now becomes a rule in the transformed grammar G' if it is not an epsilon rule.

Example 4 Assume a rule in G of the form:

$$\pi : A \rightarrow g(A_1, A_2, A_3), \text{ where}$$
$$g(\langle x_1 \rangle, \langle x_2 \rangle, \langle x_3 \rangle) = \langle x_3 a x_1 x_2 \rangle$$

Further assume that E_G includes A_1 and A_2 but not A_3, and $\overline{E}_G$ includes A_1 and A_3 but not A_2. Then G' will contain:

$$\pi_{\{2\}} : A \rightarrow g_{\{2\}}(A_1, A_3), \text{ where}$$
$$g_{\{2\}}(\langle x_1 \rangle, \langle x_3 \rangle) = \langle x_3 a x_1 \rangle$$
$$\pi_{\{1,2\}} : A \rightarrow g_{\{1,2\}}(A_3), \text{ where}$$
$$g_{\{1,2\}}(\langle x_3 \rangle) = \langle x_3 a \rangle$$

□

In the case of a PLCFRS $\mathcal{G} = (G, p)$ being transformed to $\mathcal{G}' = (G', p')$, we have:

$$p'(\pi_{\mathcal{U}}) = p(\pi) \cdot \prod_{i \in \mathcal{U}} \sum_{\substack{\zeta \in D_G(A_i) : \\ yield(\zeta) = \langle \varepsilon, \ldots, \varepsilon \rangle}} L_{\mathcal{G}}(\zeta)$$

The summation of all derivations with yields consisting only of empty strings is difficult in general, and involves the solution of a system of polynomial, nonlinear equations, a topic which we addressed in Section 2.

However, there is a special case that can be easily dealt with, namely that $E_G \cap \overline{E}_G = \emptyset$ and for each $A \in E_G$:

$$\sum_{\substack{\zeta \in D_G(A) : \\ yield(\zeta) = \langle \varepsilon, \ldots, \varepsilon \rangle}} L_{\mathcal{G}}(\zeta) = 1$$

This means that there is precisely one possible set $\mathcal{U}$ for each rule π, and $p'(\pi_{\mathcal{U}})$ will always be identical to $p(\pi)$. In this case the overall construction of elimination of nullable rules from PLCFRS $\mathcal{G}$ can be implemented in time linear in $|G|$. It is this special case that we will encounter in Section 6.

Now we turn to elimination of unit rules from a PLCFRS $\mathcal{G}$. We investigate sequences of applications of unit rules, multiplying the probabilities of all rule occurrences, and adding the probabilities of all such sequences between each pair of nonterminals. Formally, for each pair A and B of nonterminals, we have a value $\Delta_{\mathcal{G}}(A, B)$, and we write:

$$\Delta_{\mathcal{G}}(A, B) = \delta(A = B) + \sum_{\substack{\pi : A \rightarrow g(A_1), \text{ where} \\ g(\langle x_1, \ldots, x_{\phi(A_1)} \rangle) = \\ \langle x_1, \ldots, x_{\phi(A_1)} \rangle}} p(\pi) \cdot \Delta_{\mathcal{G}}(A_1, B)$$

where $\delta(A = B)$ is defined to be 1 if $A = B$ and 0 otherwise. This forms a system of linear equations in the unknown variables $\Delta_{\mathcal{G}}(\cdot, \cdot)$. Such a system can be solved in polynomial time in the number of variables, for example using Gaussian elimination.

In order to construct the transformed grammar $\mathcal{G}'$, we exhaustively choose a rule from $\mathcal{G}$:

$$\pi : A \rightarrow g(A_1, A_2, \ldots, A_r)$$

[2]Removal of epsilon rules is also investigated by Seki et al. (1991, Lemma 2.2(N2), pg. 197) for multiple context-free grammars, a syntactic variant of LCFRSs. Here we extend the result to the probabilistic version of LCFRSs.

and choose B such that $\Delta_{\mathcal{G}}(B, A) > 0$, and let $\mathcal{G}'$ contain the rule:

$$\pi_B : B \rightarrow g_B(A_1, A_2, \ldots, A_r)$$

where g_B is defined to be identical to g. The probability of π_B is $p'(\pi_B) = p(\pi) \cdot \Delta_{\mathcal{G}}(B, A)$.

The size of $\mathcal{G}'$ is quadratic in $\mathcal{G}$. The time complexity is dominated by the computation of the solution of the linear system of equations. This computation takes cubic time in the number of variables. The number of variables in this case is $\mathcal{O}(|\mathcal{G}|^2)$, which makes the running time $\mathcal{O}(|\mathcal{G}|^6)$.

6 Prefix Probabilities

In this section we gather all the constructions that have been presented in the previous sections, and provide the main result of this paper.

Let $\mathcal{G}$ be a reduced, proper and consistent PLCFRS. We assume $\mathcal{G}$ does not contain any epsilon rules, and therefore the empty string is not in the generated language.

The first step towards the computation of prefix probabilities is the construction of a FST M_{pref} that maps any string w over an assumed input alphabet to any non-empty prefix of w. In other words, its transduction is the set of pairs $\langle wv, w\rangle$, for any non-empty string w and any string v, both over the alphabet Σ of $\mathcal{G}$. The reason why we do not consider empty prefixes w is because this simplifies the definition of M_{pref} below, assuming there can be only one final state. The restriction is without loss of generality, as the computation of the prefix probability of the empty string is easy: it is always 1.

The transducer M_{pref} has two states, q_s and q_f, which are also the start and final states, respectively. The transitions have the following forms, for each $a \in \Sigma$:

$$q_s \overset{a,a}{\mapsto} q_s$$
$$q_s \overset{a,a}{\mapsto} q_f$$
$$q_f \overset{a,\varepsilon}{\mapsto} q_f$$

In words, symbols are copied unchanged from input to output as long as the automaton is in the start state. After it jumps to the final state, no more output can be produced.

Note that if we consider any pair of states s and s', such that the automaton can reach s' from s, then precisely one of the following two cases is possible:

- On any path through the automaton, the empty string is produced in the output. This applies when $s = s' = q_f$.
- On any path through the automaton, a non-empty string is produced in the output. This applies when $s = s' = q_s$, or $s = q_s$ and $s' = q_f$.

Note that in the first case, for $s = s' = q_f$, any string can be consumed in the input, in exactly one way. This has an important implication for the composition $\mathcal{G}' = \mathcal{G} \circ M_{pref}$, namely that all nullable nonterminals in $\mathcal{G}'$ must be of the form $A' = A(\langle q_f, q_f\rangle, \ldots, \langle q_f, q_f\rangle)$. By the construction of $\mathcal{G}'$, and by the assumption that $\mathcal{G}$ is reduced, proper and consistent we have:

$$\sum_{\substack{\zeta \in D_{\mathcal{G}'}(A') :\\ yield(\zeta) = \langle\varepsilon, \ldots, \varepsilon\rangle}} L_{\mathcal{G}'}(\zeta) = \sum_{\zeta \in D_{\mathcal{G}(A)}} L_{\mathcal{G}}(\zeta) \quad = \quad 1$$

Therefore, we can apply a simplified procedure to eliminate epsilon rules, maintaining the probability of a rule where we eliminate nullable nonterminals from its right-hand side, as explained in Section 5.

After also unit rules have been eliminated, by the procedure in Section 5, we obtain a grammar $\mathcal{G}''$ without epsilon rules and without unit rules. For a given prefix w we can now construct $\mathcal{G}'' \circ M_w$, and apply the inside algorithm, by which we obtain $L_{\mathcal{G}''}(w)$, which is the required prefix probability of w by $\mathcal{G}$.

Computation Consider the PLCFRS $\mathcal{G}' = \mathcal{G} \circ M_{pref}$; assume $\mathcal{G}'$ is subsequently reduced. Due to the special topology of M_{pref} and to the assumption that G is monotonic, it is not difficult to see that all nonterminals of G' have the form $A(\langle s_1, s_2\rangle, \ldots, \langle s_{2\phi(A)-1}, s_{2\phi(A)}\rangle)$ such that, for some $k \in [2\phi(A)]_0$, we have $s_i = q_s$ for each $i \in [k]$ and $s_i = q_f$ for each $i \in [2\phi(A)] \setminus [k]$. Related to this, for each rule π of G, there are only $\mathcal{O}(|\pi|)$ many rules in G' (as opposed to a number exponential in $|\pi|$, as in the general case discussed in Section 3). Since each new rule in G' constructed from π has size proportional to $|\pi|$, we may conclude that $|G'| = \mathcal{O}(|G|^2)$. Furthermore, $\mathcal{G}'$ can be computed in quadratic time.

The simplified procedure for eliminating epsilon rules and the procedure for eliminating unit rules both take polynomial time, as discussed in

Section 5. This results in a PLCFRS $\mathcal{G}''$ such that $|G''|$ is polynomially related to $|G|$, where G is the source LCFRS. Note that $\mathcal{G}''$ can be computed off-line, that is, independently of the specific input string for which we need to compute the prefix probability.

Finally, computation of $\mathcal{G}'' \circ M_w$, for a given prefix w, can take exponential time in $|w|$. However, the exponential time behaviour of our algorithm seems to be unavoidable, since the problem at hand is more general than the problem of parsing of w under a LCFRS model, which is known to be NP-hard (Satta, 1992). As already discussed in Section 3, the problem can be solved in polynomial time in case we can cast the source LCFRS G in a normal form where each rule has length bounded by some constant.

7 Discussion

Our findings subsume computation of the prefix probability:

- for probabilistic context-free grammars in time $\mathcal{O}(n^3)$ (Jelinek and Lafferty, 1991),
- for probabilistic tree-adjoining grammars in time $\mathcal{O}(n^6)$ (Nederhof et al., 1998), and
- for probabilistic synchronous context-free grammars (Nederhof and Satta, 2011b).

The latter becomes clear once we see that a synchronous context-free grammar can be expressed in terms of a restricted type of LCFRS. All nonterminals of this LCFRS, except the start symbol, have fan-out 2, and all generated strings are of the form $w\$v$, where w functions as input string, v functions are output string, and \$ is a separator between the two, which does not occur in the input and output alphabets of the synchronous context-free grammar. The rules of the LCFRS are of two forms. The first form is a single rule with the start symbol $S^\dagger$ in the left-hand side:

$$\pi^\dagger : S^\dagger \rightarrow g^\dagger(S), \text{ where}$$
$$g^\dagger(\langle x_{1,1}, x_{1,2}\rangle) = \langle x_{1,1}\$x_{1,2}\rangle$$

The other rules all have a form that ensures that variables associated with the input string are never combined with variables associated with the output string:

$$\pi : A \rightarrow g(A_1, \ldots, A_r), \text{ where}$$
$$g(\langle x_{1,1}, x_{1,2}\rangle, \ldots \langle x_{r,1}, x_{r,2}\rangle) =$$
$$\langle y_{1,1} \cdots y_{1,m_1}, y_{2,1} \cdots y_{2,m_2}\rangle$$

and each $y_{1,l}$, $l \in [m_1]$, is either a terminal (from the input alphabet) or a variable of the form $x_{1,j}$, and each $y_{2,l}$, $l \in [m_2]$, is either a terminal (from the output alphabet) or a variable of the form $x_{2,j}$.

Let $\mathcal{G}$ be a PLCFRS mimicking a probabilistic synchronous CFG as outlined above. We can define an unambiguous FST M of which the transduction is the set of pairs $\langle w_1v_1\$w_2v_2, w_1\$w_2\rangle$ for any strings w_1, v_1 over the input alphabet and any strings w_2, v_2 over the output alphabet of the synchronous CFG, where w_1 and w_2 are non-empty. The FST has states s_0, s_1, s_2, s_3, of which s_0 and s_3 are the start and the final state, respectively. The transitions are of the form:

$$s_0 \overset{a,a}{\mapsto} s_0 \qquad s_0 \overset{a,a}{\mapsto} s_1$$
$$s_1 \overset{a,\varepsilon}{\mapsto} s_1 \qquad s_1 \overset{\$,\$}{\mapsto} s_2$$
$$s_2 \overset{a,a}{\mapsto} s_2 \qquad s_2 \overset{a,a}{\mapsto} s_3$$
$$s_3 \overset{a,\varepsilon}{\mapsto} s_3$$

We can now proceed by constructing $\mathcal{G} \circ M$, and eliminating its epsilon and unit rules, to give $\mathcal{G}'$, much as in Section 6. Let w_1 and w_2 be two strings over the input and output alphabets, respectively. The prefix probability can now be effectively computed by constructing $\mathcal{G}' \circ M_{w_1\$w_2}$ and computing the inside algorithm.

We can use a similar idea to compute prefix probabilities for probabilistic extensions of the generalized multitext grammars of Melamed et al. (2004), a formalism used to model translation for which no prefix probability algorithm was previously known.

A seemingly small variation of the problem considered in this paper is to compute **infix probabilities** (Corazza et al., 1991; Nederhof and Satta, 2008). It is straightforward to define a FST M of which the transduction is the set of pairs $\langle v_1wv_2, w\rangle$. However, it does not seem possible to construct an *unambiguous* FST that achieves this. Therefore $\mathcal{G} \circ M$ does not have the required probabilistic properties that would allow a correct computation by means of the inside algorithm. The problem of infix probabilities for probabilistic context-free grammars was also considered by Nederhof and Satta (2011a).

References

S. Abney, D. McAllester, and F. Pereira. 1999. Relating probabilistic grammars and automata.

In *37th Annual Meeting of the Association for Computational Linguistics, Proceedings of the Conference*, pages 542–549, Maryland, USA, June.

Y. Bar-Hillel, M. Perles, and E. Shamir. 1964. On formal properties of simple phrase structure grammars. In Y. Bar-Hillel, editor, *Language and Information: Selected Essays on their Theory and Application*, chapter 9, pages 116–150. Addison-Wesley, Reading, Massachusetts.

J. Berstel. 1979. *Transductions and Context-Free Languages*. B.G. Teubner, Stuttgart.

A. Corazza, R. De Mori, R. Gretter, and G. Satta. 1991. Computation of probabilities for an island-driven parser. *IEEE Transactions on Pattern Analysis and Machine Intelligence*, 13(9):936–950.

J. Earley. 1970. An efficient context-free parsing algorithm. *Communications of the ACM*, 13(2):94–102, February.

K. Etessami and M. Yannakakis. 2009. Recursive Markov chains, stochastic grammars, and monotone systems of nonlinear equations. *Journal of the ACM*, 56(1):1–66.

C. Gómez-Rodríguez and G. Satta. 2009. An optimal-time binarization algorithm for linear context-free rewriting systems with fan-out two. In *Proceedings of the Joint Conference of the 47th Annual Meeting of the ACL and the 4th International Joint Conference on Natural Language Processing of the AFNLP*, pages 985–993, Suntec, Singapore, August.

M.A. Harrison. 1978. *Introduction to Formal Language Theory*. Addison-Wesley.

Liang Huang, Hao Zhang, Daniel Gildea, and Kevin Knight. 2009. Binarization of synchronous context-free grammars. *Computational Linguistics*, 35:559–595, December.

F. Jelinek and J.D. Lafferty. 1991. Computation of the probability of initial substring generation by stochastic context-free grammars. *Computational Linguistics*, 17(3):315–323.

L. Kallmeyer and W. Maier. 2010. Data-driven parsing with probabilistic linear context-free rewriting systems. In *The 23rd International Conference on Computational Linguistics*, pages 537–545, Beijing, China, August.

Laura Kallmeyer. 2010. *Parsing Beyond Context-Free Grammars*. Springer-Verlag.

Y. Kato, H. Seki, and T. Kasami. 2006. RNA pseudoknotted structure prediction using stochastic multiple context-free grammar. *IPSJ Digital Courier*, 2:655–664.

S. Kiefer, M. Luttenberger, and J. Esparza. 2007. On the convergence of Newton's method for monotone systems of polynomial equations. In *Proceedings of the 39th ACM Symposium on Theory of Computing*, pages 217–266.

M. Kracht. 2003. *The Mathematics of Language*. Mouton de Gruyter, Berlin.

M. Kuhlmann and G. Satta. 2009. Treebank grammar techniques for non-projective dependency parsing. In *Proceedings of the 12th Conference of the European Chapter of the Association for Computational Linguistics*, pages 478–486, Athens, Greece.

B. Lang. 1994. Recognition can be harder than parsing. *Computational Intelligence*, 10(4):486–494.

W. Maier and T. Lichte. 2009. Characterizing discontinuity in constituent treebanks. In P. de Groote, M. Egg, and L. Kallmeyer, editors, *Proceedings of the 14th Conference on Formal Grammar*, volume 5591 of *Lecture Notes in Artificial Intelligence*, Bordeaux, France.

W. Maier and A. Søgaard. 2008. Treebanks and mild context-sensitivity. In P. de Groote, editor, *Proceedings of the 13th Conference on Formal Grammar*, pages 61–76, Hamburg, Germany. CSLI Publications.

C.D. Manning and H. Schütze. 1999. *Foundations of Statistical Natural Language Processing*. MIT Press.

I. Dan Melamed, Giorgio Satta, and Ben Wellington. 2004. Generalized multitext grammars. In *Proceedings of ACL-04*.

J. Michaelis. 2001. *On Formal Properties of Minimalist Grammars*. Ph.D. thesis, Potsdam University.

M.-J. Nederhof and G. Satta. 2008. Computing partition functions of PCFGs. *Research on Language and Computation*, 6(2):139–162.

M.-J. Nederhof and G. Satta. 2011a. Computation of infix probabilities for probabilistic context-free grammars. In *Conference on Empirical Methods in Natural Language Processing, Proceedings of the Conference*, pages 1213–1221, Edinburgh, Scotland, July.

M.-J. Nederhof and G. Satta. 2011b. Prefix probability for probabilistic synchronous context-free grammars. In *49th Annual Meeting of the Association for Computational Linguistics, Proceedings of the Conference*, pages 460–469, Portland, Oregon, June.

M.-J. Nederhof, A. Sarkar, and G. Satta. 1998. Prefix probabilities from stochastic tree adjoining grammars. In *36th Annual Meeting of the Association for Computational Linguistics and 17th International Conference on Computational Linguistics*, volume 2, pages 953–959, Montreal, Quebec, Canada, August.

O. Rambow and G. Satta. 1999. Independent parallelism in finite copying parallel rewriting systems. *Theoretical Computer Science*, 223:87–120.

B. Sagot and G. Satta. 2010. Optimal rank reduction for linear context-free rewriting systems with fan-out two. In *Proceedings of the 48th Annual Meeting of the Association for Computational Linguistics*, pages 525–533, Uppsala, Sweden, July.

G. Satta. 1992. Recognition of linear context-free rewriting systems. In *30th Annual Meeting of the Association for Computational Linguistics, Proceedings of the Conference*, pages 89–95, Newark, Delaware, USA, June–July.

H. Seki, T. Matsumura, M. Fujii, and T. Kasami. 1991. On multiple context-free grammars. *Theoretical Computer Science*, 88:191–229.

S. Sippu and E. Soisalon-Soininen. 1988. *Parsing Theory, Vol. I: Languages and Parsing*, volume 15 of *EATCS Monographs on Theoretical Computer Science*. Springer-Verlag.

A. Stolcke. 1995. An efficient probabilistic context-free parsing algorithm that computes prefix probabilities. *Computational Linguistics*, 21(2):167–201.

K. Vijay-Shanker, D.J. Weir, and A.K. Joshi. 1987. Characterizing structural descriptions produced by various grammatical formalisms. In *25th Annual Meeting of the Association for Computational Linguistics, Proceedings of the Conference*, pages 104–111, Stanford, California, USA, July.

D. Wojtczak and K. Etessami. 2007. PReMo: an analyzer for Probabilistic Recursive Models. In *Tools and Algorithms for the Construction and Analysis of Systems, 13th International Conference*, volume 4424 of *Lecture Notes in Computer Science*, pages 66–71, Braga, Portugal. Springer-Verlag.

D.H. Younger. 1967. Recognition and parsing of context-free languages in time n^3. *Information and Control*, 10:189–208.

Efficient Matrix-Encoded Grammars and Low Latency Parallelization Strategies for CYK

Aaron Dunlop, Nathan Bodenstab and Brian Roark
Center for Spoken Language Understanding
Oregon Health & Science University
Portland, OR
[aaron.dunlop,bodenstab,roarkbr]@gmail.com

Abstract

We present a matrix encoding of context-free grammars, motivated by hardware-level efficiency considerations. We find efficiency gains of 2.5–9× for exhaustive inference and approximately 2× for pruned inference, resulting in high-accuracy parsing at over 20 sentences per second. Our grammar encoding allows fine-grained parallelism during chart cell population; we present a controlled study of several methods of parallel parsing, and find near-optimal latency reductions as core-count increases.

1 Introduction

Constituent parsers are important for a number of information extraction subtasks — e.g., anaphora and coreference resolution and semantic role labeling — and parsing time is often a bottleneck for such applications (Bjrne et al., 2010; Banko, 1999). Most constituent parsers leverage the dynamic programming "chart" structure of the CYK algorithm, even when performing approximate inference. The inner loop of the CYK algorithm computes an *argmax* for each constituent span by intersecting the set of observed child categories spanning adjacent substrings with the set of rule productions in the grammar. This 'grammar intersection' operation is the most computationally intensive component of the algorithm. Prior work has shown that the grammar encoding can greatly affect parsing efficiency (c.f Klein and Manning (2001), Moore (2004), Penn and Munteanu (2003)); in this paper we present a matrix encoding that can encode very large grammars to maximize inference efficiency.

This matrix grammar encoding allows a refactoring of the CYK algorithm with two beneficial properties: 1) the number of expensive grammar intersection operations is reduced from $O(n^3)$ to $O(n^2)$; and 2) since grammar intersection is reduced to a set of matrix operations, the resulting algorithm is amenable to fine-grained parallelization.

Most discussion of parallel parsing concentrates on *throughput*, the aggregate number of sentences parsed per second on a particular machine. In this study, we are also interested in applications for which response time is of interest (e.g., real-time speech recognition and machine translation), and thus consider *latency*, the time to parse a single sentence, as a primary objective. Given ideally efficient algorithms and hardware, there would be no tradeoff between the two — that is, we would be able to parallelize each sentence across an arbitrary number of processor cores, reducing latency and increasing throughput linearly with core-count. Unfortunately, hardware constraints and Amdahl's law ensure that we will never achieve that ideal speedup; in practice, we are likely to see some tradeoff. We will demonstrate interesting patterns of the tradeoff between throughput and latency with various parallelization methods, allowing consumers to tailor parsing strategies to particular application requirements.

Our grammar intersection method is amenable to graphics processors (GPUs) and similar massively-parallel architectures. In this work, we perform our analysis on a multicore CPU system. We demonstrate the utility of this approach using a number of different grammars, including the latent variable grammar used by the Berkeley parser (Petrov et al., 2006). We show large speedups compared to a traditional CYK implementation for serial inference, parsing over 20 sentences per second with the Berkeley grammar. Parallelizing this algorithm reduces average latency to .026 seconds.

The remainder of this paper is organized as follows: we begin in Section 2 with background on the CYK algorithm and various general and CYK-specific parallelization considerations. In Section 3 we provide a detailed presentation of our grammar encoding, data structures, and intersection method. In Section 4, we demonstrate their effectiveness on a single core and present controlled experiments comparing several parallelization strategies.

2 Background

2.1 CYK

Algorithm 1 shows pseudocode of the widely used CYK algorithm. Briefly, constituents spanning longer substrings are built from shorter-span constituents via a chart structure, as shown in Figure 1. Span-1 cells (the bottom row of the chart) are initialized with all part-of-speech (POS) tags, and with unary productions spanning a single word. At higher span cells in the chart, such as the dark grey cell in Figure 1, new constituents are built by combining constituents spanning adjacent substrings, guided by the productions in the grammar. With a probabilistic context-free grammar (PCFG) the maximum likelihood solution is found by storing, in each cell in the chart, the highest probability for each category in the non-terminal set V along with a backpointer to where that solution came from. Dynamic programming reduces this potentially exponential search to $O(n^3)$ complexity.

2.2 Parallelism

Since smooth parallelization is one of the benefits of the algorithm we will present in Section 3.2, we begin with background on some of the barriers to efficient parallelism. The overhead of parallelism takes many forms.[1] The operating system consumes processor cycles in thread scheduling; coordination and synchronization of concurrent tasks can leave processors idle; and (more importantly to memory-bound applications such as parsing) context switching between threads often requires flushing the CPU cache, resulting in more memory contention and stalls.

Further, some multi-core architectures share L2 or L3 caches between CPU cores, and nearly all share bandwidth to memory (the 'front-side bus', or FSB). Parallel execution threads compete for those resources, and may stall one another. Thus, parallelism can introduce considerable hardware overhead, even if OS- and task-level overhead are minimal, but this impact can be minimized if concurrent threads share common data structures.

[1] We are concerned primarily with parallelism within a single machine. Cluster-level parallelism incurs network latency, shared filesystem, and other forms of overhead that do not concern us here.

2.3 Low-Latency Parallel CYK

We observe that CYK parsing can be parallelized in (at least) three distinct ways, each likely to have different advantages and disadvantages vis-à-vis the bottlenecks just discussed:

Sentence-level: The simplest way to parallelize parsing is to parse sentences or documents independently on separate cores. This approach is well-understood, simple to implement, and quite effective. Total throughput should scale roughly linearly with the number of cores available, at least until we reach the limits of memory bandwidth, but latency is not improved — and may actually increase.

Cell-level: In most forms of CYK iteration, we populate each cell separately, leading to a straightforward form of cell-level parallelism. For example, in bottom-up cell iteration order, we populate one chart row fully before proceeding to the next. The cells on each row are independent of one another, so we can process all cells of a row in parallel. Unfortunately, as we move higher in the chart, there are fewer cells per row, and we must leave CPU cores idle. The highest cells in the chart are often the most densely populated (and require the most processing), an inherent limitation of this form of parallelism.[2]

Ninomiya et al. (1997) explored cell-level parallelization on a 256-processor machine. Their method incurred an overhead of 6–10× vs. their baseline serial algorithm (depending on sentence length). That is, their parallel algorithm ran 6–10 times slower on a single core than a simpler serial implementation. So even if their approach scaled ideally, many cores would be required to match their serial baseline performance. In practice, their algorithm did not scale linearly and required approximately 64 CPUs to equal their baseline single-CPU performance, and the total speedup observed on 256 CPUs was only 2–4×.

Grammar-level: Parallelization within a chart cell is more difficult to implement, but may avoid some of the weaknesses of the first two methods described. If we can fully parallelize cell population, we can make use of all available cores re-

[2] If optimizing for throughput, those idle threads could be reassigned to subsequent sentences, but cache- and FSB-contention is likely to further increase latency.

Algorithm 1 CYK($w_1 \ldots w_n$, $G = (V, T, S^\dagger, P, \rho)$) PCFG G must be in CNF.
α represents the population of the current cell.

for $t = 1$ to n **do** ▷ span = 1 (Words/POS tags)
  for $j = 1$ to $|V|$ **do**
    $\alpha_j(t,t) \leftarrow \mathrm{P}(A_j \rightarrow w_t)$
for $s = 2$ to n **do** ▷ All spans > 1 (rows in the chart)
  for $e = s$ to n **do** ▷ All end-points (cells in a row)
    $b \leftarrow e - s + 1$ ▷ begin-point for cell
    $\forall i \in V \mid \alpha_i(b,e) \leftarrow argmax_{j,k,m} \mathrm{P}(A_i \rightarrow A_j A_k)\alpha_j(b, m-1)\alpha_k(m,e)$

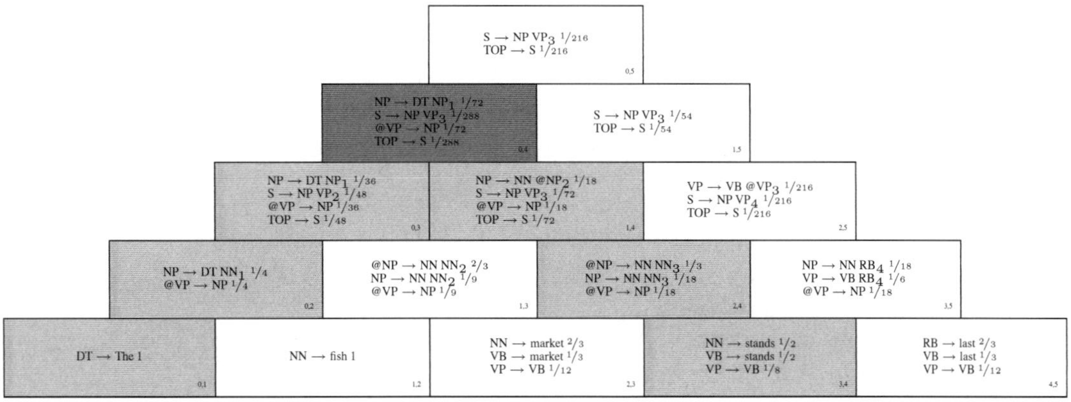

Figure 1: Example CYK chart, with target cell 0,4 highlighted in dark gray and the child cells involved in populating it highlighted in light gray.

gardless of the cell iteration order or the current position in the chart.[3] Because each thread is operating on the same cell, their working sets may align more closely than in other forms of parallelism, reducing context-switch overhead. However, this method implies very fine-grained task divisions and close coordination between threads—when we split a single grammar intersection operation across many threads, each task is quite small. At this fine granularity, locking of shared data structures is impractical, so we must divide tasks such that they share immutable data (the grammar and current cell population) but do not simultaneously mutate the same target data structures (e.g., individual threads may populate separate ranges of non-terminals in the target cell, but must not attempt to populate the same range). Even with careful task division, the task management may overwhelm the potential gains. Youngmin et al. (2011) presented one approach to this problem; we present another approach in Section 3.2.

3 Methods

3.1 Matrix Grammar Encoding

Retrieval of valid grammar rules and their probabilities is an essential component of context-free parsing. High-accuracy grammars can exceed millions of productions, so efficient model access is critical to parsing performance. Prior work on encoding the grammar as a finite state automaton (Klein and Manning, 2001) and prefix compacted tries (Moore, 2004) demonstrated that model encoding can lead to significant efficiency gains in parsing.[4] Motivated to address hardware bottlenecks and constraints, we present a novel encoding in matrix form.

Given a binarized probabilistic context-free grammar (PCFG) defined as the tuple $(V, T, S^\dagger, P, \rho)$ where V is the set of non-terminals, T is the set of terminals, $S^\dagger$ is a special start symbol, P is the set of grammar productions, and ρ is a mapping of grammar productions to probabilities, we subdivide P into binary rules, P_b, and unary rules, P_u.

We encode P_b in matrix form, where the rows of the matrix $1..|V|$ represent a production's left-

[3] Of course, we can utilize sentence-level and cell-level parallelism as well.

[4] All grammar encodings discussed, including our own, only alter efficiency; accuracy remains unchanged.

hand-side non-terminal, and the columns represent a tuple of all possible right-hand-side non-terminals (pairs in a binarized grammar). This forms a matrix of $|V|$ rows and $|V|^2$ columns. Figure 2 shows a simple grammar represented in this format.

In theory, this matrix could contain $|V|^3$ entries, but most grammars of interest are incredibly sparse, populating only a very small fraction of the possible matrix cells. For example, the Berkeley latent-variable grammar defines 1134 non-terminals, so a fully populated binary rule matrix would contain 1.49 billion rules, but the grammar only populates 1.73 million. Thus, we choose a 'compressed sparse column' sparse matrix representation (Tewarson, 1973). This storage structure is quite dense — we store the binary rules of the Berkeley grammar in approximately 10.5 MB of memory. Further, the rules are stored contiguously in memory and in order of access, so the grammar intersection operations should be very cache-efficient.

3.2 Matrix-Vector Grammar Intersection

We now present a novel intersection method, based on the grammar encoding from Section 3.1, which decouples midpoint iteration from grammar intersection, and can reduce the cell population cost considerably. We begin by pointing to Algorithm 1, the standard CYK algorithm. The $argmax$ on line 7 intersects the set of observed child categories spanning adjacent substrings (stored in chart cells) with the set of rule productions found in the grammar. Algorithms 2 and 3 show two possible grammar intersection methods, one which loops over productions in the grammar (Alg. 2) and one which loops over left-children prior to looking for grammar productions (Alg. 3). Song et al. (2008) explored a number of such grammar intersection methods, and found Algorithm 3 to be superior for right-factored grammars. We now present a novel intersection method based on the grammar encoding from Section 3.1. The description in this section is informal, with midpoints omitted for clarity. In Section 3.3, we will formalize the method as an application of a lexicographic semiring.

We represent the population of each chart cell α as a vector in $\mathbb{R}^{|V|}$. Each dimension of this vector represents the (log) probability of a non-terminal

Algorithm 2 Grammar intersection via full grammar loop (backpointer storage omitted). $\alpha(b,e)$ represents the population of the cell spanning words b to e.

$\alpha(b,e) \leftarrow 0$
for $m = b+1$ to $e-1$ **do**
  for $A_i \rightarrow A_j A_k \in P$ **do**
    $x \leftarrow \mathrm{P}(A_i \rightarrow A_j A_k)\alpha_j(b,m-1)\alpha_k(m,e)$
    if $x > \alpha_i(b,e)$ **then**
      $\alpha_i(b,e) \leftarrow x$

Algorithm 3 Grammar intersection via left child grammar loop

$\alpha(b,e) \leftarrow 0$
for $m = b+1$ to $e-1$ **do**
  for $j \in \alpha(b,m-1)$ **do**
    for $A_i \rightarrow A_j A_k \in P$ **do**
      $x \leftarrow \mathrm{P}(A_i \rightarrow A_j A_k)\alpha_j(b,m-1)\alpha_k(m,e)$
      if $x > \alpha_i(b,e)$ **then**
        $\alpha_i(b,e) \leftarrow x$

in that cell. To perform the $argmax$, we populate a temporary vector **c** of $|V|^2$ dimensions with the cartesian product of all observed non-terminals from the left and right child cells *over all midpoints*. That is, each dimension of this vector represents an ordered pair of non-terminals from the grammar, and its length (score) is the product of the inside probabilities of the respective children. For any child pairs which occur at multiple midpoints, we record only the most probable.

For example, when populating the highlighted cell (0,4) in Figure 1, the first midpoint (m=1) adds (DT,NP), (DT,S), and (DT,@VP) to **c**; the second midpoint (m=2) will add (NP,@NP), (NP,@VP), (@VP,@NP), and so on. If we observe the same pair at multiple midpoints, we retain only the maximum score.

Given a matrix-encoded grammar, G, and the child-cell vector, **c**, we simply multiply G by **c** to produce $\boldsymbol{\alpha}$, the population of the target cell. In Viterbi search, we perform this operation in the $\langle T, T \rangle$ lexicographic semiring, thus computing the maximum probability instead of the sum (described more fully in Section 3.3). Figure 2 demonstrates this Sparse-Matrix $\times$ Vector multiplication (SpMV). The SpMV is the only portion of our algorithm which must access the grammar. We perform that operation once per cell, rather than once per midpoint, reducing the num-

G

	(DT,NP)	(DT,NN)	(NN,NN)	...
NP	1/4	1/4	-	
S	-	1/32	1/32	
@VP	-	-	-	
@NP	-	-	1	
...				...

$\times$

$\mathbf{c}$

Child Pair	Prob
(DT,NP)	1/18
(DT,NN)	0
(NN,NN)	0
...	
(NP,VP)	1/72
(DT,S)	1/72
(NP,@NP)	1/12
(NP,NN)	1/72
...	...

$=$

α

Parent	Prob
NP	1/72
S	1/288
@VP	1/72
@NP	0
...	

Figure 2: Example matrix-vector multiplication for cell 0,4 in Figure 1. The grammar G encodes binary rules as a $|V| \times |V|^2$ matrix, with rows representing parents and columns representing child pairs. The vector $\mathbf{c}$ contains non-terminal child pairs observed across all possible midpoints. The matrix-vector product of $G \times \mathbf{c}$ produces the target cell population, α. Factored categories are prefixed with '@', and backpointers are omitted for clarity.

Algorithm 4 Grammar intersection via Sparse Matrix $\times$ Vector Multiplication. $h(l, r)$ maps $l, r \in V$ to an index of $\mathbf{c}$

$\mathbf{c} \leftarrow 0$
for $m = b + 1$ to $e - 1$ **do**
  for $j = 1$ to $|V|$ **do**
    for $k = 1$ to $|V|$ **do**
      $i \leftarrow h(\alpha_j(b, m-1), \alpha_k(m, e))$
      if $\alpha_j(b, m-1)\alpha_k(m, e) > \mathbf{c}_i$ **then**
        $\mathbf{c}_i \leftarrow \alpha_j(b, m-1)\alpha_k(m, e)$
$\alpha(b, e) \leftarrow G \cdot \mathbf{c}$

ber of expensive grammar operations from $O(n^3)$ to $O(n^2)$.

We note the similarity to the formalisms of Valiant (1975), which transforms parsing into boolean matrix multiplication, and Lee (1997), which inverts that transformation. However, the similarity is only superficial; Valient's algorithm populates an upper-triangular matrix, the elements of which are equivalent to CYK chart cells. Each matrix element is a subset of V, the observed population of the analogous chart cell. The matrix is populated by a transitive closure operation, which takes the place of the CYK algorithm. Our matrix operation, on the other hand, is concerned with the population of individual chart cells, the operation accomplished by Valient's $*$ operator.

Decoupling the midpoint iteration from grammar intersection is not contingent on our matrix-vector encoding. The optimization in Graham et al. (1980) also refactors the CYK algorithm to result in $O(n^2)$ grammar intersection operations by changing the dynamic programming to iterate through right (or left) child cells and build new (parent) categories in multiple chart cells at once. Similarly, the grammar-loop intersection of Algorithm 2 could be modified to first maximize over all midpoints, then iterate over grammar productions as is done in Algorithm 4. However, neither variation lends itself to straightforward parallelization, and the required synchronization would severely impact parallel efficiency.

In contrast, the cartesian product and matrix-vector operations of our SpMV method parallelize easily across many cores. We subdivide V into segments, one for each thread. Each thread iterates over its own subset of V in the left child cell and combines with all entries in the right child cell, populating an entry in $\mathbf{c}$ for each observed child pair. $\mathbf{c}$ is represented as independent segments safe for lock-free mutation by independent threads (see Section 3.4).

To perform the matrix-vector operation in parallel, we retain the same segments of $\mathbf{c}$, and segment G similarly. Each thread t multiplies its segment $G_t \cdot \mathbf{c_t}$, producing a vector $\alpha_\mathbf{t}$. We then merge the $\alpha_\mathbf{t}$ vectors into the final α. Since $|V| << |\mathbf{c}|$, this final merge is quite efficient.

3.3 Lexicographic Semiring

We now present Algorithm 4 more formally as an application of a lexicographic semiring (Golan, 1999). Roark et al. (2011) recently applied lexicographic semirings to language-model encoding. We will follow their notational conventions, and refer the interested reader to their detailed discussion.

A semiring is a ring, possibly lacking negation, defining two operations $\oplus$ and $\otimes$ and their respective identity elements $\bar{0}$ and $\bar{1}$ (Kuich and Salomaa, 1985). One common example in speech and language applications is the *tropical semiring* $(\mathbb{R} \cup \{\infty\}, min, +, \infty, 0)$. min is the $\oplus$ operation, with identity ∞, and $+$ is the $\otimes$, with identity 0. This definition is often used for Viterbi search, using negative log probabilities as costs.

A lexicographic semiring is defined over tuples of weights $\langle W_1, W_2 \ldots W_n \rangle$, with the condition that the tuples can be ordered first by W_1, then by W_2, and so on (similar to lexicographic string comparison, resulting in the name). We use the $\langle T, T \rangle$ semiring, defined as a pair of tropical weights:

$$\langle w_1, w_2 \rangle \oplus \langle w_3, w_4 \rangle = \begin{cases} \langle w_1, w_2 \rangle & \begin{array}{l} \text{if } w_1 < w_3 \text{ or} \\ (w_1 = w_3 \ \& \\ \ w_2 < w_4) \end{array} \\ \\ \langle w_3, w_4 \rangle & \text{otherwise} \end{cases}$$

$$\langle w_1, w_2 \rangle \otimes \langle w_3, w_4 \rangle = \langle w_1 + w_3, w_2 + w_4 \rangle$$

In our application, W_1 encodes the negative log probability of a production in G or of an observed non-terminal in the chart. W_2 encodes the midpoint of the maximum-probability analysis.[5] To perform grammar intersection using this semiring, we encode the grammar matrix as described in Section 3.2, and include 0 as W_2 for each grammar entry (since this weight is constant, it need not be encoded in the grammar representation).

We populate a vector of tuples $\mathbf{c}_i$ for each possible midpoint of the cell, and $\mathbf{c} = \mathbf{c_1} \oplus \mathbf{c_2} \oplus \ldots \mathbf{c_{span}}$. $\oplus$ compares with min, so the entries in $\mathbf{c}$ will be from the maximum probability midpoints and the first midpoint will 'win' in the case of a tie.

When we multiply $G \cdot \mathbf{c}$ in the $\langle T, T \rangle$ semiring, we use the $\otimes$ multiplication operator on each individual element, and the $\oplus$ addition operator for the sum. Since W_2 is 0 for all entries in G, the midpoints are simply carried over from $\mathbf{c}$, and $G \cdot \mathbf{c}$ is the minimum-cost path to each observed non-terminal.

SpMV optimizations have been explored extensively in the high-performance computing literature (c.f., for example, Williams et al. (2009), Bell and Garland (2009), Goumas et al. (2008)) Although the matrix-vector operations in the $\langle T, T \rangle$ semiring is quite distinct from SpMV in the real semiring, we anticipate that some of those algorithms will apply, and would be of particular interest if parsing with grammars more densely populated than those we explore in this study.

[5]Since W_2 represents a midpoint, we could alter the definition to specify that $W_2 \in \mathbb{N}$, but the standard tropical semiring is adequate and slightly simpler.

3.4 Vector Data Structure

We have already discussed a memory- and cache-efficient encoding of G. We must also represent $\mathbf{c}$ efficiently. Although this data structure is not a primary contribution of this work, we do note that the choice of vector representation greatly impacts overall parsing efficiency, so we will briefly describe our choices.

We represent $\mathbf{c}$ with a perfect hash of the form $h(l, r) \rightarrow [m]$, mapping left and right children to a matrix column. Since a perfect hash function ensures no collisions, this function is reversible ($h^{-1}([m]) \rightarrow (l, r)$), allowing recovery of the left and right children from their hashed representation. We construct $|V|$ different hash functions, mapping $h_i(r) \rightarrow [m_i]$. We store the data structures for these functions adjacently in memory, such that iterating over the entire range of $\mathbf{c}$ accesses memory in roughly linear order.[6] Global optimization of a perfect hash is an NP-complete problem. Even though we only create the hash once during initialization, we want to avoid exponential effort and instead use a displacement heuristic (Tarjan and Yao, 1979) to pack the hash efficiently, achieving 50-80% occupancy for most grammars. We elected not to use a minimal perfect hash, since the decrease in storage space comes at the cost of increased memory access.

4 Evaluation

We compare exhaustive and pruned parsing efficiency with several other competitive parsing implementations. We performed all matrix-encoded parsing and parallelization experiments using the open-source BUBS parser (Bodenstab and Dunlop, 2011). The parser framework is grammar agnostic, permitting experiments on grammars of various sizes, and it implements both exhaustive inference and 'Adaptive Beam Pruning', as described in Bodenstab et al. (2011). For exhaustive parsing, we use BUBS implementation of Algorithms 2 and 3 and Mark Johnson's highly optimized C implementation, `lncky` (Johnson, 2006) as baselines; for pruned inference, we compare with the Charniak parser (Charniak, 2000), the

[6]On most modern CPUs, linear memory access patterns allow aggressive and effective data pre-fetching into cache, avoiding costly CPU stalls.

	Markov-0	Markov-2	Parent	Berkeley SM6
Categories	100	3092	6971	1134
Binarized Rules	3859	13649	25229	1,725,570
F-score	60.7	71.9	77.5	89.3
BUBS Grammar loop (Algorithm 2)	0.16	1.92	23.4	29.9
BUBS Left-child loop (Algorithm 3)	0.13	0.50	0.8	63.0
Johnson (2006)	0.10	0.22	0.3	36.0
SpMV (this paper)	0.04	0.26	1.2	3.2

Table 1: Exhaustive Viterbi parse times (average seconds/sentence, lower is better) over WSJ Section 22 for various grammars. All parsers produce the same maximum-likelihood parse trees.

Berkeley parser (Petrov et al., 2006), and with the aforementioned 'Adaptive Beam Search' system implemented in BUBS. The Charniak parser is written in C and parses with a lexicalized grammar. The BUBS and Berkeley parsers are implemented in Java and parse with a latent-variable grammar.[7]

A brief note about implementation choices is appropriate here. Java has often been viewed as notoriously slow, a perception well-established when Java runtime environments were interpreted rather than compiled. Recent advances in virtual machine technology have largely eliminated the differential between Java and statically-compiled languages such as Fortran and C (c.f. Amedro et al. (2010), Kotzmann et al. (2008), Paleczny et al. (2001), Click et al. (2005), Click et al. (2007), Wrthinger et al. (2007), and Tene et al. (2009)).

We performed all trials on a 12-core Linux machine (2 × Intel® Xeon X5650 CPUs). Each core can execute 2 simultaneous threads, for a total of 24 concurrent threads. For the parsers implemented in Java, we used the Oracle 1.6.0_26 Virtual Machine.

4.1 Exhaustive Serial Search

In Table 1, we present exhaustive search results with four grammars, each induced from the Penn Treebank Sections 2-21 (Marcus et al., 1999). The Markov-order-0 and Markov-order-2 grammars were markovized as described in Manning and Schuetze (1999). The parent-annotated grammar further splits the states of the Markov-order-2 grammar by annotating each non-terminal with its parent category, as described in Johnson (1998). This expands the vocabulary greatly, but the ruleset somewhat less so. The Berkeley grammar (Petrov et al., 2006) is a high-accuracy unlexicalized grammar, learned by iteratively splitting and merging non-terminals. Its vocabulary is relatively small (particularly in comparison with the parent-annotated grammar), but the ruleset is quite large. All grammars examined are right-factored, so we evaluate Algorithm 3, per the trials in Song et al. (2008).

Johnson's C implementation outperforms the default BUBS exhaustive implementations, primarily (we believe) due to BUBS use of memory-inefficient Java objects. Our matrix grammar encoding and SpMV grammar intersection algorithm perform very well in comparison to both baseline systems; for the Markov-order-2 and Parent-annotated grammars, which have large vocabularies and relatively small rulesets, our approach performs similarly to Johnson's C implementation. For the grammars with large rulesets relative to their vocabularies (Markov-order-0 and Berkeley), our approach provides a dramatic speedup — over 9× vs. our fastest baseline using the Berkeley grammar. Other experiments not reported here indicate that the grammar representation accounts for the majority of this speedup, with the grammar intersection method accounting for an additional improvement of approximately 35%. We anticipate that potential users will primarily be interested in high-accuracy grammars, particularly for non-exact inference, so we focus all other empirical trials on the Berkeley grammar.

4.2 Pruned Serial Search

Most state-of-the-art context-free parsers resort to approximate inference techniques to decode efficiently. These methods include Coarse-to-Fine (Petrov et al., 2006), A* (Klein and Manning, 2003; Pauls et al., 2010), best-first (Caraballo and Charniak, 1998; Charniak, 2000), and beam

[7]By default, the Berkeley parser marginalizes over the latent-variables in the grammar and retrieves the Max-Rule parse tree; for fair comparison with our approach, we report timings in its simpler Viterbi-search mode.

	F-score	Sent/sec
Charniak (2000)	90.3	1.7
Berkeley (CTF Viterbi)	89.3	4.7
Adaptive Beam w/Alg. 3	89.0	10.2
Adaptive Beam w/Alg. 4	89.1	21.9

Table 2: Pruned parse times over WSJ Section 22 (average sentences/sec, higher is better).

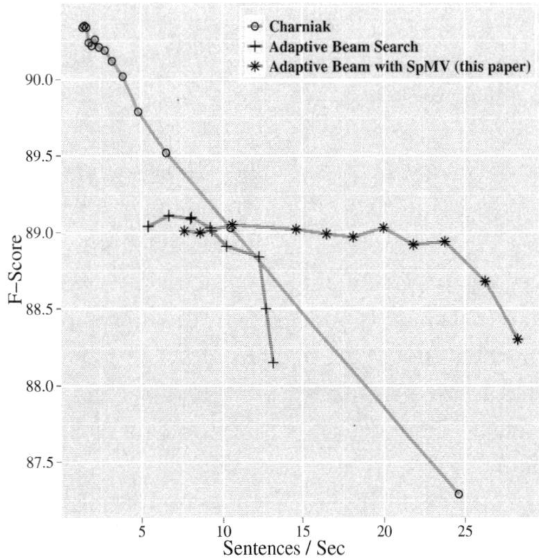

Figure 3: Comparison of F-score vs. speed over a variety of pruning parameterizations for adaptive cell pruning and for our algorithm.

search (Collins, 1999). These methods reduce the search space greatly, allowing effective search in reasonable time, although only A* guarantees finding the globally optimal solution. We take as our primary baseline, the 'Adaptive Beam Search' system implemented in BUBS. This technique predicts the appropriate population of each cell individually, allowing heavier pruning in areas of the chart in which the model predicts less ambiguity. When the lexical context is sufficient to disambiguate constituent structure, it prunes entire cells, and thus generalizes Roark and Hollingshead's linear-time chart constraint algorithm (2009). Our grammar intersection method works well with Adaptive Beam Search. Table 2 shows a speedup of over 2× vs. the baseline implementation, and an even greater advantage vs. other competitive parsers. The Charniak and Adaptive Beam pruning systems both have tunable parameters, controlling their accuracy vs. efficiency operating point. Figure 3 shows empirical results over a range of those tuning parameters for those two implementations and for our approach. For a given parameterization, the search space explored by our approach is identical to that explored by Bodenstab et al., (modulo minor differences in unary processing), so the efficiencies achieved are directly comparable. We find consistently improved speed across all pruning thresholds.

4.3 Exhaustive Parallel Search

We now move to evaluating parallelization methods. Our baseline parsers could be parallelized at a sentence-level, and possibly at a cell-level, but having already established dramatic gains vs. those approaches for serial parsing, we will focus all these trials on our own SpMV algorithm — thus, the sentence-level results reported serve as a 'baseline' of sorts, albeit one already demonstrated to be a dramatic improvement on standard baselines. We parallelize the SpMV implementation using the three parallelization strategies discussed in Section 2.3., and compare throughput and latency. To explore potential additive effects, we include a system combining cell-level and grammar-level parallelism, using several grammar-level threads for each cell-level thread, over the same range of total thread count. Note that some serial processing is required for each sentence (primarily initialization of the chart and extraction of the final parse tree), but these operations consume only 1.5% of the total time.

Executed with a single thread, the cell-level and grammar-level parallel implementations incur an overhead of less than 1%, which compares very favorably with the 500–900% overhead in Ninomiya et al. (1997). Figure 4 shows throughput and latency of each parallelization approach as thread count increases. All approaches show improved throughput with increased thread-count. Cell-level and grammar-level approaches begin to level off around 12 threads, when all physical cores are occupied; combining the two appears to benefit further from Hyper-threading, achieving throughput superior to sentence-level threading.

In Figure 4b, we see two interesting effects regarding latency: 1) We expected the sentence-parallel approach to produce fairly constant latency, but instead found that latency jumped considerably after only 4 threads; 2) Row-level and grammar-level approaches show large decreases in latency as thread count is increased, and the combination again shows additive gains — an overall reduction in latency of approximately 9× and an

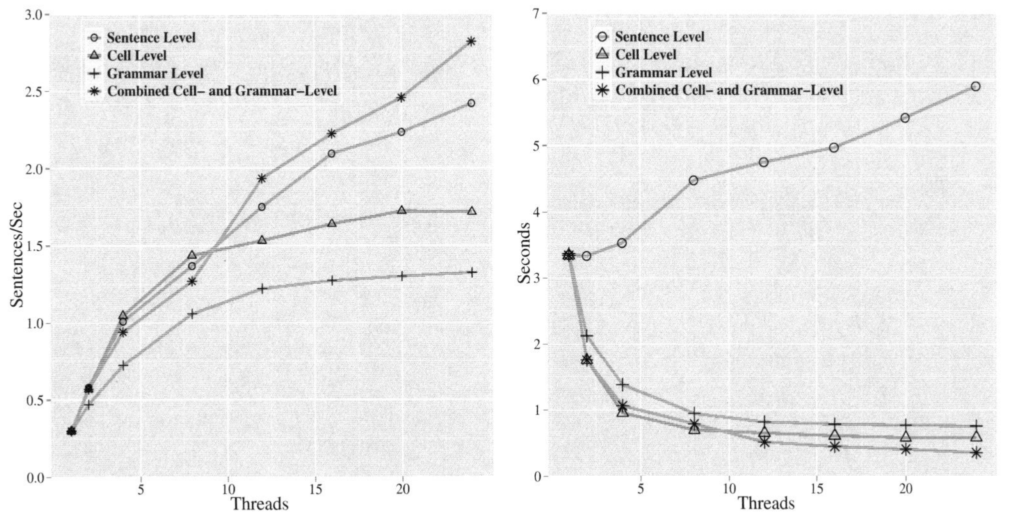

(a) Throughput, in sentences per second.

(b) Latency, in seconds per sentence.

Figure 4: Exhaustive SpMV search throughput and latency vs. thread-count.

improvement of nearly 40% vs. cell-level threading alone.

While an improvement of $9\times$ is quite impressive, we anticipate that further gains might be possible. We found that both cell-level and grammar-level methods often leave numerous threads idle, and CPU monitoring rarely shows all cores being occupied. Our observations lead us to believe that much of the 'lost' processor time is going to the task handling and inter-thread communication, and we are optimistic that hardware threading will extend the gains observed for these methods.

4.4 Pruned Parallel Search

Figure 5 presents similar trials for pruned parallel search (once again, all trials use our grammar intersection method). In this case, we find that the cell-level and combined approaches perform quite strongly— nearly optimally, in fact. In contrast to the relatively small serial portions of exhaustive search, pruned search requires some fairly expensive serial operations. The adaptive cell pruning initialization is quite costly, consuming over 35% of the total time (c.f. Bodenstab et al., 2011). In total, the serial steps account for approximately 45% of the time, so the observed 44% increase in throughput and reduction in latency, although much smaller than that of sentence-level threading, is nearly optimal. We anticipate that parallelizing the pruning initialization should further improve throughput and latency.

For grammar-level parallelism in Figure 5b, however, we find a somewhat counterintuitive result: increasing the thread-count *increases* latency. This is due to the characteristics of the grammar and the severity of pruning during inference. The Berkeley grammar has a small non-terminal set ($|V| = 1134$), but a large ruleset ($|P_b| = 1.7$ million). When performing exhaustive search, many cells are densely populated (average cell population is 450 of 1134). When performing pruned search, the cell populations are naturally much sparser (at most 30 entries, and often fewer). Thus, the grammar-level parallel tasks are much smaller. Task management overhead grows in importance as the task size shrinks, and quickly overwhelms the potential gains of additional execution threads. As already mentioned, hardware thread-management is likely to ameliorate this problem.

5 Discussion and Future Work

We have presented a novel matrix grammar encoding which has several beneficial properties. Access to grammar rules encoded in this manner is very cache-efficient, and it enables cell population using a Sparse Matrix $\times$ Vector grammar intersection. As a well-understood matrix operation, this reduction allows very fine-grained parallelism.

We demonstrated dramatic speedups on exhaustive serial parsing, and a large benefit vs. strong baselines in pruned inference. We found that the efficiency of fine-grained parallel parsing is limited by the thread management overhead, but nevertheless found considerable improvements in

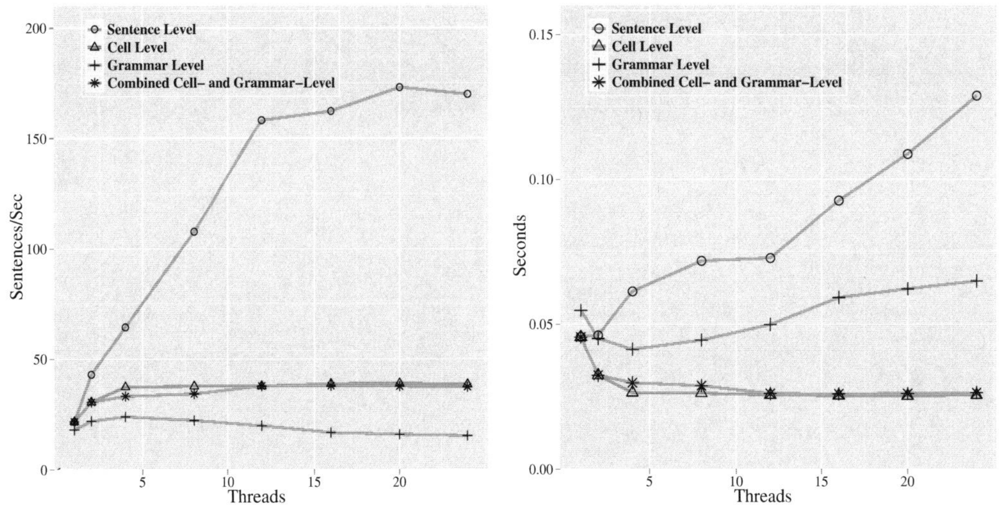

(a) Throughput, in sentences per second.

(b) Latency, in seconds per sentence.

Figure 5: Pruned search throughput and latency vs. thread-count.

throughput and latency, which may be of interest to end-user applications and others with response-time constraints.

This work is available in the open-source BUBS parser for further research or practical application. In future work, we plan to extend our approach to more parallel architectures, including graphics processing units. We also plan to parallelize the adaptive beam width pruning, and we want to explore the SpMV optimizations discussed in Section 3.3.

Acknowledgments

This research was supported in part by NSF Grant #IIS-0811745. Any opinions, findings, conclusions or recommendations expressed in this publication are those of the authors and do not necessarily reflect the views of the NSF.

References

Brian Amedro, Denis Caromel, Fabrice Huet, Vladimir Bodnartchouk, Christian Delb, and Guillermo L. Taboada. 2010. HPC in java: experiences in implementing the NAS parallel benchmarks. In *Proceedings of the 10th WSEAS international conference on applied informatics and communications and 3rd WSEAS international conference on Biomedical electronics and biomedical informatics*, page 221230.

Michele Banko. 1999. *Open Information Extraction for the Web*. PhD dissertation, University of Washington, Seattle, Washington.

Nathan Bell and Michael Garland. 2009. Implementing sparse matrix-vector multiplication on throughput-oriented processors. In *Proceedings of the Conference on High Performance Computing Networking, Storage and Analysis*, pages 1–11, Portland, Oregon. ACM.

Jari Bjrne, Filip Ginter, Sampo Pyysalo, Jun'ichi Tsujii, and Tapio Salakoski. 2010. Complex event extraction at PubMed scale. *Bioinformatics*, 26(12):382–390, June.

Nathan Bodenstab and Aaron Dunlop. 2011. BUBS parser. http://code.google.com/p/bubs-parser/.

Nathan Bodenstab, Aaron Dunlop, Brian Roark, and Keith Hall. 2011. Beam-Width prediction for efficient Context-Free parsing. In *Proceedings of the 49th Annual Meeting of the Association for Computational Linguistics*, pages 440–449, Portland, Oregon, June.

Sharon A Caraballo and Eugene Charniak. 1998. New figures of merit for best-first probabilistic chart parsing. *Computational Linguistics*, 24:275298, June.

Eugene Charniak. 2000. A maximum-entropy-inspired parser. In *Proceedings of the 1st North*

American chapter of the Association for Computational Linguistics conference, pages 132–139, Seattle, Washington. Morgan Kaufmann Publishers Inc.

Cliff Click, Gil Tene, and Michael Wolf. 2005. The pauseless GC algorithm. *Proceedings of the 1st ACM/USENIX international conference on Virtual execution environments*, page 4656.

Clifford N. Click, Christopher A. Vick, and Michael H. Paleczny. 2007. System and method for range check elimination via iteration splitting in a dynamic compiler, May. US Patent 7,222,337.

Michael Collins. 1999. *Head-Driven Statistical Models for Natural Language Parsing*. PhD dissertation, University of Pennsylvania.

Jonathan Samuel Golan. 1999. *Semirings and their Applications*. Springer, July.

Georgios Goumas, Kornilios Kourtis, Nikos Anastopoulos, Vasileios Karakasis, and Nectarios Koziris. 2008. Understanding the performance of sparse matrix-vector multiplication. In *PDP08: Proceedings of the 16th Euromicro International Conference on Parallel, Distributed and Network-based Processing*.

Susan L. Graham, Michael Harrison Ruzzo, and Walter L. 1980. An improved Context-Free recognizer. *ACM Trans. Program. Lang. Syst.*, 2(3):415–462.

Mark Johnson. 1998. PCFG models of linguistic tree representations. *Comput. Linguist.*, 24(4):613–632.

Mark Johnson. 2006. lncky. http://www.cog.brown.edu/˜mj/Software.htm.

Dan Klein and Christopher D. Manning. 2001. Parsing with treebank grammars: Empirical bounds, theoretical models, and the structure of the penn treebank. In *Proceedings of 39th Annual Meeting of the Association for Computational Linguistics*, pages 338–345, Toulouse, France, July.

Dan Klein and Christopher D. Manning. 2003. A* parsing. In *Proceedings of the 2003 Conference of the North American Chapter of the Association for Computational Linguistics on Human Language Technology (NAACL '03)*, pages 40–47, Edmonton, Canada.

Thomas Kotzmann, Christian Wimmer, Hanspeter Mssenbck, Thomas Rodriguez, Kenneth Russell, and David Cox. 2008. Design of the java HotSpot client compiler for java 6. *ACM Transactions on Architecture and Code Optimization (TACO)*, 5:7:1–7:32, May.

Werner Kuich and Arto Salomaa. 1985. *Semirings, Automata, Languages*. EATCS Monographs on Theoretical Computer Science, Number 5. Springer-Verlag, Berlin, Germany.

Lillian Lee. 1997. Fast Context-Free parsing requires fast boolean matrix multiplication. In *Proceedings of the 35th Annual Meeting of the Association for Computational Linguistics*, pages 9–15, Madrid, Spain, July. ACL.

Christopher D. Manning and Hinrich Schuetze. 1999. *Foundations of Statistical Natural Language Processing*. The MIT Press, June.

Mitchell P Marcus, Beatrice Santorini, Mary Ann Marcinkiewicz, and Ann Taylor. 1999. *Treebank-3*. Linguistic Data Consortium, Philadelphia.

Robert C Moore. 2004. Improved left-corner chart parsing for large context-free grammars. *New developments in parsing technology*, page 185201.

Takashi Ninomiya, Kentaro Torisawa, Taura Kinjiro, and Tsujii Jun'ichi. 1997. A parallel CKY parsing algorithm on Large-Scale Distributed-Memory parallel machines. In *PACLING '97*, pages 223–231, Tokyo, Japan.

Michael Paleczny, Christopher Vick, and Cliff Click. 2001. The java hotspot server compiler. *Proceedings of the 2001 Symposium on Java Virtual Machine Research and Technology Symposium*, pages 1–12.

Adam Pauls, Dan Klein, and Chris Quirk. 2010. Top-down k-best a* parsing. In *Proceedings of ACL 2010*, page 200204, Morristown, NJ, USA.

Gerald Penn and Cosmin Munteanu. 2003. A tabulation-based parsing method that reduces copying. In *Proceedings of ACL '03*, pages 200–207, Sapporo, Japan.

Slav Petrov, Leon Barrett, Romain Thibaux, and Dan Klein. 2006. Learning accurate, compact, and interpretable tree annotation. In *Proceedings of the 21st International Conference on Computational Linguistics and the 44th annual meeting of the Association for Computational Linguistics*, pages 433–440, Sydney, Australia. ACL.

Brian Roark and Kristy Hollingshead. 2009. Linear complexity Context-Free parsing pipelines via chart constraints. In *Proceedings of Human Language Technologies: The 2009 Annual Conference of the North American Chapter of the Association for Computational Linguistics*, pages 647–655, Boulder, Colorado, June. ACL.

Brian Roark, Richard Sproat, and Izhak Shafran. 2011. Lexicographic semirings for exact automata encoding of sequence models. In *Proceedings of the 49th Annual Meeting of the Association for Computational Linguistics*, Portland, Oregon, June. ACL.

Xinying Song, Shilin Ding, and Chin-Yew Lin. 2008. Better binarization for the CKY parsing. In *Proceedings of the 2008 Conference on Empirical Methods in Natural Language Processing*, pages 167–176, Honolulu, Hawaii, October. ACL.

Robert Endre Tarjan and Andrew Chi-Chih Yao. 1979. Storing a sparse table. *Commun. ACM*, 22(11):606–611.

Gil Tene, Jack H. Choquette, Scott Sellers, and Clifford N. Click. 2009. Array access, August. US Patent 7,577,801.

Reginald P. Tewarson. 1973. *Sparse Matrices. Mathematics in Science and Engineering Volume 99*. Academic Press, April.

Leslie G. Valiant. 1975. General context-free recognition in less than cubic time. *Journal of Computer and System Sciences*, 10(2):308–314, April.

Samuel Williams, Leonid Oliker, Richard Vuduc, John Shalf, Katherine Yelick, and James Demmel. 2009. Optimization of sparse matrix-vector multiplication on emerging multicore platforms. *Parallel Computing*, 35(3):178–194, March.

Thomas Wrthinger, Christian Wimmer, and Hanspeter Mssenbck. 2007. Array bounds check elimination for the java HotSpot\ client compiler. *Proceedings of the 5th international symposium on Principles and practice of programming in Java*, page 125133.

Yi Youngmin, Lai Chao-Yue, Slav Patrov, and Kurt Keutzer. 2011. Efficient parallel CKY parsing on GPUs. In *Proceedings of the 12th International Conference on Parsing Technologies*, Dublin, Ireland, October.

Efficient Parallel CKY Parsing on GPUs

Youngmin Yi[1] **Chao-Yue Lai**[2] **Slav Petrov**[3] **Kurt Keutzer**[4]

[1]University of Seoul
Seoul, Korea
ymyi@uos.ac.kr

[2,4]University of California, Berkeley
Berkeley, CA, USA
{colbylai,keutzer}
@eecs.berkeley.edu

[3]Google Research
New York, NY, USA
slav@google.com

Abstract

Low-latency solutions for syntactic parsing are needed if parsing is to become an integral part of user-facing natural language applications. Unfortunately, most state-of-the-art constituency parsers employ large probabilistic context-free grammars for disambiguation, which renders them impractical for real-time use. Meanwhile, Graphics Processor Units (GPUs) have become widely available, offering the opportunity to alleviate this bottleneck by exploiting the fine-grained data parallelism found in the CKY algorithm. In this paper, we explore the design space of parallelizing the dynamic programming computations carried out by the CKY algorithm. We use the Compute Unified Device Architecture (CUDA) programming model to reimplement a state-of-the-art parser, and compare its performance on two recent GPUs with different architectural features. Our best results show a 26-fold speedup compared to a sequential C implementation.

1 Introduction

Syntactic parsing of natural language is the task of analyzing the grammatical structure of sentences and predicting their most likely parse trees (see Figure 1). These parse trees can then be used in many ways to enable natural language processing applications like machine translation, question answering, and information extraction. Most syntactic constituency parsers employ a weighted context-free grammar (CFG), that is learned from a treebank. The CKY dynamic programming algorithm (Cocke and Schwartz, 1970; Kasami, 1965; Younger, 1967) is then be used to find the most likely parse tree for a given sentence of length n in $O(|G|n^3)$ time. While often ignored, the grammar constant $|G|$ typically dominates the runtime in practice. This is because grammars with high accuracy (Collins, 1999; Charniak, 2000; Petrov et al., 2006) have thousands of nonterminal symbols and millions of context-free rules, while most sentences have on average only about $n = 20$ words.

Meanwhile, we have entered a manycore computing era, where the number of processing cores in computer systems doubles every second year, while the clock frequency has converged somewhere around 3 GHz (Asanovic et al., 2006). This opens up new opportunities for increasing the speed of parsers. We present a general approach for parallelizing the CKY algorithm that can handle arbitrary context-free grammars (Section 2). We make no assumptions about the size of the grammar and we demonstrate the efficacy of our approach by implementing a decoder for the state-of-the-art latent variable grammars of Petrov et al. (2006) (a.k.a. Berkeley Parser) on a Graphics Processor Unit (GPU).

We first present an overview of the general architecture of GPUs and the efficient synchronization provided by the Compute Unified Device Architecture (CUDA (Nickolls et al., 2008)) programming model (Section 3). We then discuss how the hundreds of cores available on a GPU can enable a fine-grained parallel execution of the CKY algorithm. We explore the design space with different thread mappings onto the GPU and discuss how the various synchronization methods might be applied in this context (Section 4). Key to our approach is the observation that the computation needs to be parallelized over grammar rules rather than chart cells. While this might have been difficult to do with previous parallel computing architectures, the CUDA model provides us with

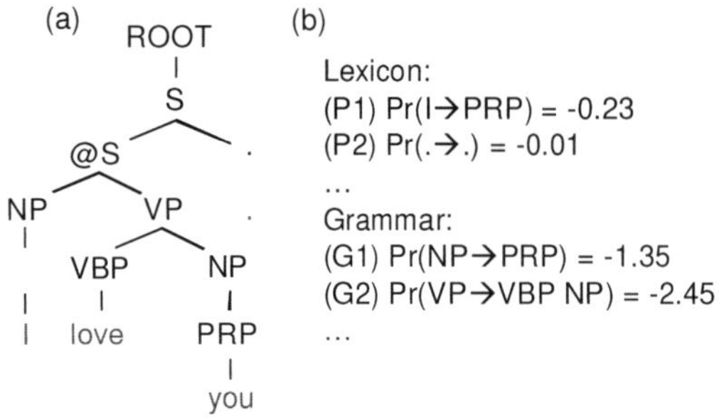

Figure 1: An example of a parse tree for the sentence "I love you ."

fine-grained parallelism and synchronization options that make this possible.

We empirically evaluate the various parallel implementations on two NVIDIA GPUs (GTX480 and GTX285) in Section 5. We observe that some parallelization options are architecture dependent, emphasizing that a thorough understanding of the programming model and the underlying hardware is needed to achieve good results. Our implementation on NVIDIA's GTX480 using CUDA results in a 26-fold speedup compared to the original sequential C implementation. On the GTX285 GPU we obtain a 14-fold speedup.

Parallelizing natural language parsers has been studied previously (see Section 6), however, previous work has focused on scenarios where only a limited level of coarse-grained parallelism could be utilized, or the underlying hardware required unrealistic restrictions on the size of the context-free grammar. To the best of our knowledge, this is the first GPU-based parallel syntactic parser using a state-of-the-art grammar.

2 Natural Language Parsing

While we assume a basic familiarity with probabilistic CKY parsing, in this section we briefly review the CKY dynamic programming algorithm and the Viterbi algorithm for extracting the highest scoring path through the dynamic program.

2.1 Context-Free Grammars

In this work we focus our attention on constituency parsing and assume that a weighted CFG is available to us. In our experiments we will use a probabilistic latent variable CFG (Petrov et al., 2006). However, our algorithms can be used with any weighted CFG, including discriminative ones, such as the ones in Petrov and Klein (2007a) and Finkel et al. (2008).[1] The grammars in our experiments have on the order of thousands of nonterminals and millions of productions.

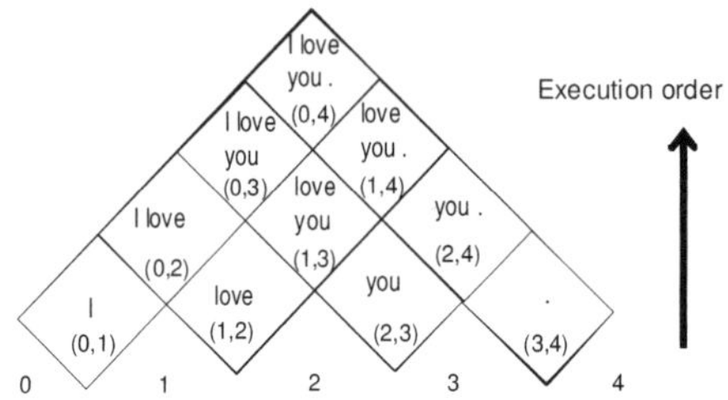

Figure 2: The chart that visualizes the bottom-up process of CKY parsing for the sentence "I love you ."

Figure 1(a) shows a constituency parse tree. Leaf nodes in the parse tree, also called terminal nodes, correspond to words in the language. Preterminals correspond to part-of-speech tags, while the other nonterminals correspond to phrasal categories. For ease of exposition, we will say that terminal productions are part of a lexicon. For example, (L1) in Figure 1(b) is a lexical rule providing a score (of -0.23) for mapping the word "I" to the symbol "PRP." We assume that the grammar has been binarized and contains only *unary* and *binary* productions. We refer to the application of grammar rules as *unary/binary relaxations*.

2.2 Sequential CKY Parsing

The CKY algorithm is an exhaustive bottom-up algorithm that uses dynamic programming to incrementally build up larger tree structures. To keep track of the scores of these structures, a chart indexed by the start and end positions and the symbol under consideration is used: *scores*[*start*][*end*][*symbol*] (see also Figure 2). After initializing the preterminal level of the chart with the part-of-speech scores from the lexicon, the algorithm continues by repeatedly applying all binary and unary rules in order to build up larger spans (pseudocode is given in Figure 3). To reconstruct the highest scoring parse tree we perform a top-down search. We found this to be more efficient than keeping backpointers.[2]

One should also note that many real-world applications benefit from, or even expect n-best lists of possible parse trees. Using the lazy evaluation algorithm of Huang and Chiang (2005) the extrac-

[1]For feature-rich discriminative models a trivially parallelizable pass can be used to pre-compute the rule-potentials.

[2]This observation is due to Dan Klein, *p.c.*

```
Algorithm: parse(sen, lex, gr)
Input: sen /* the input sentence */
       lex /* the lexicon */
       gr /* the grammar */
Output: tree /* the most probable parse tree */

scores[][][] = initScores();
nWords = readSentence(sen);
lexiconScores(scores, sen, nWords, lex);
for length = 2 to nWords
    binaryRelax(scores, nWords, length, gr);
    unaryRelax(scores, nWords, length, gr);
tree = backtrackBestParseTree(scores);
return tree;
```

Figure 3: Pseudocode for CKY parsing.

```
Algorithm: binaryRelax(scores, nWords, length, gr)
Input: scores /* the 3-dimensional scores */
       nWords /* the number of total words */
       length /* the current span */
       gr /* the grammar */
Output: None

for start = 0 to nWords − length
    end = start + length;
    foreach symbol ∈ gr
        max = FLOAT_MIN;
        foreach rule r per symbol // defined by gr
            // r is "symbol ⇒ l_sym r_sym"
            for split = start + 1 to end − 1
                // calculate score
                lscore = scores[start][split][l_sym];
                rscore = scores[split][end][r_sym];
                score = rule_score + lscore + rscore;
                // maximum reduction
                if score > max
                    max = score;
        scores[start][end][symbol] = max;
```

Figure 4: Binary relaxations in CKY parsing.

tion of an n-best list can be done with very little overhead after running a slightly modified version of the CKY algorithm. Our parallel CKY algorithm could still be used in that scenario.

3 GPUs and CUDA

Graphics Processor Units (GPUs) were originally designed for processing graphics applications, where millions of operations can be executed in parallel. In order to increase the efficiency by exploiting this parallelism, typical GPUs (Lindholm et al., 2008) have hundreds of processing cores. For example, the NVIDIA GTX480 GPU has 480 processing cores called *stream processors* (SP). The processing cores are organized hierarchically as shown in Figure 5: A group of SPs makes up a *streaming multiprocessor* (SM). A number of SMs form a single graphics device. The GTX480, for example, contains 15 SMs, with 32 SPs in each SM, resulting in the total of 480 SPs. Despite this high number of processors, it should be emphasized that simply using a GPU, without understanding the programming model and the underlying hardware architecture, does not guarantee high performance.

3.1 Compute Unified Device Architecture

Recently, Nickolls et al. (2008) introduced the Compute Unified Device Architecture (CUDA). It allows programmers to utilize GPUs to accelerate applications in domains other than graphics. CUDA is essentially the programming language C with extensions for thread execution and GPU-specific memory access and control. A CUDA *thread* is executed on an SP and a group of threads (called a *thread block*) is executed on an SM. CUDA enables the acceleration of a wide range of applications in various domains by executing a number of threads and thread blocks in parallel, which are specified by the programmer. Its popularity has grown rapidly because it provides a convenient API for parallel programming. In order to better utilize the massive parallelism in the GPU, it is typical to have hundreds of threads in a thread block and have hundreds or even thousands of thread blocks launched for a single *kernel*: a data-parallel function that is executed by a number of threads on the GPU.

3.2 Single Instruction Multiple Threads

One of the most important features of the GPU architecture is commonly known as Single Instruction Multiple Threads (SIMT). SIMT means that threads are executed in bundles (called *warps*), to amortize the implementation cost for a large number of processing cores. In typical GPUs, a warp consists of 32 threads that share the units for instruction fetching and execution. Thus, a thread cannot advance to the next instruction if other threads in the same warp have not yet completed their own execution. On the other hand, threads in different warps are truly independent: they can be scheduled and executed in any order. Inside a warp, if some threads follow different execution paths than others, the execution of the threads with different paths is serialized. This can happen for example in if-then-else structures and loop constructs where the branch condition is based on thread indices. This is called a *divergent*

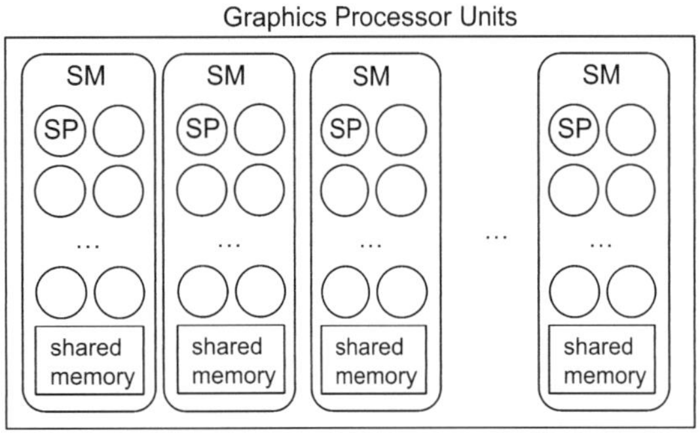

Figure 5: The hierarchical organization of GPUs.

branch and should be avoided as much as possible when designing parallel algorithms and mapping applications onto a GPU. In the programming model of CUDA, one or more warps are implicitly grouped into thread blocks. Different thread blocks are mapped to SMs and can be executed independently of one another.

3.3 Shared Memory

Generally speaking, manycore architectures (like GPUs) have more ALUs in place of on-chip caches, making arithmetic operations relatively cheaper and global memory accesses relatively more expensive. Thus, to achieve good performance, it is important to increase the ratio of Compute to Global Memory Access (CGMA) (Kirk and Hwu, 2010), which can be done in part by cleverly utilizing the different types of shared on-chip memory in each SM.

Threads in a thread block are mapped onto the same SM and can cooperate with one another by sharing data through the on-chip *shared memory* of the SM (shown in Figure 5). This shared memory has two orders of magnitude less latency than the off-chip *global memory*, but is very small (16KB to 64KB, depending on the architecture). CUDA therefore provides the programmer with the flexibility (and burden) to explicitly manage shared memory (i.e., loading a value from global memory and storing it).

Additionally, GPUs also have so called *texture memory* and *constant memory*. Texture memory can be written only from the host CPU, but provides caching and is shared across different SMs. Hence it is often used for storing frequently accessed read-only data. Constant memory is very small and as its name suggests is only appropriate for storing constants used across thread blocks.

3.4 Synchronization

CUDA provides a set of APIs for thread synchronization. When threads perform a reduction, or need to access a single variable in a mutually exclusive way, *atomic operations* are used. Atomic operation APIs take as arguments the memory location (i.e., pointer of the variable to be reduced) and the value. However, atomic operations on global memory can be very costly, as they need to serialize a potentially large number of threads in the kernel. To reduce this overhead, one usually applies atomic operations first to variables declared in the shared memory of each thread block. After these reductions have completed another set of atomic operations is done.

In addition, CUDA provides an API (*__syncthreads()*) to realize a barrier synchronization between threads in the same thread block. This API forces each thread to wait until all threads in the block have reached the calling line. Note that there is no API for the barrier synchronization between all threads in a kernel. Since a return from a kernel accomplishes a global barrier synchronization, one can use separate kernels when a global barrier synchronization is needed.

4 Parallel CKY Parsing on GPUs

The dynamic programming loops of the CKY algorithm provide various types of parallelism. While the loop in Figure 3 cannot be parallelized due to dependencies between iterations, all four loops in Figure 4 could in principle be parallelized. In this section, we discuss the different design choices and strategies for parallelizing the binary relaxation step that accounts for the bulk of the overall execution time of the CKY algorithm.

4.1 Thread Mapping

The essential step in designing applications on a parallel platform is to determine which execution entity in the parallel algorithm should be mapped to the underlying parallel hardware thread in the platform. For a CKY parser with millions of grammar rules and thousands of symbols, one can map either rules or symbols to threads. At first sight it might appear that mapping chart cells or symbols to threads is a natural choice, as it is equivalent to executing the first loop in Figure 4 in parallel. However, if we map a symbol to a thread, then it not only fails to provide enough parallelism to fully utilize the massive number of threads in

```
Algorithm: threadBasedRuleBR(scores, nWords, length, gr)
Input: scores /* the 3-dimensional scores */
       nWords /* the number of total words */
       length /* the current span */
       gr /* the grammar */
Output: None

1   for start = 0 to nWords − length in parallel
2       end = start + length;
3       foreach rule r ∈ gr in parallel
4           __shared__ int sh_max[NUM_SYMBOL] =
                                      FLOAT_MIN;
5           // r is "symbol ⇒ l_sym r_sym"
6           for split = start + 1 to end − 1
7               // calculate score
8               lscore = scores[start][split][l_sym];
9               rscore = scores[split][end][r_sym];
10              score = rule_score + lscore + rscore;
11              // local maximum reduction
12              if score > local_max
13                  local_max = score;
14          atomicMax(&sh_max[symbol], local_max);
15  // global maximum reduction
16  foreach symbol ∈ gr in parallel
17      atomicMax(&scores[start][end][symbol],
                                 sh_max[symbol]);
```

Figure 6: Thread-based parallel CKY parsing.

```
Algorithm: blockBasedRuleBR(scores, nWords, length, gr)
Input: scores /* the 3-dimensional scores */
       nWords /* the number of total words */
       length /* the current span */
       gr /* the grammar */
Output: None

for start = 0 to nWords − length in parallel
    end = start + length;
    foreach symbol ∈ gr in parallel
        __shared__ int sh_max = FLOAT_MIN;
        foreach rule r per symbol in parallel
            // r is "symbol ⇒ l_sym r_sym"
            for split = start + 1 to end − 1
                // calculate score
                lscore = scores[start][split][l_sym];
                rscore = scores[split][end][r_sym];
                score = rule_score + lscore + rscore;
                // local maximum reduction
                if score > local_max
                    local_max = score;
            atomicMax(&sh_max, local_max);
// global maximum reduction
foreach symbol ∈ gr in parallel
    atomicMax(&scores[start][end][symbol], sh_max);
```

Figure 7: Block-based parallel CKY parsing.

GPUs,[3] but it can also suffer from load imbalance due to the fact that each symbol has a varying number of rules associated with it. Since threads in the same warp execute in SIMT fashion, this load imbalance among threads results in divergent branches, degrading the performance significantly. It is therefore advantageous to map rules rather than symbols to threads.

4.1.1 Thread-Based Mapping

If we map rules to threads, the nested loops in line 3 and line 5 of Figure 4 become one flat loop that iterates over all rules in the grammar and the loop can be executed in parallel as shown in line 3 of Figure 6. Since the grammar we use has about one million rules, this mapping provides sufficient parallelism to fully utilize the GPU, without running into load imbalance issues. We call this mapping *thread-based mapping*.

Unfortunately, thread-based mapping has a major drawback. Since each rule is mapped to a different thread, threads for rules with the same parent symbol need to be synchronized in order to avoid write conflicts. In this mapping, the synchronization can be done only through atomic operations (shown in line 14 and line 17 of Figure 6), which can be costly.

[3] $\#threads/warp \times max(\#warps)/SM \times \#SM = 32 \times 48 \times 15 = 23{,}040$ threads in the GTX480.

4.1.2 Block-Based Mapping

Another mapping can be obtained by exploiting the two levels of granularity in the GPU architecture: threads and thread blocks. We can map each symbol to a thread block, and the rules associated with each symbol to threads in the respective thread block. This mapping creates a balanced load because an SM can execute any available thread block independently of other thread blocks, instead of waiting for other SMs to complete. For example, when the first SM completes the computation of a thread block (because the associated symbol has few rules), it can proceed to the next available thread block (which corresponds to another symbol). This corresponds to mapping each iteration of the loop in line 3 of Figure 4 to thread blocks and the loop in line 5 to threads. We call this mapping *block-based mapping* and provide pseudocode in Figure 7. The main advantage of this mapping is that it allows synchronization without using costly atomic operations.

Another advantage of the block-based mapping is that we can quickly skip over certain symbols. For example, the preterminal symbols (i.e. part-of-speech tags), can only cover spans of length 1 (i.e. single words). In block-based mapping, only one thread needs to check and determine if a symbol is a preterminal and can be skipped. In contrast, in thread-based mapping, every thread in the

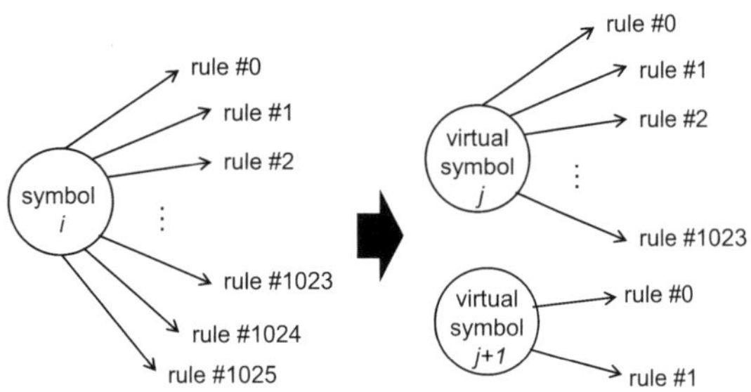

Figure 8: Creating virtual symbols whenever a symbol has too many rules.

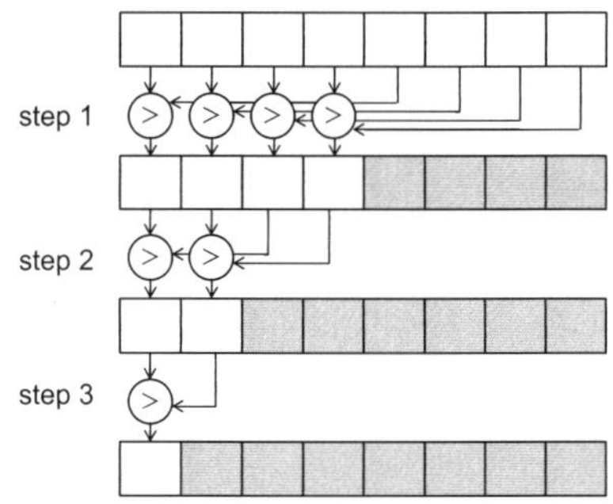

Figure 9: Parallel reduction on shared memory between threads in the same thread block with 8 threads.

thread block needs to perform the check. Since this check involves a global memory access, it is costly. Minimizing the number of global memory accesses is key to the performance of parallel algorithms on GPUs.

A challenging aspect of the block-based mapping comes from the fact that the number of rules per symbol can exceed the maximum number of threads per thread block (1,024 or 512 depending on the GPU architecture). To circumvent this limitation, we introduce virtual symbols, which host different partitions of the original rules, as shown in Figure 8. Introducing virtual symbols does not increase the complexity of the algorithm, because virtual symbols only exist until we perform the maximum reductions, at which point they are converted to the original symbols.

4.2 Span-Level Parallelism

Another level of parallelism, which is orthogonal to the previously discussed mappings, is present in the first loop in Figure 4. Spans in the same level in the chart (see Figure 2), are independent of each other and can hence be executed in parallel by mapping them to thread blocks (line 1 of Figure 6 and Figure 7). Since CUDA provides up to three-dimensional (x, y, z) indexing of thread blocks, this can be easily accomplished: we create two-dimensional grids whose X axis corresponds to symbols in block-based mapping or simply a group of rules in thread-based mapping, and the Y axis corresponds to the spans.

4.3 Thread Synchronization

Thread synchronization is needed to correctly compute the maximum scores in parallel. Synchronization can be achieved by atomic operations or by parallel reductions using *__syncthreads()* as explained in Section 3. The most viable synchronization method will of course vary depending on the mapping we choose. In practice, only atomic operations are an option in thread-based mapping, since we would otherwise need as many executions of parallel reductions, as the number of different parent symbols in each thread block. In block-based mapping, on the other hand, both parallel reductions and atomic operations can be applied.

4.3.1 Atomic Operations

In thread-based mapping, to correctly update the score, each thread needs to call the atomic API max operation with a pointer to the desired write location. However, this operation can be very slow (as we will confirm in Section 5), so that we instead perform a first reduction by calling the API with a pointer to the shared variable (as shown in line 14 of Figure 6), and then perform a second reduction with a pointer to the *scores* array (as shown in line 17 of Figure 6). When we call atomic operations on shared memory, shared variables need to be declared for all symbols. This is necessary because in thread-based mapping threads in the same thread block can have different parent symbols.

In block-based mapping we can also use atomic operations on shared memory. However, in this mapping, all threads in a thread block have the same parent symbol, and therefore only one shared variable per thread block is needed for the parent symbol (as shown in line 15 of Figure 7). All the reductions are performed on this single shared variable. Compared to thread-based mapping, block-based mapping requires a fraction of the shared memory, and costly atomic operations on global memory are performed only once (as shown in line 18 of Figure 7).

4.3.2 Parallel Reductions

Parallel reduction is another option for updating scores in block-based mapping. Each thread in the thread block stores its computed score in an array declared as a shared variable and performs parallel reduction with a binary-tree order as shown in Figure 9 (from leaves to the root). When there are N threads in a thread block, the maximum score in the thread block is obtained after $\log 2N$ steps and stored in the first element in the array. Note that when implementing the parallel reduction *__syncthreads()* needs to be called at the end of each step to ensure that every thread can read the updated value of the previous step. This approach can potentially be faster than the inherently serial atomic operations, but it comes with the cost of using more shared memory (proportional to the number of participating threads). This synchronization method is in practice only applicable to block-based mapping and cannot be applied to thread-based mapping since it assumes that all threads in a thread block perform reductions for the same parent symbol.

4.4 Reducing Global Memory Accesses

By now it should be clear that increasing CGMA and reducing global memory access is important for high GPU performance. We can approximately calculate the CGMA ratio of our kernel by counting global memory accesses and arithmetic operations per thread. There are three global memory accesses for each binary rule: the left child symbol ID, right child symbol ID, and the rule score itself. Moreover, there are two global memory accesses for referencing the scores with left child ID and right child ID in the split-point loop in line 7 of Figure 4. The loop in line 7 iterates up to the *length* of the span. The number of global memory accesses is thus $2 \cdot length + 3$. On the other hand, there are only two additions in the kernel, resulting in a very low CGMA. To improve performance, we need to increase the CGMA ratio by better utilizing the shared memory. Since shared memory is rather limited, and global memory accesses to the *scores* array in line 9 and 10 of Figure 4 spread over a wide range of memory locations, it is impossible to simply transform those global memory accesses into shared memory accesses. Instead, we need to modify the access pattern of the kernel code to meet this constraint.

If we look into the access pattern (ignoring the

(a)

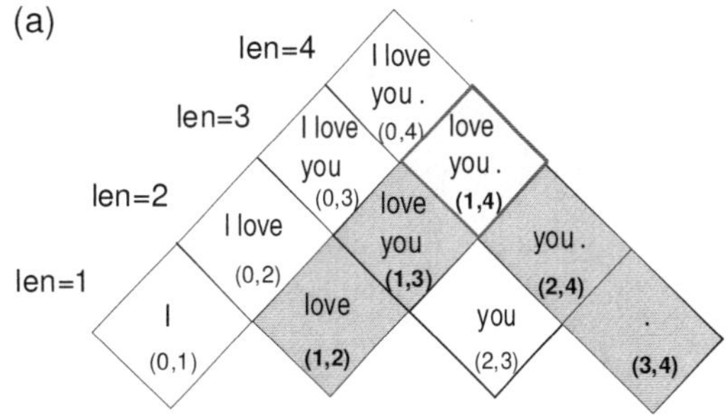

(b)

```
for split = start + 1 to end − 1
    lscore = scores[start][split][l_sym];
    rscore = scores[split][end][r_sym];
    score = rule_score + lscore + rscore;
```

⬇

```
for k = 1 to len − 1
    lscore = sh_scores_L[k][unique_l_sym];
    rscore = sh_scores_R[k][unique_r_sym];
    score = rule_score + lscore + rscore;
```

Figure 10: (a) Chart example illustrating the access patterns of the *scores* array: the shaded cells are the locations that the threads with *start* = 1, *end* = 4 accesses. (b) Better memory access patterns with the new arrays

symbol dimension of the *scores* array), we can see that the accesses actually occur only in restricted locations that can be easily enumerated. For example, the accesses are restricted within the shaded cells in Figure 10(a) when the current cell is $(1, 4)$. We can thus introduce two arrays (*sh_scores_L* and *sh_scores_R*) that keep track of the scores of the children in the shaded cells. These two arrays can easily fit into shared memory because there are only about 1000 unique symbols in our grammar and the sentence lengths are bounded, whereas the *scores* array can only reside in global memory. Figure 10(b) shows how the new arrays are accessed. For each unique left/right child symbol, we need to load the score from *scores* to *sh_scores_L* and *sh_scores_R* once through a global memory access. Thus, the number of global memory access will be reduced when multiple rules share the same child symbols.

Another way to reduce global memory accesses is to use texture memory. Recall that texture memory can be used for caching, but needs to be initiated from the CPU side and costs overhead. Moving the *scores* array to texture memory seems promising since it is frequently read to obtain the scores of children symbols. How-

CPU type	Core i7 2.80 GHz	
System memory	2GB	
GPU type	GTX285	GTX480
	648 MHz	1400 MHz
GPU memory	1GB	1.5GB
#SM	30	15
#SP/SM	8	32
Shared memory/SM	16KB	up to 64KB
L1 cache/SM	N/A	up to 64KB

Table 1: Experimental platforms specifications.

ever, as the array is updated at every iteration of binary relaxation, we need to update it also in texture memory by calling a binding API (between line 4 and 5 in Figure 3). While it can be costly to bind such a large array every iteration, we can reduce this cost by transforming its layout from *scores*[*start*][*end*][*symbol*] to *scores*[*length*][*start*][*symbol*], where $length = end - start$. With the new layout, we only need to bind the array up to size $(length - 1)$ (rather than the entire array), significantly reducing the cost of binding it to texture memory.

5 Experimental Results

We implemented the various versions of the parallel CKY algorithm discussed in the previous sections in CUDA and measured the runtime on two different NVIDIA GPUs used in a quad-core desktop environment: GTX285 and GTX480. The detailed specifications of the experimental platforms are listed in Table 1.

The grammar we used is extracted from the publicly available parser of Petrov et al. (2006). It has 1,120 nonterminal symbols including 636 preterminal symbols. The grammar has 852,591 binary rules and 114,419 unary rules. We used the first 1000 sentences from Section 22 of the Wall Street Journal (WSJ) portion of the Penn Treebank (Marcus et al., 1993) as our benchmark set. We verified for each sentence that our parallel implementation obtains exactly the same parse tree and score as the sequential implementation. We compare the execution times of various versions of the parallel parser in CUDA, varying the mapping, synchronization methods and memory access patterns.

Figure 11 shows the speedup of the different parallel parsers on the two GPUs: *Thread* stands for the thread-based mapping and *Block* for the block-based one. The default parallelizes over spans, while *SS* stands for sequential spans, meaning that the computation on spans is executed sequentially. *GA* stands for global atomic synchronization, *SA* for shared atomic synchronization, and *PR* for the parallel reduction. *SH* stands for the transformed access pattern for the *scores* array in the shared memory. *tex:rule* stands for loading the rule information from texture memory and *tex:scores* for loading the *scores* array from texture memory. *tex:both* means both the *tex:rule* and *tex:scores* are applied.

The exhaustive sequential CKY parser was written in C and is reasonably optimized, taking 5.5 seconds per sentence (or 5,505 seconds for the 1000 benchmark sentences). This is comparable to the better implementations presented in Dunlop et al. (2011). As can be seen in Figure 11, the fastest configuration on the GTX285 is *Block+PR+SS+tex:scores*, which shows a 17.4× speedup against the sequential parser. On the GTX480, *Block+PR* is the fastest, showing a 25.8× speedup. Their runtimes were 0.32 seconds/sentence and 0.21 seconds/sentence, respectively. It is noteworthy that the fastest configuration differs for the two devices. We provide an explanation later in this section.

On both the GTX285 and the GTX480, *Thread+GA* shows the worst performance as global atomic synchronization is very costly. *Thread+GA* on the GTX285 is even about 8 times slower than the sequential CKY parser. Note that although it is still the slowest one, *Thread+GA* on the GTX480 actually shows a 4.5× speedup.

On the GTX285, *Thread+SA*, *Block+SA*, and *Block+PR* show 6.4×, 8.1×, and 10.1× speedups, respectively. Perhaps somewhat surprisingly, parallelizing over spans actually hurts performance. By not serializing the computations for spans, we can get speedups of 13% for *Thread+SA+SS* over *Thread+SA* and about 40% for *Block+SA+SS* and *Block+PR+SS* over their parallel spans versions. In thread-based mapping, the atomic operations on shared memory are the bottleneck, so that sequential processing of spans makes only a small difference. On the other hand, in *Block+SA* and *Block+PR* on the GTX285, the global memory bandwidth is the major limiting factor since the same rule is loaded from the global memory redundantly for each span when we parallelize over spans. Hence, executing spans sequentially removes the redundant global memory loads and substantially improves the performance.

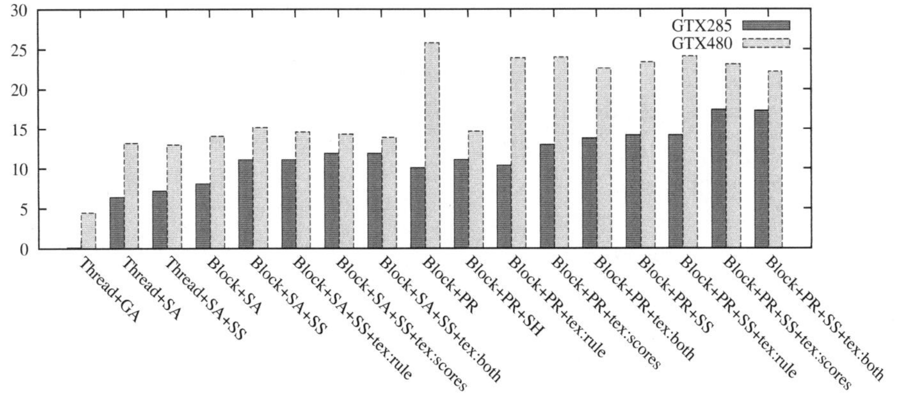

Figure 11: Speedups of various versions of parallel CKY parser that have different mappings, synchronization methods, and different memory access optimizations.

On the GTX285, the transformed access pattern for the *scores* array along with accesses to the shared memory (*Block+PR+SH*) improves the performance by about 10%, showing a 11.1× speedup. Placing the *scores* array in texture memory improves all implementations. The reduced binding cost due to the array reorganization results in additional gains of about 25% for *Block+PR+SS+tex:scores* and *Block+PR+tex:scores* against *Block+PR+SS* and *Block+PR* (for a total speedup of 17.4× and 13.0×, respectively). However, placing the rule information in texture memory improves the performance little as there are many more accesses to the *scores* array than to the rule information.

The GTX480 is the Fermi architecture (NVIDIA, 2009), with many features added to the GTX285. The number of cores doubled from 240 to 480, but the number of SMs was halved from 30 to 15. The biggest difference is the introduction of L1 cache as well as the shared memory per SM. For these reasons, all parallel implementations are faster on the GTX480 than on the GTX285. On the GTX480, parallelizing over spans (*SS*) does not improve the performance, but actually degrades it. This is because this GPU has L1 cache and a higher global memory bandwidth, so that reducing the parallelism actually limits the performance. Utilizing texture memory or shared memory for the scores array does not help either. This is because the GTX480 hardware already caches the scores array into the L1 cache.

Interestingly, the ranking of the various parallelization configurations in terms of speedup is architecture dependent: on the GTX285, the block-based mapping and sequential span processing are preferred, and the parallel reduction is preferred over shared-memory atomic operations. Using texture memory is also helpful on the GTX285. On the GTX480, block-based mapping is also preferred but sequential spans mapping is not. The parallel reduction is clearly better than shared-memory atomic operations, and there is no need for utilizing texture memory on the GTX480. It is important to understand how the different design choices affect the performance, since one different choices might be necessary for grammars with different numbers of symbols and rules.

6 Related Work

A substantial body of related work on parallelizing natural language parsers has accumulated over the last two decades (van Lohuizen, 1999; Giachin and Rullent, 1989; Pontelli et al., 1998; Manousopoulou et al., 1997). However, none of this work is directly comparable to ours, as GPUs provide much more fine-grained possibilities for parallelization. The parallel parsers in past work are implemented on multicore systems, where the limited parallelization possibilities provided by the systems restrict the speedups that can be achieved. For example, van Lohuizen (1999) reports a 1.8× speedup, while Manousopoulou et al. (1997) claims a 7-8× speedup. In contrast, our parallel parser is implemented on a manycore system with an abundant number of threads and processors to parallelize upon. We exploit the massive fine-grained parallelism inherent in natural language parsing and achieve a speedup of more than an order of magnitude.

Another difference is that previous work has often focused on parallelizing agenda-based parsers (van Lohuizen, 1999; Giachin and Rullent, 1989; Pontelli et al., 1998; Manousopoulou et al., 1997). Agenda-based parsers maintain a queue of prioritized intermediate results and iteratively refine and combine these until the whole sentence is processed. While the agenda-based approach is easy to implement and can be quite efficient, its potential for parallelization is limited because only a small number of intermediate results can be handled simultaneously. Chart-based parsing on the other hand allows us to expose and exploit the abundant parallelism of the dynamic program.

Bordim et al. (2002) present a CKY parser that is implemented on a field-programmable gate array (FPGA) and report a speedup of up to 750×. However, this hardware approach suffers from insufficient memory or logic elements and limits the number of rules in the grammar to 2,048 and the number of non-terminal symbols. Their approach thus cannot be applied to real-world, state-of-the-art grammars.

Ninomiya et al. (1997) propose a parallel CKY parser on a distributed-memory parallel machine consisting of 256 nodes, where each node contains a single processor. Using their parallel language, they parallelize over cells in the chart, assigning each chart cell to each node in the machine. With a grammar that has about 18,000 rules and 200 nonterminal symbols, they report a speedup of 4.5× compared to an optimized C++ sequential version. Since the parallel machine has a distributed-memory system, where the synchronization among the nodes is implemented with message passing, the synchronization overhead is significant, preventing them from parallelizing over rules and nonterminal symbols. As we saw, parallelizing only over chart cells (i.e., words or substrings in a sentence) limits the achievable speedups significantly. Moreover, they suffer from load imbalance that comes from the different number of nonteriminal symbols that each node needs to process in the assigned cell. In contrast, we parallelize over rules and nonterminal symbols, as well as cells, and address the load imbalance problem by introducing virtual symbols (see Figure 8).

It should be noted that there are a also number of orthogonal approaches for accelerating natural language parsers. Those approaches often rely on coarse approximations to the grammar of interest (Goodman, 1997; Charniak and Johnson, 2005; Petrov and Klein, 2007b). These coarse models are used to constrain and prune the search space of possible parse trees before applying the final model of interest. As such, these approaches can lead to great speed-ups, but introduce search errors. Our approach in contrast preserves optimality and could in principle be combined with such multi-pass approaches to yield additional speed improvements. There are also some optimality preserving approaches based on A*-search techniques (Klein and Manning, 2003; Pauls and Klein, 2009) or grammar refactoring (Dunlop et al., 2011) that aim to speed up CKY inference. We suspect that most of the ideas therein are orthogonal to our approach, and therefore leave their integration into our GPU-based parser for future work.

7 Conclusion

In this paper, we explored the design space for parallelizing the CKY algorithm for parsing, which is widely-used in constituency based natural language parsers. We compared various implementations on two recent NVIDIA GPUs. The fastest parsers on each GPU are different implementations, since the GTX480 supports L1 cache while the GTX285 does not, among other different architectural features. Compared to an optimized sequential C implementation our parallel implementation is 26 times faster on the GTX480 and 17 times faster on the GTX285. All our parallel implementations are faster on the GTX480 than on the GTX285, showing that performance improves with the addition of more Streaming Processors.

Acknowledgements

This work was supported in part by the 2010 Research Fund of the University of Seoul. This work was also supported by Microsoft (Award #024263) and Intel (Award #024894) funding and by matching funding by U.C. Discovery (Award #DIG07-10227). Additional supports comes from UC Berkeley Par Lab affiliates National Instruments, Nokia, NVIDIA, Oracle, and Samsung.

We also thank Alexander ("Sasha") Rush for valuable comments that lead to improvements of this paper.

References

K. Asanovic, R. Bodik, B. Catanzaro, J. Gebis, P. Husbands, K. Keutzer, D. Patterson, W. Plishker, J. Shalf, S. Williams, and K. Yelick. 2006. The landscape of parallel computing research: A view from berkeley. Technical report, Electrical Engineering and Computing Sciences, University of California at Berkeley.

J. Bordim, Y. Ito, and K. Nakano. 2002. Accelerating the CKY parsing using FPGAs. In *ICHPC '02*.

X. Carreras, M. Collins, and T. Koo. 2008. TAG, dynamic programming, and the perceptron for efficient, feature-rich parsing. In *CoNLL '08*.

E. Charniak and M. Johnson. 2005. Coarse-to-Fine N-Best Parsing and MaxEnt Discriminative Reranking. In *ACL '05*.

E. Charniak. 2000. A maximum–entropy–inspired parser. In *NAACL '00*.

J. Cocke and J. T. Schwartz. 1970. Programming languages and their compilers: Preliminary notes. Technical report, Courant Institute of Mathematical Sciences, New York University.

M. Collins. 1999. *Head-Driven Statistical Models for Natural Language Parsing*. Ph.D. thesis, University of Pennsylvania, Philadelphia, PA, USA.

A. Dunlop, N. Bodenstab, and B. Roark. 2011. Efficient matrix-encoded grammars and low latency parallelization strategies for CYK. In *IWPT '11*.

J. Finkel, A. Kleeman, and C. D. Manning. 2008. Efficient, feature-based, conditional random field parsing. In *ACL/HLT '08*.

E. P. Giachin and C. Rullent. 1989. A parallel parser for spoken natural language. In *IJCAL '89*.

J. Goodman. 1997. Global thresholding and multiple-pass parsing. In *EMNLP '97*.

L. Huang and D. Chiang. 2005. Better k-best parsing. In *IWPT '05*.

T. Kasami. 1965. An efficient recognition and syntax-analysis algorithm for context-free languages. Scientific Report AFCRL-65-758, Air Force Cambridge Research Lab.

David B. Kirk and Wen-mei W. Hwu. 2010. *Programming Massively Parallel Processors: A Hands-on Approach*. Morgan Kaufmann Publishers Inc., San Francisco, CA, USA, 1st edition.

D. Klein and C. Manning. 2003. A* parsing: Fast exact viterbi parse selection. In *NAACL '03*.

E. Lindholm, J. Nickolls, S. Oberman, and J. Montrym. 2008. Nvidia tesla: A unified graphics and computing architecture. *IEEE Micro*, 28(2):39–55.

A. G. Manousopoulou, G. Manis, P. Tsanakas, and G. Papakonstantinou. 1997. Automatic generation of portable parallel natural language parsers. In *Proceedings of the 9th conference on Tools with Artificial Intelligence*.

M. Marcus, B. Santorini, and M. Marcinkiewicz. 1993. Building a large annotated corpus of English: The Penn Treebank. In *Computational Linguistics*.

J. Nickolls, I. Buck, M. Garland, and K. Skadron. 2008. Scalable parallel programming with CUDA. *ACM Queue*, 6(2):40–53.

T. Ninomiya, K. Torisawa, K. Taura, and J. Tsujii. 1997. A parallel cky parsing algorithm on large–scale distributed–memory parallel machines. In *PACLING '97*.

NVIDIA. 2009. Fermi: NVIDIA's next generation CUDA compute architecture. `http://www.nvidia.com/content/PDF/fermi_white_papers/NVIDIA_Fermi_Compute_Architecture_Whitepaper.pdf`.

A. Pauls and D. Klein. 2009. Hierarchical search for parsing. In *NAACL-HLT '09*.

S. Petrov and D. Klein. 2007a. Discriminative log-linear grammars with latent variables. In *NIPS '07*.

S. Petrov and D. Klein. 2007b. Improved inference for unlexicalized parsing. In *NAACL '07*.

S. Petrov, L. Barrett, R. Thibaux, and D. Klein. 2006. Learning accurate, compact, and interpretable tree annotation. In *ACL '06*.

E. Pontelli, G. Gupta, J. Wiebe, and D. Farwell. 1998. Natural language processing: A case study. In *AAAI '98*.

M. P. van Lohuizen. 1999. Parallel processing of natural language parsers. In *ParCo '99*, pages 17–20.

D.H. Younger. 1967. Recognition and parsing of context-free languages in time n^3. *Information and Control*, 10.

CuteForce – Deep Deterministic HPSG Parsing

Gisle Ytrestøl
Department of Informatics / University of Oslo
gisley@ifi.uio.no

Abstract

We present a deterministic HPSG parser capable of processing text incrementally with very fast parsing times. Our system demonstrates an efficient data-driven approach that achieves a high level of precision. Through a series of experiments in different configurations, we evaluate our system and compare it to current state-of-the-art within the field, and show that high quality deterministic parsing is realistic even for a 'deep' unification-based precision grammar.

1 Motivation

The traditional chart parsing paradigm for text parsing has been to process one sentence at a time, and through some type of dynamic programming algorithm derive the most probable analysis. For a formalism like HPSG, even short sentences can license hundreds of valid (i.e. grammatical) analyses, and at some point a statistical model has to be employed to reduce and pin down an n-best candidate list. In order to circumvent a costly extraction of the full parse forest, deterministic incremental parsing has enjoyed an increased interest in the research community. Deterministic parsing can mitigate both the time and space complexity challenges often associated with probabilistic chart parsing methods. The deterministic incremental approach is attractive both from a computational and a cognitive standpoint. Whereas traditional chart parsing approaches require the entire sentence as input before producing an analysis, an incremental algorithm will incrementally expand a syntactic/semantic derivation as it reads the input sentence one word/token at a time. There are several attractive features to this approach. The time-complexity will be linear when the algorithm is deterministic, i.e. when it does not allow for later changes to the partial derivation. For a number of applications, e.g. speech recognition, the ability to process input on the fly per word, and not per sentence, can also be vital.

This paper introduces a 'deep' incremental deterministic HPSG parser, dubbed *CuteForce*. It has an optional unification mode, ensuring that all parse derivations are valid HPSG analyses. Unification is a costly operation, and for certain applications it may be a desirable trade-off to gain a significant speed-up by replacing unification with less expensive constraint checking.

2 Related Work

While there is a rich research tradition in statistical parsing, the predominant approach derives from chart parsing and is inherently non-deterministic. In the following, we review alternative approaches to statistical parsing, with a focus on deterministic and incremental processing.

2.1 Deterministic Parsing

Deterministic parsing aims to derive one single analysis provided the input string and the grammar. As almost any medium to long sentence carries substantial inherent ambiguity given even a moderately simple grammar, this would in practice mean to disambiguate on the fly by making a sequence of local choices that continuously pursue the globally optimal derivation.

Dependency Grammar Kudo and Matsumoto (2002) introduced an efficient deterministic dependency parser for Japanese. Their parser outperformed previous probabilistic models with respect to accuracy and efficiency. Yamada and Matsumoto (2003) applied a similar method for English, and received a near state of the art accuracy compared to other dependency grammar parsers.

The method was further investigated with MaltParser (Nivre et al., 2007; Nivre and Scholz, 2004). MaltParser is a platform for data-driven dependency parsing, which can induce a parsing model from treebank data and parse new input using a pre-compiled parsing model. The parser is formalized as a transition-based instantiation of a shift-reduce parser. It has been applied to a range of different languages, and Nivre et al. (2007) report that dependency accuracy consistently ranges from 80 to 90 %, "usually with less than a 5% increase in error rate compared to state-of-the art parsers for the language in question."

CFG Sagae and Lavie (2005) present a deterministic CFG parser grounded in the same classifier-based strategy that was pursued by MaltParser. Given that the search-space of constituent trees is larger than for dependency trees, the potential efficiency gain of deterministic parsing could be higher than for dependency parsing, but the margin of error would also be larger, given that a deterministic CFG parse is likely to reach more decision points, with more alternative paths than the same sentence would have encountered in dependency parsing. Although they do not reach the same precision/accuracy as 'classic' state-of-the-art parsers (e.g. Collins (1997), Charniak (2000), Charniak and Johnson (2005)), "the simplicity and efficiency of deterministic parsers make them attractive in a number of situations requiring fast, light-weight parsing, or parsing of large amounts of data." (Sagae and Lavie, 2005)

HPSG The increased complexity of unification-based grammars like HPSG could potentially license a substantial increase in efficiency by parsing deterministically, but the inherent hard constraints of unification-based grammar could cause a high number of parse failures. Parallel to the development of the CuteForce parser, Ninomiya et al. (2010; 2009) provide a deterministic shift-reduce parser for HPSG where this issue is addressed. To mitigate the problem of parse failures, they suggest default unification (Ninomiya et al., 2002; Copestake, 1993; Carpenter, 1993) by overwriting inconsistent constraints in the grammar, outlining a deterministic and a non-deterministic configuration.

Ninomiya et al. (2010) evaluate their parser on Enju2.3ß, an HPSG for English, which is extracted from Section 02-21 of the Penn Treebank (Miyao and Tsujii, 2005; Miyao et al., 2004). Their deterministic parser using default unification reaches a coverage of 95%. They further conclude that "[t]he experiments revealed that deterministic parsing with default unification achieved a high degree of accuracy of 87.6 per cent for the Penn Treebank with gold part-of-speech (POS) tags." (Ninomiya et al., 2010)

Further, Matsuzaki et al. (2007) provide a fast, partially deterministic shift-reduce HPSG parser. The parser requires a preceding non-deterministic supertagging and CFG-filtering stage prior to the unification-based parsing which is done through a deterministic shift-reduce algorithm, and gives "comparable accuracy with a speed-up by a factor of six (30 msec/sentence) compared with the best published result using the same grammar." (Matsuzaki et al., 2007)

2.2 Traditional Unification-Based Parsing

Whereas the parser proposed by Ninomiya et al. (2010; 2009) is to our knowledge the only other effort to deterministically parse HPSG, traditional chart parsing approaches for unification-based grammars have been presented in a number of research efforts (e.g. Riezler et al. (2000), Kaplan et al. (2004), Malouf and van Noord (2004), Miyao and Tsujii (2005), Toutanova et al. (2005)). Since unification is a destructive, hence non-reversible operation, a non-deterministic parsing algorithm will need to preserve the original feature structure in order to keep the entire parse forest intact. Keeping the parse forest intact is crucial when constructing an n-best list over the most probable HPSG analyses that is licensed by the grammar, as the individual parse tree will contain diverging feature structures. This has been addressed in several research papers, as this could potentially be a major bottleneck for non-deterministic HPSG parsing (Callmeier, 2000; Oepen and Carroll, 2000; Zhang et al., 2007).

PET HPSG Parser The PET platform was developed as a tool for experimentation with HPSG processing and implementation techniques (Callmeier, 2000). It has further been developed through subsumption-based packing (Oepen and Carroll, 2000), selective unpacking and statistical parse ranking (Zhang et al., 2007). It is maintained by DELPH-IN[1], which is a cooperation between academic institutions and researchers working with deep linguistic processing in HPSG.

The PET HPSG Parser will for each input sentence use a hand-crafted grammar (e.g. LinGO ERG) to retrieve the candidate analyses that are

[1] `http://www.delph-in.net/`

grounded in the grammar, thus being *well-formed*. During parsing it attempts to create the full packed parse forest for each input sentence, and produces an *n*-best list based on statistical parse ranking. Parsing will fail if the full parse forest cannot be constructed within a preset time limit (normally 60 seconds).

3 LinGO ERG and Redwoods Treebank

There exists a number of different HPSG grammars used for automatic parsing. The parser presented in this paper uses LinGO (Linguistic Grammars Online) ERG (English Resource Grammar), which is a broad-coverage, linguistically precise handcrafted grammar for English (Flickinger, 2000). It is continuously being developed and expanded to increase coverage for new domains.

The Redwoods treebank is a collection of annotated corpora from a variety of domains, including tourism guides, transcribed scheduling dialogs, ecommerce emails and Wikipedia articles (Oepen et al., 2002). Each analysis in the treebank is manually disambiguated and assigned an HPSG analysis in accordance with ERG. Its use in this project is recorded in Table 1. HPSG signs corresponding to lexical types are developed manually and assigned in accordance with the lexical coverage of the grammar. Each derivation within Redwoods is grounded in ERG, ensuring that the analyses from each individual treebank are kept consistent with the overall grammar.

WikiWoods WikiWoods is a collection of automatically annotated Wikipedia articles, in total 1.3 million articles and 55 million utterances. WeScience (*ws*) can be seen as a manually annotated subset of WikiWoods (Flickinger et al., 2010; Ytrestøl et al., 2009). The WikiWoods corpus is parsed with the PET HPSG parser using the 1010 release of ERG, and will contain a proportion of incorrect analyses. In a manual inspection of 1,000 random utterances, roughly 82 % of the analyses were deemed correct or nearly correct (Flickinger et al., 2010).

In this paper we augment the training data with derivations from WikiWoods, using the derivations from Section 2000 and onwards. As demonstrated in this paper, both the supertagger as well as CuteForce benefits greatly from the augmented training data.

3.1 Statistics and Example

Table 1 provides an overview of the Redwoods treebanks which are used in this paper.

Name	#Sent	~Length	Usage
ws1-11	7636	14.4	train
ws12	601	15.6	dev
ws13	785	14.1	test
logon	8501	13.3	train
vm	11116	6.8	train
sc	2564	15.1	train

Table 1: The corpora in Redwoods treebank used for training and testing in this paper.
#Sent refers to the number of sentences. ~Length is the average number of tokens per sentence for the treebank.
ws – WeScience, Wikipedia articles
logon – Tourism guides
vm – Verbmobil corpus, transcribed dialogs
sc – SemCor, subset of English Brown Corpus

Figure 1 presents an HPSG derivation for a simple sentence. This tree of ERG rules can be presented as a feature structure, and a semantic MRS representation can be derived directly from its structure.

Lexical Rules and Lexical Types The derivation in Figure 1 is composed of lexical and syntactic rules. Further, each token is assigned a lexical type, which is conceptually equivalent to a supertag (see Section 4). From the leaves in Figure 1 we see that punctuation is considered a part of the token, e.g. for *RSS-*. The lexical types end with the *_le* suffix. The lexical type for "RSS-", *n_-_pn_le*, provides the HPSG sign template for a proper noun. The conceptual sign is further augmented by the lexical ERG rules, which end with **lr*. The hyphen in "RSS-" is hence annotated with *w_hyphen_plr*.

For "specialized" the lexical type *v_np*_le* denotes the lexical category verb (*v*), with an optional noun phrase subcategorization argument. *v_pas_odlr* denotes a passive verb, and *v_j-nb-pas-tr_dlr* derives an attributive adjective from a transitive passive verb. Altogether there are 50 lexical rules in the ERG, and around 1,000 lexical types.

Syntactic Rules Syntactic ERG rules have a *_c* suffix. The rules can be unary or binary. The root node in Figure 1, *sb-hd_mc_c*, denotes the conventional *head-subject* main clause in HPSG, in

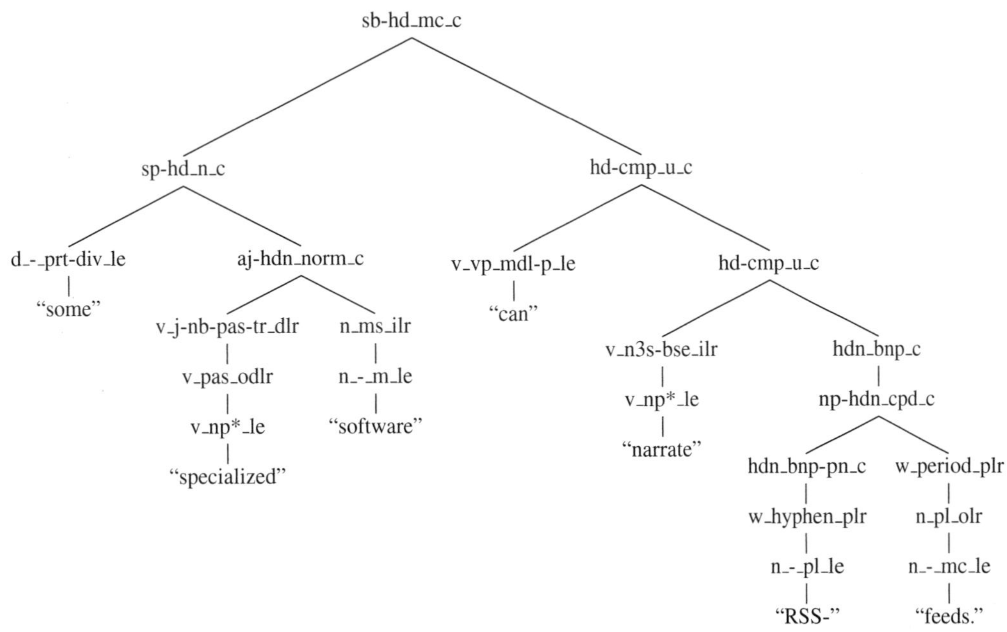

Figure 1: HPSG derivation from WeScience.

turn connecting a *head+specifier* (*sp-hd_n_c*) and a *head+complement* (*hd-cmp_u_c*) phrase in a binary production. There are in total 145 binary and 55 unary syntactic rules in the ERG.

4 Preprocessing and Supertagging

CuteForce assumes an input buffer consisting of the tokenized words, part-of-speech tags and lexical types. For tokenization we use the gold standard ERG tokenization provided by the treebank. HPSG lexical types are supertags providing a lexical template for the input token (Bangalore and Joshi, 1999). Currently, there are 1186 lexical types in the grammar, and these templates can be seen as an extension to the token, enriching the word with HPSG lexical information, corresponding to the HPSG sense of a word sign.[2] Dridan (2009) showed that supertagging contributes to both speed-up and increased coverage for the PET HPSG Parser. Although it would be feasible to integrate supertagging into the parsing oracle, assigning supertags incrementally during parsing, we have opted for a pre-processing stage for performance reasons, a design choice which is parallel to MaltParser.

Dridan (2009) investigated supertagging of lexical types within ERG. The thesis concludes that the TnT tagger (Brants, 2000) performs better than C&C Tagger (Clark and Curran, 2007) when trained on the limited training data that was available in 2009. However, the learning curve for the TnT tagger seemed to flatten out at around 150,000 tokens, whereas the learning curve for C&C was still rising.

We trained the C&C tagger on the Redwoods treebank, and augmented it with sentences from the WikiWoods corpus (see Table 1). The findings in Dridan (2009) suggest that non-gold standard data may improve the C&C tagger. Additionally we developed a customized feature model trained with SVM^{hmm}, which is an implementation of structural SVMs for sequence tagging which learns a hidden Markov model (Joachims et al., 2009). Whereas the C&C tagger is optimized for supertagging, and has a relatively fixed configuration, SVM^{hmm} requires that the user designs features specifically aimed for the classification task. This allows the user to address certain unconventional aspects of ERG supertagging, most especially the tokenization that includes punctuation. On smaller sets of training data, SVM^{hmm} outperformed C&C. However, C&C trains much faster, and is capable of training on much larger amounts of data than SVM^{hmm}.

Results The best single tag accuracy in Dridan (2009) refers to Section 2 of WeScience, since this was released prior to the final release of WeScience. In Table 2 we present the lexical type accuracies (*lt acc.*) on WeScience Section 13 for the

[2] 892 different lexical types are found in the training data.

best configurations for SVM^{hmm} and the C&C tagger, along with the best single lexical type accuracy for WeScience 2 reported in Dridan (2009). *# sent* refers to the number of sentences in the training data, and *cpu hours* is the number of hours it took to train the model. Although we were able to train even larger models for the C&C tagger, the accuracy seemed to flatten out at approximately 6,800,000 tokens on our development set, so we have applied this model. For the C&C tagger, we used the default parameter settings.

	TnT [3]	C&C	SVM^{hmm}
lt acc.	0.864	0.953	0.934
# sent	≈10,000	6,800,000	300,000
cpu hours	<0.1	314	480

Table 2: Single tag accuracy on WeScience Section 2 (TnT) and Section 13 (C&C and SVM^{hmm}).

Consistent with the assumption in Dridan (2009), augmenting the training data contributes substantially to the performance of the tagger. C&C and SVM^{hmm} (Table 2) are trained on 6,800,000 and 300,000 sentences respectively, approximately 94 million/4 million tokens. C&C has a comparatively low accuracy when the amount of training data is limited. We assume the punctuation regime in ERG works is C&C's disadvantage when the training data is limited, since it will result in a large lexicon with comparatively low frequency per lexical entry. When increasing the training data, this sparsity problem will have less impact – it is even plausible that this contributes to the overall performance of C&C when the amount of training data is high, because the punctuation provides enriched information about the token.

Part-of-speech tags are assigned prior to supertagging. POS tags are not part of the final HPSG derivation, but are used both by the parsing oracle in CuteForce and by the supertagger. The POS tags used in training and test data are tagged using the TnT POS tagger, applying the pre-compiled English WSJ model bundled with the tagger.

[3]From the best single tag accuracy reported in Dridan (2009) on Section 2 of *ws*. Training time is not stated in Dridan (2009), but in TnT it should only be a matter of minutes for such a small data set. This model is trained on 1,941 sentences from WeScience, and additional data from the Redwoods treebank, approximately 10,000 sentences, and WeScience should hence be considered (mostly) out-of-domain for this model, compared to the models used in the training of the C&C and SVM^{hmm} tagger.

5 CuteForce – Deterministic Incremental HPSG Parsing

Our parser, CuteForce, employs a classifier-based *oracle* to guide the shift-reduce parser that incrementally builds a syntactic/semantic HPSG derivation that conforms to the LinGO English Resource Grammar (ERG).

Parser Layout The sentence input buffer β is a list of tuples with token, part-of-speech tags and HPSG lexical types (supertags).

Given a set of ERG rules R and a sentence buffer β, a parser configuration is a tuple $c = (\alpha, \beta, \iota, \pi)$ where:

- α is a stack of "active" edges[4]
- β is a list of tuples of word forms W, part of speech tags POS and lexical types LT derived from a sentence $x = ((W_1, POS_1, LT_1), ...(W_n, POS_n, LT_n))$.
- ι is the current input position in β
- π is a stack of passive edges instantiating an ERG rule

The stack of passive edges π makes up the full HPSG representation of the input string if the string is accepted.

Transition System The shift-reduce parser has four different transitions, two of which are parameterized with a unary or binary ERG rule, which are added to the passive edges, hence building the HPSG structure. The four transitions are:

- ACTIVE – (adds an active edge to stack α, and increments ι)
- UNIT(R^1) – (adds unary passive edge to π instantiating unary ERG rule (R^1))
- PASSIVE(R^2) – (pops α and adds binary passive edge to π instantiating binary ERG rule (R^2))
- ACCEPT – (terminates the parse of the sentence. π represents the HPSG derivation of the sentence)

[4]An "active" edges in our sense is a hypothesis of an application of a binary rule where the left daughter is known (an element of π), and the specific binary ERG rule and the right daughter is yet to be found.

Parsing Configuration Mode The parser can operate in three oracle configurations: HPSG Unification mode, CFG approximation mode and unrestricted mode.

In HPSG Unification mode, the parser validates that each transition implies a valid unification. This is done through an XML-RPC interface to LKB (Copestake, 2002). We expect that a substantial speedup could be obtained if this implementation was done natively in CuteForce[5]. All UNIT and PASSIVE transitions are implicit unifications. For each parsing stage, the parsing oracle returns a ranked list of transitions. The highest-ranked transition not violating a unification constraint will be executed. If no transitions yield a valid unification, parsing fails for the given sentence. All non-failing parses (i.e. parses that terminates with the ACCEPT transition) are ensured to produce a valid HPSG derivation.

In CFG mode, a naive CFG approximation of the ERG is employed to guide the oracle. The CFG approximation consists of CFG rules harvested from the parser's training data, augmented with derivations from WikiWoods, in total 300,000 sentences. Each ERG rule instantiation, using the identifiers shown in Figure 1 as non-terminal symbols, will be treated as a CFG rule, and each parser action will be validated against the set of CFG rules. If the parser action yields a CFG projection not found among the valid CFG rules in the CFG approximation, the CFG filter will block this transition. If the parser arrives at a state where the CFG filter blocks all further transitions, parsing fails.

In unrestricted mode, the oracle chooses the highest scoring transition without any further restrictions imposed. In this setting, the parser typically reaches close to 100 % coverage – the only sentences not covered in this setting are instances where the parser enters an infinite unit production loop, and the sentence is dismissed.[6]

[5] Specifically, the current unification back-end performs non-destructive unification, i.e. it does not take advantage of the deterministic nature of CuteForce.

[6] One would require additional heuristics to avoid unary loops in an incremental parsing scheme that allows for such productions. In Sagae and Lavie (2005) they force a non-unary production after three consecutive unary transitions in order to break a potential loop.

5.1 Machine Learning Model

A discriminative machine learning model is used to predict the parser action. The model is trained and tested on the WeScience Treebank, a branch of the hand-annotated LinGO Redwoods treebank (Ytrestøl et al., 2009; Oepen et al., 2002). Section 1-11 is used for training, Section 12 is used in development and Section 13 is held-out for testing. The training data is further augmented with additional sentences from other Redwoods treebanks (see Table 1), and derivations from the automatically annotated Wikiwoods corpus. Parsing results for CuteForce initially improve when the size of the training data increases, but the full extent of the effect of training on partially incorrect training data is not yet clear. Section 3 provides a more in-depth presentation of the training data used in this paper. The parsing is reduced to a classification problem. Each HPSG analysis is a derivation from one unique sequence of parser actions $T = t_1, t_2 \ldots t_n$ The input histories are feature vectors representing a parser state, and the output class is a transition t. This can be seen as a deterministic implementation of a History-based model, introduced by Black et al. (1993). Formally, a derivation D is a sequence of the highest scoring transitions T:

$$\arg\max_{t_i} P(t_i \mid \Phi(t_1, .., t_{i-1}))$$

The function Φ maps the current state, or *history*, to a feature vector. The vector is further defined through a set of feature functions, see Section 5.2.

For training we use LibLinear (Fan et al., 2008), which provides a number of solvers. In CuteForce, we have used the implementation of SVM multi-class classification of Crammer and Singer's formula (Vapnik, 1995; Keerthi et al., 2008; Crammer and Singer, 2002), which has given better results than other learners evaluated during the development.

5.2 Feature Model

CuteForce is equipped with a rich feature model optimized for a large (100,000+) set of training derivations. In our training data of 150,000 training derivations, we have approximately 6 million training instances, where each instance represents a parser action and is mapped to a feature vector. We distinguish between *static* and *dynamic* features, where the static features are defined prior to parsing and only depend on the properties of the input buffer, whereas the dynamic features are defined by the HPSG derivation that is partially built during parsing. Part-of-speech tags and ERG lexical types (supertags) are annotated in a preprocessing stage.

For the history-based model, we expand the formal parser definition in Section 5 with a position index j for α and π, where 0 denotes the top of the stack, -1 denotes the next stack element etc.

Feature Functions We define a set of feature functions to describe the features used in the feature vector:

- $\beta_{(\iota)}$ is the ιth $W/POS/LT$ tuple in the input buffer, where ι denotes the current buffer position.
- BL is the length of buffer β
- $W_{(\iota)}$ is the ιth word form in β.
- $LT_{(\iota)}$ is the ιth lexical type in β.
- $POS_{(\iota)}$ is the ιth Part-of-Speech tag in β, annotated by the preprocessor (TNT).
- $LC_{(\iota)}$ is the lexical category tag derived from $LT_{(\iota)}$.
- $SubCat_{(\iota)}$ is the Subcategorization field derived from $LT_{(\iota)}$.
- $IP_{(\iota)}$ and $FP_{(\iota)}$ denote word-initial and word-final punctuation in the word $W_{(\iota)}$, respectively.
- $\alpha_{(j)}$ is the jth unification candidate edge from the top of the active edge stack.
- $\pi_{(j)}$ is the jth edge from the top of the passive edge stack.
- $l_{(e)}$ is the left-branched daughter of the edge e.
- $r_{(e)}$ is the right-branched daughter of the (passive) edge e.
- $h_{(e)}$ is the HPSG head of the edge e. $h^*_{(e)}$ denotes the head-relation down to the preterminal.
- $ER_{(e)}$ is the ERG rule of the (passive) edge e.
- $S_{(\alpha/\pi)}$ denotes the size of the α and π stacks.

Feature Templates Each training instance maps 70 features to the feature vector. In this paper we limit ourselves to presenting the feature functions corresponding to the atomic features extracted for each parsing state (see Table 3). In the feature vector, most of the atomic features occur in conjunction with other features, and only a few of the features will occur by themselves. A combination of two or more features is necessary to represent the inherent dependence many features have on one another, given that we train the model linearly. For our model derived from 150,000 sentences, we extracted approximately 6 million features, using a frequency cutoff of 3.

SF	$W_{(\iota-1,\iota,\iota+1)}$,$POS_{(\iota-1,\iota,\iota+1,\iota+2)}$ $LC_{(\iota-1,\iota,\iota+1,\iota+2)}$,$\iota$, $BL-\iota$ $LT_{(\iota-1,\iota,\iota+1,\iota+2)}$,$FP_{(\iota)}$,$IP_{(\iota)}$ $SubCat_{(\iota,\iota+1,\iota+2)}$
DF	$S_{(\alpha)}$,$ER_{(\pi_{(0)})}$,$ER_{(h_{(\pi_{(0)})})}$,$ER_{(h_{(h_{(\pi_{(0)})})})}$ $ER_{(h^*_{(\pi_{(0)})})}$,$ER_{(h_{(l_{(\alpha_{(0)})})})}$,$ER_{(h_{(h_{(l_{(\alpha_{(0)})})})})}$ $ER_{(h^*_{(l_{(\alpha_{(0)})})})}$,$ER_{(l_{(\pi_{(0)})})}$,$ER_{(r_{(\pi_{(0)})})}$ $ER_{(l_{(l_{(\alpha_{(0)})})})}$,$ER_{(r_{(l_{(\alpha_{(0)})})})}$,$ER_{(l_{(\alpha_{(-1)})})}$

Table 3: Static and dynamic features.

5.3 Training Data

Given the available treebanks and corpora we have at our disposal (see Section 3), we evaluated a number of different training data configurations. In addition to corpora from the Redwoods treebank, we can extend the training model with WikiWoods data.

In Figure 2 we observe that the accuracy of CuteForce improves when extending the number of training derivations. Figure 2 presents results for parsing without CFG or Unification filtering using gold standard lexical types.

Training data from the WeScience treebank amounts to 7,636 sentences. When training on the same amount of sentences from other (out of domain) treebanks from Redwoods, we see a clear drop in precision – both the in-domain WeScience treebank, and maybe more surprisingly, the annotated WikiWoods corpus is a better source for training than the out-of-domain, yet gold standard, Redwoods data.

Training solely on WikiWoods annotation yields lower performance when the amount of training data is limited, but from 30,000 sentences there are only minor differences in the per-

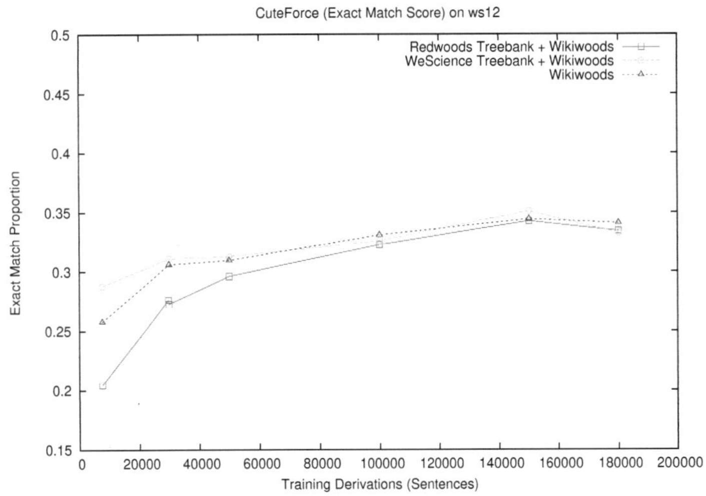

Figure 2: The exact match proportion (proportion of sentences with an HPSG analysis identical to the gold standard) increases when adding more training sentences. The WeScience Treebank augumented with WikiWoods derivations, totally 150,000 sentences, reaches the highest accuracy.

formance for the two in-domain configurations. There are at least two trends in Figure 2 that seem obvious: First, in-domain data is a better training source than out-of-domain data – even when the training data contains a proportion of errors. Second, when the amount of training data is very limited, training on the WeScience treebank yields the best results. However, when we extend the amount of WikiWoods derivations in the training data, these differences diminish, and from 100,000 training sentences onwards, there seems to be no substantial differences between the training data configurations. At about 150,000 derivations, the curve appears to flatten out, and even starting to decline. For the remainder of the paper, we continue using the model trained on WeScience, augmented with Wikiwoods annotation, totally 150,000 derivations, as this configuration achieved the highest accuracy on the development data set.

In this iteration we have indiscriminately used WikiWoods sentences from Section 2000 and onwards. It could prove beneficial to reject sentences in the training data that are obvious outliers. This could be very short (one word) sentences, very long sentences, sentences partially or completely in a foreign language[7], or sentences that have other properties that may imply that they are unsuited to use as training data. This will be subject for further research.

[7]Certain articles in the English Wikipedia contain large amount of foreign texts, for example articles concerning a specific language.

6 Evaluation

CuteForce is evalutated on Section 13 from WeScience (*ws13*), and the experiments were carried out on an Intel Xenon(R) server with 2 GHz CPU.

6.1 Deterministic HPSG Parsers

To our knowledge, the parser outlined in Ninomiya et al. (2010) is the only effort in incremental deterministic unification-based parsing, along side with CuteForce. However, a complete head-to-head comparison of the parse analyses produced by the parsers is not possible due to formal and technical difference in the underlying grammars. Whereas the HPSG Enju grammar used by Ninomiya et al. (2010) is induced from the Penn Treebank, the ERG is a handcrafted grammar. Where the granularity of an induced grammar like Enju is largely determined by information available in the treebank, the ERG includes more fine-grained and richer analyses, for example with respect to subcategorization patterns (including relational nouns and adjectives), multi-word expressions and other subtle linguistic properties that cannot easily be extracted from a treebank with heuristics alone.

Even if the parser proposed by Ninomiya et al. (2010) had been publicly available, adapting it to ERG would not be straightforward, because the typed feature structure logic assumed in the ERG is formally richer than that of Enju. Alternatively, one could opt for a partial evaluation of the analyses generated by the two parsers, e.g. by extracting dependency relations (Clark and Curran (2007), Cahill et al. (2008)). This would be subject for further investigation.

Instead of directly comparing the two deterministic parsers, we can however see how they relate to traditional non-deterministic parsers. Ninomiya et al. (2010) present an extensive evaluation of their deterministic parser, compared to other non-deterministic Enju HPSG parsers. In the following, we will compare CuteForce to the PET HPSG Parser, which is the de facto HPSG parser for the DELPH-IN consortium.

6.2 CuteForce vs PET HPSG Parser

The PET HPSG Parser is the most widely used parser for ERG. Its design is distinctly different from CuteForce (see Section 2.2). Comparing the two parsers based on available testing data is non-trivial: Whereas Ytrestøl et al. (2009) report a parsing coverage of 86 % for the sentences annotated in WeScience, it is only the sentences that were actually covered that appear in the WeScience Treebank. Hence, the PET Parser will have a 100 % coverage in all the test sentences we are able to evaluate. To accommodate for this, we have evaluated the parsers on test sentences where the coverage overlaps for both parsers, hence we have divided the results according to the parser mode in which CuteForce is operating. Table 4 presents the parser scores on *ws13* when CuteForce is using gold standard supertags, whereas Table 5 presents the same score when CuteForce is applying supertagged input.

6.3 Parsing Results

The oracle mode determines the coverage for CuteForce, hence the subset of the test data that is evaluated for each configuration. *M* in Table 4 and 5 refers to the CuteForce oracle mode, where *N* in unrestricted, *C* is CFG approximation mode, and *U* is unification mode. *Ex* is the proportion of sentences that was parsed identically to the gold standard derivation. *Cov* refers to the corresponding coverage, only relevant for CuteForce[8]. *F1* is the Parseval F1-score when treating the gold standard and the parsed analysis as a CFG tree structure. *TA* is the lexical type (supertag) accuracy. All tree derivation scores are computed by *evalb*[9].

Val is the proportion of the parsed analyses that are valid HPSG derivations, and $\sim$*SL* refers to the average sentence length for the subset. *mps* is the average number of millisecond per sentence used by the parser (this excludes preprocessing time done by the supertagger).

In Table 4 and 5 we see that with gold standard supertags, CuteForce is comparable, and even more accurate than PET in certain validation matrices. When parsing with supertagged input, PET is in overall better. However, when considering the F1-score, it seems clear that the parse derivations produced by CuteForce have high quality. Parsing time is consistently 15 msec/sentence unless we apply unification. This is to our knowledge the fastest parsing time reported by a parser on a major HPSG grammar.

We see that the proportion of sentences that are well-formed HPSG derivations are in the range from 0.47-0.59, depending on the configuration. Although a fairly high share of the derivations will not yield a unifiable HPSG derivation, it is however likely that one could extract a partially well-formed semantic structure through robust unification (Fouvry, 2003). This is also addressed in Zhang and Krieger (2011), and will be evaluated in further studies.

7 Future Work

There are alternative paths that could be pursued to attempt to improve on the current configuration. Instead of using single tags, one could let the supertagger assign multiple supertags. Zhang and Clark (2011) present a shift-reduce parser for CCG where the parsing oracle chooses between a set of candidate supertags assigned by the supertagger. Hence they are able to take syntactic information into account when choosing the supertag. A similar approach could be beneficial for CuteForce.

Allowing for non-determinism would open for a number of strategies. Ytrestøl (2011) evaluated a backtracking algorithm where ranking is applied to locate and redo an incorrect transition done by CuteForce. Alternatively, one could consider a beam-search strategy in line with Ninomiya et al. (2010). This will be subject for further study.

[8]Since the treebanks only consist of sentences that the PET parser was able to parse, PET will have 100 % coverage in all configurations.

[9]`http://nlp.cs.nyu.edu/evalb/`

	M	Cov	Ex	F1	TA	Val	~SL	mps
CF	N	0.99	0.42	0.86	1	0.51	14.1	15
PET	-	1	0.48	0.87	0.965	1	14.1	2.3k
CF	C	0.81	0.52	0.89	1	0.59	12.0	15
PET	-	1	0.55	0,88	0.966	1	12.0	2.3k
CF	U	0.57	0.77	0.94	1	1	8.6	1.6k
PET	-	1	0.66	0.90	0.972	1	8.6	2.3k

Table 4: Parsing results for CuteForce (gold standard lexical types) and PET HPSG Parser on *ws13*, evaluated on sentences where the coverage overlaps for both parsers.

	M	Cov	Ex	F1	TA	Val	~SL	mps
CF	N	0.99	0.36	0.82	0.953	0.47	14.0	15
PET	-	1	0.48	0.87	0.965	1	14.0	2.3k
CF	C	0.79	0.45	0.85	0.959	0.59	11.9	15
PET	-	1	0.55	0.88	0.966	1	11.9	2.3k
CF	U	0.52	0.70	0.92	0.974	1	8.1	1.6k
PET	-	1	0.69	0.90	0.976	1	8.1	2.3k

Table 5: Parsing results for CuteForce (supertagged lexical types) and PET HPSG Parser on *ws13*, evaluated on sentences where the coverage overlaps for both parsers.

8 Concluding Remarks

We have presented an efficient deterministic parsing approach to HPSG. Whereas unification-based parsing traditionally has been associated with non-deterministic parsers, we have demonstrated a deterministic system capable of achieving a high level of precision with very fast parsing times. Although it is questionable if a deterministic system could ever reach the same precision-level as state-of-the-art non-deterministic systems, deterministic parsing would be attractive for applications where it is desirable to trade some precision for high-speed incremental parsing.

Acknowledgement

The author would like to thank the anonymous reviewers for their helpful suggestions, and Stephan Oepen (University of Oslo) and Joakim Nivre (Uppsala University) for their valued input and inspiring feedback during the writing of this paper, and in the PhD project in general. Experimentation and engineering was made possible through access to the TITAN high-performance computing facilities at the University of Oslo (UiO), and we are grateful to the Scientific Computation staff at UiO, as well as to the Norwegian Metacenter for Computational Science.

References

Srinivas Bangalore and Aravind K. Joshi. 1999. Supertagging: an approach to almost parsing. *Computational Linguistics*, pages 237–265.

Ezra Black, Fred Jelinek, John Lafferty, David M. Magerman, Robert Mercer, and Salim Roukos. 1993. Towards history-based grammars: Using richer models for probabilistic parsing. In *Proceedings of the 31st Meeting of the Association for Computational Linguistics*, pages 31–37.

Thorsten Brants. 2000. TnT - a statistical part-of-speech tagger. In *Proceedings of the 6th ACL Conference on Applied Natural Language Processing*, pages 224–231.

Aoife Cahill, Michael Burke, Ruth O'Donovan, Stefan Riezler, Josef van Genabith, and Andy Way. 2008. Wide-coverage deep statistical parsing using automatic dependency structure annotation. 34:81–124.

Ulrich Callmeier. 2000. PET — A platform for experimentation with efficient HPSG processing techniques. *Natural Language Engineering*, 6 (1) (Special Issue on Efficient Processing with HPSG):99 – 108.

Bob Carpenter. 1993. Skeptical and credulous default unification with applications to templates and inheritance. In *Inheritance, defaults and the lexicon*, pages 13–37. Cambridge University Press.

Eugene Charniak and Mark Johnson. 2005. Coarse-to-fine n-best parsing and maxent discriminative reranking. In *Proceedings of the*

43th Meeting of the Association for Computational Linguistics, pages 173–180.

Eugene Charniak. 2000. A maximum-entropy-inspired parser. In *Proceedings of the 1st Conference of the North American Chapter of the ACL*, pages 132–139. Morgan Kaufmann Publishers Inc.

Stephen Clark and James Curran. 2007. Formalism-independent parser evaluation with ccg and depbank. In *Proceedings of the 45th Meeting of the Association for Computational Linguistics*, pages 248–255.

Michael Collins. 1997. Three generative, lexicalised models for statistical parsing. In *Proceedings of the 35th Meeting of the Association for Computational Linguistics and the 7th Conference of the European Chapter of the ACL*, pages 16–23.

Ann Copestake. 1993. Defaults in lexical representation. In *Inheritance, defaults and the lexicon*, pages 223–245. Cambridge University Press.

Ann Copestake. 2002. *Implementing Typed Feature Structure Grammars*. CSLI Publications.

Koby Crammer and Yoram Singer. 2002. On the algorithmic implementation of multiclass kernel-based vector machines. *The Journal of Machine Learning Research*, 2:265–292.

Rebecca Dridan. 2009. *Using Lexical Statistics to Improve HPSG Parsing*. Ph.D. thesis, Saarland University.

Rong-En Fan, Kai-Wei Chang, Cho-Jui Hsieh, Xiang-Rui Wang, and Chih-Jen Lin. 2008. Liblinear: A library for large linear classification. *The Journal of Machine Learning Research*, 9:1871–1874.

Dan Flickinger, Stephan Oepen, and Gisle Ytrestøl. 2010. Wikiwoods: Syntacto-semantic annotation for english wikipedia. In *Proceedings of the 7th International Conference on Language Resources and Evaluation*. European Language Resources Association (ELRA).

Dan Flickinger. 2000. On building a more efficient grammar by exploiting types. *Natural Language Engineering*, 6 (1):15 – 28.

Frederik Fouvry. 2003. *Robust Processing for Constraint-Based Grammar Formalisms*. Ph.D. thesis, Univeristy of Essex.

Thorsten Joachims, Thomas Finley, and Chun-Nam John Yu. 2009. Cutting-plane training of structural SVMs. *Machine Learning*, 77:27–59.

Ronald M. Kaplan, Stefan Riezler, Tracy H. King, John T. Maxwell III, and Er Vasserman. 2004. Speed and accuracy in shallow and deep stochastic parsing. In *Proceedings of the main conference on Human Language Technology Conference of the North American Chapter of the Association of Computational Linguistics*.

S. Sathiya Keerthi, S. Sundararajan, Kai-Wei Chang, Cho-Jui Hsieh, and Chih-Jen Lin. 2008. A sequential dual method for large scale multi-class linear SVMs. In *Proceeding of the 14th ACM SIGKDD international conference on Knowledge discovery and data mining*, KDD '08, pages 408–416. ACM.

Taku Kudo and Yuji Matsumoto. 2002. Japanese dependency analysis using cascaded chunking. In *Proceedings of the 6th conference on Natural language learning - Volume 20*, COLING-02, pages 1–7. Association for Computational Linguistics.

Robert Malouf and Gertjan van Noord. 2004. Wide coverage parsing with stochastic attribute value grammars. In *Proceedings of the IJCNLP workshop Beyond Shallow Analysis*.

Takuya Matsuzaki, Yusuke Miyao, and Jun'ichi Tsujii. 2007. Efficient HPSG parsing with supertagging and cfg-filtering. In *Proceedings of the 20th International Joint Conference on Artificial Intelligence*, pages 1671–1676.

Yusuke Miyao and Jun'ichi Tsujii. 2005. Probabilistic disambiguation models for wide-coverage hpsg parsing. In *Proceedings of the 43rd Annual Meeting on Association for Computational Linguistics*, pages 83–90. Association for Computational Linguistics.

Yusuke Miyao, Takashi Ninomiya, and Jun ichi Tsujii. 2004. Corpus-oriented grammar development for acquiring a head-driven phrase structure grammar from the penn treebank. In

Proceedings of the 1nd International Joint Conference on Natural Language Processing, pages 684–693.

Takashi Ninomiya, Yusuke Miyao, and Jun'ichi Tsujii. 2002. Lenient default unification for robust processing within unification based grammar formalisms. In *Proceedings of the 19th International Conference on Computational Linguistics*, pages 1–7.

Takashi Ninomiya, Nobuyuki Shimizu, Takuya Matsuzaki, and Hiroshi Nakagawa. 2009. Deterministic shift-reduce parsing for unification-based grammars by using default unification. In *Proceedings of the 12th Conference of the European Chapter of the ACL*, pages 603–611. Association for Computational Linguistics.

Takashi Ninomiya, Takuya Matsuzaki, Nobuyuki Shimizu, and Hiroshi Nakagawa. 2010. Deterministic shift-reduce parsing for unification-based grammars. *Natural Language Engineering*, pages 1–35.

Joakim Nivre and Mario Scholz. 2004. Deterministic dependency parsing of English text. In *Proceedings of the 20th International Conference on Computational Linguistics*. Association for Computational Linguistics.

Joakim Nivre, Johan Hall, Jens Nilsson, Atanas Chanev, Gülsen Eryigit, Sandra Kübler, Svetoslav Marinov, and Erwin Marsi. 2007. Maltparser: A language-independent system for data-driven dependency parsing. *Natural Language Engineering*, 13(2):95–135.

Stephan Oepen and John Carroll. 2000. Ambiguity packing in constraint-based parsing. Practical results. In *Proceedings of the 1st Conference of the North American Chapter of the ACL*, pages 162 – 169.

Stephan Oepen, Kristina Toutanova, Stuart Shieber, Chris Manning, Dan Flickinger, and Thorsten Brants. 2002. The LinGO Redwoods treebank. Motivation and preliminary applications. In *Proceedings of the 19th International Conference on Computational Linguistics*.

Stefan Riezler, Detlef Prescher, Jonas Kuhn, and Mark Johnson. 2000. Lexicalized stochastic modeling of constraint-based grammars using log-linear measures and EM training. In *Proceedings of the 38th Meeting of the Association for Computational Linguistics*, pages 480 – 487.

Kenji Sagae and Alon Lavie. 2005. A classifier-based parser with linear run-time complexity. In *Proceedings of the 9th International Workshop on Parsing Technologies*, pages 125–132. Association for Computational Linguistics.

Kristina Toutanova, Christopher D. Manning, Dan Flickinger, and Stephan Oepen. 2005. Stochastic HPSG Parse Disambiguation using the Redwoods Corpus. In *Research in Language and Computation*.

Vladimir N. Vapnik. 1995. *The nature of statistical learning theory*. Springer.

Hiroyasu Yamada and Yuji Matsumoto. 2003. Statistical dependency analysis with support vector machines. In *Proceedings of the 8th International Workshop on Parsing Technologies*, pages 195–206.

Gisle Ytrestøl, Dan Flickinger, and Stephan Oepen. 2009. Extracting and Annotating Wikipedia Sub-Domains — Towards a New eScience Community Resource. In *Proceedings of the 8th Workshop on Treebanks and Linguistic Theories*, pages 185 – 197.

Gisle Ytrestøl. 2011. Optimistic backtracking: a backtracking overlay for deterministic incremental parsing. In *Proceedings of the ACL 2011 Student Session*, HLT-SS '11, pages 58–63.

Yue Zhang and Stephen Clark. 2011. Shift-reduce ccg parsing. In *Proceedings of the 49th Meeting of the Association for Computational Linguistics*, pages 683–692.

Yi Zhang and Hans-Ulrich Krieger. 2011. Large-scale corpus-driven pcfg approximation of an hpsg. In *Proceedings of the 12th International Workshop on Parsing Technologies*.

Yi Zhang, Stephan Oepen, and John Carroll. 2007. Efficiency in unification-based n-best parsing. In *Proceedings of the 10th International Workshop on Parsing Technologies*, pages 48–59. Association for Computational Linguistics.

Large-Scale Corpus-Driven PCFG Approximation of an HPSG

Yi Zhang
LT-Lab, DFKI GmbH
Saarbrücken, Germany
yizhang@dfki.de

Hans-Ulrich Krieger
LT-Lab, DFKI GmbH
Saarbrücken, Germany
krieger@dfki.de

Abstract

We present a novel corpus-driven approach towards grammar approximation for a linguistically deep Head-driven Phrase Structure Grammar. With an unlexicalized probabilistic context-free grammar obtained by Maximum Likelihood Estimate on a large-scale automatically annotated corpus, we are able to achieve parsing accuracy higher than the original HPSG-based model. Different ways of enriching the annotations carried by the approximating PCFG are proposed and compared. Comparison to the state-of-the-art latent-variable PCFG shows that our approach is more suitable for the grammar approximation task where training data can be acquired automatically. The best approximating PCFG achieved ParsEval F_1 accuracy of 84.13%. The high robustness of the PCFG suggests it is a viable way of achieving full coverage parsing with the hand-written deep linguistic grammars.

1 Introduction

Deep linguistic processing technologies have been evolving closely around the development of rich formalisms which typically introduce mild context-sensitivity. Examples of well-adopted frameworks include various Tree Adjoining Grammars, Combinatory Categorial Grammars, Lexical Functional Grammars (with untyped Features Structures in F-structures), and Head-Driven Phrase Structure Grammars (with Typed Featured Structures). Such formalisms have been successfully powering the modern formal linguistic studies. However, the intrinsic complexity of *deeper formalisms*[1] hinders the deployment of such resources in language technology applications.

Take HPSG for example. The linguistic framework is built on top of the typed feature logic formalisms (e.g., Carpenter (1992)). The monostratal representation integrates various syntactic and semantic information concerning a linguistic object (and all its sub-components) in a single typed features structure. And the integration of information and compatibility checking is achieved by the *unification* operation. Such a formalism is especially suitable for developing and implementing a linguistic theory. But the lack of a polynomial upper-bound time complexity in unification-based parsing raises concerns of the processing efficiency.

Meanwhile, from the grammar engineering perspective we see grammar developers constantly joggling between two somewhat conflicting goals: on the one hand, to describe the linguistic phenomena in a precisely constrained way; on the other hand, to achieve broad coverage when parsing unseen real-world texts. As a result, many of these large-scale grammar implementations are forced to choose to either compromise the linguistic preciseness, or to accept the low coverage in parsing.

In this paper, we propose PCFG approximation as a way to alleviate some of these issues in HPSG processing. While HPSG framework is great for linguistic description, we show that when carefully designed, a much simpler approximating probabilistic context-free grammar can be extracted automatically, and is capable of achieving good parsing accuracy while maintaining high robustness and efficiency.

The rest of the paper is organized as the following: Section 2 gives an overview of HPSG as an linguistic theory and its application in parsing;

[1] In the context of this paper, by deeper formalism we mean formalisms which are at least mildly context-sensitive, in a comparative sense to the context-free grammars.

Section 3 reviews the previous related work on CFG approximation of HPSG; Section 4 presents the corpus-driven PCFG approximation with both internal and external annotations; Section 5 describes the evaluation setup and results; Section 6 compares our approach with other related work on parsing (such as self-training), and foresees the application of the approximating PCFGs; Section 7 concludes the paper.

2 Parsing with Head-Driven Phrase Structure Grammars

Head-Driven Phrase Structure Grammar (Pollard and Sag, 1994) is a constraint-based highly lexicalized non-derivational generative grammar framework. Based on a typed feature structures formalism, the HPSG theory describes a small set of highly generalized linguistic principles, with which the rich information derived from the detailed lexical types interacts to produce precise linguistic interpretations.

Several large-scale HPSG-based NLP parsing systems have been built in the past decade. Among them are the Enju English & Chinese parser (Miyao et al., 2004; Yu et al., 2010), the Alpino parser for Dutch (van Noord, 2006), and the LKB & PET (Copestake, 2002; Callmeier, 2000) for English, German, Japanese and a dozen more other DELPH-IN[2] grammars of various languages. These systems are successful showcases of where modern grammar engineering contributes to the state-of-the-art parsing systems. With the modern processing techniques such as quasi-destructive unification (Tomabechi, 1991), quick check (Kiefer et al., 1999), ambiguity packing (Oepen and Carroll, 2000) and selective unpacking (Zhang et al., 2007), the practical parsing efficiency has been greatly improved. But none of these changes the underlying formalism, therefore the parser still can run into exponential parsing time in theory.

Another disadvantage of deep grammar lies in the difficulty of proper statistical modeling of the richer representation. For example, Abney (1997) shows that naïve MLE is not consistent for unification-based grammars, and proposes random fields as an alternative. In practice, we see most HPSG parsing systems opt for a discriminative *Maximum Entropy Model* (MEM) for parse ranking on top of the hypothesis space licensed by the HPSG grammar (Miyao and Tsujii, 2002; Malouf and van Noord, 2004; Toutanova et al., 2005). For further efficiency, the hypothesis space of the HPSG parses is pruned with supertagging or symbolic CFG filtering rules (Matsuzaki et al., 2007) at early stages. It is however unclear how these separate models can be unified to guide the best-first construction of HPSG parses without an exhaustive creation of the (packed) parse forest or ad hoc pruning.

Moreover, the heavily constraint-based nature of the grammar poses a difficult choice between linguistic preciseness and practical parsing robustness. As a result, many HPSG parser implementations have to sacrifice on the linguistic side in trade for a decent parsing coverage.

3 Related Work

Previous work in the direction of HPSG approximation has seen two major approaches: grammar-based approach and the corpus-driven approach.

The grammar-based approach (Kiefer and Krieger, 2004) tries to compile out a huge set of categories by flattening the TFSes into atomic symbols. This approach can in theory guarantee the equivalence of the grammars in both parsing and generation. However, in practice it generates billions of CFG productions. Even when carefully choosing a subset of the HPSG features, the resulting grammar is too large to be useful for parsing or generation.

The corpus-based approach (Krieger, 2007), on the other hand, builds the approximating CFG by observing the growth of the chart when parsing texts with the HPSG. Passive edges on the chart represent the successful application of HPSG rules, hence are modeled by an approximating CFG production. Also, the symbols in CFG only carry partial information from a small set of feature-paths used in *quick check* (Kiefer et al., 1999), i.e., the frequently failed feature-paths in unification, hence the most discriminating ones.

Both approaches are symbolic in the sense that there is no probabilistic model produced to disambiguate the CFG parses. In the case of corpus-based approach, one can also acquire frequency counts for each CFG rule. But since not all passive edges occur in a full parse tree, and not all parses are correct, the statistics obtained is not suitable for the parsing task.

Kiefer et al. (2002) propose to use a PCFG in a

[2] http://www.delph-in.net/

two-stage parsing setup, where the PCFG predicts derivations in the first step, followed by the replay of unification. The experiment was carried out on a relatively small grammar. And due to the unavailability of large-scale treebank at the time, unsupervised Inside-Outside algorithm was used for the probability estimation.

Cahill et al. (2004) reported an application of the PCFG approximation technique in LFG parsing and the recovery of long distance dependencies on the f-structures. Two main differences between their work and the one presented in this paper should be noted. First, the approximation target for Cahill et al. (2004) is a treebank-induced grammar, while this paper targets for a large-scale hand-crafted grammar. Second, the monostratal representation in HPSG entails that a correct derivation tree will also guarantee the correct recovery of unbounded dependencies represented by the underlying feature structures, while in the LFG universe these have to be resolved on the f-structures instead of the c-structures.

4 Probabilistic Context-Free Approximation of HPSG

Unlike the approaches in previous work which approximates the symbolic HPSG alone, we propose a PCFG approach which approximates the combination of the grammar and its disambiguation model. This allows us to closely model the deep parser behavior with a single approximation PCFG.

For the experiments in this paper, we use the English Resource Grammar (ERG; Flickinger (2002)) and the accompanying treebanks (see Section 5.1 for detailed descriptions). But the technique presented in this section can be easily applied to other languages and HPSG grammar implementations.

4.1 Derivation Normalization

A complete HPSG analysis is recorded in a derivation tree. The terminals of the tree are surface tokens in the sentence. The preterminals are the names of the activated lexical entries. The non-(pre)terminal nodes (except for the root) correspond to grammar rules applied to create the HPSG signs. An extra root node denotes the *"root"* condition fulfilled to license a complete HPSG parse. An example derivation of ERG is given in Figure 1.

Before extracting the approximation grammar, we perform several normalizing transformations on the original derivations. First, in order to acquire an unlexicalized grammar, we replace the lexical entry names on the preterminal with their corresponding lexical type defined in the ERG lexicon. Second, we collapse the unary chain of morphological rules together with the preterminal lexical types to form the so-called *"supertag"*. As shown in Figure 1, these unary rules always occur above the preterminals and below any syntactic constructional rules. Practice shows that this helps improve the parsing accuracy of the PCFG. The last normalization concerns with the treatment of punctuations. In ERG (as for release 1010), punctuations are treated as affixes instead of independent tokens by themselves. For better compatibility with other annotations, we convert the original punctuation-attaching unary rule (applied above the morphological rules and below the syntactic rules) into a binary branch. The normalized derivation tree of the previous example is shown in Figure 2. It is worth noting that all the normalizing steps can be reversed without introducing ambiguity. The approximating PCFGs will be extracted from the normalized derivations, while the evaluation will be reported on the original derivations (though the tagging accuracy will be calculated on the lexical types).

4.2 PCFG with External Annotation

Although the derivation tree records all necessary information to recover the complete HPSG analysis (i.e. carrying out unification on each node of the tree with corresponding grammar rules and lexical entries), it does not always encode the necessary information in an explicit way, due to the fact that rules in HPSG are highly generalized (see Section 2). For example, the rule *"hd-cmp_u_c"* in ERG can be used to express a head-complement composition without specifying the syntactic category of the head. Thus a node marked only with *"hd-cmp_u_c"* could be a VP, PP, or $\overline{\text{NP}}$. Therefore it will be difficult to accurately predict the derivation without such information. To compensate for the lack of information in the derivation tree, we add additional *annotations* to the non-terminals. We further differentiate external annotation, i.e., additional information from the context of the tree node, and internal annotation, i.e. infor-

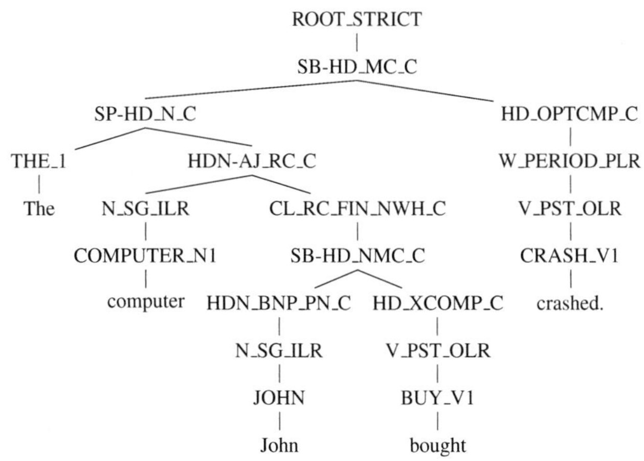

Figure 1: Example of an original ERG derivation tree

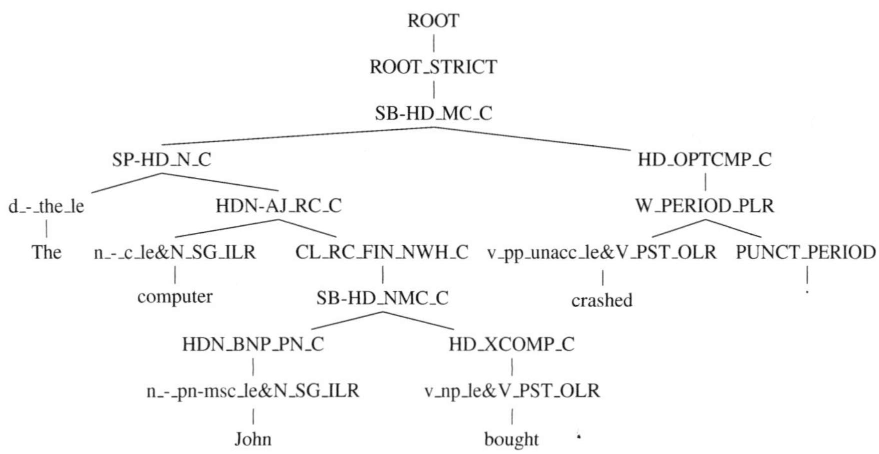

Figure 2: Example of a normalized derivation tree

mation coming from the HPSG sign.[3]

For the external annotation, we mark each non-terminal node with up to n grandparents. This is an effective technique used in both PCFG parsing (Klein and Manning, 2003)[4] and HPSG parse disambiguation (Toutanova et al., 2005). As ERG rules are either unary or binary, we do not annotate nodes with sibling information, though for a grammar with flat rules this could potentially help, as shown by Klein and Manning (2003) (so-called *horizontal markovization*). We choose not to annotate the preterminal supertags with grandparents, for the overly fine-grained tagset hurts the parsing coverage.

4.3 PCFG with Internal Annotation

While the external annotation enrich the derivation tree by gathering context information, the internal annotation explores the detailed HPSG sign associated with the tree node. Note that an average ERG sign contains hundreds of feature-paths and their corresponding values, it is important to pick a suitable small yet effective subset of them as annotation. Following the practice of (Krieger, 2007), we choose to use up to six top-ranked *quick-check* paths (see Table 1), which are the most frequently failed feature-path in unification.

To access the HPSG sign, feature structures are reconstructed by unifying the corresponding TFS of the HPSG rule with the instantiated TFSes of its daughters. This can be done efficiently even with naïve unification algorithms, for there is no search involved. And the unification never fails when the original derivation tree is produced by the ERG. Next, the value of the annotation is determined by the *type* of the TFS at the end of each given feature-path (or **undef** in case the path was not defined in the TFS). For example, for feature-path SYNSEM.LOCAL.CAT.COMPS (the remaining list of complements for the sign), value **null** denotes an empty list, while **olist** denotes a list with only optional complements. Figure 3 shows an example of an annotated tree with 1-level grandparent and HEAD feature-path annotation.

[3]Our notion of *internal* and *external* annotation is slightly different to that of (Klein and Manning, 2003). In our notion, *internal* annotation refers to the information from the local HPSG sign.

[4]This technique is called *vertical markovization* in (Klein and Manning, 2003).

	Feature-Path
1	SYNSEM.LOCAL.CAT.HEAD
2	SYNSEM.LOCAL.CONJ
3	SYNSEM.LOCAL.AGR.PNG.PN
4	SYNSEM.LOCAL.CAT.VAL.COMPS
5	SYNSEM.LOCAL.CAT.HEAD.MOD
6	SYNSEM.LOCAL.CAT.VAL.COMPS.FIRST.OPT

Table 1: Top feature-paths used for internal annotation

4.4 Grammar Extraction & Probability Estimation

To extract the approximating PCFG, we need a disambiguated treebank annotated with HPSG derivations. The treebank is constructed by first parsing the input sentences with the HPSG parser, then disambiguated either manually or automatically by the parse selection model. The CFG symbols and production rules are extracted directly from the annotation enriched derivation trees from the treebank. Each tree node contributes to one frequency count of the corresponding CFG rule with the parent's symbol as the LHS, and the symbols of its daughters as the RHS. For the experiments in this paper, we do not prune the CFG symbols or rules. The rule probability is calculated with *Maximum Likelihood Estimate* (MLE) without smoothing.

$$P_r(A \to \beta) = P(A \to \beta|A) = \frac{\#(A \to \beta)}{\#A} \quad (1)$$

The lexical model, however, does receive smoothing for unknown word handling. More specifically, words are assigned a signature ($sig(w)$) based on their capitalization, suffix, digit and other character features. We then use the MLE estimate of $P(T|sig(w))$ as a prior against which observed taggings T were taken:

$$P(T|w) = \frac{\#(T, w) + \alpha \cdot P(T|sig(w))}{\#T + \alpha} \quad (2)$$

$P(T|w)$ is then inverted to give $P(w|T)$.

The grammar extraction procedure is very efficient. The time required is linear to the size of the treebank. Even with the richest annotations (with unification operations involved), the procedure marches through thousands of trees per minute. This allows us to scale up the extraction with millions of trees.

4.5 Hierarchically Split-Merge PCFG

For comparison we also trained a hierarchically split-merge latent-variable PCFG with the Berkeley parser (Petrov et al., 2006). The latent-variable

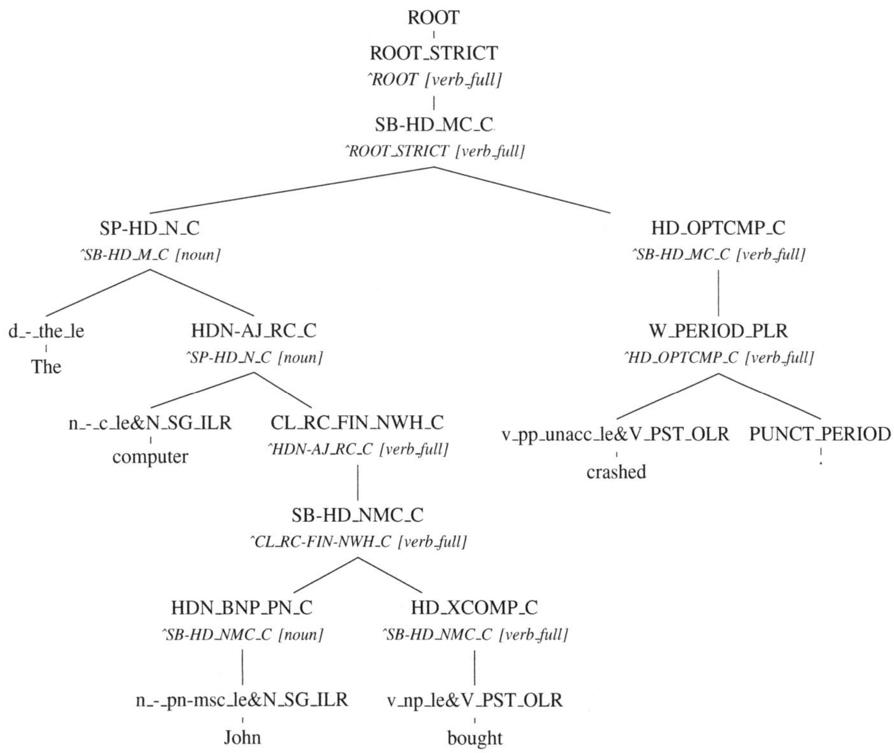

Figure 3: Example tree with 1-level grandparent and HEAD feature-path annotation

approach has proven to deliver state-of-the-art parsing performance for multiple languages. The key advantage is that it automatically induces subcategories from the treebank and produces a finer grained grammar without manual intervention. On treebanks with coarse-grained categories (which is typical for manually annotated treebanks), this is particularly effective.

In our experiment, we train the split-merge latent-variable PCFG on the derivation trees. The *Expectation-Maximization* training process is much more expensive than our MLE-based PCFG extraction. Also, given that the categories in the normalized derivations are already quite fine-grained (hundreds of non-terminal symbols and thousands of tags), the grammar stopped improving after only three rounds of split-merge iterations.

5 Experiments

5.1 Grammar & Data

We use the 1010 release of the *English Resource Grammar* for the approximation experiments. This version of the ERG contains a total of 200 syntactic constructional rules, and 50 lexical/inflectional rules. 145 of the 200 syntactic rules are binary, while the remaining 55 are unary. All lexical/inflectional rules are unary. In addition, the grammar contains a hand-compiled lexicon with around 1000 leaf lexical types and over 35K base-form entries.

Several large treebanks have been developed with the ERG. Unlike the traditional manually annotated treebanks, these are referred to as the Redwoods-style dynamic treebanks (Oepen et al., 2002). Sentences from the corpus are first parsed by the ERG, and then manually disambiguated (mostly by the grammarian himself). For the experiments in this paper, we use the manually disambiguated WeScience Treebank (Ytrestoel et al., 2009), which currently contains a totally of over 11K sentences from a selection of Wikipedia articles in the domain of Natural Language Processing with an average length of 18 tokens per sentence, pre-processed to strip irrelevant markups, and divided into 13 sections. Of all the sentences, about 78% received exactly one "gold" analysis. The rest either fail to be parsed by the ERG, or there is no single acceptable reading. We will only use the subset of sentences with a *"gold"* parse for the experiment. More specifically we keep *"ws12"* for development and *"ws13"* for the final testing. Sections *"ws01"* to *"ws11"* contain a total of 7,636 "gold" trees, which are used for training.

Apart from the WeScience, we also use the large-scale automatically disambiguated WikiWoods Treebank (Flickinger et al., 2010). Currently, WikiWoods contains about 55M English sentences extracted from the English Wikipedia articles. The corpus is parsed with the 1010 version of the ERG, and automatically disambiguated with a Maximum Entropy model trained with the manually disambiguated trees. Only 1 top-ranked reading is preserved. Since the correctness of the parse is unchecked, the dataset is potentially noisy. The total amount of trees available for training is about 48M.

5.2 The Parser

The approximating PCFG tends to grow huge when rich annotations and large corpora are used. For efficient application of the resulting grammar, we implemented a CKY-style parser with bit-vector-based algorithm as the one proposed by Schmid (2004). The algorithm shows its strength in extensibility for grammars with millions of rules and hundreds of thousands of non-terminal symbols.

A slight deviation of our implementation from the BitPar algorithm is that, after constructing the bit-vector-based recognition chart, we do not apply the top-down filtering routine before calculating the Viterbi probabilities. Practice shows that in our case the recognition chart is normally sparse, and the filtering routine itself costs more time than what it saves from the additional calculations in the Viterbi step.

For correctness checking, we reproduced the unlexicalized PCFG parsing accuracy reported by Klein and Manning (2003) on PTB with our bit-vector parser while achieving better efficiency (in both training and testing) than the Stanford Parser. Even though our parser is implemented in Java (for better cross-platform compatibility), the low-level bit-vector-based operations make our system competitive even in comparison to the BitPar implemented in C++.

As mentioned early, we do not prune the PCFG rules during parsing. For the lexical look-up, we allow the lexical model to propose multiple tags (cut by certain probability threshold). In case a full parse is not found, a partial parsing model tries to recover fragmented analysis according to the Viterbi probabilities of the constituents. With careful design of the PCFG and sufficient training data, the parser normally delivers close to full parsing coverage even without the fragmented partial parsing mode.

5.3 Evaluation & Results

For the evaluation of our approximating PCFGs, we compare the top-1 parses produced by the PCFG with the manually disambiguated gold trees in *"ws13"*. We assume the inputs have been pre-tokenized but not tagged. All comparisons are done on the original derivations. Several accuracy measures are used, including the ParsEval labeled bracketing precision, recall, F_1 and exact match ratio. Since the ParsEval scores ignore the preterminal nodes, we also report the (lexical type) tagging accuracy. Several different training sets are used.

ws contains 7636 *"gold"* trees from the sections *"ws01-ws11"* of the WeScience. The MEM parse selection model is trained with this dataset. The dataset is too small to acquire high coverage PCFGs with heavy annotations. Therefore, only PCFG(0) and PCFG(FP1) results are reported here.

ww000 contains 85,553 automatically parsed and disambiguated trees from the WikiWoods (all fragments with 000 as suffix). This is less than 0.2% of the entire WikiWoods, but close to the limit for the latent-variable PCFG training with the Berkeley Parser.

ww00 contains about 482K sentences (all fragments with 00 as suffix), roughly 1% of the entire WikiWoods. We were able to successfully train PCFGs with relatively rich annotations.

ww contains the complete WikiWoods with ~48M parsed tress. With feature-path annotations, the training of the models takes too long. Also, excessive annotation makes it difficult to parse with the resulting huge grammar. We stop at two levels of grandparent annotation, a PCFG with almost 4M rules and over 128K non-terminal symbols.

Table 2 summarizes the results of the accuracy evaluation. All results are reported on the 785 trees from the section *"ws13"* of the WeScience. MEM is the accuracy of the HPSG parser disambiguation model given the candidate parse forest. PCFG(0) is the unannotated PCFG read off the bare (normalized) derivation trees. PCFG(GPm,FPn) is the annotated PCFG model with m-levels of grandparents and n feature-paths. And PCFG-LA(SM3) is the latent-variable PCFG after three split-merge iterations.

With the small WS training set, the baseline PCFG without annotation achieved F_1 of merely 60.96. Even one level of grandparent annotation, the parsing coverage drops by over 10%. With 1 feature-path annotation, F_1 improved significantly to 66.45.

On the larger WW-000, the performance of the baseline PCFG decreases by two 2% of F_1, most likely due to the noise introduced by the automatic disambiguation. However, the larger training set enables 1-level grandparent annotation, which brings F_1 up to 71.42. The latent-variable PCFG also performs well, delivering the best F_1 at 71.87 after three split-merge iterations. But the learning curve of the Berkeley parser has already flatten out at this point, and we were unsuccessful in further scaling up the training set.

With our annotated PCFGs, significant improvements are achieved on the even larger WW-00. The baseline PCFG seems to have recovered from the previous drop, and outperforms the one trained with the *"gold"* trees. With the mixture of 1-level of grandparent and some feature-path annotations, F_1 reached over 80. The best performance on WW-00 is achieved with PCFG(GP1,FP5). 2-levels of grandparents alone outperforms 1-level of grandparent, but the grammar quickly reaches its size limit on this training set and starts to loose coverage when more feature-path annotations are added.

Finally, with the complete WikiWoods, both PCFG(GP1) and PCFG(GP2) improved further, with PCFG(GP2) reaching the highest F_1 at 84.13. It is interesting to note that this is even higher than the F_1 of the MEM disambiguation model. This is partially due to the self-training effect on the huge corpus. Another explanation is that the objective function of the discriminative MEM was optimized on the complete parse match instead of individual constituents, which will explain its high exact match ratio at 43.57%.

6 Discussion

It is important to note that the grammar approximation task we take on in this paper is different from the traditional treebank-based parsing. Although the accuracy evaluation for both tasks are done on a fixed set of *"gold"* trees, in the grammar approximation task we have access to the theoretically infinite pool of training data automatically generated by the original grammar. Some complex grammar extraction algorithms which work fine on a small training corpus fail to scale up to handle millions of trees. On the other hand, our MLE-based PCFG extraction shows its advantage in extensibility.

The approach of training a PCFG with automatically annotated treebank is in a sense similar to the self-training approach in semi-supervised parsing (McClosky et al., 2006). However, instead of parsing the unlabeled data with the PCFG directly, we rely on the HPSG grammar and its disambiguation model. The highly constrained ERG analyses on unseen data allow us to obtain high quality trees. And the penalty on introducing noisy data is quickly compensated by the huge amount of data.

The approximating PCFG is much less constrained than the ERG. From the linguistic point of view, it is difficult to interpret the huge set of PCFG rules. And unlike the ERG, the PCFG is unsuited in making grammaticality judgment. However, for the parsing task, the approximating PCFG has its advantage in being flexible and robust, needless to mention its cubic parsing time complexity. One can choose various combinations of annotations for a balanced efficiency, accuracy and coverage. Although the experiments reported in Section 5 are only testing on sentences which the ERG can parse, we have also applied the PCFGs on the remaining ~20% texts and got close to full parsing coverage (less than 1% failure). Although the derivation tree constructed by the PCFG does not guaratee a unifiable HPSG analysis with typed feature structures, it provides an approximate prediction on how the HPSG analysis should look like. It is conceivable that with robust unification under the open-world assumption of the type hierarchy (Fouvry, 2003), one can get a partially well-formed semantic structure with the guidance of the approximating PCFG. Also, it would be interesting to evaluate its impact on the overall parser performance based on the semantic structures instead of the theory-specific derivations.

		#Rule	#NT	#T	P	R	F_1	Ex	TA
WS	MEM	-	-	-	82.70	82.91	**82.80**	43.57	96.87
	PCFG(0)	10,251	208	1,152	63.53	58.59	60.96	19.49	86.19
	PCFG(FP1)	12,178	669	1,152	70.02	63.22	66.45	20.51	86.20
WW-000	PCFG(0)	25,859	236	1,799	60.18	57.34	58.73	14.14	85.33
	PCFG(GP1)	64,043	3,983	1,799	72.61	70.28	71.42	21.02	86.92
	PCFG-LA(SM3)	*	*	*	73.12	70.66	**71.87**	23.18	89.81
WW-00	PCFG(0)	61,426	247	2,546	63.61	61.14	62.35	16.56	88.59
	PCFG(GP1)	187,852	5,828	2,546	77.87	77.41	77.64	24.84	91.83
	PCFG(GP1,FP4)	271,956	16,731	2,546	80.60	79.84	80.22	29.04	93.20
	PCFG(GP1,FP5)	319,511	21,414	2,546	80.94	80.32	**80.63**	28.54	93.33
	PCFG(GP1,FP6)	320,630	21,694	2,546	80.92	80.31	80.61	28.41	93.33
	PCFG(GP2)	489,890	45,658	2,546	79.68	79.56	79.62	28.92	92.01
	PCFG(GP2,FP2)	559,006	66,218	2,546	79.78	79.46	79.62	32.23	92.71
WW	PCFG(GP1)	1,007,563	8,852	4,472	80.34	79.60	79.97	28.79	93.45
	PCFG(GP2)	3,952,821	128,822	4,472	84.27	83.98	**84.13**	37.71	94.39

Table 2: Parsing Accuracy on *'ws13'* with various models and training sets. Reported are grammar size (#Rule, #NT, #T); ParsEval precision (P), recall (R), F_1, and exact match ratio (Ex) on the original derivation tree; and tagging accuracy (TA) on the lexical types.

Looking at the specific annotation strategies, we compared the internal annotations with the external ones. Experiment result shows that when the grandparent annotation is added, the grammar size grows quickly. On a huge training set, this is rewarded with significant accuracy gain. On the smaller training set though, over-annotating with grandparents results in a decrease in accuracy due to data sparseness. Instead, annotating with feature-path information increases the grammar size moderately, allowing one to approach the optimal granularity of the PCFG.

In comparison to the linguistic annotations used by Klein and Manning (2003) for PTB parsing, our annotations are less language or treebank specific. This is due to the fact that the ERG rules are relatively fine-grained in treating various linguistic constructions. And the most relevant annotations can be gathered from either the grandparents or the internal feature structure. Such general design allows us to experiment with other deep HPSG grammars in the near future.

For the clarity of the experiment, we have chosen not to do constructional pruning or smoothing, and focused our evaluation mostly on parsing accuracy. This leaves much room for future investigation. For instance, we observe that a large portion of the grammar rules have very low frequency counts and almost no impact on the parsing accuracy. On the other hand, even with the simple PCFG(GP1), after training with 45M sentences, the grammar continues to pick up new rules at a rate of one rule per 160 sentences. Most of these new rules are the combination of low frequency supertags.

Last but not the least, given the promising parsing accuracy of the approximating PCFG, we believe it is worth reconsidering the role of the hand-written grammars in the deep linguistic processing. In the past, manual grammar engineering has been taking on the dual role of offering concise and accurate linguistic description on the one hand, while attending the efficiency and robustness in parsing on the other. The conflicting goal has hindered the development of large-scale linguistic grammars. The technique as the one presented in this paper shows one way of liberating grammarians from the concerns over the processing difficulties.

7 Conclusion

We presented a corpus-driven approach to approximate a large-scale hand-written HPSG with a PCFG for robust and accurate parsing. Different annotations are used to enrich the derivation trees. And with the 48M sentence from the English Wikipedia automatically parsed and disambiguated by the ERG, a MLE-based PCFG achieved F_1 of 84.13, higher than the performance of the discriminative MEM parse selection model (which has access to the candidate HPSG parse forest). The obvious robustness and potential efficiency advantages of the approximating PCFG suggest its promising applications in deep linguistic processing.

Acknowledgments

We thank Stepehn Oepen, Bernd Kiefer and Dan Flickinger for enlightening discussions related to the work presented in this paper. We also thank the anonymous reviewers for their comments. The first author thanks the DFG-funded *Excellence Cluster of MMCI* and the *Deependance* project funded by the BMBF for their support of the work. The second author thanks project CogX (FP7 ICT 215181), NIFTi (FP7 ICT 247870) and Monnet (FP7 ICT 248458) for their support.

References

Steven Abney. 1997. Stochastic attribute-value grammars. *Computational Linguistics*, 23:597–618.

Aoife Cahill, Michael Burke, Ruth O'Donovan, Josef Van Genabith, and Andy Way. 2004. Long-distance dependency resolution in automatically acquired wide-coverage PCFG-based LFG approximations. In *Proceedings of the 42nd Meeting of the Association for Computational Linguistics (ACL'04), Main Volume*, pages 319–326, Barcelona, Spain.

Ulrich Callmeier. 2000. PET – a platform for experimentation with efficient HPSG processing techniques. *Journal of Natural Language Engineering*, 6(1):99–108.

Bob Carpenter. 1992. *The Logic of Typed Feature Structures*. Cambridge University Press, Cambridge, UK.

Ann Copestake. 2002. *Implementing Typed Feature Structure Grammars*. CSLI, Stanford, USA.

Dan Flickinger, Stephan Oepen, and Gisle Ytrestl. 2010. WikiWoods: Syntacto-semantic annotation for English Wikipedia. In *Proceedings of the Seventh conference on International Language Resources and Evaluation (LREC'10)*, Valletta, Malta.

Dan Flickinger. 2002. On building a more efficient grammar by exploiting types. In Stephan Oepen, Dan Flickinger, Jun'ichi Tsujii, and Hans Uszkoreit, editors, *Collaborative Language Engineering*, pages 1–17. CSLI Publications.

Frederik Fouvry. 2003. *Robust processing for constraint-based grammar formalisms*. Ph.D. thesis, Gradudate School, University of Essex, Colchester, UK.

Bernd Kiefer and Hans-Ulrich Krieger. 2004. A context-free superset approximation of unification-based grammars. In *New Developments in Parsing Technology*. Kluwer. http://www.wkap.nl/prod/b/1-4020-2293-X.

Bernd Kiefer, Hans-Ulrich Krieger, John Carroll, and Rob Malouf. 1999. A Bag of Useful Techniques for Efficient and Robust Parsing. In *Proceedings of the 37th Annual Meeting of the Association for Computational Linguistics*, pages 473–480, Maryland, USA.

Bernd Kiefer, Hans-Ulrich Krieger, and Detlef Prescher. 2002. A novel disambiguation method for unification-based grammars using probabilistic context-free approximations. In *Proceedings of the 19th International Conference on Computational Linguistics (COLING'02)*, Taipei, Taiwan.

Dan Klein and Christopher D. Manning. 2003. Accurate unlexicalized parsing. In *Proceedings of the 41st Annual Meeting of the Association for Computational Linguistics*, pages 423–430, Sapporo, Japan.

Hans-Ulrich Krieger. 2007. From UBGs to CFGs: A practical corpus-driven approach. *Natural Language Engineering*, 13(4):317–351. Published online in April 2006.

Robert Malouf and Gertjan van Noord. 2004. Wide coverage parsing with stochastic attribute value grammars. In *Proceedings of the IJCNLP-04 Workshop: Beyond Shallow Analyses - Formalisms and Statistical Modeling for Deep Analyses*, Hainan Island, China.

Takuya Matsuzaki, Yusuke Miyao, and Jun'ichi Tsujii. 2007. Efficient HPSG parsing with supertagging and CFG-filtering. In *Proceedings of the 20th International Joint Conference on Artificial Intelligence (IJCAI 2007)*, pages 1671–1676, Hyderabad, India.

David McClosky, Eugene Charniak, and Mark Johnson. 2006. Effective self-training for parsing. In *Proceedings of HLT-NAACL-2006*, pages 152–159, New York, USA.

Yusuke Miyao and Jun'ichi Tsujii. 2002. Maximum entropy estimation for feature forests. In *Proceedings of the Human Language Technology Conference*, San Diego, USA.

Yusuke Miyao, Takashi Ninomiya, and Jun'ichi Tsujii. 2004. Corpus-oriented grammar development for acquiring a Head-Driven Phrase Structure Grammar from the Penn Treebank. In *Proceedings of the 1st International Joint Conference on Natural Language Processing (IJCNLP 2004)*, pages 684–693, Hainan Island, China.

Stephan Oepen and John Carroll. 2000. Ambiguity packing in constraint-based parsing — practical results. In *Proceedings of the 1st Annual Meeting of the North American Chapter of Association for Computational Linguistics (NAACL 2000)*, pages 162–169, Seattle, USA.

Stephan Oepen, Kristina Toutanova, Stuart Shieber, Christopher Manning, Dan Flickinger, and Thorsten Brants. 2002. The LinGO Redwoods treebank: motivation and preliminary applications. In *Proceedings of COLING 2002: The 17th International Conference on Computational Linguistics: Project Notes*, Taipei, Taiwan.

Slav Petrov, Leon Barrett, Romain Thibaux, and Dan Klein. 2006. Learning accurate, compact, and interpretable tree annotation. In *Proceedings of the 21st International Conference on Computational Linguistics and 44th Annual Meeting of the Association for Computational Linguistics*, pages 433–440, Sydney, Australia.

Carl J. Pollard and Ivan A. Sag. 1994. *Head-Driven Phrase Structure Grammar*. University of Chicago Press, Chicago, USA.

Helmut Schmid. 2004. Efficient parsing of highly ambiguous context-free grammars with bit vectors. In *Proceedings of Coling 2004*, pages 162–168, Geneva, Switzerland.

Hideto Tomabechi. 1991. Quasi-destructive graph unification. In *Proceedings of the 29th Annual Meeting of the Association for Computational Linguistics (ACL 1991)*, pages 315–322, Berkeley, USA.

Kristina Toutanova, Christoper D. Manning, Dan Flickinger, and Stephan Oepen. 2005. Stochastic HPSG parse selection using the Redwoods corpus. *Journal of Research on Language and Computation*, 3(1):83–105.

Gertjan van Noord. 2006. At Last Parsing Is Now Operational. In *Actes de la 13e Conference sur le Traitement Automatique des Langues Naturelles (TALN 2006)*, pages 20–42, Leuven, Belgium.

Gisle Ytrestoel, Dan Flickinger, and Stephan Oepen. 2009. Extracting and annotating Wikipedia sub-domains: Towards a new escience community resource. In *Proceedings of the Seventh International Workshop on Treebanks and Linguistic Theory*, pages 185–197, Groningen, the Netherlands.

Kun Yu, Miyao Yusuke, Xiangli Wang, Takuya Matsuzaki, and Junichi Tsujii. 2010. Semi-automatically developing chinese hpsg grammar from the penn chinese treebank for deep parsing. In *Proceedings of the 23rd International Conference on Computational Linguistics (Coling 2010)*, pages 1417–1425, Beijing, China.

Yi Zhang, Stephan Oepen, and John Carroll. 2007. Efficiency in unification-based N-best parsing. In *Proceedings of the 10th International Conference on Parsing Technologies (IWPT 2007)*, pages 48–59, Prague, Czech.

Features for Phrase-Structure Reranking from Dependency Parses

Richárd Farkas, Bernd Bohnet, Helmut Schmid
Institute for Natural Language Processing
University of Stuttgart
{farkas,berndbh,schmid}@ims.uni-stuttgart.de

Abstract

Radically different approaches have been proved to be effective for phrase-structure and dependency parsers in the last decade. Here, we aim to exploit the divergence in these approaches and show the utility of features extracted from the automatic dependency parses of sentences for a discriminative phrase-structure parser. Our experiments show a significant improvement over the state-of-the-art German discriminative constituent parser.

1 Introduction

Both phrase-structure and dependency parsers have developed a lot in the last decade (Nivre et al., 2004; McDonald et al., 2005; Charniak and Johnson, 2005; Huang, 2008). Different approaches have been proved to be effective for these two parsing tasks which has implicated a divergence between techniques used (and a growing gap between researcher communities). In this work, we exploit this divergence and show the added value of features extracted from automatic dependency parses of sentences for a discriminative phrase-structure parser. We report results on German phrase-structure parsing, however, we note that the reverse direction of our approach – i.e. defining features from automatic phrase-structure parses for discriminative dependency parsers – is also manifest which we will address as future work.

Some generative parsing approaches exploited the difference between phrase-structure and dependency parsers. For instance, Klein and Manning (2003) introduced an approach where the objective function is the product of the probabilities of a generative phrase-structure and a dependency parsers. Model 1 of Collins (2003) is based on the dependencies between pairs of head words. On the other hand, the related work on this topic for discriminative parsing is sparse, we are only aware of the following works. Carreras et al. (2008) and Koo et al. (2010) introduced frameworks for joint learning of phrase-structure and dependency parsers and showed improvements on both tasks for English. These frameworks require special formulation of – one or both – parsing approaches while our simple approach allows the usage of arbitrary dependency parsers and any feature-based phrase-structure parser. Wang and Zong (2010) used automatic dependency parses for pruning the chart of a phrase-structure parser and reported a significant improvement. One of our feature templates can be regarded as the generalization of this approach.

2 Feature-Rich Parse Reranking

The most successful supervised phrase-structure parsers are feature-rich discriminative parsers which heavily depend on an underlying PCFG (Charniak and Johnson, 2005; Huang, 2008). These approaches consists of two stages. At the first stage they apply a PCFG to extract possible parses. The full set of possible parses cannot be iterated through in practice, and is usually pruned as a consequence. The *n-best list parser*s keep just the 50-100 best parses according to the PCFG. Other methods remove nodes and hyperedges whose posterior probability is under a predefined threshold from the forest (chart).

The task of the second stage is to select the best parse from the set of possible parses (i.e. rerank this set). These methods employ a large feature set (usually a few millions features) (Collins, 2000; Charniak and Johnson, 2005). The n-best list approaches can straightforwardly employ local and non-local features as well because they decide at the sentence-level (Charniak and Johnson, 2005). Involving non-local features is more complicated in the forest-based approaches. The conditional random field methods usually use only local features (Miyao and Tsujii, 2002; Finkel et al., 2008). Huang (2008) introduced a beam-search and average perceptron-based procedure for incorporating them, however his empirical results show only minor improvement from incorporating non-local features. In this study, we experiment with n-best list reranking and a packed-forest based model as well along with local features exclusively. Our goal is to investigate the extension of the standard feature set of these models by features extracted from the automatic dependency parse of the sentence in question.

3 Dependency Parse-Based Features for Phrase-Structure Parsing

Given the automatic (1-best) dependency parse of the sentence in question, we defined three feature templates for representing hyperedges (i.e. a CFG rule applied over a certain span of words). We illustrate them on two hyperedges E_1 = *(NP die Inseln (PP von Rußland))* and E_2 = *(VP fordern (NP die Inseln) (PP von Rußland))*. Let's assume that the corresponding dependency subtree consists of the following arcs: ROOT→fordern, Inseln$\xrightarrow{DET}$die, fordern$\xrightarrow{OBJA}$Inseln, von$\xrightarrow{PN}$Rußland, fordern$\xrightarrow{PP}$von.

outArc features are counting the dependency arcs which "go out" from the constituent in question. More precisely we count the words within the span whose parent in the dependency tree lays outside the span of words in question. We use the absolute count and the ratio of outArcs among the words of the span. The more arcs go out, the further away is the dependency subtree over the words of the constituent from a dominating subtree. Hence, these features try to capture the "phraseness" of the span of words in question based on the dependency tree. For E_1 we have `outArc=2` and `outArcRatio=2/4` as the parent of *Inseln* and *von* lay outside the constituent. For E_2 we have `outArc=1` and `outArcRatio=1/5`.

POSRel features intend to tune daughter attachments to the dependency parse based on the POS tags of the lexical heads. For this we gather the daughter constituents whose lexical head is linked in the (undirected) dependency tree to the head of the parent constituent. We define features from them using the pair of the two head's POS tag and a triplet using the POS tags and the corresponding dependency label. For E_1 we cannot extract features as the lexical head of the parent (*Inseln*) and the lexical head of the daughter (*von*) are not linked in the dependency tree. For E_2 we have the following binary valued features: `VVFIN-NN`, `VVFIN-NN-OBJA`, `VVFIN-APPR`, `VVFIN-APPR-PP` as both daughter attachments have the corresponding arcs in the dependency tree.

ConstRel features are similar to `POSRel` but use the constituent labels rather than the POS tags of the heads. Thus, once again we do not have any positive feature for E_1, but for E_2 we extract: `VP-NP`, `VP-NP-OBJA`, `VP-PP`, `VP-PP-PP`.

We also investigated the role of case and grammatical functions and extended the `POSRel` and `ConstRel` feature sets by adding this information to the labels. For instance besides `VVFIN-NN-OBJA` and `VP-NP-OBJA` from our example E_2 we also used `VVFIN-NN-Acc-OBJA` and `VP-NP-OA-OBJA`.

Note that the value of `outArc` is 1 iff the word span in question has a dominating dependency subtree in the automatic parse. Wang and Zong (2010) prune hyperedges with `outArc`$\neq$ 1 thus this feature can be regarded as a generalization of their approach.

4 Two-Stage Parsing of German

As a **first-stage** parser, we used BitPar (Schmid, 2004), a fast unlexicalized PCFG parser based on a first pass where non-probabilistic bottom-up parsing and top-down pruning is efficiently carried out by storing the chart in bit vectors. Bitpar constructs the probabilistic forest only after top-down pruning, i.e. after computing the posterior probability of each hyperedge given the input sentence. The forest is pruned by deleting hyperedges whose posterior probability is below some threshold.

We used a treebank grammar enriched with case information, lexicalization of selected prepositions, conjunctions, and punctuation symbols, coarse parent category features for adverbs, adverbial phrases, prepositions, PPs and special markers for non-verbal phrases containing a *wh* expression, phrases without a head and clauses without a subject. We applied a second-order markovization of rules below a frequency threshold_1, but infrequent second-order Markov symbols are replaced by first-order Markov symbols if the frequency is below threshold_2. We used simple regular expressions for unknown word clustering and estimated POS probabilities for unknown words of each cluster based on the word suffix. The relative frequency estimates of the POS probabilities of known words were interpolated with the respective unknown word POS probabilities using

Witten-Bell smoothing. To the best of our knowledge Bitpar with this grammar is the state-of-the-art German generative parser.

At the **second stage**, we used n-best list and forest-based rerankers as well. The feature values of a full possible parse is the sum of the local feature vectors (for the hyperedges) (Charniak and Johnson, 2005). Learning is guided by the so-called oracle parse which is the full parse in the set of possible parses most similar to the gold standard tree. Our oracle extraction method is an extension of Huang (2008)'s dynamic programing procedure which takes into consideration POS tag and grammatical function matches as well and selects hyperedges with higher posterior probability for tie-breaking. For a detailed description of the training and supporting algorithms please refer to Charniak and Johnson (2005) and Huang (2008).

5 Experiments

We evaluate our approach on the Tiger corpora of the Parsing German Shared Task (PaGe) (Kübler, 2008). Its training, development, and test datasets consist of 20894, 2611 and 2611 sentences respectively. We decided to use these corpora to be able to compare our results with other results.

We used the **dependency parser** of Bohnet (2010) to generate the parses for the feature extraction. We selected the parser since it had top scores for German in the CoNLL Shared Task 2009. The parser is a second order dependency parser that models the interaction between siblings as well as grandchildren. The parser was after the Shared Task enhanced by a Hash Kernel, which leads to significantly higher accuracy. We generated the dependency structures by 10-fold cross-validation training of the training corpus. The model for the annotation of the test set and development set was trained on the entire training corpus.

We evaluated the dependency parses themselves in line with PaGe. Table 1 shows the labeled (LAS) and unlabeled attachment scores (UAS) of the dependency parser and compares it with the Malt parser (Nivre et al., 2004; Hall and Nivre, 2008), which was the only and therefore best dependency parser that participated in the PaGe's dependency parsing track. Bohnet's parser reaches higher labeled and unlabeled scores. The last row shows the parsing accuracy with predicted Part-of-Speech. We used the parses with predicted pos tags for our reranking experiments.

Table 1: Dependency parser accuracy. [1]Gold Part-of-Speech tags;[2]Predicted Part-of-Speech tags.

	Test		Dev.	
	UAS	LAS	UAS	LAS
Malt[1]	92.63	90.80	-	-
Bohnet[1]	94.49	92.64	94.80	92.64
Bohnet[2]	93.69	91.71	93.68	91.70

Regarding the **phrase-structure parser**, our grammar extractor used markovization $\text{threshold}_1 = 20$ and $\text{threshold}_2 = 10$ resulting in a grammar with over fifty thousand of rules. Our prior experiments found the forest pruning threshold to be optimal at the order of 10^{-2} which resulted in packed forests with average node number of 108. The oracle scores were 87.1 and 91.4 for the 100-best lists and packed forests, respectively.

At the second stage, we filtered out rare features (which occurred in less than 5 sentences). The new dependency parse-based feature set consists of 9240 and 5359 features before and after filtering. We employed the ranking MaxEnt implementation of the MALLET package (McCallum, 2002) and the average perceptron training of the Joshua package (Li et al., 2009). The update mechanism of the latter one was extended by using the F-score of the candidate full parse against the oracle parse as a loss function (see MIRA (Crammer and Singer, 2003) for the motivation). We used the state-of-the-art feature set of the German phrase-structure parse reranker of Versley and Rehbein (2009) as a baseline feature set. This feature set is rich and consists of features constructed from the lexicalized parse tree and its typed dependencies along with features based on external statistical information (like the clustering of unknown words according to their context of occurrences and PP attachment statistics gathered from the automatic POS tagged DE-WaC corpus, a 1.7G words sample of the German-language WWW). This feature set consists of 1.7 and 0.2 million of features before and after filtering and enables the direct comparison of our results with state-of-the-art discriminative results on German. We use the `evalb` implementation of PARSEVAL as evaluation metric hereafter on basic constituent labels (noGF) and on the conflation of these labels and grammatical functions (GF). We have to mention that our F-values are not comparable to the official results of PaGe – which was our original goal – because the evaluation metric there was a special im-

Table 2: Results achieved by dependency feature-based reranking.

	noGF	GF
Baseline	78.48	66.34
outArc	79.19	67.21
POSRel	79.99	68.13
ConstRel	79.67	67.72
All	80.20	68.32
All+Case	80.35	68.48

plementation for calculating F-value (which differs from evalb for example in handling punctuation marks) and it used gold-standard POS tags in the input (which we thought to be unrealistic). On the other hand, our results are comparable with results of Rafferty and Manning (2008) and Versley and Rehbein (2009).

Table 2 shows the **results** achieved by the MaxEnt 100-best list reranker using one out of the three feature templates alone and their union (`All`) on the development set. `All+Case` refers to the enriched feature set incorporating case information for POS tag and grammatical functions for labels. `Baseline` here refers to the top parse of Bitpar (the first stage parser). We note that the inside probability estimation of Bitpar for an edge is always in our feature set.

Each of the three feature templates achieved significant improvements over a strong baseline – note that our first-stage parser is competitive with Versley and Rehbein (2009)'s two-stage parser – . On the other hand, as the `All` results are just slightly better than `POSRel` (the best individual feature template), the three templates seem to capture similar patterns. The introduction of case information also improved the results, thus we incorporate them into our final feature set. Table 3 illustrates the added value of the dependency features (`Dep=All+Case`) over the reranking feature set of Versley and Rehbein (2009) (`RR`). We also cite here previously published results on the same dataset by Rafferty and Manning (2008) (a generative parser) and Versley and Rehbein (2009) (a conditional random field-based discriminative parser). The rows `RR`, `Dep` and `RR+Dep` show the results achieved by the MaxEnt 100-best list parser while the AvgPer row show the results of the forest-based average perceptron approach using the `RR+Dep` feature set. We report numbers only at this feature configuration due to the lack of space and because the difference between this and n-best list approaches is similarly moderate at other configurations as well.

Table 3: Results achieved by the enriched feature set.

	Develop.		Test	
	noGF	GF	noGF	GF
Rafferty'08	77.40	–	–	–
Versley'09	78.43	67.90	–	–
Baseline	78.48	66.29	79.21	66.63
RR	80.51	68.55	80.95	68.67
Dep	80.35	68.48	80.56	68.39
RR+Dep	81.34	69.73	81.49	69.44
AvgPer	81.41	69.67	81.68	69.42

The results of Table 3 show that our simple features constructed from the automatic dependency parse of the sentence are as useful as the state-of-the-art rich feature set for German. Moreover these two features sets have a certain level of diversity as their union could achieve significantly better results than any of them alone. This is probably due to fact that most of the `RR` features are lexicalized while `Dep` features are unlexicalized. Regarding the two discriminative approaches, our findings are similar to Huang (2008), i.e. the packed forest-based and n-best list procedures achieved similar results by using only local features. We found that the improvements by applying the dependency features are similar at the two evaluation metrics (with and without grammatical functions).

6 Conclusions and Future Work

We presented experimental results on exploiting automatic dependency parses in a discriminative phrase-structure parser. Our simple feature templates achieved around 1.8 points of improvement in terms of F-score over Bitpar, the state-of-the-art generative parser for German and 0.8 when we extended a rich feature set. Although these results are promising, we consider them as the first step on a long road. In the future, we will implement more sophisticated features derived from dependency parses (like dependency paths rather than single edges and non-local ones) and investigate the reverse direction, i.e. whether automatic constituent parses can help dependency parsers.

Acknowledgement

We would like to thank Yannick Versley for his support on reimplementing their feature set and clarifying evaluation issues of German phrase-structure parsing. This work was funded by Deutsche Forschungsgemeinschaft grant SFB 732.

References

Bernd Bohnet. 2010. Top accuracy and fast dependency parsing is not a contradiction. In *Proceedings of the 23rd International Conference on Computational Linguistics (Coling 2010)*, pages 89–97.

Xavier Carreras, Michael Collins, and Terry Koo. 2008. Tag, dynamic programming, and the perceptron for efficient, feature-rich parsing. In *CoNLL 2008: Proceedings of the Twelfth Conference on Computational Natural Language Learning*, pages 9–16.

Eugene Charniak and Mark Johnson. 2005. Coarse-to-fine n-best parsing and maxent discriminative reranking. In *Proceedings of the 43rd Annual Meeting on Association for Computational Linguistics*, ACL '05, pages 173–180.

Michael Collins. 2000. Discriminative reranking for natural language parsing. In *Proceedings of the Seventeenth International Conference on Machine Learning*, ICML '00, pages 175–182.

Michael Collins. 2003. Head-driven statistical models for natural language parsing. *Comput. Linguist.*, 29:589–637, December.

Koby Crammer and Yoram Singer. 2003. Ultraconservative online algorithms for multiclass problems. *J. Mach. Learn. Res.*, 3:951–991.

Jenny Rose Finkel, Alex Kleeman, and Christopher D. Manning. 2008. Efficient, feature-based, conditional random field parsing. In *Proceedings of ACL-08: HLT*, pages 959–967.

Johan Hall and Joakim Nivre. 2008. A dependency-driven parser for german dependency and constituency representations. In *In Proceedings of the ACL Workshop on Parsing German*, pages 47–54.

Liang Huang. 2008. Forest reranking: Discriminative parsing with non-local features. In *Proceedings of ACL-08: HLT*, pages 586–594.

Dan Klein and Christopher D. Manning. 2003. Fast exact inference with a factored model for natural language parsing. In *Proceedings of Advances in Neural Information Processing Systems*, volume 15.

Terry Koo, Alexander M. Rush, Michael Collins, Tommi Jaakkola, and David Sontag. 2010. Dual decomposition for parsing with non-projective head automata. In *Proceedings of the 2010 Conference on Empirical Methods in Natural Language Processing*, pages 1288–1298.

Sandra Kübler. 2008. The PaGe 2008 shared task on parsing german. In *Proceedings of the Workshop on Parsing German*, pages 55–63.

Zhifei Li, Chris Callison-Burch, Chris Dyer, Juri Ganitkevitch, Sanjeev Khudanpur, Lane Schwartz, Wren N. G. Thornton, Jonathan Weese, and Omar F. Zaidan. 2009. Joshua: an open source toolkit for parsing-based machine translation. In *Proceedings of the Fourth Workshop on Statistical Machine Translation*, StatMT '09, pages 135–139.

Andrew Kachites McCallum. 2002. Mallet: A machine learning for language toolkit. http://mallet.cs.umass.edu.

Ryan McDonald, Fernando Pereira, Kiril Ribarov, and Jan Hajic. 2005. Non-projective dependency parsing using spanning tree algorithms. In *Proceedings of Human Language Technology Conference and Conference on Empirical Methods in Natural Language Processing*, pages 523–530.

Yusuke Miyao and Jun'ichi Tsujii. 2002. Maximum entropy estimation for feature forests. In *Proceedings of the second international conference on Human Language Technology Research*, HLT '02, pages 292–297.

Joakim Nivre, Johan Hall, and Jens Nilsson. 2004. Memory-based dependency parsing. In Hwee Tou Ng and Ellen Riloff, editors, *HLT-NAACL 2004 Workshop: Eighth Conference on Computational Natural Language Learning (CoNLL-2004)*, pages 49–56.

Anna Rafferty and Christopher D. Manning. 2008. Parsing three German treebanks: Lexicalized and unlexicalized baselines. In *Proceedings of the Workshop on Parsing German*, pages 40–46.

Helmut Schmid. 2004. Efficient parsing of highly ambiguous context-free grammars with bit vectors. In *Proceedings of Coling 2004*, pages 162–168.

Yannick Versley and Ines Rehbein. 2009. Scalable discriminative parsing for german. In *Proceedings of the 11th International Conference on Parsing Technologies (IWPT'09)*, pages 134–137.

Zhiguo Wang and Chengqing Zong. 2010. Phrase structure parsing with dependency structure. In *Coling 2010: Posters*, pages 1292–1300.

Comparing the Use of Edited and Unedited Text in Parser Self-Training

Jennifer Foster, Özlem Çetinoğlu, Joachim Wagner and Josef van Genabith
National Centre for Language Technology/Centre for Next Generation Localisation
School of Computing
Dublin City University
Ireland
{jfoster,ocetinoglu,jwagner,josef}@computing.dcu.ie

Abstract

We compare the use of edited text in the form of newswire and unedited text in the form of discussion forum posts as sources for training material in a self-training experiment involving the Brown reranking parser and a test set of sentences from an online sports discussion forum. We find that grammars induced from the two automatically parsed corpora achieve similar Parseval f-scores, with the grammars induced from the discussion forum material being slightly superior. An error analysis reveals that the two types of grammars do behave differently.

1 Introduction

There have been several successful attempts in recent years to employ automatically parsed data in semi- and unsupervised approaches to parser domain adaptation (McClosky et al., 2006b; Reichart and Rappaport, 2007; Huang and Harper, 2009; Petrov et al., 2010). We turn our attention to adapting a Wall-Street-Journal-trained parser to user-generated content from an online sports discussion forum. The sentences on the discussion forum are produced by a group of speakers who are communicating with each other about a shared interest and are discussing the same events, but, who, given the open, unedited nature of the medium itself, do not follow an in-house writing style. Our particular aim in this paper is to compare the use of discussion forum comments as a source of unlabelled training material to the use of edited, professionally written sentences on the same theme. We hypothesise that the well-formed sentences will be more suitable as training material since they are likely to be closer syntactically to the source domain Wall Street Journal (WSJ) sentences than the noisier discussion forum sentences, while at the same time, remaining lexically close to the target domain, thus acting as a type of "self-training bridging corpus" (McClosky et al., 2006b).

2 Related Work

McClosky et al. (2006b) demonstrate that a WSJ-trained parser can be adapted to the fiction domains of the Brown corpus by performing a type of self-training that involves the use of the two-stage Brown reranking parser (Charniak and Johnson, 2005). Their training protocol is as follows: sentences from the LA Times are parsed using the first-stage parser (Charniak, 2000) and reranked in the second stage. These parse trees are added to the original WSJ training set and the *first-stage* parser is retrained. The sentences from the target domain, in this case, Brown corpus sentences are then parsed using the newly trained first-stage parser and reranked using the original reranker, resulting in a Parseval f-score increase from 85.2% to 87.8%.

McClosky and Charniak (2008) later show that the same procedure can be used to adapt a WSJ-trained parser to biomedical text. They also try an experiment which is very similar to the experiment described in this paper. Instead of using Medline abstracts as training material, they use sentences from a biology textbook under the assumption that the parses produced for these sentences will be more accurate (and thus more reliable as training data) than the sentences in the abstracts since they are closer to the source domain. They find, however, that the textbook sentences are less effective than the target domain material. We attempt to repeat the experiment with Web 2.0 data, believing that the two setups are sufficiently different for our experiment to be worthwhile — our bridging corpus is closely related in subject matter to our target corpus (both referring to the same events) but quite different in form (professionally edited versus an unedited mix of writing styles), whereas their bridging corpus is less closely related in content (biology textbooks versus Medline abstracts) and more closely related in form (both professionally edited and syntactically well-formed).

3 Data

Our dataset, summarised in Table 1, consists of a small treebank of hand-corrected phrase structure parse trees and two larger corpora of unannotated sentences.

Discussion Forum Treebank The treebank is an extension of that described in Foster (2010). It contains 481 sentences taken from two threads on the BBC Sport 606 discussion forum in November 2009.[1] The discussion forum posts were split into sentences by hand. The sentences were first parsed automatically using an implementation of the Collins Model 2 generative statistical parser (Bikel, 2004). They were then corrected by hand using as a reference the Penn Treebank (PTB) bracketing guidelines (Bies et al., 1995) and the PTB trees themselves (Marcus et al., 1994). For more detail on the annotation process, see Foster et al. (2011). The development set contains 258 sentences and the test set 223. The experiments in this paper are carried out on the development set (which we refer to as *FootballDev*).

Discussion Forum Corpus The same discussion forum used to create the treebank was scraped during the final quarter of 2010. The content was stripped of HTML markup and passed through an in-house sentence splitter and tokeniser, resulting in a corpus of 1,009,646 sentences. We call this the *FootballTrainDiscussion* corpus.

Edited Text Corpus In order to compare the use of edited versus unedited text, we also collected a corpus of professionally written news articles on the same theme as the discussion forum sentences, namely, the English Premier League. Content was scraped from the online BBC sports site[2] and articles dating from April 2010 to February 2011 retrieved. Similar preprocessing was carried out on these as was carried out on the *FootballTrainDiscussion* content, i.e. HTML-stripping, sentence splitting and tokenisation. The resulting corpus, which we will refer to as *FootballTrainEdited*, contains 209,014 sentences.

[1] `http://www.bbc.co.uk/dna/606/F15264075?thread=7065503&show=50` and `http://www.bbc.co.uk/dna/606/F15265997?thread=7066196&show=50`

[2] `http://www.bbc.co.uk/search/sport/football` and `http://www.bbc.co.uk/search/news/football`

4 Experiments

We retrain the Brown parser using the self-training protocol of McClosky et al. (2006b), that is, we retrain the first-stage parser using combinations of trees produced by the reranking parser for sentences from Sections 2 to 21 of the WSJ section of the Penn Treebank and from *FootballTrainEdited|Discussion*. We then parse the sentences in *FootballDev* using the retrained first-stage parser and the original reranker.

Because we have approximately five times the number of sentences in *FootballTrainDiscussion* than in *FootballTrainEdited*, we first train five different *FootballTrainDiscussion* grammars. The graph in Figure 1 shows the results on *FootballDev* when the training data contains disjoint subsections of *FootballTrainDiscussion*, each containing 200,000 sentences, along with varying amount of *WSJ2-21* trees. This gives us an idea of the amount of variation we might expect within one training set source — the f-score noise is roughly 1.5 points wide (= 3 boxes in the graph).

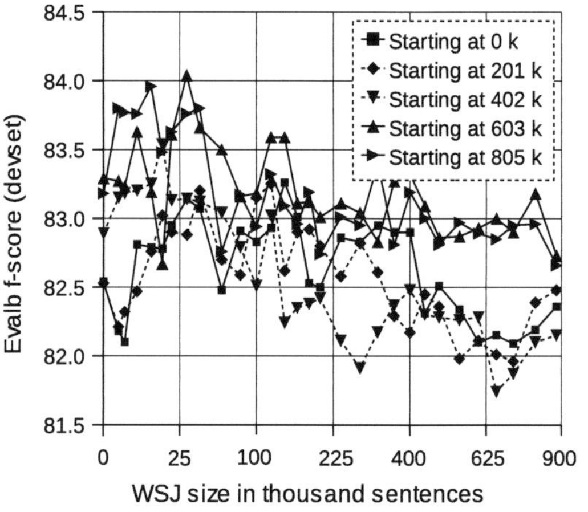

Figure 1: Comparing the performance of five grammars trained on disjoint 200k subsections of *FootballTrainDiscussion* in a Brown self-training experiment. Results are on *FootballDev*.

We now turn to the main experiment of the paper, i.e. the comparison of *FootballTrainDiscussion* and *FootballTrainEdited*. The graph in Figure 2 compares the performance of the *FootballTrainEdited* grammars with the performance average over the five types of *FootballTrainDiscussion*

Corpus Name	*#Sen*	*SL Mean*	*SL Med.*	σ
FootballDev	258	17.7	14	13.9
FootballTest	223	16.1	14	9.7
FootballTrainDiscussion	1,009,646	15.4	12	13.3
FootballTrainEdited	209,014	17.7	17	11.4

Table 1: Basic Statistics on the Web 2.0 datasets: number of sentences, average sentence length, median sentence length and standard deviation

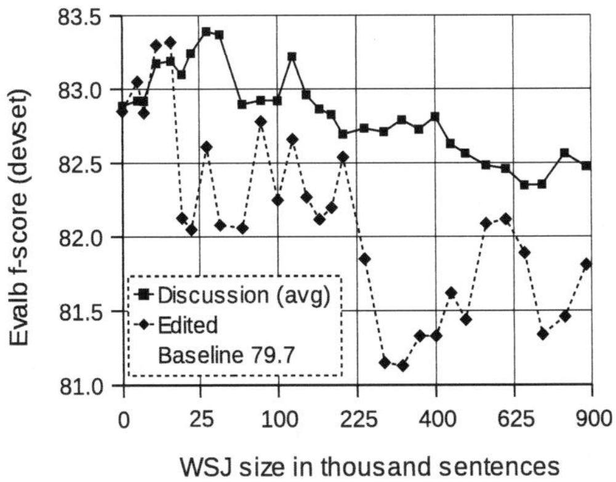

Figure 2: Comparing the use of discussion forum material (*FootballTrainDiscussion*) and newswire articles (*FootballTrainEdited*) in a Brown self-training experiment. Results are on *FootballDev*.

grammars on *FootballDev*. Note that a baseline grammar which is trained on one copy of *WSJ02-21* and no automatically parsed data achieves a Parseval f-score of 79.7. The results in Figure 2 appear to refute our original hypothesis, suggesting that there is very little difference between the two corpora, with the user-generated content of *FootballTrainDiscussion* emerging as slightly superior on our development set.[3] The only time that the *FootballTrainEdited* curve is above the *FootballTrainDiscussion* is when the size of the original WSJ training set is restricted. This is an intuitively appealing result — in this scenario, the sentences in the *FootballTrainEdited* corpus are making up for the lack of WSJ trained material, although it is not clear whether this is because the *FootballTrainEdited* sentences are slightly longer than the *FootballTrainDiscussion* sentences (see Table 1) or because they contain more WSJ-like constructions.

[3]Keeping the *WSJ02-21* dataset size constant, we test whether the difference between a *FootballTrainEdited* grammar and its five corresponding *FootballTrainDiscussion* grammars is statistically significant. Of the 150 pairs, 42 differences are statistically significant ($p < 0.05$).

5 Analysis

We next attempt to determine the strengths and weaknesses of the two types of training material by classifying our development set items into those that have improved as a result of self-training, those that have remained unchanged and those that have deteriorated. We examine all edited grammars shown in Figure 2, i.e. the thirty grammars obtained using 200,000 sentences from *FootballTrainEdited* and varying sized copies of *WSJ02-21*. For the discussion grammars, we examine the grammars trained using one of the five disjoint 200,000-sentence subsets of *FootballTrainDiscussion* and varying sized copies of *WSJ02-21* — we randomly choose the grammars marked with squares in Figure 1. Following McClosky et al. (2006a), we present a breakdown of our results according to sentence length, number of co-ordinating conjunctions (`CC`) in the sentence, and, number of unknown words[4] in the sentence. The results are shown in Tables 2, 3 and 4. Sentence counts are provided along with average f-score differences between a self-trained grammar and the baseline grammar.

It is not possible to discern strong patterns in the breakdown of results but we do observe the following subtle differences between the two types of grammars:

- The *FootballTrainEdited* grammars are more conservative than the *FootballTrainDiscussion* grammars, with a larger number of sentences unchanged by self-training.
- The *FootballTrainDiscussion* grammars outperform the *FootballTrainEdited* grammars for short sentences.

[4]A word is considered to be unknown if it does not appear at all in *WSJ02-21*.

Table 2: Effect of Self-Training Broken Down by Sentence Length

Discussion	1-9		10-19		20-29		30-39		40-59		>= 60		TOTAL	
Better	339	(+21.4)	761	(+14.7)	643	(+11.0)	229	(+9.6)	271	(+12.5)	65	(+5.7)	2308	(+13.6)
No Change	1853		1760		444		119		27		7		4210	
Worse	118	(-26.6)	329	(-8.3)	443	(-7.7)	192	(-7.0)	92	(-7.1)	48	(-5.3)	1222	(-9.4)
TOTAL	2310	(+1.8)	2850	(+3.0)	1530	(+2.4)	540	(+1.6)	390	(+7.0)	120	(+1.0)	7740	(+2.6)
Edited	**1-9**		**10-19**		**20-29**		**30-39**		**40-59**		**>=60**		**TOTAL**	
Better	237	(+20.6)	667	(+12.3)	543	(+10.8)	218	(+10.4)	213	(+9.2)	97	(+7.5)	1975	(+12.1)
No Change	1985		1934		656		202		29		1		4807	
Worse	88	(-18.5)	249	(-6.8)	331	(-9.4)	120	(-5.8)	148	(-6.3)	22	(-2.5)	958	(-8.5)
TOTAL	2310	(+1.4)	2850	(+2.3)	1530	(+1.8)	540	(+2.9)	390	(+2.6)	120	(+5.6)	7740	(+2.0)

Table 3: Effect of Self-Training Broken Down by Number of Coordinating Conjunctions in a Sentence

Discussion	0		1		2		3		4		TOTAL	
Better	1286	(+16.5)	631	(+11.1)	312	(+9.1)	0	(—)	79	(+5.5)	2308	(+13.6)
No Change	3061		981		131		30		7		4210	
Worse	573	(-10.8)	518	(-8.3)	97	(-8.8)	0	(—)	34	(-4.6)	1222	(-9.4)
TOTAL	4920	(+3.0)	2130	(+1.3)	540	(+3.7)	30		120	(+2.3)	7740	(+2.6)
Edited	**0**		**1**		**2**		**3**		**4**		**TOTAL**	
Better	1052	(+14.5)	561	(+10.0)	234	(+9.8)	18	(+5.2)	110	(+6.3)	1975	(+12.1)
No Change	3414		1168		212		12		1		4807	
Worse	454	(-9.6)	401	(-8.0)	94	(-5.4)	0	(—)	9	(-3.6)	958	(-8.5)
TOTAL	4920	(+2.2)	2130	(+1.1)	540	(+3.3)	30	(+3.1)	120	(+5.5)	7740	(+2.0)

Table 4: Effect of Self-Training Broken Down by Number of Unknown Words in a Sentence

Discussion	0		1		2		3		4		5		>=6		TOTAL	
Better	488	(+16.2)	865	(+10.8)	360	(+11.2)	319	(+19.1)	91	(+15.8)	107	(+11.9)	78	(+17.2)	2308	(+13.6)
No Change	2028		1277		584		223		58		30		10		4210	
Worse	274	(-14.0)	408	(-7.5)	406	(-9.5)	58	(-6.3)	31	(-5.3)	13	(-4.2)	32	(-5.7)	1222	(-9.4)
TOTAL	2790	(+1.5)	2550	(+2.5)	1350	(+0.1)	600	(+9.6)	180	(+7.1)	150	(+8.1)	120	(+9.7)	7740	(+2.6)
Edited	**0**		**1**		**2**		**3**		**4**		**5**		**>=6**		**TOTAL**	
Better	330	(+14.9)	758	(+11.1)	329	(+8.8)	328	(+15.7)	55	(+14.0)	94	(+9.5)	81	(+10.4)	1975	(+12.1)
No Change	2291		1352		800		241		91		32		0	(—)	4807	
Worse	169	(-13.5)	440	(-7.0)	221	(-8.6)	31	(-3.8)	34	(-7.4)	24	(-1.6)	39	(-11.2)	958	(-8.5)
TOTAL	2790	(+1.0)	2550	(+2.1)	1350	(+0.8)	600	(+8.4)	180	(+2.9)	150	(+5.7)	120	(+3.4)	7740	(+2.0)

- The *FootballTrainEdited* grammars appear to perform better than the *FootballTrainDiscussion* grammars when there are a relatively high number of coordinating conjunctions in a sentence (greater than two).
- Self-training with both *FootballTrainDiscussion* and *FootballTrainEdited* data tends to benefit sentences containing several unknown words, with the discussion grammars being superior.

6 Conclusion

We compare the use of edited versus unedited text in the task of adapting a WSJ-trained parser to the noisy language of an online discussion forum. Given the small size of our development set, we have to be careful how we interpret the results. However, they do seem to suggest that the two corpora are performing at similar levels of effectiveness but exhibit differences. For example, if we take the best performing *FootballTrainEdited* and *FootballTrainDiscussion* grammars from those used in our error analysis of Section 5, we get two grammars with a Parseval f-score of 83.2 on *FootballDev*. Assuming the existence of a perfect classifier, which, given an input sentence, can predict which of the two grammars will produce the higher-scoring tree, the f-score for *FootballDev* increases from 83.2 to 85.6. When we include the baseline grammar (f-score: 79.7), this increases to 86.4. This suggests that the next step in our research is to build such a classifier including as features the sentential properties we examined in Section 5, as well as the features described in McClosky et al. (2010) and Ravi et al. (2008).

Acknowledgements

This research has been supported by Enterprise Ireland (CFTD/2007/229) and by Science Foundation Ireland (Grant 07/CE/ I1142) as part of the CNGL (www.cngl.ie) at the School of Computing, DCU.

References

Ann Bies, Mark Ferguson, Karen Katz, and Robert MacIntyre. 1995. Bracketing guidelines for Treebank II style. Technical report, University of Pennsylvania.

Daniel Bikel. 2004. Intricacies of Collins parsing model. *Computational Linguistics*, 30(4).

Eugene Charniak and Mark Johnson. 2005. Course-to-fine n-best-parsing and maxent discriminative reranking. In *Proceedings of the 43rd ACL.*

Eugene Charniak. 2000. A maximum-entropy-inspired parser. In *Proceedings of NAACL.*

Jennifer Foster, Özlem Çetinoğlu, Joachim Wagner, Joseph Le Roux, Joakim Nivre, Deirdre Hogan, and Josef van Genabith. 2011. From News to Comment: Resources and benchmarks for parsing the language of Web 2.0. In *Proceedings of IJCNLP.*

Jennifer Foster. 2010. "cba to check the spelling" Investigating parser performance on discussion forum posts. In *Proceedings of HLT NAACL.*

Zhongqiang Huang and Mary Harper. 2009. Self-training PCFG grammars with latent annotations across languages. In *Proceedings of EMNLP.*

Mitchell Marcus, Grace Kim, Mary Ann Marcinkiewicz, Robert MacIntyre, Ann Bies, Mark Ferguson, Karen Katz, and Britta Schasberger. 1994. The Penn Treebank: Annotating predicate argument structure. In *Proceedings of the ARPA Speech and Natural Language Workshop.*

David McClosky and Eugene Charniak. 2008. Self-training for biomedical parsing. In *Proceedings of ACL:HLT.*

David McClosky, Eugene Charniak, and Mark Johnson. 2006a. Effective self-training for parsing. In *Proceedings of NAACL.*

David McClosky, Eugene Charniak, and Mark Johnson. 2006b. Reranking and self-training for parser adaptation. In *Proceedings of ACL.*

David McClosky, Eugene Charniak, and Mark Johnson. 2010. Automatic domain adaptation for parsing. In *Proceedings of NAACL-HLT.*

Slav Petrov, Pi-Chuan Chang, Michael Ringgaard, and Hiyan Alshawi. 2010. Uptraining for accurate deterministic question parsing. In *Proceedings of EMNLP.*

Sujith Ravi, Kevin Knight, and Radu Soricut. 2008. Automatic prediction of parser accuracy. In *Proceedings of EMNLP.*

Roi Reichart and Ari Rappaport. 2007. Self-training for enhancement and domain adaptation of statistical parsers trained on small datasets. In *Proceedings of ACL.*

Beyond Chart Parsing: An Analytic Comparison of Dependency Chart Parsing Algorithms

Meixun Jin, Hwidong Na and Jong-Hyeok Lee
Department of Computer Science and Engineering
Pohang University of Science and Technology (POSTECH)
San 31 Hyoja Dong, Pohang, 790-784, Republic of Korea
meixunj,leona,jhlee@postech.ac.kr

Abstract

In this paper, we give a summary of various dependency chart parsing algorithms in terms of the use of parsing histories for a new dependency arc decision. Some parsing histories are closely related to the target dependency arc, and it is necessary for the parsing algorithm to take them into consideration. Each dependency treebank may have some unique characteristics, and it requires for the parser to model them by certain parsing histories. We show in experiments that proper selection of the parsing algorithm which reflect the dependency annotation of the coordinate structures improves the overall performance.

1 Introduction

In data-driven graph-based parsing, a chart parser is frequently combined with a learning method to derive and evaluate the parse forest and output the optimal parse tree (Chen et al., 2010; Koo and Collins, 2010). The proper selection of a parsing algorithm is important for efficiency and correctness.

Chart parsing is the realization of dynamic programming for syntactic analysis. It is suitable for ambiguous grammars, for example, the grammars of natural languages. Practically, according to the diverse implementations of dynamic programming for dependency syntactic analysis, there are a number of dependency chart parsing algorithms. In this paper, we list a number of bottom-up dependency chart parsing algorithms in terms of their use of the *parsing histories* (section 2).

Incorporating parsing histories into parse tree decoding requires changes to the parsing algorithm. For instance, when decoding a dependency by including the most recently detected *sibling* arc, a modified parsing algorithm has been used in (McDonald et al., 2006) in contrast to the algorithm used in (McDonald et al., 2005). Parsing histories are partial results generated from previous parsing steps. In a chart parser, these histories can be used in subsequent parsing steps. Previous works have shown that the use of parsing histories helps to resolve syntactic ambiguities (Yamada and Mastumoto, 2003; Nivre et al., 2007b; McDonald et al., 2006; Carreras, 2007; Chen et al., 2010). Obviously, using more histories provides better parsing disambiguation. However, there is a trade-off between using more histories and parsing efficiently. One option is to incorporate only important histories. The selection of different histories requires changes to the parsing algorithm.

Another reason for the careful selection of parsing algorithms is from the diverse dependency annotation strategies. The dependency annotations for the same linguistic structures, i.e., coordinate structures can vary (Section 3.1). Additionally, in our opinion, some linguistic or corpus-oriented characters exist for each training data set. Different parsing algorithms are required to deal with the diversity of the corpus.

2 Dependency Chart Parsing Algorithms

A chart parser is the realization of dynamic programming for syntactic analysis. It parses all the substrings of the input sentence and stores the corresponding sub-parse-trees in a data structure called a chart. Dependency chart parsers can be categorized into *constituent*-based and *span*-based parsers depending on the type of substring each cell of the chart yields.

The main difference between constituent-based and span-based algorithms lies in the type of substrings they process. A constituent-based algorithm identifies and parses substrings corresponding to *constituents* and a span-based algorithm does on substrings corresponding to *spans*.

A constituent-based algorithm is a modification

of a phrase-structure (PS) chart parsing algorithm. In a constituent-based dependency parser, the head word of the substring is derived instead of the non-terminal of PS parsing, and information related to the head word is stored in corresponding cell of the chart. In a modified CYK algorithm(Younger, 1967), the cell reserves the possibility for each word of the substring to be the head. Thus, n kinds of sub-dependency-trees are reserved for processing a substring of length n. The space complexity for a cell is O(n), and the overall space complexity is O(n^3) and time complexity is O(n^5) for parsing of a sentence of length n. For a detailed description, refer to (Nivre, 2006).

A *span* is a *half*-constituent that is formed by splitting a constituent at the position of its *head* (Eisner and Satta, 1999). The span is characterized by the head being located either on the left or right edge. In the span-based dependency chart parser proposed by (Eisner and Satta, 1999), there are two kinds of subtrees reserved in each cell of the chart, i.e., the head is the left-most word or the right-most word. Given this condition, Eisner's algorithm can parse with a time complexity of O(n^3) and a space complexity of O(n^2).

In bottom-up parsing, either a constituent-based or a span-based algorithm derives parse tree for a sequence by combining two (or more) subsequences with a new dependency arc. These subsequences have been parsed in earlier steps, and they are called as *parsing histories*. These histories are frequently used for a better evaluation of the new dependency arc (Chen et al., 2010). Table 1 lists a number of dependency chart parsing algorithms. Each of them adopts different method to derive a new parse tree from couple of smaller sequences. In the following, we discuss in detail how these algorithms differ in their use of the parsing histories for the new dependency arc decision.

2.1 Constituent-Based Algorithms

Table 1 lists the step for various dependency chart parsing algorithms to decide a new dependency arc connecting h(ead) and d(ependent). and present the constituents dominated by h and d respectively.

The derivation of the new constituent in Alg. 1 (Table 1) is processed in one-step, and the one-step processing can be defined as the function f of Alg. 1, which involves three parameters: two constituents and and the evaluation of the dependency arc . The dependency between (h, d) is evaluated by $score(h, d, (\cdot, \cdot))$ defined in Table 1. Here, (,) is the context of parsing histories, which are available for the new dependency arc detection in Alg. 1.

Algs. 2-4 listed in Table 1 are variants of Alg. 1, and the derivation of the new constituent over smaller constituents in these algorithms is processed in *two* steps. In Alg. 2, the first step combines one constituent with the detection of the dependency arc, and the process is represented by the function $f(\cdot, \cdot)$; the combination of the second constituent represented as $f(\cdot)$, is processed at the second step (Table 1, Alg. 2). With such a two-step operation, parsing histories available for the decision of the arc in Alg. 2 is $(h, \cdot)$. Comparing to Alg.1 of (,), the histories included in is not available in Alg.2. One benefit of such a two-step operation is that it reduces the time complexity O(n^5) of Alg. 1 to O(n^4).

In Algs. 3 and 4, one of the constituents is divided into two parts (spans). The first step combines the constituent with the closer span and makes a decision about the new dependency arc. The other span is attached to the result of the first step. The available parsing histories is (,) for Alg.3, and (,) for Alg.4.

The two-step processing requires the reservation of the partial results generated at the first step: for Alg. 2, for Alg. 3, and for Alg. 4 (Table 1). Reserving these partial results in the chart in addition to the constituent , only increases the *constant factor*, the overall space complexity remains as O(n^3).

For more information on Algs. 2 and 3 see (Eisner and Satta, 1999). and Alg. 4 see (Jin, 2011).

2.2 Span-Based Algorithms

Alg. 5 is the span-based algorithm proposed by (Eisner, 1996). The algorithm has been widely used in data-driven graph-based dependency parsers, because of its efficiency by parsing with a complexity of O(n^3). When combined with a learning method, the training for a data-driven parser involves repeatedly decoding of parse trees. Parsing efficiency is an important factor in such an approach. Some extensions to Alg. 5 have been proposed (Carreras, 2007; McDonald et al., 2006) with the aim of enriching the information available for new dependency arc detection. The work

	Chart combinations	Combination function / Score function for new dependency arc	Time / Space Complexity
Alg. 1	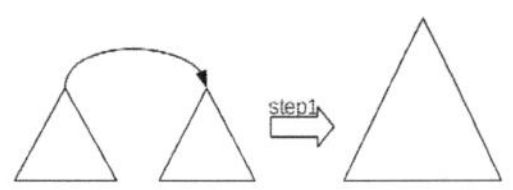	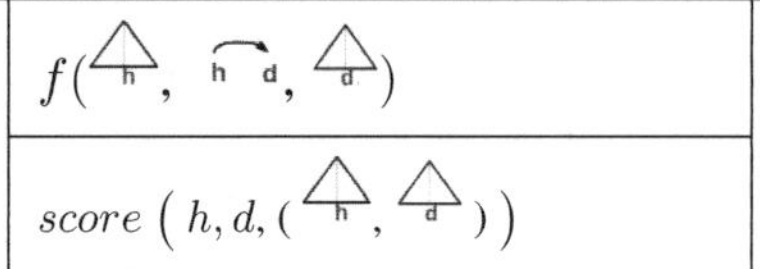	$O(n^5)/O(n^3)$
Alg. 2	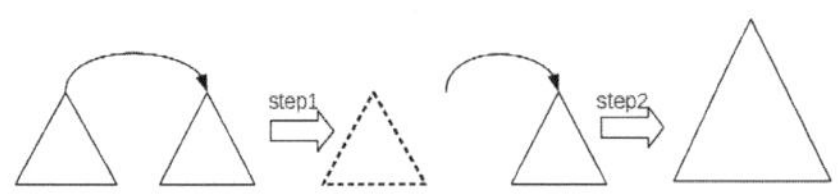	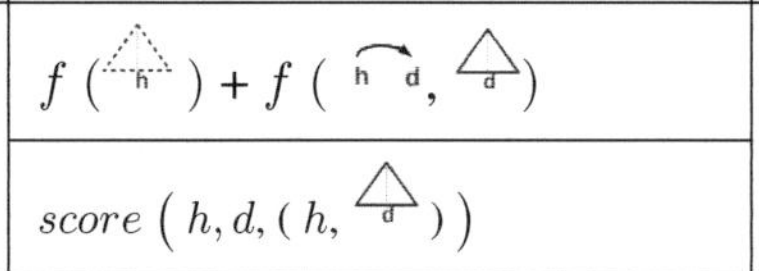	$O(n^4)/O(n^3)$
Alg. 3	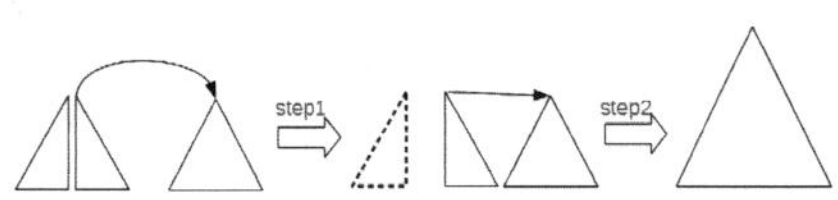	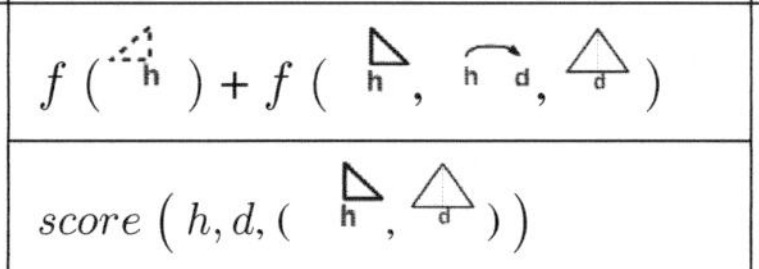	$O(n^4)/O(n^3)$
Alg. 4	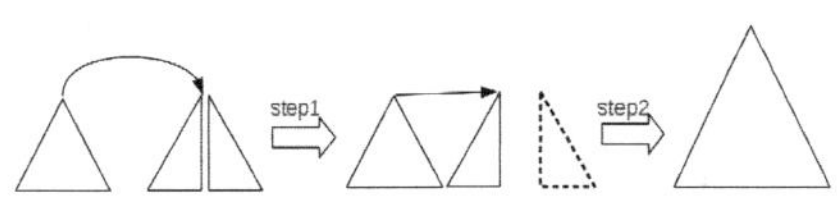	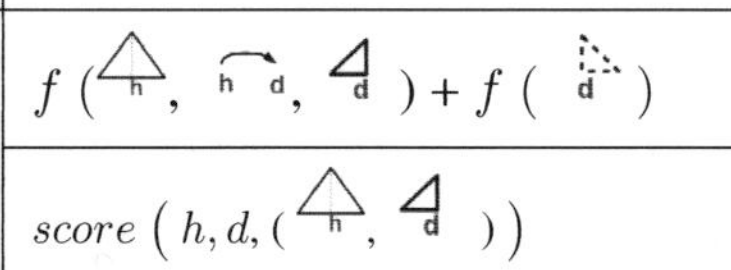	$O(n^4)/O(n^3)$
Alg. 5		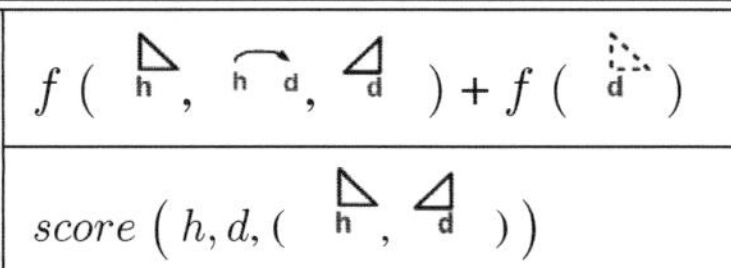	$O(n^3)/O(n^2)$
Alg. 6	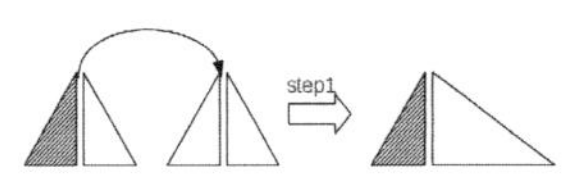	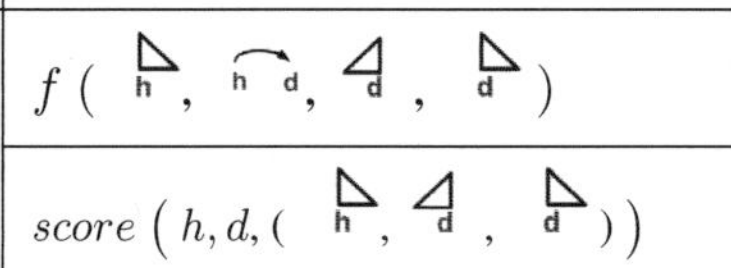	$O(n^4)/O(n^2)$

Table 1: Comparison of various dependency chart parsing methods. The dashed part is attached in step2. Algs. 5-6 are *span-based* algorithms, during the step of right-side span construction, the shadowed left-side span remains *un*change.

of (Koo and Collins, 2010) is a similar propose of the method of Alg. 2 on span-based algorithms.

In terms of the use of the parsing histories, the amount of information available for a new dependency arc decision with Alg. 5 is ($\triangle_h$, $\triangle_d$), which is about *half* of ($\triangle_h$, $\triangle_d$) of Alg.1. Some common but important relations between pair of dependents for some corpora, such as the relation between the left and right dependents of a head (the pair of dependency arcs shown in Fig. 1(a)), cannot be modeled using such an algorithm.

Alg. 6 (Table 1), is an alternative to Alg. 5. The two-step operation in Alg. 5 merges and becomes a one-step operation in Alg. 6 by direct processing over three spans ($\triangle_h$, $\triangle_d$, $\triangle_d$) . Such a *ternary*-span combination increases the parsing histories from ($\triangle_h$, $\triangle_d$) of Alg.5 to *three* spans as ($\triangle_h$, $\triangle_d$, $\triangle_d$) (see the score function of Alg. 6 in Table 1). However, the time complexity of Alg.6 increases from $O(n^3)$ of Alg.5 to $O(n^4)$. Comparing to other $O(n^4)$ algorithms, Algs.2-4, Alg. 6 is more efficient with a small constant factor. The space complexity is also modest as $O(n^2)$ which is the same as that for Alg. 5.

The relation between the left and right dependents of a head can be modeled using Alg. 6. In span-based algorithms, the left and right spans sharing the head are treated independently, and the relations between the left and right dependents are often ignored in previous span-based algorithms. To our knowledge, Alg. 6 is the first span-based algorithm to model this. For detailed implementation of Alg.5 refer to (Eisner and Satta, 1999), and Alg.6 to (Jin, 2011).

3 Diverse Dependency Annotation Strategies

Since the CoNLL'06 shared tasks for *multilingual dependency parsing* (Buchholz and Marsi, 2006),

(a) CCH (b) CCD.I (c) CCD.II

Figure 1: (a) CCH; (b) and (c) two cases of CCD, with *left* conjunct as head.

it has become common to construct a *universal* parser to derive parse trees of diverse languages in a *unified* way, with less consideration about the varieties among corpora.

In addition to the variations of different language, there are some variations because of the diverse strategies for dependency annotations. It is clear that a *subject* or an *object* takes a verb as its head. However, for the case of *preposition* vs. *noun*, or *complementizer* vs. *verb* in sub-clauses, there are various dependency annotation strategies. Such diversities of dependency annotation need corresponding changes for parsing algorithms. Since the same linguistic structures are presented differently with different annotation strategies. In section 3.1, we discuss for such changes required for the case of coordinate structures.

3.1 Diversity for Denpendency Annotation of Coordinate Structures

There are various strategies for annotating dependencies of coordinate structures. These include, *coordinate conjunction as head* (CCH), and *coordinate conjunction as dependent* (CCD) strategies (McDonald and Nivre, 2007), and CCD can further be categorized into two cases illustrated in Figures 1(b) and 1(c).

Coordinate structures are characterized by symmetries between conjuncts. The symmetries are important clues for the disambiguation of coordinate structure. The different dependency annotation strategies for coordinate structures require different methods to model the symmetry sharing between conjuncts. For CCH-type coordinate structures, it is essential for the parser to model the pair of dependents shown in Figure 1(a). Existing span-based approaches (McDonald et al., 2006; Carreras, 2007; Koo and Collins, 2010) do not model such relations. That explains why the average performance for CCH-type coordinate structures is about 15% to 20% lower than that of CCD-type in the work of (McDonald et al., 2006), according to the analysis given in (McDonald and Nivre, 2007). Considering the frequent use of coordinate structures among sentences, for hight performance parsing, it is crucial to select a parsing algorithm that can parse such structures well.

Corpus	2nd-order[1] (McDonald et al., 2006)		Alg. 6	
	overall	coord.	overall	coord.
Chinese	88.29%	81.66%	89.41%	85.09%
Slovene	78.93%	58.79%	80.32%	74.06%

[1] The results of MSTParser(V0.2), which is available from http://www.seas.upenn.edu/~strctlrn/MSTParser/MSTParser.html

Table 2: Results of experiment.

4 Experiments

We conduct our experiments on two data sets, the Chinese corpus of CoNLL'07 (Nivre et al., 2007a), and the Slovene corpus of CoNLL'06 (Buchholz and Marsi, 2006) shared task for *multilingual dependency parsing* track. Both corpora are of the CCH-type.

Table 2 lists the performance of two systems, i.e., the 2nd-order system of (McDonald et al., 2006) and the proposed system with Alg. 6 (Table 1) as the parse tree decoder. As the discussions given in the previous section, the 2nd-order gives low performance for coordinate structures compared to the overall parsing results. The proposed system gives better coordinate disambiguation by modeling the relation between dependents located on different-sides of the head.

5 Conclusion

In this paper, we categorize bottom-up dependency chart parsing algorithms into constituent-based and span-based algorithms according to the strings each identifies and parses. We further categorize algorithms in terms of the use of parsing histories for new dependency arc detection. We show that proper selection of the parsing algorithm helps to improve the overall parsing performance.

Acknowledgments

This work was supported in part by the Korea Science and Engineering Foundation (KOSEF) grant funded by the Korean government (MEST No. 2011-0017960), and in part by the BK 21 Project in 2011.

References

Sabine Buchholz and Erwin Marsi. 2006. Conll-x shared task on multilingual dependency parsing. In *Proceedings of the 10th Conference on Natural Language Learning(CoNLL-X)*, New York City, USA, June. Association for Computational Linguistics.

Xavier Carreras. 2007. Experiments with a higher-order projective dependency parser. In *Proceedings of the CoNLL Shared Task Session of EMNLP-CoNLL 2007*, pages 957–961, Prague, Czech Republic, June. Association for Computational Linguistics.

Wenliang Chen, Jun'ichi Kazama, Yoshimasa Tsuruoka, and Kentaro Torisawa. 2010. Improving graph-based dependency parsing with decision history. In *Coling 2010: Posters*, pages 126–134, Beijing, China, August. Coling 2010 Organizing Committee.

Jason M. Eisner and Giorgio Satta. 1999. Efficient parsing for bilexical context-free grammars and head automaton grammars. In *Proceedings of the 37th Annual Meeting of the Association for Computational Linguistics*. Association for Computational Linguistics.

Jason M. Eisner. 1996. Three new probabilistic models for dependency parsing: An exploration. In *Proceedings of the 34th Annual Meeting of the Association for Computational Linguistics*, pages 340–345. Association for Computational Linguistics.

Meixun Jin. 2011. Dependency chart parsing algorithms. *Technical Report, POSTECH*.

Terry Koo and Michael Collins. 2010. Efficient third-order dependency parsers. In *Proceedings of the 48th Annual Meeting of the Association for Computational Linguistics*, pages 1–11, Uppsala, Sweden, July. Association for Computational Linguistics.

Ryan McDonald and Joakim Nivre. 2007. Characterizing the errors of data-driven dependency parsing models. In *Proceedings of the 2007 Joint Conference on Empirical Methods in Natural Language Processing and Computational Natural Language Learning (EMNLP-CoNLL)*, pages 122–131.

Ryan McDonald, Fernando Pereira, Kiril Ribarov, and Jan Hajic. 2005. Non-projective dependency parsing using spanning tree algorithms. In *Proceedings of Human Language Technology Conference and Conference on Empirical Methods in Natural Language Processing*, pages 523–530, Vancouver, British Columbia, Canada, October. Association for Computational Linguistics.

Ryan McDonald, Kevin Lerman, and Fernando Pereira. 2006. Multilingual dependency analysis with a two-stage discriminative parser. In *Conference on Natural Language Learning (CoNLL)*.

Joakim Nivre, Johan Hall, Sandra Kübler, Ryan McDonald, Jens Nilsson, Sebastian Riedel, and Deniz Yuret. 2007a. The CoNLL 2007 shared task on dependency parsing. In *Proceedings of the CoNLL Shared Task Session of EMNLP-CoNLL 2007*, pages 915–932, Prague, Czech Republic, June. Association for Computational Linguistics.

Joakim Nivre, Johan Hall, Jens Nilsson, Atanas Chanev, Gulsen Eryigit, Sandra Kubler, Svetoslav Marinov, and Erwin Marsi. 2007b. Maltparser:a language-independent system for data-driven dependency parsing. *Natural Language Engineering*, 2(13):95–135.

Joakim Nivre. 2006. Inductive dependency parsing. *Text, Speech and Language Technology*, 34.

Hiroyasu Yamada and Yuji Mastumoto. 2003. Statistical dependency analysis with support vector machines. In *Proceedings of the 8th International Workshop on Parsing Technologies(IWPT)*, pages 195–206.

Daniel H. Younger. 1967. Recognition and parsing of context-free languages in time n3. *Information and Control, 12(4)*, 4(12):361–379.

Parser Evaluation Using Elementary Dependency Matching

Rebecca Dridan
NICTA Victoria Research Laboratory
Dept. of Computer Science and Software Engineering
University of Melbourne
rdridan@csse.unimelb.edu.au

Stephan Oepen
Department of Informatics
Universitetet i Oslo
oe@ifi.uio.no

Abstract

We present a perspective on parser evaluation in a context where the goal of parsing is to extract meaning from a sentence. Using this perspective, we show why current parser evaluation metrics are not suitable for evaluating parsers that produce logical-form semantics and present an evaluation metric that is suitable, analysing some of the characteristics of this new metric.

1 Introduction

A plethora of parser evaluation metrics exist, which evaluate different types of information, at different levels of granularity, using different methods of calculation. All attempt to measure the syntactic quality of parser output, but that is not the only goal of parsing. The DELPH-IN consortium[1] has produced many grammars of different languages, as well as a number of parsers, all with the aim of extracting meaning from text. In order to drive development, we need a parser evaluation metric that evaluates against that goal. That is, we require a metric that measures semantic rather than syntactic output. In the following section, we reflect on and categorize the semantic information we wish to evaluate, and discuss how current metrics partially overlap with this framework. We then, after describing some of the specifics of the tools we work with, present an evaluation metric that fits within the given framework, and show, using a couple of case studies, some characteristics of the metric.

2 Semantic Information

Our primary goal in parsing is to extract meaning from text. To evaluate progress towards this goal in a granular fashion, one needs to break up the semantic information into discrete elements. For this purpose, we distinguish three broad classes of information that contribute to meaning:

- **class 1** core functor – argument structure, whether syntactic or semantic
- **class 2** predicate information, such as the lemma, word category, and sense
- **class 3** properties of events and entities, such as tense, number, and gender

The widely-used PARSEVAL metric (Black et al., 1991) evaluates phrase structure, which covers none of these classes directly. Dependency-based evaluation schemes, such as those used by MaltParser (Nivre et al., 2004) and MSTParser (McDonald et al., 2005) evaluate **class 1** surface information. The annotation used in the Briscoe and Carroll (2006) DepBank for parser evaluation also describes just **class 1** syntactic information, although the relationships are different to those that MaltParser or MSTParser produce. The annotation of the original King et al. (2003) PARC700 DepBank does describe all three classes of information, but again in terms of syntactic rather than semantic properties.

A common element between all the dependency types above is the use of grammatical relations to describe **class 1** information. That is, the dependencies are usually labels like SUBJ, OBJ, MOD, etc. While these grammatical functions allow one to describe the surface linguistic structure, they do not make the underlying deep structure explicit. This deep structure describes semantic rather than syntactic arguments and can be seen in resources such as the Prague Dependency Treebank (Böhmová et al., 2003) and the Redwoods Treebank (Oepen et al., 2004b). Using this semantic argument structure for parser evaluation not only gets closer to the actual sentence meaning that we are trying to extract, but is potentially more general, as there is generally wider agreement on semantic arguments than on, for example, whether the main verb depends on the auxiliary, or

[1] See http://www.delph-in.net for background.

vice versa.[2]

3 Background

The parser that we will be evaluating in this work encodes its semantic output in the form of Minimal Recursion Semantics (Copestake et al., 2005), although the derivation that we use for the evaluation metric should be compatible with any parser that produces information in classes given in the previous section.

3.1 Minimal Recursion Semantics

Minimal Recursion Semantics (MRS) is a flat semantic formalism that represents semantics as a bag of *elementary predications* and a set of underspecified scopal constraints. An elementary predication can be directly related to words in the text, or can reflect a grammatical construction, such as compounding. Each elementary predication has a relation name, a label and a distinguished variable (designated ARG0). Arguments of a predication are identified by 'bleached' ARG*n* roles (which are to be semantically interpreted for classes of predicates). Figure 1 shows the MRS analysis of *He persuaded Kim to leave*. Here we see six elementary predications, four with text referents and two as construction-specific covert quantifiers. The ARG1, ARG2 and ARG3 roles of the verbal predicates describe the predicate–argument relations and demonstrate co-indexation between the ARG2 of *persuade* and the ARG1 of *leave*. Entity and event variables carry properties such as gender or tense. An evaluation scheme based on MRS therefore allows us to evaluate **class 1** information using the roles, **class 2** information through predicate names and **class 3** information from the properties of the distinguished variables.

3.2 Setup

We will use the PET parser (Callmeier, 2000) and associated grammars as our test environment to evaluate. The traditional accuracy metric for PET has been sentence accuracy which requires an exact match against the very fine-grained gold analysis, but arguably this harsh metric supplies insufficient information about parser performance on its own. In order to evaluate a parser for its use in an application, we are also interested in knowing how good the top ranked parse is, rather than only whether it is the very best parse possible. Even if the goal of evaluation were just parser development, a nuanced granular evaluation may help reveal what types of mistakes a parser is making.

4 EDM: Elementary Dependency Match

In addition to our focus on semantic information, we considered two other requirements for an effective parser evaluation metric. It should be:

1. understandable not just by parser developers, but also potential users of the parser.
2. configurable to suit the level of detail required for a particular scenario.

4.1 Elementary Dependencies

The metric we have devised to satisfy these requirements is Elementary Dependency Match (EDM), based on so-called Elementary Dependencies (EDs), a variable-free reduction of MRS developed by Oepen and Lønning (2006).[3] In our work, we use sub-string character spans (e.g. <3:12>) to identify nodes in the dependency graph, to facilitate alignment of corresponding elements across distinct analyses. In keeping with our information classes, this allows us to separate the evaluation of **class 2** information from **class 1**. Our EDM metric hence consists of three triple types which align with the three information classes:

ARGS:	$span_i$	$role_j$	$span_k$
NAMES:	$span_i$	NAME	$relation_i$
PROPS:	$span_i$	$property_j$	$value_j$

In these forms, $relation$ is the predicate name of an elementary predication from the MRS, $role$ is an argument label such as ARG1, $property$ refers to an attribute such as TENSE or GEND and $value$ is an appropriate instantiation for the respective property. Figure 2 shows the triples produced for the MRS in Figure 1. The text segment associated with each character span is shown for illustrative purposes, but is not part of the triple.

During evaluation, we compare the triples from the gold standard analysis with that ranked top by

[2] At the same time, we wish to focus *parser* evaluation on information determined solely by grammatical analysis, i.e. all contributions to interpretation by syntax, and only those. For these reasons, the task of semantic role labeling (SRL) against PropBank-style target representations (Kingsbury et al., 2002) is too far removed from parser evaluation proper; Copestake (2009) elaborates this argument.

[3] In more recent work, Copestake (2009) shows how essentially the same reduction can be augmented with information about the underspecified scope hierarchy, so as to yield so-called Dependency MRS (which unlike EDs facilitates bidirectional conversion from and to the original MRS).

$\langle h_1,$

h_3:pron<0:2>(ARG0 x_4\{PERS *3*, NUM *sg*, GEND *m*, PRONTYPE *std_pron*\}),
h_5:pronoun_q<0:2>(ARG0 x_4, RSTR h_6, BODY h_7),
h_8:_persuade_v_of<3:12>(ARG0 e_2\{SF *prop*, TENSE *past*, MOOD *indicative*\}, ARG1 x_4, ARG2 x_{10}, ARG3 h_9),
h_{11}:proper_q<13:16>(ARG0 x_{10}\{PERS *3*, NUM *sg*\}, RSTR h_{12}, BODY h_{13}),
h_{14}:named<13:16>(ARG0 x_{10}, CARG *Kim*),
h_{15}:_leave_v_1<20:26>(ARG0 e_{16}\{SF *prop-or-ques*, TENSE *untensed*, MOOD *indicative*\}, ARG1 x_{10}, ARG2 p_{17})

$\{ h_{12} =_q h_{14}, h_9 =_q h_{15}, h_6 =_q h_3 \} \rangle$

Figure 1: MRS representation of *He persuaded Kim to leave.*

"He"	<0:2>	ARG0	<0:2>	"He"
"persuaded"	<3:12>	ARG1	<0:2>	"He"
"persuaded"	<3:12>	ARG2	<13:16>	"Kim"
"persuaded"	<3:12>	ARG3	<20:26>	"leave."
"Kim"	<13:16>	ARG0	<13:16>	"Kim"
"leave."	<20:26>	ARG1	<13:16>	"Kim"
"He"	<0:2>	NAME	pronoun_q	
"He"	<0:2>	NAME	pron	
"persuaded"	<3:12>	NAME	_persuade_v_of	
"Kim"	<13:16>	NAME	proper_q	
"Kim"	<13:16>	NAME	named	
"leave."	<20:26>	NAME	_leave_v_1	
"He"	<0:2>	GEND	*m*	
"He"	<0:2>	NUM	*sg*	
"He"	<0:2>	PERS	*3*	
"He"	<0:2>	PRONTYPE	*std_pron*	
"persuaded"	<3:12>	MOOD	*indicative*	
"persuaded"	<3:12>	SF	*prop*	
"persuaded"	<3:12>	TENSE	*past*	
"Kim"	<13:16>	NUM	*sg*	
"Kim"	<13:16>	PERS	*3*	
"leave."	<20:26>	MOOD	*indicative*	
"leave."	<20:26>	SF	*prop-or-ques*	
"leave."	<20:26>	TENSE	*untensed*	

Figure 2: Gold triples for *He persuaded Kim to leave.*

the parser, and calculate precision, recall and F_1-score across all triples, as well as across the three separate triple types (NAME, ARG and PROP).

4.2 Alternate Configurations

The full EDM metric weights each triple equally which may not be ideal for all scenarios. The division by triple type gives one alternative view that provides a more complete picture of what sort of mistakes are being made by the parser. For particular applications, it might be that only **class 1** information will be used, and in that case just measuring ARGs might be a better metric. Further fine-tuning is possible by assigning weights to individual predicate types via a configuration file similar to the parameter files used with the EvalB PARSEVAL script (Sekine and Collins, 1997). This will allow a user to, for example, assign lower weight to entity properties, or only evaluate ARG1 and ARG2 roles. One particular configuration we have found useful is to assign zero weight to the PROP triples and only evaluate ARGs and NAMEs. While the **class 3** information is useful for applications such as machine translation, and ideally would be evaluated, some applications don't make use of this information, and so, in certain scenarios, it makes sense to ignore these triples in evaluation. This configuration produces a metric broadly similar to the CCG dependencies used by Clark and Curran (2007) and also to the predicate argument structures produced by the Enju parser (Miyao and Tsujii, 2008), in terms of the information classes included, although the CCG dependencies again encode syntactic rather than semantic structure.

5 Analysis

To get some idea of the numeric range of the different EDM configurations, we parsed a section of the SemCor corpus (Miller et al., 1994) using the English Resource Grammar (ERG: (Flickinger, 2000)), and then calculated the average F_1-score for each rank, as ranked by the statistical model packaged with the ERG. Figure 3 shows the relative differences between five configurations: all triples together (EDM), the NAME, ARG and PROP triple types separately (EDM_N, EDM_A and EDM_P, respectively) and measuring just the NAME and ARG types together (EDM_{NA}).

We can see that all configurations show approximately the same trends, and maintain their relative order. EDM_P is consistently higher, which follows from the fact that many of the properties are inter-dependent, and that the parser enforces agreement. Most difficult to identify correctly is the ARG type, which represent the core semantic arguments. All of the scores are quite high, even at the 40th rank parse, which is due to using a highly constrained grammar with fine-grained analyses that can vary in only small details.

To get a different view of the information that EDM provides, we looked at different scenarios

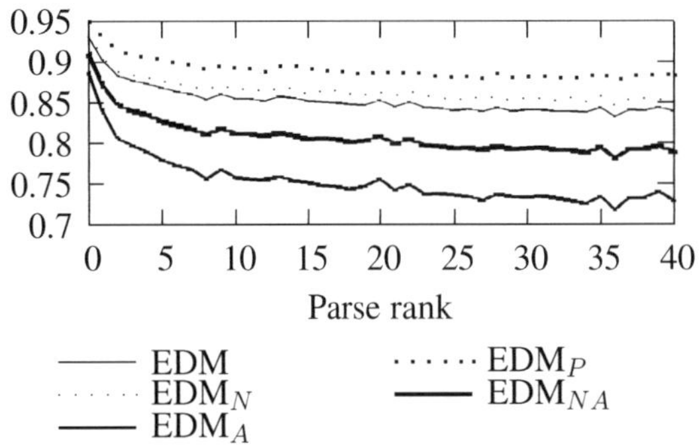

Figure 3: Average F_1 score at each rank (up to 40).

	Config 1			Config 2		
Sent. Acc.	0.095			0.093		
	P	**R**	**F**	**P**	**R**	**F**
EDM	0.847	0.677	0.753	0.847	0.693	0.763
EDM$_{\text{NA}}$	0.796	0.635	0.707	0.798	0.652	0.717
EDM$_{\text{A}}$	0.778	0.620	0.690	0.780	0.637	0.701
EDM$_{\text{N}}$	0.815	0.651	0.724	0.815	0.668	0.734
EDM$_{\text{P}}$	0.890	0.714	0.792	0.890	0.729	0.801

Table 1: Comparing unknown word handling configurations.

that allow us to see relative differences in parser performance, measured using EDM and variants, as well as the traditional sentence accuracy.

5.1 Cross-Configuration

One possible evaluation scenario involves changing a parameter in the parser and measuring the effect. The results in Table 1 come from parsing a single corpus using a variant of the ERG with a much smaller lexicon in order to test two unknown word handling configurations.

The sentence accuracy figures are very low, since the grammar has been limited, and show no real difference between the two configurations. In the EDM results, we can see that, while the precision between the two configurations is very similar, recall is consistently lower for Config 1 (which had a slightly better sentence accuracy).

5.2 Cross-Grammar

In this comparison, we look at two different grammars, over parallel test data.[4] The Spanish Resource Grammar (SRG: (Marimon et al., 2007)) also produces MRS, although properties are treated differently, so we leave out the EDM

[4]The MRS test suite was constructed to represent a range of phenomena and consists of 107 short sentences which have been translated into multiple languages, maintaining parallel MRS analyses as far as possible.

	SRG			ERG		
Sent. Acc.	0.95			0.85		
	P	**R**	**F**	**P**	**R**	**F**
EDM$_{\text{NA}}$	0.97	0.97	0.97	0.92	0.93	0.92
EDM$_{\text{A}}$	0.96	0.95	0.95	0.90	0.91	0.90
EDM$_{\text{N}}$	0.98	0.98	0.98	0.93	0.95	0.94

Table 2: Comparing between the SRG and ERG grammars over a parallel test suite. PROP type triples are excluded for compatibility.

and EDM$_P$ metric for compatibility and compare to ERG performance over the same small test set.

While the SRG is a less mature grammar, and does not analyse the full range of constructions that the ERG parses, EDM allows us to compare over items and information types that both grammars cover, and in Table 2 we can see that the SRG ranking model performs better over this data.

6 Conclusion

The current range of parser evaluation metrics all evaluate the syntactic quality of parser output, which makes them unsuitable to evaluate parsers which aim to output semantic analysis. The EDM metric we describe here allows us to evaluate the semantic output of any parser that can encode information in the Minimal Recursion Semantic framework, and indeed, the derivation that we use should be generalisable to any logical-form semantic output. This metric can measure three different classes of deep semantic information, and can be configured to evaluate whatever level is suitable for the potential application, or for the parser being evaluated. We have demonstrated that EDM and its variants, together with sentence accuracy, can give a detailed picture of how accurately a parser can extract meaning from text, allowing useful comparisons in a variety of circumstances. Furthermore, since MRS is used in applications and other semantic research (Oepen et al., 2004a; Dridan, 2007; Schlangen and Lascarides, 2003; Fuchss et al., 2004), the metric we have described here may prove useful in other areas where semantic comparison is required.

Acknowledgements

NICTA is funded by the Australian Government as represented by the Department of Broadband, Communications and the Digital Economy and the Australian Research Council through the ICT Centre of Excellence program.

References

Ezra Black, Steve Abney, Dan Flickinger, Claudia Gdaniec, Ralph Grishman, Phil Harrison, Don Hindle, Robert Ingria, Fred Jelinek, J. Klavans, Mark Liberman, Mitch Marcus, S. Roukos, B. Santorini, and Tomek Strzalkowski. 1991. A procedure for quantitatively comparing the syntactic coverage of English grammars. In *Proceedings of the Workshop on Speech and Natural Language*, pages 306–311, Pacific Grove, USA.

Alena Böhmová, Jan Hajič, Eva Hajičová, and Barbora Hladká. 2003. The Prague Dependency Treebank: A three level annotation scenario. In Anne Abeill, editor, *Treebanks: building and using parsed corpora*. Springer.

Ted Briscoe and John Carroll. 2006. Evaluating the accuracy of an unlexicalised statistical parser on the PARC DepBank. In *Proceedings of the 44th Annual Meeting of the ACL and the 21st International Conference on Computational Linguistics*, pages 41–48, Sydney, Australia.

Ulrich Callmeier. 2000. PET - a platform for experimentation with efficient HPSG processing techniques. *Natural Language Engineering*, 6(1):99–107.

Stephen Clark and James R. Curran. 2007. Wide-coverage efficient statistical parsing with CCG and log-linear models. *Computational Linguistics*, 33(4):493–552.

Ann Copestake, Dan Flickinger, Ivan A. Sag, and Carl Pollard. 2005. Minimal Recursion Semantics: an introduction. *Research on Language and Computation*, 3(4):281–332.

Ann Copestake. 2009. Invited talk: Slacker semantics: Why superficiality, dependency and avoidance of commitment can be the right way to go. In *Proceedings of the 12th Conference of the European Chapter of the ACL (EACL 2009)*, pages 1–9, Athens, Greece.

Rebecca Dridan. 2007. Using Minimal Recursion Semantics in Japanese question answering. Master's thesis, The University of Melbourne.

Dan Flickinger. 2000. On building a more efficient grammar by exploiting types. *Natural Language Engineering*, 6(1):15–28.

Ruth Fuchss, Alexander Koller, Joachim Niehren, and Stefan Thater. 2004. Minimal recursion semantics as dominance constraints: Translation, evaluation, and analysis. In *Proceedings of the 42nd Annual Meeting of the ACL*, pages 247–254, Barcelona, Spain.

Tracy Holloway King, Richard Crouch, Stefan Riezler, Mary Dalrymple, and Ronald M. Kaplan. 2003. The PARC 700 Dependency Bank. In *Proceedings of the LINC-03 Workshop*, pages 1–8, Budapest, Hungary.

Paul Kingsbury, Martha Palmer, and Mitch Marcus. 2002. Adding semantic annotation to the Penn treebank. In *Proceedings of the Human Language Technology 2002 Conference*, pages 252–256, San Diego, California.

Montserrat Marimon, Núria Bel, and Natalia Seghezzi. 2007. Test-suite construction for a Spanish grammar. In *Proceedings of the GEAF 2007 Workshop*, pages 224–237, Stanford, USA.

Ryan McDonald, Fernando Pereira, Kiril Ribarov, and Jan Hajič. 2005. Non-projective dependency parsing using spanning tree algorithms. In *Proceedings of Human Language Technology Conference and Conference on Empirical Methods in Natural Language Processing (HLT/EMNLP)*, pages 523–530, Vancouver, Canada.

George A. Miller, Martin Chodorow, Shari Landes, Claudia Leacock, and Robert G. Thomas. 1994. Using a semantic concordance for sense identification. In *Proceedings of ARPA Human Language Technology Workshop*, pages 240–243, Plainsboro, USA.

Yusuke Miyao and Jun'ichi Tsujii. 2008. Feature forest models for probabilistic HPSG parsing. *Computational Linguistics*, 34(1):35–80.

Joakim Nivre, Johan Hall, and Jens Nilsson. 2004. Memory-based dependency parsing. In *Proceedings of the 8th Conference on Natural Language Learning (CoNLL-2004)*, pages 49–56, Boston, USA.

Stephan Oepen and Jan Tore Lønning. 2006. Discriminant-based MRS banking. In *Proceedings of the Fifth International Conference on Language Resources and Evaluation (LREC 2006)*, pages 1250–1255, Genoa, Italy.

Stephan Oepen, Helge Dyvik, Jan Tore Lønning, Erik Velldal, Dorothee Beermann, John Carroll, Dan Flickinger, Lars Hellan, Janne Bondi Johannessen, Paul Meurer, Torbjørn Nordgård, and Victoria Rosén. 2004a. Somå kapp-ete med trollet? Towards MRS-based Norwegian—English machine translation. In *Proceedings of the 10th International Conference on Theoretical and Methodological Issues in Machine Translation*, pages 11–20, Baltimore, USA.

Stephan Oepen, Dan Flickinger, Kristina Toutanova, and Christopher D. Manning. 2004b. LinGO redwoods: a rich and dynamic treebank for HPSG. *Journal of Research in Language and Computation*, 2(4):575–596.

David Schlangen and Alex Lascarides. 2003. A compositional and constraint-based approach to non-sentential utterances. In *Proceedings of the 10th International Conference on Head-Driven Phrase Structure Grammar*, pages 380–390, East Lansing, USA.

Satoshi Sekine and Michael Collins. 1997. EvalB: a bracket scoring program. `http://nlp.cs.nyu.edu/evalb/`.

Parsing of Partially Bracketed Structures for Parse Selection

Mark-Jan Nederhof
School of Computer Science
University of St Andrews
St Andrews, United Kingdom

Ricardo Sánchez-Sáez
Instituto Tecnológico de Informática
Universidad Politècnica de Valencia
Valencia, Spain

Abstract

We consider the problem of parsing a sentence that is partially annotated with information about where phrases start and end. The application domain is interactive parse selection with probabilistic grammars. It is explained that the main obstacle is spurious ambiguity. The proposed solution is first described in terms of appropriately constrained synchronous grammars, and then in terms of a computational model for parsing. Experiments show the feasibility for a practical grammar.

1 Introduction

In interactive parse selection, the objective is to obtain correct parses of sentences in a corpus, by means of an iterative process, alternately drawing upon a language model and human linguistic judgement. In a first step, the most likely parse is computed on the basis of the model. This parse is displayed to the human annotator, who looks for possible errors and enters corrections. Each correction takes the form of an occurrence of a phrase that the parse should contain. The model is then consulted anew, to recompute the most likely parse, but now under the constraint that all occurrences of phrases entered previously by the linguist must be included. This process is repeated until no more errors remain. Applications can be found in creation of treebanks (Marcus et al., 1993) and computer-assisted translation (Barrachina et al., 2009).

Apart from the exact language model used in the process, there are various ways to implement interactive parse selection. One obvious approach is to demand that errors are corrected strictly from left to right. That is, where the occurrence of a phrase is asserted by the annotator, it is implicitly assumed that all phrases in the latest proposed parse that are wholly contained in the preceding prefix are correct. This means that these structures in a left-hand portion of the parse tree can no longer change in future iterations.

Another degree of freedom in the design of interactive parse selection is the exact information that the human annotator provides about occurrences of phrases. The most obvious choice would be a triple consisting of the beginning, the end, and the syntactic category ('noun phrase', 'prepositional phrase', etc.). If desired, the category could be omitted or underspecified. This approach has been implemented for example by Sánchez-Sáez et al. (2009; 2010).

The main motivation for interactive parse selection is that it saves the human annotator manual labour, by automatic prediction of at least parts of parses that very often are correct. With the criterion of minimizing human effort, it not clear however that the optimal design of interactive parse selection is of the kind outlined above, with a strictly left-to-right strategy, and with specification of both the beginning and the end for each corrected phrase. One objection against the left-to-right strategy is that errors may be temporarily overlooked. Typical implementations may allow backtracking to deal with this situation, but backtracking entails that work needs to be redone.

One objection against having to specify the beginning as well as the end of a corrected phrase is firstly that this requires more mouse clicks or keyboard strokes than if, say, only the correct beginning of a phrase were specified. Furthermore, for long and complex sentences, it may be tedious to determine both phrase boundaries.

For these reasons we explore a less rigid alternative, namely to allow the human annotator to specify only the beginning of a phrase, or only the end of a phrase. This is formalized in the remainder of this paper as an unmatched open bracket, or an unmatched close bracket. Such a bracket may be labelled with a category or not. Parse selection is not constrained to be unidirectional, and at each iteration, brackets can be placed at arbitrary positions in the input sentence, and thereupon the most likely parse is (re-)computed that is consistent with the provided brackets so far.

In our notation, the unmatched brackets are written as square brackets. We refer to them as 'unmatched' because the user need not specify both the beginning and end of a phrase. However, users *may* specify both the beginning of a phrase and the end of the same phrase, by a square open and a square close bracket, if they so choose.

Next to unmatched brackets, we also allow matched brackets in the input, which in our notation are written as round brackets. These must always occur in pairs of one open bracket and one close bracket, specified together by the user. Unlike square brackets, pairs of round brackets must be properly nested. As square brackets, round brackets may be labelled by categories or may be unlabelled. Sentences enriched with matched and unmatched brackets will be called *partially bracketed* strings.

As we will informally illustrate in the following section, parsing of partially bracketed strings by context-free grammars causes particular problems. The main issue is spurious ambiguity, by which one input string may be parsed in different ways all corresponding to one and the same parse tree by the input grammar. Where the language model is used to compute the most likely parse, performance may suffer from having one computation computed in more than one way. A more serious consequence is that computation of inside probabilities is hindered by subparses being represented more than once. Also n-best parsing algorithms no longer work correctly without further refinements.

The main contribution of this article is to offer a solution to avoiding all spurious ambiguity. Our theoretical framework is that of order-preserving synchronous context-free grammars, to be summarized in Section 3. With this machinery, mappings between unbracketed, bracketed and partially bracketed strings will be presented in Section 4. A sketch of a proof that spurious ambiguity is avoided as claimed is the subject of Section 5. The actual parsing process, which is based on Earley's algorithm, is presented in Section 6.

Section 7 discusses an implementation. The practicality of our approach is demonstrated by experiments measuring running time. In addition, some possible optimizations are proposed. We end our paper with conclusions, in Section 8.

The issue of avoiding spurious ambiguity was considered before by (Wieling et al., 2005). Our treatment differs in that the solution is at the same time more precise, in terms of synchronous CFGs rather than grammar transformations, and more succinct, using simpler constraints on allowable structures. Also novel is our parsing algorithm, which is versed towards practical application. Earlier work on partially bracketed strings, such as that by Pereira and Schabes (1992), has involved matching brackets only.

2 Informal Illustration

Let us consider the following example context-free grammar:

$$\begin{array}{lcl} NP & \rightarrow & Adj\ NP \mid N \\ Adj & \rightarrow & \textbf{big} \mid \textbf{angry} \\ N & \rightarrow & \textbf{dog} \end{array}$$

(The vertical bar separates alternative right-hand sides for the same left-hand side nonterminal symbol.)

The language of all fully bracketed strings is generated by the following grammar:

$$\begin{array}{lcl} NP & \rightarrow & (_{NP}\ Adj\ NP\ )_{NP} \mid (_{NP}\ N\ )_{NP} \\ Adj & \rightarrow & (_{Adj}\ \textbf{big}\ )_{Adj} \mid (_{Adj}\ \textbf{angry}\ )_{Adj} \\ N & \rightarrow & (_{N}\ \textbf{dog}\ )_{N} \end{array}$$

We can make such bracketed strings less precise by:

1. omitting labels of categories at brackets, and/or
2. replacing a matching pair of round brackets by a pair of square brackets, of which zero, one or both may then be omitted.

For example, we can 'fuzzify' a fully bracketed string:

$$(_{NP}\ (_{Adj}\ \textbf{big}\ )_{Adj}\ (_{NP}\ (_{Adj}\ \textbf{angry}\ )_{Adj}\ (_{NP}\ (_{N}\ \textbf{dog}\ )_{N}\ )_{NP}\ )_{NP}\ )_{NP} \quad (1)$$

by a partially bracketed string:

$$\textbf{big angry (dog)]}_{NP} \quad (2)$$

Note there is little point in omitting the label of one round bracket from a pair of matching brackets without also omitting it from the other bracket in the pair. This is because the one omitted label could be reconstructed from the remaining label by casual inspection of the string.

The language of all partially bracketed strings can thus be naively specified by a context-free grammar where next to a rule of the form:

$$A \rightarrow (_A\ \alpha\ )_A$$

we also have a rule of the form:

$$A \rightarrow (\ \alpha\ )$$

and nine rules of the form:

$$A \rightarrow y^{(l)}\ \alpha\ y^{(r)}$$

where $y^{(l)}$ is one of $[_A$, $[$, or the empty string ε, and $y^{(r)}$ is one of $]_A$, $]$, or ε.

However, with the resulting grammar, the partially bracketed string in (2) can be parsed in five different ways, four of which are illustrated in Figure 1. The trees in (a) and (b) differ in the placement of $]_{NP}$ to the right of a right-most path in the parse tree with more than one node labelled *NP*; in fact, there are three different nodes to which $]_{NP}$ can be attached. The trees in (c) and (d) differ from those in (a) and (b) in the placement of the pair of unlabelled round brackets on either side of a path in the parse tree involving only unit rules (that is, rules with right-hand sides of length one).

Because the original grammar was unambiguous, the existence of five different parse trees for the partially bracketed string should be seen as spurious ambiguity, given the task of finding parses of "**big angry dog**" that are consistent with the collection of brackets inserted into that string. As we will explain in more detail later in this article, this problem of spurious ambiguity is avoided by demanding that brackets occur as high as possible. In the example, this means that the round brackets are placed around "*N*" as in (c) or (d) rather than around "**dog**" as in (a) or (b). Further, $]_{NP}$ is attached to the highest possible node labelled *NP* as in (d) rather than (c). Thus, our parser would return only the tree in (d). It is not difficult to see there is always a unique way of placing brackets as high as possible.

3 Preliminaries

In order to formalize the main problem and its solution, we turn to a restricted type of synchronous context-free grammar (SCFG), in notation similar to that in Satta and Peserico (2005). A SCFG $\mathcal{G}$ defines a relation between a source language generated by a context-free grammar $\mathcal{G}_1$ and a target language generated by a context-free grammar $\mathcal{G}_2$. In the general case, each 'synchronous' rule in $\mathcal{G}$ has the form $\langle A \rightarrow \alpha, B \rightarrow \beta \rangle$, where $A \rightarrow \alpha$ is a rule in $\mathcal{G}_1$ and $B \rightarrow \beta$ is a rule in $\mathcal{G}_2$. The number of nonterminal symbols in α must equal that in β.

Each such synchronous rule $\langle A \rightarrow \alpha, B \rightarrow \beta \rangle$ is also associated with a bijection from the nonterminal occurrences in α to the nonterminal occurrences in β. By this bijection, one may express a reordering of constituents between source and target structures. In this paper, we will consider a restricted type of SCFG without such reordering, or put differently, the bijection implicitly maps the i-th nonterminal occurrence in α to the i-th nonterminal occurrence in β. We will call this restriction OP-SCFG (*order-preserving* SCFG).

Let $\mathcal{G}$ be an OP-SCFG as above, with S_1 the start symbol of $\mathcal{G}_1$ and S_2 the start symbol of $\mathcal{G}_2$. We first define relations $\mathcal{T}_{\mathcal{G}}^{(A,B)}$ between pairs of languages, for A a nonterminal in $\mathcal{G}_1$ and B a nonterminal in $\mathcal{G}_2$, to be the smallest relations such that:

1. existence of a synchronous rule
$$\langle A \rightarrow w_0 A_1 w_1 \cdots w_{n-1} A_m w_m, \\ B \rightarrow v_0 B_1 v_1 \cdots v_{m-1} B_m v_m \rangle \quad (3)$$
2. existence for $1 \leq i \leq m$ of strings x_i and y_i such that $x_i\ \mathcal{T}_{\mathcal{G}}^{(A_i,B_i)}\ y_i$

together imply that:

$$w_0 x_1 w_1 \cdots x_m w_m\ \mathcal{T}_{\mathcal{G}}^{(A,B)}\ v_0 y_1 v_1 \cdots y_m v_m$$

The transduction $\mathcal{T}_{\mathcal{G}}$ generated by $\mathcal{G}$ is now defined to be $\mathcal{T}_{\mathcal{G}}^{(S_1,S_2)}$.

For each 4-tuple (x, A, B, y) such that $x\ \mathcal{T}_{\mathcal{G}}^{(A,B)}\ y$ we can build at least one derivation tree that shows in reverse how $x\ \mathcal{T}_{\mathcal{G}}^{(A,B)}\ y$ was obtained. More precisely, such derivation trees can be inductively defined as follows. Let there be a synchronous rule as in (3), and let each t_i, with $1 \leq i \leq m$, be a derivation tree associated with a 4-tuple (x_i, A_i, B_i, y_i) such that $x_i\ \mathcal{T}_{\mathcal{G}}^{(A_i,B_i)}\ y_i$.

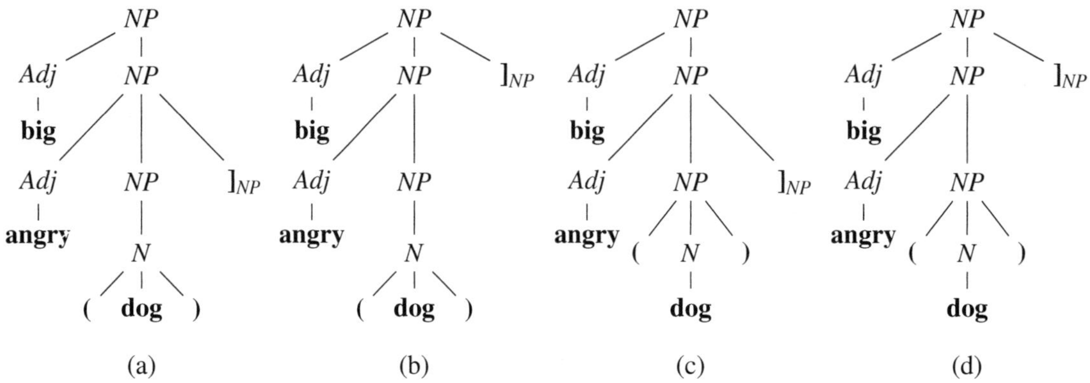

Figure 1: Four parses of the same partially bracketed string.

Then a derivation tree can be constructed for the 4-tuple (x, A, B, y), where $x = w_0 x_1 w_1 \cdots x_m w_m$ and $y = v_0 y_1 v_1 \cdots y_m v_m$, by a root node labelled by the above synchronous rule, and its (ordered) children are the roots of t_i.

Similar to the notion of ambiguity in CFGs, we say that a pair (x, y) is ambiguous for a fixed SCFG if more than one derivation tree can be associated with the 4-tuple (x, S_1, S_2, y). We say the SCFG is ambiguous if there is at least one ambiguous pair (x, y). For an example of these concepts, see the following section.

In this paper, we will assume there are no epsilon rules, i.e., rules with empty right-hand sides.

4 Bracketed and Partially Bracketed Strings

The parsing problem for a CFG $\mathcal{G}$ can be described in terms of a transduction from unbracketed strings to fully bracketed strings, by means of the OP-SCFG $\mathcal{G}_{bracket}$ that has one synchronous rule:

$$\langle A \rightarrow \alpha, A \rightarrow (_A\ \alpha\ )_A \rangle$$

for each rule $A \rightarrow \alpha$ in $\mathcal{G}$. The strings y such that $x\ \mathcal{T}_{\mathcal{G}_{bracket}}\ y$ each describe one parse of x according to the input CFG $\mathcal{G}$.

A naive transduction to fuzzify fully bracketed strings can be defined in terms of a SCFG $\mathcal{G}_{naive}$ of which the synchronous rules are, for each rule $A \rightarrow \alpha$ in the input grammar:

- $\langle A \rightarrow (_A\ \alpha\ )_A, A \rightarrow (_A\ \alpha\ )_A \rangle$,
- $\langle A \rightarrow (_A\ \alpha\ )_A; A \rightarrow (\ \alpha\ ) \rangle$,
- $\langle A \rightarrow (_A\ \alpha\ )_A, A \rightarrow y^{(l)}\ \alpha\ y^{(r)} \rangle$, for all nine combinations of $y^{(l)} \in \{[_A, [, \varepsilon\}$ and $y^{(r)} \in \{]_A,], \varepsilon\}$.

The problem with spurious ambiguity that was the subject of discussion in Section 2 can now be expressed in formal terms, as ambiguity of SCFG $\mathcal{G}_{naive}$. Concretely, one and the same fully bracketed string can be mapped to one and the same partially bracketed string in different ways. This is particularly relevant if the transduction is used in reverse, mapping a given partially bracketed string to fully bracketed strings, or in other words, building parse trees according to the input grammar. As explained in the introduction, the problems this causes include increased running time, and failure of probabilistic models and n-best algorithms.

To illustrate this, let us revisit the example from Figure 1, which corresponds to the following input/output pair:

$$\begin{aligned}(\ &(_{NP}\ (_{Adj}\ \textbf{big}\ )_{Adj}\ (_{NP}\ (_{Adj}\ \textbf{angry}\ )_{Adj} \\ &\qquad (_{NP}\ (_N\ \textbf{dog}\ )_N\ )_{NP}\ )_{NP})_{NP}\ , \\ &\textbf{big angry (dog)}\ ]_{NP}\ )\end{aligned} \quad (4)$$

With $\mathcal{G}_{naive}$, there are five different derivation trees through which this pair can be obtained. For example, the tree in Figure 1 (d), which we regard as the preferred one, corresponds to application of the following rules:

$\langle\ NP \rightarrow\ (_{NP}\ Adj\ NP\ )_{NP}\ ,\ NP \rightarrow\ Adj\ NP\ ]_{NP}\ \rangle$,
$\langle\ Adj \rightarrow\ (_{Adj}\ \textbf{big}\ )_{Adj}\ ,\ Adj \rightarrow\ \textbf{big}\ \rangle$,
$\langle\ NP \rightarrow\ (_{NP}\ Adj\ NP\ )_{NP}\ ,\ NP \rightarrow\ Adj\ NP\ \rangle$,
$\langle\ Adj \rightarrow\ (_{Adj}\ \textbf{angry}\ )_{Adj}\ ,\ Adj \rightarrow\ \textbf{angry}\ \rangle$,
$\langle\ NP \rightarrow\ (_{NP}\ N\ )_{NP}\ ,\ NP \rightarrow\ (\ N\ )\ \rangle$,
$\langle\ N \rightarrow\ (_N\ \textbf{dog}\ )_N\ ,\ N \rightarrow\ \textbf{dog}\ \rangle$

As solution we propose a refined SCFG $\mathcal{G}_{fuzzy}$. It specifies the same transduction as $\mathcal{G}_{naive}$, but now without ambiguity. Intuitively, we ensure that any brackets in a partially bracketed string are attached as high as possible. Because there can be at most one way of doing this that corresponds to a fully bracketed string, the implication is that there can be at most one derivation tree for each combination of a source string x and a target string y.

The SCFG $\mathcal{G}_{fuzzy}$ conceptually keeps records of where brackets are attached by replacing nonterminals A in all possible ways by nonterminals $A(s^{(l)}, s^{(r)})$, where the values $s^{(l)}$ and $s^{(r)}$ are either ϵ or a bracket. If such a value is a bracket, that means that this bracket was attached to the nearest descendant to which it could be attached, in the left-most (for $s^{(l)}$) or right-most (for $s^{(r)}$) path downwards in the parse tree. The definition of $\mathcal{G}_{fuzzy}$ disallow situations where this bracket could be moved to the current node, because that would imply that the bracket is not attached as high as possible. Note that there is a finite number of choices for $s^{(l)}$ and $s^{(r)}$, so that the rules are still within context-free power.

The synchronous rules of $\mathcal{G}_{fuzzy}$ are specified in Table 1. As expressed by (5) and (6), the round brackets from the source language can be replaced with unlabelled or square brackets. If in the target language there is an open round bracket, either labelled or unlabelled, then the close bracket must be of the same form, and vice versa.

As is clear from (7), only nonterminals are extended with two arguments. Terminals in Σ are copied unchanged from source language to target language. The first line of (8) says that if the current rule is a unit rule, and if a pair of round brackets were attached to a node further down, possibly along more occurrences of unit rules, then there must be a reason why these brackets cannot be attached to the current node, and the only reason can be that other brackets $y^{(l)} \neq \varepsilon$ or $y^{(r)} \neq \varepsilon$ are already attached to the current node. The second and third lines similarly exclude situations where a square bracket was placed further down, while it could be attached to the current node.

The information about brackets attached to the current node, or brackets from further down if no brackets are attached to the current node, is passed on bottom-up, as expressed by (9). For technical reasons, we need to augment the grammar with a new start symbol, as shown in (10).

5 Correctness

Two properties of $\mathcal{G}_{fuzzy}$ are of interest. The first is that $\mathcal{T}_{\mathcal{G}_{fuzzy}}$ equals $\mathcal{T}_{\mathcal{G}_{naive}}$, and the second is that $\mathcal{G}_{fuzzy}$ is unambiguous. The first proof is tedious, but the intuition is simple: if we are given a derivation tree associated with 4-tuple (x, S, S, y) where $x\ \mathcal{T}_{\mathcal{G}_{naive}}\ y$, for a fully bracketed string x and partially bracketed string y, then we can systematically change this derivation tree, to preserve x and y but move brackets to be attached as high as possible in the parse tree of y. With this attachment of brackets, we can straightforwardly map this derivation tree into a derivation tree associated with $(x, S^\dagger, S^\dagger, y)$ where $x\ \mathcal{T}_{\mathcal{G}_{fuzzy}}\ y$, ensuring that the constraint in (8) is satisfied. Conversely, if $x\ \mathcal{T}_{\mathcal{G}_{fuzzy}}\ y$ then clearly $x\ \mathcal{T}_{\mathcal{G}_{naive}}\ y$.

The unambiguity of $\mathcal{G}_{fuzzy}$ can be argued as follows. First, if $\mathcal{G}_{fuzzy}$ were ambiguous, then there would be a pair (A, B) of nonterminals and a pair (x, y) of strings, with the length of xy minimal and AB minimal according to some fixed lexicographical ordering, such that two or more different derivation trees can be associated with 4-tuple (x, A, B, y) where $x\ \mathcal{T}^{(A,B)}_{\mathcal{G}_{fuzzy}}\ y$. Because of the minimality of xy and AB, the two derivation trees must differ in the synchronous rule at the root, each of which must be of the form in (5). The remainder of the proof consists of a large number of case distinctions, and in each the task is to show a contradiction, by violation of (8). For example, suppose y starts with [and the two synchronous rules differ in that one has $y^{(l)} =$ [and the second has $y^{(l)} = \varepsilon$. Then in the second case, the [must be generated by a rule further down in the derivation tree, which would violate (8).

6 Parsing

In this section we simplify the discussion by looking only at the context-free rules in the right parts of the synchronous rules defined in Table 1. These rules generate the right projection of $\mathcal{T}_{\mathcal{G}_{fuzzy}}$. We will discuss a recognition algorithm on the basis of these rules, with the tacit assumption that this can be extended to a parsing algorithm, to obtain fully bracketed strings as output, for a given partially bracketed strings as input.

Naively, one could use any parsing algorithm instantiated to the set of rules in the right parts of (5). For example, one could use the classical Earley algorithm (Earley, 1970; Stolcke, 1995). This manipulates items of the form $[\![\langle A \rightarrow \alpha \bullet$

For given CFG $\mathcal{G}$, with set N of nonterminals, set Σ of terminals, and start symbol $S \in N$, the SCFG $\mathcal{G}_{fuzzy}$ has one synchronous rule:

$$\langle\, A \rightarrow (_A\, X_1 \cdots X_m\,)_A,\;\; A(s_0^{(l)}, s_0^{(r)}) \rightarrow y^{(l)}\, Y_1 \cdots Y_m\, y^{(r)} \,\rangle \tag{5}$$

for each rule $A \rightarrow X_1 \cdots X_m$ in $\mathcal{G}$, for each choice of the pair:

$$(y^{(l)}, y^{(r)}) \in \{((_A,)_A), ((,))\} \cup \{[_A, [, \varepsilon\} \times \{]_A,], \varepsilon\} \tag{6}$$

and for each choice of pairs:

$$(s_i^{(l)}, s_i^{(r)}) \in \{((_B,)_B) \mid B \in N\} \cup \{((,))\} \cup (\{[_B \mid B \in N\} \cup \{[, \varepsilon\}) \times (\{]_B \mid B \in N\} \cup \{], \varepsilon\})$$

for each i ($1 \leq i \leq m$) such that $X_i \in N$, and $(s_i^{(l)}, s_i^{(r)}) = (\varepsilon, \varepsilon)$ for each i such that $X_i \in \Sigma$, and:

$$Y_i = \begin{cases} X_i(s_i^{(l)}, s_i^{(r)}) & \text{if } X_i \in N \\ X_i & \text{if } X_i \in \Sigma \end{cases} \tag{7}$$

under the following constraints:

$$\begin{array}{l} m = 1 \wedge (s_1^{(l)}, s_m^{(r)}) \in \{((_A,)_A), ((,))\} \;\rightarrow\; (y^{(l)} \neq \varepsilon \;\vee y^{(r)} \neq \varepsilon) \;\wedge \\ (s_1^{(l)} = [_A \vee s_1^{(l)} = [) \;\rightarrow\; y^{(l)} \neq \varepsilon \;\wedge \\ (s_m^{(r)} =]_A \vee s_m^{(r)} =]) \;\rightarrow\; y^{(r)} \neq \varepsilon \end{array} \tag{8}$$

and:

$$(s_0^{(l)}, s_0^{(r)}) = \begin{cases} (y^{(l)}, y^{(r)}) & \text{if } (y^{(l)}, y^{(r)}) \in \{((_A,)_A), ((,))\} \\ (s_1^{(l)}, s_m^{(r)}) & \text{if } m = 1 \wedge y^{(l)} = y^{(r)} = \varepsilon \;\wedge (s_1^{(l)}, s_m^{(r)}) \in \{((_B,)_B) \mid B \in N \setminus \{A\}\} \\ (s^{(l)}, s^{(r)}) & \text{otherwise, where:} \\ & \quad s^{(l)} = \begin{cases} y^{(l)} & \text{if } y^{(l)} \in \{[_A, [\} \\ s_1^{(l)} & \text{if } y^{(l)} = \varepsilon \wedge s_1^{(l)} \in \{[_B \mid B \in N \setminus \{A\}\} \\ \varepsilon & \text{otherwise} \end{cases} \\ & \quad s^{(r)} = \begin{cases} y^{(r)} & \text{if } y^{(r)} \in \{]_A,]\} \\ s_m^{(r)} & \text{if } y^{(r)} = \varepsilon \wedge s_m^{(r)} \in \{]_B \mid B \in N \setminus \{A\}\} \\ \varepsilon & \text{otherwise} \end{cases} \end{cases} \tag{9}$$

$\mathcal{G}_{fuzzy}$ further has one synchronous rule:

$$\langle\, S^\dagger \rightarrow S,\;\; S^\dagger \rightarrow S(s^{(l)}, s^{(r)}) \,\rangle \tag{10}$$

for each choice of the pair:

$$(s^{(l)}, s^{(r)}) \in \{((_B,)_B) \mid B \in N\} \cup \{((,))\} \cup (\{[_B \mid B \in N\} \cup \{[, \varepsilon\}) \times (\{]_B \mid B \in N\} \cup \{], \varepsilon\})$$

where $S^\dagger$ is a new symbol.

Table 1: The SCFG $\mathcal{G}_{fuzzy}$ constructed out of CFG $\mathcal{G}$.

$\beta\rangle, i, j]\!]$, which means that of a rule $A \to \alpha\beta$ from the grammar, the first part α has been processed and was found to generate the substring $a_{i+1} \cdots a_j$ of a fixed input string $a_1 \cdots a_n$.

The problem is that there is a very large number of rules as in the right parts of (5). This number is in fact exponential in the length m of the largest rule from the original grammar $\mathcal{G}$. Casual inspection of the constraints on the rules in Table 1 reveals however that only the values of $s_0^{(l)}$, $s_0^{(r)}$, $y^{(l)}$, $s_1^{(l)}$, $s_m^{(r)}$, $y^{(r)}$ are ever used in the current rule. The values of $s_i^{(l)}$ for $1 < i \leq m$ and the values of $s_i^{(r)}$ for $1 \leq i < m$ can be safely ignored.

We therefore let the parser manipulate items of the form $[\![\langle A(s_0^{(l)}, s_0^{(r)}) \to \alpha' \bullet \beta'\rangle, [s_1^{(l)}, s_m^{(r)}], i, j]\!]$ where $\alpha'\beta' = y^{(l)}; \alpha; y^{(r)}$ and $A \to \alpha$ is a rule in $\mathcal{G}$. Each such item can be seen as an abbreviation of an item for the Earley algorithm for the right parts in (5), leaving out fields that are not useful. The values of $s_0^{(l)}$, $s_0^{(r)}$, $y^{(l)}$, $s_1^{(l)}$, $s_m^{(r)}$, $y^{(r)}$ are initially the empty string, and are gradually filled in as these values become known.

The recognition algorithm is presented as deduction system in Table 2. Step (11) is the initialization step of Earley's algorithm and Step (12) straightforwardly corresponds to the predictor step. Steps (14), (15) and (17) correspond to the scanner step of Earley's algorithm. In the side condition of (17), the constraints on the allowable combinations of $y^{(l)}$, $s_1^{(l)}$, $s_m^{(r)}$, $y^{(r)}$ are checked, and $s_0^{(l)}$ and $s_0^{(r)}$ are determined on the basis of the other values.

The steps (13) and (16) have no direct equivalent in Earley's original algorithm. They are motivated by the intention to give uniform treatment to context-free rules with and without brackets. Step (18) straightforwardly corresponds to the completer step of Earley's algorithm, given the abbreviated form of our items, as explained above. Acceptance is expressed by step (19).

Deduction systems like this have a common algorithmic interpretation; see for example McAllester (2002). The time complexity of our algorithm is $\mathcal{O}(n^3 \cdot |\mathcal{G}|^2)$, where $|\mathcal{G}|$ is the size of the input grammar. This can be brought down as usual to $\mathcal{O}(n^3 \cdot |\mathcal{G}|)$ using techniques from Graham et al. (1980), which bring the complexity in line with the best known practical parsing algorithms for context-free grammars. Note that if the values of $s_0^{(l)}$, $s_0^{(r)}$, $y^{(l)}$, $s_1^{(l)}$, $s_m^{(r)}$, $y^{(r)}$ in an item $[\![\langle A(s_0^{(l)}, s_0^{(r)}) \to \alpha' \bullet \beta'\rangle, [s_1^{(l)}, s_m^{(r)}], i, j]\!]$, with $\alpha'\beta' = y^{(l)}; \alpha; y^{(r)}$, are anything other than ϵ, then they are uniquely determined by i and j. It is for this reason that the number of possible labelled and unlabelled brackets does not contribute an extra factor to the time complexity.

The recognition algorithm can also be straightforwardly extended to compute the most likely parse or the inside probability, similarly to how this is done by Jelinek et al. (1992). Note that unambiguity is essential in the latter case. The probabilities manipulated by the parser would then be based on the probabilities of rules from the original grammar, similarly to how this is normally done in probabilistic parsing algorithms based on Earley's algorithm (Stolcke, 1995; Nederhof, 2003).

7 Experiments

We have implemented the construction from Table 1 and the parsing algorithm from Table 2. Our aim was to assess the feasibility in practical terms. The latter algorithm was based on an implementation of the standard Earley algorithm, which we used as a base line. The implementation language is C++ and the experiments were performed on a laptop computer with a 2.66 GHz Intel Core 2 Duo processor.

First, a context-free grammar was extracted from sections 2-21 of the Penn Treebank, with NoTransform and NoEmpties as in (Klein and Manning, 2001), and unary rules were collapsed. This grammar has 84613 rules, 372 nonterminals and 44389 terminals (words). With this grammar, we parsed the (unbracketed) sentences from section 23 that had length 10 or less. Of these, 92 sentences were outside the language generated by the grammar and were discarded. Parsing of the remaining 178 sentences using the standard Earley algorithm took 8m27s in total.

Next, we tried to construct a context-free grammar that generates partially bracketed sentences without spurious ambiguity, as the right-projection of the construction in Table 1. Predictably, this was found to be infeasible for any but very small subsets of our input grammar, because of the exponential behaviour in the length of right-hand sides.

Lastly, the extended Earley algorithm from Table 2 was applied on the same 178 sentences, but now in partially bracketed form. We started with the fully bracketed sentences, as they appear in

Initialize

$$\frac{}{\llbracket\langle S(\varepsilon,\varepsilon) \rightarrow \bullet; \alpha; \rangle, [\varepsilon,\varepsilon], 0, 0\rrbracket} \left\{(S \rightarrow \alpha) \in \mathcal{G}\right. \tag{11}$$

Predict

$$\frac{\llbracket\langle A(\varepsilon,\varepsilon) \rightarrow y^{(l)}; \alpha \bullet B\beta; \rangle, [s_1^{(l)}, s_m^{(r)}], i, j\rrbracket}{\llbracket\langle B(\varepsilon,\varepsilon) \rightarrow \bullet; \gamma; \rangle, [\varepsilon,\varepsilon], i, i\rrbracket} \left\{(B \rightarrow \gamma) \in \mathcal{G}\right. \tag{12}$$

No open

$$\frac{\llbracket\langle A(\varepsilon,\varepsilon) \rightarrow \bullet; \alpha; \rangle, [\varepsilon,\varepsilon], i, i\rrbracket}{\llbracket\langle A(\varepsilon,\varepsilon) \rightarrow ; \bullet\alpha; \rangle, [\varepsilon,\varepsilon], i, i\rrbracket} \tag{13}$$

Open

$$\frac{\llbracket\langle A(\varepsilon,\varepsilon) \rightarrow \bullet; \alpha; \rangle, [\varepsilon,\varepsilon], i, i\rrbracket}{\llbracket\langle A(\varepsilon,\varepsilon) \rightarrow y^{(l)}; \bullet\alpha; \rangle, [\varepsilon,\varepsilon], i, i+1\rrbracket} \left\{y^{(l)} = a_{i+1} \in \{\mathbf{(}_A, \mathbf{(}, \mathbf{[}_A, \mathbf{[}\}\right. \tag{14}$$

Scan

$$\frac{\llbracket\langle A(\varepsilon,\varepsilon) \rightarrow y^{(l)}; \alpha \bullet a\beta; \rangle, [s_1^{(l)}, s_m^{(r)}], i, j\rrbracket}{\llbracket\langle A(\varepsilon,\varepsilon) \rightarrow y^{(l)}; \alpha a \bullet \beta; \rangle, [s_1^{(l)}, s_m^{(r)}], i, j+1\rrbracket} \left\{a = a_{j+1}\right. \tag{15}$$

No close

$$\frac{\llbracket\langle A(\varepsilon,\varepsilon) \rightarrow y^{(l)}; \alpha\bullet; \rangle, [s_1^{(l)}, s_m^{(r)}], i, j\rrbracket}{\llbracket\langle A(s_0^{(l)}, s_0^{(r)}) \rightarrow y^{(l)}; \alpha; \bullet\rangle, [s_1^{(l)}, s_m^{(r)}], i, j\rrbracket} \begin{cases} \text{the constraint in (8) with } y^{(r)} = \varepsilon \\ (s_0^{(l)}, s_0^{(r)}) \text{ defined by (9)} \end{cases} \tag{16}$$

Close

$$\frac{\llbracket\langle A(\varepsilon,\varepsilon) \rightarrow y^{(l)}; \alpha\bullet; \rangle, [s_1^{(l)}, s_m^{(r)}], i, j\rrbracket}{\llbracket\langle A(s_0^{(l)}, s_0^{(r)}) \rightarrow y^{(l)}; \alpha; y^{(r)}\bullet\rangle, [s_1^{(l)}, s_m^{(r)}], i, j+1\rrbracket} \begin{cases} y^{(r)} = a_{j+1} \in \{\mathbf{)}_A, \mathbf{)}, \mathbf{]}_A, \mathbf{]}\} \\ \text{the constraint in (8)} \\ (s_0^{(l)}, s_0^{(r)}) \text{ defined by (9)} \end{cases} \tag{17}$$

Complete

$$\frac{\begin{array}{c}\llbracket\langle A(\varepsilon,\varepsilon) \rightarrow y^{(l)}; \alpha \bullet B\beta; \rangle, [s_1^{(l)}, s_m^{(r)}], i, j\rrbracket \\ \llbracket\langle B(t_0^{(l)}, t_0^{(r)}) \rightarrow z^{(l)}; \gamma; z^{(r)}\bullet\rangle, [t_1^{(l)}, t_{m'}^{(r)}], j, k\rrbracket\end{array}}{\llbracket\langle A(\varepsilon,\varepsilon) \rightarrow y^{(l)}; \alpha B \bullet \beta; \rangle, [u_1^{(l)}, u_m^{(r)}], i, k\rrbracket} \begin{cases} u_1^{(l)} = \begin{cases} t_0^{(l)} & \text{if } \alpha = \varepsilon \\ s_1^{(l)} & \text{otherwise} \end{cases} \\ u_m^{(r)} = \begin{cases} t_0^{(r)} & \text{if } \beta = \varepsilon \\ s_m^{(r)} & \text{otherwise} \end{cases} \end{cases} \tag{18}$$

Accept

$$\frac{\llbracket\langle S(s_0^{(l)}, s_0^{(r)}) \rightarrow y^{(l)}; \gamma; y^{(r)}\bullet\rangle, [s_1^{(l)}, s_m^{(r)}], 0, n\rrbracket}{\textit{accept}} \tag{19}$$

Table 2: Recognition of partially bracketed strings.

p	time
0.0	25m33s
0.2	68m08s
0.4	51m07s
0.6	34m36s
0.8	21m02s
1.0	11m48s

Table 3: CPU time for recognition of sentences of length ≤ 10 from section 23 of the Penn Treebank, for a varying probability p.

the treebank, and then randomly omitted a varying percentage of brackets and category labels.

This process of 'fuzzifying' a fully bracketed sentence proceeds in stages, with one potential step turning a bracket pair $(_A\ )_A$ into $[_A\ ]_A$. If this step does not happen, there is another potential step turning $(_A\ )_A$ into ( ). For each labelled square bracket individually, a step may remove the label, which is then optionally followed by a step removing the bracket altogether. The process is parameterized with a value p, which expresses the probability that a step of fuzzifying does not happen. Hence, $p = 0$ means that all annotation is removed and $p = 1$ means that all brackets and labels are kept.

The results are given in Table 3. The first row of the table corresponds to the sentences in unannotated form. The running time is higher than the baseline of the standard Earley algorithm. This was to be expected, as there are some extra steps in Table 2, introduced for handling of brackets, and these steps are performed even if the input contains no brackets at all. Nonetheless, the running time is of the same order of magnitude.

In the next few rows of the table we see that the running time increases further. Again, this is to be expected, as the presence of brackets induces multiple instances of parsing items where there would be only one in the unbracketed case. When close to 100 % of the brackets are maintained, the running time again decreases. This is because the brackets reduce ambiguity.

One may object that the parsing of fully bracketed sentences should take close to 0 seconds, as those sentences are already parsed. However, we have not introduced any further optimizations to the Earley algorithm apart from those presented in Table 2, and the predictive nature of the algorithm leads to many steps creating different partial analyses at an open bracket of which all but one is discarded upon finding the matching close bracket.

The main objective was to investigate to which extent parsing of partially bracketed structures is possible, under the constraint that no spurious ambiguity should arise. Our experiments show that the running time is of the same order of magnitude as parsing of unbracketed strings using the standard Earley algorithm. Further refinements can be expected to reduce the running time.

For example, we found a straightforward optimization that is realized by letting parts of the check from condition (8) happen as soon as possible, rather than delaying them until completion of an item in (16) or (17). In concrete terms, the compatibility of an open bracket $y^{(l)}$ and the value of $s_1^{(l)}$ coming from the first member in the right-hand side can be checked as soon as that first member is known. This and other optimizations lead to a more involved formulation however, and for presentational reasons we abstain from further discussion.

Further note that the general ideas that led to Table 2 starting from the construction in Table 1 can as easily be used to derive other parsing algorithms for partially bracketed strings, using any other parsing strategy such as the bottom-up Earley algorithm (Sikkel, 1997) and left-corner parsing (Rosenkrantz and Stearns, 1970).

8 Conclusions

This paper has introduced a sound and elegant theoretical framework for processing partially bracketed strings. That is, an input string may contain any combination of matched or unmatched and labelled or unlabelled brackets.

Our theory, which uses synchronous CFGs, led us to a procedure based on Earley's algorithm. Its effectiveness was shown in experiments using a practical grammar. Despite having implemented few optimizations, we found that the time measurements show promising results, and considerable speed-ups may be expected by further refinement of the implementation. Use for the purpose of interactive parse selection therefore seems feasible. Further work will be needed to determine to which extent linguists benefit from being able to specify partially bracketed structures.

Acknowledgements

This work is partially supported by the Spanish MICINN under the MIPRCV Consolider Ingenio 2010 (CSD2007-00018), MITTRAL (TIN2009-14633-C03-01), and Prometeo (PROMETEO/2009/014) research projects, and the FPU fellowship AP2006-01363.

References

S. Barrachina, O. Bender, F. Casacuberta, J. Civera, E. Cubel, S. Khadivi, A. Lagarda, H. Ney, J. Tomás, E. Vidal, and J.-M. Vilar. 2009. Statistical approaches to computer-assisted translation. *Computational Linguistics*, 35(1):3–28.

J. Earley. 1970. An efficient context-free parsing algorithm. *Communications of the ACM*, 13(2):94–102, February.

S.L. Graham, M.A. Harrison, and W.L. Ruzzo. 1980. An improved context-free recognizer. *ACM Transactions on Programming Languages and Systems*, 2:415–462.

F. Jelinek, J.D. Lafferty, and R.L. Mercer. 1992. Basic methods of probabilistic context free grammars. In P. Laface and R. De Mori, editors, *Speech Recognition and Understanding — Recent Advances, Trends and Applications*, pages 345–360. Springer-Verlag.

D. Klein and C.D. Manning. 2001. Parsing with treebank grammars: Empirical bounds, theoretical models, and the structure of the Penn treebank. In *39th Annual Meeting and 10th Conference of the European Chapter of the Association for Computational Linguistics, Proceedings of the Conference*, pages 338–345, Toulouse, France, July.

M.P. Marcus, B. Santorini, and M.A. Marcinkiewicz. 1993. Building a large annotated corpus of English: The Penn treebank. *Computational Linguistics*, 19(2):313–330.

D. McAllester. 2002. On the complexity analysis of static analyses. *Journal of the ACM*, 49(4):512–537.

M.-J. Nederhof. 2003. Weighted deductive parsing and Knuth's algorithm. *Computational Linguistics*, 29(1):135–143.

F. Pereira and Y. Schabes. 1992. Inside-outside reestimation from partially bracketed corpora. In *30th Annual Meeting of the Association for Computational Linguistics, Proceedings of the Conference*, pages 128–135, Newark, Delaware, USA, June–July.

D.J. Rosenkrantz and R.E. Stearns. 1970. Properties of deterministic top-down grammars. *Information and Control*, 17:226–256.

R. Sánchez-Sáez, J.A. Sánchez, and J.M. Benedí. 2009. Interactive predictive parsing. In *Proceedings of the 11th International Conference on Parsing Technologies*, pages 222–225, Paris, France, October.

R. Sánchez-Sáez, J.A. Sánchez, and J.M. Benedí. 2010. Confidence measures for error discrimination in an interactive predictive parsing framework. In *The 23rd International Conference on Computational Linguistics, Posters Volume*, pages 1220–1228, Beijing, China, August.

G. Satta and E. Peserico. 2005. Some computational complexity results for synchronous context-free grammars. In *Human Language Technology Conference and Conference on Empirical Methods in Natural Language Processing*, pages 803–810.

K. Sikkel. 1997. *Parsing Schemata*. Springer-Verlag.

A. Stolcke. 1995. An efficient probabilistic context-free parsing algorithm that computes prefix probabilities. *Computational Linguistics*, 21(2):167–201.

M. Wieling, M.-J. Nederhof, and G. Van Noord. 2005. Parsing partially bracketed input. In *Computational Linguistics in the Netherlands*, pages 1–16.

Detecting Dependency Parse Errors with Minimal Resources

Markus Dickinson and **Amber Smith**
Indiana University
Bloomington, IN USA
{md7,smithamj}@indiana.edu

Abstract

To detect errors in automatically-obtained dependency parses, we take a grammar-based approach. In particular, we develop methods that incorporate n-grams of different lengths and use information about possible parse revisions. Using our methods allows annotators to focus on problematic parses, with the potential to find over half the parse errors by examining only 20% of the data, as we demonstrate. A key result is that methods using a small gold grammar outperform methods using much larger grammars containing noise. To perform annotation error detection on newly-parsed data, one only needs a small grammar.

1 Introduction and Motivation

There is a need for high-quality dependency annotation for the training and evaluation of dependency parsers (Buchholz and Marsi, 2006), ideally large amounts of annotated data. This is a lofty goal for any language, especially languages with few, if any, annotated resources. Citing Abeillé (2003), Hwa et al. (2005) say: "it appears that acquiring 20,000-40,000 sentences — including the work of building style guides, redundant manual annotation for quality checking, and so forth – can take from four to seven years." As pointed out by Dickinson (2010), a major bottleneck in obtaining annotation involves the need for human correction, leading to the following process: 1) automatically parse corpora (van Noord and Bouma, 2009), which will contain errors, and 2) identify problematic parses for human post-processing. We develop this second step of detecting errors.

In particular, there is the problem of having little annotated data to work with, as in the cases of: lesser-resourced languages (e.g., Ambati et al., 2010; Simpson et al., 2009), new annotation schemes, and new domains with limited in-domain annotated data (e.g., Plank and van Noord, 2010). In these situations, there is a large cost to annotate data, and parsing results are worse than in cases with more annotated training data (Nivre, 2010).

We develop error detection methods based on a coarse grammar, comparing parsed rules to rules in a grammar in order to identify anomalies, as outlined in section 2. This is akin to theoretically-driven work in treebanking, where a grammar is used to guide treebank annotation (e.g., Oepen et al., 2004; Rosén et al., 2005; Bond et al., 2004), but it shares an insight with work incorporating grammatical information to improve parsing, namely that even simple grammatical information can inform parse output (e.g., Plank and van Noord, 2010; Ambati, 2010; Seeker et al., 2010).

Our methods are simple and efficient, requiring no additional parsing technology. This is especially beneficial for lesser-resourced languages, and, as we describe in section 3, makes the methods applicable to any treebanking scenario. Also, we want to know "which linguistic constructs are hard to analyze" (Goldberg and Elhadad, 2010a). Framing parse failures in terms of grammatical anomalies makes them easily interpretable, leading to quicker annotation decisions, as systematic problems can be seen at a glance (cf. Wallis, 2003; Hara et al., 2009) and perhaps also helping unearth latent theoretical decisions (cf., e.g., Leech, 2004).

We improve upon previous methods in two ways, as described in section 4. First, we streamline the different sources of information by adding the counts for all n-grams within a rule: this balances concerns over sparse data for longer n-grams with the fact that longer n-grams are more informative. Secondly, taking the scores initially assigned by our methods, we compare them with scores for possible parse revisions. This checks whether the parser could have made a better decision and more directly connects to parse revision work (e.g., Attardi and Ciaramita, 2007). As we show in section 5, these methods have the potential to help annotation quality go from, e.g., 65% accuracy to 85% by presenting annotators with cases highly likely to be erroneous. Based on the results using a noisy grammar in section 6, we also conclude that a small gold grammar is more effective than a large noisy one, a useful result since such resources can quickly be developed manually.

2 Error Detection

We build from methods for detecting *ad hoc*, or anomalous, rules in dependency parses (Dickinson, 2010). Dependency *rules* represent a head with its arguments and adjuncts, and ad hoc rules are "used for specific constructions and unlikely to be used again," indicating annotation errors and rules for ungrammaticalities (Dickinson, 2011).

To understand a dependency rule, consider figure 1 from the Talbanken05 corpus (Nilsson and Hall, 2005), for the Swedish sentence in (1).[1]

(1) Det går bara inte ihop .
it goes just not together
'It just doesn't add up.'

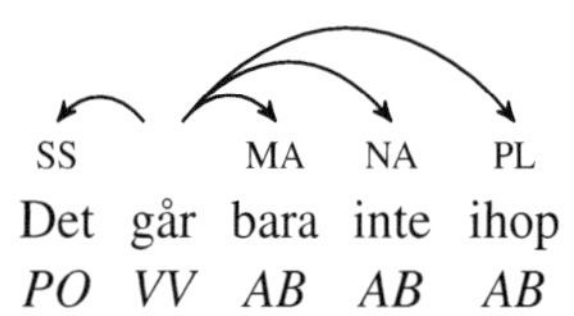

Figure 1: Dependency graph example

A grammar *rule* is comprised of a dependency relation rewriting as a head with its sequence of POS-dependent pairs, as in figure 2.

1. TOP → root ROOT:VV
2. ROOT → SS:PO VV MA:AB NA:AB PL:AB
3. SS → PO
4. MA → AB
5. NA → AB
6. PL → AB

Figure 2: Rule representation for (1)

The error detection methods work by comparing an individual parsed rule to rules in a (training) grammar. Based on comparisons to similar rules, a score is assigned to each individual element of a rule, and elements with the lowest scores are flagged. The intuition is that there should be regularities in dependency structure; non-conformity to regularities indicates a potential problem.

Dickinson (2010) compares pairs of dependency relations and POS tags (instead of using only, e.g., dependencies), and we follow suit. Relatedly, although scores can be obtained for each unit in its role as a dependent or as a head, we score elements based on how they function as dependents (see also section 2.1). In figure 2, for instance, the PO position is scored with respect to its role in rule #2, where it is a dependent, and not rule #3, where it is a head.

As Dickinson (2010) says, "We do not want to compare a rule to all grammar rules, only to those which *should* have the same valents." For a given parse rule, we can compare it to rules with the same head or rules which have the same "mother" (left-hand side (LHS)) dependency relation. We follow Dickinson (2010) in comparing to rules *either* with the same LHS or with the same head, taking the greater value of scores; this gives a rule more chances to prove its validity. The formula is given in (2), where e_i refers to the ith element in a rule ($r = e_1...e_m$) and the score is based on having the same head (h) or the same LHS (lhs).

(2) $S(e_i) = \max\{s(e_i, h), s(e_i, lhs)\}$

Most importantly, there is the method of comparison itself. Dickinson (2010) explores the *bigram* and *whole rule* methods. To see how these work, consider the bigram method for the rule in (3), with implicit START and END tags. To score AT:AJ, the bigram method counts up how often the bigrams DT:PO AT:AJ and AT:AJ VN appear in all OO (LHS) or VN (head) rules in the grammar. The whole rule method works similarly, but comparing full subsequences. We develop more general methods in section 4, with the same rough idea: rules with low scores are likely errors.

(3) OO → DT:PO **AT:AJ** VN

The formula for the bigram method is given in (4), where c = comparable item (head or LHS), and $C(x, c)$ refers to the count of x, c in the grammar. Which grammar we use is discussed in section 3.

(4) $s(e_i, c) = C(e_{i-1}\mathbf{e_i}, c) + C(\mathbf{e_i}e_{i+1}, c)$

2.1 Unary Rules

Consider again the "unary" rules in the grammar, as in SS → PO in figure 2. Dickinson (2010) included these rules, as this captures the fact that,

[1]Category definitions are in appendix A.

e.g., PO has no dependents. However, for the way rules are scored, we can remove these unary rules.

Because unary rules only contain heads, only items which are the heads in rules are actually affected by such rules. For example, with SS $\rightarrow$ PO, only PO-headed rules will be affected. But, as mentioned above, we score elements by how they function *as dependents*. We can thus ignore such rules. Removing them from a grammar also gives a better indication of the size of a rule set.

3 Scenarios

As there are different scenarios for building annotated corpora—corpora for new languages, corpora of a much larger nature than previously created, corpora in a new domain, etc.—the assumptions of one's resources can be quite different. We sketch different possibilities here.

3.1 Types of Grammars

Our methods are based on having a grammar to compare parse rules to. Automatically-parsed data can be obtained in different ways, affecting grammar resources. First, parsed data can be obtained from a parser trained on gold data. In this case, a GOLD GRAMMAR can be extracted from the gold data. For error detection, we can then compare the parsed data to this fixed grammar (section 5).

One subtype of this is the situation where the gold grammar is small (SMALL GRAMMAR). To be in this situation, one could develop a small treebank and extract a grammar from it, or one could manually write (coarse) grammar rules. We work with corpus-extracted grammars, but one advantage of the type of approach we take—unlike more theoretically grammar-driven ways of treebanking (e.g., Oepen et al., 2004; Rosén et al., 2005; Bond et al., 2004)—is that grammar-writing is simpler, using only very coarse categories.

The second type of situation (NOISY GRAMMAR) arises when not all the rules in the grammar are valid, as when rules are extracted straight from automatically-parsed data. If the data has been parsed, some parser exists, but it may be the case that: a) data is exchanged, but the technology is not; or b) the data is partially hand-corrected. In either case, a NOISY GRAMMAR can be extracted from the parsed data (section 6).

This leads to the possibility of hybrid grammars, where some rules have been hand-checked and others have not—i.e., a concatenation of a gold and a noisy grammar. Since gold and noisy grammars are more primary, we focus on them.

Finally, there may be a hand-crafted or specialized parser, tuned to a particular annotation scheme. This can arise from continual development in a large project (e.g., the Alpino project (Plank and van Noord, 2010)) or when one uses a parser without having access to the corpus it was trained on. If the parser has an accessible grammar, there is a GOLD GRAMMAR; otherwise, a NOISY GRAMMAR can be extracted.

3.2 Grammar-Based Error Detection

The reason we phrase error detection in terms of grammars is that some grammar is always available, whereas we cannot always assume a modifiable parser. Error detection based on coarse grammars is applicable to any of these scenarios, as opposed to, e.g., methods which rely on details of how a parser is likely to fail (e.g., Attardi and Ciaramita, 2007; Goldberg and Elhadad, 2010b).[2] Additionally, because we can always obtain a grammar from parsed data, we will have access to the frequency of occurrence of each rule.[3]

4 Methods of Comparison

In this section, we develop the best methods of rule comparison (section 4.1) and introduce a new, orthogonal way of flagging possible errors (section 4.2). In order to compare directly to the previous work, we use the Swedish Talbanken corpus (Nilsson and Hall, 2005) with the same data split as in the CoNLL-X Shared Task (Buchholz and Marsi, 2006); in section 5 and beyond, we switch the training and testing data. In all experiments, we use gold standard POS tags.

To keep the data sets clear across different training regiments, we refer to them as the *large* and *small* Talbanken data sets. The large Talbanken data has 11,042 sentences, 191,467 words, 96,517 (non-unary) rule tokens and 26,292 rule types. The small data set has 389 sentences, 5,656 words, 3,107 rule tokens and 1,284 rule types. As we show in section 5, even such a small grammar can be highly effective in detecting parse errors.

[2]Those methods are of course well-suited to the issue of improving parsing technology.

[3]Even for hand-written grammars, the methods we develop can be altered to be type-based instead of token-based.

4.1 Method Improvement

As discussed in section 2, the main previous methods of flagging errors look for anomalous bigrams or anomalous "whole rules." Each method has its limitations, looking only at local context (bigram) or only at the whole context (whole rule). Yet there is a straightforward, principled way to combine the methods: add together all n-gram parts of a rule (cf. Zhao et al., 2010; Bergsma et al., 2009).

To do this, during training we break a rule down into its component n-grams (cf. steps 1 and 2 below) and store the frequency of the rule for each n-gram. For rule scoring, we then:

1. Add START and END context tags to the list of elements in a rule.
2. Calculate all (contiguous) bigrams, trigrams, etc., up to the length of the whole rule.
3. Calculate the frequency of all n-grams (based on a training set) containing a given element.

This is encapsulated in the formula in (5).

(5) $s(e_i, c) = \sum_{ngram: e_i \in ngram \wedge n \geq 2} C(ngram, c)$

For example, focusing on AT:AJ back in rule (3) with the head VN as the comparable item (c), we count up the grammar frequencies of n-grams, as in (6). A benefit of this method is that, by using local and global contexts, equally-frequent bigrams, for example, are sorted out by whether they continue to occur in longer forms.

(6) s(AT:AJ, VN) = C(DT:PO **AT:AJ**, VN)
+ C(**AT:AJ** VN, VN)
+ C(START DT:PO **AT:AJ**, VN)
+ C(DT:PO **AT:AJ** VN, VN)
+ C(**AT:AJ** VN END, VN)
+ C(START DT:PO **AT:AJ** VN, VN)
+ C(DT:PO **AT:AJ** VN END, VN)
+ C(START DT:PO **AT:AJ** VN END, VN)

We refer to the new method as the *all-gram* (*All.*) method, and results are reported in table 1 using MaltParser (Nivre et al., 2007). Our goal is to improve annotation post-editing, and so we report precision (P) and recall (R) of error detection, for positions below the threshold. Either an attachment or labeling error counts as an error. Precision is thus the complement of a labeled attachment score (LAS); for example, by using no score, the parser has an LAS of 82.0% and error detection precision of 18.0%. Two F-scores are provided—F_1 and $F_{0.5}$, which weights precision twice as much—and the best value of each is reported. We favor precision, so as to prevent annotators from sorting through false positives.

Score	Thr.	pos.	P	R	F_1	$F_{0.5}$
None	n/a	5,656	18.0%	100%	30.5%	21.5%
All.	0	56	92.9%	5.1%	9.7%	21.0%
	60	479	61.8%	29.1%	39.6%	50.5%
	390	1,234	42.5%	51.7%	46.7%	44.1%
Tri.	0	215	77.2%	16.3%	27.0%	44.2%
	5	478	66.3%	31.2%	42.4%	54.1%
	49	1,202	44.1%	52.2%	47.8%	45.5%
High.	0	215	77.2%	16.3%	27.0%	44.2%
	5	424	69.6%	29.0%	41.0%	**54.4%**
	90	1,373	42.2%	57.0%	**48.5%**	44.5%

Table 1: Talbanken error detection results for different scores: parser = MaltParser trained on large data; grammar = large gold; evaluation data = small data (*pos.* = positions below threshold (*Thr.*))

Comparing the results here on the same data in Dickinson (2010), we have a slightly higher F_1 score than the previous best method (46.7% vs. 46.4% [whole rule]) and a higher $F_{0.5}$ than the best method (50.5% vs. 49.9% [bigram]).

4.1.1 Excluding Bigrams

The methods are still very close, so we attempt to improve further. Consider the tree in figure 3, for the example in (7), where there is no verb, and a preposition (PR) is the sentence's root. The resulting rule, which occurs 79 times in the training data, is TOP → *root* ROOT:PR.

(7) Ur giftermålsbalken 5 kap < 1 och < 2
From marriage act 5 ch. < 1 and < 2
'From the marriage act, ch. 5, para. (?) 1 and 2'

When bigram information is included in calculating scores, both *root* ROOT:PR and ROOT:PR END get counted 79 times, leading to high scores for both PRs in (8), when only the first is correct. Bigrams do not distinguish the correct first PR from the incorrect second PR attachment in (8): both have 79 pieces of supporting evidence.

(8) TOP → *root* ROOT:PR ROOT:PR

We need both left and right contexts in rule scoring. We thus experiment with using both trigram information as a model of its own (*Tri.*) and a model which uses all trigrams and above (i.e., the

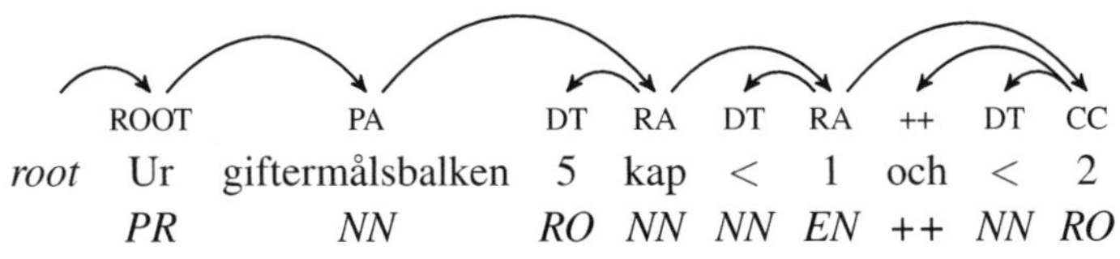

Figure 3: Preposition-rooted sentence (from large Talbanken data set)

same as (5), but with $n \geq 3$), which we refer to as the *high-gram* method (*High.*). These are included in table 1, where we can see improvements in precision and recall. For example, with a threshold of 5, we find 29% of all errors by examining 424 instances (i.e., 7.5% of the parsed corpus).

Trigrams are the minimum length to obtain contextual information on each side, and longer n-grams (for the high-gram method) give more precise indication that the rule context is valid. Even though long n-grams are rare, they are useful, leading to a positive, albeit small, improvement.

4.1.2 Notes on Evaluation

The intended use of the scores is for annotators to start with the lowest-scoring positions (i.e., tokens) and work upwards. The F-measures give some sense of this, but we need a way to evaluate across different corpora. To account for this, we do two things: first, we report the values for the lowest threshold, so that one can get a sense of the precision for the highest-priority cases. Secondly, we use Talbanken for development, finding the best $F_{0.5}$ score and calculating the percentage of the test corpus that the threshold identifies. In the case of evaluating on the small test corpus, $\frac{424}{5{,}656} = 7.5\%$, so other experiments with a similar large/small split would be evaluated with a threshold identifying as close to 7.5% of the evaluation corpus as possible. We reset thresholds for experiments where the large corpus is the test corpus, as these behave differently, due to differing parser quality; in section 5.1, we will set this at 23%. The bottom two lines of table 7, for instance, present results for the lowest threhold (0) and the one which identifies as close to 23% of the tokens as possible (25). Also, as we emphasize precision, in future tables we report $F_{0.5}$ and ignore F_1.

4.2 Revision Checking

The n-gram models discussed so far are not very sophisticated. Low scores conflate two issues: 1) the element in question is anomalous, or 2) there was no better attachment or labeling for this element, i.e., the parser could not have made a better decision. Identifying the latter cases could reduce false positives, i.e., correct low-scoring positions.

For example, for (9), the parser correctly attaches *hållas* ('hold') to *måste* ('must') in a VG relation, as in figure 4. The high-gram scoring method assigns a score of 0, because UK:UK MV VG:VV and MV VG:VV END were never observed in the grammar, but there is no better attachment in this instance. By determining that attaching to *som* or *hemligt* is no better, we can overcome some limitations of the original scoring. We refer to the process of checking for a better-scoring attachment or labeling as a *revision check*.

(9) Du kommer under din utbildning att få
You come under your education to get
se och höra sådant som måste hållas
see and hear such as must be held
hemligt .
secret .

'You will during your education see and hear things that must be kept secret.'

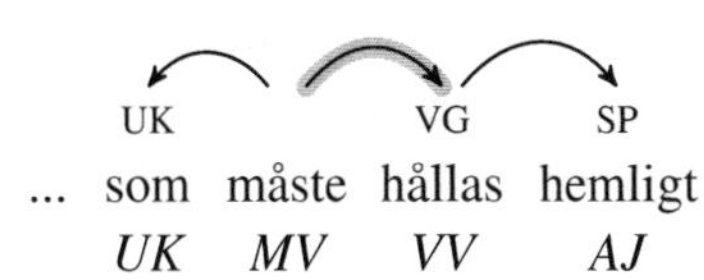

Figure 4: Correct low-scoring dependency structure

What a better-scoring revision means depends to a great extent on parser quality. Trained on a small gold corpus, the parser has not seen much data. If other attachments or labelings result in better scores, the parser may not have had enough information to select the revision and perhaps should have given it more weight. For a parser with high accuracy (e.g., trained on large gold data), on the other hand, the parser should have considered the revision and rejected it on the basis of good evidence. The elements which do not have a better revision are ones which may represent new types of constructions. Thus, the parser may do worse if there are no reasonable revisions—just the opposite of the expectation for a small corpus.

4.2.1 Revision Checking Algorithm

For an element e_i in a rule r ($lhs \rightarrow e_1 e_2, ..., e_n$), where e_i is a (pos_i, dep_i) pair:

1. Score e_i, e_{i-1} (left context), and e_{i+1} (right context) within r, using, e.g., the high-gram method.
2. Check a different labeling in the original rule.
   (a) Replace (pos_i, dep_i) with all relevant (pos_i, dep_j) pairs (where $dep_i \neq dep_j$)
      - **Relevant** dependency labels occurred in training with pos_i; other labels will result in a score of 0.

   (b) Score the modified rule.
   (c) Flag the rule if a different labeling results in an **improvement**, namely:
      i. The modified element's score increases, and left/right context scores improve or stay the same.
      ii. The modified element's score stays the same, and context scores increase.
3. Check different re-attachments (and re-labelings) by placing the element in question (e_i) into other rules (x), if appropriate.
   (a) Remove e_i from the original rule:
      i. Remove e_i from r to obtain r'.
      ii. Score r' and extract scores for positions to the left/right of where e_i used to be.
      iii. If e_{i-1} or e_{i+1} is worse than originally scored, skip next step and do not flag.

   (b) Modify and score other rules (x):
      i. Insert element into the appropriate position within x, following linear ordering.
      ii. Determine whether this is an appropriate **candidate attachment site**:
         A. Inserting e_i does not introduce a cyclic structure.
         B. Inserting e_i does not create a non-projective structure.

      iii. Try all **relevant** dependency labelings for this element to obtain different x'.
      iv. Score each modified rule x', in particular e', e'_{-1}, and e'_{+1}.
      v. **Flag** the original rule if a different atttachment+labeling results in an **improvement** (as defined above).

While the idea is straightforward, there are several points to note. First, the output is that we flag an element if *any* revision shows improvement, but do not keep track of which revision is better. Secondly, in step #3bii we use a strict notion of where an element may be inserted—ensuring no cyclicity or non-projectivity—but either of these conditions may be relaxed. Further, we do not check rootedness, as we do not enforce a globally optimal tree. Finally, the algorithm can check any element in any order; if one were to perform rule revision, the ordering of elements would matter, as scores would change based on previous revisions.

4.2.2 Using the Flagged Elements

Once rules are flagged as having a better-scoring revision or not, we can use: a) the original (high-gram) score, and b) the revision check flag (yes = a better revision exists). These can be used independently or in conjunction. We will evaluate by reporting error detection precision and recall for the lowest-scoring flagged and unflagged positions, as well as for all flagged and unflagged positions. We can also view the process as: correct all the flagged positions and then move to the unflagged ones, and so we report combinations of all flagged positions plus some amount of unflagged positions.

In table 2, we report results using the large gold grammar on the small parsed data. We note first that the highest precision is recorded for the lowest unflagged position (82.8% vs. 77.2% without the flagged/unflagged distinction). As mentioned, when the parser is high quality, the cases where we cannot find a better attachment or labeling may be the most difficult. This gives us some promise of being able to use these techniques for active learning (e.g., Sassano and Kurohashi, 2010). Secondly, the F-scores are lower than the best ones obtained on this data ignoring the revision flagging. Thus, when the parser is of a high quality, we want to prioritize the initial high-gram scores over a revision check. As we will see in section 5.2, smaller grammars present a different picture.[4]

5 Small Gold Grammars

Turning to a small gold grammar, we perform two sets of experiments: in the first, we use MaltParser[5] on the Swedish Talbanken data (sections 5.1 and 5.2). Then, in section 5.3, we use MSTParser (McDonald et al., 2006)[6] on the

[4]Determining at what point one switches from "low quality" to "high quality" is a question for future research.

[5]`http://maltparser.org/`

[6]`http://sourceforge.net/projects/mstparser/`

Score	Thr.	pos.	P	R	$F_{0.5}$
L	0	215	77.2%	16.3%	44.2%
LF	0	70	65.7%	4.5%	17.7%
AF	1,269	670	43.1%	28.4%	39.1%
LU	0	145	**82.8%**	11.8%	37.6%
AU	31,987	4,986	14.6%	71.6%	17.3%
AF+U0	n/a	815	50.2%	40.3%	47.8%
AF+U5	n/a	931	51.5%	47.1%	**50.5%**

Table 2: Revision checking: same set-up as in table 1, using high-gram method for checking. (L=lowest, A=all, F=flagged, U=unflagged, Ux=unflagged up to threshold x)

dependency-converted English Wall Street Journal (WSJ) data (Marcus et al., 1993),[7] and we vary the size and appropriateness of the gold grammar. With these permutations, we demonstrate the wide applicability of our methods. With little annotated training data, parser results are worse than before, placing more priority on error detection.

5.1 Working with a Small Gold Grammar

Swapping the Talbanken data, the training data is now approximately 10% of the corpus (small data) and the test data 90% (large data). The results are given in table 3, where the first thing to note is the overall worse parser performance, reflected in a much higher baseline precision (*None*) of 35.4% (=64.6% LAS), significantly higher then with the normal split (P=18.0%, LAS=82.0%, table 1).

Score	Thr.	pos.	P	R	$F_{0.5}$
None	n/a	191,467	35.4%	100%	40.7%
Freq.	0	116,847	48.1%	82.7%	52.5%
Bi.	0	21,110	85.2%	26.5%	59.0%
	6	48,890	70.0%	50.4%	65.0%
Tri.	0	44,297	72.7%	47.5%	**65.7%**
High.	0	44,297	72.7%	47.5%	**65.7%**
All.	0	21,110	85.2%	26.5%	59.0%
	9	48,690	70.3%	50.4%	65.2%

Table 3: Talbanken error detection results for different scores: parser = MaltParser trained on small data; grammar = small gold; evaluation data = large data

With low parser accuracy, baseline F measures are higher: by going over every instance, an annotator will, in principle, find every error (100% recall), with 35% precision. However, that means going through over 190,000 words by hand. To improve the corpus with less effort, we want to identify errors with high precision. Indeed, in the results in table 3, we find precision around 70% with recall around 50%.[8]

Consider the high-gram method, which has the highest $F_{0.5}$, 65.7%, at a score of 0—i.e., no rules in the grammar with any trigrams or longer n-grams supporting a given rule.[9] First, this is much higher than the 54.4% for the standard data split (table 1), partly due to the fact that the parser accuracy is lower. Secondly, 44,297 positions are flagged—23% of the corpus—with 32,209 erroneous; annotators could correct nearly 3 out of every 4 flagged dependencies, fixing 47% of the errors. We will use 23% of the corpus for other experiments with large data (cf. section 4.1.2). Finally, if 32,209 corrections are added to the original 123,595 correct positions, the resulting corpus will have correct dependencies 81.4% of the time (vs. 64.6% LAS), making the corpus more suitable for, e.g., training parsers (cf. Nivre, 2010).

Note also that at the lowest threshold, the bigram method is the most precise (85.2%). What we observed before (cf. example (8) in section 4.1.1) is true—positive evidence of bigrams may be misleading—but *negative* evidence from bigrams may be useful (cf. Dickinson, 2011). If a position has no bigram support, this is worse than no trigrams. One can thus consider splitting the zero high-gram elements into two classes: those which never occurred as bigrams (more likely to be erroneous) and those which did.

To gauge an upper bound on error detection, we use the large gold grammar for an oracle experiment. This helps sort out the effect of the grammar (and its size) from the effect of the comparison methods. We can see the results in table 4.

In comparing to table 3, we see that the results with the much larger grammar are a few points better. The best $F_{0.5}$ measure goes from 65.7% to 69.6%, despite the grammar sizes being 1,284 and 26,292 rule types, respectively (section 4). Even a small gold grammar is extremely useful for error detection. Furthermore, the small grammar here is based on data which is disjoint from the evaluation data, whereas the large grammar comes from (gold) annotation for the evaluation data.

[7]We used the LTH Constituent-to-Dependency Conversion Tool (Johansson and Nugues, 2007), selecting options for CoNLL 2007 format and no NP rebracketing.

[8]Since errors are often inter-related (Hara et al., 2009), it is likely an annotator would actually have a higher recall, but we do not explore inter-relatedness here.

[9]The trigram method performs identically here because no trigrams means no higher n-grams.

Score	Thr.	pos.	P	R	$F_{0.5}$
None	n/a	191,467	35.4%	100%	40.7%
Freq.	0	84,067	57.5%	71.2%	59.8%
Bi.	84	33,197	80.5%	39.2%	66.6%
Tri.	18	39,707	78.8%	46.1%	69.0%
High.	23	39,278	79.8%	46.2%	**69.6%**
All.	203	39,846	77.0%	45.2%	67.5%

Table 4: Talbanken oracle error detection results: same set-up as table 3, but grammar = large gold

5.2 Small Gold Grammar Revision Checking

Turning to flagging positions by whether they have better-scoring possible revisions, we report the results for Talbanken in table 5. With a previous best $F_{0.5}$ of 65.7% for all zero-scoring element, we observe improvement here (68.2%), obtained by going over all (21,670) flagged positions and then including the (34,343) lowest unflagged positions.

Score	Thr.	pos.	P	R	$F_{0.5}$
L	0	44,297	72.7%	47.5%	65.7%
LF	0	9,954	**73.8%**	10.8%	34.1%
AF	72	21,670	69.1%	22.0%	48.4%
LU	0	34,343	72.4%	36.6%	60.5%
AU	1233	169,797	31.2%	77.9%	35.4%
AF+U0	n/a	56,013	71.1%	58.7%	**68.2%**

Table 5: Revision checking: same set-up as in table 3, using high-gram method for checking

This matches the intuition that, when the quality of the parse is low, such a sanity check can improve parse error detection. Note in this case that 69.1% of all flagged (AF) cases need revision, not much lower than the overall (lowest) precision of 72.7%. No matter the rule score, if it is flagged, then it is quite likely to be in need of revision. To evaluate in other situations with large evaluation corpora, we will take all flagged positions and then the lowest-scoring unflagged positions.

Consider the practical effect: 56,013 positions are identified, with 39,825 (71.1%) erroneous. Fixing these cases would correct 58.7% of the errors, resulting in 85.4% corpus accuracy ($\frac{163,420}{191,467}$).

False Negatives We investigate some of the false negatives—i.e., cases which the revision check does not flag but which are low-scoring—in order to discover the limitations of the method. In general, the underflagging often results from the conservative nature of candidate selection. Because we do not allow cycles to be introduced, for example, it is nearly impossible to revise a ROOT element. The most frequent false negatives are those with multiple ROOTs, e.g., the erroneous IP position in TOP → root ROOT:NN ROOT:IP (not flagged 82 times). Extremely long rules (e.g., over 10 dependents) are also underflagged. Because we do not permit non-projectivity, if an element is between two sister elements, those are often the *only* positions which can serve as alternate heads; otherwise, branches have to cross. This is schematized in figure 5, where revisions for D could only include C and E as heads.

Figure 5: Schematic for sister relations

5.3 Grammar Size and Quality

As with the Talbanken data, we want to test these methods on English data using a small amount of training data and a large amount of test data. To do this, we train different parser models. We use the default training options for MSTParser and train one model on section 00 of the WSJ data, one on section 24, and one on both. All three models are then used to parse sections 02-21, with results in table 6. We use the default settings, as this is a good fit for using the methods in the real world.[10]

Par.	Tokens	Size	UAS	LAS
00	46,451	7,250	81.7%	73.4%
24	32,853	5,797	80.5%	71.8%
0024	79,304	11,095	83.5%	76.0%

Table 6: Parser accuracies for WSJ models with different training data (*Par.*), including number of training *Tokens* and *Size* of grammar (non-unary rule types)

In addition to varying the parser, we also vary the grammar, running tests for each model using gold standard grammars derived from different sections. This set-up allows us to see the effect of varying the size of the parser training data, the size of the grammar, and the different grammars across data sets—i.e., error detection using a grammar from a different section than the one the parser is trained on. The results are in table 7.

[10]In development, we also tested parser models with the optimized settings used for McDonald et al. (2005), but there was little impact on accuracy: 73.7%, 72.1%, and 76.2% LAS for the respective training data situations in table 6.

Par.	Gram.	Thr.	pos.	P	R	$F_{0.5}$
00	None	n/a	950,022	26.6%	100%	31.2%
	00	0	143,365	79.5%	45.1%	**68.9%**
		9	217,804	70.8%	61.0%	68.6%
	24	0	152,281	78.0%	47.0%	**68.9%**
		6	219,712	69.4%	60.2%	67.3%
	0024	0	130,724	**81.0%**	41.9%	68.3%
		16	217,628	70.7%	60.9%	68.5%
24	None	n/a	950,022	28.2%	100%	32.9%
	00	0	155,889	79.7%	46.4%	69.7%
		6	218,227	73.4%	59.8%	**70.2%**
	24	0	157,733	79.1%	46.6%	69.4%
		5	217,751	72.6%	59.0%	69.4%
	0024	0	139,604	**81.3%**	42.3%	68.6%
		12	218,207	73.3%	59.7%	70.1%
0024	None	n/a	950,022	24.0%	100%	28.3%
	00	0	127,667	77.7%	43.6%	**67.2%**
		14	219,362	64.6%	62.3%	64.1%
	24	0	133,596	76.3%	44.8%	66.9%
		9	216,826	64.0%	60.9%	63.3%
	0024	0	114,486	**79.7%**	40.1%	66.5%
		25	218,731	64.4%	61.9%	63.9%

Table 7: WSJ: high-gram scores for lowest and 23% thresholds: parser = default MST trained on different data (*Par.*); grammar = gold from section listed (*Gram.*); evaluation data = sections 02-21

Looking at the results for the parser trained on section 00, there are 252,700 errors (26.6%) in over 950,000 words. By using the high-gram method and a grammar extracted from the gold data for section 00, we obtain a precision of 70.8% and recall of 61.0% at the 23% threshold: thus, one could correct 61% of the errors by looking at only 23% of the corpus (217,804 positions, with about 154,000 of them erroneous). Alternatively, using a threshold score of zero on the same data results in higher precision (79.5%) and lower recall (45.1%). This pattern of higher precision at the lowest threshold and higher recall for the 23% threshold is consistent across all testing scenarios, showing the effectiveness of correcting by working up from the lowest-scoring items.

Within the results for each parser, the grammar based on section 00 is more effective at sorting out the errors (i.e., has a higher $F_{0.5}$ score) than the other grammars—although the differences are small. This is true even for the parser trained on section 24 (70.2% vs. 69.4%), and the reverse situation (parser=00, grammar=24) even performs on a par with the other grammars. This indicates that a grammar from a different (albeit, related) corpus can be effective in error detection. Future work can explore applying this work across domains.

As for grammar size, the differences in $F_{0.5}$ between the smallest (section 24) and the largest (both sections) for all experiments is <1%. Even with a small gold grammar, we again conclude that this method can effectively sort out a majority of the errors with high precision.

5.3.1 Revision Checking

To gauge the results of revision checking, we report results for the WSJ parser trained only on section 00, as shown in table 8. The results for the other two parsers are not shown for space reasons, but they follow exactly the same trends, namely a consistent improvement, verifying the Talbanken results (section 5.2). For example, comparing to the 00 parser results without revision checking in table 7, we observe a greater $F_{0.5}$ value for all grammars by taking all flagged positions and the lowest-scoring unflagged positions (AF+U0). With the section 00 grammar, for instance, we see an improvement in $F_{0.5}$ from 68.9% to 71.6%.

Gr.	Score	Thr.	pos.	P	R	$F_{0.5}$
00	LF	0	78,805	**92.2%**	28.8%	66.4%
	AF	1,325	141,914	79.7%	44.8%	68.9%
	AF+U0	n/a	206,474	74.8%	61.1%	**71.6%**
24	LF	0	79,755	**91.9%**	29.0%	64.1%
	AF	1,167	138,912	79.4%	43.6%	68.2%
	AF+U0	n/a	211,438	73.7%	61.6%	**70.9%**
0024	LF	0	76,570	**92.0%**	28.0%	63.3%
	AF	3,200	144,041	80.3%	45.8%	69.8%
	AF+U0	n/a	198,195	76.1%	59.7%	**72.1%**

Table 8: WSJ revision checking results, using the high-gram method, for the parser trained on section 00; same set-up as in table 7

Perhaps the most notable feature of these results is the precision of the lowest-scoring flagged positions, around 92% for all grammars. This means that for this type of data, annotators could go over 80,000 positions, with very few false positives, providing much potential for efficient correction.

6 Noisy Grammar

In this section, we switch to using a noisy grammar, i.e., one extracted from the parsed data itself. Using the same parser for Swedish as in section 5.1 and parsing the large corpus, we extract a grammar from the parsed data and obtain the results for the high-gram method in table 9. As the parsed rules are from the grammar, this can be seen as an internal consistency check.

Score	Thr.	pos.	P	R	$F_{0.5}$
None	n/a	191,467	35.4%	100%	40.7%
No-Rev.	3	267	88.4%	0.3%	1.7%
	76	44,274	68.4%	44.6%	61.8%
AF	2,784	12,769	67.9%	12.8%	36.4%
AF+U55	n/a	44,155	68.8%	44.7%	62.1%

Table 9: Talbanken error detection results for the high-gram method: parser = MaltParser trained on small data; grammar = large noisy; evaluation data = small data (*No-Rev.* = No revision checking)

These results are noticably lower than when using a small gold grammar (tables 3 and 5). Without revision checking, the high-gram $F_{0.5}$ score goes from 65.7% to 61.8%, in spite of the fact that the noisy grammar has 95,900 rule tokens and 25,904 types, compared to 3,107/1,284 in the gold grammar. That is, a small set of high-quality rules outperforms a large set of more questionable rules, possibly because of parser bias in the grammar.

As for the impact of revision checking, the precision for all 12,769 flagged positions is 67.9%—on a par with the precision without revision checking. Indeed, for all flagged positions combined with many lowest-scoring unflagged positions (up to the 55 threshold, or 23% of the corpus), the $F_{0.5}$ score is slightly improved, though still well below the small gold grammar case.

Comparing the noisy grammar in table 10 to the small gold grammars in table 7, the trend in English is more pronounced. For example, for the parser trained on section 00 (and the 00 grammar), the $F_{0.5}$ goes from 68.9% to 56.9%. Each noisy WSJ grammar has over 85,000 rules, yet the noise greatly pulls down the accuracy, thereby confirming our preference for (small) gold grammars.[11]

7 Summary and Outlook

Taking into account different ways in which automatic dependency parses are obtained, we have advocated for a grammar-based method of detecting parse errors and have illustrated the gains that can be made by using such methods, including the incorporation of revision checking. Methods using a small gold grammar outperform the methods using much larger grammars with noise in them. Thus, to employ such methods on new data, one needs a small grammar, perhaps from a small hand-annotated corpus. Using our methods can improve the resulting annotation of large amounts of parsed data, allowing annotators to focus on problematic parses and not correct ones.

In the future, one can test these methods on real-world corpus-building efforts, integrating them into a particular annotation workflow. Because the method of scoring parses is very general, one can also explore using the scores in different contexts, such as scoring the validity of parse structures in a parser combination model (e.g., Surdeanu and Manning, 2010; Sagae and Tsujii, 2007; Sagae and Lavie, 2006); sorting sentences for active learning (cf. Sassano and Kurohashi, 2010); or selecting parse structures for parsing (Chen et al., 2009).

[11]We also tried concatenating the small gold and large noisy grammars to make a hybrid grammar (section 3), but the results were hardly better than in tables 9 and 10.

Par.	Thr.	pos.	P	R	$F_{0.5}$
00	3	315	90.5%	0.1%	0.6%
	460	218,497	58.7%	50.7%	56.9%
24	3	400	90.5%	0.1%	0.7%
	438	218,612	61.1%	49.8%	58.4%
0024	3	377	91.8%	0.2%	0.8%
	479	218,512	55.7%	53.5%	55.3%

Table 10: WSJ: high-gram scores: parser = default MST trained on different data (*Par.*); grammar = extracted from appropriate parsed 02-21; evaluation data = 02-21

Acknowledgments

We would like to thank Jennifer Foster, the IU CL discussion group, and the three anonymous reviewers for useful feedback; and thanks to Yvonne Adesam for translation help.

A Some Talbanken05 categories

POS tags	
++	coord. conj.
AB	adverb
AJ	adjective
EN	indef. article
FV	*få* (get)
NN	noun
PO	pronoun
PR	preposition
RO	numeral
VN	verbal noun
VV	verb

Dependencies	
++	coord. conj.
AT	nominal pre-modifier
CC	sister of first conjunct (binary branching coordination)
DT	determiner
FS	dummy subject
MA	attitude adverbial
NA	negation adverbial
PA	preposition comp.
PL	verb particle
RA	place adverbial
SS	subject
VG	verb group

References

Abeillé, Anne (ed.) (2003). *Treebanks: Building and using syntactically annoted corpora*. Dordrecht: Kluwer Academic Publishers.

Ambati, Bharat Ram (2010). Importance of Linguistic Constraints in Statistical Dependency Parsing. In *Proceedings of the ACL 2010 Student Research Workshop*. Uppsala, Sweden, pp. 103–108.

Ambati, Bharat Ram, Mridul Gupta, Samar Husain and Dipti Misra Sharma (2010). A high recall error identification tool for Hindi treebank validation. In *Proceedings of The 7th International Conference on Language Resources and Evaluation (LREC)*. Valletta, Malta.

Attardi, Giuseppe and Massimiliano Ciaramita (2007). Tree Revision Learning for Dependency Parsing. In *Proceedings of NAACL-HLT-07*. Rochester, NY, pp. 388–395.

Bergsma, Shane, Dekang Lin and Randy Goebel (2009). Web-Scale N-gram Models for Lexical Disambiguation. In *Proceedings of the International Joint Conference on Artificial Intelligence (IJCAI)*. Pasadena, California, pp. 1507–1512.

Bond, Francis, Sanae Fujita et al. (2004). The Hinoki Treebank: Toward Text Understanding. In *Proceedings of the 5th International Workshop on Linguistically Interpreted Corpora (LINC-04)*. Geneva, pp. 7–10.

Buchholz, Sabine and Erwin Marsi (2006). CoNLL-X Shared Task on Multilingual Dependency Parsing. In *Proceedings of CoNLL-X*. New York City, pp. 149–164.

Chen, Wenliang, Jun'ichi Kazama, Kiyotaka Uchimoto and Kentaro Torisawa (2009). Improving Dependency Parsing with Subtrees from Auto-Parsed Data. In *Proceedings of EMNLP-09*. Singapore, pp. 570–579.

Dickinson, Markus (2010). Detecting Errors in Automatically-Parsed Dependency Relations. In *The 48th Annual Meeting of the Association for Computational Linguistics (ACL-10)*. Uppsala, Sweden.

Dickinson, Markus (2011). Detecting Ad Hoc Rules for Treebank Development. *Linguistic Issues in Language Technology* 4(3).

Goldberg, Yoav and Michael Elhadad (2010a). An Efficient Algorithm for Easy-First Non-Directional Dependency Parsing. In *Human Language Technologies: The 2010 Annual Conference of the North American Chapter of the Association for Computational Linguistics*. Los Angeles, California, pp. 742–750.

Goldberg, Yoav and Michael Elhadad (2010b). Inspecting the Structural Biases of Dependency Parsing Algorithms. In *Proceedings of the Fourteenth Conference on Computational Natural Language Learning*. Uppsala, Sweden, pp. 234–242.

Hara, Tadayoshi, Yusuke Miyao and Jun'ichi Tsujii (2009). Effective Analysis of Causes and Inter-dependencies of Parsing Errors. In *Proceedings of the 11th International Conference on Parsing Technologies (IWPT'09)*. Paris, France: Association for Computational Linguistics, pp. 180–191.

Hwa, Rebecca, Philip Resnik, Amy Weinberg, Clara Cabezas and Okan Kolak (2005). Bootstrapping parsers via syntactic projection across parallel texts. *Natural Language Engineering* 11, 311–325.

Johansson, Richard and Pierre Nugues (2007). Extended Constituent-to-dependency Conversion for English. In *Proceedings of NODALIDA 2007*. Tartu, Estonia.

Leech, Geoffrey (2004). Adding Linguistic Annotation. In Martin Wynne (ed.), *Developing Linguistic Corpora: a Guide to Good Practice*, Oxford: Oxbow Books, pp. 17–29.

Marcus, M., Beatrice Santorini and M. A. Marcinkiewicz (1993). Building a large annotated corpus of English: The Penn Treebank. *Computational Linguistics* 19(2), 313–330.

McDonald, Ryan, Koby Crammer and Fernando Pereira (2005). Online Large-Margin Training of Dependency Parsers. In *Proceedings of the 43rd Annual Meeting of the ACL*. AnnArbor, pp. 91–98.

McDonald, Ryan, Kevin Lerman and Fernando Pereira (2006). Multilingual Dependency Analysis with a Two-Stage Discriminative Parser. In *Proceedings of the Tenth Conference on Computational Natural Language Learning (CoNLL-X)*. New York City, pp. 216–220.

Nilsson, Jens and Johan Hall (2005). *Reconstruction of the Swedish Treebank Talbanken*. MSI report 05067, Växjö University: School of Mathematics and Systems Engineering.

Nivre, Joakim (2010). Harvest Time - Explorations of the Swedish Treebank. *The Ninth Treebanks and Linguistic Theories Workshop*, Invited Talk. Tartu, Estonia. December 4, 2010.

Nivre, Joakim, Johan Hall, Jens Nilsson, Atanas Chanev, Gulsen Eryigit, Sandra Kübler, Svetoslav Marinov and Erwin Marsi (2007). MaltParser: A language-independent system for data-driven dependency parsing. *Natural Language Engineering* 13(2), 95–135.

Oepen, Stephan, Dan Flickinger and Francis Bond (2004). Towards holistic grammar engineering and testing—grafting treebank maintenance into the grammar revision cycle. In *Beyond Shallow Analyses—Formalisms and Statistical Modelling for Deep Analysis (Workshop at The First International Joint Conference on Natural Language Processing (IJCNLP-04))*. Hainan, China.

Plank, Barbara and Gertjan van Noord (2010). Grammar-Driven versus Data-Driven: Which Parsing System Is More Affected by Domain Shifts? In *Proceedings of the 2010 Workshop on NLP and Linguistics: Finding the Common Ground*. Uppsala, Sweden, pp. 25–33.

Rosén, Victoria, Koenraad de Smedt, Helge Dyvik and Paul Meurer (2005). TREPIL: Developing Methods and Tools for Multilevel Treebank Construction. In *Proceedings of the Fourth Workshop on Treebanks and Linguistic Theories (TLT 2005)*. Barcelona, Spain, pp. 161–172.

Sagae, Kenji and Alon Lavie (2006). Parser Combination by Reparsing. In *Proceedings of the Human Language Technology Conference of the NAACL, Companion Volume: Short Papers*. New York City, USA, pp. 129–132.

Sagae, Kenji and Jun'ichi Tsujii (2007). Dependency Parsing and Domain Adaptation with LR Models and Parser Ensembles. In *Proceedings of the CoNLL Shared Task Session of EMNLP-CoNLL 2007*. Prague, Czech Republic, pp. 1044–1050.

Sassano, Manabu and Sadao Kurohashi (2010). Using Smaller Constituents Rather Than Sentences in Active Learning for Japanese Dependency Parsing. In *Proceedings of the 48th Annual Meeting of the Association for Computational Linguistics*. Uppsala, Sweden, pp. 356–365.

Seeker, Wolfgang, Ines Rehbein, Jonas Kuhn and Josef Van Genabith (2010). Hard Constraints for Grammatical Function Labelling. In *Proceedings of the 48th Annual Meeting of the Association for Computational Linguistics*. Uppsala, Sweden, pp. 1087–1097.

Simpson, Heather, Kazuaki Maeda and Christopher Cieri (2009). Basic Language Resources for Diverse Asian Languages: A Streamlined Approach for Resource Creation. In *Proceedings of the 7th Workshop on Asian Language Resources*. Suntec, Singapore, pp. 55–62.

Surdeanu, Mihai and Christopher D. Manning (2010). Ensemble Models for Dependency Parsing: Cheap and Good? In *Human Language Technologies: The 2010 Annual Conference of the North American Chapter of the Association for Computational Linguistics*. Los Angeles, pp. 649–652.

van Noord, Gertjan and Gosse Bouma (2009). Parsed Corpora for Linguistics. In *Proceedings of the EACL 2009 Workshop on the Interaction between Linguistics and Computational Linguistics: Virtuous, Vicious or Vacuous?*. Athens, pp. 33–39.

Wallis, Sean (2003). Completing Parsed Corpora. In Abeillé (2003), pp. 61–71.

Zhao, Yanyan, Bing Qin, Shen Hu and Ting Liu (2010). Generalizing Syntactic Structures for Product Attribute Candidate Extraction. In *Human Language Technologies: The 2010 Annual Conference of the North American Chapter of the Association for Computational Linguistics*. Los Angeles, California, pp. 377–380.

Author Index